Pricing Systems, Indexes, and Price Behavior

Pricing Systems, Indexes, and Price Behavior

Nancy D. Ruggles and Richard Ruggles

Foreword by James Tobin

Edward Elgar
Cheltenham, UK • Northampton, MA, USA

Published by
Edward Elgar Publishing Limited
Glensanda House
Montpellier Parade
Cheltenham
Glos GL50 1UA
UK

Edward Elgar Publishing, Inc.
136 West Street
Suite 202
Northampton
Massachusetts 01060
USA

A catalogue record for this book
is available from the British Library

Library of Congress Cataloguing in Publication Data

Ruggles, Nancy D., 1922–1987
    Pricing systems, indexes, and price behavior / Nancy D. Ruggles and Richard Ruggles : foreword by James Tobin.
    A selection of 16 essays written between 1940 and 1990.
    1. Prices—United States. 2. Price indexes. 3. Pricing—United States. I. Ruggles, Richard, 1916– . II. Title.
HB235.U6R84 1999
338.5'2'0973—dc21   99–17051

ISBN 1 85898 993 0

Printed and bound in Great Britain by Bookcraft (Bath) Ltd.

Contents

PART THREE   PRICE BEHAVIOR

Foreword

James Tobin

For me, it is a great pleasure and a signal honor to introduce this volume of the collected essays of Nancy Dunlap Ruggles and Richard Ruggles, my good friends and colleagues over many decades. The Ruggles and Ruggles partnership was, from their marriage in 1946 to Nancy's tragic accidental death in 1987, a husband–wife team unsurpassed, at least in economics, in its unity and its scientific and professional contributions. Most of their work, regardless of formal attribution, was at bottom joint between them.

The sixteen essays in this volume cover an extensive range of microeconomics, devoted to economic theories, their applications to important issues of policy, and their consistency with detailed empirical data. The topics differ, but the essential characteristics of the approaches to them remain the same. The authors are accomplished, resourceful and focussed practitioners of a style of economic research and exposition that is, unfortunately, out of fashion today. Here are its main features: Nancy and Richard Ruggles always selected socially important problems and issues, and they concentrated on logic and fact relevant to them. Whatever their topic, they exhaustively, sympathetically, and critically surveyed the past literature, and took off from the existing state and uncertainty of knowledge. They rarely used mathematics or wrote down equations, and they relied sparingly on formal statistics and econometrics. Yet they were able to state and explain theoretical propositions and debates clearly and accurately, and they skillfully and tellingly brought empirical data to bear. These essays were written between 1940 and 1990 but almost all of them are very relevant to issues of great importance in 2000.

It is fitting that the volume begins with three essays that constituted the bulk of Nancy's Harvard Ph.D. dissertation. Economic life is rife with cases of increasing returns to scale involving significant fixed costs, in long runs as well as short runs. These cases are ever an embarrassment to pure theory, which is most comfortable with constant or decreasing returns to the scale of inputs and with competition among sellers and buyers who individually have no control over prices. How to introduce scale economies (including public goods) into formal general equilibrium models of the Arrow–Debreu type is still an active but unsuccessful pursuit of formal theorists. When Nancy Ruggles tackled this subject half a century ago, it had already for many years challenged the best theoretical minds of the profession. The holy grail, many thought and hoped, was somehow to impose the marginal cost pricing principle, for which optimality could be claimed in ordinary competitive circumstances. But who would pay the fixed costs? Nancy Ruggles reviewed thoroughly and expertly the large literature on this problem, and she showed conclusively that there is no answer to this key question that does not involve arbitrary relative valuations of utility outcomes of different individuals. Thus, there is no way to separate marginal cost pricing as *the* efficiency condition from the distributional consequences of paying for it. Current-day theorists struggling with such questions, including the roles of price discrimination and multipart price formulas, could profit from reading these papers.

Richard Ruggles's skeptical call for operationally meaningful tests of economists' basic assumptions of value theory — marginal revenue equals marginal cost — is a fitting conclusion to Part One on Price Theory. He prescribed and practiced the use of disaggregated microdata, surveys and censuses of business establishments.

Price Measurement, the topic of Part Two, is a subject on which Richard Ruggles has been a leading contributor during his long career. Today his contributions are again central, as economists, statisticians, politicians, government agencies and the general public worry about the accuracy of index numbers and their suitability for their various uses, especially in adjusting social security pensions, taxes, wages and other outlays and incomes. Characteristically he undertook a thorough history of index number theory, and he was importantly involved in official reviews of the Consumer Price Index and Wholesale Price Index. Measuring quality change is a key issue in index number construction today; Richard was perceptively worrying about it in 1961. He and Nancy were also concerned, both conceptually and practically, with measurement of geographical differences in prices and welfare.

Richard Ruggles's earliest economics publication (1940), the opening essay in Part Three, was an entry in a statistical debate about a conjecture in Keynes's *General Theory,* namely that, while money wage rates move procyclically, real wage rates move countercyclically. John Dunlop, then a young Harvard faculty member, challenged Keynes's conjecture with empirical evidence. Ruggles, writing before his graduation from Harvard College in 1939, convincingly questioned Dunlop's findings by means of simple but ingenious statistical tests.

The use of microdata on a macroissue was to become typical Ruggles methodology, exemplified in the remaining three articles in Part Three. One took up the issue of price flexibility in cyclical depression. Richard first converted a popular, but vague hypothesis, that price inflexibilities in concentrated industries make recessions worse, into an economically meaningful question.

He then found, taking account of structural differences among industries, no evidence that concentration or monopoly made prices rigid.

The remaining two essays use disaggregated Social Security files and Current Population Surveys to obtain informative descriptions of earnings profiles and of employment, unemployment and labor force participation. These articles are living demonstrations of the worth of the Ruggles research strategy.

Preface

Prices are the *sine qua non* of economists and the bread and butter issue for politicians. Only in a timeless and spaceless world where tastes and technology remain unchanged can prices be identified. Yet paradoxically, for both the pure and impure theorist, prices provide the core for analyzing highly generalized worlds that do not exist. For more mundane economists and for politicians, prices are basic for measuring change over time and space. The essays in this volume are divided into three parts. Part One is concerned with three pricing systems and the role of prices in the theories of value and income distribution. Part Two focuses on the problems of measuring price change over time and space. Part Three examines the behavior of prices, costs, wage rates and earnings in the economy.

PART ONE   PRICE THEORY

The Welfare Basis of the Marginal Cost Pricing Principle, Recent Developments in the Theory of Marginal Cost Pricing and **Discriminatory and Competitive Pricing** are the initial three essays in Price Theory and they are all drawn from the doctoral dissertation of Nancy D. Ruggles. In 1946–47, when she entered Radcliffe as a first-year graduate student in economics, the 'new welfare economics' and 'marginal cost pricing' had gained wide acceptance. In order to understand these doctrines more fully, she chose for her doctoral thesis the topic *Resource Allocation and Pricing Systems* under the direction of Edward Mason in industrial organization and Wassily Leontief in economic theory. The thesis was completed in July 1948 in New Haven, and Paul Samuelson was designated as the third examiner. As a member of the editorial board of the *Review of Economic Studies*, Samuelson recommended publishing the chapters of the dissertation concerned with marginal cost pricing. The chapter on discriminatory pricing has never been published. Yet, Nancy viewed discriminatory pricing as a central topic in the analysis of both resource allocation and the distribution of income.

The Value of Value Theory was written for a session on 'Industrial Pricing' at the 1953 meetings of the American Economic Association. This paper is based on previous research relating to the behavior of prices and wages (see

Part Three on Price Behavior), and a proposed research project on the price–cost behavior of manufacturing establishments in the Census of Manufactures. This 'Price–Cost Project' was subsequently funded by the Social Science Research Council and the Bureau of the Census. The data processing was programmed in machine language by Nancy Ruggles on the Univac I at the Census Bureau. Thousands of computer tapes were involved, and the price–cost project absorbed much of the research activity during the following decade and again in the early 1980s when, with the help of Orin Hansen and Catherine Viscoli at Yale, we finally managed to develop the 'Longitudinal Establishment Data' (LED) file of microdata at the Bureau of the Census.

PART TWO   PRICE MEASUREMENT

During the late 1950s both politicians and economists became greatly concerned with the problem of inflation and questions were raised as to whether the price indexes developed by the federal government correctly measured price change in the economy. Congressional hearings were held, and a review of price indexes was undertaken.

The Wholesale Price Index was written as Part V of the Stigler Committee report in 1961 on *The Price Statistics of the Federal Government: Review, Appraisal and Recommendations*. The Stigler Committee consisted of George Stigler, chairman, Dorothy Brady, Edward Denison, Philip McCarthy, Albert Rees, Richard Ruggles and Boris Swerling. The report covered all price data collected by the federal government, and made many recommendations. Several studies were undertaken by the National Bureau on behalf of the Committee. In particular, Zvi Griliches undertook a study of automobile prices in which he introduced the concept of hedonic price indexes. Thirty-five years later, the upward bias of the cost of living index was again investigated by the Boskin Committee. The focus was on the possible overstatement of inflation, and on whether the Consumer Price Index overstated price increases from the point of view of indexing social security payments. The findings of the Boskin Committee were quite consistent with those of the Stigler Committee, but the conclusions drawn from them were more readily accepted by both politicians and economists.

Measuring the Cost of Quality was written for the magazine *Challenge* in 1961, and included, in a more popular form, testimony relating to the Consumer Price Index that had been presented in hearings before the Joint Economic Committee of Congress during 1958 and 1959.

Domestic Price Statistics: Their Reliability as History and Their Usefulness for Economic Policy was written for hearings on this topic held by the Joint Economic Committee in 1966. This was five years after the Stigler

Committee report, and the problem of using price indexes as a basis for economic policy continued to be controversial.

Redundancy in Price Indexes for International Comparisons: A Stepwise Regression Analysis (1966) was a progress report by Nancy Ruggles when she was a research associate at the Yale Economic Growth Center and a Consultant to the Agency for International Development. This analysis of international price comparisons involved using data provided by the United Nations Economic Commission for Latin America, the United States Department of State and the Brookings Institution. Orin Hansen at Yale did much of the computer programming that was required. The objective of this research was to develop more efficient methods for constructing international price comparisons. This line of research was terminated when Nancy and Richard Ruggles moved their research activity from the Yale Economic Growth Center to the National Bureau of Economic Research in New York and Washington, DC. This technique of examining redundancy was subsequently used by Richard Ruggles in *The Wholesale Price Index: Review and Evaluation,* in 1970.

Price Indexes and International Price Comparisons had its origin in research undertaken for the Agency for International Development, the Yale Growth Center and the United Nations Economic Commission for Latin America (ECLA) in Santiago, Chile. ECLA had collected price and quantity data from 20 Latin American countries on 270 commodities for the period 1960–62. In 1968 a memorial volume was being undertaken in honor of Irving Fisher's 100th birthday. Given Fisher's extensive work on price indexes, it seemed appropriate that a project exploring international price indexes using the ECLA data be published in such a volume.

The Wholesale Price Index: Review and Evaluation (1977) took place a decade after the original review by the Stigler Committee. It was initiated by Albert Rees who was the Director of the Council on Wage and Price Stability under President Nixon, and who had served on the original Stigler Price Review Committee. The Bureau of Labor Statistics cooperated fully with this study, making available the original price observations collected from individual producers. Much of the computer processing of data was done at Yale University by Orin Hansen and at the National Bureau of Economic Research in New York under the supervision of Charlotte Boshan. It was found that the Wholesale Price Index was grossly inadequate and that the Bureau of Labor Statistics had done little to implement the Stigler Committee's recommendations.

PART THREE   PRICE BEHAVIOR

The Relative Movements of Real and Money Wage Rates was written by

Richard Ruggles in 1939–40 for a course taught by Joseph Schumpeter. At that time, the neo-classical and Keynesian view that wages were 'sticky' relative to other prices in the economy was being challenged by a number of empirical studies — including a study by John Dunlop at Harvard. The paper concluded that the three studies examined did not successfully refute the neo-classical and Keynesian views with respect to wage and price behavior in the economy.

The Nature of Price Flexibility and the Determinants of Relative Price Changes in the Economy was written for a National Bureau of Economic Research Conference on 'Business Concentration and Price Policy' in 1955. The essay is based primarily on the unpublished Ph.D. dissertation of Richard Ruggles, 'Price Structure and Distribution over the Cycle'. The thesis was written under Joseph Schumpeter (Business Cycles) and Edward Mason (Industrial Organization), with Wassily Leontief (Economic Theory) as the third examiner. Although the Ph.D. thesis had its origin in the controversy about the stickiness of wages relative to prices, it was greatly influenced by Kalecki's *Essays on Economic Fluctuations*, and Lange's *Price Flexibility and Employment*. This essay attempted to demonstrate how prices changed relative to costs in different industries and kinds of economic activity.

Price Stability and Economic Growth in the United States (1962) was written primarily for German and Latin American audiences who were interested in the economic developments in the United States. The article was intended to summarize much of the material relating to price measurement, price behavior, output and employment in the United States since World War II that had been presented in various reports and testimony by Richard and Nancy Ruggles.

Chronic Inflation in the United States, 1950–73 was written for a volume honoring Felipe Pazos in 1976. We had become well acquainted with Pazos during the Alliance for Progress and the 'Committee of Nine'. Pazos had published a study on *Chronic Inflation in Latin America*, and it seemed highly appropriate to apply the same type of analysis in 'Chronic Inflation in the United States, 1950–73', analyzing the price behavior of the United States economy in the post-World War II period.

The Anatomy of Earnings Behavior (1977) was developed as part of a larger project at Yale on 'The Measurement of Economic and Social Performance' (MESP) — (see **Macro–Micro Analysis**) supported by the National Science Foundation. This project had as its objective the utilization of micro- and macrodata in a more integrated manner for understanding how the behavior of individuals and enterprises related to the behavior of the macroeconomic system. For the project on the longitudinal analysis of earnings, 50 large reels of computer tapes of 'Longitudinal Employer–Employee Data' (LEED file) on the earnings for 700,000 individuals were obtained from the Social Security Administration — with changes in computer technology, within a year the complete set of data shortly fitted on five computer tapes. (In terms of 1998 personal computers, such a data set would fit easily on a single CD-ROM.) These longitudinal microdata made it possible to analyze how the earnings changed for individuals of different age, sex and race. William Parke at Yale was responsible for much of the computer programming of the LEED data.

The Measurement of the Supply and Use of Labor (1979) represented a further attempt to utilize microdata in the development of macroeconomic information. By reprocessing the Current Survey of Population samples, it was feasible to take into account individuals who were working part time and wanted to work full time and other individuals who had given up looking for work. Since the microdata reported data for individuals in different Standard Statistical Metropolitan Areas, it was also possible to examine the change in wage rates in local areas in relation to the levels of unemployment in those areas.

I am particularly indebted to Glena Ames and Kevin Foster for their valuable assistance in preparing the volumes of essays of Nancy D. Ruggles and myself. Glena Ames, of the Cowles Foundation at Yale, helped scan into the computer a large volume of reprints and manuscripts for the various volumes. She redrew diagrams and reformatted tables and texts. Kevin Foster, in the Economics Department at Yale, helped select the essays to be included in the various volumes, prepared abstracts of the essays and edited the prefaces. The volumes of essays could not have been completed without them.

Richard Ruggles, May 1998

Abstracts

PART ONE   PRICE THEORY

1. The Welfare Basis of the Marginal Cost Pricing Principle
   Nancy D. Ruggles (1949)

An examination of nineteenth-century utility theory and the treatment of decreasing cost industries by Marshall and Pigou reveals that the marginal cost pricing principle had its intellectual roots in neo-classical economic theory. However, it was Pareto's attempt to escape the necessity for inter-personal comparisons in the formulation of optimum welfare that led to the 'new' welfare economics. A critical review of the lively debate that took place on this topic during the 1930s indicates that by 1938, despite the varying views, the new welfare economics became well established and was accepted as the basis for the marginal cost pricing principle.

2. Recent Developments in the Theory of Marginal Cost Pricing
   Nancy D. Ruggles (1949)

Hotelling's 1938 article on 'The General Welfare in Relation to Problems of Taxation and Railway and Utility Rates' served as the basis for what became known as the 'marginal cost pricing principle'. A wide spectrum of economic theorists, general economists and specialists in applied fields, such as public utilities, became involved in the controversy about marginal cost pricing. A critical review of this literature reveals, however, that setting prices equal to marginal cost in decreasing cost industries such as public utilities would result in the violation of the marginal conditions elsewhere in the economic system. Every pricing system results in some income distribution, and no substantial re-distribution of income is possible without changing that price system, for instance, by altering the marginal conditions on labor and leisure, in the case of an income tax. For this reason, it is imperative that the question of interpersonal valuations be taken specifically into account.

of the wholesale price reporting is inadequate and subject to error. As a consequence, it is recommended that the wholesale price index be revised to take account of the universe of total sales and purchases of commodities other than at the retail level, organized around an input–output framework at the 5-digit level of commodity classification.

6. Measuring the Cost of Quality
   Richard Ruggles (1961)

   The Consumer Price Index is used to measure the amount of inflation taking place in the economy. However, due to its failure to take quality change and new products into account, it overstates the rate of inflation and gives readings that may result in policies of slow growth and high unemployment. The defects in the Consumer Price Index are also inherent in the other price indexes that are used to measure the change in real national output and economic growth.

7. Domestic Price Statistics: Their Reliability as History and Their Usefulness for Economic Policy
   Richard Ruggles (1966)

   Price indexes have proved to be woefully inadequate as long-run historical indicators. In an economy where product change and new products are the hallmark of economic progress, price indexes that do not and cannot take such changes into account are bound to provide misleading information. Furthermore, in even the short run, the existing aggregate price indexes are not adequate for taking into account the special circumstances of individual groups in society. The apparent trade-off between price inflation and unemployment may not in fact exist. On the other hand, the attempt to increase the minimum wage to offset rising prices may also result in wage and price spiral. Other solutions might be undertaken, such as indexing social security to the cost of a basket of goods that the elderly consume or providing indexed bonds to compensate fixed income groups whose cost of living has increased.

8. Redundancy in Price Indexes for International Comparisons: A Stepwise Regression Analysis
   Nancy D. Ruggles (1966)

   Improved international price comparisons are essential for understanding the process of economic growth, planning for economic development, and analyzing balance of payments problems. The basic purpose of this essay is methodological. It is designed to develop techniques and methods for price measurements which will, for a given cost, produce the best possible price measurements. This study develops price relatives or price ratios as an alternative to the market basket approach. The familiar Paasche and Laspeyres indexes can be treated as weighted averages of price ratios, where the weights are specified functions of market baskets. But other weights that give the importance of different price relatives can be used as well, for instance expenditure shares. Possible price indexes are constructed with the administrative data used to determine cost-of-living allowances by the US Department of State and the United Nations in conjunction with data provided by the Economic Commission for Latin America and the Brookings Institution. These show that many price items are redundant, and stepwise regression analysis can be useful in exploring this problem, reducing the redundancy and providing weighting systems.

9. Price Indexes and International Price Comparisons
   Richard Ruggles (1968)

   Traditional price indexes (including those of Irving Fisher) have focused on measuring price change in a given country. It is possible, however, to use price indexes to analyze the difference in prices across different countries. Using data collected by ECLA on 270 commodities for 19 Latin American countries in 1960 to 1961, a variety of different index number formulas were computed — including the Fisher Ideal, Laspeyres, Paasche, Palgrave and Walsh index formulas. These computations show that, while the different indexes show only minor differences over time (although quality changes are poorly measured, so only over short periods of time), there is substantial variation across countries. The Paasche and Laspeyres indexes give substantially different results because there is much more substitution of goods between countries than within a country over time. Arbitrary weightings of these two indexes, such as Fisher's ideal index, do not satisfy the circularity conditions vital to cross-country comparisons. A system based on averaging expenditure weights seems more reasonable.

10. The Wholesale Price Index: Review and Evaluation
    Richard Ruggles (1977)

    This study was commissioned by the Council on Wage and Price Stability and was based on a detailed analysis of the Wholesale Price Index published by the Bureau of Labor Statistics. Its conclusions are: (1) the scope and coverage of the index is inadequate, (2) the classification system used is inappropriate, (3) the lack of integration between the wholesale price data and other economic data impairs its usefulness, (4) the intermingling of order and shipment prices results in data that are difficult to interpret, (5) the mixed use of both purchasers' and producers' prices, combined with insufficient accounting for discounts, rebates, and special prices, obscures cyclical fluctuations, (6) the use of specification pricing omits most of the quality change taking place in the economy, (7) the system of weighting used by BLS results in misleading price indexes and (8) the lack of probability sampling prevents the estimation of sampling errors and reduces the efficiency of the collection effort.

PART THREE   PRICE BEHAVIOR

11. The Relative Movements of Real and Money Wage Rates
    Richard Ruggles (1940)

    Three empirical studies by Dunlop, Richardson and Tarshis concerning the relative movement of real and money wage rates are analyzed. It was found that (1) on the basis of statistical relationships and (2) on conceptual grounds, none of these studies has successfully refuted the relationship between real wages and prices as formulated by Keynes and Marshall, that real and money wages would move in opposite directions. The data from two of the studies are reexamined and it appears that the movement of money wage rates is such that the degree of variation upward is greater than that downward, so wages are more flexible up than down. Money wage rates also tend to rise in prosperity, while cost-of-living changes do not follow the business cycle so closely. There seems no clear relationship between money wage rates and the cost of living.

12. The Nature of Price Flexibility and the Determinants of Relative Price Changes in the Economy
    Richard Ruggles (1955)

    A critical review of the literature on price flexibility is presented, and an empirical analysis is provided of the wage and price behavior of the different sectors of the United States economy during the Depression of the 1930s. On the basis of the analysis of the data for the different sectors, it was found that the prices of producers tend to move in accordance with their directs costs, computed as the weighted average of labor and material costs. In agriculture, prices were determined primarily by the shape of marginal costs and demand for agricultural products. The prices of coal and other mineral products were related to the changes in wage costs since wages are a large fraction of total costs. Manufacturing prices were directly related to wage and material costs. The distributive industries passed along the increases in their costs. There was no evidence to support Gardiner Means' theory that industrial concentration or monopoly was responsible for rigid prices in the economy.

13. Price Stability and Economic Growth in the United States
    Richard Ruggles and Nancy D. Ruggles (1962)

    Examining the data on prices, wages, and productivity since the Depression, in most industries prices followed labor and materials costs, as there is a general tendency for gross margins to remain constant. Broadly speaking, when productivity changes are small, prices depend upon the level of demand and the behavior of wages. Productivity rises make possible rising wages with falling producer costs. Too much political attention has been given to price stability rather than the maintenance of employment, but the two goals are related. With high employment and capacity utilization, there are greater incentives for businesses to make productivity-enhancing investments. While the automatic stabilizers in place have moderated recessions, they have also strangled the booms and so kept down productivity. Policies to stop prices should not be concerned with keeping demand low but rather encouraging investment that will lead to rises in productivity that will dampen cost pressures.

14. Chronic Inflation in the United States, 1950–73
    Nancy D. Ruggles and Richard Ruggles (1976)

    Felipe Pazos published a study about chronic inflation in Latin America and observed that price increases in Latin America were not merely temporary disturbances — rather they were chronic phenomena. Over the period from 1950 to 1970, the annual price increases were not closely related to the fluctuations in output, and generally it was not excess demand that triggered price rises. Wage changes were not very sensitive to the level of employment, rather the wage–price spiral. These findings about the nature of chronic inflation were found to be relevant to the experience of the United States over the period from 1950 to 1973. The US also saw a continual rise in prices and wages, even when output and employment declined. Wages rose despite unemployment, and were not related to the change in output. Further, there is a strong positive relation between changes in output and in productivity, while prices rise most in the sectors with low productivity growth.

15. The Anatomy of Earnings Behavior
    Nancy D. Ruggles and Richard Ruggles (1977)

    The Longitudinal Employer–Employee Data (LEED) file consists of a 1 percent longitudinal sample of individual social security records. Quarterly data on wages and salaries are provided for approximately 700,000 individuals over the period from 1957 to 1969. These data are analyzed to show the differences in wages and salaries received by individuals of different ages, sex and race and the pattern of changes over time. The age–earnings profiles for individual years are quite different from the cohort earning patterns over time. Sharp differences are found in the level and change in earnings over time for individuals classified by sex and race.

16. The Measurement of the Supply and Use of Labor
   Richard Ruggles (1979)

The data contained in the Current Population Surveys over the period 1973–77 that were used to estimate the level of unemployment in the economy were re-tabulated to calculate the unemployment rate in terms of 'man-hours' rather than in terms of the number of unemployed workers. This involved taking into account part-time workers who wanted to work full time and discouraged workers who had given up looking for work. The level of unemployment by this measure is approximately twice the percentage of the labor force that are reported as unemployed. In addition, an analysis of the relation between the level of unemployment in Standard Metropolitan Areas to the change in average hourly earnings showed no significant relationship — this suggested that at the level of local labor markets there was no trade-off between the level of unemployment and the change in wage rates. The paper also discusses the measurement of productivity and advances the hypothesis that the slowdown in productivity growth is due mainly to the recession, as well as a shift of economic activity to the services, where the productivity measures are poorer.

List of Tables and Figures

TABLES

FIGURES

PART ONE

PRICE THEORY

1. The Welfare Basis of the Marginal Cost Pricing Principle

Nancy D. Ruggles
Radcliffe College

Marginal cost pricing has frequently been advocated in recent years as the one system of pricing which will yield an optimum allocation of resources. This prominence of marginal cost pricing in recent economic literature springs partly from the political significance of using marginal cost as a basis of price policy, and partly from the nicety of the theoretical apparatus involved. As it is usually conceived, the essence of marginal cost pricing is that producers will price their products so that each consumer is permitted to purchase all products at the marginal cost of production, without regard to whether or not total costs are covered by receipts from sales. The system thus necessarily involves subsidizing all producers who operate under conditions of decreasing costs. This article will attempt to evaluate the validity of the theoretical apparatus and in addition will explore some of its practical implications.

Present-day proponents of marginal cost pricing almost universally couch their arguments in terms of the precepts of the 'new' welfare economics. To speak of any pricing principle outside of a welfare context is in the last analysis of doubtful meaning, since fundamentally methods of resource allocation can only be evaluated in welfare terms. For this reason, this paper will begin with a restatement in bare outline of those principles of modern welfare economics which are basic to the consideration of pricing systems. This section will serve to point out the specific assumptions which underlie almost all current discussions of marginal cost pricing; it is intended only as a brief summary statement of the current position. A bare restatement of the present formulations of points involved is not sufficient, however, to give meaningful content to a field which has as long and complex a history as has welfare theory. This can only be done by setting the present welfare framework into the context of its historical development. By tracing the evolution of the welfare principles,

This chapter first appeared in *Review of Economic Studies*, **17** (2), 1949.

their meaning as criteria for judging pricing systems becomes much clearer. Section 1 is concerned entirely with the development of these general welfare considerations.

But marginal cost pricing has not always been advocated on welfare grounds. Welfare considerations provide all the tools which are necessary to make an abstract analysis of the current statement of the marginal cost pricing principle, but their history alone does not show how and why the marginal cost pricing principle evolved or what its implications for practical policy are. Section 2 is concerned with marginal cost pricing in its narrower sense, tracing its gradual evolution from the increasing and decreasing cost theories of Marshall and its shift to reliance on welfare arguments. A further article, that will appear in a forthcoming issue of this journal, will bring the history up to date and will evaluate it in terms of the assumptions upon which it is based.

1. THE WELFARE BASIS OF THE MARGINAL COST PRICING PRINCIPLE

Summary Statement

The new welfare economics starts with the basic premise that it is impossible to make interpersonal comparisons of utility. It then considers what statements can be made regarding the efficiency of the resource allocating mechanism, taking care to avoid any necessity for interpersonal comparisons. An increase in the general welfare, on this basis, is defined as a change which will improve the positions of some persons (in their own estimation), without worsening anyone else's position. This definition is not as restrictive as might at first appear. By making use of the 'compensation principle', the number of situations about which judgments can be made is considerably broadened. In a situation in which, by some proposed change, some individuals would gain and others would lose, it may be possible for those who gain to recompense the losers for all of their loss, and still have some gain left over. If, then, the change is made and such compensation is carried out, the situation becomes one in which there are gainers but not losers, and a judgment regarding efficiency can be made. As will be brought out below, this argument does not imply that the change and the compensation should both be carried through.

The implementation of these welfare assumptions in the form of the marginal conditions for maximum welfare springs directly from the basic definitions themselves. These marginal conditions can be divided into two sets: those relating to production and those relating to exchange.

The marginal production conditions are those ensuring that the factors of production will be used in the most efficient manner. In the first place, the use of an input factor by any one firm must, at the margin, yield the same amount of a specific product as its use by any other firm. Otherwise, it would be possible by shifting factors among firms to produce more of that product with the same quantity of input factors. The first condition, therefore, is that the marginal rate of transformation, or in monetary terms the marginal cost, must be equal for all firms producing the same product.

Second, with regard to interrelations among the different input factors, it must not be possible to rearrange the combination of factors used so as to yield a greater total production. Within the limits of technical requirements, specific types of production can often be carried out by a number of different combinations of the factors of production. When two factors are used in several types of production, maximum efficiency will have been obtained only if the marginal productivities of the two factors bear the same relationship to each other for every use where both are employed. Where this condition is not met, it would be possible, without changing the total quantity of the two factors, to increase output in one line of production without decreasing it in any other line simply by recombining the factors employed in producing the different products. The failure to meet this condition would be reflected in monetary terms in a free exchange economy by the fact that costs could be reduced by substituting one factor for the other.

The marginal conditions of exchange require that the goods, which are produced in this most efficient manner, be in accordance with consumers' preferences. In the first place, the marginal utility to each consumer of the factors of production transformed into consumers' goods must be equal in all uses. If it were not, it would be possible to increase welfare by shifting the factors of production from producing one type of consumers' good to another. In the second place, every individual must allocate his time between earning income and enjoying leisure in such a way that he cannot increase his satisfaction either by reducing his leisure and increasing his income or by reducing his income and extending his leisure.

All of these marginal conditions of maximum welfare lie within the restrictions of the new welfare economics and proceed directly from the definition of an optimum as a situation in which no one can be made better off without making someone else worse off. The implications of these marginal conditions, and the implications of the assumptions upon which they are based, can best be demonstrated if the system is considered within the context of its historical development. The next section will be devoted to a brief discussion of the more important contributors to this line. Most of the argument will be very familiar to many readers, but it is useful to put it down in one place in order to trace the development of the ideas and to establish the basic assumptions involved.

The Development of the New Welfare Economics

The major difference between the older welfare economics and the so-called new welfare economics lies in the treatment of interpersonal comparisons of utility. Many of the early writers in the field of welfare recognized the difficulty involved in making such comparisons, but argued that even though the comparison of utilities between individuals involved ethical judgments, such judgments were necessary if economic analysis was to be significant. For some time, assumptions about interpersonal comparisons of utility were an essential part of the existing body of economic and social doctrine. Bentham's utilitarianism, which proposed the greatest sum total of happiness as the proper criterion of social policy, not only assumed that individuals' utilities were additive, but further postulated that the utility of each individual should count equally. Mill (1896, Book II, Ch. 2, para. 4; Book V, Ch. 9, para. 2), brought up on Bentham, advocated the diffusion of wealth on the utilitarian ground of equality of individuals, although he nowhere examined the comparability of individual utilities in detail. Marshall's concept of consumers' surplus was also essentially based on the addition of individual utilities. He recognized in passing that consumers' surplus only affords a measure of surplus satisfaction if the fact that the same sum of money represents different amounts of pleasure to different people is disregarded — but he then proceeded as if this difference in the utility of money to different individuals could, in fact, be disregarded (Marshall, 1936, p. 128). In similar fashion, virtually all of the literature of this period either assumed away or ignored the problem of interpersonal comparison of utilities.

A somewhat more explicit handling of utility is to be found in those writers who discussed the theory of taxation, of whom Edgeworth is perhaps the prime example. In a series of articles on the theory of taxation, Edgeworth (1897) argued that taxation of individuals should be differentiated according to size of income, permanence of income, marital status, number of children, age and other attributes. But nowhere did Edgeworth suggest that the utility of individuals possessing the same attributes might not be comparable. In fact, in considering the effect of different incomes he introduced a discourse on the subject of whether or not Bernoulli's law (that utility diminishes in inverse ratio to income) understates or overstates the true situation (Edgeworth, 1897, pp. 557 ff.), and his discussion of the question of whether each taxpayer should sacrifice an equal absolute amount of utility or an equal proportion of total utility implicitly assumed that the comparison of individuals' utilities is valid.

Wicksell (1934, pp. 77–93) considered the problem of the comparability of individual marginal utilities in a manner remarkably similar to Edgeworth's. He recognized that the problem of the comparability of utilities between different persons exists, and that in special cases it would have to be taken into account. In general, however, he believed that it would be possible to abstract from individual variations in all respects except social differences and the distribution of property.

Wicksell's welfare system was one of the first to contain an explicit development of the set of marginal conditions necessary to attain maximum welfare. These marginal conditions obviously did not all originate with him; there were many contributors to the line, and from it emerged the exchange conditions to which almost all economists agreed and which they all integrated into their systems of thought. To trace the actual development of these exchange conditions would, in fact, involve studying the origin and development of marginal utility theory in conjunction with the theory of value and exchange. The marginal conditions of *exchange* which Wicksell (1934, pp. 37 ff.) developed did not depend on interpersonal utility; in fact in this connection he even discussed the difficulty of measuring utility and the meaninglessness of any measure which can be developed, and he was very careful to point out that his exchange conditions were dependent only on *intra*personal comparisons. Some of the other marginal conditions which he developed, however, did depend directly on the assumption that interpersonal comparisons are possible. For example, he pointed out that a rich man carries his consumption so far that the marginal utility of the last unit consumed is little or nothing to him, whereas a poor man must discontinue his consumption of practically all commodities at a point where they possess for him a very high marginal utility, and Wicksell (1934, p. 77) agreed with Bohm-Bawerk that an exchange of income between the rich man and the poor man might lead to a much greater total utility for both together (and therefore for society as a whole). In other words, he argued that unless the marginal utility of income is identical for all individuals, welfare could be increased by shifting income from those having low marginal utilities to those with higher marginal utilities. On this ground, he was able to advocate such measures as minimum wages and tariffs, even though these measures may interfere with the marginal conditions of exchange. The fact that people have different incomes, he felt, imposes limitations on the effectiveness of the marginal conditions of exchange in producing maximum welfare.

With this background, it is not surprising that Pigou wove into the fabric of his analysis the assumption that interpersonal comparisons of utility are possible. Although he never actually discussed the matter, his use of the concept of social net product implied that individual satisfactions are additive fully as much as did Marshall's use of consumers' surplus. Pigou used the size and the distribution of the national dividend to indicate aggregate economic welfare. Provided that the dividend accruing to the poor is not diminished, he argued, increases in the aggregate national dividend of the community (unless they result from coercing people to work more than they wish to) carry with them increases in economic welfare. Furthermore, he argued that changes in the distribution of the national dividend in favor of the poor (except in very special circumstances) will also increase economic welfare. He mentioned in passing that an essential condition for the latter to be true is the similarity of temperament among members of the community, but apparently considered this condition so obviously true as to require no further discussion (Pigou, 1929, Chs 7, 8, esp. p. 91).

Pigou in effect implied a set of marginal conditions of production when he said that the marginal social net product of resources in each use must be equal in order to maximize the national dividend. His proof is the demonstration that if these marginal conditions are not met, the aggregate national dividend could be increased by removing resources from uses in which the marginal social net product is low and employing them in uses with higher marginal social net products (Pigou, 1929, p. 138). That this concept is based on interpersonal comparisons is evident, since it rests on the use of the national dividend as an indicator of welfare.

The various assumptions with regard to interpersonal comparisons of utility which were made by the earlier writers on welfare economics do not necessarily invalidate the structure which they erected under these assumptions, but the conclusions which are derived from their analysis must be deemed the result of the special assumptions which were made, not of the analytical framework of the system alone. At an early stage in the development of welfare economics, attempts were made to separate the general framework of welfare analysis from these special assumptions with regard to interpersonal comparisons of utility. One of the first such attempts was Pareto's. His efforts and those of his successors have yielded a welfare structure which undertakes to determine what conclusions can be reached analytically without any assumptions at all with respect to interpersonal comparisons.

Pareto (1909, pp. 354 ff.), in order to escape the necessity for interpersonal comparisons of utility, formulated a special definition of the general welfare. He defined a point of maximum welfare as a position from which there is no possible movement which would make everyone in the system better off. If a given displacement from the original position which would increase the welfare of some persons would necessarily result in a decrease in the welfare of others, it is not possible with his definition to determine whether aggregate welfare would be increased or decreased by the change. In other words, once both positive and negative increments of individual welfare have taken place, the situations before and after the change become noncomparable, and are outside the scope of the Paretian welfare system.

Basic to Pareto's definition of the welfare optimum is his explanation of it in terms of the well-known indifference diagram relating to exchange between two individuals. A similar diagram is shown in Figure 1.1. For the first individual, the axes are OX and OY; for the second, $\omega\alpha$ and $\omega\beta$. The indifference

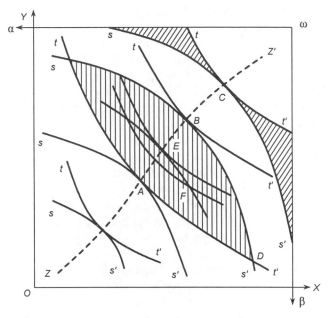

Figure 1.1 Indifference Diagram

curves *tt'* pertain to the first individual, and the curves *ss'* pertain to the second. An increase in satisfaction for the first individual is represented by proceeding in the direction from *O* to ω; for the second person, satisfaction increases in the direction from ω to *O*. Under these conditions, point *C*, located at a point where the indifference curves of the two individuals are tangent, represents a position of maximum welfare in Pareto's sense. Any movement away from *C*, no matter what the direction, would result in a loss for at least one of the individuals. A movement in the direction of ω involves a gain for the first individual, but at the same time a loss for the second. A movement in the direction of *O*, of course, reverses this situation: the second individual gains but the first loses. Finally, any movement in the direction of *X* or *Y* will make both individuals worse off. Point *D*, on the other hand, does not represent such an optimum. From this point, a movement into the area which is vertically shaded would increase the welfare of both individuals. But there is no one special position within this area which represents, relative to point *D*, the best of all possible positions. A series of optima exists, at the points of tangency of the various indifference curves — points *E*, *A* and *B*. These optimum points cannot be compared with each other because they represent positions in which one person is better off at the expense of the other, but all of them have one thing in common: they are all superior to point *D*. Pareto did not elaborate further on the nature of the optima, but it will facilitate later analysis if several points are brought out somewhat more clearly at this stage.

Each point on the line Z-Z' connecting the various points of tangency of the two sets of indifference curves (known as the contract line because of its use in another connection) represents a position of maximum welfare, according to Pareto's definition. But each point on this line can only be said to be superior to points within a certain limited area. Point C, for example, is only superior to points lying within the shaded area. Only if the starting position lies in this area can a movement to C improve the general welfare.

With respect to point D, all points on the line Z-Z' between A and B are optimum points. Point F represents an improvement over D, since it leaves both individuals on higher indifference curves, but it is not an optimum. It does not follow from this, however, that positions A and B are superior to position F. Point F is not comparable with either A or B, even though all three are comparable with point D. The fact that points A and B are relative optima and point F is not, is irrelevant. There is an area within which lie positions which are superior to F, but A and B do not lie within this area. Likewise, there are positions for which A and B represent relative optima, but F is not one of them. In common sense terms, all this means is that two situations can exist which cannot be compared with each other, even though each of them can be compared with the same third situation. Simple examples of this phenomenon are easily constructed. For instance, suppose that two individuals, A and B, are both to be given an increase in income. If A is given $50 and B is given $25, both are undoubtedly better off than before. Alternatively, if B had been given the $50 increase while A got the $25, each would still have considered himself better off than before the increase. Each of these moves can thus be compared with the original situation without resorting to interpersonal comparisons. But, any judgment about whether A or B should get the larger increase necessarily involves interpersonal comparisons and, therefore, the two alternative moves cannot be compared with each other without making such interpersonal comparisons.

The Paretian welfare system, by not admitting interpersonal comparisons, thus does not arrive at any one point of maximum welfare; rather, it sets up an infinite number of noncomparable optima. Under this system, it is only possible to evaluate changes when they either make all individuals better off or else make all individuals worse off. A situation can be called superior to another only if the change results in advantage to some and disadvantage to none. This aspect of Pareto's welfare system will be important in the evaluation of the marginal cost pricing principle in the second part of this paper.

Enrico Barone (1935), writing on production in a collectivist state, set forth as the criteria of general welfare about the same conditions as those suggested by Pareto, but he went further than the simple statement of the optimum by introducing the idea that an increase in the welfare of an individual (if prices are constant) can be expressed in terms of the excess money income he would have over what was necessary to maintain his original level of welfare. Similarly, a decrease in an individual's welfare could be measured by the amount of money income which would be needed to return him to his former welfare level. This device does not increase the comparability of different situations, of course, but it does open up the possibility of further analysis. For example, suppose that a change occurs which affects only three individuals: the welfare of *A* and *B* is increased by the change, but that of *C* is decreased. If the assumptions of Pareto and Barone with respect to interpersonal comparisons are followed, this situation is not comparable with that which existed before the change. But it can be made comparable by transferring the gain (in terms of income) of individuals *A* and *B* to individual *C*. If, when this transfer has been made, individual *C* is more than recompensed for his loss, the general welfare can be said to have increased; no one is worse off than he originally was, and individual *C* is now better off. If, on the contrary, when the gains of *A* and *B* are transferred to *C*, they are not sufficient to bring him back to his original level, there has been a decrease in the general welfare. This principle of using transfers of income to bring incomparable situations into the area of comparability will become very important in the examination of the later developments of welfare economics. It should be noted at this stage that it is the actual transfer of income which makes comparison possible; the mere existence of the possibility of such transfer is not sufficient. In Barone's discussion (1935, pp. 256, 271), this distinction was not always made clear. At times, he seemed to indicate that a change which produces both positive and negative increments of welfare can be evaluated by determining whether there is an excess of positive over negative increments. Such a procedure is equivalent to declaring that the same amount of income would yield equivalent utility to all of the individuals involved and this, of course, involves interpersonal comparisons of utility.

Both Pareto and Barone developed some of the marginal conditions under the assumption that interpersonal comparisons are not possible. Pareto defined the marginal conditions of exchange in his demonstration of the meaning of an optimum. The demonstration that the indifference curves of two individuals between whom exchange is taking place would be tangent to each other at any point of optimum is equivalent to saying that the marginal rates of substitution between the two commodities are equal for the two individuals. Barone did not develop the marginal conditions explicitly, but they are implicit in his development of the 'collective maximum', in which he showed that the conditions for maximum welfare in a collective state are the same fundamental conditions of allocation and exchange as those which are characteristic of free enterprise. Both Pareto and Barone were most concerned with the proof that free competition will yield an optimum within the restrictions of the welfare system which does not admit interpersonal comparisons. Although Barone pointed out that free competition is not the only optimum or necessarily the best, he did not stress the point. Both writers (Pareto, 1909, p. 359; Barone, 1935, p. 283), in analyzing the possibility of multiple prices, indicated that with falling costs the utilization of differentiated prices may yield greater welfare than would a uniform price.

One of the earliest English language treatments of welfare which excluded interpersonal comparisons of utility was that of A.P. Lerner (1933). Lerner not only defined maximum welfare as a situation which would show itself in the impossibility of any individual being put into a preferred position without putting some other individual into a worse position, but he also stated that this situation was the social optimum relative to a given distribution of income among individuals. By setting up the optimum conditions in this form, Lerner provided the final element that was needed to build the structure of the new welfare economics. Lerner's treatment leads to a separation of the problems relating to the efficiency with which resource allocation is carried out from those relating to the desirability of given distributions of income. According to his view, the efficiency problem does not require interpersonal comparisons of utility, but the question of the distribution of income does.

Lerner's definition of the social optimum, relative to the given distribution of income, in effect contains the marginal conditions of production: the optimum, he said, is a situation in which the resources which are to be devoted to satisfying the wants of each individual are so allocated among the things he wants that his total satisfactions would not be increased by any transference of resources from the provision of any one of the things he gets to any other thing he wants. The marginal conditions of exchange Lerner expressed by the proviso that the situation is not an optimum as long as an individual can, by changing his pattern of consumption, move to a preferred position without placing any other individual on a lower indifference curve. His analysis is the same as that previously developed by Pareto. Incidentally, there is no recognition in Lerner's work of the previous contributions of Pareto and Barone on this subject, so that his exposition may very well represent an independent development, not merely an extension of what went before.

The work of Pareto and Barone was taken over directly, however, by Harold Hotelling (1938). The same definition of maximum welfare is applied directly to the problem of marginal cost pricing. Hotelling made one distinct contribution to the theory of interpersonal comparisons. This was the furthering of the concept of compensation — that an optimum can be achieved by a process of change plus a system of collections and compensations such that everyone will be better off than before. As a practical matter, however, he argued that in some cases the compensation need not necessarily be paid to those who suffer a decrease in welfare, i.e., that the general welfare can be purchased at the expense of sacrifices by some. Of course, this represents a departure from the original definition of the optimum which he had adopted; as long as some individuals do make sacrifices and others do gain, no judgment can be made about the general welfare without introducing interpersonal comparisons.

This question of whether or not compensation must be paid has been the subject of considerable controversy. Both Harrod (1938) and Robbins (1938) maintained that the gain of one group can be said to exceed the loss of others only if the individuals involved are treated as in some sense equal. The statement that social welfare is increased even though compensation is not paid to those whose welfare is lessened involves the proposition that there is an equal capacity for satisfaction on the part of economic subjects. The argument centered specifically around whether it could be said that an earlier repeal of the corn laws would have increased the general welfare. By the repeal the landlords would have suffered, but consumers in general would have benefited because of the lower price of grain. Harrod and Robbins argued that, under the given conditions, it could not necessarily be said that the repeal would have increased the general welfare, but Kaldor (1939) maintained that since it would have been possible to make everyone better off than before by paying some form of compensation to the landlords, it was unnecessary that the compensation actually be paid. The economist's case for repeal was valid, he said, and the fate of the landlords was irrelevant. On this basis, Kaldor suggested that welfare economics be divided into two parts, the first relating to production and the second to distribution. Hicks (1939) supported Kaldor's position by saying that sound policy with respect to efficiency is independent of interpersonal comparisons, and that questions of income distribution alone depend upon the valuation of utility.

In elaboration of the Kaldor–Hicks position, Scitovsky (1941a,b) presented an analysis which is more precise in its development. The criterion of an increase in welfare which he set up is a double one. To be able to say that a given change has increased the general welfare, he said, it must in the first place be possible, after the specified change has taken place, so to redistribute income that everyone is better off than before. In the second place, it must not be possible just by redistributing income without making the specified change to reach a position superior to that which would exist after that change. Applying this double criterion to Kaldor's argument, Scitovsky said that Kaldor's standard is one-sided. It considers only the original income distribution, but the test of increased welfare should also be made by using the income distribution which would result after the change. It may well be that a change will appear desirable according to the Kaldor criterion, but that once the change has been made the original position will appear to have been preferable after all. Because of this paradoxical possibility, Scitovsky thought that the double criterion would be necessary, but that when both parts of it were met the new situation could be said to be better than the old.

Scitovsky pointed out that by this criterion the change need not actually improve everyone's position; it is only necessary that for every possible distribution of income the change would improve everyone's position if it were to leave distribution unchanged. By so defining efficiency, Scitovsky felt that he had accomplished the separation of efficiency from distribution that Kaldor set out to make. The question of distribution, Scitovsky said, is a matter of ethics, not economics, and for analytical purposes must be kept strictly separate (although, of course, it cannot be disregarded). All statements concerning the national welfare are subject to modification by considerations of social justice, but these considerations of social justice should not be allowed to interfere with the analysis of questions of efficiency.

The implications of Scitovsky's work become somewhat clearer in connection with his statement that the problem of establishing a double criterion for welfare is essentially the same as the problem which is met in index number theory, and that the welfare comparisons made using it are valid in the same sense that the index number comparisons are valid. It will, therefore, be useful to consider in exactly what sense the development of the double criterion in the index number problem is similar and whether the argument is equally applicable to a system which rules out interpersonal comparisons of utility.

The type of index number problem to which Scitovsky refers can be illustrated by the problem of determining whether the set of goods consumed by an individual in one period represents a higher or lower standard of living (assuming no change in the individual's preferences) than the set of goods he consumes in a second period. If the quantities of goods change but their prices do not, the problem is, of course, a simple one. It is only necessary to compare the values of the goods consumed in the two periods; it follows directly that the standard of living is higher in the second period if the value of the goods consumed is greater. The individual could have reached his original standard of living by spending less, so that the fact that he spends more in the second period must mean that he prefers the second combination of goods. The changed and increased expenditure is evidence of some increase in welfare. The same reasoning, of course, works in reverse if the value of the goods consumed in the second period is lower.

The problem arises in index number theory when the prices of the goods consumed, as well as their quantities, have changed between the two periods. In terms of the conventional symbols, the question is to compare $\Sigma p_1 q_1$ with $\Sigma p_2 q_2$. A direct comparison of the magnitude of the two value figures obviously provides no answer, since price changes, as well as quantity changes, are included. But in some cases it is possible to make an indirect comparison by using constant prices as weights. This is where the double criterion is necessary; two questions must be asked before a complete answer can be obtained. In the first place, it is necessary to ask whether the goods consumed in Period 2 have greater value than the goods consumed in Period 1, if both sets of goods are valued in terms of Period 1 prices. (For example, is $\Sigma p_1 q_1 < \Sigma p_1 q_2$?) In the second place, it is also necessary to ask whether it will still be true that the goods consumed in Period 2 have a greater value than those consumed in Period 1 if both are now valued in terms of Period 2 prices. (For example, $\Sigma p_2 q_1 < \Sigma p_2 q_2$?) Only if the answer to both questions is affirmative, higher in the second period than it was in the first, can it truly be said that the individual's standard of living is higher in the second period than it was in the first, i.e., that $\Sigma p_2 q_2 > \Sigma p_1 q_1$.

There is one step in this analysis which requires an assumption that has not yet been made explicit. It is not possible to proceed from the statements that $\Sigma p_1 q_1 < \Sigma p_1 q_2$ and $\Sigma p_2 q_1 < \Sigma p_2 q_2$ to the conclusion that $\Sigma p_1 q_1 > \Sigma p_2 q_2$ without establishing some relationship between the first two statements. Such a relationship can be established if it is assumed that the individual's satisfaction is a function only of the quantities of goods he gets, not of their prices. It then follows that, as far as the individual's welfare is concerned, $\Sigma p_1 q_1 = \Sigma p_2 q_1$ and $\Sigma p_1 q_2 < \Sigma p_2 q_2$. By substituting the appropriate equalities in the original statements the conclusion can be reached that $\Sigma p_1 q_1 < \Sigma p_2 q_2$.

Returning to Scitovsky's question of the general welfare in the economy, it is apparent that just as in the index number example above a change in price prevents direct comparisons, so, in the Kaldor case, the change in the distribution of income between the two situations also prevents direct comparisons. As is done in the index number problem, Scitovsky proposes to consider the direction of the change in welfare, using both the original distribution of income and the distribution of income resulting after the change as weighting systems; he is again attempting to compare indirectly that which cannot be compared directly. Like the index number case again, however, an assumption is required to connect the two statements which will exist for the two different income distributions. If the double criterion is to be adequate, this assumption must be that the general welfare is not a function of the weighting system used, i.e., the distribution of income — or to put it another way, any change in the distribution of income will leave total welfare unchanged. A shift in income from one individual to another, by this assumption, would not affect total welfare. Such an assumption not only admits interpersonal comparisons, but specifically requires that the utility of income be identical for all individuals in the system.

In spite of the elaborate system which has been erected, Pareto's original restrictions regarding specific changes, which involve one individual gaining at another's expense, have not been circumvented. Scitovsky removed one element of ambiguity from the previous welfare constructs. In addition he introduced the concept of a comparison of all possible distributions of income without a specific proposed feature with all possible distributions of income with that specific feature. This concept may prove to be an exceedingly useful one for studying the nature of economic systems, but it must be remembered that it applies only to the comparison of points with corresponding distributions of income. Situations with differing distributions of income still cannot be compared without making interpersonal comparisons.

Coming back to Kaldor and the corn laws, the final conclusion must be that it is impossible to tell whether a repeal of the corn laws alone would have increased total welfare; it is still not possible to say whether the loss to the landlords is or is not greater than the gain to the other sectors of the economy. It can be said with certainty that the repeal of the corn laws with compensation of the landlords would have increased total welfare over what it was with the corn laws in effect — but this, of course, does not mean that repealing the corn laws with compensation would necessarily have been better from a welfare point of view than repealing them without compensation. No economic judgment can be made on the latter without introducing interpersonal comparisons.

The question at issue can perhaps be made more readily apparent by passing from the corn laws to a somewhat different example. It might well be possible to demonstrate that, by Scitovsky's definition, allocating efficiency in the economy would be increased by a repeal of income taxes and the substitution of a head tax (since the head tax would have no adverse effect upon the incentive to work) and that it would be possible for those who gain by the change to compensate those who would lose. Few people would argue, however, that such a change in the tax structure *without compensation* is defensible on the ground that it would increase the general welfare.

Paul Samuelson (1938), Melvin Reder (1947), and most recently, Kenneth Arrow (1948a,b), have all recognized the necessity for paying compensation if an economic policy is to be advocated on the basis of the criteria established by the new welfare economics. Samuelson, in addition to considering the compensation problem, pointed out that the classical arguments regarding the desirability of free trade rest on the same sort of fallacious assumption that the particular optimum point reached on the contract curve is the best position; these arguments, he said, involve the comparison of different individuals' utilities about which it is assumed that nothing can be said. Arrow considered specifically the Scitovsky form of the compensation principle. Although he said that the Scitovsky form might lead to at least a partial ordering that would cover more cases than would the requirement that compensation actually be paid, his final conclusion is that the possibility of a consistent answer becomes more and more remote when the alternatives are expanded beyond two and this strongly suggests that unaccomplished redistributions are irrelevant.

The insistence that compensation be paid before the economist can make any judgment on welfare grounds does not imply that failure to compensate might not yield a greater increase in welfare, but it does mean that no decision can be made on this question without also making some assumption about interpersonal comparisons of utility. The economist cannot say that it is essential for compensation to be paid; rather, he must profess his ignorance about the situation where compensation is not paid. It may well be that if interpersonal comparisons are made on any reasonable basis the case for omitting the compensation will be very great — but should this be true the change can only be advocated in terms of interpersonal comparisons, not on the ground of its efficiency in allocating resources. In some absolute sense the loss in welfare by some must be considered to be outweighed by the gains of others.

At the same time that these explorations of the implications of the fundamental assumptions about interpersonal comparisons were taking place, the development of a set of marginal conditions based upon these assumptions was also progressing. As shown above, Pareto, Barone, and Lerner had already largely derived these conditions within the framework of the new welfare economics. In Bergson's (1938) treatment, the marginal conditions of production and exchange reached essentially their present development. He set them forth with greater elegance than had his predecessors, and examined them, not only in terms of the new welfare economics, but also in the welfare system of Marshall and Pigou. From this point onward, the expression of the marginal conditions, as a part of welfare economics, has not changed significantly. A precise statement of the basic assumptions and propositions of the new welfare economics in mathematical terms was contributed by Lange (1942). One of the most compact nonmathematical statements is Samuelson's. Of the marginal conditions of production, Samuelson says (1947, p. 233):

> Productive factors are correctly allocated if the marginal productivity of a given factor in one line is to the marginal productivity of the same factor in a second line as the marginal productivity of any other factor in the first line is to its marginal productivity in the second line. The value of the common factor of proportionality can be shown to be equal to the marginal cost of the first good in terms of the (displaced amount of the) second good.

The marginal conditions of exchange are quite analogous to the marginal conditions of production. The ratio of the marginal utilities of any two goods for any one individual must be the same as their ratio for any other individual, and must be equal to the transformation ratio between the two goods in a production sense. Combining these two sets of marginal conditions, Samuelson (1947, p. 238) arrives at one summary statement:

> (1) We must have a common marginal rate of indifference between any two goods for every individual; this common indifference ratio must, moreover, be equal to

the ratio at which one of these goods can be transformed into the other in a production sense, the transformation to come about as the result of transferring any resource from one good's production to the other's. (2) We must have for all individuals a common ratio of indifference between supplying more of any factor of production and enjoying more consumption of a given good; this common ratio must be equal to the rate at which supplying more of that factor results in greater production of the good in question.

Reder's (1947, Ch. II) treatment of the question, in terms of corollaries to the marginal conditions, makes their implications somewhat clearer, but the basic principles are identical with those of Samuelson's summary statement.

The history of the development of these aspects of the new welfare economics shows, somewhat more clearly than a bare statement of the present concepts, the problems which are involved and the solutions which are implied. It also, as will become evident in the next section, provides a background for the study of the development of the marginal cost pricing thesis. The issues which were and are important in the marginal cost pricing controversy make sense only in light of the accompanying development of welfare economics itself. In the consideration of marginal cost pricing which follows, it should again be remembered that there is nothing in the marginal conditions themselves which, without recourse to interpersonal comparisons, can specify one optimum position; there is an infinite number of relative optima among which the economist cannot choose within the bounds of his restricted assumptions. In terms of some concept of absolute welfare, furthermore, one position which is a relative optimum may well be less satisfactory than another position which is not a relative optimum. Moving to an optimal position by a process which requires that some individuals sacrifice in order that others may gain does not necessarily yield a position of greater welfare. Greater welfare in terms of the assumptions of the new welfare economics can only positively be said to be achieved when no one loses and someone gains. If the compensation which must be paid to those who lose by a given change is less than the gain to those who benefit, it can be said that welfare will be increased if the change is made and compensation is paid. This, of course, does not mean that the payment of compensation itself will increase welfare but it does mean that the payment of compensation is necessary if the economist is to be able to make any positive statements without recourse to interpersonal comparisons.

2. THE EVOLUTION OF THE MARGINAL COST PRICING PRINCIPLE

Although arguments in favor of marginal cost pricing are now based on the concepts of the new welfare economics, the idea of treating industries differently according to the nature of their costs had its roots as far back as Marshall. On the basis of his concept of consumers' surplus, Marshall (1936, p. 468) reasoned that maximum satisfaction could be achieved by taxing commodities which were produced under conditions of increasing costs and paying bounties on commodities produced under conditions of decreasing costs. The proof which Marshall offered for this conclusion was the purely geometrical demonstration that in the increasing cost case the loss in consumers' surplus from a tax would be much smaller than the gross receipts from the tax and in the decreasing cost case the bounty paid for increased production would be smaller than the gain in consumers' surplus. From this observation it was a simple step to note that by taxing the increasing cost industries and by giving bounties to decreasing cost industries, consumers' surplus could be increased.

Pigou (1912, p. 178) further developed this argument in his early book, *Wealth and Welfare*. As he later stated (1922, pp. 458–65) in a reply to Robertson, his analysis at this time was based entirely on Marshall, and was intended only to be a translation of the Marshallian analysis on this point into the terminology of marginal social net product. Proceeding from his definition of the *social* net product, Pigou maintained that the marginal social net product must be equal in all uses if welfare is to be maximized. Under a system of free exchange, however, the marginal *private* net product rather than the marginal social net product will determine the point where production will take place. In an increasing cost industry, Pigou argued, marginal private net product will be larger than marginal social net product, since the private product does not take into account the increase in the costs of the rest of the industry which would be attendant upon an increase in the output of a particular firm. From this it followed, according to Pigou, that production was carried too far in increasing cost industries, since their marginal social net products would be lower than in other industries. By applying a uniform tax of an appropriate amount to these industries, their output could be reduced and the marginal social net product of the industry could be raised to the point where it was just equal to that of other industries. By similar reasoning, Pigou argued that decreasing cost industries operate at a point below the social optimum, since in such industries the marginal social net product is greater than the marginal private net product. For these industries, a bounty was advocated in order to increase production and thereby reduce marginal social net product to that of resources in general.

Allyn Young (1913), in his review of *Wealth and Welfare*, did not let this analysis pass unchallenged. He pointed out that the basic causes of changes in costs were not symmetrical for increasing and decreasing cost industries. In increasing cost industries, increased prices for the use of land and other factors accompanying increased production do not represent a using up of resources; they are only transferences of purchasing power. The increase in cost for the industry occasioned by a producer increasing his output and so creating a greater demand for the factors of production does not, therefore, result in a social cost. To be consistent, Pigou (and Marshall) should have taken into account the increase in producers' surplus (economic rent) caused by the greater demand for scarce resources, as well as the increased prices of the factors to their users. But the decreasing cost case, Young pointed out, is different: it actually does represent an economizing in the use of factors. He qualified his statement by saying that he did not see how decreasing costs were compatible with the assumptions of competition which Pigou had set up, but agreed that anything except a monopoly practicing perfect price discrimination would produce at a level of output which would fall short of the ideal.

Ten years later, this subject was reopened by J.H. Clapham (1922), but it remained for Robertson (1924) to criticize effectively the analysis with regard to decreasing cost industries. Robertson divided the causes of external decreasing costs into two groups: internal economies in some industries appearing as external economies in other industries and dynamic factors of improvement such as inventions and changes in technology. Assuming that Pigou intended his analysis to apply to the static case only, Robertson argued that all external economies could be reduced to internal economies elsewhere in the system. For this reason, he went even further than Young had in criticizing Pigou: he not only did not favor taxing increasing cost industries, but also opposed subsidies for decreasing cost industries. The bounty which would have to be paid under the Pigou–Marshall hypothesis would subsidize all costs above marginal cost, which, he said, was equivalent to paying the whole burden of the fixed costs — and this policy could not possibly be sound! This interpretation was at least partially the result of confusion regarding the nature of marginal cost. Since Robertson's article was written some time before the development of the Viner system of envelope curves, it is not surprising that some confusion should have existed on this point. Pigou (1922) himself later vigorously rejected, as a 'grotesque misunderstanding', the implication that he advocated subsidizing decreasing cost enterprises to the extent of the whole burden of the fixed original plant.

At about this same time, F.H. Knight (1923), in a much more elaborate analysis, showed that Pigou's case of increasing cost industries was nothing more or less than the allocation mechanism working in conjunction with rents. Although his discussion was in content no different from the analysis made by Young 11 years earlier, Knight covered the question with much greater generality, showing that rent is a result of the price mechanism operating so as to allocate resources correctly. He also demonstrated again that, in the static case, external decreasing costs are purely the result of internal decreasing costs in some other industry.

The concept of external economies was, to some extent, rescued by P. Sraffa (1926, p. 525). He pointed out that decreasing costs could come about for reasons other than the lowering of raw material or commodity prices. An economy is not static and, as an industry grows, its greater importance in the economy may, for example, bring with it greater supplies of trained and mobile labor or new producers' services may spring up where none existed before. These are, of course, nothing but Robertson's second category of causes of decreasing costs. The importance of Sraffa's (1943) discussion should not be minimized, however; 17 years later the same subject merited a leading article in the *American Economic Review*, in which the same conclusions were again developed.

Knight (1925) pointed out both in his 1923 article and in a later article that decreasing costs mean monopoly, but it is highly significant that he took no part in the discussion of whether or not these decreasing cost industries should produce at marginal cost.

This early period saw a considerable shift in the nature of the controversy regarding pricing policy in increasing and decreasing cost industries. Marshall's original argument had been based almost entirely on the concept of consumers' surplus in industries operating under external increasing or decreasing costs. Pigou's translation of these ideas into the terminology of social net product in *Wealth and Welfare* was essentially in the same context. Although Allyn Young had pointed out the errors of such an approach, Pigou did not change his position substantially in *The Economics of Welfare*. It was only after the Robertson and Knight criticisms appeared that Pigou shifted the basis of his arguments. However, in recognition of the points established in this controversy a reorientation of the problem did emerge by the end of this period. The major writers in the field gradually began to turn away from the increasing cost case, and to focus on internal rather than external decreasing costs. Thus the basic elements of the marginal cost pricing thesis started to appear in recognizable form.

One of the first evidences of this transition was an article by H.D. Dickinson (1933) on price formation in a socialist economy. Dickinson's article was in many respects a hybrid: it had many of the faults of the previous constructs (in that he failed to recognize that increasing cost industries would in their own self-interest produce at the proper point), but he did introduce the use of marginal cost as the pricing criterion. His proposal was that all industries with increasing costs should have added to their costs a uniform unit tax, and that all industries with decreasing costs should have a deduction from costs in the form of a subsidy. The amount collected from the tax on increasing cost industries would go into a 'marginal cost equalization fund', and from this fund subsidies would be paid to the decreasing cost industries. The balance would provide a surplus or deficit to be added to or made up from general taxation funds. This procedure would, according to Dickinson, provide the maximum amount of production for the economy.

Dickinson's article elicited a reply by M. Dobb (1933). He said that more than one possible maximum may exist, and that it may not be of such prime importance to reach a specific one of these relative maxima. But his treatment makes it somewhat difficult to discover exactly what he meant by this statement, and it is not clear whether or not his purpose was to bring to bear Barone's observation that an infinite number of optima will exist in a system which excludes interpersonal comparisons. Dobb (1933, p. 594) did state that after a maximum has been reached by the method Dickinson proposed it would still not be at all clear just what had been maximized — in the oft-quoted passage 'one is tempted to the suspicion that to strive after such a maximum is very like looking in a dark room for a black hat that may be entirely subjective, after all'.

Lerner (1934a) immediately rushed to the support of Dickinson's proposals in an article on economic theory in relation to the socialist economy. He argued that the maximum in question is intended to be a maximum only in the sense that when this point has been reached, it is no longer possible to increase the output of one industry without diminishing the output of other industries — in other words, that this is one relative maximum of production, but by no means the only one. In all fairness to Dobb's original criticism, however, it should be pointed out that Lerner was starting a new argument, rather than continuing the old one. Dickinson's article had simply conceived of the marginal cost pricing system as a device for reaching the absolute maximum of total production in value terms, and he had not realized that this concept involved any ambiguities, any necessity for choice among many optimal positions, or any necessity for making interpersonal comparisons.

This article of Lerner's was promptly commented upon by Dobb (1934), and this time he was very much more explicit in his criticism. This time, Dobb charged that the maximization proposed by Lerner, although only one of many maxima, was still essentially a maximization of total output in value terms, and had meaning only on the basis of a certain scale of relative valuations. This charge is equivalent to saying that, in spite of the care taken to recognize the existence of many maxima, Lerner's conclusions still involved interpersonal comparisons of utility. In effect, Dobb said that by maintaining that the maximum in question was desirable, Lerner was arguing that this particular maximum was in some sense better than any other — and that this last statement could not be made without introducing interpersonal valuations. Lerner (1934b), in turn, stoutly denied this accusation and maintained that the desirability of attaining the maximum in question was entirely aside from all value judgments. The similarity between this Dobb–Lerner controversy and the Harrod–Robbins–Hicks–Kaldor controversy over the compensation principle is striking. The welfare elements involved are precisely the same, and in both controversies all the participants retired feeling strongly convinced that their original positions were correct.

The Dobb–Lerner controversy brought up for explicit consideration one new point, even though it did not arrive at any generally accepted conclusion on it. This was the question of whether or not interpersonal comparisons of utility are involved in advocating marginal cost pricing. Up to this time, the old welfare concepts which took interpersonal comparisons for granted had been implicitly assumed by all of the writers who had discussed the problems of pricing with increasing or decreasing costs.

The first attempt to examine the effects of the taxation which would be required to subsidize decreasing cost industries was made by L.M. Fraser (1933). His particular treatment was not very useful, however, for several reasons. One of the major difficulties is that Fraser believed it to be to the self-interest of entrepreneurs in decreasing cost industries to expand to the socially most desirable point. Joan Robinson's (1933) reply charged that in disproving Marshall's point on the taxation of increasing cost industries, Fraser was only 'flogging a dead horse' and she further pointed out the obvious fact that a firm with decreasing costs will operate at the socially most desirable point only when it receives a subsidy equal to the difference between average and marginal cost, so that it can charge marginal cost to its customers and at the same time cover its total expenses. However, the question of whether such subsidies are desirable or feasible, Joan Robinson felt, was quite a different story, and she did not offer any answer to it.

At this point, the problem of the appropriate level of output in increasing and decreasing cost industries became closely interwoven with the theory of monopoly and monopolistic competition. Chamberlin (1933, pp. 10, 77), in the first edition of his book, pointed out that the monopolistic influence was generally toward prices higher than they would be under pure competition, and that the effect of monopoly on the individual's adjustment characteristically would lead to smaller scales of output. Chamberlin was always very careful not to draw any sweeping conclusions from these observations, but others were not. Lerner (1933) immediately seized upon the divergence between price and marginal cost as a measure of the social loss caused by a monopolist. The only point of production which would maximize social welfare, he said, is the point where marginal cost is equal to price. Any other point would contravene the marginal conditions and, therefore, is automatically a point of less than maximum welfare.

A synthesis of the decreasing-cost-industry arguments and the monopolistic competition arguments was provided by R.F. Kahn (1935). He did not attempt to develop his arguments on the basis of a welfare system which excludes interpersonal comparisons. From the first, he emphasized that his work was based on the Pigovian concepts of social net product and the national dividend, and necessarily assumed the marginal utility of money to be equal for everyone. On this basis, he could state that decreasing cost industries, such as public utilities, should be subsidized in order to permit them to expand and operate at the point where price equals marginal cost. The case of firms in imperfect competition, he said, is directly analogous to this; the degree of imperfection takes the place of the decreasing cost and it would be socially desirable to expand these industries. Kahn made one further advance over his predecessors: he drew attention to the fact that if all industries have similarly decreasing costs or similarly imperfect competition, the payment of subsidies or bounties would not be useful or successful, and there would be no case for interference. Kahn's (1936) article stimulated replies by C.L. Paine (1936a,b), but these responses centered mainly on issues other than those under discussion here. In a later article, Paine (1937) did discuss marginal cost pricing, but the subject was treated in a very cursory manner which did not consider any of the fundamental issues raised by Kahn.

During the next few years, the development of the theory of marginal cost pricing was given a new twist by a number of writers who concerned themselves with the relation between the marginal cost pricing principle and the price system of a socialist economy. Lerner (1937), in particular, gave impetus to this turn of the controversy, writing a lengthy criticism of E.F.M. Durbin's (1936) analysis of price systems for a planned economy. Durbin had advocated an average cost pricing system. Lerner dissented from this opinion, saying that the one contribution pure economic theory has to make to the building up of a socialist economy is that price must be made equal to marginal cost. Lerner's article was one of the first general explanations of the marginal cost pricing principle which adequately treated the problem of defining marginal cost. His presentation of the Viner envelope curves showing explicitly the relationship between long- and short-run marginal cost served a very useful purpose. Although Viner's article (1931) on the subject had been written six years before, many of the writers (Durbin included) had no very clear conception of what was meant by marginal cost.

About this same time, Meade (1937) also advocated the principle of marginal cost pricing in the planning of industry. Meade proposed both the control of monopoly so as to force production to take place at the point where marginal cost is equal to price, and the extension of subsidies to all those cases where marginal cost pricing would not cover total costs. From Meade's point of view, the principle of marginal cost pricing was by this time no longer a controversial question, but rather something to be explained in a popular manner. Lange (1938, esp. p. 76) writing at about the same time, adopted the same attitude: the scale of output in a socialist economy, he indicated, should be fixed so that marginal cost is equal to the price of the product.

Thus, by 1938, the marginal cost pricing principle had by stages evolved out of the original Marshallian premise with reference to increasing and decreasing cost industries. Along the way, the basis of the argument had shifted from the assumption of equal marginal utilities of income to the claim that interpersonal comparisons need not be made, and the conclusions had shifted from the simple Marshallian premise concerning increasing and decreasing costs, based on a comparison of geometrical areas, to a fairly subtle proposition of pricing at marginal cost. Although there still was not full agreement on all of the reasoning involved — for instance, Dobb's question with regard to what it was that was being maximized — there was a fairly general agreement among the majority of those writing on this subject that the principle of marginal cost pricing was a valid principle for the achievement of an optimum allocation of resources, and even, in the view of some, the only optimum. This history of the origin and development of the marginal cost pricing thesis is largely ignored by present-day writers on welfare economics, even though it has played a very real part in shaping the present form of the theory. There is a considerable gulf between the marginal cost pricing thesis up to 1938 and its development after that period.

REFERENCES

Arrow, Kenneth J. (1948a), 'The possibility of a universal social welfare function. Abstract and Notation', *Cowles Commission Discussion Paper* 238.

―――― (1948b), 'Second thoughts on social welfare indices' and Corrigendum, *Cowles Commission Discussion Papers* 237 and 237R.

Barone, Enrico (1935), 'The ministry of production in the collectivist state', reprinted in F.A. Hayek (ed.), *Collectivist Economic Planning*, London, pp. 245–90.

Bergson, Abram (1938), 'A reformulation of certain aspects of welfare economics', *Quarterly Journal of Economics*, **52**, 310–34.

Chamberlin, Edward (1933), *The Theory of Monopolistic Competition*, Cambridge.

Clapham, J.H. (1922), 'Of empty economic boxes', *Economic Journal*, **22**, 305–14.

Dickinson, H.D. (1933), 'Price formation in a socialist community', *Economic Journal*, **43**, 237–50.

Dobb, M. (1933), 'The problems of a socialist economy', *Economic Journal*, **53**, 588–98.

―――― (1934), 'Economic theory and socialist economy: A reply', *Review of Economic Studies*, **2**, 144–51.

Durbin E.F.M. (1936), 'Economic calculus in a planned economy', *Economic Journal*, **46**.

Edgeworth, F.Y. (1897), 'The pure theory of taxation', *Economic Journal*, **7**, 46–70.

Fraser, L.M. (1933), 'Taxation and returns', *Review of Economic Studies*, **1**, 45–59.

Harrod, R.F. (1938), 'Scope and method of economics', *Economic Journal*, **48**, 396–97.

Hicks, J.R. (1939), 'The foundations of welfare economics', *Economic Journal*, **64**, 696–712.

Hotelling, Harold (1938), 'The general welfare in relation to problems of taxation and of railway and utility rates', *Econometrica*, **6**, 242–69.

Kahn, R.F. (1935), 'Some notes on ideal output', *Economic Journal*, **45**, 1–35.

_____ (1936), 'Mr. Paine and rationalisation: A note', *Economica*, n.s., **3**, 327–9.

Kaldor, Nicholas (1939), 'Welfare propositions of economics and interpersonal comparisons of utility', *Economic Journal*, **49**, 549–52.

Knight, F.H. (1923), 'Fallacies in the interpretation of social cost', *Quarterly Journal of Economics*, **38**, 582–606.

_____ (1925), 'Decreasing cost and comparative cost', *Quarterly Journal of Economics*, **39**, 331–3.

Lange, Oscar (1938), *On the Economic Theory of Socialism*, Minneapolis.

_____ (1942), 'The foundations of welfare economics', *Econometrica*, **10**, 215–28.

Lerner, A.P. (1933), 'Monopoly and the measurement of monopoly power', *Review of Economic Studies*, **1**, 157–75.

_____ (1934a), 'Economic theory and socialist economy', *Review of Economic Studies*, **2**, 51–61.

_____ (1934b), 'A reply to Mr. Dobb', *Review of Economic Studies*, **2**, 152–4.

_____ (1937), 'Statics and dynamics in socialist economics', *Economic Journal*, **47**, 253–70.

Marshall, Alfred (1936), *Principles of Economics*, 8th edition, London, Book III.

Meade, J.E. (1937), *An Introduction to Economic Analysis and Policy*, 2nd edition, London, pp. 188–94.

Mill, J.S. (1896), *Political Economy*, Book II, Chapter 2, Book V, Chapter 9.

Paine, C.L. (1936a), 'Rationalisation and the theory of excess capacity', *Economica*, n.s., **3**, 46–60.

_____ (1936b), 'Rejoinder to Mr. Kahn', *Economica*, n.s., **3**, 330–34.

_____ (1937), 'Some aspects of discrimination by public utilities', *Economica*, n.s., **4**, 425–39.

Pareto, W. (1909), *Manuel d'économie politique*, Paris, pp. 354–59.

Pigou, A.C. (1912), *Wealth and Welfare*, London.

_____ (1922), 'Economic boxes: A reply', *Economic Journal*, **22**, 458–65.

_____ (1929), *The Economics of Welfare*, 3rd edition, London.

Reder, Melvin W. (1947), *Studies in the Theory of Welfare Economics*, New York.

Robbins, Lionel (1938), 'Interpersonal comparisons of utility: A comment', *Economic Journal*, **38**, 635–41.

Robertson, D.H. (1924), 'Those empty boxes', *Economic Journal*, **34**, 16–31.

Robinson, Joan (1933), 'Mr. Fraser on taxation and returns', *Review of Economic Studies*, **1**, 137–43.

Samuelson, P.A. (1938), 'Welfare economics and international trade', *American Economic Review*, **28**, 261–66.

_____ (1947), *The Foundations of Economic Analysis*. Cambridge, pp. 249–52.

Scitovsky, Tibor (1941a), 'A note on welfare propositions in economics', *Review of Economic Studies*, **9**, 77–88.

_____ (1941b), 'A reconsideration of the theory of tariffs', *Review of Economic Studies*, **9**, 89–110.

Sraffa, P. (1926), 'The laws of returns under competitive conditions', *Economic Journal,* **36**, 525.

_____ (1943), 'External economies and diseconomies', *American Economic Review,* **33**, 493–511.

Viner, J. (1931), 'Cost curves and supply curves', *Zeitschrift für Nationalökonomie, 3,* 23–46.

Wicksell, Knut (1934), *Lectures on Political Economy,* London (E. Classen, tr.), Vol. I, pp. 77–93.

Young, Allyn (1913), 'Pigou's *Wealth and Welfare*', *Quarterly Journal of Economics,* **26**, 672–86.

2. Recent Developments in the Theory of Marginal Cost Pricing

Nancy D. Ruggles
Radcliffe College

In a previous article, which appeared in an earlier issue of this journal, the origins of the marginal cost pricing hypothesis and its welfare basis were examined. This paper will be concerned with the more recent formulations of the marginal cost pricing principle, the controversy surrounding it and an evaluation of the general argument in terms of its welfare basis.

1. HOTELLING'S STATEMENT OF THE MARGINAL COST PRICING PRINCIPLE

Most of the present-day discussions of marginal cost pricing take for their basis the work of Harold Hotelling (1938). His presentation consists of both a mathematical treatment of the problem and a detailed explanation of the implications of the principle. It is directed both toward those who understand an argument based on a rigorous mathematical proof and toward those who must be shown the common sense applications. The following summary of Hotelling's view on marginal cost pricing will serve as a basis for the discussion of the marginal cost controversy which it evoked, and also as a starting point for the last section of this paper, the general evaluation of the marginal cost pricing thesis within the framework of the new welfare economics. Hotelling did not refer at all to the development of the marginal cost pricing principle in the period just prior to that in which he wrote. Instead, he chose to go back to the work of an engineer, Jules Dupuit (1932), who wrote on the subject of utility in about the year 1844, in connection with an analysis of such public works as roads and bridges. He defined the total benefit of a public work such as a road or a bridge as the aggregate of the maximum prices which a perfectly

This chapter first appeared in *Review of Economic Studies*, **17** (2), 1949.

discriminating monopolist could charge equal to the costs of the best alternatives to its use. Applying this definition to the search for a method of maximizing the total benefit, he reasoned that charging a toll, however small, would cause some individuals to do without these services. The services of an already existing road or bridge have no real cost, so that any diminution in its use would represent a net loss of benefits. The greatest benefit would be obtained from a bridge if its services were free, and the higher the toll which was charged the greater would be the damage done. Dupuit's argument was based upon a concept of measurable utility and free interpersonal comparison, but Hotelling maintained that, by virtue of the analysis made possible by modern mathematical methods, the essence of Dupuit's propositions could be substantiated without any necessity for such dependence.

As a start on his modernization of Dupuit, Hotelling postulated an economy in which products are priced at marginal cost, and the difference between this amount and total cost is made up by taxation. He then derived algebraically the fundamental theorem that 'if a person must pay a certain sum of money in taxes, his satisfaction will be greater if the levy is made directly on him as a fixed amount than if it is made through a system of excise taxes which he can to some extent avoid by rearranging his production and consumption'. The truth of this theorem is evident, both from the mathematical proof and from an analysis of indifference curves. Hotelling then extended the analysis from one individual to the whole community, postulating that 'if government revenue is produced by any system of excise taxes, there exists a possible distribution of personal levies among the individuals of the community such that the abolition of the excise taxes and their replacement by these levies will yield the same revenue while leaving each person in a state more satisfactory to himself than before'. On this basis, he recommended a system of pricing at marginal cost. The deficits which would occur in decreasing cost industries should be made up out of the public treasury, he said, with the requisite funds collected by means of lump-sum taxes.

Hotelling next considered what sources of revenue are of the nature of lump-sum taxes, and whether such sources of revenue would be adequate to cover the deficits as a result of the marginal cost pricing system. He recommended income taxes, taxes on inheritances and taxes on the site value of land, since all of these, he said, are lump-sum taxes which do not affect the price of any commodity. There is also, he pointed out, one other source of revenue available to the state which would not impair the marginal conditions; this is to be found in the price of commodities available in limited quantity. Such a scarce commodity is space on trains during holiday periods. If the total demand for rail travel during the year is not sufficient to provide enough cars to accommodate all who wish to travel during holiday periods, the limited space in existing cars will acquire a rental value similar to that of land. The appropriate way to handle this situation is to set the price high enough to limit demand to the amount of space available. This solution, Hotelling said, would be more satisfactory than either permitting overcrowding or selling tickets at marginal cost only to those who happen to be first in line. Using these sources of revenue, he thought that it would always be possible to obtain enough revenue to finance the marginal cost pricing system. Hotelling recognized that for reasons of political expediency it may not be feasible to raise all of the revenue from these sources, so that excise taxes may have to be resorted to; in this event the excise taxes should be so distributed as to minimize the resulting loss. With an appropriate system of compensations and collections, Hotelling thus argued, a change from an average cost pricing system to the marginal cost pricing system can increase everyone's satisfaction.

Hotelling recognized that the 'system of collections and compensations' is an essential element if the change to marginal cost pricing is to increase everyone's satisfaction, but in practice he thought it probably would not be feasible to carry through all of the collections and compensations. The general well-being would have to be purchased at the expense of sacrifices by some. For example, it might be that the introduction of cheap electricity into a region would raise the level of its economic existence so much that the benefits received by the individuals in the region would far exceed the money cost of the development. Yet, it might not be possible to devise a system of lump-sum taxes on the inhabitants of the region which would cover total costs. Rather than forgo the investment, Hotelling argued, it would be better to sell the electricity at its marginal cost and make up the difference from revenues derived from other parts of the country — a procedure which, of course, involves a shift in the distribution of income. Hotelling defended his recommendation on the grounds that, in the first place, the benefits from such regional development are not confined to the area most immediately affected, and in the second place, considering many projects together, the benefits of all of them may be so widespread that most persons in all parts of the country would be better off as a result of the program as a whole. Hotelling believed that the latter condition would probably in general be met by a system of marginal cost pricing, although he recognized that at least two groups of persons — those in the highest income groups and landowners — could be expected on balance to suffer a loss.

In order to illustrate the application of marginal cost pricing, Hotelling considered two cases, one relating to tolls on bridges and the other to railway rates. With respect to bridges, for the use of which marginal cost is zero, Hotelling pointed out, as Dupuit originally had, that the bridge will be used more if there are no tolls and the cost is paid by taxes on the site value of land and on incomes and inheritances. If the bridge services are not sold at marginal cost, i.e., if tolls are charged, the total amount of benefit will be decreased by the decreased use. The returns to society will be greater if the bridge is financed by either land or income taxes, for then only the distribution of income will be affected, not its total amount. It is sometimes argued, Hotelling said, that if tolls are not charged, the benefits will go to people who do not pay for them, whereas those whose taxes do pay for the bridge do not necessarily benefit from it, and furthermore, that payment for the bridge by tolls would injure no one, since everyone who uses the bridge does so willingly and is better off thereby. But, he replied, the surrounding landowners may also have benefited from the increase in land values occasioned by the bridge, and the bridge would get very much more use if it were free. The attempt to make such projects self-liquidating, he maintained, will greatly reduce the total benefit.

The railroad rate case is similar. The current running costs of railroads are only a small fraction of their total costs and the actual extra costs of marginal use are even smaller. In a rational economic system, Hotelling said, rates should be set in such a fashion that they would even out the traffic over the year, ensuring full utilization of capacity at all times. In practice, he argued, the exact opposite is true, and furthermore both freight and passenger rates are extremely complex and remote from marginal cost. The present rate structures are presumably based on the estimated elasticity of the different demands, but it cannot be assumed, Hotelling maintained, that the rate differentials have been determined accurately even for the purpose of maximizing revenue, much less for that of maximizing utility. And from the point of view of the users of the railroads, the very complexity of the rates is an impediment to the accurate distribution of budgets so as to maximize satisfactions.

Hotelling admitted that a number of problems would arise in an actual application of marginal cost pricing. Aside from the purely technical problems of determining costs (which it is assumed could be solved), problems of interpretation would also exist. For instance, when a train is completely full the marginal cost of carrying an additional passenger is equal to the cost of running another train, but in the more normal situation when a train is not full the extra cost of carrying an extra passenger is very small. A sharp increase in rates to the unlucky first passenger on each train can be avoided by an averaging of rates according to the probability of having to run another train. If it is not feasible to run another train, a fare should be charged (as was pointed out above) which is of sufficient magnitude to distinguish between the purchasers, enabling those who are willing to pay the most to ride.

A second special problem arises with respect to expenditures which are not for consumption. The usual criterion for private investment is whether or not it will pay for itself, but this criterion obviously becomes inapplicable with marginal cost pricing. Hotelling offered instead the criterion that the investment should be undertaken if some distribution of the burden is possible such that everyone concerned would be better off than without the new investment.

He stressed that it is not necessary that any such distribution of the burden be practicable, but did agree that compensation should be paid to those who are injured by the new investment when the failure to compensate would cause undue hardship. Anticipating the objection that the overhead of an industry must be met in order to determine whether the investment was a wise policy, Hotelling maintained that such a method of testing is absurd. The question of whether it was wise to build the Union Pacific Railroad is an interesting historical problem, but the attempt to solve it now by charging rates high above marginal cost is too costly, since it may in the process ruin the territory the Union Pacific was designed to serve. Furthermore, it would probably give the wrong answer, since what a perfectly discriminating monopolist would charge and what the Union Pacific can charge are two entirely different matters. It would be far better, he said, to operate the railroads for the benefit of the present-day population, and let dead men and dead investments lie in their graves. It may well be that under present conditions no distribution of the burden exists which would make the investment in a particular railroad worth while, but this does not mean that it would be wise to let the investment, which has already been made, go unutilized.

This is Hotelling's presentation of the marginal cost pricing principle, with the reasoning which supports it. As such, it constitutes the credo of those who advocate marginal cost pricing on the grounds of the new welfare economics. Hotelling's position actually represents one of the more conservative statements of the principle, and he took care to protect himself on a number of issues regarding which some of his followers have not been as careful. Few, if any, of the advocates of the marginal cost pricing principle have taken a less extreme position on the issue than has Hotelling, and for this reason its fate may legitimately be identified with the fate of his presentation of it.

2. THE MARGINAL COST PRICING CONTROVERSY

Up to 1938, the development of the marginal cost pricing principle had for the most part been on a highly theoretical plane concerned with the basic welfare principles, with some attention to the problems of designing an optimum price system for a socialist state. At about this time, the emphasis of the discussion shifted to more concrete considerations of pricing systems. This shift was to a large extent due to Hotelling, since much of the later work in the field was stimulated by his article.

Almost simultaneously with the appearance of Hotelling's article, however, at least one other writer was advocating that marginal cost pricing be applied in specific situations. R.H. Montgomery (1939a,b), in two articles on government ownership and operation of railroads and electric utilities, independently reached almost the same conclusions as Hotelling, although the basis of his reasoning was essentially the welfare economics of Marshall and Pigou rather than the 'new' welfare economics. On the basis of his analysis, he recommended that both of the industries he discussed charge only incremental costs (i.e., price at marginal cost), without attempting to maximize profits.

One of the earliest comments specifically directed at Hotelling's article was Frisch's (1939a,b). He raised four objections. In the first place, he undertook to demonstrate that it was not necessary for prices actually to equal marginal cost provided they were proportional to it. Hotelling (1939a), in his reply to Frisch, agreed that proportionality is all that would be necessary. But, as a number of people, including Lerner (1944, pp. 102–4) and Samuelson (1947, p. 240), have since pointed out, Frisch and Hotelling were both wrong on this point. Exact equality really is necessary for consistency in the system as a whole, taking account of the prices of the factors of production. It is apparent that if the prices of consumers' goods were not equal to marginal cost, but factor payments were maintained equal to the marginal products of the factors, the relationship between work and leisure would be altered and the marginal conditions throughout the system would not be met. On the other hand, if prices of factors as well as finished goods were all raised proportionally, nothing would be accomplished; it would still be found that prices were *equal* to marginal costs. In his reply to Frisch, Hotelling did recognize in connection with another point that an income tax is an excise tax on a factor of production, but he never fully integrated this point into the proof that *equality* of price to marginal cost is necessary.

The second objection which Frisch raised related to Hotelling's criterion of the welfare of the country as a whole. Hotelling advocated marginal cost pricing on the ground that it would increase the general welfare, even though he admitted that some classes would lose by it. Frisch correctly drew attention to the fact that this conclusion is at variance with Hotelling's original definition of welfare, which had been taken over from Pareto and was designed to avoid the need for interpersonal comparisons. Frisch pointed out that in the analysis of any change which would make the welfare indicators of different individuals move in different directions (which Hotelling admitted would happen as a result of the introduction of marginal cost pricing), no general indicator of welfare can be used without dependence upon interpersonal comparisons. For this reason, Frisch claimed that Hotelling's conclusions with regard to the desirability of marginal cost pricing do not follow from the mathematical propositions he had proved. In his first reply to Frisch, Hotelling did not answer this charge, and Frisch did not repeat it in his second note.

In addition to these two points, Frisch raised two more objections which Hotelling did effectively refute. First, Frisch maintained that there was nothing in the actual mathematics which related in any way to marginal cost. A non-proportional change in prices (i.e., by an excise tax), he said, would diminish satisfactions irrespective of whether or not marginal cost pricing was in effect before the imposition of the taxes. Hotelling (1939b) showed in his second rejoinder that the mathematical proof requires either that the original prices be set at marginal cost or that the quantities taken be completely unaffected by the change in price, and he considered the second alternative trivial. Secondly, Frisch argued that the gain in utility resulting from the government's spending the tax revenue should be taken into account, as well as the loss in utility resulting from the tax itself. Hotelling rightly replied to this objection that his argument was concerned not with the question of whether the collection of any tax at all would increase welfare, but rather with the question of whether, once the amount to be collected had been determined on some other basis, welfare would be greater if it were collected by an income or an excise tax.

Unfortunately, not all of the other points which were made in the marginal cost controversy were as brief or as clear-cut as Frisch's. For instance, H.W. Robinson (1939) entered the fray with great vigor, but the issue which he brought up was almost an irrelevant one. He was concerned about the fact that income taxes were collected at the end of the year, so that the consumer might have great difficulty in arranging his budget so as to maximize his satisfactions and still be able to meet the income tax at the end of the year. This difficulty, Robinson claimed, might more than offset the increase in welfare which would otherwise be expected to result from the substitution of income for excise taxes. The pertinence of this point is reduced, however, with the introduction of current payment income tax plans, and in any case it does not bear upon any of Hotelling's basic issues.

Not only negative reactions were stimulated by Hotelling's work; among writers in the field of public control and public utility economics, there were positive reactions as well (Bonbright, 1940; Wallace, 1939, 1941). No less an authority in the field than Bonbright hailed Hotelling's work as 'one of the most distinguished contributions to rate-making theory in the entire literature of economics'. Unfortunately, after this laudatory comment, Bonbright showed that he did not fully grasp the relation of Hotelling's marginal cost pricing principle to utility rate-making. He indicated that the striking discrepancies between marginal and average costs of public utilities are not due primarily to long-run decreasing costs, but rather to the temporary or chronic presence of excess plant capacity. Thus, according to Bonbright, it is not the difference between long-run average and marginal cost which makes average cost pricing unsatisfactory, but rather the existence of off-peak periods in the short run. Bonbright did not seem to realize that Hotelling's marginal cost pricing thesis does not necessarily imply the use of the same rate for both peak and off-peak periods. Hotelling's system adequately allowed for short-run problems of this nature by the use of commodity rents. He had recommended adjusting prices in such a way as to even out peak loads, by charging a rent in addition to marginal cost whenever the demand at marginal cost would exceed the available supply. Bonbright's misinterpretation of Hotelling's thesis again resulted from the misunderstanding of long- and short-run marginal cost.

This prevalent confusion between long- and short-run marginal cost was pointed out by E.W. Clemens (1941), in an article on the subject of price discrimination in decreasing cost industries. He showed that Montgomery (1939b, p. 143) had misunderstood the nature of marginal costs when he laid down the principle that the extension of capacity should continue 'as long as the output which would be taken at incremental cost can be produced at lower average cost'. Clemens showed that since the lowest point on the long-run average cost curve coincides with both the long- and short-run marginal cost curves, only the single criterion of marginal cost is needed, and the condition that average cost be a minimum is superfluous. However, Clemens vigorously dissented from both Montgomery's and Hotelling's conclusions that pricing at marginal cost is the only satisfactory solution. He maintained that this solution is necessary only if a one-price system is postulated, but that a system of price discrimination could also arrive at the point of ideal output. He had no adequate discussion of what he meant by price discrimination, however; apparently he believed that the use of a block system of rates could achieve the ideal solution. This argument is not necessarily valid, since the use of block rates for different customers could violate the marginal conditions for some of the customers. Hotelling had recognized that perfect price discrimination would satisfy the marginal conditions, but rejected it on the basis of its impossibility in actual practice. To be consistent, Clemens would have had either to advocate perfect price discrimination or to maintain that discontinuities in demand exist such that the use of block rates will not lessen the total amount bought by each consumer below that which would be bought at marginal cost.

Further exploration of price discrimination as an alternative to marginal cost pricing was undertaken by W.A. Lewis (1941a,b). The conclusions Lewis reached are similar to those Clemens had arrived at. In addition, he went on to point out that the issue between the marginal cost pricing system and price discrimination is one of social justice, not economics — but he did not explain what he meant by this statement. He also said that in peak periods the proper rate should not be determined by the previous level of marginal cost, but rather by whatever can be obtained maintaining capacity operation, thus agreeing with Hotelling's commodity rent principle.

The final contribution of the public utility economists to the controversy was an exchange between Emery Troxel (1943, 1944) and D.F. Pegrum (1944, pp. 58–60). Pegrum pointed out that 'the equating of gains to consumers against the losses of those called upon to bear the fixed costs would not represent any problem if the consumers and taxpayers were identical and if

Price Theory

their incomes were the same or inequalities a matter of indifference'. This is, of course, the same objection to marginal cost pricing as that raised by Frisch in mathematical terms. Troxel's answer on this point was that he recognized that 'the public authorities cannot always accept dispassionate reasoning when they want to stay alive politically'. In other words, Troxel refused to admit that the conclusions of the marginal cost pricing system involve any logical problem of interpersonal comparison.

It was not only the public utility economists who took part in the controversy on marginal cost pricing in this period. An examination of some of the budgetary implications of the marginal cost pricing principle was carried out by J.E. Meade (1944a,b), along with the development of a criterion of price and output policy for state enterprise. Meade stated that it is entirely possible for the operation of socialized industries at marginal cost to involve losses commensurate with the total income earned on property in the rest of the economy. At this point, Meade recognized what Hotelling had ignored: that if the amount of funds which must be raised is substantial, the necessary income tax might have to be high enough to interfere seriously with the achievement of the best balance between work and leisure. This point is an important qualification to Hotelling's thesis that income taxes are superior in all instances to divergence from the marginal cost conditions elsewhere in the economy. For this reason, Meade felt that the operation of decreasing cost industries at marginal cost should be accompanied by some measure of public ownership of property.

In answer to Meade's proposals for public ownership, J.M. Fleming (1944) brought up several points, some of which are valid and some are not. First, he pointed out that increasing cost industries which operate to capacity will cover their overhead and in addition may yield competitive rents; for this reason it is not true that all of the overhead in the economy will have to be subsidized. Meade, in his reply, recognized this point as valid, and admitted that he had not considered the possibility of marginal cost curves becoming discontinuous at capacity. A second point made by Fleming, one which is much less well taken, was that a general indirect tax on all output would have no net effects on incentive or income distribution since it is only necessary for price to be proportional to marginal cost, not equal to it. Meade, in his reply, agreed, but, as has been pointed out above, the point is not valid. The Fleming proposition of a general indirect tax on output is in effect an expenditures tax; it not only has the defects outlined in the discussion of Frisch, but in addition would violate the marginal conditions between spending and saving.

A.P. Lerner (1944, pp. 174–240), in *The Economics of Control*, developed the theory of marginal cost pricing in a more general form than had, until then, been done. He recognized the necessity for meeting all of the marginal conditions, including those of work and leisure — but then, having recognized it, he proceeded to erect a structure which does not meet them. As Samuelson has pointed out, it is not easy to devise a tax or subsidy which will not affect the marginal conditions, so that it is extremely difficult to change the distribution of income from that which a pricing system automatically yields without violating the marginal conditions. Taxes cannot be related to actual performance, since this will alter the relation between work and leisure — a somewhat similar point is made by Meade (1946, pp. 47–69) in his review of Lerner's book; instead they would have to be adjusted to an individual's capabilities or potentialities, and as Lerner himself seems to realize, this would be an impossible task. But Lerner was not willing to accept the income distribution which would necessarily result from his system as socially right or desirable; in Chapter 3, he advocated equality of income among individuals. Whether he intended to achieve this equality of income by departing from marginal productivity as the criterion of wage payments or by superimposing a system of income taxes and subsidies is not made clear, but in either case the end result would be the same. The marginal conditions relating to the factors of production would not be met — and the failure in this case would be great enough so that it would certainly affect the supply of the factors. In Lerner's system, therefore, the allocation mechanism for labor (as well as for the other factors) would tend to break down, since no means would be available to lure labor from one occupation to another. If, as Lerner advocated, all money incomes were equal, people would choose the work they preferred, or for that matter no work at all, and there would be a scarcity of labor for unpleasant or tedious jobs. Thus, for Lerner, as for the other advocates of marginal cost pricing, the problem of obtaining the desired income distribution would interfere with satisfying the marginal conditions of work and leisure.

A practical question concerning the workability of marginal cost pricing was brought up at about this time by T. Wilson (1945). He raised the objection that in making investment decisions under the marginal cost pricing system there would be no test of the accuracy of the forecast. Hotelling, of course, covered this question from a theoretical point of view when he said that there is little interest in the wisdom of making an investment after it has been made, since then the question is purely academic. But as Wilson pointed out, it is true that past experience can provide a guide for the laying of future plans. A successful enterprise of one type encourages duplication, whereas one that is a failure serves as a warning. Requiring an investment to pay for itself is undoubtedly overconservative, but where estimation of the outcome is difficult Wilson felt that some such criterion is necessary.

Another dissent from the view of Meade, Fleming, and Lerner was expressed by R.H. Coase (1945). He did not disagree with the thesis that price should equal marginal cost, but argued that total cost would also have to be covered if there was not to be a redistribution of income in favor of the consumers of products in which fixed costs form a high proportion of total costs. He was in effect again pointing out that marginal cost pricing without compensation leads to a change in the income distribution, so its result cannot be compared in welfare terms with that of average cost pricing. The method of exposition is different, but the argument is essentially the same as that set forth by Frisch and Pegrum. Correct price discrimination, Coase said, would permit both the marginal and the total conditions to be met — but the advocates of marginal cost pricing would probably reply to this that in practice price discrimination could not be correctly adjusted to meet the marginal conditions and that, therefore, its abolition in favor of marginal cost pricing would increase welfare.

Coase (1946) further extended his arguments against marginal cost pricing in a later article. In this article, he developed an example of a situation in which average costs are different from marginal costs, yet all costs are directly assignable to specific consumers. The example is that of purchases from a centrally located store by customers located in a radial pattern, so that delivery to each customer must be made individually. The cost of supplying goods to any customer would then be the store cost of the goods plus the cost of delivery. Together these make up total cost. The charge, he argued, should be a delivery fee plus the store cost of the goods. This device Coase referred to as multi-part pricing. He maintained that Hotelling and Lerner had overlooked this possibility in favor of a system in which all delivery charges would be paid by the public at large through taxation. The adoption of the marginal cost pricing system, he said, would involve a redistribution in favor of those to whom the cost of delivery was greatest — i.e., those who lived farthest away.

Two fundamental conditions for an optimum pricing system were laid down in this article. In the first place, Coase said, for each individual consumer the same factor should have the same price wherever it is employed or else the price system will misallocate resources, i.e., the usual marginal conditions of production and exchange must be satisfied. In the second place, Coase said that the price of a factor should be the same for all consumers, since otherwise one consumer would be obtaining more for the same amount of money than another consumer. This is the first instance in which the criterion of price uniformity had been held up as a welfare principle. Coase used it because of his concept of the distribution of income; he stipulated uniform prices to different consumers so that the distribution of money income would be equivalent to the distribution of income in terms of the factors of production. (In no place has he recognized that the question of the utility of the income is also relevant.) But this stipulation of uniform prices is inconsistent with Coase's own earlier statement that correct price discrimination would meet both the marginal and the total conditions. Multi-part pricing, Coase maintained, would satisfy both the marginal conditions and the criterion of uniform factor pricing, and Hotelling and Lerner, by considering only average and marginal cost pricing, omitted the one satisfactory solution.

With respect to the alternative merits of marginal and average cost pricing, Coase emphasized that both systems have advantages and disadvantages. He recognized that if consumers are not allowed to buy additional units at marginal cost there will be a maldistribution of the factors of production, and he also admitted that production which is worth undertaking can sometimes be carried out with marginal cost pricing when it could not with average cost pricing. The disadvantages of marginal cost pricing lie, according to him, in the fact that the income taxes which must be levied to subsidize the decreasing cost industries impose a tax on effort and on waiting, and in the fact that taxing some individuals to provide factors of production for the use of other individuals involves a redistribution of income which cannot be avoided in any way except by levying excise taxes on the products of decreasing cost industries — a self-defeating measure, since it would only result in a return to average cost pricing. With reference to investment, Coase repeated the objections originally raised by Wilson that the market test is necessary as a guide, even if it is more conservative than might be wished. Finally, Coase claimed that the marginal cost pricing principle destroys the guide to policy, making it exceedingly easy to make errors.

Considerable controversy was stirred up by Coase's article. Both G.F. Thirlby (1947) and H. Norris (1947) criticized the multi-part pricing solution on the ground of its limited applicability. Thirlby suggested that Coase discuss certain elements which are inherent in the multi-part pricing model, for instance, the costs of administration and credit, which create problems if such costs are to be included as a part of charges made to individual purchasers. Norris also pointed out that it is the common or joint costs which cause the trouble. J.A. Nordin (1947), in another reply to Coase, suggested again that it was not necessary to have prices equal to marginal cost, provided they were proportional to it. Coase (1947) rightly criticized Nordin for this statement and, in addition, pointed out that such a price system would still alter the distribution of income in favor of those consuming the products of decreasing cost industries.

Most of the participants in the discussion on the general merits of marginal cost pricing implicitly agreed with Hotelling that the income tax provided the best method of raising revenue to finance the marginal cost pricing system. One or two people — Meade, for example — had realized that if the amounts in question were large the departure from the marginal conditions on the factor side occasioned by the use of the income tax might be serious, but in general very little attention was paid to this aspect of the problem. At the same time, however, a parallel discussion was going on which was not concerned with the issue of marginal cost pricing at all, but dealt solely with the problem of the alternative merits of the income and excise tax (Wald, 1945; J.R. Hicks, 1938; Ursula Hicks, 1936; Joseph, 1939). Hotelling, in agreement with the whole classical theory of taxation, had assumed that an income tax would in welfare terms be exactly the same as a lump-sum tax. It was now shown by a number of writers that under certain circumstances excise taxes are not more burdensome to the individual than are income taxes. H.P. Wald's demonstration of the question is perhaps the clearest. He pointed out again that, unlike a lump-sum tax, an income tax is an excise tax on work. In cases where a commodity excise tax does not affect the amount which is purchased, such a commodity excise tax will therefore be superior to an income tax. An excise tax upon a commodity whose demand is inelastic with respect to both price and income would fulfill this condition, and would therefore be less burdensome than an income tax which produced an economic effect by altering the marginal conditions between work and leisure. Hotelling's implicit assumption that what he had proved mathematically for a lump-sum tax would also hold for income taxes is therefore untenable; following Wald's analysis, there may exist a number of types of excise taxes which are superior to general income taxes in terms of welfare.

One of the most complete discussions of marginal cost pricing, aside from Lerner's, is to be found in Melvin Reder's (1947) book on welfare economics. There is, however, an implicit contradiction in Reder's work. First, as has been pointed out earlier, he maintained that the existence of the possibility of paying compensation to those harmed by a given class of reorganization is not sufficient; this compensation must actually be paid if the economist is to be able to advocate policies on welfare grounds. The economist's entire argument for the policy, he said, may be formally incorrect if compensation is not paid (Reder, 1947, p. 97). But, on the other hand, in his discussion of monopoly he indicated several times that the introduction of marginal cost pricing will increase welfare, since compensation *could* be paid (Reder, 1947, pp. 51–4). Nowhere in this section did he indicate that the compensation must be paid before any judgment can be made about the change in welfare. Yet, if a new product priced at marginal cost and requiring subsidization were brought on to the market, people who were taxed but did not consume the product would suffer. According to Reder's compensation principle, it would seem that the taxes should be borne only by those who consume the product — but, as Coase has pointed out, an excise tax on these commodities would only result in raising the price back to average cost. Reder got out of this dilemma by using a partial analysis which failed to consider the source of the funds with which to subsidize the decreasing cost industries.

One of the most recent contributions to this field of literature is an article by William Vickrey (1948). This article considered a number of diverse objections to marginal cost pricing, in the end disposing of all of them. One of these related to the problem of making investment decisions under a marginal cost pricing system. This problem arises, he said, not because of the use of marginal cost pricing, but because of the existence of decreasing cost industries. In these industries, average cost pricing does not provide an adequate guide for investment decisions either, since average cost pricing would prevent many worthwhile projects from being undertaken. Vickrey also considered price discrimination as an alternative means of reaching an optimum, but concluded that although price discrimination would represent an improvement over average cost pricing, it still would result in a failure to meet the marginal conditions for some people, and therefore would not achieve a proper allocation of resources. Finally, Vickrey argued that marginal cost is in most cases no more elusive as a basis for pricing than average cost — a point which is probably well taken. In this article again, marginal cost pricing was advocated without any examination of the source or nature of the subsidies it would require, even though there is an implicit assumption that whatever method is used to obtain the subsidies will meet the marginal conditions. The use of the concept of consumers' surplus was an important part of Vickrey's discussion; in fact, his treatment was much closer to that of Pigou than it was to the later welfare economists.

Such is the history of the marginal cost controversy. It is apparent that not all of the contributors to it have had an adequate appreciation of the previous development of welfare economics in general or the marginal cost pricing principle in particular. For the most part, the contributions of the mathematical economists have not been integrated with those of the nonmathematical economists, and those in the special field of public utilities have not been completely aware of the theoretical framework within which the discussion was set by the other writers. More than anyone else, Samuelson has adequately covered all of the major points at issue. These points appear in scattered form throughout Samuelson's discussion of welfare economics, but they are not integrated into a form which would show their relevance to questions of pricing policy. To the casual observer, the whole controversy may seem to have lacked any common ground or to have failed to reach any accepted conclusion. Yet as a result of it, the advocates of marginal cost pricing have gained a large following — larger, in all probability, than that of their opponents. The next section will bring together the threads of the story, and will attempt to evaluate its contribution to the theory of the operation of different pricing systems as mechanisms for resource allocation.

3. SUMMARY

The advocates of marginal cost pricing maintain that in any situation in which all prices are not equal to marginal cost the general welfare can be increased by setting these prices equal to marginal cost. Furthermore, they say that this conclusion can be reached without requiring any judgments comparing the utilities of different persons. This claim for the superiority of marginal cost pricing is based on the argument that it meets the marginal conditions for maximizing welfare, and that for this reason it represents an optimum. In evaluating marginal cost pricing, it is therefore necessary to consider three questions: Is meeting these marginal conditions a sufficient basis for recommending a pricing system? Does the marginal cost pricing system meet these marginal conditions? Does the marginal cost pricing system, in fact, avoid any necessity for interpersonal comparisons? This paper has surveyed the literature dealing with these questions; it will now be useful to summarize briefly the findings of this literature.

The use of marginal analysis for reaching a maximum is, of course, a fundamental part of the methodology of economic analysis. In one form or another it has been applied to the specific field of welfare economics from almost the earliest writers in this field onward. Pigou and Wicksell, on the one hand, and Pareto and Barone, on the other, firmly established marginal analysis as a tool for finding a maximum of the social welfare. The marginal conditions in relation to welfare have by now been developed to a great degree of refinement by a number of mathematical economists. Bergson, Lange, Samuelson, and Arrow have all contributed to this development. As is true with any marginal analysis, however, it must be remembered that the marginal conditions provide a mechanism for finding a relative maximum, but not an absolute maximum. Within this limitation, the literature which has been discussed in the preceding part of this paper adequately demonstrates that, other things being equal, a pricing system which meets the marginal conditions will yield greater welfare than a pricing system which fails to meet the marginal conditions.

Marginal cost pricing is supported on the ground that it would meet these marginal conditions, and so would yield a maximum of welfare. This is the argument that has been put forth throughout the development of the marginal cost pricing principle, from its first appearance in Dickinson's article through the work of Lerner, Meade, and Lange, to Hotelling and on through Troxel, Reder, and finally Vickrey. And to the extent that prices are actually set equal to marginal cost, it is obvious that marginal cost pricing will meet the marginal conditions. But, although the argument has sometimes been left at this point, the question is not quite so simple. Marginal cost pricing would, of course, make necessary the payment of subsidies to producers with decreasing costs, since otherwise they could not cover their total costs. Before the system can be considered complete, some consideration must be given to the method of financing these subsidies. Many of the supporters of marginal cost pricing have failed to consider this question. Lerner and Meade among the earlier writers, Troxel among the public utility economists and more recently Reder and

Vickrey, all fall into this group. All of their arguments are partial, since they do not provide any mechanism in their systems for supplying the revenue necessary to finance the subsidies. A number of writers have considered this necessity for financing the system, however, and a number of suggestions have been made.

In the first place, it has been suggested that the need for subsidies can be avoided altogether, by making prices proportional to rather than equal to marginal cost. The marginal conditions of exchange will be just as well satisfied, it is argued, and at the same time it will be possible to cover total cost. This view was put forth by Frisch in his reply to Hotelling, and agreed to by the latter. It was again proposed by Fleming in answer to Meade, and Meade agreed. Finally, it was suggested by Nordin in reply to Coase. But the fallacy of the argument has also repeatedly been pointed out, among others, by Lerner, Samuelson, and Coase. Unless the prices paid to the factors of production, as well as the prices paid for consumers' goods, are included in the set which is raised proportionally to marginal cost, the marginal conditions with respect to the factors of production will be violated. If factor prices, as well as commodity prices, are included, nothing will be accomplished by the proportional increase; it will be found that marginal costs will have risen in the same proportion and that prices will still be equal to marginal costs.

Hotelling's original presentation of the marginal cost pricing thesis included the provision that the necessary revenue be raised by taxes on inheritances, rent of land, and incomes, since, he argued, all of these are lump-sum taxes and therefore would not interfere with the marginal conditions. A true lump-sum tax is, by definition, one which falls on either producers' or consumers' surplus and therefore does not violate the marginal conditions. Taxes on inheritances and taxes on the rent of land in all probability do fall into this category, and should the revenue derivable from them be sufficient to meet the subsidies, Hotelling's system would meet the marginal conditions. But even Hotelling does not expect this to be true, and income taxes are a different matter. As Meade and Samuelson have pointed out, income taxes are in effect excise taxes on the supply of certain factors of production, and if they are at all substantial they will prevent the marginal conditions of production from being met. Coase has also pointed out that income taxes are, as he put it, taxes on effort and waiting. Finally, Wald has demonstrated that the income tax will not only violate the marginal conditions, but furthermore that in certain instances excise taxes on specific commodities would diminish the welfare of the individual paying the tax less than would a generalized income tax.

Finally, because of this difficulty in raising the revenue required to finance the subsidies, pricing systems which would in themselves meet total costs have been proposed as alternatives to marginal cost pricing. Price discrimination, for instance, was suggested by Clemens, Lewis, and Coase. Coase also offered multi-part pricing, but it was quickly pointed out that the latter covered only a very special case. All such proposals, of course, represent departures from marginal cost pricing. For the most part, they have been rejected by the advocates of marginal cost pricing on the grounds of complexity and impossibility of actual operation. It thus becomes apparent that none of the variants of the marginal cost pricing system which have as yet been proposed actually do meet all of the marginal conditions for maximizing welfare. And, furthermore, it has been shown by some writers that it is not necessarily more important, from the point of view of increasing welfare, to meet the marginal conditions relating to the pricing of consumers' goods than it is to meet those conditions relating to payments to the factors of production.

The question which remains to be considered is that of whether or not the marginal cost pricing principle can be supported without reliance on interpersonal comparisons of utility. The interpretation of this question has given rise to considerable difference of opinion. The early writers who set out to establish a welfare system which was independent of interpersonal judgments — Pareto and Barone — defined such a system as one in which decisions about specific measures could only be made if everyone who would lose as a result of each measure were fully compensated for his loss. It would not be sufficient, they said, to consider what the results of such compensation would be if it were made; it must actually be made. This view of the meaning of the compensation principle was maintained later by Harrod and Robbins. Kaldor and Hicks, on the other hand, suggested that it was not necessary actually to pay compensation to determine whether or not a given measure would be beneficial. If the measure would increase welfare with compensation paid, they said, it would also increase welfare even if the compensation were not paid, and requiring the payment of the compensation would constitute an undue sanctification of the *status quo*. Since the economist cannot decide without making interpersonal comparisons whether the income distribution which preceded the change or that which would result from it would be preferable, he cannot say that it would be better to pay the compensation, so returning to the initial distribution of income. This concept of the compensation principle was further refined and extended by Scitovsky, who, by introducing a double criterion of increased welfare, removed a certain degree of ambiguity from it. Since then, however, it has been effectively demonstrated by Samuelson, Reder, and Arrow, among others, that compensation must actually be paid if interpersonal comparisons are to be avoided. It is true that no choice can be made between the income distribution existing before a proposed change and that which would result afterward, but it is for this very reason that no opinion can be offered on the desirability of the change, unless the compensation necessary to return to the original income distribution is actually paid. As Samuelson has said, the economist cannot say that the change should be made and the compensation paid; he can only say that the change could be made and the compensation could be paid with an increase in welfare. He cannot say that it is better to pay the compensation than not to; he simply cannot say anything at all about the case in which compensation is not paid.

The advocates of marginal cost pricing have, in general, not explicitly discussed the question of interpersonal comparisons — except to the extent of stating that marginal cost pricing would not require them — and they have, therefore, never specified whether their arguments depend upon the looser or the stricter form of the compensation principle. But it is apparent that implicit in the arguments of virtually all of the proponents of marginal cost pricing (for instance, Meade, Lange, Hotelling, Reder, and Lerner) is the idea that it is only necessary that compensation be possible, not that it be paid, in order to be able to say that a change to the marginal cost pricing system is desirable. Hotelling came the closest to an explicit consideration of the matter in his statement that certain groups in the economy would probably suffer as a result of the introduction of marginal cost pricing — namely, landowners and those in the upper income groups — but that the general well-being would have to be purchased at the cost of sacrifices by some. That the general well-being cannot be purchased at the cost of sacrifices by some without requiring the interpersonal judgment that the loss in utility by those who sacrifice is less than the gain in utility by those who gain was immediately pointed out by Frisch, and was again brought up by Pegrum and Coase. Even if it were possible, therefore, to finance the necessary subsidies entirely by means of lump-sum taxes, the arguments in favor of the marginal cost pricing system would still be dependent upon interpersonal comparisons of utility.

From this summary of the literature, it is evident that the Hotelling version of the marginal cost pricing principle is formally inconsistent on at least two points. Because it is proposed to finance the necessary subsidies by means of revenue derived from an income tax, the system fails to meet the marginal conditions relating to the factors of production. And, because the tax is not necessarily collected from the people who receive the benefit of the subsidies, support of the marginal cost pricing principle must be based on interpersonal comparisons of utility. The Reder–Lerner version of the principle, which fails to specify how the subsidies would be financed, is also inconsistent on two counts. It still requires interpersonal comparisons, in that it favors those who consume the products of decreasing cost industries over those who do not. And, second, the failure to consider the method of financing does not avoid the necessity for raising the revenue in some way or other. The system in this form is partial and would break down if made general. The following section will consider the practical importance of these points: whether because of these inconsistencies the whole idea must be rejected or whether, in spite of them, marginal cost pricing still would be advantageous.

4. EVALUATION

Since the marginal cost pricing system does not meet the standard its advocates claim, an evaluation of the proposal must consider the significance of this failure. As a first step in this direction, it will be useful to determine what changes would be needed to make the marginal cost pricing system conform to that standard, and also exactly what conditions and assumptions are involved in the system as it stands.

In order to make the marginal cost pricing system fulfill the requirements claimed for it, a method of financing would have to be provided that would meet the marginal conditions, and the compensation that has been omitted from the plan would have to be introduced. Introducing the compensation would in effect mean that the revenue for subsidizing any given product would have to be derived from the people who consumed that product, and not from anyone else. To do this without violating the marginal conditions, the tax would have to fall on the consumers' surplus derived by the purchasers from the consumption of that specific product. It could not bear upon the marginal unit purchased by any consumer, so any form of per-unit tax would be inadmissible. A tax that must fall upon the consumption of a specific product, but not upon the marginal unit, would of necessity yield a form of price discrimination. The marginal units to each consumer would have to be sold at marginal cost, with the difference between marginal cost and average cost made up by charging more than average cost on pre-marginal units. In order, therefore, to reach a pricing system which does actually meet the conditions which the advocates of marginal cost pricing claim their system meets, it would be necessary to abandon marginal cost pricing altogether, and adopt instead a special form of price discrimination. The proponents of marginal cost pricing have argued that price discrimination which is properly designed to meet the marginal conditions would be impossible to achieve in practice. If this objection were well founded, it would then have to be concluded that this line of analysis yields no one consistent and feasible system of pricing which will meet the marginal conditions and at the same time avoid any necessity for interpersonal comparisons of utility.

The assumptions upon which the marginal cost pricing system actually is based are easily derived. With respect to interpersonal comparisons, marginal cost pricing involves a redistribution of income from those who do not consume the products of decreasing cost industries to those who do. If this redistribution is to be either a matter of indifference or a net contribution to total utility, one of two conditions must be met: either the distribution of income, whatever it be, must be a matter of indifference, or this particular redistribution of income must not lessen welfare. To meet the first of these conditions, the original Pigovian assumption is necessary — the utility of income must be the same to all individuals, and therefore for all practical purposes constant. If the marginal utility of money is the same for all people, marginal transfers of income among individuals become a matter of indifference. The total utility of the community would not then be altered by a change in the distribution of income, even though the distribution of that total utility would be different. The manner in which the burden of financing the necessary subsidies is distributed would be a matter of indifference, and on this score, marginal cost pricing would be acceptable. As for the second condition (that this particular redistribution be acceptable even though others might not be), the redistribution in question would not be systematic with respect to income so that the only assumptions about the utility of income which would meet this condition are trivial. It thus becomes apparent that with regard to interpersonal comparisons of utility marginal cost pricing depends upon the same assumption as the old welfare economics of Marshall and Pigou. Like Pigou, it of necessity defines an increase in welfare as an increase in total output, somehow determined, and it does not even make the elementary restrictions with regard to distribution that Pigou did. If this definition of welfare is accepted, marginal cost pricing will not on this count interfere with the reaching of a maximum. In any other case it will.

The second implicit assumption made by the advocates of marginal cost pricing is to be found in the consideration of the marginal conditions. The financing of the Hotelling version of marginal cost pricing is based upon the income tax, and for this reason involves a violation of the marginal conditions relating to the factors of production. This violation of the marginal conditions would have no effect upon the allocation of resources, however, if it did not change the supply of the factors of production. Therefore, it is necessary, if the marginal cost pricing system is to meet all of the marginal conditions, to assume that the supply of the factors of production is fixed. The price received by the factors of production would then be a matter of indifference from the point of view of resource allocation, since it would have no effect upon their utilization, and the marginal conditions of production would be met regardless of what the net return to the factors might be. In other words, the income tax would be the same as a true lump-sum tax if it did not alter the supply of any of the factors of production.

These, then, are the assumptions which are implicit in the marginal cost pricing system: that, in the first place, the marginal utility of income is constant, and, in the second place, the supply of the factors of production is fixed. The reasonableness of these particular assumptions is of prime importance in assessing the practical merits of marginal cost pricing. Obviously, no unique decision can be made about the reasonableness of a set of assumptions; the question is one of personal opinion and each person is entitled to base his recommendations regarding the pricing system upon whatever assumptions seem to him to be most acceptable. It should be recognized, however, that advocacy of marginal cost pricing does involve these two particular assumptions, and that it does not rest upon the assumptions that its champions maintain.

In these circumstances, there are certain additional comments which seem relevant to the question of the desirability of marginal cost pricing. In the first place, it would seem to be true, as has been pointed out above, that it is not possible to design a pricing system upon the basis of some criterion of efficiency, and then to alter the income distribution in any desired way without affecting the efficiency of the pricing system. No such separation of the problem is possible. Every pricing system results in some sort of income distribution and no substantial redistribution of income is possible without changing that pricing system. For this reason, it is imperative that the question of interpersonal valuations be taken specifically into account. It is because of the failure to recognize this necessity, in maintaining that no interpersonal comparisons are involved, that objections can be raised to the marginal cost pricing thesis. Had the specific set of interpersonal valuations which is implicit in marginal cost pricing been chosen deliberately, one would have been entitled to differ with the choice but one could not have accused the thesis of inconsistency. In choosing a pricing system, it thus becomes necessary to make specific assumptions about interpersonal comparisons of utility, and then to judge the pricing system in relation to these assumptions as well as in relation to the marginal conditions.

In practice, for the design of a specific pricing system with interpersonal comparisons taken into account, the framework of marginal cost pricing would in many instances be found too restrictive. For example, assuming that a redistribution of income from the wealthy to the poor is desirable — as would be implied by the use of the income tax to finance marginal cost pricing — it is not always true that the income tax is the most efficient means of accomplishing this purpose and at the same time achieving an efficient allocation of resources. In certain situations, it has been demonstrated in the literature that excise taxes are more efficient in raising revenue than equivalent income taxes. The necessary conditions for this to be true are in all probability met by many luxury goods. Excise taxes on such luxury goods would therefore constitute an important source of revenue, which in cases of products for which the demand is inelastic could be obtained without significant violation of the marginal conditions. Reliance solely upon the income tax, insisting that the prices of all consumers' goods be set at marginal cost, thus neglects a device which would help to provide necessary revenue in a manner which would tend to alter the income distribution in the desired direction. The practical significance of such alternative sources of revenue becomes greater if the objective is not primarily that of achieving a certain specified distribution of income by lowering those at the top, but rather that of raising the level of the lower groups so that no one falls below some minimum. If a system of income taxes on income above a certain level is used to collect revenue to redistribute to persons with incomes below that level, there will, of course, be some limit to the amount that can be collected. A high tax rate will eventually restrict the supply of the factors of production offered by the group which is taxed, but excise taxes of equivalent amount might have no such restrictive effect. The total amount of revenue which could be collected (and so the total amount of productive factors freed for redistribution), might, therefore, be greater with excise taxes than with income taxes alone. With such an objective, a system which included excise taxes might produce greater general welfare than would income taxes alone, even if it did not add to the welfare of the taxpayers themselves.

A second problem, in addition to that of integrating specific interpersonal comparisons into the pricing system, relates to the practical problems to which any proposed pricing system would give rise. It was, in fact, upon this very basis that the advocates of marginal cost pricing rejected perfect price discrimination in favor of a system of constant pricing at marginal cost. Perfect price discrimination, they argued, would be too complex and too difficult to apply in practice, and marginal cost pricing would be much simpler. On this same basis it is evident that marginal cost pricing would also raise difficulties; there are a number of sectors of the economy in which for technological reasons marginal cost pricing would be unsatisfactory. This is particularly true of the distributive trades. By their very nature, distributive firms operate with marginal costs considerably below average cost. Operation of all retailing and wholesaling units with marginal cost pricing would pose almost insoluble problems with regard to entry, and therefore with regard to the correct operation of the whole distributive industry. Marginal cost pricing, in other words, does not satisfactorily solve many of the problems which are now disturbing the economy, and there is reason to believe that the adoption of marginal cost pricing might make some of the existing flaws even more troublesome. In many such instances, other methods — price discrimination itself, for instance — would prove far more workable. And if these alternatives should not prove adequate, it is frequently a moot question whether violating the marginal conditions by raising price slightly above marginal cost would diminish welfare any more than would the necessity for coping with the technological problems involved in marginal cost pricing.

Furthermore, it is quite likely that in certain sectors of the economy price discrimination which would meet the marginal conditions would not be difficult to arrive at, despite the protestations to the contrary of the proponents of marginal cost pricing. Demand curves are not smooth and continuous and single-valued, they contain many discontinuities, and there are many products for which demand is almost perfectly inelastic within the relevant range. Taking advantage of such discontinuities and inelasticities, the construction of work-able systems of price discrimination which will not violate the marginal conditions is quite feasible. For example, it is probably true that the use of block systems of rates for electricity does not appreciably interfere with the meeting of the marginal conditions, since it is to be doubted whether house-holders greatly reduce their consumption of electricity because they cannot obtain additional amounts at the industrial rate. Similarly, with respect to many large items of consumers' expenditures — household appliances, for example — many consumers are quite willing to pay average cost for one unit, and the fact that they cannot buy a second unit at marginal cost has no effect upon their purchases, since they would not buy an additional unit even if it were priced at marginal cost. And whether or not they buy the first unit may be primarily a question of the distribution of income, rather than of pricing alone. Such dis-continuities make it possible to meet total costs in many decreasing cost industries without violating the marginal conditions appreciably. In other in-stances, inelasticities perform the same function. Price discrimination between different lines of a product produced by one firm, for instance, is a device to cover total costs by charging more than average cost on some lines and less than average cost on others. Examples of such price discrimination are to be found in the pricing of consumers' durables — radios, for instance. Some con-sumers are willing to pay more for a radio in a fancy case, but no consumer who can pay even marginal cost will go without one, since a low-priced line in a plain case is also available. The consumer who buys the more expensive radio will pay a price which is greater by far more than the actual difference in marginal cost of the two radios — in other words the low-priced line may be sold at very nearly marginal cost, and most of the overhead recovered on the high-priced line. Such devices for covering total costs and at the same time approaching the marginal conditions are prevalent in the economy today, and especially so in those industries which would technologically lend themselves best to marginal cost pricing. The abolition of all presently existing price discrimination in favor of constant marginal cost pricing would therefore not necessarily represent a net gain. The existence of high or inelastic demand may even limit the application of the marginal cost pricing principle in the specific case most often used as an example by the advocates of marginal cost pricing, that of tolls on bridges. Hotelling himself would recognize that if the traffic is greater than the capacity of the bridge a rental charge may properly be made, in order to assure that the privilege of utilizing the existing capacity will go to those who most desire it. On this basis, the tolls on the Hudson River bridges and tunnels (to which Hotelling so vigorously objects) may not be so objec-tionable after all, at least at certain periods of the day. Furthermore, if the toll is small in comparison with the other costs incurred by the individuals making use of the service, demand may be sufficiently inelastic so that the toll will have little or no effect upon use. Such, for instance, may be the case with respect to the tolls on the New York parkway system. Gasoline costs and the difference in time saved in comparison with the size of the toll may make for considerable inelasticity in demand over the relevant range. The social cost (reduction in use) involved in allocating the cost of the highway to those who make use of it thus may be very small in relation to the total revenue involved.

Finally, it should be pointed out that there is a whole set of arguments advanced by the advocates of marginal cost pricing which can be used equally well to support pricing at other than marginal cost levels. Hotelling, for instance, supported the pricing of power projects at marginal cost on the ground that others besides those directly involved would benefit. This is a very good argument for pricing many commodities below, rather than at, marginal cost. Milk for children, subway transportation in large cities, and many other commodities and services might better be so priced. The nation has a stake in healthy children, and the benefits accrue to others besides the children and those upon whom they are dependent for support. Similarly, it can be argued that the subways benefit landowners, automobile drivers, and employers in large cities. There is, therefore, no necessary reason why the price charged to those who ride the subways should be equal to marginal cost — some part of that marginal cost might well be borne by the others who benefit from each person's riding, or, if the benefit is widespread, by general taxation.

Thus it appears that, since the distribution of income must be taken into account, there is no one general pricing system which will be more efficient than all others for all sectors of the economy. Different pricing principles are economic tools which find applicability in different circumstances. The task of the economist in designing price systems is not so much one of finding a general panacea, but rather one of the systematic analysis of the special problems which arise in different sectors of the economy. Marginal cost pricing may very well increase welfare in certain specific situations. The fact that it is not applicable as a general system does not mean that it should be disregarded altogether. Certain railway and utility rates do provide an area in which marginal cost pricing would increase welfare. Hotelling was undoubtedly right in pointing out that the gain enjoyed by those who benefit from the lower price is frequently greater than the loss borne by those helping to subsidize the industry, and the attempt to assess the burden carefully may lead to greater diseconomy than allocating it incorrectly (even though in so stating he contradicted his original assumptions).

In summary, then, the design of a pricing system must take into account the conditions which do exist in the economy. The various sectors of the economy differ from one another in the restrictions which they impose on the pricing system, and what is appropriate for one sector may be completely inappropriate for another. No one formula can be established which will be valid as a general

Price Theory

principle. But one statement can be made: the search for a panacea, for a single simple rule by which to guide all conduct is, because of the technological requirements of the different parts of the economy and because of the problems of redistribution, a vain search and even a foolish one. A set of tools is available with which to accomplish a complicated job. A better job can be done if each tool is used where it is appropriate, instead of throwing away all but one and expecting it to serve all purposes.

REFERENCES

Bonbright, J.C. (1940), 'Major controversies as to the criteria of reasonable public utility rates', *Papers and Proceedings of the American Economic Association,* **30,** 379–89.

Clemens, E.W. (1941), 'Price discrimination in decreasing cost industries', *American Economic Review,* **31,** 794–802.

Coase, R.H. (1945), 'Price and output policy of state enterprise: A comment', *Economic Journal,* **55,** 112–13.

———— (1946), 'The marginal cost controversy', *Economica,* n.s., **33,** 169–82.

———— (1947), 'The marginal cost controversy: Some further comments', *Economica,* n.s., **14,** 150–53.

Dupuit, Jules (1932), 'De l'Utilité et de sa Mesure', Collected and reprinted with comments by Mario di Bernardi and Luigi Einaudi, *La Reforma Sociale,* Turin.

Fleming, J.M. (1944), 'Price and output policy of state enterprise: A comment', *Economic Journal,* **54,** 328–37.

Frisch, Ragnar (1939a), 'The Dupuit taxation theorem', *Econometrica,* 7, 145–50.

———— (1939b), 'A further note on the dupuit taxation theorem', *Econometrica,* 7, 150–57.

Hicks, J.R. (1938), *Value and Capital,* London, pp. 40–41.

Hicks, Ursula (1936), *The Finance of British Government, 1920–1936,* London.

Hotelling, Harold (1938), 'The general welfare in relation to problems of taxation and of railway and utility rates', *Econometrica,* 6, 242–69.

———— (1939a), 'The relation of prices to marginal costs in an optimum system', *Econometrica,* 7, 151–5.

———— (1939b), 'A final note', *Econometrica,* 7, 158–60.

Joseph, M.W.F. (1939), 'The excess burden of indirect taxation', *Review of Economic Studies,* 6, 226–31.

Lerner, A.P. (1944), *The Economics of Control,* New York.

Lewis, W.A. (1941a), 'The two-part tariff', *Economica,* n.s., **8,** 249–70.

———— (1941b), 'The two-part tariff: A reply', *Economica,* n.s., **8,** 399–408.

Meade, J.E. (1944a), 'Price and output policy of state enterprise', *Economic Journal,* **54,** 321–8.

———— (1944b), 'Rejoinder', *Economic Journal,* **54,** 337–9.

———— (1946), 'Review of Lerner's *Economics of Control*', *Economic Journal,* **55,** 47–69.

Montgomery, R.H. (1939a), 'Government ownership and operation of the electric industry', *Annals of the American Academy of Political and Social Science*, **201**, 43–9.

_____ (1939b), 'Government ownership and operation of railroads', *Annals of the American Academy of Political and Social Science*, **201**, 137–45.

Nordin, J.A. (1947), 'The marginal cost controversy: A reply', *Economica*, n.s., **14**, 134–49.

Norris, H. (1947), 'State enterprise and output policy and the problem of cost imputation', *Economica*, n.s., **14**, 54–62.

Pegrum, D.F. (1944), 'Incremental cost pricing: A comment', *Journal of Land and Public Utility Economics*, **20**, 58–60.

Reder, M.W. (1947), *Studies in the Theory of Welfare Economics*, New York.

Robinson, H.W. (1939), 'Consumer's surplus and taxation: Ex-ante or ex-post?', *South African Journal of Economics*, **7**, 270–80.

Samuelson, P.A. (1947), *The Foundations of Economic Analysis*, Cambridge.

Thirlby, G.F. (1947), 'The marginal cost controversy: A note on Mr. Coase's model', *Economica*, n.s., **14**, 48–53.

Troxel, E. (1943), 'Incremental cost determination of utility prices', *Journal of Land and Public Utility Economics*, **19**, 292–9.

_____ (1944), 'Incremental cost pricing: A further comment', *Journal of Land and Public Utility Economics*, **20**, 60–63.

Vickrey, William (1948), 'Some objections to marginal cost pricing', *Journal of Political Economy*, **56**.

Wald, H.P. (1945), 'The classical indictment of indirect taxation', *Quarterly Journal of Economics*, **59**, 577–96.

Wallace, Donald (1939), 'Kinds of public control to replace or supplement anti-trust laws', *Papers and Proceedings of the American Economic Association*, **29**, 194–212.

_____ (1941), *Economic Standards of Price Control*, Monograph No. 32, Temporary National Economic Committee, 76th Congress, 3rd Session, pp. 414–15.

Wilson, T. (1945), 'Price and output policy of state enterprise: A comment', *Economic Journal*, **55**, 454–61.

3. Discriminatory and Competitive Pricing

Nancy D. Ruggles
Radcliffe College

1. DISCRIMINATORY PRICING

The Definition of Discriminatory Pricing

In the following discussion, the terms discriminatory pricing, price discrimination and price differentiation are used interchangeably, all in the sense which is defined in this following section.

Discriminatory pricing has, in economic literature, ordinarily been considered to be a function of monopoly over a single commodity. Pigou, for instance, discussed discriminatory pricing in a chapter entitled 'Discriminating Monopoly', which described the pricing of a single commodity. In taking this approach, he was following the traditional treatment of price discrimination in the previous literature. His discussion represents the culmination of the classical development of the subject, and therefore, will be taken as a starting point for this discussion.

Pigou based his definition of discriminatory pricing on the concept of an identical commodity which, at one point in time, is sold at different prices. He distinguished three degrees of price discrimination. Price discrimination of the first degree involves charging a different price for each unit of the commodity sold in such a way that the price exacted for each is equal to the demand price for it and no consumers' surplus is left to the buyers. In later economic literature, this type of price discrimination is termed 'perfect'. Perfect price discrimination does not violate the marginal conditions, since each buyer has an opportunity to buy at marginal cost when he is no longer willing to pay more than marginal cost. Price discrimination of the second degree would exist if a monopolist were to charge x separate prices in such a way that all units with a

---

This chapter was part of the author's 1949 Ph.D. thesis and was unpublished.

demand price greater than x were sold for x, all with a demand price less than x but greater than y and so forth. This type of price discrimination also meets the marginal conditions, but does not exact the full amount that consumers would be willing to pay. The price for some units of the commodity will be below that which could be exacted, but any buyers who are willing to buy any units of the commodity at or above marginal cost will be satisfied. Price discrimination of the third degree would exist if a monopolist were able in some way to separate his customers into different groups, and if for each of these groups the monopolist could charge a different monopoly price. This system of price discrimination does not meet the marginal conditions, since some individuals will not be able to buy additional units at marginal cost.

These definitions of discriminatory pricing proved not to be as clear-cut as they at first seemed. A controversy arose between Pigou (1912b) and Taussig (1912) on the question of whether under this definition railroad freight rate structures represent discrimination. Pigou's (1929, pp. 290–303) final views were that the railroad is selling one commodity, transportation, and charging different rates to different groups, and that this is price discrimination of the third degree. Taussig's view was that the transportation of each different commodity represents a different product, so that the railroad is selling different services to the different buyers. The situation then is one of joint products rather than of price discrimination. Both Pigou and Taussig based their definitions of discrimination on the concept of product homogeneity, and although other writers (Watkins, 1916) in this period felt that this basis was insecure no satisfactory alternative was developed.

Lerner (1933) was one of the first to explicitly reject physical similarity of products as a basis for the classification of commodities. He recognized that the same things at different places are different commodities, saying that the definition of a commodity should be based on economic rather than on physical considerations. 'In calling the same thing at different places different commodities', he said, 'we have rejected the criterion of physical similarity as a basis for the recognition or classification of commodities and have put in its place substitutability at the margin.' Triffin (1940, pp. 90–95) applied this concept to a general definition, such that every unit of an item is in essence a different commodity, since it fills different needs. The same kind of cloth sold to different customers cannot, in an economic sense, be said to be the same commodity, since it fills different needs. Even when a number of units of a given product are sold to one individual, these different units represent different commodities to him, since the marginal unit will of necessity fill a need different from that filled by the first unit. Lerner admits that such a concept of a commodity is so abstract and elusive as to be unusable, but he points out that this is really an advantage, since it prevents the misuse of inconsistent definitions based on physical similarities; inadequate definitions may well lead to more confusion than the avoidance of any definition at all.

A consistent definition of price discrimination was finally developed by John Miller (1941, pp. 122–5). His treatment recognizes the commodity definition of Lerner and Triffin, and his final definition is in no way dependent on homogeneity of commodities such as had been assumed by Pigou and Taussig. He pointed out that the use of the term 'discrimination' with reference to industrial practice was extremely confused, and that while it usually referred to differences in price or quality there seemed to be little consistent basis to the definition. More differences in price or quality would not be sufficient evidence of discrimination, unless all of the variables in a sale (price, quality, services, terms, marginal cost, etc.) except one were identical. In other words, discrimination can be said to occur when a seller charges different prices for two or more identical units sold at the same moment of time under identical conditions. This definition is more restricted than Pigou's and Taussig's, but at the same time it is more capable of being generalized. Miller goes on to point out that cases in which only one variable differs are very rare; it is far more likely that two or more variables will be different between two sales. Strictly speaking, under the Pigovian definition there were only two ways out of this dilemma. Either the differences had to be ignored (the solution Pigou took) or the concept of price discrimination had to be declared irrelevant since more than one commodity was involved (Taussig's argument). But for purposes of public policy neither of these alternatives is very satisfactory. Even when two or more commodities are involved, it is often important to be able to determine whether price discrimination exists between two markets. Miller, therefore, extends the definition to cover the case in which both the prices and the costs of production of two products are different. On the basis of the marginal costs of producing the two commodities, a specific differential would be expected in their prices. If this differential is not found to exist, the prices of the two commodities can be said to be discriminatory with reference to each other. For example, an aluminum company might be expected to sell aluminum ingot at one price and fabricated aluminum at another price. A specific differential would be expected between the two on the basis of the difference in marginal cost, but price differentials which are either greater or less than this amount can be considered discriminatory. If a firm charges marginal cost for all of its products, the prices which result cannot be said to be discriminatory between customers. Furthermore, if two prices bear the same proportion to marginal cost, neither can be considered more discriminatory than the other, though both may be more discriminatory than another price which is equal to marginal cost. Measuring price discrimination by the relation of price to marginal cost is equivalent to Lerner's measure of the degree of monopoly power [(price − marginal cost)/price]. Miller maintains that this measure is an appropriate one since discrimination, by its very nature, implies some monopoly power, and discriminatory prices are the same as monopoly power. Although the exact meaning of monopoly power in this sense is somewhat obscure, it is certainly true that this relationship of price to marginal cost does yield an operational definition of price discrimination between different commodities.

Before going on to consider different types of price discrimination, it is necessary to clarify the exact meaning of the definition in certain specific situations. In the first place, where the factors of production are limited, an increase in demand will cause prices to rise without increasing the quantity supplied. This price rise does not create a disparity between price and marginal cost, but rather represents the accrual of rents to the factors of production; price may still equal marginal costs. Translated into curve analysis, in Figure 3.1, the new demand curve $(D'-D')$ would still intersect the (discontinuous portion of) marginal cost curve at a point representing the same output, and a price equal to marginal cost at the point of intersection would not be discriminatory. Production at capacity yields rents, which must be included in marginal cost, so that marginal cost becomes the amount at which the purchaser with the lowest reservation price is willing to resell. If some individuals are charged more than this price, there is price discrimination, since with a free market it would be possible to obtain the unit of the marginal individual by slightly outbidding his reservation price. Rent will exist in a market in which there is free interchange of goods, but price discrimination cannot. For price discrimination to exist, monopoly control such that some individuals do not have access to certain units of the product at their marginal supply price is essential.

In the second place, under this definition of price discrimination, a monopolist may be engaging in discriminatory pricing even though he charges the one single price which maximizes his profit to all comers. In a situation such as that illustrated by Figure 3.2, for instance, any single price above the constant marginal cost would be discriminatory. Within the relevant range, capacity will not be reached and the marginal cost curve will not become discontinuous, so that rents cannot exist in the sense that they do in Figure 3.1.

Applying this definition to the Pigou–Taussig controversy about railroad rates, it becomes evident that railroad rate structures do, in fact, represent discriminatory pricing, both as between the transportation of different commodities (since all of the rates do not bear the same relation to marginal cost) and with respect to any other goods and services which are priced at marginal cost. Pigou, thus, was correct with regard to railroads, but a second example which he cited, the case of a hotel which charges different rates in different seasons, does not necessarily fit into this definition. If, when the demand is high, the hotel charges a rate which will just fill it to capacity and, when the

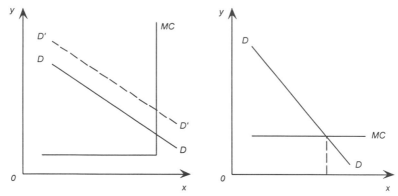

Figure 3.1 No price discrimination   *Figure 3.2 Price discrimination*

demand is low, it charges marginal cost, there will be no discrimination between the two rates, even though they may be very different. When demand is
high, the hotel will be receiving economic rent, but will still be pricing at the
marginal supply price. The change in demand, therefore, produces a change
in the rental payment, but does not produce price discrimination. Had the
example been cast in the traditional theory of land rents instead of hotel rates,
this conclusion probably would have been obvious to Pigou. Rents will exist
with competitive marketing of products, but price discrimination can exist only
with monopoly.

Discriminatory pricing is extremely widespread in the economy as it exists
today. Almost all public utilities by their very nature make use of it. Not only
railroads, but also streetcars and buses, gas and electric companies, water-
works, and even taxicabs use discriminatory pricing as a device to cover their
costs. In most of these industries, of course, marginal cost pricing could not
cover total costs, and discrimination as between customers yields greater
revenue than would any one uniform price. Municipal transit companies, for
instance, often sell passes entitling the holder to unlimited rides within a fixed
time period for a given sum, or they sell a given number of tokens at a discount
from the regular fare. Other utilities — gas, electric and water companies —
usually manage to charge different prices for different units sold to the same
consumer. A fixed charge or a higher rate on the first units taken enables the
company to offer marginal services at a low rate, and so encourages utilization;
such a procedure yields a greater total revenue for them than would a division
of the customers into groups in each of which a uniform price is charged.
Taxicabs in some localities similarly charge differential rates according to the
number in the group carried, and the differences ordinarily do not correspond
to any differences in costs.

Product price discrimination is evident in many other industries besides public utilities. Product differentiation is, of course, primarily designed to permit price discrimination, and conventional methods of selling often produce this result even when it is not consciously intended. Manufacturers often put out several models or brands of their products in which the price differential does not correspond to the cost differential. In the usual practice, a deluxe model is priced relatively higher with respect to its cost than a utility model. Packaging, branding and advertising all similarly serve to separate products into different markets and to enable manufacturers to make price differentials which do not correspond to differences in factor cost. Price discrimination is widespread, also, in the distributive trades. Manufacturers sell their products at different discounts to different groups of distributors, and in most cases the discounts are not directly proportional to any differences in costs. (This procedure is considered a fair trade practice, although discrimination between members of the same group is considered unfair.) Both wholesalers and retailers indulge in probably unconscious price discrimination, by virtue of the practice of charging mark-ups which are based on the value of the item sold. There is usually very little relation between the cost of selling a good and its value; the cost of selling an inexpensive item may be greater than the cost of selling more expensive items, so that the items of greater value bear more than their share of the selling costs in the economy.

Excise taxes also lead to price discrimination, since the producer will treat the tax as a part of his marginal cost in calculating his price and output, but from the point of view of the economy as a whole the added amount of the excise tax does not represent factor cost. Subsidies likewise can lead to price discrimination, since they may alter the producer's conception of his marginal cost. (The discrimination resulting from subsidies, of course, may balance existing price discrimination in the opposite direction, so that the effect of the subsidy may be to reduce the amount of price discrimination.)

Finally, prices of factors of production, as well as those of products, may be discriminatory. Whenever a factor does not receive the value of its marginal product, price discrimination exists. Of necessity, therefore, factor price discrimination will exist wherever there is product price discrimination. When marginal factor cost differs from price — i.e., when there is price discrimination with respect to products — not all of the factors can be receiving the value of their marginal products, so that, by definition, factor price discrimination must also exist. Factor price discrimination may also exist even when there is no product price discrimination. Social insurance contributions, corporate profits taxes and personal income taxes all result in a difference between what is paid to the factor and what the factor receives, so that even though the factor may be paid the value of its marginal product, the amount it actually receives will be different.

Discriminatory pricing, therefore, is absent only when products sell for amounts which are equal to the marginal costs of their production, and when the factors of production receive for their contributions the full value of their marginal products. The complete absence of discriminatory pricing, of course, would also imply that all prices are equal to average cost as well as marginal cost, since no source other than receipts from sales would be available for meeting total costs which would not involve price discrimination somewhere in the economy. It also requires, therefore, the complete absence of decreasing cost industries.

It should be noted at this point that marginal cost pricing does involve discrimination if decreasing costs exist anywhere in the economy. Marginal cost pricing, it is true, prices products at their marginal factor cost, but the subsidization of decreasing cost industries means that some at least of the factors of production will be receiving more than the value of their marginal product. If an industry is not used to capacity — as a decreasing cost industry by definition is not — the marginal cost of using certain of its overhead items will be zero, and zero is what they should receive under a rigorous system of pricing according to marginal productivity. The marginal cost pricing system, recognizing that production would be impossible without the fixed factors even though their marginal productivity is zero, departs from uniform pricing to provide subsidies for decreasing cost industries. For this reason, however, the conclusions which apply to uniform pricing systems do *not* apply to the marginal cost pricing system.

Price Discrimination and the Distribution of Income

In a uniform pricing system — one in which there is no price discrimination — the distribution of income will have economic significance. An individual's income under such a pricing system would represent a given quantity of the factors of production, valued at marginal cost. It would be a matter of indifference to the economy how an individual distributed his income among various expenditures, since any pattern of choices would represent the same value of productive factors used. A given level of income, irrespective of how it is spent, would be equivalent to a specific quantity of the factors of production. The distribution of income would determine the distribution of factors in their marginal uses. Assuming that the choices of individuals are rational, the resource allocation pattern would be an optimum relative to the given income distribution, since individuals will always use their incomes (and in this case, the factors of production) in such a way that the greatest welfare will result. Economizing of income, under a uniform price system, would automatically result in economizing of the factors of production.

Although with a uniform pricing system there is a direct relation between income and the factors of production, it does not, of course, follow that there is a direct relation between income and satisfactions. The same quantity of the factors of production may very well mean differing satisfactions for different individuals. If one individual wears a larger size of clothes than another, he will need more cloth, even assuming that one suit of clothes will yield the same satisfaction to both. Differences in tastes, family size, occupation, locality, and many other factors will all lead to differences in the amount of satisfaction which an individual can derive from a given income, even when that income implies a definite quantity of the factors of production. Income distribution, therefore, is by no means equivalent to the distribution of satisfactions, even in this limited case.

This distribution of income which exists under a system of uniform pricing must follow directly from the relative productivity of the different factors of production. Less productive individuals will receive less income and more productive individuals will receive more. Furthermore, there can be no systematic redistribution *of income* from those with higher incomes to those with lower incomes without destroying the uniformity of the pricing system, since such a redistribution would alter the return to the factors, and prices would no longer be uniform. Whenever the income of individuals does not follow directly from their productivity, discriminatory pricing exists, at least on the factor side.

When prices are not all equal to marginal factor cost, the nominal distribution of income loses much of what meaning it has under uniform pricing. If prices do not equal marginal factor costs, the same income spent in different patterns will use up different quantities of the factors of production. An individual who spends his income on commodities with prices above marginal cost will get less for his money in terms of productive factors than he would if he spent it for commodities priced at marginal cost. Prices, as well as the nominal distribution of income, become important in determining the distribution of the factors of production among different individuals. Income — i.e., command over the factors of production — is in effect transferred from those who buy products priced above factor cost to those who sell these products (or, when taxes cause the discrepancy, to the government). Discriminatory pricing thus involves a transfer of income over and above factor cost, and this transfer essentially constitutes a redistribution of income.

Discriminatory pricing has a redistributive effect, as well as the expected allocative effect, but in certain instances the allocative effect of discriminatory pricing may be identical with that of uniform pricing. This is true, for instance, of first-degree (perfect) and second-degree (marginally correct) price discrimination. Both of these meet the marginal conditions of exchange, since in both the marginal price which each individual pays for his marginal unit of a product would be equal to marginal cost. The discrimination applies only to the pre-marginal units. It will not alter the choices of individuals with respect to the marginal units. In other words, price discrimination of the first and second degree differs from uniform pricing in its distributive effect only; its effect on the allocation of resources is the same. The choices of individuals would differ under uniform pricing and price discrimination of the first and second degree because of an income effect, but not because of any substitution effect. Such price discrimination is similar, in this respect, to the levying of lump-sum taxes. The basis upon which the redistribution is carried out may be different, but the restriction to distributive effects is the same.

Price discrimination of the third degree — that in which a producer's sales are divided into different groups, within which different prices are charged — does contravene the marginal conditions of exchange. It differs from uniform pricing, therefore, both in its distributive effects and in its allocative effects. Under certain plausible circumstances, the effect of price discrimination of the third degree may be identical to that of price discrimination of the first or second degree; whenever the demand curve is discontinuous over the relevant range of prices, the technical failure of the price system to meet the marginal conditions will have no bearing upon the allocation of resources. In the more usual case, price discrimination of the third degree will alter the choices of individuals at the margin, as well as effecting a redistribution of income.

Price discrimination of the third degree may accomplish a given redistribution (if it is systematically designed for the purpose, as it would be if the price discrimination resulted from the introduction of taxes), but it will do it at the cost of using more factors of production than are necessary to permit a given level of satisfactions to be reached. If a person spends all of his income on commodities which have discriminatory prices because of commodity taxes, he will consume fewer factors of production than he would if he consumed commodities priced at factor cost, and the difference will be available for redistribution. However, price discrimination on the marginal unit, if demand is not discontinuous or very inelastic, will lead individuals to shift some of their consumption to other commodities, some of which are priced more nearly at marginal cost. The final level of satisfaction which the individual reaches, therefore, will be one which with uniform pricing he could have reached using a smaller quantity of the factors of production, and the quantity of the factors of production available for redistribution will be smaller by this amount than they would have been had the redistribution been effected by lump-sum taxation. The use of price discrimination of the third degree as a method of redistributing income thus entails a cost; the level of satisfaction reached by the individuals from whom income is taken is less than it might be with the same quantity of the factors of production, or, what is the same thing from a different point of view, the quantity of the factors of production available for redistribution is less than it might have been leaving the taxed individuals with the same level of satisfaction.

Price discrimination of the third degree for the purpose of redistribution may be imposed either on the factor side (income or profits taxes) or on the product side (excise taxes). Systematic redistribution of income from those with the highest standards of living to those with lower standards thus may be accomplished either on the basis of the incomes which these individuals receive or on the basis of their patterns of expenditure. Ideally, of course, redistribution should be accomplished by methods which are similar in their effects to lump-sum taxes — i.e., by price discrimination of the first and second degree. But such methods are not always adequate for the particular systematic redistribution which is desired, and other methods must be employed. Any third-degree price discrimination will involve violation of the marginal conditions either on factors or on products, and it is not possible *a priori* to say whether price discrimination which departs from uniform pricing because of excise taxes on certain types of luxury, for instance, is more or less desirable as a method of redistribution than price discrimination which departs from uniform pricing because of an income tax. Unless it is assumed that the marginal utility of income is equal for all individuals, the seriousness of violating the marginal conditions will depend in large part upon for what particular individuals in the economy the marginal conditions are violated. The problem thus becomes one of maximizing total welfare rather than one of maximizing individual welfare, and interpersonal comparisons are necessary. Some of the factors bearing upon the relative efficiency in redistributing income of income and excise taxes were pointed out in the discussion of marginal cost pricing, but they are of sufficient importance to be worth restating with specific reference to discriminatory pricing systems.

The income tax maintains the marginal conditions of exchange: the individual does get the greatest possible satisfaction out of the quantity of the factors of production which he receives; but his preferences between income and leisure are altered. In order to reach an effective rate of taxation on large incomes which is high enough to accomplish the desired redistribution, the marginal rate may have to be high enough to lower seriously the incentive to work. Income taxes which are as high as would be necessary to accomplish the redistribution thus may defeat their own purpose if they lead individuals to consume leisure instead of taxable income. An income tax would actually increase the amount of work which would be offered only when an individual sacrifices leisure in order to maintain more nearly his current standard of living, and this would occur ordinarily only where the marginal utility of income is relatively high, such as it might be among the lower income groups. An income tax designed to maximize the supply of the factors of production, therefore, would conflict with the redistributive aim, and an income tax designed purely for redistribution would seriously limit the supply of the factors of production. This conflict is all the more important when a large portion of the population is below an adequate standard of living, and it is essential for the achievement of the maximum welfare for the group that the redistribution not seriously impair the factor supply. When taxation involves 20 or 30 percent of the national income, the question ceases to be one of taxing only really wealthy individuals — say the upper 1 or 2 percent; individuals whose income amounts to no more than two or three times the average may be called on for contributions substantial enough to affect their incentive to work. The fact that the income tax bears first on the supply of the factors of production and only second on the consumption of individuals may then become significant.

With excise taxes on specific commodities, it may be possible to tax individuals according to their patterns of consumption. Individuals with higher standards of living consume different types of commodities from those consumed by individuals with lower standards of living, not simply more of the same commodities. A family which is well off will consume different kinds of foods, and will purchase different types of consumers' durable goods, than will a family which is less well off. Excise taxes which take these patterns into account can in effect redistribute income according to the standard of living enjoyed by the consumer. Excise taxes, like income taxes, may be sufficiently high to price commodities out of the market and so defeat their purpose, but a well-designed system of excise taxes on specific goods might create a demand for income among upper income groups rather than discourage it; the demand for specific commodities may still be inelastic even though the demand for generalized income — the supply of labor — is not. Under these circumstances, more rather than less of the factors of production would be available for redistribution. An income tax, to operate similarly, would have to be designed to tax individuals according to the elasticity of their demand curves for leisure — and this, besides being impracticable, would usually defeat the purpose of the redistribution. Excise taxes, therefore, may offer greater selectivity and flexibility, they can be levied on different commodities with respect to the price and income elasticity of the different income groups, and so can be shaped with regard to the considerations both of the effect on the supply of the factors of production and of the relative amount of redistribution made possible. It is probable, therefore, that a system which attempts to achieve an optimum distribution of income within the welfare framework will obtain better results if both income and excise taxes are utilized.

Likewise, a pricing system involving discrimination other than that due to taxation may yield results superior to a uniform pricing system if the problem of altering the distribution of income is taken into account. The pricing system as it now exists places more of the burden of overhead and selling costs on persons consuming more expensive goods than on persons consuming cheaper goods, so that lower income groups get a greater quantity of the factors of production for a given outlay than do the upper income groups. A correction of this situation by pricing entirely in accord with marginal factor cost might decrease welfare instead of increasing it, if the problem of redistribution between income groups is difficult to solve.

Considering the pricing system only as it affects the allocation of resources, therefore, neglects an essential part of the problem. Assuming that the patterns of consumers' preferences and the productivity functions of factors are fixed, any complete system of pricing carries with it a specific distribution of income, and prescribing a complete price system will therefore at least initially dictate the type of income distribution which will exist. If this distribution of income is considered undesirable, the economic problems involved in designing a system of redistribution will involve alteration of the prescribed pricing system itself and of the allocation of resources which follows from it. Disregarding the problems related to redistributing income overlooks but does not avoid the difficulties which exist. The problems of redistribution which accompany different price systems will be quite different, and some systems will lend themselves to redistributing techniques which are ruled out of other systems. In a system which admits price discrimination, for instance, redistribution may be simpler than in a uniform pricing system. The economist, therefore, does not fulfill his task when he gives attention only to the allocation side of the problem. Technical economic knowledge is required to achieve any given desired income distribution in a manner which is compatible with efficient resource allocation, and the price system must be shaped to both problems. It is not up to the economist to decide what the income distribution should be, but once that decision has been made by the society, the economist should know how to achieve it.

Price Discrimination in Decreasing and Increasing Cost Industries

It has been pointed out in the previous chapters that the marginal cost pricing system rests upon interpersonal comparisons, comparing the gain achieved by those purchasing a commodity with the loss sustained by those subsidizing the industry, and that in effect this system rests upon the implicit assumption that the marginal utility of income is the same for all individuals regardless of their level of income or other characteristics. It is now possible to reinterpret this same point in terms of the above discussion of the income distribution.

It has already been pointed out that marginal cost pricing is more than just a system of resource allocation; it involves a systematic redistribution of the factors of production in favor of those who consume the products of decreasing cost industries. This principle of distribution must be accepted by anyone who advocates the marginal cost pricing principle, since redistribution necessarily involves an abandonment of the marginal cost pricing system. If the total costs of decreasing cost industries are actually covered by the people consuming the products of the industries, the system becomes one of product price discrimination, not constant marginal cost pricing. All of this has been discussed before, but the objection may have been raised that there has been a lack of symmetry between the treatment of decreasing and increasing cost industries. If individuals buying the products of decreasing cost industries should pay the total costs of their products, it may be argued, individuals buying the products of increasing cost industries should symmetrically get the benefit of the surplus created in these industries. Alternatively, if it is correct that the surplus of increasing cost industries should not be given back to the consumers of the specific products of these industries, it has been suggested that this surplus can be used as a subsidy for the decreasing cost industries.

The lack of symmetry between the treatment of decreasing and increasing cost industries is directly attributable to the definition of the distribution of income. Welfare is said to increase whenever some individuals are better off and no individuals are worse off; regardless of how the surplus is distributed, the basic distribution of income is not considered to have changed. But a decrease in welfare is by definition impossible without a change in the distribution of income. It cannot be definitely said that a decreasing cost industry is worth operating if those who consume the products do not pay all of the costs, but in an increasing cost industry it may be true that everyone who consumes the product will be better off than if the industry did not exist and no one will be worse off even though those consuming the product do not receive *all* of the benefits of the industry. A decreasing cost industry operating at marginal cost would cause a change in the income distribution, and interpersonal comparisons would be needed to make an adequate evaluation of the merits of this pricing system. With an increasing cost industry, a surplus will arise which the marginal cost pricing system will distribute in some specific way, but *any* distribution of the gain will increase welfare over what it would be without the industry, and interpersonal comparisons are not required to say that there has been a gain.

The surplus which would be created by pricing the products of increasing cost industries at marginal cost would become rent to the factors of production, and for the fixed factors taxation of a portion of this rent might not affect resource allocation. The appropriate distribution of this portion of the surplus is then not determinable by welfare considerations. But it does not follow that such surplus should be used to subsidize the decreasing cost industries. A simultaneous introduction of an increasing and a decreasing cost industry, with the costs of the decreasing cost industry fully covered by the surplus of the increasing cost industry would, of course, increase welfare, but the introduction of the increasing cost industry alone would also increase welfare, and it cannot be demonstrated that combining it with a decreasing cost industry would produce the greater increase. This would perhaps be more evident if the criterion for saying that, without doubt, the industry is a factor increasing welfare be stated in the form that the removal of an industry should make some people worse off and no one better off. Increasing cost industries priced at marginal cost meet this test, regardless of what is done with the surplus, but decreasing cost industries do not. Those who had bought the product would be worse off, but those who no longer had to pay the subsidy (or who now received it) would be better off.

In like manner, as a consequence of the definition of the distribution of income, it can be said that a decreasing cost industry operating with discriminatory pricing in such a way as to meet the marginal conditions and cover its total costs is preferable to the nonexistence of the industry, but it is not possible to say without introducing interpersonal comparisons how the discrimination should be applied (except in the one special case that only perfect price discrimination will meet total costs). The method of price discrimination adopted must be one which either meets the marginal conditions or because of discontinuities in demand has the same effect, if an optimum is to be reached without resorting to interpersonal comparisons. This is a necessary condition, but it is by no means sufficient to yield a principle of pricing on any but the marginal units. Whenever perfect price discrimination would more than cover the total costs of the industry, the problem becomes essentially one of determining which of the individuals making the gain should pay over some or all of this gain to cover costs or to be redistributed to others.

For a similar reason, it is not always possible to say that price discrimination would be better than a single monopoly price, even though with price discrimination output would be greater. Joan Robinson (1933, p. 204) recognizes this fact when she points out that when some output would be produced even if discrimination were forbidden, it is only possible to say definitely whether price discrimination is damaging to the interests of the customers if we identify ourselves with one or the other group of customers. In comparison with a single-price monopoly, discrimination will always be to the disadvantage of those buyers for whom the price is raised and to the advantage of those for whom the price is lowered, and it is impossible to set the gains of the group against the losses of the other. This point has not been realized by many of the more recent writers in the field of welfare economics — Vickrey, for example. If output under price discrimination more nearly approaches what it would be under marginal cost pricing, he assumes that price discrimination is, of necessity, superior to average cost pricing (and, of course, to any higher single monopoly price). Price discrimination actually can be said to be superior to average cost pricing only when the average price charged to each consumer is equal to or lower than the single price which would be charged otherwise. This situation may occur in certain fields such as public utilities.

Long before the new welfare economics was born, the problems raised by decreasing cost industries and the place of price discrimination in solving them were well treated by J.M. Clark (1923), in *The Economics of Overhead Costs*. In his terms, decreasing costs are the result of overhead costs and of incomplete utilization of capacity. His conclusion (p. 416) bears repeating here.

> If one had to choose a motto of six words, expressing the most central economic consequence of overhead cost, the first choice might fall upon some such phrase as: 'Full utilization is worth its cost', but a close second would be: 'Discrimination is the secret of efficiency'. This last, to be sure, needs to be taken with a proviso: one must know where to stop. . . . For discrimination is not solely an economic fact. It raises moral and social issues: it is the tool of favoritism and greed and the vehicle of the highest social justice. It may rouse our righteous resentment or our admiring commendation. So far as overhead costs are concerned, the role they play is passive; they permit discrimination: the pursuit of maximum profit impels man to discriminate, and most of the other motives known to man join in at one time or another, playing a part and modifying the character of the result.

2. COMPETITIVE PRICING

In the literature of economics, it has long been recognized that competition postulates a specific pricing system. The term 'competition' means different things to different people; 'perfect', 'pure', and 'free' competition are all different, and may all yield different pricing systems. But competition and free competition are most widely used to mean perfect competition and, in the following discussion, this is the concept which will be considered. Perfect competition, as Chamberlin (1933, p. 11) points out, relates to the description of a type of market, and not to a pricing system. Nevertheless, if every individual, both in his capacity as a seller of the factors of production and of commodities and as a purchaser of them, has full knowledge and no monopoly power, a specific pricing system will result. The doctrine of self-interest will yield maximization of individual welfare in accordance with the marginal conditions of production and exchange. The explanation of this mechanism has been developed and refined from the time of Adam Smith onward; and with this development belief in the competitive system as *the* optimum has prevailed, not only among economists, but also among sizable segments of the public at large. In some periods, this belief in the competitive system was reinforced by the erection of the 'economic laws' as natural and immutable: the Malthusian doctrines recognized and explained the existence of human misery with an air of inevitability; and the Darwinian concept of 'the survival of the fittest' was applied to the economic system as a justification of free competition. As a rationalization in defense of the existing organization of the economy, free competition is frequently held to be the framework of the current economic system, despite the obvious discrepancies between the theoretical models and reality. For this reason, if for no other, competitive pricing must be included in any study of pricing systems. It should be noted that it is only as a system of resource allocation that competition will be investigated here; of course, it has many other facets, but these are not pertinent to the present study.

Competitive Pricing as an Optimum System

That perfect competition, under certain circumstances, will yield an optimum system of pricing has been recognized by a long line of economists. Most of the current views on the subject derive from the neo-classicists. Walras, as Wicksell (1934, p. 74) pointed out, never doubted that under conditions of uniform pricing free competition would yield maximum welfare, and he even maintained that each individual is made best off by free competition. As Samuelson (1947, p. 205, n) points out, Walras's exact position is not clear, since his basic assumptions are not clear. Furthermore, Walras sometimes adds one further condition — given the existing distribution of wealth. Marshall in general considered that a competitive system would be optimal, although he pointed out that difficulties would arise in increasing and in decreasing cost industries, and he did not consider that the distribution of income which would result from competition was necessarily good. The most extreme position was perhaps that taken by J.B. Clark (1899, p. 3), based upon the observation that 'the share of income that attaches to any productive function is gauged by the actual product of it'. The assumption that every productive unit *should* be paid its marginal product, and that the distribution which results is in some sense ethically correct, is implicit in all of Clark's work. As far as he was concerned, perfect competition not only yields a commodity pricing system which is correct, but also a distribution of income which is correct.

Although both Pareto and Barone developed the concept of multiple optima excluding interpersonal comparisons, both of them still seemed to consider that in some sense the particular optimum yielded by a competitive pricing system is better than any other. When Pareto (1909, p. 361) finally stated that free competition will give the greatest welfare, he ignored the concept of multiple optima which had developed earlier, and spoke instead of *the* optimum. Barone (1935, p. 257) was more careful, pointing out that it is incorrect to state that under a regime of perfect competition every individual obtains a higher scale of choice than is possible under any other regime, but he then went on to follow his general conclusions about free competition with two corollaries. The first of these is that 'each substitution of other conditions, for one or more of the characteristic conditions of free competition is a *destruction of wealth*, in the sense that wealth which could have been produced with the available resources is not obtained.' The second is that 'if it is considered desirable to benefit some at the expense of others, it is much better — rather than altering the conditions of free competition to obtain such a result *indirectly* — to make direct transfers from the latter to the former, because by such a method the harm inflicted on the latter is less, in proportion to the gain made by the former'. To this second corollary, he made one important qualification: it only remains true insofar as the method of direct transfer does not noticeably alter the conditions of production. Barone recognized that the older economists had a vague idea of all this, but he said that they did not have a precise conception of it which could be supported by rigorous demonstration, and that although the conclusions they arrived at by intuitive judgment were substantially correct, their arguments were essentially rationalizations of what they believed rather than the logical basis for these beliefs.

Wicksell's (1934, pp. 78–83) formulation of the question was somewhat more exact than Barone's. He said that free competition would achieve maximum welfare if the marginal utility of all commodities were the same for all individuals, since welfare would then be invariant with a shift in the distribution of income. In cases where a change in the distribution of income could increase welfare, Wicksell did not, like Barone, suggest that free competition be preserved and direct transfers be made. He recognized that free competition includes paying the factors their marginal products, and that any restriction or compulsion is an encroachment on free competition. Furthermore, by making use of the commodity 'labor' and its price 'wages', Wicksell showed that a rise in wages with shorter hours could benefit labor at the expense of the propertied class, and that under certain circumstances such a shift in the distribution of income might increase welfare over that which would obtain under free competition. His analysis was general, and would have applied equally well to commodity prices as to factor prices, so that it amounted to a demonstration that pricing at other than factor cost will not necessarily yield less welfare than a system of free competition. Yet, in his conclusion, he separated the problem of the distribution of income from the allocative function of the price system in much the same way that Barone had in his second corollary. His final statement was that, *disregarding* the distribution of income, free competition does really lead to a maximization, in the usual and proper sense, of the means of satisfying human wants.

Competitive Pricing and Marginal Cost Pricing

From Pigou onward, one branch of the theory of competitive pricing became closely connected with the marginal cost pricing hypothesis, the evolution of which has already been traced in detail by Ruggles (1938, Ch. III). It will be useful, therefore, to examine the exact relation of marginal cost pricing to the competitive pricing system as it is usually envisaged. Barone had conceived of competitive pricing as a system in which all of the marginal conditions would be met: under perfect competition, the prices of commodities would coincide with both their average and their marginal costs (including normal profits). As has frequently been point out (see Ruggles, 1938, Ch. III; Knight, 1923, pp. 582–606), however, decreasing costs are not compatible with perfect competition; if competition is effective, the size of the productive unit will grow until no further economies are obtainable or until there is only one establishment left in the industry. Perfect competition thus is a special case of the marginal cost pricing system, in which decreasing cost industries are ruled out. The marginal cost pricing principle represents an attempt to extend the marginal conditions to decreasing cost industries so that it will be applicable to the economy as it actually exists.

The marginal cost pricing principle is thus an outgrowth of the welfare principles which underlie the choice of the competitive system as optimum. The advocates of marginal cost pricing would recognize that perfect competition is an optimum system as far as it goes; their only objection would be that it does not cover the full range of possibilities. They would argue that their system would be more general and comprehensive than perfect competition but would achieve the same sort of optimum.

Competitive Pricing and the Problem of Income Distribution

The analytic approaches of those who hold that perfect competition is an optimum and of those who hold that marginal cost pricing is desirable are quite similar. Both break the welfare problem into two parts, resource allocation and the distribution of income, and direct their attention only to the first of these problems. The distribution question is avoided either by saying that it is not the function of the economist to pass upon what is essentially an ethical problem or else by saying that the desirable distribution can be obtained by superimposition of taxes after the price system has been decided upon on resource allocation grounds.

It is, of course, true that the question of the appropriate form of income distribution is not one which the economist *qua* economist can decide, but, as has been pointed out in the previous chapters, this does not mean that the price systems which the economist designs can disregard the problem of the distribution of income. The method of obtaining the desired income distribution is an economic problem, and one which is closely bound up with the price system. To disregard the effect of a given price system upon the income distribution is no more legitimate than it would be to disregard the allocation effects of a wage and price system designed primarily to yield a particular distribution of income. Contrary to the view, both of those supporting competitive pricing (Marshall, Pareto, Barone, and Wicksell) and those supporting the newer forms of welfare economics (Lerner, Hicks, Scitovsky, and Hotel-ling), the problem of resource allocation cannot be separated from the problem of income distribution; an optimum price system superior to all other price sys-tems cannot be said to exist without reference to the distribution of income. Such a separation ignores the redistributive effects of pricing systems, failing to recognize that factor payments are a part of the price system and, at the same time, assuming that redistribution by changing the prices of factors is neces-sarily superior to redistribution by changing the prices of products. The last two chapters have indicated that there seems to be little theoretical or practical basis for this belief.

Perfect competition as a pricing system, is thus subject to some of the same objections as those which were raised in connection with marginal cost pricing. The price system is not independent of the distribution of income, and therefore in the absence of a decision regarding what the income distribution should be no one optimum price system can be designated. Perfect competition, like marginal cost pricing, is necessarily optimal only when the marginal utility of income is the same for all individuals, since only then will welfare be un-affected by the distribution of income.

Competitive Pricing and Industrial Organization

Competition postulates a system of industrial organization, as well as a system of pricing, and a second branch of the theory of competitive pricing has con-cern itself with this aspect. Marginal cost pricing is an outgrowth of the welfare pricing principles of the competitive system, but it has given up a substantial part of the competitive system: the advocates of marginal cost pricing have substituted a rule of pricing for the automatic mechanism of competitive industrial organization. As far as Lerner, Meade, and their fol-lowers are concerned, industrial organization is of no consequence as long as each producer prices his products at marginal cost. The competitive system, on the other hand, specifies a particular industrial organization, from which the desired pricing system will automatically follow. In this sense, marginal cost pricing represents an abandonment of the basic principles of perfect competition. But not all of the proponents of competition have proceeded in the direction of marginal cost pricing; there are a great many people who still emphasize the industrial organization aspects of competition, arguing that a desirable pricing system will result if the industrial organization is appro-priate.

The whole literature of anti-trust legislation is concerned essentially with the problem of industrial organization, and there have been many statements of the philosophy behind it. One of the best, in perhaps the strongest form, is to be found in the writings of Henry Simons (1948). He advocated specific reforms aimed at more nearly achieving a competitive industrial organization. Feeling that the real enemies of liberty were the advocates of a managed economy and national planning, Simons wished to establish and maintain conditions such that there would be no need to regulate prices. Given the correct conditions, Simons felt there would be no need for Lerner's rule, and without these conditions, the introduction of such a rule would be equivalent to the institution of a managed economy.

There remain a number of similarities between the marginal cost pricing approach and Simons's institutional approach, beside the obvious one, that both spring from the ideas originally contained in the neo-classical competitive theory. Simons broke the problem of achieving an optimum into two parts in the same way that Hicks, Lerner, and Scitovsky did. He used the concept of commutative justice as a norm in all voluntary economic associations. Commutative justice dictates that each factor of production shall receive according to its contribution to production, and simply takes for granted the existing distribution of property and personal capacity. From any given initial position, all participants must be better off with cooperative production, division of labor, and exchange, or else the production, division of labor, or exchange must not take place, if commutative justice is to be maintained. This concept is, of course, the same as the marginal conditions of production and exchange. In stressing commutative justice, Simons said that he had no intention of ignoring distributive justice; he simply wanted to urge that the two problems be distinguished in analysis, discussion and action. The virtue of a free exchange society, he felt, is that it invites separation of these problems. Such a society permits the progressive mitigation of inequality and affords the largest possibility of substantial equality. But the primary problem, he still maintained, is production. The common man has a far greater stake in the size or the aggregate income than in any possible redistribution of income. Like Pigou, Simons (1948, p. 46) maintained that the size of the social product valued in market terms is a measure of economic efficiency, and that the highest level of production, and therefore, of economic efficiency, requires a close approximation to the norm of commutative justice. For Simons, therefore, what is most important is that free exchange be preserved. Egalitarian measures should be superimposed on the economic process, effecting redistribution afterward, not in the immediate course of productive and commercial transactions. Simons did state that this is only a minimal prescription since redistribution presents a difficult task in devising measures which will lessen inequality without inordinately adverse effects on production. The best means, he said, must be applied with caution and restraint, but he offered no further discussion of the matter. In all of Simons's writings, remarkably little attention is given to this problem of how to redistribute income — it is simply assumed that the proper means is the income tax, and that no adverse effects will follow from its use. Like the new welfare economists, Simons focused his attention almost entirely on production and exchange.

As a consequence of his basic philosophy, Simons considered monopoly to be the most important problem involved in designing a free enterprise economy. His primary objection to monopoly was that it prevents the efficient utilization of resources. Simons also objects to monopoly because of its political effects — but the consideration of problems of political power is outside the scope of this paper. The main purpose of monopoly is to maintain an abnormally high return, and to prevent the influx of resources which would reduce monopoly profits to normal levels (Simons, 1948, p. 47). Thus monopoly means the diversion of resources from more highly valued uses to less highly valued uses. In terms of welfare economics, monopoly is equivalent to an interference with the marginal conditions of production and exchange. Even in cases when enterprise monopoly does not succeed in making large profits, it may cause inefficiency (p. 48). The cartel or trade association form of monopoly, for example, may be able to force price or output limitations on existing firms, but it is seldom possible to restrict the growth of new firms. This form of monopoly will therefore lead to a wastage of investment as well as to exploitation of consumers. There will be new investment as long as returns are high, and as this new capacity comes into production the output of existing producers will have to be further restricted until finally no higher return is realized than in competitive fields. Equilibrium when cartels and trade associations exist thus means equality between price and average cost, despite the enormous discrepancy between marginal cost and price.

But enterprise monopoly, Simons's belief, is not the most serious of the monopoly problems. As yet, the specific industrial monopolies are not a serious evil, and by themselves could be easily remedied. The major monopoly problem is that of labor organizations (Simons, 1948, p. 35). Labor monopolies are organized like armies rather than like businesses, and they encounter no diseconomies of size because they produce nothing. Strong labor monopolies, if they do not die in the early stages of their development, would, Simons felt, grow into intolerable monopolies which would tend to combine with enterprise monopolies in maximizing joint exactions from the public, at the same time fighting with the enterprise monopolies over the division of the spoils. As is true for trade associations and cartels, the numbers in labor organizations may increase until the members are no better off than they would have been without any union at all (Simons, 1948, p. 48), yet the products of all industries will be priced higher because a large part of the community's labor resources will be wasted — such a waste occurring, Simons felt, whenever the level of wages is raised above the competitive level with the result that employment in the field is lessened and laborers are diverted to less remunerative employments. Simons (1948, p. 121) recognized that his position would evoke little sympathy — saying that 'questioning the virtues of the organized labor movement is like attacking religion, monogamy, motherhood, or the home. Among the modern intelligentsia any doubts about collective bargaining admit of explanation only in terms of insanity, knavery, or subservience to the "interests".' But he still believed that the labor monopoly was actually injurious to the interests of labor.

In addition to the various forms of monopoly, Simons also discussed certain other questions which he felt should have an important place in the attempt to design a free enterprise economy which would approximate the mechanism of perfect competition. These are monetary controls, taxation, tariffs and subsidies and advertising expenses. The first of these does not enter directly into the pricing system, and so will not be discussed here. Taxation and the question of tariffs and subsidies are all related directly to resource allocation and, therefore, will be considered in detail. Finally, Simons considered the question of advertising and merchandising to be separate from the monopoly problem, and so it will be considered separately here. He pointed out that the type of advertising and selling expense will vary with industrial organization, and that the existence of such expenses provides a great incentive to combination, but did not think that combination would reduce the amount of such expenses greatly.

In developing his positive program for *laissez-faire*, Simons deals with each of these problems in turn. With respect to monopoly, the positive program for *laissez-faire* is very explicit. To avoid the necessity for overall regulation, each and every industry either should be effectively competitive or should be completely socialized. The government should definitely plan (see Simons, 1948, pp. 57–8) on the socialization of railroads, utilities, and every other industry where effective competitive conditions cannot be maintained — i.e., industries with markedly decreasing costs. But one of the main objectives of government policy should be to prevent the development of conditions which would necessitate socialization, and with respect to the sectors of the economy where competition is possible, Simons did have very definite ideas about how to proceed. In the first place, the incorporation laws should be amended so as to give the federal government, rather than the states, complete control. There should then be a strict limitation on the amount of property one corporation could own, so that no single company would be large enough to dominate an industry. Simons recognized the difficulty of defining industries and commodities, but he did not think it insoluble. As a tentative rule, he suggested that no ownership unit should produce or control more than 5 percent of the total output of any commodity. Horizontal combinations should be prohibited and vertical integrations should be permitted only insofar as they are clearly not incompatible with the maintenance of real competition. In his view, few of the gigantic corporations which now exist can be defended on the ground that their present size is necessary to achieve production economies.

Simons (1948, p. 82) did not approve of the methods at present in use for combating monopoly, although he agreed that there should be vigorous and vigilant prosecution of conspiracy in restraint of trade. He said at one point (p. 99), 'I do not like the rule of reason (either Mr. Arnold's or the Court's); I am skeptical about this talk of the Sherman Act as a broad constitutional principle of government, and I am diffident about turning our monopoly problems over to a profession which has demonstrated almost an infinite capacity to mis-understand them.' He further charged (p. 102) that 'Arnold comes disquiet-ingly near to saying that all industries should be treated as public utilities and the Anti-Trust Division transformed into a super public utility commission with power not to fix prices (rates), but to harass those who charge unreasonably until they abandon the practice'. It is the regulative function of the government which Simons feared most, and he was anxious to establish a form of industrial organization which will not require any governmental regulation. Decon-centration was his solution; there is no need to break up productive units, but both vertical and horizontal combinations must be broken up. Selling must be divorced from manufacturing, and industrial research must be disassociated from particular operating firms. Furthermore, Simons was not willing to make any compromise with special cases unless technological efficiency is involved, and he felt that technological efficiency would rarely be involved except in the outstanding cases of public utilities and railroads.

The labor monopoly, although it is somewhat more complex, should be treated in essentially the same way as enterprise monopoly. If there were real competition among employers, there would be no danger in the application of the general prohibitions on restraint of trade to labor organizations. But the best that can be hoped for in this direction, Simons (1948, p. 61) thought, is that labor monopolies, if not fostered and supported by the state, will cease to grow and may even decline in power. Competitive conditions among em-ployers and an efficient system of labor exchanges would reduce the labor monopoly's public favor, and it then might be possible to lessen the power of labor organizations.

In the sectors of the economy where competition is not feasible (i.e., the public utilities), socialization is preferable to government regulation of private monopolies. Unregulated extra-legal monopolies Simons (1948, p. 87) con-siders to be tolerable evils, but when private monopolies have the blessing of the state they threaten the existence of the system. The real monopoly problem arises because the state will rarely permit private monopoly to bear the brunt of its own actions. Competition, when long suppressed, would cause too much disturbance if it were allowed to reappear and therefore, for the general welfare the government is likely to be drawn into the enforcement of 'fair prices' and 'just rates'. Regulation, Simons feels, would seldom be regulation in the interests of the public at large, but rather in the interests of the particular group which is regulated. The only way to avoid this outcome is to abolish the interest group concerned by the establishment of complete socialization. It is for this reason that Simons favors actual state ownership, rather than mere government regulation. Socialization, thus, is Simons's answer to the problem of decreasing cost industries, but nowhere did he face the question of how socialization would solve the problems of such industries. Making private monopolies public does not obviate the necessity for running them and the problem of how their products should be priced still remains — the marginal cost pricing system at least has the virtue that it does specify what constitutes ideal pricing.

Simons's concern with taxation was twofold. He considered taxation both as a means of redistributing income and as affecting the allocation of resources — but he never considered the interrelation between the two. Reduction in inequality among individuals, Simons (1948, p. 65) believed, is immensely important; and progressive taxation not only is an effective means to this end, but within the existing framework the only effective means. He believed that gains to those at the bottom of the income scale could be realized without any real loss to those at the top, so long as the latter could maintain their relative rank in the income scale. Progressive taxation thus could achieve a drastic reduction in inequality without a loss of efficiency in the system, and without impairing the attractiveness of the economic game. Although Simons formed his opinions at a time (1934) when the level of income taxation was low enough so that it probably did not have any effect upon the incentive to work, he maintained the same position in later articles (1944), saying that progressive taxation could handle the problem in inequality without serious diseconomies (Simons, 1948, p. 148).

Simons (1948, p. 83) recommended the abolition of all excise taxes except the gasoline tax, and his opposition is obviously based upon the principle that such taxes interfere with the efficient allocation of resources. He did not discuss his reasons for favoring the gasoline tax, but probably considered that it constitutes payment for benefit received, since it pays for the use of roads by those who travel them. With this one exception, Simons's position on taxation is similar to that of the advocates of marginal cost pricing. Both Hotelling and Lerner advocated the income tax for redistributive purposes, and condemned all excise taxes.

Simons (1948, p. 69) considered tariffs and subsidies to be essentially the same as positive and negative excise taxes, and subject to the same disabilities. With free foreign trade, it would be easier to maintain effective competition in domestic markets, and therefore the limitations on the size of corporations would need to be less severe (p. 84). Likewise, Simons believed that the abolition of subsidies and production control in agriculture would yield a pricing structure more in accord with competitive pricing. Simons did not elaborate upon the question of what he would do to solve the problems of agriculture which originally led to the institution of the subsidy programs, but merely assumed that it could be done within the framework of a completely competitive pricing system.

The final point in Simons's (1948, p. 71) program concerns merchandising. He recognized that much of the vaunted efficiency of production in the modern economy is dissipated in the wastes of merchandising. Producers are forced to spend enormous amounts on selling expenses to counteract the expenditures of their competitors, and the economies gained by mass production are often lost in the struggle for outlets. It is interesting to note that Simons did not attribute this waste to monopoly control in distribution, but on the contrary to the 'absurd proliferation of small retail establishments which spring up to exact on small volumes of trade the large percentage tribute which existing arrangements allow to those who can classify as dealers rather than consumers'. This merchandising problem does encourage combination among producers, however, since by acting cooperatively they may save themselves the expenses of competitive selling activities. Yet such combination, Simons felt, will not in practice save the consumer anything. The battle of selling would only become one between organized groups, in which fully as much would be spent. Simons's solution lies primarily in consumer education and in research carried out by cooperatives, but he feels that the problem is both more difficult and less important than the other reforms he proposed.

The reforms which Simons suggests are far more realistic and consistently complete than those of most theorists who have advocated a competitive industrial organization, but they are still not as direct as the proposals of those lawyers and economists who have made specific industry studies with reference to anti-trust action. No systematic attempt can be made here to canvass the literature of this field, but it may be useful to mention briefly one recent study as representative. Eugene Rostow's (1948) recent study of the oil industry is based on premises which are almost completely in line with Simons's. Rostow points out that 20 firms control 80 percent of all oil production in the United States, and argues that since the current monopolistic form of organization is not technologically advantageous, it would be better to reorganize the industry on a more competitive basis. Such reorganization, he believes (p. 117), would eliminate some of the 'astronomic' wastes of monopolistic competition, and would release competitive energies now restricted by monopoly interests. Effective competitive reform in the oil industry would involve the separation of the major companies into different units controlling the four main functions, production, transportation, refining, and distribution. Further horizontal division of some of the major companies which survived the vertical dissolution might also be necessary. With respect to the actual production in the oil fields, Rostow (p. 119) recognizes that competition cannot yield an optimum, and so for this part of the industry, he recommends unitization of the oil fields. Under this plan, the rate of output of each oil field would be governed as a whole by a federal agency which would give consideration to such things as geological problems. Once effective dissolution had been achieved in the remaining parts of the industry, administrative control of the market would not be necessary; competitive forces would prevent all of the restrictive monopolistic practices without any of the costs of detailed administrative supervision (p. 123). This view is of course virtually identical with Simons's.

Rostow (1948, p. 125) recognizes that there is some problem involved in defining a monopoly, but he points out that monopolistic competition (he really means oligopoly) is on the verge of being recognized under the Sherman Act as the offense of monopoly. He cites the aluminum case as evidence of this, in that Judge Hand indicated that the control of 90 percent of supply was certainly monopoly, 60 percent was doubtful, and 33 percent was definitely not (p. 127). The tobacco case, in Rostow's opinion, was a further step in the right direction, in that the percentage of control required was reduced: each of the three major companies produced between 20 and 30 percent of American cigarettes, and in 1939 their total output was only 68 percent of the total (pp. 129–30). On a basis similar to that used in the tobacco case, Rostow feels that the existence of monopoly in the oil industry can be proved, even though the control of 80 percent of the industry is split up among 20 firms. Thus Rostow believes that both the basic reason for introducing a program of competitive reorganization of the oil industry and the means for achieving it are at hand; all that remains to be done is to implement the program in order to obtain the advantages of competitive industrial organization in this field.

Evaluation of Industrial Reorganization to Achieve Competitive Pricing

The problem of defining monopoly

Before it is possible to make use of industrial reorganization to achieve an optimum allocation of resources, it is necessary to arrive at some means of recognizing a desirable or undesirable form when it occurs. Both law and economics have experienced marked difficulties in their attempts to define competition and monopoly in a way which is usable for the purpose of remedial action. The greatest share of attention has been directed toward the characteristics of monopoly; it is a fairly simple matter to discover when an industry does not possess all of the attributes of perfect competition, but, since few if any industries could pass this test, it alone is not a sufficient basis for policy. It is, therefore, generally held that only those industries which have the specific characteristics of flagrant monopoly, somehow defined, should be reorganized. Among the specific characteristics which have most frequently been offered as tests are the level of profits, the elasticity of demand, the stability of demand, price rigidity, and the share of the market controlled. Each of these merits a brief consideration.

The profit measure still retains its popular appeal and profits are often cited (as they are by Simons, for instance) as the main purpose and one of the chief evils of monopoly, but the existence of profits higher than is usual cannot be used as a proof of monopoly. Profits frequently contain in them elements of rent: if a producer is more efficient than his competitors, or if he has some unique advantage, his profits may be larger than normal. As John Ise (1940, pp. 33–45) has pointed out, the separation of monopoly profits and rental income is not only empirically difficult, but in many cases theoretically impossible. On the statistical side, Bain (1941, pp. 271–93) has shown that the accounting statements of firms give an absolutely unreliable indicator either of monopoly power or of excess profits. The profit rate depends on valuations, changes in price levels and similar elements which are not related to the existence of monopoly, and furthermore, since these elements are not comparable for different firms, profit figures are not comparable between firms. Finally, even if profit rates were comparable between firms, the indicator would discover only the reasonably efficient monopolies. Monopolies which result in a gross waste of resources and so do not make excessive profits would go undetected.

The inverse of the elasticity of demand was originally offered by Lerner (1933, pp. 157–75) as a measure of monopoly power. By this measure, a producer faced with an inelastic demand for his products would be very much more of a monopolist than a producer faced with an elastic demand. There are several reasons why this result is unsatisfactory. In the first place, even though a producer is faced with an inelastic demand curve, he may be very much at the mercy of his competitors' actions. His demand curve may shift violently over a period of time and yet retain its inelastic characteristics. A producer with a more elastic demand curve may, on the other hand, be fairly independent of his competitors, and if freedom of entry is restricted he may be able to reap large profits by selling at a price far above his average cost. Second, even between producers whose demand curves are equally stable, it is difficult to see why the elasticity of demand is related to monopoly *per se*. The statistical attempts to test the degree of monopoly by using Lerner's measure [(price – marginal cost)/price] have not met with any very great degree of success. John Dunlop (1939, pp. 522–34) made such a statistical study, using approximations of marginal cost. Aside from the statistical problems involved in finding marginal cost, the measurement of elasticity of demand by this technique assumes that the producer actually is equating marginal cost and marginal revenue. Furthermore, should the producer be operating at capacity, marginal cost would be discontinuous and so could not be used to measure elasticity.

A definition of monopoly which attempts to take into account the relationship among the demand curves of various producers was suggested by Paul Sweezy (1937). Sweezy defined a monopolist as a producer whose demand curve is independent both of the prices he charges and the level of his profits. In such a situation, Sweezy pointed out, the producer does not have to worry about the reactions of his competitors; he can charge the price which will maximize his profit without fearing that new competitors will enter the field or that old competitors will react to his prices. This definition does exclude oligopolistic interdependence of demand, but it is not applicable for distinguishing between pure competition and monopoly. Pure competition would meet the definition as well as monopoly, since a producer in pure competition neither fears the reaction of his competitors to his own price changes nor influences by his own profit rate the entry of new firms into the industry. In actual practice, this definition has never had very much use by those seeking tests of monopoly, since it would be difficult to devise any statistical application of it.

Price rigidity is frequently held to be an indication of monopoly control. Much of the basis for the use of price rigidity as a measure of monopoly comes from Gardiner Means's (1935) study of price flexibility. He found that prices of agricultural products were flexible and prices of manufactured products were inflexible. From this evidence he assumed that, since agriculture is a competitively organized industry and manufacturing is monopolistic, price inflexibility is highly related to monopolistic practices. It has been correctly pointed out by Tibor Scitovsky (1941), however, that prices of producers with inelastic demands should not for maximum profit be any less flexible than prices of producers in perfect competition. There is, therefore, no theoretical reason for believing that monopoly causes inflexible prices. On the statistical side, Alfred Neal (1942) has shown that there is no particular relation between price flexibility or inflexibility and industrial concentration. The causal factors affecting price changes are numerous, but they do not seem to be highly related to what are generally conceived to be monopoly elements.

One of the most widely used measures of monopoly is the percentage of market control which is exercised by a firm or a group of firms. This quantity has the advantage of being measurable in many cases, but problems arise as to the exact interpretation of the magnitudes which are derived. As was pointed out above in connection with the controversy between Pigou and Taussig on the definition of price discrimination, the concept of a commodity or a market is not a very clear-cut or useful tool of analysis. Whenever the question of monopoly arises, there is almost sure to be a question about the definition of the pertinent market. The Aluminum Company, for instance, controlled at one time over 90 percent of the virgin aluminum produced in this country, but this figure does not take into account scrap aluminum or imported aluminum, or the other metals which are close substitutes for aluminum in many uses. If the definition of a commodity is made narrow enough, every producer of a branded product will be found to control 100 percent of the supply, but on the other hand, if the definition is made wide enough and is applied to a large category of goods, few if any producers would be found to control any significant percentage of the total. Not only is this measure difficult to apply, furthermore, but it is also subject to the theoretical disadvantage that it does not take account of the producer's position within his market. Such things as freedom of entry and nature of competitors are not taken into account.

Finally, there is implicit in most discussions of monopoly a concern with the absolute size of a producer. Simons gives this criterion explicit recognition by including in his program an absolute size limitation on corporations. Sheer size almost invariably carries with it power, and it is to this as much as to anything else that the opponents of monopoly react. Few of the people who are in favor of strong anti-trust action are concerned with the multitude of small monopolies to be found in every town — the corner grocery store, the town bank or the local newspaper. Opposition to these monopolies is weak not because they are unimportant to those who are affected by them, but because they are small in relation to the whole economy and it is difficult to find any solution to them.

Economic significance of monopolistic influences

A great deal more attention has been given to the problem of proving the existence of monopoly than to interpreting its practical economic significance. In two of the specific industries which have already been mentioned, however, there has been some analysis along these lines. The study of the aluminum industry by Donald Wallace (1937, p. 365) came to the conclusion that 'it has not been possible to determine whether undesirable consequences of existing types of control attain a magnitude which is worth bothering about'. Profits were not excessive throughout the company's history, and there was some indication that the company sold at low prices to encourage demand. Also, there was some expansion prompted by nonprofit motives. In the utensil industry, Wallace believed, the constructive activities of the Aluminum Company may have overbalanced the results of any uneconomic behavior. The company's dealings with independent utensil makers seemed to him fair and helpful, if somewhat arbitrary and dictatorial. With respect to scrap and sand castings, not enough evidence was available to reach complete conclusions, but some of the charges of unfair practices were shown to be without foundation. This does not, of course, mean that the Aluminum Company had obtained ideal results in all of its management policies, but it is open to question whether either of the proposed remedies — splitting the field up into an oligopolistic organization on this one hand, or providing government competition by a publicly owned plant on the other hand — would have substantially improved the situation from the point of view of resource allocation.

Tobacco, again, is an industry which is commonly agreed to be highly monopolistic: three producers control a substantial proportion of the output of cigarettes. The economic significance of this monopolistic situation has been analyzed in a study by Richard Tennant (1948). Profits were found to be higher in relation to investment in this field than they were in more competitive fields, but there did not appear to be exploitation either of labor or of raw materials producers. A reduction in price sufficient to lower profits to the competitive level would not have amounted to more than a fraction of a cent a pack, and therefore, taking the elasticity of demand into account, the effect of abnormal profits on the level of output was probably negligible. Thus, from the point of view of pricing and resource allocation, Tennant does not feel that the form of industrial organization which exists can be charged with inefficiency. This does not mean that Tennant is in favor of doing nothing about the tobacco industry — he recommends that the industry be deconcentrated, on the grounds of political power. His position on this aspect of monopoly is quite similar to Simons's. No technical advantage is gained by the large companies, so Tennant feels that no loss would be involved in breaking them up. One gain which he would hope to obtain by deconcentration would be a limitation of advertising. As Simons has pointed out, however, it is doubtful whether total selling costs with many producers would be much different from total selling costs with few. Although much of the national advertising might be abolished, advertising by individual companies might still affect their demand curves favorably, and the struggle for outlets by the multitude of small producers would be greatly intensified.

In his study of the oil industry, Rostow (1948), like many others, has concentrated upon attempting to prove that monopoly exists, by using most of the measures described above. Although Bain's study (1945) had already shown that from 1929 onward the overall profits of the industry (excepting those of the nonintegrated producers) provided no more than a normal return on investment, Rostow hastens to point out that this does not prove that the industry is competitive, since inefficiency, wasteful investment, and unnecessary advertising or distribution expenses might cover up the true significance of profits. Rostow himself gives no evidence on whether the industry is inefficient in this sense, but the possibility that it might be in his view discredits the validity of the profit measure. Unfortunately, the measures which Rostow does use are no more helpful in this respect. He explores the possibility of using price flexibility, but reaches no general conclusion about this measure, since the TNEC (US Temporary National Economic Committee, 1940) investigation of the subject showed that petroleum prices were among the more flexible of commodity prices. He also attempts to compute marginal cost and with it to show that the divergence of marginal cost from price indicates that there is monopoly by Lerner's measure. But, because of the crudeness of his statistical measure, he actually succeeds only in measuring the amount of overhead costs. If the latter were technologically given, no amount of deconcentration would alter the degree of monopoly given by this measure. In the last analysis, Rostow's charge of monopoly rests almost exclusively on the fact that 20 companies control 80 percent of the output. Although in his preface Rostow says that it is because of the effect that monopoly has on prices and resource allocation that the industry should be reorganized, he spends most of his time trying to prove the existence of monopoly, and nowhere gets around to the economic significance of monopoly. He seems to feel, as do so many writers in this field, that a demonstration of the existence of monopoly is a full and sufficient proof that resources are being misallocated and that deconcentration will cure it.

Nature of modern industrial organization

A modern economy embraces different sectors, and these different sectors are entirely different in their industrial organization. Agriculture, manufacturing, services and distributive trades are all different from each other and, even within these sectors, there are special factors which condition the type of industrial organization which exists in specific areas. The concept of perfect competition is applicable only to certain areas of agriculture and manufacturing. Perfect competition not only is not found in the service and distributive industries, but in many instances would be impossible. Imperfect competition characterizes all retail trade and most services, and no amount of increase in the number of firms in these areas will produce perfect competition.

In some industries, it is generally recognized that larges number of producing units would be uneconomic, and most advocates of competitive industrial organization have made exceptions of these natural monopolies, suggesting either regulation or government ownership. The most familiar example of this sort of industry is, of course, those public utilities which have decreasing costs dues to technological factors. There are, however, somewhat more subtle cases in which the factor of decreasing costs for the industry as a whole is absent. An excellent example of the latter is to be found in the history of the New York taxicab industry (based upon the discussion of this industry in C.O. Ruggles, 1938). An investigation of the taxicab industry before it was publicly regulated revealed that the number of cabs was far in excess of the number needed to provide cheap and efficient transportation. As the number of cabs increased, the available number of passengers were split up among more and more companies, with each cab cruising a larger percentage of the time and carrying fewer passengers. The cost per passenger naturally rose as the number of cabs increased. But rising costs did not discourage the increase in the number of cabs, because it was still possible by working long hours to make a profit even with low utilization. Restricting the number of taxicabs would not have solved the problem since the remaining cabs would have been able to charge the same or even higher rates, and so make more than competitive profits. The industry is not a decreasing cost industry within the traditional meaning of this term; in fact, due to the factor of traffic congestion an increase in taxi services can only be obtained at increasing cost. Yet, by public regulation, both of the number of cabs and the rates which they were permitted to charge, a very much improved situation was obtained. A smaller number of cabs handled the same amount of business, so that wages and profits in the industry improved. Service was not reduced, since the number of cabs had previously been excessive. Because of the reduction in congestion, and consequently in accidents, general conditions in the industry improved. This, therefore, is a case in which the competitive solution did not provide ideal resource allocation, even though the industry is not, like most public utilities, a natural monopoly.

What is true of the taxicab industry is more or less true of all retail trade. Perfect competition is not possible in the distributive trades, and the attempt to achieve it or to allow the competitive forces which do exist full play may result only in increasing numbers and increasing costs without benefit either to the producers or the consumers. In the marketing of gasoline, for example, gasoline stations cluster at the point of largest demand, with the result that they often only manage to split up a given amount of business among an increasing number of outlets. Of course, if all of these outlets were in perfect competition such a situation would not exist, but since imperfect rather than perfect competition is the rule it not only can exist but can be stable. Gasoline stations can compete with each other in many different ways. They can offer different facilities, services, or such free goods as maps; and in some instances, there may even be price differences. There is no reason, therefore, why the competitive mechanism should offer the correct amount of distributive capacity to consumers. Other types of retail trade follow much the same pattern, with the result that retail mark-ups are forced higher and higher as more firms enter the industry; more and more outlets are splitting up the available amount of consumers' expenditures, and the share of each becomes less. It might seem that this duplication of distributive facilities would offer consumers more convenience, but it does so only at an exorbitant price and without giving the consumers any choice in the matter. Furthermore, as the number of outlets increases there is a tendency for each of them to grow smaller, so that the number of lines of goods and the amount of stock they can carry decreases. The result is to make fewer choices available to the consumer, because he individually is presented with more limited stocks, even though there are larger stocks in the distributive channels.

In such a situation, distributors find that they can increase their sales volume more easily by increasing their selling expenses than by lowering prices, and competition frequently is on this basis rather than that of price.

When margins can be drastically reduced, however, a large volume of sales can be gained — this has been notably true in the growth of grocery super-markets in recent years. Consumers are not very sensitive to small price differences, so that a small amount of increase in selling expense will bring in a greater volume of trade than an equivalent price reduction. But as the amount of selling expense grows, it becomes relatively less effective, since the majority of advertising channels are subject to decreasing returns. As price differentials become larger, on the other hand, they become relatively more effective. When both margins and selling expenses are high, therefore, it may profit a retailer to eliminate most of his selling expenses and offer instead a substantial price differential. This, combined with other innovations, is what has happened in the field of food retailing; supermarkets have managed to cut their selling expenses sufficiently to attract customers because of the difference in price.

From the point of view of its effect upon the manufacturers who supply the products, as well as its effect upon consumers, the free play of competition may result in misallocation of resource. Any one distributor can carry only a limited variety of products, and it is to each manufacturer's interest not only to have his product included in this number but to have the products of other manufacturers excluded. As a result, manufacturers go to a great deal of expense to tie outlets to themselves and to develop new outlets. Large sales and marketing forces are created in the effort to penetrate rivals' markets. National advertising is utilized not only to attract customers but even more to persuade outlets to carry such well-known products. Producers often will supply capital, store equipment, and displays in order to persuade outlets to carry their products. When these practices become competitive between producers, a great deal of expenditure goes into channels which cannot be said to be the direct result of consumers' choice. On the other hand, when producers try to develop new outlets, consumers are again split up among a larger number of outlets, and the end result is that the necessary margin between producer and consumer is raised. Thus, the struggle for outlets again is a type of competition which contributes little to the efficiency of resource allocation.

Simons's view of industrial organization assumes that the classical theory of perfect price competition is applicable to all sectors of the economy, if only the industrial organization is appropriate. But as long as production, distribution and consumption remain separated from one another in the organization of economic activity, the situations described above will exist, even though there are a large number of small firms within each sector. The problems are deeper than the simple question of the number of firms in an industry and the power of each.

Deconcentration of industries and its economic effect
The deconcentration of industry will have a number of effects which Simons

and Rostow have neglected in their analysis, in addition to those which they have considered. In the first place, changes or fluctuations in demand will have very different repercussions in deconcentrated industries from those which will result in industries where multiple plant firms are the rule. In the second place, deconcentration may result in excess plant capacity, rather than in operation more nearly at capacity. In the third place, with deconcentration the pricing system itself will undergo a change, especially if producers charge a single price to all customers. Finally, deconcentration will have an effect upon the struggle for outlets, and may not decrease selling expense. The following discussion can only suggest what these effects are; it cannot in the space allowed develop a complete analysis of them.

The problem of multiple-plant firms has not received the attention which is due to it in light of its very great importance in modern economic systems. One recent article by Don Patinkin (1947) has highlighted certain aspects of multiple-plant firms in relation to imperfect competition. He recognized that under certain cost conditions dissolution as an answer to monopoly is open to criticism. The monopolist with many plants under his control will divide production among these plants in the most economic manner possible. When a monopolist controls a number of plants, there will be only one demand curve for all of the plants as a group, but if each of the plants were separately operated each would have its own demand curve. If the analysis is extended to include a change in demand, the multiple-plant case will yield far different results from the individually operated plant case, provided that different plants have different cost curves. With separately operated plants, there is no assurance that the more efficient plants will continue to operate at a higher rate than the less efficient plants; all of them may suffer an equal decline in demand.

With respect to the full utilization of capacity, it is quite possible and even probable that deconcentration would result in greater excess capacity in many industries. Individual producers need a margin of capacity in order to be in a favorable competitive position within the industry. But if the industry is integrated, such excess capacity as a competitive safeguard is not necessary, and a monopolist may be content with a smaller total capacity for a given level of output than would independent producers taken as a group. This is especially true when fluctuations in demand are frequent. When there are many producers in the industry, each has an incentive to expand whenever demand increases, even though he knows the increase is temporary, because he hopes thereby to be able to capture a larger share of the market. But where competition is less intense, excess capacity may not be created in periods of peak demand if producers do not feel that it will pay for itself in the future.

There is an even more subtle effect which deconcentration may have upon the pricing system. With vertically integrated production, the costs which are considered from one stage of production to the next are *marginal* costs. For instance, when a grocery chain is considering whether or not to introduce another store into a given area, the costs of distribution and warehousing, of which account would need to be taken, would only be the additional costs which the new store would involve. But if the chain did not exist and the warehousing, distributing and retail selling stages of selling food were separated under different managements, any new firm deciding whether or not to enter an area would have to make its decision on the basis of the charges to it of warehousing and distribution services. If the price system in effect were a single-price one, these charges would represent *average* rather than marginal cost. An integrated industry thus operates on marginal costing, whereas deconcentrated, unintegrated industry will have to operate (considering the industry as a whole) on the basis of average costs, unless primary producers discriminated among their customers in the later stages of the industry. This difference between the two systems may become important if there is any lumpiness of factors which results in discontinuities or in decreasing costs.

Finally, it has already been pointed out that the struggle for outlets is an extremely important factor in modern economic systems, and that it may lead to less than optimal resource allocation. The existence of many producers may make it difficult for one to penetrate the sales area of another, thus not only increasing selling expenses but also limiting consumers' choice.

Deconcentration, therefore, would yield a different system of imperfect competition from that which had existed, but there is no assurance that the new system would be an improvement, as far as short-run resource allocation is concerned. This, of course, does not mean that a high degree of industrial concentration is always to be countenanced — there may be a great many other reasons why monopoly *per se* is bad. The scope of this study, however, excludes consideration both of dynamic considerations (so that arguments based on the concept of evolutionary changes in the economic system are not relevant here) and of noneconomic considerations (political power arguments). Considering only short-run resource allocation, a concentrated industrial organization is not necessarily always worse than a deconcentrated organization. The increase of numbers in imperfect competition can give rise to undesirable resource allocation, since there is no automatic mechanism in imperfect competition which will ensure that the number of firms is in accord with consumers' preferences. One of the major errors which both Simons and Rostow make is the assumption that decreasing concentration will be equivalent to approaching perfect price competition more closely. Actually, it is often possible that a highly concentrated industry will more closely fulfill the requirements of workable competition than will imperfect competition with large numbers. In any case, there seems to be little ground, on the basis of short-run resource allocation, for supporting an economic policy directed solely at deconcentration, as an end in itself.

3. CONCLUSION

Pricing systems in relation to resource allocation have been considered in this paper within the framework of certain restrictive assumptions, which must be recalled in considering the conclusions to be drawn from this study. One of these assumptions was that the problem of full employment is not related to the design of a pricing system, and so need not be taken into account. This assumption is of course highly restrictive, and makes the conclusions based upon it inapplicable to the majority of real situations. A second major assumption was that the dynamic problems relating to the patterns of evolution in the economic system can be disregarded. The analysis in this paper is essentially static, and is not relevant to the problems of growth and change.

Within the limits of these assumptions, pricing and resource allocation have been considered in terms of certain welfare criteria. An examination of the basic assumptions of both the older and the newer welfare economics reveals that the usual procedure of separating the question of the efficiency of resource allocation from considerations of the distribution of income is a technique of more limited application than is generally realized. Contrary to most of the existing applications of this technique, it is not possible to compare the efficiency of two positions in which the distribution of income is different without resorting to interpersonal comparisons of utility. An optimum pattern of resource allocation with reference to one distribution of income may or may not be more efficient than a less-than-optimum pattern which has a different income distribution. Ruling out interpersonal comparisons of utility, the term efficiency has meaning only within a specific distribution of income: if some individuals are made better off and none are made worse off, the efficiency of resource allocation has increased. It is not sufficient that it be possible to meet this condition by redistributing income; it must actually be met by carrying through the redistribution if it is to be legitimately maintained that the efficiency of resource allocation has increased. A closer approach to the marginal conditions of production and exchange, therefore, can be said with certainty to represent an increase in welfare only if the distribution of income remains unchanged or if, abandoning the restrictions of the new welfare economics, certain specific assumptions are made regarding the marginal utilities of income of the different people involved.

These, in brief, are the welfare considerations which are pertinent to the question of pricing systems. With reference to them, marginal cost pricing, discriminatory pricing and competitive pricing were examined in the attempt to discover what pricing system will most nearly fulfill the requirements of an optimum method of resource allocation — in other words, what is the nature of an ideal pricing system.

Marginal Cost Pricing

The marginal cost pricing system, because it involves a random redistribution of income, will yield an optimum allocation of resources only if the marginal utilities of income of all individuals in the economy are equal. If this were true, it would be the total market value of goods produced which would be important, and their distribution would have no bearing. No change in the income distribution would then affect the total welfare of the economy. At first glance, it might appear that marginal cost pricing would yield an optimum if only the factors of production were fixed in supply or at least did not respond to changes in factor prices, since it would then be possible to redistribute income to correct the random effects without altering the total value of wealth in the economy. The proponents of marginal cost pricing would argue that the necessary redistribution should be undertaken after prices are set at marginal cost. But in order to do this, the redistribution would have to be related to the purchase of commodities and the end result would be, not marginal cost pricing, but discriminatory pricing. For example, suppose that a new commodity is introduced into the economy, and that the marginal cost of this commodity is far below average cost. If the marginal utility of income to all individuals is not assumed to be equal, the introduction of the commodity with pricing at marginal cost can positively be said to represent an increase in welfare only if no one is made worse off by the introduction of the new commodity. The difference between average and marginal cost cannot be made up, therefore, by any method which would place the burden on persons who do not consume the commodity — in other words, meeting the deficits of decreasing cost industries by general taxation is ruled out. But if those who do not consume the product are not to contribute to paying for it, those who do consume it must pay its total cost in some way or other. If the marginal conditions are to be met, this is equivalent to discriminatory pricing.

The question of how to redistribute income (without altering the price system in the process) is never adequately considered by the proponents of marginal cost pricing. It is usually assumed that the only proper method, where substantial quantities are involved, is the income tax. This procedure, of course, involves the abrogation of the marginal conditions on the factors of production, and from the point of view of the general welfare it cannot be shown that it is always better to violate the marginal conditions with respect to the factors of production than with respect to commodities. It is quite possible, for example, that due to differences in elasticity of demand certain specific excises on commodities would be a useful method of redistribution, and when the level of income taxes is already high, such excises might well be superior to a further increase in the marginal income tax rate.

Many of the arguments used by the advocates of marginal cost pricing can be used equally well to support pricing at other than marginal cost levels. Hotelling, for instance, supported the pricing of power projects at marginal costs on the ground that others besides those directly involved would benefit. This is a very good argument for pricing many commodities below, rather than at, marginal cost. Milk for children, subway transportation in large cities, and many other commodities and services might better be priced below marginal cost. The nation has a stake in healthy children, and the benefits accrue to others besides the children and those upon whom they are dependent for support. Similarly, it can be argued that the subways benefit landowners, automobile drivers and employers in large cities. There is, therefore, no necessary reason why the price charged to those who ride the subways should be equal to marginal cost — some part of that marginal cost might well be borne by the others who benefit from each person's riding, or, if the benefit is widespread, by general taxation.

In his theoretical analysis of toll charges on bridges, Hotelling is probably quite correct, but the application of this analysis is perhaps not quite so general as might appear. Hotelling, himself, would recognize that if the tariff is greater than the capacity of the bridge a rental charge may properly be made, in order to assure that the privilege of utilizing the existing capacity will go to those who most desire it. On this basis, the tolls on the Hudson River bridges and tunnels (to which Hotelling so vigorously objects) may not be so objectionable after all, at least at certain periods of the day. Furthermore, if the toll is small in comparison with the other costs incurred by the individuals making use of the service, demand may be sufficiently inelastic so that the toll will have little or no effect upon use. Such, for instance, may be the case with respect to the tolls on the New York parkway system. Gasoline costs and the difference in time saved in comparison with the size of the toll may make for considerable inelasticity in demand over the relevant range. The social cost (reduction in use) involved in allocating the cost of the highway to those who make use of it thus may be very small in relation to the total revenue involved.

Finally, there are sectors of the economy in which marginal cost pricing is not really feasible, from an administrative point of view. This is particularly true of the distributive trades. By their very nature, distributive firms operate with marginal costs considerably below average cost. Operation of all retailing and wholesaling units with marginal cost pricing would pose almost insoluble problems with regard to entry, and therefore with regard to the correct operation of the whole distributive industry. Marginal cost pricing, in other words, does not satisfactorily solve many of the problems which are now disturbing the economy, and there is reason to believe that the adoption of marginal cost pricing might make the existing flaws in the distributive sector even more troublesome.

The marginal cost pricing system is thus based essentially on the same assumptions as the older welfare economics of Pigou, and is not consistent with the postulates of the new welfare economics. Marginal cost pricing can only be made consistent with the new welfare economics if it is assumed that there are no decreasing cost industries in the economy. Marginal cost would then equal average cost, and the system, as far as pricing is concerned, would be the same as perfect competition. In order to bring marginal cost pricing within the boundaries of the new welfare economics in a manner which would fit the existing technology in which decreasing cost industries play an important role, discriminatory pricing is necessary and the system ceases to be one of constant marginal cost pricing.

Discriminatory Pricing

Discriminatory pricing has been defined to exist whenever price is set at other than marginal cost on any unit of a product, or whenever a factor receives other than the value of its marginal product for any unit of its services; thus, even an income tax would involve discriminatory pricing on the factor side. All price discrimination involves redistributive as well as allocative effects, and in many instances the redistributive effects are undesirable. This, for instance, would be true of some prices based on what the traffic will bear — necessities could successfully be priced far above their marginal cost. Likewise, a flat *ad valorem* tax such as a sales tax yields a discriminatory pricing system which will have unfavorable redistributive effects. The pertinent literature, insofar as price discrimination on commodities is concerned, has been concerned primarily with these unfavorable types of redistribution, and such price discrimination is, therefore, generally held in disfavor. Price discrimination on the factors of production, on the other hand, has frequently been condoned, since the firms in which it has usually occurred have more often effected a redistribution in the right direction. It does not follow that price discrimination with respect to the factors of production is always superior to price discrimination on commodities, however. Excise taxes on luxury commodities may be used to redistribute income in the desired direction, and in certain cases such excise taxes might not have as great an effect in reducing the supply of the factors of production as would an equivalent income tax. When this is true, it is impossible to say that the income tax, for the economy as a whole, is superior to certain excise taxes.

Price discrimination is much more prevalent in the present-day economy than is generally recognized. The distributive trades, by utilizing percentage mark-ups, are essentially indulging in discriminatory pricing, since the costs of distribution of more expensive items are not necessarily proportionally greater than those for less expensive items. Another form of price discrimination, which is perhaps more generally recognized as discrimination, is that which is combined with product differentiation. Luxury commodities sell for proportionally more above factor cost than do utility models, and often carry a larger share of the overhead.

The method of price discrimination which is used will have an influence upon the extent to which capacity is utilized. Discrimination such that the marginal price is equal to marginal cost will, in decreasing cost industries, ordinarily result in a greater utilization than will average cost pricing, and it has long been recognized that such discrimination will sometimes yield an increase in welfare for everyone concerned. If costs are decreasing rapidly and demand in one group is very elastic, it may be possible by lowering the price to this group to increase production sufficiently so that even the highest price charged is less than it would be with a single average cost price. Unless the price to all consumers is lowered by charging multiple prices, it is not possible, without introducing interpersonal comparisons, to determine whether a system of multiple prices is better than a single price equal to average cost. Thus the question of whether the discriminatory practices currently employed by railroads and public utilities are desirable cannot be settled by any general theoretical conclusion. Just because certain forms of price discrimination can improve a situation does not mean that any system of price discrimination is justifiable. It is ordinarily true that an optimum system of price discrimination cannot be determined without utilizing interpersonal comparisons, so that the problem cannot be said to lie within the boundaries of new welfare economics.

Discriminatory pricing does not designate a specific price system in the same sense that marginal cost pricing and competitive pricing does. Rather, it designates a large family of pricing systems — including, among others, marginal cost pricing. Uniform pricing, under the definition developed above, is inapplicable to the economy as it exists, so that the pricing system must represent some form of price discrimination. Some forms of price discrimination are more useful than others in solving the problems of resource allocation and redistribution, and ruling any of them out without considering their effects unduly restricts the design of an optimum price system. Specifically, restricting the pricing system to a single price for each commodity or factor service (somehow defined), or restricting discrimination to the factor side only, is equivalent to throwing away useful tools. This is not to say, of course, that multiple pricing should always be used for every commodity, or that discrimination should be entirely on the commodity side; rather, it is simply an argument that no general class of pricing systems should be ruled out without good reason either in terms of violation of the marginal conditions or in terms of difficulties of practical application.

Competitive Pricing

The price system which results from a perfectly competitive market structure is a special case of marginal cost pricing, requiring that no decreasing cost industries exist in the economy. Like marginal cost pricing, therefore, it necessarily represents an optimum only when the marginal utilities of income are equal for all individuals, or, since decreasing cost industries are here ruled out, when supply of the factors of production is fixed in relation to factor payments. The problem of redistribution, as has been pointed out above, is not necessarily a separate problem from that of the design of the pricing system, so that it cannot be argued that redistribution by the income tax is necessarily preferable to some other alteration of the pricing system. Unless one or both of these conditions is met, therefore, competitive pricing even on the commodity side will not necessarily represent an optimum.

Unlike marginal cost pricing, perfect competition arrives at a pricing system through the operation of a specific system of industrial organization. In order to meet the marginal conditions of production and exchange, the system of industrial organization must be one of perfect, not imperfect, competition; it is easily shown that imperfect competition may yield a pricing system which is less desirable than that yielded by monopoly. Believing that it is possible to arrive at such a perfectly competitive industrial organization, a great many people have considered monopoly to be the chief obstacle in the way of efficient resource allocation. But it is difficult to find a satisfactory definition of what monopoly is in this connection, and it is even more difficult to evaluate the economic significance of monopoly. Many measures of monopoly have been suggested, but no one of them seems fully satisfactory — and if all the characteristics of the different measures were required, monopoly would almost never be found to exist. The seriousness of the failure of monopoly to meet the marginal conditions may not be very great in welfare terms; a problem arises of deciding in what circumstances it is worthwhile to change the nature of the system to achieve a somewhat problematical gain.

Deconcentration as a solution to the monopoly problem is not entirely satisfactory in all instances. Modern industrial organization is based largely on imperfect competition, and deconcentration, by substituting a larger for a smaller number of firms, keeping them still in imperfect competition, will not necessarily approach the conditions of perfect competition any more closely. Rather, deconcentration may serve to raise selling expenses, increase the number of outlets, reduce consumers' choice, lead to excess plant capacity or uneconomic use of capacity and, where there are lumpy factors of production, prevent marginal costing. In very large sectors of the economy, the concept of perfect competition is simply inapplicable, and there is no automatic mechanism which will ensure that the increase in numbers in imperfect competition will yield a more desirable system of resource allocation. Because the processes of production, distribution and consumption are separated in the economy, and because not all competition is price competition, the misallocation of resources may be more serious when there is a large number of firms than it is when there is a smaller number.

For these reasons, the policy of overall deconcentration as a method of obtaining an optimum pricing system seems to have its drawbacks. There are undoubtedly specific instances in which deconcentration may have a beneficial effect upon resource allocation, but it does not follow that deconcentration can be recommended on this ground as a general policy. On other grounds, political or moral ones, for instance, it is possible to raise serious objections to monopoly *per se*, but such analysis is outside the scope of this study.

The Nature of an Optimum Pricing System

The problem of designing an optimum pricing system is highly related to the theory of international trade, and some of the problems involved would be more generally recognized if considered in this framework. In the first place, on much the same grounds that perfect competition is held to yield an optimum, free trade is held to be *the* optimum (see Scitovsky, 1941, p. 79). Not all writers in the field of international trade have fallen into this error, however; some have realized that there are many optima of which free trade is only one, and that without specific interpersonal comparisons it is impossible to say that free trade does represent maximum welfare (see Samuelson, 1938, p. 265). In addition, to suggest that free trade should exist, but that there should be a tax on exports to redistribute income between countries is obviously a contradiction in terms — yet this is exactly what has been advocated in the design of price systems, in the use of a competitive price system with an income tax to redistribute income. Redistribution of income is an economic problem involving the pricing system, and advocating income taxes alone for this purpose is the same as stating a preference for taxes on exports, to the exclusion of taxes on imports.

In order to determine a single optimum, therefore, a pricing system must take into account the desired distribution of income, and in order to decide upon a distribution of income interpersonal comparisons of utility are necessary. This reasoning has led some economists to feel that the new welfare economics is overly pretentious (see Stigler, 1943, p. 357). Such a charge is not entirely unjustified, in view of the attempts which have been made to base the marginal cost pricing hypothesis solely upon it, but there is nothing inherent in the new welfare economics which leads automatically to such perversion. As Samuelson (1943, p. 605) has pointed out, the new welfare economics is not intended as a substitute for the old, but rather attempts to 'derive *necessary* conditions whose validity is independent of value judgements as between individuals. . .'.

From the discussion in the preceding sections, it appears that, no matter what distribution of income is considered desirable, there is no one specific pricing system which will be more efficient that all others. Different pricing principles are economic tools which find applicability in different circumstances. The task of the economist in designing price systems is not so much one of finding a general panacea, but rather one of the systematic analysis of the special problems which arise in different sectors of the economy.

Marginal cost pricing, for instance, may very well increase welfare in certain specific situations. The fact that it is not applicable as a general system does not mean that it should be discarded altogether. Certain railway utility rates undoubtedly provide an area in which marginal cost pricing would increase welfare. As Hotelling pointed out, the gain enjoyed by those who benefit from the lower price is frequently greater than the loss borne by those helping to subsidize the industry, and the attempt to assess the burden carefully may lead to greater diseconomy than allocating it incorrectly.

An approximation of the competitive mechanism, likewise, is in certain sectors essential for the operation of the economy. But this does not mean that everything which can be termed monopoly or oligopoly should be eradicated and a large number of firms set up in its stead. Such a procedure may be far more wasteful than the existence of a certain degree of concentration. Even the most monopolistic firms face considerable competition from producers who sell somewhat substitutable goods and services. The industrial organization of the economy is almost always a form of imperfect competition, but some forms of imperfect competition are more workable than others. From the point of view of resource allocation, the object of industrial reorganization should be to make the competitive mechanism workable; in some specific instances, deconcentration will aid in achieving this end, but overall deconcentration is not likely to be a very efficient tool.

In summary, then, the pricing system must be designed to fit the conditions which do exist in the economy. Different parts of the economy differ from one another in the restrictions they impose on the pricing system, and what is appropriate for one sector may be completely inappropriate for another. The pricing system will, of necessity, be one which involves price discrimination; the question to be solved is what form of price discrimination should be employed. No one answer can be given which will be valid as a general principle. But one statement can be made: the search for panaceas, for simple rules by which to guide all conduct, is, because of the technological requirements of the different parts of the economy and the problem of redistribution, a vain search and even a foolish one. The economist is given a kit of tools with which to accomplish a complicated job. A better job can be done if each is used where it is appropriate, instead of throwing away all but one, and expecting it to serve all purposes.

REFERENCES

Bain, J.S. (1941), 'The profit rate as a measure of monopoly power', *Quarterly Journal of Economics*, **55**, 271–93.

Bain, J.S. (1945), *The Economics of the Pacific Coast Petroleum Industry, Part II, Price Behavior and Competition*, Berkeley.

Barone, E. (1935), 'The ministry of production in the collectivist state', in F.A.V. Hayek (ed.), *Collectivist Economic Planning*, London, Appendix A.

Chamberlin, E. (1933), *The Theory of Monopolistic Competition*, Cambridge.

Clark, J.B. (1899), *The Distribution of Wealth*, New York.

Clark, J.M. (1923), *The Economics of Overhead Costs*, Chicago.

Dunlop, J. (1939), 'Price flexibility and the degree of monopoly', *Quarterly Journal of Economics*, **53**, 522–34.

Ise, J. (1940), 'Monopoly elements in rent', *American Economic Review*, **30**, 33–45.

Knight, F.H. (1923), 'Fallacies in the interpretation of social cost', *Quarterly Journal of Economics*, **38**, 582–606.

Lerner, A.P. (1933), 'The concept of monopoly and the measurement of monopoly power', *Review of Economic Studies*, **1**, 157–75.

Marshall, A. (1936), *Principles of Economics*, 8th edition, London.

Means, G. (1935), 'Industrial prices, their relative inflexibility', *Senate Document No. 13*, 74th Congress, 1st Session, Washington.

Miller, J.P. (1941), *Unfair Competition*, Cambridge, MA.

Neal, A.C. (1942), *Industrial Concentration and Price Inflexibility*, New York.

Pareto, V. (1909), *Manuel d'économique politique*, Paris.

Patinkin, D. (1947), 'Multiple-plant firms, cartels, and imperfect competition', *Quarterly Journal of Economics*, **61**, 173–205.

Pigou, A.C. (1912a), *Wealth and Welfare*, London.

_____ (1912b), 'Railway rates and joint costs', *Quarterly Journal of Economics*, **27**, 535–6, 687–92.

_____ (1929), *The Economics of Welfare*, 3rd edition, London.

Robinson, J. (1933a), *Imperfect Competition*, London.

Rostow, E. (1948), *A National Policy for the Oil Industry*, New Haven, CT.

Ruggles, C.O. (1938), *Problems in Public Utility Economics and Management*, New York.

Samuelson, P.A. (1938), 'Welfare economics and international trade', *American Economic Review*, **28**, 261–6.

_____ (1943), 'Further comment on welfare economics', *American Economic Review*, **33**, 604–6.

_____ (1947), *The Foundations of Economic Analysis*, Cambridge, MA.

Scitovsky, T. (1941), 'Prices under monopoly and competition', *Journal of Political Economy*, **49**, 663–85.

Simons, H. (1948), *Economic Policy for a Free Society*, Chicago.

Stigler, G.L. (1943), 'The new welfare economics', *American Economic Review*, **33**, 355–9.

Sweezy, Paul (1937), 'The economist's place under socialism', in *Explorations in Economics*, Cambridge, MA.

Taussig, F.W. (1912), 'Railway rates and joint costs once more', *Quarterly Journal of Economics*, **27**, 378–84.

Tennant, R.B. (1948), 'The American cigarette industry', unpublished; submitted as a doctoral dissertation, Yale University.

Triffin, R. (1940), *Monopolistic Competition and General Equilibrium Theory*, Cambridge, MA, pp. 90–95.

US Temporary National Economic Committee (1940), *Price Behavior and Business Policy*, Monograph 1, Washington, DC.

Wallace, D.H. (1937), *Market Control in the Aluminum Industry*, Cambridge, MA.

Watkins, G.P. (1916), 'The theory of differential rates', *Quarterly Journal of Economics*, **30**, 682–703.

Wicksell, K. (1934), *Lectures on Political Economy*, translated by E. Classen, London.

4. The Value of Value Theory

Richard Ruggles
Yale University

An evaluation of any body of theory requires some sort of implicit or explicit definition of the objectives of that theory. If the objectives are conceived of at a very concrete and specific level, the evaluation will be simpler and less vague but will lack the broad perspective which might be gained if the immediate objectives are put into a more general framework. To provide such a general setting, this paper will first consider the role of value theory in the actual analysis of economic problems. Once this has been done, the examination of the more specific objectives of value theory will take on greater significance. With respect to these more specific objectives, a number of fairly common charges regarding the limitations of value theory will be discussed, and from these, as a third part of the paper, some possible suggestions for future work in this area will be developed.

1. THE PLACE OF VALUE THEORY IN ECONOMIC ANALYSIS

For the purpose of this evaluation, it is convenient to divide economic problems into three general areas. I realize at the outset that such a division is highly arbitrary and that many other kinds of division would be equally valid. Insofar as economics is coincident with its literature, however, it is useful to observe implicit divisions which occur in that literature. Economics, like other fields of knowledge, does not develop evenly; certain areas of research progress faster and farther than others, so that they acquire a separate identity of their own. The general areas I have chosen to delineate are: the determination of the level of economic activity, the evolution or growth of economic systems, and the evaluation of the efficiency of resource allocation.

This chapter first appeared in *American Economic Review*, **44** (2), 1954

Level of Economic Activity

The analysis of the level of activity in an economy has developed in the last two decades largely along aggregative lines. Such aggregative economic constructs as gross national product, disposable income, consumer expenditures and gross capital formation have been utilized, both theoretically and empirically, to build models of aggregative economic behavior. Although these models have in them assumptions about the behavior of producers and consumers, value theory is rarely used explicitly. In the theory of the consumption function, perhaps, there has been some attempt to lean on that part of value theory concerned with consumer behavior but, in general, these attempts have not made much explicit use of formal value theory tools, nor have they been notably successful in developing an aggregative theory of consumer behavior. Indeed, it would seem that casual empiricism rather than analytic value theory has been the basis of most model-making relating to the level of activity in an economic system.

Evolution of Economic Systems

Analysis concerned with the evolution and growth of economic systems is, in general, less formally developed than analysis of the level of economic activity. Work in this area has gone along two principal lines. The first has been the development of simplified abstract growth models involving a relatively small number of variables such as capital stock and technological change. These models are usually closely related to those used in the analysis of the level of economic activity. It is even truer here, however, that the relationships employed are either assumed or else derived from conventional time series data; formal value theory contributes very little. The second approach in this area is more institutional and historical, analyzing the rise and fall of specific institutions: such things as the growth of unionism, the development of countervailing power, the effect of the system of taxation and the impact of atomic power are examined in the context of the existing institutions and operation of the economy. There is no particular reason why this sort of analysis should not utilize the tools of value theory, yet because of the concern of these discussions with political and social institutions it rarely seems appropriate to bring in the abstract concepts that are involved in value theory. Here, again, casual empiricism is substituted for analytic tools.

Efficiency of Resource Allocation

In the area of the efficiency of resource allocation, in contrast with the preceding areas, considerable use actually has been made of value theory, as a tool in analyzing the behavior of producers and consumers under given sets of circumstances and in evaluating and comparing the consequences of such behavior. Even the most elementary course in economics spends considerable time showing the determinants of price and output under different market conditions, in order to demonstrate the social efficiency or inefficiency of certain forms of industrial organization.

The marginal conditions of production and exchange used by some welfare economists to develop a criterion for optimum output are derived directly from value theory concepts. The area of efficiency of resource allocation is, in fact, the area in which value theory has played its major role. I do not wish at this time to digress to give my own personal views regarding the proper nature of this area of research. The extent of the controversy in the welfare economics literature of the last two decades has amply indicated that there are wide differences of opinion about just what the nature of this area ought to be. In its widest sense, of course, this area includes both of the fields discussed above: the full utilization of resources and economic growth.

For the purpose of this paper, however, a precise definition of the field is not necessary. Nor is it necessary to take the further step of asking whether work in the area has in fact added to the general fund of useful knowledge. For the present stage of evaluation, it is only necessary to establish that value theory is actually utilized in this area.

2. USEFULNESS OF VALUE THEORY AS A TOOL OF ANALYSIS

With this consideration of the relevance of value theory to economic analysis, it is now appropriate to proceed to the second phase of the evaluation: the consideration of the efficiency of value theory as a tool of analysis. Without this second step, no final evaluation of the contribution of value theory is possible. Even though value theory may have an important function, if it fulfills this function very inadequately, it cannot be considered to be making a significant contribution to economics.

The objective of value theory as a tool of analysis is the explanation of producer and consumer behavior at the level of the individual decision-making unit, as opposed to the aggregative behavior pattern for the economy as a whole which represents the combined results produced by the actions of a large number of different decision-making units. Since I cannot, within the short space of this paper, hope to cover both the producer and consumer aspects of value theory, I will restrict myself to an explicit consideration of the theory of the firm. Much of what is said will, of course, also be applicable to the theory of consumer behavior. Although there are marked differences between the theory of producer behavior and the theory of consumer behavior, there is also an underlying similarity. This arbitrary procedure of singling out the theory of the firm for consideration is especially appropriate since the topic of this session is industrial pricing. Specifically, this section of the paper will consider the adequacy of the theory of the firm in supplying a meaningful method of analyzing industrial pricing.

The charges commonly made against the theory of the firm bear a striking family resemblance. Most of them are variants on the theme that in some manner or other the theory is unrealistic or irrelevant. In the following section, I will try to be somewhat more concrete about the charges, but I must confess that all of those I shall mention are basically the same kind of objection. The specific charges I shall cover are: that value theory is tautological, that many of the concepts of value theory have no empirical counterparts, that the necessity of using rigid *ceteris paribus* assumptions paralyzes the analysis so that it can say little about any concrete situation, that many important factors influencing economic behavior are omitted from the analysis, and finally that value theory has been designed to consider only a single-product plant producing a durable, storable good, so that the theory is incapable of dealing with the complex situations found in most industrial firms.

The validity of the first charge — that the theory of the firm is tautological — depends, in large part, on whether profit maximization is taken to be the basic motive of producers' behavior or whether profit maximization is viewed as only one of many possible courses of action. To the extent that the profit maximization principle is considered to be indeed the basic determinant of producers' behavior, the theory of the firm is truly a theory. But if it is maintained that profit maximization is only an assumption that may or may not be true, the theory of the firm does reduce to a set of definitional statements.

The situation is not unlike that famous discussion of the quantity equation versus the quantity theory. As long as none of the variables in the equation is given behavior characteristics, the quantity equation remains purely definitional. But once it is held, for instance, that velocity tends to remain constant, the equation becomes a theory. The charge that value theory is tautological in this sense, of course, does not condemn the theory; for analytical purposes definitional frameworks can be very useful, even aside from the value of any single specific theory which is developed to interrelate the variables defined. National income accounting, for example, sets up an empirical framework which is useful for many analytic purposes and in numerous theoretical contexts.

Another sort of meaning, however, can be attached to the charge of tautology. This interpretation involves the basic nature of the concepts used in the theory of the firm: specifically, the coverage of the concepts of marginal cost and marginal revenue. If marginal cost and marginal revenue are defined to take into account all factors, actual or implied, that the producer considers, including such things as expectations, risk-bearing, frictions and psychological predilections toward large or small output, it will be true that by definition every producer, because he is doing what he wants to do, is in fact maximizing profits, and that any apparent evidence to the contrary is misleading because it does not take into account all of the implicit components of cost and revenue. Stated in this extreme manner, the profit maximization premise of value theory would by definition always obtain. But since the concepts used in the analysis would not be independent of the results they were attempting to explain, no new or useful information would be added by using such a framework to study the behavior of the firm.

Although a theory of the firm expressed in such blatant terms would find few supporters, I fear that there is in most of us a tendency to make theory more general by subsuming more and more of the variables we are trying to explain in the very concepts used to make the explanation. I think it is a legitimate charge that value theory too often, in the attempt to attain theoretical generality, loses its analytic significance.

The second charge — that the concepts used in value theory have no measurable empirical counterparts — requires some investigation of the nature of these concepts. If the value theory concepts were tautologically derived from the principle of profit maximization in the manner just described, these concepts would certainly be unmeasurable. But even where the concepts are conceptually independent of what they seek to explain, it does not always follow that they will be measurable. For example, consider the concepts of price and quantity. These concepts have meaning only when the product itself does not change. Where product characteristics have changed, resort must be had to some sort of index number solution, and this is usually not theoretically satisfactory. Similarly, the elasticity of demand is a useful concept for empirical analysis only if the demand curve does not shift in the period under consideration or if, despite shifts, elasticity remains fairly constant both over a range of output and over time. Empirical measurements of elasticity have to operate upon these assumptions, so that at best they can result only in an idea of magnitude rather than in exact measurement.

Marginal cost does not fare much better. Statistical measurements of marginal cost have been singularly unsuccessful, for the most part attempting to measure the marginal by fitting a regression to adjusted total cost figures. The problem here, like the problem with the demand curve, is that shifts in costs and random factors introduce a wide variability into the observed total cost figures, so that it is not easy to trace the exact course of the cost function.

The theory of the firm is even less satisfactory when it comes to the concept of factor payments. The factors of production are generally conceived of as either three or four in number: land, labor, and capital, with or without entrepreneurship or risk-taking as a fourth. These factors, the theory states, will be utilized in production in such a manner as to equate the price of each with its marginal revenue product. Unfortunately, in empirical terms there is no way to separate the payments for these factors from one another. Wages paid may or may not cover the total payment for labor. In a small owner-operated firm, for instance, it is entirely possible for the labor contributed by the owner and his family to far outweigh any purchased labor.

Rent is even less meaningful in an empirical context. A business may control a great many factors which produce a rental income and yet receive no rental payment. Thus a farmer who owns his own land should theoretically be paying himself a rent for this land, and it might appear proper to impute such a payment even though none is made. To do so empirically, however, is usually impossible, and the situation becomes correspondingly worse in more complex firms where there are no ready market prices for the factors owned.

Profit is the most perplexing concept of all, because in any empirical measurement, it must be a residual and probably contains some of each of the other factors as well as true profit. This is readily observable for farmers and small shopkeepers, but is equally true for more complex firms.

Thus, it must be admitted that the concepts used in the theory of the firm do not have any simple, convenient empirical counterparts. The consequences of this charge are quite serious when one considers the degree to which this impairs the usefulness of the theory of the firm for explaining actual industrial pricing. Unless the theoretical concepts correspond fairly closely to their empirical counterparts, no rigorous analytic explanation of what actually does take place in industrial pricing is possible. In fact, unless the concepts match, it is impossible even to express in theoretical terms what is happening in any given actual situation, much less explain it.

The third charge — that using rigid *ceteris paribus* assumptions paralyzes the theory of the firm so that little can be said about any concrete situation — is only partially justified. Quite often objections of this nature result from a misunderstanding of the function of *ceteris paribus* assumptions, with the consequent misconception that the theory of the firm should be able to explain a particular producer's behavior in a particular situation. The theory of the firm is concerned with the effect of certain specific variables upon the behavior of the firm. It does not deny that other factors may also affect the behavior of the firm. When other behavior-determining factors are present, the effect of the given variables may be obscured or distorted, thus producing an error term in the empirical analysis. Only by repeated trials can the theory be tested; if the error term then appears to be random, the theory may be considered satisfactory despite the fact that it does not provide a complete explanation of any one particular case.

Although the use of *ceteris paribus* assumptions is thus a necessary and useful part of the analytic method, it must be admitted that it can, in certain circumstances, limit the application of the theory to such a degree that no meaningful empirical analysis can be made. When the concepts of value theory are defined in such a manner that they are observable only in very special circumstances, the error term may be so large that empirical testing can only be inconclusive. It is probably true that the concepts of value theory which usually are used can be indicted on these grounds, but this is only a reiteration of the preceding charge that value theory concepts have no convenient empirical counterparts rather than a legitimate attack on the use of *ceteris paribus* assumptions.

The fourth charge — that many important factors influencing economic behavior are omitted from the theory of the firm — is sometimes only a restatement of the objection to the use of *ceteris paribus* assumptions. Also, it is not always clear that those who make this objection realize that factors influencing economic behavior can implicitly be included in the analysis in terms of their effect on explicit factors. The theory of the firm is quite correct in omitting from explicit analysis many major factors which affect the behavior of the producer through their effect on cost or revenue. For example, the distance between a producer and his supplier may affect costs, but by using costs of materials delivered to the producer, this factor is implicitly covered. Such factors are not really excluded from consideration; they are part and parcel of the forces which determine the cost and revenue functions and are, therefore, implicitly included in them. A mere taxonomic listing of such determinants would do little to further an analytic approach to producer behavior.

On the other hand, it must also be admitted that there are factors which may have an important influence on producers' behavior that do not get included either implicitly or explicitly in the theory of the firm. Such things as the government's attitude toward industrial concentration or toward excessive profits for certain large firms may have an important bearing on the decisions of these firms. This is another way of saying that if the theory of the firm could be applied to empirical situations, the error terms which would result might be large and nonrandom. Unfortunately, since the theory of the firm cannot be tested empirically on any significant scale at this time, such charges can be neither substantiated nor denied.

Finally, the charge that value theory is designed to consider only a single-product plant producing a durable, storable good and is incapable of dealing with the complex situations found in most industrial plants is again in part a reflection of the charge that the concepts used in the theory of the firm are applicable only to a small number of extremely simplified empirical situations. The full blame for the restricted application of the theory of the firm cannot be laid at the door of ill-constructed concepts, however, since academic economists seem to have bent over backwards in restricting their theoretical analyses to a manufacturing plant of a very simple variety and omitting from consideration producers operating in distributive trade, mining, services, etc.

The concepts of the theory of the firm may be fairly useless for empirical applications, but they are by no means as inoperable theoretically as they have been made to appear by traditional textbook presentations. Nevertheless, I must confess that the value theory concepts available would not be satisfactory for analyzing highly competitive situations.

In summary, I believe it is fair to say that although value theory does have an important role in the analysis of resource allocation problems, there are very serious defects in the manner in which it fills this role. In all the charges against value theory, one major element stands out. The concepts of the theory of the firm are not set up to be operable in empirical terms, and this in turn prevents the theory of the firm from being tested empirically or from being used to analyze empirical situations.

Over and above this particular criticism of the inherent limitations of value theory for analyzing problems in the field of resource allocation, there still remains the criticism that was indicated in the first section of this paper, namely, that value theory is not used to any significant degree as a tool of analysis in the other areas of economics. Fundamentally, I feel that this failure also is directly traceable to the nature of the value theory concepts as traditionally defined. Because the microconcepts used in value theory are basically different from the macroconcepts used in aggregative analysis, there is a wide gap between micro- and macrotheory. From a theoretical point of view, this gap is very unfortunate, because it means that value theory must remain a partial rather than a general equilibrium analysis and that aggregative theory, because of its different concepts, cannot use microbehavior theory to check the implicit propositions about producer and consumer behavior inherent in the aggregative behavior patterns which are posited or observed.

3. SUGGESTIONS FOR FUTURE WORK

On the basis of this evaluation of the extent to which value theory is used in various areas of economics and the efficiency with which it fulfills these uses, I shall now bring up four related suggestions for the future development of work in this area.

First, I believe that it should be explicitly recognized that the concepts of value theory as traditionally stated are not empirically operable, and in consequence that a separate conceptual framework must be erected for classifying empirical information about the individual firm. Second, I would hope that such a conceptual framework would be of a very general nature and would take into account the requirements of macrotheory as well as those of microtheory.

Third, I feel that the classification scheme adopted in this framework should have as its basic criterion empirical operability, but within this criterion both functional and institutional characteristics should be observed as much as possible. Finally, I would suggest that such a framework should be used in conjunction with orthodox value theory rather than substituted for it.

Recognition that the conceptual framework of value theory as traditionally stated is not, by itself, sufficient for analyzing the empirical behavior of producers has important implications. It does not mean that value theory should be completely rejected. Value theory is still useful as a part of the research process; understanding the basic formal relationships of the major determinants of behavior and building models to study such relationships are necessary steps in the research process, and the concepts that are best adapted to this use may well not be adapted to the study of empirical material. The recent methodological history of macroeconomics provides an excellent illustration of this point.

The theory of income and employment contains many empirically inoperable concepts such as liquidity preference, the marginal efficiency of capital and the propensity to consume. Even the definitional framework of the theory of income and employment, the equation $Y = C + I$, as originally stated was not particularly meaningful in empirical terms.

Nevertheless, the basic ideas contained in this equation were capable of being developed into the empirical framework of national income accounting. I am citing the example of macrotheory not merely as an analogy but rather to demonstrate a principle of methodological design. If this principle were applied to value theory, certain concepts such as the elasticity of demand and marginal cost might not appear directly in the empirical framework, any more than the propensity to consume or the marginal efficiency of capital appears in national accounts. The less measurable aspects of value theory are useful for analytic purposes and should influence the classification scheme, but they should not be an explicit part of the empty boxes we wish to fill. In the past, overemphasis on theory has all too often resulted in the proliferation of unfillable empty boxes, thus creating an unbridgeable gap between theoretical and empirical analysis.

This first suggestion leaves open the question of the nature of the empirical framework which we seek to erect. In developing this framework, again taking heed of the experience with national income accounting, I would suggest the desirability of making it as all-embracing as possible. All producing and consuming units in the economy, for example, should be capable of being fitted into the analysis conveniently and be capable of being interrelated with each other in meaningful terms.

The basic principle of national income accounting and money flows analysis, that is, the use of transactions and the concept of money flows, would, I

believe, meet this objective. The behavior of the firm would thus be thought
of in terms of the transactions in which it engages. Following the basic
principle of national accounts and money flows a little further, the microframework would concern itself with the classification of all the receipts and outlays
of producers and consumers. By these suggestions, I do not mean that the
classifications currently used in national income accounting or money flows
analysis should be directly transferred as a framework for microanalysis; quite
on the contrary, I feel that the erection of a framework for microanalysis might
well lead to the changing of many of the classifications which are now used in
national income accounting and money flows analysis. What I would like to
suggest, however, is that some sort of common classificatory framework be set
up for both micro- and macrodata so that analyses can be carried out at varying
levels of aggregation and disaggregation.

As my third suggestion, I think that, within the general framework of receipts and outlays, the basic criterion of classification should be that the
transactions grouped together should, in some sense, be homogeneous and
easily distinguishable as such. The wage bill paid by the firm, materials purchased by the firm and receipts from sales of goods are all classifications of this
type. Both functional and institutional characteristics will be very useful as a
basis for classifying flows. Thus purchases of materials can be distinguished
from purchases of labor and social security tax payments can be distinguished
from corporate tax payments. Institutional classifications such as the separation
of salary payments from wage payments may be useful for certain kinds of
analyses.

Despite the comprehensiveness of such a receipts and outlays framework,
many of the variables which are extremely useful for analytic purposes would
not enter directly into it. This has also been found true in the field of national
income accounting. Here such things as price and output indexes and the distribution of manpower among industries are all treated separately from the
formal system of accounts. I should imagine that in the microframework, too,
such things as prices, output and man-hours, perhaps sometimes in index form,
would be required in addition to the formal framework itself.

Once the framework and its auxiliary information have been set up, the
question of precisely how this framework is to be utilized in analyzing the behavior of the firm arises. As indicated in the discussion of the first suggestion,
it should be emphasized that such a framework is not a substitute for value
theory but is to be used in conjunction with it. What it does make possible is
the analysis of the behavior of the flows within the firm under varying conditions. It is the purpose of the empirical framework to set forth such behavior
relationships and to indicate their variation over time and from group to group.
It is the function of value theory to analyze the conditions under which such
behavior would emerge. Until an empirical framework is set up to be used in

conjunction with value theory, the progress that will be possible both in empirical work and in value theory will be very limited.

In conclusion, I would like to take up a specific example of the type of empirical–theoretical analysis to which I have been referring. We all know that the Census of Manufactures contains a great deal of useful information, and I have always been somewhat perplexed as to why this wealth of information has not been utilized to a greater extent than it has. The Census of Manufactures gives certain data in classifications which correspond quite closely to some of the concepts I have been discussing for an empirical framework. For example, it gives for various industries value of product, cost of materials, and direct wages paid. These particular classifications do not by themselves yield a highly refined or complex conceptual framework, but if we look at the other side of the picture and ask what can be done empirically with such an array, a number of interesting possibilities present themselves.

In many industries, the value of products, the wage bill, and materials purchased relate generally to the same body of goods, namely, the output of the plant during the year. The valuation of inventories creates a real problem in some industries, but for other industries the problem is not too serious. It is interesting to study, industry by industry, the movement of the value of product, the wage bill, and materials purchased relative to each other, on the grounds that the relative movements among these would reflect the same relative movements among the realized price of the product, wage cost, and materials cost; thus giving a picture of the changes in price–cost structure that occur in different industries with changes in income and employment. At this juncture, it should be pointed out that the realized price is not necessarily the same as the quoted price. Such things as discounts and rebates will affect the realized price. Also, in some industries, sales of goods as seconds in order to dump them will be reflected in realized price but not in conventional price indexes.

Wage cost, similarly, is not the same thing as the wage rate. Wage cost would reflect changes in the productivity of the worker, due either to technological change or changes in the scale of output, as well as any change in the wage rate. Similarly, materials cost may rise or fall, not only because the prices of materials have risen or fallen, but also because more or less materials are utilized per unit of output.

The results one gets from studying the interrelations of these particular flows and what they indicate about prices, wage costs and materials costs in various industry groups are rather interesting. As one would anticipate, in those industries which process agricultural materials such as food and textiles, the cost of materials fluctuates much more widely than does wage cost. In theoretical terms this is to be expected, since output in the agricultural sector does not fluctuate widely with changes in the aggregate level of income, so that the effect of income changes is reflected almost entirely in changes in the price of agricultural output. Wage rates are traditionally stickier than agricultural prices, so that in these industries, in the absence of violent change in technology or in productivity, materials cost would rise faster in times of rising income and fall further in periods of falling income than wage cost. In many of the mineral processing industries, however, the prices of raw materials do not fluctuate as widely as those of the agricultural raw materials. The amplitude of the fluctuation of material cost is often approximately the same as that of the fluctuation in wage cost. There are exceptions to this rule, and they are generally located in those sectors of the economy where materials are derived from mineral industries in which the mineral deposits in themselves are quite valuable.

Probably the most interesting point of this whole analysis is that realized prices in the vast majority of industries tend to fluctuate with almost exactly the same amplitude as the weighted average of wage cost and materials cost, irrespective of whether the industries process agricultural or mineral products. Wage cost and material cost together represent a kind of direct cost of production, and the difference between this direct cost and total receipts can be thought of as a gross margin over direct costs. This gross margin shows remarkable stability for different industries, even when there are large changes in income and employment in the economy such as occurred between 1929 and 1931.

I cannot, in the confines of this paper, go into the ramifications of this particular analysis, but I do wish to point out that it has wide implications for the study of such things as the behavior of income flows in the various sectors of the economy and the effect of industrial organization on pricing. With respect to this latter point, for example, the form of industrial organization appears to have no significant effect, as far as I have been able to ascertain, upon the behavior of these gross margins, and thus price–cost behavior, in the economy. The traditional case for price inflexibility in certain sectors, because of the industrial organization of these sectors is, therefore, quite unfounded.

I have not meant to present in this paper an embryonic theory of industrial pricing; this is the function of the other speaker on the program. I have introduced the above analysis merely to illustrate that empirical analysis could be developed in a transactions framework and to point out that without some sort of empirical framework our theory of industrial pricing may indeed be just more empty boxes which we never can fill.

PART TWO

PRICE MEASUREMENT

5. The Wholesale Price Index

Richard Ruggles
Yale University

---

1. THE ORIGINAL CONCEPT

The Wholesale Price Index has been published as a continuous series since 1890. It was originally intended as a measure of price movements taking place in primary markets (i.e., other than at the retail level). At the time it was first constructed, economics was very much concerned with the concept of the price level, and it was believed that the Wholesale Price Index more correctly reflected the behavior of the price level — the purchasing power of the dollar — than did the traditionally more sticky retail prices. It was recognized, of course, that the index was only an approximation to price behavior at the wholesale or primary market level, since it was based on a relatively small sample of the many commodities which flow through these markets. Not only were many commodities excluded because price quotations were difficult to obtain, but it was recognized that there were some real price changes which could not be measured — for example, some improvements in quality, hidden discounts, differences in delivery schedules, etc. In spite of these difficulties, it was felt that the Wholesale Price Index did adequately represent the prices of all transactions in commodities taking place at other than the retail level.

Although the major emphasis of the wholesale price work in the early period was on the behavior of the aggregate price index, price series or specific commodity groups were also given, and considerable use was made from the start of the prices of these so-called leading commodities. The leading commodities were grouped into nine categories of a somewhat mixed nature, partly reflecting an industrial classification, partly classes of commodities bought by consumers and partly goods at various stages of fabrication. These early categories were farm products, foods, cloth and clothing, fuel and lighting, metals and metal products, building materials, chemicals and drugs, house furnishings

---

This chapter first appeared as a Report of the Price Review Committee, Joint Economic Committee, 1961.

and miscellaneous. This classification suggests that the Wholesale Price Index was intended to be a comprehensive, general purpose index reporting the general price behavior of the economy.

The Development of the Index

Since the initiation of the Wholesale Price Index, many changes have been made both in the content and in the methods of calculating the index. Originally, prices of some 250 commodities were collected, but this number has gradually increased until at the present time prices of some 1,900 commodities are included. As new commodities were added, they tended to be commodities with a higher degree of fabrication and generally more stable prices. The increased coverage of the Wholesale Price Index, therefore, had the effect of making the index, and hence the economy, appear to be more stable than it would have under the previous coverage. Increasing the size of the sample and increasing the proportion of more stable items both contributed to minimizing the fluctuation of the index (see McAllister, 1961).

With the development of other kinds of price indexes, e.g., the cost-of-living indexes, consumer price indexes, and most recently the gross national product deflator, the Wholesale Price Index has ceased to be a general purpose measure used to indicate the basic price behavior of the economy. More effort has been directed toward presenting price indexes by specific sectors of the economy and by stage of processing. For example, indexes of prices of crumple materials for further processing are given for the food industry, for manufacturing and for construction. Prices of intermediate materials, supplies and components are reported for the same groups. As less emphasis has been placed upon the overall price index, more attention has been directed toward the calculation of subindexes which are useful to those concerned with specific sectors of the economy.

The Present Wholesale Price Index

The present Wholesale Price Index complex consists of a comprehensive monthly index, a weekly index intended to represent what the monthly index would be if all the prices in the monthly index were collected and tabulated each week, and a daily index based on prices of 22 commodities traded on organized markets or exchanges.

The monthly index, as already indicated, covers some 1,900 items from 2,000 companies who supply about 4,500 individual reports. Additional data are secured from trade sources and other governmental agencies, for example, questionnaires are generally used and specification pricing is used so far as possible. In those instances where specifications change or new commodities are introduced, elaborate effort is made to see that only price changes affect the index.

The monthly index still contains the type of subgrouping which was used in the 1890 index, but the number of categories has been increased to 16. There has been some redefinition of categories, e.g., foods have been changed to processed foods, and cloth and clothing to textile products and apparel; and new categories reflecting specific industries have been added, e.g., tobacco and bottled beverages, rubber and rubber products, lumber and wood products, pulp, paper and allied products, machinery and motive products, and non-metallic minerals (structural). These changes reflect a movement toward a more purely industrial classification system. Behind these subgroup indexes, there are indexes for product classes and individual commodities, with a total of 1,340 item series. As already indicated, the indexes have also been classified by stage of processing. The indexes are further amplified by classifications showing the durability of goods and the economic sector for which the goods are destined, for example, consumers, producers, etc. Finally, there is a series of special wholesale price indexes which are of special interest: thus fish, soaps, detergents, steel mill products, industrial valves, abrasive grinding wheels and construction materials are all represented by special indexes.

Weights for the monthly index are based upon value of shipments data from the Industrial Censuses for 1954, but interplant transfers are excluded from these weights where possible. Each commodity price series is considered to be representative of a class of prices and is assigned the weight proper to the whole class. The class of commodities, in turn, is usually defined in terms of similarity of manufacturing processes, thus embodying the assumption that prices of commodities produced under similar conditions behave in the same way. The assumption that prices reflect conditions of cost more closely than they do conditions of demand is presumably more accurate over long periods than in the short run.

The Uses of the Wholesale Price Index

The utilization of the Wholesale Price Index as a general price index has changed with the passage of time, as we have noted. The preference that has developed for the use of the Consumer Price Index and the deflators of the national income accounts to measure changes in the value of the dollar had several causes. One major cause of the shift was the realization that the Wholesale Price Index was not a true sample of prices in the system, and that it was not particularly pertinent to any particular group of consumers or businesses in the economy. In contrast, the Cost-of-Living Index, and later the Consumer Price Index had a more exact frame of reference in terms of the market basket of goods purchased by a given class of consumers.

Just as the development of the Cost-of-Living and Consumer Price Indexes replaced the Wholesale Price Index as a general measure of the value of the dollar from the viewpoint of consumers, so also did the development of the implicit price deflators in the national income accounts replace the Wholesale Price Index as an overall measure of price behavior. The implicit deflator of gross national product has the advantage that it is considerably more comprehensive than the Wholesale Price Index, and the weighting system refers to a definable universe of final goods and services.

The factor of timing has prevented the abandonment of the aggregate Wholesale Price Index, however. The implicit price deflators of the gross national product are only available on a yearly and quarterly basis. The monthly Wholesale Price Index together with the Consumer Price Index is, therefore, still used as an indicator of how prices in the economy are moving on a current month-to-month basis. The weekly and daily Wholesale Price Indexes are still widely used as economic indicators which may help to show how the economy is moving over shorter periods of time. In this context, however, they are used in the same manner as freight car loadings, stock prices and other short-term indicators.

Manufacturers and trade associations are interested mainly in the group indexes, product class indexes and individual commodity indexes. A survey made by the Department of Labor indicated that 75 percent of the users wanted the price indexes by commodity groups and that half of all users considered the prices for individual commodities essential. One-third of the manufacturers questioned used the index to adjust materials contract prices, and one major industry adjusts all its materials contracts on the basis of changes in the index. There can be little doubt that the considerable amount of detail provided within the Wholesale Price Index is found to be very valuable by businesses which are concerned with the price behavior that is taking place in those markets in which they are producing goods or buying materials. For these users, the general Wholesale Price Index aggregate is not useful, but the highly detailed and specific information on individual industries, product classes and commodities is very valuable.

One of the major uses of wholesale price data is in the production of other basic economic data by government agencies. Thus the implicit price deflators of the gross national product lean heavily upon the product and commodity price data contained in the Wholesale Price Index. Any improvement in this Index aimed at more comprehensive coverage and better price reporting would substantially aid the deflation of gross national product by final product. Two examples may be cited. At the present time it is not possible to provide deflations of gross national product by industry of origin; improvement in the Wholesale Price Index coverage would make this extension possible. The price data necessary to value changes in inventories are notably deficient.

The Census Bureau, the Bureau of Labor Statistics and the Federal Reserve Board use the wholesale price data to estimate output by industry and to analyze productivity on an industry basis. These are, of course, different aspects of the same problem, and are directly related to the implicit price deflators by industry. Adequate wholesale price data are therefore the basic information on industrial activity and commodity output required for a large number of different uses.

Thus the use of the general price index as an aggregate has declined except in those instances where it is used as a short-term economic indicator (see below). At the same time, however, there has been a demand by industry, by other parts of the statistical system and by the academic world for more detailed and comprehensive wholesale price data on industries and commodities.

The Structure of the Wholesale Price Index

The behavior of the Wholesale Price Index is highly dependent on the universe of transactions it covers. It is somewhat paradoxical, then, that the universe of the WPI has never been clearly defined, and that ease of collection has been a major determinant of which prices to include. In reviewing the requirements for a Wholesale Price Index, therefore, it will be useful to examine what the Wholesale Price Index as an aggregate should measure, what universe of prices should be covered, what the substructure of the index should be and what kind of weighting system should be employed.

From the viewpoint of economic analysis, the Wholesale Price Index does not appear to be a meaningful economic construct. The transaction coverage is not descriptive of any definable set of producers or purchasers in the economy. Nor does the present WPI universe have a logical structure of subclasses which are appropriate to the analysis of economic developments: for example, indexes of buying and selling prices of industries, which would allow analysis of changes in 'value added'. There is no principle to determine how many steps in the fabrication of a raw material should be included.

The Committee believes that the structure of the wholesale price area should be revised to meet several objectives. The basic objective is comprehensiveness: there is need for price information on every important sector of the economy dealing in commodities, and a good structure will reveal gaps in our price information. A second objective is maximum detail in price reporting: the individual prices are the basic need for most business and scientific uses. And a third objective is the development of price indexes for the subgroups of commodity transactions which are most useful in economic analyses.

The framework for the universe should consist of the total sales and purchase of commodities other than at the retail level. Care should be taken to see that no important commodity class is omitted from coverage. This suggests that commodities should be priced at a number of different points in the distribution system, and to the extent feasible, separate indexes constructed for the pricing at these different points. Thus coal of a type sold to power companies may be different in its price behavior from coal of a type sold to dealers for retail distribution. An attempt should be made to cover pricing of every major body of commodity sales in the economy. It is recognized, of course, that in some areas price information may be very difficult to obtain, and substitute kinds of pricing may have to be developed in order to represent such areas fully. Other areas may be covered better because it is relatively easy and inexpensive to obtain price quotations on even quite minor categories.

From the point of view of completeness of price data, it is important that the Wholesale Price Index coverage be integrated with other price measurements. At the present time, the Wholesale Price Index covers agriculture and mining, as well as manufacturing. Although construction materials are covered as a part of manufacturing, construction itself is not included, nor is transportation. Exports and imports are partly covered by the Wholesale Price Index, but they are not systematically segregated. It should be recognized, of course, that on our comprehensive view of the Wholesale Price Index universe, portions of the universe will lie in areas in which data are now collected by other agencies. This is also true at present; however, the agricultural and mineral prices now in the WPI are collected in part by other agencies. We do not attempt to decide whether all of the price data falling in our proposed universe for the Wholesale Price Index should be compiled or analyzed by the BLS or whether the integrated system of price indexes is achieved through inter-agency collaboration. Analytically and conceptually, the same problems will have to be faced and the same price information will have to be collected.

The purpose of giving the Wholesale Price Index extremely broad coverage is to obtain price data which will be useful for the many purposes for which industry and other government agencies use such price data. To achieve maximum usefulness, the system of subclassification should be such that it meshes with other kinds of information available about the economy. Thus it should be possible to integrate information available from the Census of Manufactures, from the OASI and the Internal Revenue Service, as well as from other parts of the Bureau of Labor Statistics. For this reason, it seems desirable that the subclassification should aim at fitting into the Standard Industrial Classification. At the present time, BLS has joined with the Census Bureau to produce price indexes classified by 5-digit commodity groups and by broader SIC industry categories. This represents a very considerable step forward, and if it can be carried out to its logical conclusion, would achieve the general structure of wholesale prices we recommend.

If adequate coverage of the economy at the Census 5-digit commodity level can be obtained, these commodity indexes could be combined in a large number of different ways to produce other meaningful price measurements. Commodities could be grouped according to the industry which produces them, thus forming a price index covering the sales of that industry. Similarly, the commodity price indexes could be combined so as to yield price indexes of inputs purchased by industries for use in production. Such input and output price indexes would be highly useful in studying productivity changes and in measuring product (value-added) originating by industry. Combination of commodity groups into economic classes would also be possible. Thus price indexes of goods purchased by the government or of goods purchased by producers as capital goods could be calculated. Price indexes could further be calculated according to the durability of commodities or according to other characteristics which are desired for economic analysis. In other words, price indexes for a basic commodity classification at the Census 5-digit level could be used as building blocks to create a large number of useful and meaningful price indexes.

The ability to combine the basic commodity indexes into meaningful groups depends upon the availability of adequate weighting schemes. In order to build a price index for the output of a given industry from commodity price indexes, it is necessary to know precisely what commodities an industry produces and how much of each commodity is produced. This information is given in the industrial censuses and presents no very great problem. For the input price indexes, however, it is necessary to know what commodities are used by each industry, and the amount of each commodity used. This information is not readily available at the present time, and would require an additional collection program. What is required is a knowledge of the commodity input and the commodity output of each industry, preferably at the Census 4-digit level. This would involve the creation of a large input–output table to provide the basis for weighting, which would have to be revised periodically (say, at five-year intervals) to keep the weighting system up to date. If an input–output table were available, the commodity price indexes could be used for deflating the input–output relations to yield the volumes of inputs and outputs of each industry.

The underlying schemata can be illustrated with a simple input–output table, as shown in Table 5.1. In this table, the sectors producing commodities are shown as rows. Sectors purchasing commodities are shown as columns. Commodities produced by agriculture may be sold either to agriculture itself, to mining, manufacturing, or others such as retailers, government or exports. The price index of total agricultural goods sold would be an average of these price indexes weighted by the relative amount of goods sold to each purchaser, i.e., A → T. Similarly, the goods which agriculture buys from agriculture, mining and manufacturing constitute the commodity inputs to agriculture, and a price index of these purchases (i.e., I → A) yields the input price index of agriculture. Both the output and the input price indexes referred to above are

Price Measurement

Table 5.1 Input–Output Sectors Purchasing Commodities

Sectors producing commodities	Sectors Purchasing Commodities				
	Agriculture	Mining	Manu-facturing	Other, e.g., retailers gvt exports	Total
Agriculture	$A \to A$	$A \to E$	$A \to M$	$A \to O$	$A \to T$
Mining	$E \to A$	$E \to E$	$E \to M$	$E \to O$	$E \to T$
Manufacturing	$M \to A$	$M \to E$	$M \to M$	$M \to O$	$M \to T$
Total	$I \to A$	$I \to E$	$I \to M$	$I \to O$	$I \to T$ (WPI)

gross, in that they cover transactions between firms in the same industry. It would be quite possible to compute a net output price index and net input price index by omitting the infra-industry transactions (those enclosed in the boxes in the table). In effect, the present BLS weighting procedure for the 4-digit manufacturing industries yields a net output price index since it excludes the interplant transfers within the industry. Probably both gross output and net output price indexes are needed. For the process of deflation, a gross output price index is often more pertinent, since in collecting data on manufacturers' sales it is often not feasible to collect the additional information required to obtain net sales to purchasers outside the industry.

The general Wholesale Price Index in such a scheme would be constructed with the weights resulting from combining the columns or rows, i.e., the corner of the table, $I \to T$. A Wholesale Price Index, so defined, would meet the definition of an index of prices of commodities bought and sold other than at the retail level, and the prices of these commodities would be weighted by their relative importance in total sales. Such a definition would give the WPI a definite universe and a specific form of weighting, so that changes in scope and weighting would not be so important in the future in affecting the behavior of the index as they have been in the past. It should be recognized, of course, that the industrial organization of the economy itself will affect the number of transactions taking place in the various industrial sectors and this, in turn, will bring into the index either more or fewer price observations, with proportionally more or less weight being given to each area of the economy. Vertical integration, for example, would transform what previously were purchases and sales of commodities between previously separate companies into transfers between departments within the same company with no price indicator attached. Conversely, increased vertical specialization might result in the sale of intermediate goods which before had entered no distinguishable market. There is no way of insulating the Wholesale Price Index from such changes in industrial organization, as long as it is supposed to be a fairly complete representation of the universe of commodity transactions. Changes in growth and in the industrial structure of the economy will, therefore, be important determinants which alter the behavior of the Wholesale Price Index.

Implementation of the Proposed Revision of the WPI

The present BLS program for the expansion of the WPI and its reclassification on a 5-digit commodity basis seems definitely in the correct direction. Priorities for adding new items should probably be determined largely by the needs of other statistical agencies in the government that require wholesale price data to compute deflators and to aid in the measurement of output. This strongly suggests that BLS should continue to work closely with the National Income Division of the Department of Commerce, the Bureau of the Census and the Federal Reserve Board in making the Wholesale Price Index a better tool for their specific needs.

To implement the proposed weighting system, it will be necessary to utilize the 1958 industrial censuses to construct an input–output table. Experience gained in this effort should be directed toward obtaining better basic information at the time of the next industrial censuses. It may be necessary to approach a detailed input–output table through steps of progressively finer industrial classification.

Since the present Wholesale Price Index can be continued during the transition and in any event is not an important index, considerable flexibility is possible in the timing and sequence of the improvements. As soon as improvements are made they should be included in the index. In terms of analytic importance, it would probably be most useful if a first approximation could be made to the 5-digit commodity classification and the other consequent SIC industrial categories at an early date.

Not all parts of the full system of prices we propose will be available currently for the monthly index of wholesale prices. An abbreviated input–output system, with full industrial detail where the data permit, will suffice for the monthly reports, and a comprehensive report covering the entire system can then be published annually.

Sensitive Price Indexes

The literature abounds with statements of the need for a sensitive price index which measures the immediately current or prospective movements of wholesale prices, as a guide in policy formation and in predicting business movements. This literature, however, is much less emphatic about the nature of 'sensitivity'. Often what seems to be implied is that the index number should be based upon prices which change often or by relatively large amounts, but these mechanical criteria have no direct relevance to the measurement of short-run business conditions. Even more often, what seems to be sought is an index which will predict the future course of prices or of business.

The ambiguity of the discussions of sensitive price indexes, and the ambiguity of such indexes, is due to the failure to specify exactly what the index is to measure. If the index is to measure the current price situation, then presumably the full, regular Wholesale Price Index is what should be used. It is true that this index contains prices which do not change often (although in good part this is a defect in the price data; see Section 2), but to the extent that such prices are valid they are part of the current price situation which is to be measured. (The problem raised by mere delay in reporting prices is discussed below.) Sensitivity, in this context, means only exaggeration, and it is difficult to see any purpose in exaggerating current price movements.

If the index in question is to measure the impending movements of prices — and no one denies that such a measure would be useful — mere volatility of prices is, of course, irrelevant. For this purpose, those prices should be included in the index which reflect estimates of the state of the commodity markets (say) three or six months in the future. There are two important sets of prices which do attempt to estimate market conditions in the near future. The first set consists of futures prices on organized exchanges; they are at present excluded from the Wholesale Price Index. The second set consists of prices on goods to be produced and delivered a considerable time after the contract is made. The WPI index now contains a substantial number of such prices: many 'built to order' items have fairly distant delivery dates; and a considerable number of prices cover contracts which run for specified periods.

We believe an index of this latter type has enough interest and potential usefulness to justify at least a serious experimental program. The basic data, namely, futures prices and identification of prices covering deliveries well in the future, are not now collected, but certainly could be. The experimental work and, given its success, the continuing program, might well be undertaken by the Federal Reserve System in cooperation with the BLS.

As far as the currency of price information is concerned, the present delay is not great: prices as of the middle of one month are published by the second week of the following month. The weekly index of the WPI provides a more current estimate of the entire index. The present weekly index does not perform especially well as a predictor of the monthly index, but this deficiency can probably be remedied by drawing a more appropriate sample.

2. THE QUALITY OF THE PRICE DATA

Some of the wholesale price quotations are collected from government bodies and exchanges, but the largest part is collected from individual manufacturers or their trade associations, primarily by mail. The question that must be posed is: How good are these price quotations — how accurately do they measure the terms on which transactions actually take place? The answer is not readily given, for obviously, if a comprehensive body of transaction prices were at hand, the BLS would use it. But several types of evidence very strongly suggest that the price quotations obtained from manufacturers do not faithfully measure the movements of prices, quite aside from the usual problems of quality change.

Table 5.2 Comparison of Monthly and Weekly WPI Prices

	Monthly Index		Errors in Weekly Index*			
	Jan.	Dec.		Less than		Mean
Category	1954	1955	Positive	±0.1	Negative	absolute
All commodities	110.8	111.3	3	7	14	0.1
All except farm and food	114.5	119.7	4	4	16	0.1
Farm products	97.9	83.4	13	1	10	0.2
Processed foods	106.2	98.2	7	5	12	0.2

*The median errors are considerably larger than the average monthly change in the monthly index, and in the *three*-year period, 1953–55 inclusive, the weekly index reported no change for three decades and three rises in the monthly index and reported one rise as a change. Large movements of the monthly index are consistently predicted correctly.

Weighty evidence of a spurious short-run rigidity in the behavior of BLS prices is afforded by Flueck (1961). When frequency of price change is tabulated against number of reporters from whom the prices are collected, it is found that the frequency of price change for intermediate and finished manufactures is twice as great if there are three or more price reporters than if only one price report is collected. Yet more than 400 price indexes in the WPI are based upon single reports.

It is impossible to believe, therefore, that the extreme short-run rigidity of many WPI prices represents the true behavior of even the quoted prices in the market. This rigidity introduces a systematic lag in the index relative to changes in average price quotations.

When average receipts of producers are compared with price quotations, there are important and unexpected differences in trend. Thus the WPI index of steel prices rose 101.5 percent from 1947 to 1957, whereas the index of receipts per ton (calculated from numerous subclasses of steel products, with constant weights) rose only 89.3 percent. One must make allowance for minor differences in coverage but the main source of difference (changes of the product mix within the subclasses of steel) should probably have led to a greater rise of unit values because better qualities of steel were being used. A variety of such examples are reported in McAllister (1961); no one is very convincing but the ensemble sheds doubt on the validity of the price quotations, particularly with respect to their lack of responsiveness to cyclical fluctuations.

There exists one large body of publicly available price data which has not been used on any scale to test the BLS quotations: the bids on government purchase orders. A sample of such prices during the past decade has been compared with BLS quotations, and the comparisons are fairly consistent in showing that the BLS prices are both higher and more rigid than the average of bid prices (Flueck, 1961). The example in Table 5.3 will illustrate this evidence (dollars per gallon).

Table 5.3 Gasoline Bid Prices and WPI Price

Date of Bid Opening	Bid Prices on Gasoline			WPI Price
	Low	Mean	High	
November 6, 1954	$0.0933	$0.0996	$0.1033	$0.105
May 4, 1955	0.0948	0.0991	0.1075	0.105
August 3, 1955	0.0992	0.1038	0.11	0.105
October 25, 1995	0.0844	0.0855	0.0875	0.105
April 25, 1956	0.099	0.105	0.11	0.105
October 9, 1956	0.09585	0.0997	0.10495	0.105

86+ octane gasoline, Gulf coast, f.o.b. refinery, for bids; WPI, 87 Gulf coast, f.o.b. refinery, minimum of 20,000 barrels.

In summary, the evidence that the BLS company price quotations are not valid transaction prices is highly persuasive. The quotations now collected are at best the initial base for negotiation in many cases, and often represent only the hopes of sellers or the snares of inexperienced buyers.

We recommend that a major shift be made to the collection of buyers' prices. Large and continuous buyers of manufactures should be able to supply prices which truly represent the effective terms on which transactions are made. We do not believe that this shift to buyers' prices will be simple or free of new difficulties, but it is the most promising source of comprehensive, continuous, and reliable price quotations.

Where buyers' prices are not available, we recommend extensive use of unit values, at least as benchmarks to which the monthly prices are adjusted. Unit values are inferior to specification *transaction* prices, but when unit values are calculated for fairly homogeneous commodities, they are more realistic than quoted prices in a large number of industrial markets.

REFERENCES

Flueck, John (1961), 'A study in validity: BLS wholesale price quotations', Joint Economic Committee, 87th Congress, 1st Session, Staff Paper No. 9.

McAllister, Harry E. (1961), 'Statistical factors affecting the stability of the wholesale and consumers' price indexes', Joint Economic Committee, 87th Congress, 1st Session, Staff Paper No. 8.

6. Measuring the Cost of Quality

Richard Ruggles
Yale University

The bogy of inflation is with us again. This cry, which was chronic during the 1950s, has been a major factor in determining our monetary and fiscal policies. Since these policies are based on the movements in the price indexes, it is time to consider whether our confidence in these indexes is justified.

Since 1948, the Consumer Price Index has increased by approximately 25 percent. A large part of this increase — about one-third of it — occurred in the brief space of one year, at the beginning of the Korean War. The other two-thirds was spread more or less evenly over the other 12 years — an average increase of about 1.5 percent a year.

In view of these statistics, policy-makers might have concluded that we had relative price stability in the 1950s, except at the beginning of the Korean War when scare buying forced prices up. Instead, we hear much about a continual and insidious price creep. When price indexes continued to rise during periods of recession, such as in 1958, many policy-makers concluded that rising prices stemmed from increasing costs due to excessive wage demands and administered prices of monopolies.

To understand what has *really* been happening to prices, we must first examine the factors responsible for the rises in the index. For this purpose, let us take a look at the 12 percent increase in the Consumer Price Index that has occurred since the Korean War. There are major segments of consumer purchases for which prices have not risen at all since that time. The price index for consumer durables, for example, shows a decline of approximately 3 percent. On the other hand, the index for medical care rose by more than 30 percent. On the average, the prices of services rose a substantial 23 percent while those of commodities rose only 6 percent.

This difference in behavior largely reflects the fact that the price of a service is generally the rate of compensation of those performing it. And these wages naturally rise as per capita income rises. In the last 50 years, the prices

This chapter first appeared in *Challenge*, **10** (2), 1961.

of services relative to those of commodities have risen continually as a consequence of such general rises in living standards. On the other hand, commodity prices can sometimes reflect increased productivity. If the increase in output per man-hour is greater than in the wage rate, the cost of production may actually fall, thus permitting lower commodity prices despite higher wages.

The identification of price indexes with rates of pay in the service industries involves the implicit assumption that the productivity of the service industries has remained unchanged. In some instances, this assumption may be correct, but in others quite wide of the mark.

In the case of medical care, for example, the apparent 30 percent price increase of the last eight years must be qualified by considering the increase in medical knowledge, better drugs and the new preventive medicines. Certainly the Salk vaccine was a tremendous medical advance which, in addition to sparing many lives, will save consumer dollars that would have gone for the treatment of polio.

The measurement of price changes comes down to a question of whether one gets more or less for one's money. In the field of medical care it can be argued that most people would rather pay today's prices for today's medical care than yesterday's prices for yesterday's medical care. The fact that diseases were treated more cheaply in yesterday's world is more than offset by the increased knowledge and new drugs available for curing disease today. Although it is difficult to measure improvement in the *quality* of medicine in quantitative terms, there is no justification for ignoring it — which is what our present method of computing price indexes does.

The problem of measuring changes in quality also arises in the commodity components of the Consumer Price Index. In the Congressional hearings on government price statistics conducted earlier this year, Zvi Griliches of the University of Chicago reported on the effect that changes in specifications had upon automobile prices. Dr Griliches computed the value of specifications such as size, automatic transmission, horsepower, etc., by taking the price differences for a given year among cars with these varying specifications. Automobile prices were then adjusted to take into account the different features included as standard equipment in each year.

On this basis, using the value of specifications given by the 1954 price schedule, the prices of the 'low priced three' dropped 27 percent from 1954 to 1960, although their unadjusted list price rose 34 percent, and the Consumer Price Index for these automobiles reported a rise of 11 percent. The significance of this study is not that the Consumer Price Index for automobiles needs some minor adjustment to reflect the true price situation, but rather that the overemphasis on price change is itself in question. Instead of an 11 percent price increase over this period, there may have been a price reduction of as much as 27 percent.

This same kind of analysis could, of course, be applied to other major kinds of consumer durables, such as home laundry equipment, refrigerators and freezers, portable radios, cameras and hi-fi equipment. Almost all of these have shown considerable change in recent years. If the change in *quality* were taken into account, the price index for consumer durables would have fallen far more than the 3 percent now reported.

Besides the quality change in existing goods, we should also take into account the effect of the introduction of totally new commodities upon the consumer's purchasing power. The index of consumer prices is purposely designed so that the introduction of new goods or the dropping of old ones will have no effect. Thus the introduction of such things as television, synthetic fibers and plastic products has had no effect upon the index.

But the introduction of new products obviously *does* have an influence upon the consumers' standard of living, just as do quality improvements in existing products. It is quite possible to imagine an economic system which obtains its higher standard of living through the introduction of new products which are superior to the old ones they replace. In such a system, the consumer might continuously get more value for his dollar, even though the prices of the old products rose steadily due to rising wage and material costs.

Yet, conventional price indexes would show this situation as one in which prices are rising and consumers are getting less for their dollars. Although, of course, in our economy not all of the improvement in the standard of living comes about through the substitution of new products for old, it does seem clear that much of it has been achieved in this way, despite the systematic exclusion of this factor from price indexes.

Innovations and new products are not restricted to the durable goods field. They have, for instance, been highly significant in the food industry over the last decade. Meals are much easier to get and the choice available to the housewife is much greater. There will be those who claim that the additional packaging and processing now common is an undesirable element of cost, and that the personal contact between the individual proprietor and the customer has been lost. Conversely, it can be argued that increased attention to packaging not only standardizes the merchandise, but it raises the level of sanitation and grading. In addition, the freedom to examine goods allows the customer to make comparisons before buying in a way that would not have been possible before.

It is, of course, not possible to measure accurately the dimensions of quality and product change. Nevertheless, one can safely suggest that, given the size of the average yearly increase in the Consumer Price Index since Korea, quality and product improvements may well have been much greater, so that we may actually have had declining rather than increasing prices.

This does not mean that price indexes are completely invalid. Price indexes are useful in that they can show the relative differences in price behavior over time or between countries. For example, the 8 percent increase in the price index at the beginning of the Korean War indicates that prices were rising more rapidly in this period than at any other time in the decade of the 1950s.

In periods of hyperinflation, such as have been experienced by some Latin American countries in recent years, where the price index may rise by as much as 80 percent in a single year, the indexes give a good indication of what is happening since such large increases cannot be offset by quality change. It is only in periods when price changes are relatively small that it becomes a serious error to use the indexes as an exact measure of what is taking place in the economy. In such periods, the systematic biases of the price index may well be greater than the reported price change.

The defects of the Consumer Price Index are also inherent in the other price indexes which are used to deflate the gross national product to measure the change in real output. Two major categories of goods are produced by the economy besides consumer goods. These are goods and services purchased by the government, ranging from school teaching to missiles, and plant and equip-ment purchased by producers for use in later production. To measure the quantity of output in these categories, we need price indexes to calculate it in noninflationary terms. In measuring the output of government, it is assumed — as it is throughout the service sector — that the productivity of civil servants never changes. The price indexes for this area are merely based on the changes in pay of government employees. While one may be tempted to agree with this evaluation of civil servants, the fact is that the introduction of computers, office machines and other automatic equipment has greatly increased the effectiveness of the individual worker. For example, the 1960 census data were processed by microfilming the original schedules and automatically producing magnetic tape for electronic computers. Automatic equipment performed jobs which took thousands of clerks in previous censuses. Not only was the payroll re-duced, but more information was made available in a much shorter space of time and output per census employee rose very considerably.

Similar examples of the increased output of government employees can be cited at the local level. Policemen, for example, have been provided with radio-equipped patrol cars, and more recently, transistorized walkie-talkies. Street cleaners have been given mechanical equipment. In some areas — edu-cation, for instance — progress is more difficult to measure. Yet most of us would be unwilling to have our children given the same education as we re-ceived, especially in the area of science and mathematics.

In producers' durable equipment, once again, the price indexes leave out quality change and new products, but there are probably very few industries in which producers in 1960 would have been willing to buy 1950 models of machines, even if they could get them at 1950 prices. According to the WPI,

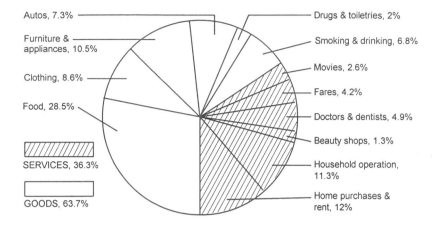

Source: Relative weights of goods and services used by Bureau of Labor Statistics to prepare the Consumer Price Index.

Figure 6.1 Make-up of the Consumer's Market Basket

the 1960 price of producers' durable equipment was 23 percent above the 1950 price; if producers' durable equipment showed as much quality change as was shown in the study referred to above for automobiles, it seems probable that, in fact, prices actually fell.

For construction, both industrial and residential, the index is computed on the basis of wage rates and material costs. Thus again it is assumed that productivity does not change. While the construction industry is notorious for its lack of progressiveness, if we consider the new methods of off-the-site fabrication of components it is obvious that this assumption is not entirely valid.

Once again, it seems that price indexes have greatly exaggerated the actual price rise. Thus we see that for almost every category of goods, whether purchased by consumers for household consumption, by government for public services or by producers for plant and equipment, the conventional price indexes do not reflect the effects of the introduction of new products and the improvement of existing products or the increased productivity of those providing services. These omissions mean that all the price indexes are higher than they should be. And since the indexes are used to deflate the value of current output and calculate its worth in noninflationary terms, our rate of growth is thus considerably understated.

The fact that our growth rate has probably been higher than we thought does not mean, however, that we should be any happier *vis-à-vis* the Russians. These elements would also have at least as much effect upon the Russian figures. As we well know, the Soviet rate of technological progress in some areas has exceeded ours, but even in the areas where they are still well behind us, the *rate* at which they introduce new technology might be faster than ours.

A half-century ago, many more industries were producing the kind of output that could be measured quite satisfactorily in quantity terms. Today, new major industries such as electronics, chemicals, machinery and household appliances account for an increasingly important share of our output. In all these industries, the changes in prices and output are very difficult to measure, since the nature of the products is continually changing. It may mean, therefore, that the national concern over a sagging economic growth rate is really not warranted. The problem may be our inability to measure growth represented by product changes and increased productivity in the service industries. The inadequacy of the price indexes will become even more glaring in the years ahead.

It is interesting to speculate on what will happen to our measurement of output when further growth does not take the form of additional consumption of identical items, but rather goods of improved quality, the substitution of new products for old, and the consumption of higher quality services. In such a world our conventional price indexes would fail to catch the quality improvement, they would not recognize that the substitution of new products for old was any increase in the standard of living, and they would report the continued increase in the use of services solely in terms of the rates of remuneration. Thus they might show an economy with constant output and rising prices, even though the standard of living was increasing rapidly. What is perhaps more serious, the conventional price and output indexes would fail completely to distinguish between a dynamic economy and one that was truly stagnant.

The single-minded pursuit of price stability, coupled with the false soundings given by our present price indicators, is likely to lead our economic policy-makers astray. The tragedy of the postwar period is not so much the slow rate of growth (which we cannot measure anyway), but rather the underutilization of our resources and the low level of investment to which the continuous existence of excess capacity leads.

At the quiver of a decimal point in the Consumer Price Index, the government has instituted restrictive monetary and fiscal policies. Its objective has been to restrain demand so that producers would find themselves with excess capacity and thus not raise prices, and the labor unions would be deterred by the existence of unemployment from seeking wage increases. The economy has been in either a depressed state, or under restraining monetary and fiscal policies throughout almost all the period since Korea. It is small wonder that in such an environment the rate of investment is low. In an economy where a false fear of inflation continually holds demand in check, even a low level of investment creates capacity which cannot be fully utilized.

With this in mind, it is appropriate to inquire what a faster rate of growth and better utilization of our capacity would do to our price indexes.

Historically, if we look at any period of upward change in the general level of activity, we find that the price indexes rise. Thus, for example, in the recovery from the Depression of the 1930s, prices in certain sectors responded sharply to the increase in demand. Farm prices rose by about 85 percent in the five years from 1932 to 1937. Even in the metals industry, prices went up about 30 percent. At the same time, unemployment dropped from 25 percent to about 14 percent. It cannot very well be argued that these price rises were the result of excess demand pressing on fully employed resources.

In other words, growth and the increase in real income tend to produce price increases in certain sectors irrespective of the pressure on resources. If the price index is to remain stable, the increases in such sectors would have to be balanced by lower prices in other sectors, where productivity increases would permit prices to fall. Given the imperfections of our price indexes, however, economic growth will almost inevitably result in an upward movement of the price index irrespective of the pressure of demand.

Despite the relatively high unemployment rate of close to 7 percent, there is a tendency to minimize the underutilization of our resources which has resulted from too much concern with small movements in the price index. It is argued that at least 4 percent of this unemployment is frictional, and thus we are operating at 97 percent of full employment — a high level in anybody's vocabulary. Such a computation, however, is very misleading. The unemployment rate is not very closely related to the economy's excess capacity. The spread of automation and the increase in the number of white-collar employees means that many industries can expand their output considerably without hiring more workers. Thus a steel company operating at 50 percent capacity might be able to double its output by adding 10 or 20 percent more employees. This is even more true for such sectors of the economy as electric power, communications, finance, insurance and retail trade — all sectors whose activity (and thus output) increases with an increase in the general level of activity of the economy without requiring any substantial manpower increase.

This relationship between the increase in man-hours employed and the increase in output shows up clearly in the overall statistics. In the recoveries from all of our past recessions, output has risen much faster than man-hours employed. On average, output tends to rise during economic recoveries about three times as fast as the man-hours required to produce it. In the first six months of the present recovery, if we are to believe the figures, an increase in output of approximately 5 percent has been accompanied by an increase in man-hours of less than 1 percent.

Much of the increase in manpower that is needed, furthermore, does not come from the reservoir of the unemployed. Unutilized manpower within firms is drawn upon and cuts in the work week which may have been put into effect during the recession are restored. With increasing employment opportunities, the labor force itself tends to expand, thus providing additional resources. Even allowing for frictional unemployment, it seems reasonable that there could be an increase of 10 or 12 percent in man-hours.

The Council of Economic Advisers has estimated that in early 1961 the economy was operating at a level some 10 percent below full capacity. This figure seems far too conservative when one takes into account the additional man-hours available and their relation to potential output. If past performance is a guide, it would not seem unreasonable to suppose that the 10 or 12 percent additional man-hours which were available in the spring of 1961 could have been utilized to produce 25 percent more output. This seems all the more likely since, by late summer of 1961, output had risen by about 5 percent and unemployment had not fallen at all.

It is true, of course, that an increase in real output of 25 percent, even though it created no pressure on resources, would cause our price indexes to rise. Under present anti-inflation policy, we would then move quickly to prevent such real output increases from occurring. In fact, that is exactly what we are doing even though the increase in real output has been less than this. As already suggested, the price indexes have quivered, and there is talk of putting the brakes on. Those wishing to restrict demand have labeled the unemployment 'structural', and thereby have succeeded in removing it from their own consciences. This rationalization may satisfy them, but it is not much help for the unemployed — since it is obvious that the only cure for unemployment, whether structural or any other kind, is more jobs, and you don't get more jobs by restricting demand, no matter how much retraining you do.

The loss in potential output does not seem to be very impressive when expressed as a percentage of total output, but, in fact, we waste through under-utilization an amount equal in size to two or three times what we now spend on defense, or 20–25 times as much as we are now giving in foreign aid. These wasted resources could rebuild our cities and automate our factories within a few short years; they could raise our rate of growth to equal or surpass that of any other nation.

This, then, is the cost of taking our price indexes too seriously. They inhibit real growth, because growth by its very nature must lead to increases in the price indexes. And because this inhibited growth in output does not keep up with the growth in our capacity to produce, we have ever-present excess capacity. The excess in machines is self-limiting; producers soon learn when investment is unprofitable. But the excess in manpower is harder to dispose of — the unemployed are there, and you can't really make the problem go away by saying that they don't exist.

7. Domestic Price Statistics: Their Reliability as History and Their Usefulness for Economic Policy

Richard Ruggles
Yale University

1. INTRODUCTION

Price indexes are one of the major tools of the economist and a basic economic indicator for the policy-maker, not only as indexes to show the extent to which the dollar has been devalued and the cost of living increased, but also because they underlie two other basic economic indicators: the measurement of output and the measurement of productivity change. The question I wish to examine today is whether price indexes perform their function adequately by giving a reliable picture of what has occurred in the past and how the interpretation of past price behavior should affect future economic policy decisions.

As long-run historical indicators, price indexes continue to be woefully inadequate. Price change can be measured unambiguously only by observing the *same* commodity at two points of time. Strictly speaking, if a commodity changes in any of its specifications, no price change can be calculated. Similarly, if a new product comes on the market, its price cannot be taken into account since it had no counterpart in the previous period. In an economy where changes in products and the development of new products were relatively minor, these factors might not seriously interfere with the calculation of indexes of price change. But to say that we are, in the American economy today, producing substantially the same items we produced in, say, 1929, is some distance from the truth. In almost every line of production — for example, food processing, textiles, chemicals, electronics, appliances, building construction, space exploration and military equipment — spectacular

---

This chapter was a Statement before the Subcommittee on Economic Statistics of the Joint Economic Committee, May 26, 1966.

improvements in products and totally new products are continually being introduced.

If we use for our historical price indicators only the measured change in prices of those commodities which existed in the previous period and whose specifications have not changed, when in fact large parts of our resources are being channeled into the creation of new technologies and new products, and into changing the nature of old products, the result may be highly misleading. The price changes we can measure are not a random sample of what is happening to prices throughout the economy; they are a sample of that stagnant portion of the economy where the lack of technological improvement is most apparent. This sample is then used as a yardstick for the economy as a whole. Because the price indexes are incapable of taking into account the most important elements of technological change, they necessarily overstate the price rise and seriously understate the real output change which has taken place.

In the shorter run, however, data on relative price movements of different parts of the economy and year-to-year differences in price behavior do provide a wealth of information about the economic system, if correctly analyzed. But even for short-run analysis one cannot rely on any total price index as a basis for economic policy decisions. All prices do not behave alike and there are systematic differences in behavior among various groups of prices. An aggregate price index, since it is only one figure, cannot throw any light on these differences in behavior, yet they are directly relevant to an understanding of the past and to the development of policy for the future. For the development of such policy we need to have some appreciation of the forces which impinge upon different groups of prices, and an understanding of how the price system can be expected to behave with the growth of the economic system.

2. FACTORS INFLUENCING PRICE INDEXES

To understand the major factors influencing the movement of price indexes, it is useful to consider three sectors of the economy which, although highly interrelated, have rather different characteristics with respect to price behavior. These sectors are: service, agriculture and manufacturing. Almost all economic activity can be classified broadly under one of these three headings, so that their combined behavior will determine the behavior of the aggregate price index.

One of the most striking characteristics of our price system over the past 150 years has been rising wages and salaries, so that people, through a rise in their money income, participate directly in the increased productivity of the system as a whole. In the United States, where people are free to enter any occupation they wish, the wage or salary rate is one of the major devices used to attract people into specific jobs. New industries which are making high profits pay high wages and salaries in order to attract workers. Older industries wishing to retain their labor must compete in the labor market, and raise their wages accordingly. In declining industries wages rarely fall; rather it is the jobs themselves which disappear. The people who do remain employed are generally paid the going rate. Except under widespread conditions of extreme duress, it is psychologically and institutionally difficult to lower a person's wage or salary. Thus, due to the constant appearance of new industries, increased productivity and increased profits for the economy as a whole, wage and salary rates show a secular rise.

This increase in wages and salaries is not only an increase in income; it is also an increase in the cost of labor. In those sectors of the economy where labor is the primary input — i.e., the service industries — prices will rise directly with the increase in wages and salaries. This, as we all know, has been reflected in the cost of such things as education, medical care, government services, urban transportation, domestic servants, etc. In computing the price index for most of these sectors, it is assumed that productivity does not change, since there is no way to measure it. Thus any increase in wages and salaries paid must result in an increase in the price index for these services. During the last ten years, the price index for consumer services has, in fact, risen by more than 20 percent due to the continued rise of wages and salaries. To obtain stability of prices in this sector, therefore, it would be necessary also to require constancy of wages and salaries.

A second important characteristic of our price system is the role of agriculture and farm prices. The amazing growth of productivity of the farm sector has enabled the United States to reduce the number of people employed in agriculture today to half of what it was 50 years ago, and at the same time to double agricultural output. This is an achievement which is without parallel in the annals of economic development. But it is essentially a long-run process, involving such factors as the mobility of the population, the use of fertilizers, the creation of hybrids and the development of farm machinery. In the short run, agricultural output is affected mainly by the weather and agricultural prices are affected by the relation between the level of demand and the available supply. If demand in the economy, as a whole, expands faster than agricultural output, agricultural prices will rise. For example, with the expansion of demand caused by the Korean War, agricultural prices rose by more than 20 percent in less than two years. If the increase in agricultural output matches the increase in demand, prices will remain stable. If total demand in the economy moves forward more slowly than the increase in agricultural output, agricultural prices will decline; it was this situation which led to the development of the system of price supports in order to prevent undue hardship to the farmer. Agricultural prices were virtually stable or declining during the period from the end of the Korean War until last year. Within the last year, however, there has been a sharp rise in agricultural prices, and this, coupled with the price increases in services, has convinced many economists that a demand inflation is imminent.

The final sector which must be considered is manufacturing. It is probably true that when most people think of prices they generally have in mind the price behavior of commodities which are produced by the manufacturing sector. The manufacturing sector is, of course, subject to many of the forces I have already mentioned. It must pay the going wages and salaries in order to hire labor, and many producers purchase agricultural products to use as raw materials. It does not follow, however, that the prices of manufactured goods are merely a reflection of wages and agricultural prices. Within manufacturing, the use of new technology and the substitution of machines for labor have resulted in continual cost reductions, so that in spite of increases in wage rates and raw material prices, productivity gains have in many periods been more than sufficient to lead to a reduction in costs per unit of output. Unlike the service industries, some of the increase in productivity in manufacturing industries can be measured, insofar as it relates to improved production methods for the same products. As a result, the price index for consumer durables has fallen, despite the fact that it does not take into account the improved quality of the goods which are produced or the introduction of new products. In real terms, which would include the quality improvement, prices have probably fallen rather substantially in this sector of the economy.

It should be noted, however, that productivity increases most rapidly in the manufacturing sector when the economy is growing most rapidly. In part, this is due to the fact that firms are able to spread their fixed costs over a larger number of units and utilize their capacity more efficiently. But this is not the only factor. Generally speaking, periods of high output are also periods of high profits, so producers find it possible and profitable to make new investments which provide them with more efficient plant and equipment, leading to still further increases in productivity. There is little statistical evidence that the manufacturing sector as a whole runs into higher costs as it expands output. What evidence does exist suggests quite the opposite: that the gains in productivity come to an end only when output begins to slacken, demand grows flaccid and investment drops. It is an interesting question as to whether a period of continued labor shortage would result in an eventual decline in productivity, or whether instead it would encourage producers to use labor more efficiently and introduce labor-saving devices and automation at a faster rate. This topic might well bear investigation.

3. THE BEHAVIOR OF PRICE INDEXES

Given this thumbnail sketch of the role of wages and salaries, agricultural prices and prices of manufactured goods in price indexes, it is possible to develop conclusions concerning price behavior in both the long run and short run. These conclusions serve as useful guidelines to see whether the economy is performing as might be expected given its underlying characteristics.

In the long run, price indexes for the American economy can be expected to rise. The increases in wages and salaries which take place over time will be directly reflected in the price indexes of services. In agriculture, we cannot expect to see any offsetting price decline; for reasons of equity, the government considers that it is unfair to let agricultural prices drop significantly and for the farmer to be forced to accept a lower standard of living as the result of the increased productivity of agriculture. In manufacturing, price indexes will continue to be measured by those commodities which remain substantially the same from period to period. These commodities will generally be ones which are made with the same materials and employ approximately the same techniques of production and will include, of course, the most stagnant items produced. Items where technological change is the greatest will be omitted. Only the technological change which is involved in producing the same good more efficiently will be taken into account. In the past, even this type of technological change has been sufficient to keep price indexes for manufactured goods from rising significantly but this may or may not be true in the future. To the extent that new products become more important, however, the price index for this sector becomes more and more meaningless.

Even with the increase in conventional price indexes for different sectors of the economy, continued economic growth has other price implications. The value of land in cities and in desirable spots in the country, at the seashore and in the mountains will rise as the population grows and people have more income. The prices of rare books, art objects, stamp collections and anything else which is in scarce supply will also be bid up. To stabilize prices of such goods would require not only that money income be held constant, but also that real income not be allowed to rise. Anyone looking to the future, therefore, must, if we accept our present economic system, realize that prices as measured by price indexes will show a continuous rise.

4. THE PROBLEMS OF MAINTAINING EQUITY

It is well recognized that a continuous price rise causes substantial inequities to individuals living on fixed incomes or on accumulated savings. This is, of course, the major reason why price stability is considered to be an important objective of economic policy. Individuals who have invested their savings in insurance, government bonds, or savings banks have found on retirement that the value of these assets has eroded to the point where they are no longer the bulwark for their old age that they expected. Similarly, pension plans which when initiated seemed generous may 20 or 30 years later under changed economic conditions seem pitifully small.

The Consumer Price Index, furthermore, does not really measure the change in the cost of living for such groups. Retired people living on fixed incomes are less likely to purchase items such as consumer durables which may fall in price, but instead their expenditures are more likely to be for such things as rent, property taxes, urban transportation, medical care and other personal services, all of which have risen faster than the average of consumer prices. The fact that the quality of goods and services has improved does not necessarily make the increase in the cost of living for a retired individual any less real. If a bus ride increases from 15 to 25 cents, the cost of living for the person using the bus will increase from 15 to 25 cents for transportation, even though the new buses may be air conditioned, quieter, more comfortable and more frequent. In general, I would expect that the cost of living for the retired population has risen very much faster than the Consumer Price Index. Indeed, it seems unfortunate that at the same time the rest of the economy is enjoying prosperity, growth and increases in income, this group may face an outlook of continuous retrenchment brought about by relatively fixed income and an ever-rising cost of living.

5. THE PROBLEM OF STOPPING THE PRICE RISE

For many, the solution to this problem seems simple. If prices rise, this is taken to be an indication that there is too much money chasing too few goods, and that if the government will stop spending, or tax increases will be put into effect, or banks will restrict credit for investment, the balloon can be punctured and the economy deflated to its proper level. Basically this doctrine comes down to the statement that there is too much spending taking place, and if consumers, government and investors can be persuaded to reduce their spending, prices will not rise. In order to evaluate the validity of this proposition, we must examine exactly how such a price reduction might be expected to be brought about, in the light of the discussion earlier of wages, agriculture and manufacturing.

In recent years, it has been popular to assume that the rate of wage increase which will take place is directly dependent upon the level of unemployment. Under this doctrine, when an economy approaches too near the full employment level, the wage rate will start to rise precipitously. There is assumed to be some equilibrium level of unemployment which will lead to a wage increase just equal to the productivity gains being realized in the economy, thus ensuring price stability. A related but somewhat different approach to wage determination alternatively suggests that it is the climate of expansion, large profits and increasing output which emboldens labor to ask for larger and larger increases, and that it is necessary to change the economic climate, increasing the amount of unemployment and reducing profits, in order to make labor more hesitant about asking for wage increases and management firmer in resisting them. This theory of wage determination does not depend upon the level of unemployment but rather upon the direction of change. Under such a theory, only deteriorating conditions can hold wages in check, and any recovery may generate excessive increases in wages. A considerable amount of research has been done on the question of wage determination, both in the United States and for European countries, but the results have not led to any clear conclusion. Since World War II, some of the periods with greatest wage increases have been those periods when unemployment levels were highest. On the other hand, the dramatic reduction in the level of unemployment in recent years has been accompanied by smaller than average wage increases. Furthermore, the periods marked by recessions have, in most cases, had little effect upon the rate of wage increase. On the basis of present evidence, one could not expect that reasonable reductions in investment, curtailment of expenditure on the part of the government, or increase in taxes would have any significant effect on the next round of wage increases.

In agriculture, the situation is different but it is equally unclear that a reduction in total demand is called for. During the last year the rise of about 13 percent in the prices of farm products has had a sharp impact on both the Wholesale Price Index and the Consumer Price Index. Looking within agriculture, one finds that meat animals rose over one-third in price, due mainly to increased money income in the economy and stepped-up military purchases. In recent weeks, however, the Council of Economic Advisers has pointed out that agricultural production increases are already under-way or in prospect for both livestock and crops, and these increases point to some decline in farm prices as larger supplies move to market. According to this analysis, the index of prices received by farmers has apparently passed its peak. If this is the case, it would be foolish to reduce the level of spending in the economy in order to curtail the demand for agricultural products, only to have the increasing supply pile up again in the form of government surpluses. To the extent that military purchases of agricultural goods are a major factor and may become more important in the future, some form of price control in this sector might be preferable to trying to reduce domestic demand for food by cutting back the level of all other economic activity and employment.

In manufacturing, a dampening of demand will not, in all probability, result in the reduction of prices. Recent softening in demand in the automobile industry, for example, has merely resulted in cutbacks in output and employment. In fact, if manufacturing output begins to level off, the rate of productivity change will also level off, as it has always done during other periods of output stability. Under such circumstances, as has been pointed out above, wages can be expected to continue to increase, and the increase in wages will be translated into higher unit costs. It is quite possible that the result would be increases in manufacturing prices due to rising costs, just as in the period from 1956 to 1958. The expansion of output over the last five years, with its consequent reduction in unemployment and high level of investment, has suggested to some observers that we must be pressing on capacity in the manufacturing sector. If capacity were, in fact, a fixed and invariant limit, this would, of course, be the case. But the high level of investment itself breeds new capacity at a high rate. If output falters now, capacity will race ahead of utilization. Once it is obvious that output is not going to continue to expand, producers will cut back investment, and we will once more be faced with the familiar leveling off and decline in investment which was so characteristic of the 1950s, and which thus far we have managed to avoid in the 1960s.

Taking all three price sectors into consideration, therefore, there is no reason to believe that a deliberately planned recession will now slow down the secular rise of the price indexes, any more than did the recessions of the 1950s.

6. FIXED INCOMES VS UNEMPLOYMENT: EQUITY CONSIDERATIONS

As has already been indicated, a rise in the cost of living involves a loss in welfare by individuals who have fixed incomes, savings and pensions. In a similar way, even a mild recession will result in a loss in welfare for those individuals who are laid off and become unemployed. In order to appraise the importance of these effects, it will be useful to examine the number of people who may be directly affected by increases in the cost of living and/or a recession.

Currently there are approximately 18 million people in the United States who are of age 65 or over; approximately 14 million of these are no longer in the labor force and are living on their past savings, pensions and social security. Studies of the income distribution of this group have shown, furthermore, that over two-thirds of them have a total income of less than $3,000 per year, and one-third of them less than $2,000.

In terms of those who suffer from unemployment, we are accustomed to thinking that only the particular people who are unemployed at one moment of time are affected by the problem of unemployment. The fact that we have managed to reduce the level of unemployment from almost 7 percent of the labor force to less than 4 percent has made many people feel that the problem is no longer one of major consequence, and that the remaining unemployed are either a hard core of unemployable or else people who are merely changing jobs and happen to be unemployed for a few weeks. The manpower data, however, present a substantially different picture.

During 1964, for example, when unemployment averaged 3.8 million, over 14 million people were in fact unemployed and looking for work at some period during the year. For most of these people, the period of unemployment meant a substantial reduction in their annual income. For each family involved, the reduction in money income is considerably greater than the loss which would be caused by the erosion of price increases. Even if a man is out of work for only five or six weeks, this would mean a loss of 10 percent or more of his annual income. Unemployment often hits the same people several times within a year, and they are often people who are in the lowest income groups. On average, in fact, the income of the people who are unemployed is more than one-third lower than it would have been if they had been fully employed. Unemployment compensation makes up for only 20 percent of the average loss in income incurred through unemployment. From an equity point of view, of course, such unemployment compensation is very important, since the family responsibilities of the unemployed and their lack of other sources of income may make their position very difficult indeed in the short run.

Although, as I pointed out earlier, I do not personally believe that there is a trade-off between the rise in the price index and the level of unemployment, those who do hold such a belief would do well to consider the equity problems involved in this trade-off. If it is necessary to increase the level of unemployment by any significant degree to achieve stability in the price index, the number of people who are adversely affected may be larger, and the damage done to their way of life may be much greater than would result from permitting the price increase to take place. The equity problem becomes even more difficult when there is no real assurance that dampening economic activity will prevent the secular price increase. Under such circumstances it seems very unwise to make what is in real terms a substantial sacrifice and obtain nothing for it.

So far, I have discussed the question of equity almost entirely in terms of the two specific groups who are most hurt by a price rise or unemployment. In actual practice, however, there are many other costs and benefits to be considered. A reduction in spending and cutback in output means that the economy produces less, profits are less, investment for the future is less, and the real income of those who are employed is less. It is important that we view things in their proper perspective, and take those actions which will make the best real use of our resources.

7. OTHER POSSIBLE SOLUTIONS

If we reject slowing the economy down as an effective method of bringing prices into line, what other solutions are possible? One question which we should consider more carefully than in the past is whether we might not compensate for the inequities caused by rising prices, much in the same way we have compensated for some of the inequities caused by unemployment.

First, special attention should be given to measuring more carefully the actual changes in the cost of living of fixed income groups over time. As already indicated, our present Consumer Price Index is not constructed for this purpose, and is not adequate for it. Such a cost-of-living index would take into account the types of goods and services actually consumed by retired people, and instead of using specification prices, would take into account the actual outlays required to maintain a given standard of living.

Once such a cost-of-living index was constructed, the problem of compensating for the rise in living costs could be attacked directly. Social security payments might be tied to such an index, to ensure that they do not lag behind the increase in the cost of living and thus erode away. Provision could also be made for a safe form of asset which could be held by lower income groups whose members may not have the experience and knowledge to invest wisely in the stock market, real estate, or other business ventures. At the present time, many people lean heavily on savings accounts and government bonds to provide them with a stock of assets for their old age. But in the past, increases in the cost of living have meant that individuals who hold their financial assets in this form have lost a significant part of their equity and arrived at their old age with considerably less financial security than they had reason to expect. Although the amount of financial assets normally accumulated by lower and middle income families is not large, these financial assets are very important to the individuals involved. In order to avoid having the affluent take advantage of a measure designed to protect those in modest circumstances, the same device could be used for these financial assets as is currently used for the insurance of bank deposits: a limit could be placed on the absolute amount involved. The government could sell bonds whose value and rate of return would be tied to the cost of living, with a limit of $10,000 for any one individual. Such a limit would cover the total assets (excluding homes) owned at the present time by more than three-quarters of all retired people in the country.

A similar type of bond could be provided for insurance companies and private pension plans to use as a basis for the provision of cost-of-living payments for insurance and retirement pensions. Here again, maximum levels of insurance and pensions could be specified.

It is interesting to note that wages and farm prices have already been linked to price indexes, even though they are readily adjusted upward without such a linkage. From the point of view of the economy as a whole, cost-of-living bonds and cost-of-living pensions would be much less inflationary than cost-of-living wage contracts and farm parity prices, because they would not raise the costs of production of the economy. They would, of course, add to purchasing power; that is their purpose. If excess demand should develop, it would be proper to attack this by taxing those sectors of the economy which were receiving the benefits of the price rise in terms of capital gains caused by rising values and increased income levels due to prosperity. It is no contradiction to say that the economy should simultaneously try to use all the resources at its command, correct the inequities caused by either unemployment or cost-of-living changes, and levy taxes in as equitable a manner as possible in the amount necessary to achieve these objectives. This approach is far better than trying to make the economy discipline itself by chastising both workers and employers through unemployment and low profits, or by controlling them with wage and price controls.

From the point of view of the price behavior of the economy, there is a second major question which requires careful reexamination. This question involves the problem of whether the government can successfully legislate minimum wage levels as a device for raising income levels without causing adverse price behavior. Currently a proposal is before the Congress to raise the minimum wage from $1.25 to $1.40 next year, and to $1.60 the year after. Such a wage increase would be inflationary, not because it would provide additional purchasing power, but rather because it would raise the costs of production and thus prices both in the industries directly affected and in other industries where increases in the minimum wage will be looked upon as a guide. It is quite possible, as we have seen both in the United States and other countries, for increasing wage costs to raise prices in spite of the existence of unemployment and excess capacity. Those who believe that prices rise solely because there is too much money chasing too few goods have not studied the historical record either in the United States or in other countries. Most price rises originate from the cost side and in the process can well fail to develop the purchasing power which is required even to maintain previous levels of output.

What is the solution, then, to this dilemma? If $1.25 an hour is considered to be below the poverty line, the government should recognize this directly and make allowance for it in the tax system. It is far better to handle the problem of low income directly through a negative income tax than it is to set an artificial minimum wage level. For this reason, therefore, I would strongly urge that the minimum wage not be raised. To raise it poses a real threat to the future price stability of the economy.

Is the prospect of long-run price stability as bleak as might be suggested in view of the foregoing discussion? There can be little doubt, I think, that for certain kinds of prices increases are inevitable over time, as long as we have increases in money income, economic growth and population increase. Land and other scarce resources will be bid up in the future, just as they have been ever since Manhattan was bought for $24. Relatively speaking, man's labor will also become more valuable relative to commodities as he is able to produce more. Therefore, anyone wishing to use human services directly must inevitably pay the higher prices involved. On the other side, we will of course have the tremendous increases in productivity, new technology and products emerging from an economy which is ever growing. Under such circumstances, aggregate price indexes are not really meaningful statistical measurements. Given our present methods of measurement, the rise in the aggregate price index is inevitable, but its significance remains highly doubtful.

8. CONCLUSION

In conclusion, I would like to summarize the major points I have made.

Neither the Wholesale Price Index nor the Consumer Price Index correctly reflects the actual price behavior of the economy, since they do not take into account technological improvements and the introduction of new products. The amount of price increase is grossly overstated, and as a consequence the record of real output change is very much understated.

The Consumer Price Index is not a suitable instrument for measuring the change in the cost of living of those individuals who are forced to live on fixed incomes and accumulated savings. Paradoxically, the rise in cost of living for these groups (mainly retired persons) has probably been very much sharper than the increase shown by the Consumer Price Index. As a consequence of the continued rise in the cost of living, those with fixed incomes and with savings in the form of bank accounts or government bonds face a serious problem in the erosion of their standard of living. This situation will continue to be important, and cannot be cured by altering the rediscount rate, exhorting unions to live within the guidelines, or asking business to cut back investment. It should be recognized as a long-run economic problem, and attacked by such measures as tying social security payments to a properly constructed cost-of-living index and providing cost-of-living government bonds as a form of safe, nonerodible savings for moderate and lower income groups.

The increases in price indexes will be further intensified if the government attempts to ensure adequate levels of income by raising minimum wage rates, which result in increased costs. A negative income tax would not raise costs and prices as much and would be more equitable.

The attempt to limit the current rise in consumer prices by dampening the economy would increase hardship through additional unemployment far more than it could possibly benefit the fixed income groups.

Instead of trying to hold prices and wage rates down by depressing demand, a maneuver which is unlikely to be successful in any case, a more hopeful approach would be to strive to reduce wage costs by increasing productivity. Every attempt should be made to stimulate productivity gains by encouraging automation and the substitution of capital for labor. This would allow the economy to expand its output without running into increasing costs and consequent rising prices.

Except for the development of a war situation, there is very little danger that a price inflation will result from demand outracing supply. Rather, as is now becoming increasingly apparent, we may soon again be in the position where without further tax reduction we will be unable to purchase the amount the economy can and would like to produce. The most immediate threat to the peace-time American economy is that the rapid increase of industrial capacity will outstrip demand, and that our automatic stabilizers (profits and taxes) will limit our economic growth below the potential which we would achieve if we were able to take full advantage of our real resources.

8. Redundancy in Price Indexes for International Comparisons: A Stepwise Regression Analysis

Nancy D. Ruggles
Yale University

Since World War II, there has been a growing realization that improved international price comparisons are essential for understanding the process of economic growth, planning for economic development and analyzing balance of payments problems. Knowledge of comparative price structures between countries is necessary for the comparison of real levels of per capita output or consumption; the measurement of purchasing power of different currencies in terms of commodities which enter international trade is necessary to analyze the degree to which current exchange rates reflect equilibrium conditions; and examination of a given country's prices compared with those of other countries is necessary to evaluate comparative advantages.

International price comparisons by themselves cannot, of course, provide answers to these problems. The comparison of real output and consumption levels, the determination of equilibrium exchange rates and the analysis of comparative advantage require, in addition, information on the substitutability of products, their elasticities of supply and income elasticities, the importance of technological change and the effect of the learning process which continually goes on. International price measurements are just one element in any model designed to analyze these problems, but even though they do not yield specific answers, they are basic to any consideration of these problems.

This chapter first appeared as a Progress Report for the Agency for International Development and the Yale Growth Center, November 15, 1966.

1. RECENT RESEARCH ON INTERNATIONAL PRICE MEASUREMENT

Systematic measurement of relative prices in different countries is difficult to carry out since it requires a systematically integrated and coordinated project involving research activities in different countries. The first major project on international price comparisons was the Gilbert and Kravis study undertaken by the OEEC in 1952. This study involved comparison of various European countries with the United States. It was aimed primarily at the comparison of the real national product and the purchasing power of the currencies of the countries involved. The approach taken was that of establishing price deflators for the expenditures on gross national product. This research, together with its extension in a subsequent study by Gilbert and Associates, constitutes the classic work done to date with respect to European countries.

In 1960, the Economic Commission for Latin America undertook a very comprehensive study designed to measure purchasing power of the Latin American countries compared with each other and with the United States. This study had as its major purpose the comparison of actual exchange rates with the measurement of exchange rates based on purchasing power.

More recently, another examination of the problem of measuring relative per capita income was undertaken by Beckerman and Bacon. This approach utilized regression techniques to relate 'indicators' such as numbers of automobiles per capita, telephones, letters mailed, etc., to real income, and thus, to obtain for countries where price and output information is not available an indirect measure of the level of real income.

2. PURPOSE AND SCOPE OF PRESENT PROJECT

Although the present project recognizes the importance of arriving at answers to major questions, its basic purpose is methodological. It is designed to develop techniques and methods for price measurement which will, for a given cost, produce the best possible price measurements. In line with this objective, an attempt will be made to see whether data which are the byproduct of administrative procedures, can be utilized for international price comparisons, and it will investigate the effect of classification systems and numbers of commodities or observations on the quality of the measurements.

The project was started under the sponsorship of the Agency for International Development and the Yale Economic Growth Center. The UN Economic Commission for Latin America has cooperated in very large degree by providing their original worksheets containing price and quantity data for 21 cities, so that different experiments could be performed on these basic data.

The US Department of State provided data on prices collected in 19 Latin American countries in connection with determination of cost-of-living allowances for foreign service officers. Finally, the Brookings Institution has provided information on the commodity content and weights used in cost-of-living indexes for five Latin American countries.

The first phase of the project involved analyzing the ECLA data to see what difference the use of different countries' weights made in the measurement of relative prices. Binary comparisons were made for each pair of Latin American countries, using different weighting systems. These price indexes were, first, the Laspeyres price index based on the quantity of the specific items consumed in the first country; second, the Paasche price index based on the quantity of the specific items consumed in the second country; third, the Fisher Ideal Price Index based on the geometric mean of these two indexes; and fourth, a price index based on the average quantity of specific items consumed in Latin America, as a whole.

This phase of the research was completed approximately a year ago. It was determined that in the comparison of the purchasing power of two countries the Laspeyres price index yielded estimates of purchasing power parity exchange rates which were on the average about 35 percent lower than the Paasche price index. The use of the Fisher Ideal Price Index understandably gave a purchasing power measurement halfway between the two extremes, and the price index based on average Latin American quantity weights gave almost precisely the same result as the Fisher Ideal Index. These results agree with the Gilbert and Associates findings, although that study did not go as fully into this specific problem.

The present phase is concerned with a number of related problems and focused on the development of price relatives or price ratios as an alternative to the market basket approach. It involves a reexamination of weighting systems and methods of computation, the designation of commodities to be priced and the estimation of weights to be assigned and the testing of alternative computation procedures and methods of commodity selection.

It is anticipated that later phases of the project will introduce a time dimension into the cross-section analysis. In addition, different techniques of price collection will be examined; in this context the prices collected by the Department of State for post-allowance indexes will be related to the prices collected by ECLA. Finally, partly as a byproduct and partly as one of the major objectives of the project, it is hoped that useful and reasonable classification systems can be developed for international price comparisons which can relate the microprice information directly to the various breakdowns used in more aggregative data such as the national accounts.

3. USE OF PRICE RELATIVES FOR PRICE MEASUREMENT

Traditionally, price indexes have used the 'market basket' approach to make comparisons of prices over time or space. The most familiar formulation is the Laspeyres index which uses the quantity of commodities in the base period or country as weights for prices. This formulation for comparing two countries is as follows:

$$\overline{LP}_{ko} = \sum_{i=1}^{n} P_{ik} q_{io} \bigg/ \sum_{j=1}^{n} P_{jo} q_{jo} \tag{8.1}$$

where $\overline{LP}_{ko}$ represents the Laspeyres price index for country k with country o equal to 1; P_{ik} represents the price of commodity i in country k; and q_{io} represents the quantity of commodity i in country o.

The Paasche index is similar but uses k country's quantities as price weights instead of o country's quantities. This formulation for the same index would be:

$$\overline{PP}_{ko} = \sum_{i=1}^{n} P_{ik} q_{ik} \bigg/ \sum_{j=1}^{n} P_{jo} q_{jk} \tag{8.2}$$

where $\overline{PP}_{ko}$ represents the Paasche price index for country k with country o equal to 1. As has already been indicated in the case of Latin America, the Laspeyres index is, on average, approximately 35 percent lower than the Paasche index for the comparison of pairs of countries.

The Fisher Ideal Index, which is the geometric mean of the Laspeyres and Paasche indexes, is:

$$\overline{FP}_{ko} = \sqrt{\left(\sum_{i=1}^{n} P_{ik} q_{io} \bigg/ \sum_{j=1}^{n} P_{jo} q_{jo} \right) \cdot \left(\sum_{i=1}^{n} P_{ik} q_{ik} \bigg/ \sum_{j=1}^{n} P_{jo} q_{jk} \right)} \tag{8.3}$$

where $\overline{FP}_{ko}$ represents the Fisher Ideal Price Index for country k with country o equal to 1.

The use of average Latin American quantity weights yields the following:

$$\overline{AQP}_{ko} = \sum_{i=1}^{n} P_{ik} q_{ia} \bigg/ \sum_{j=1}^{n} P_{jo} q_{ja} \tag{8.4}$$

where $\overline{AQP}_{ko}$ represents a price index for country k with country o equal to 1, and with prices in each country weighted by average quantities. For Latin America, this index yielded approximately the same results as the Fisher Ideal Index.

All of the formulations discussed so far conceive of the price index as a comparison of different market baskets of commodities. It would, however, be equally possible to interpret $\bar{P}_{ko}$ as an average of the price relatives of the two countries. Recasting the Laspeyres index in this form yields the following index:

$$LP\bar{}_{ko} = \sum_{i=1}^{n} [(p_{ik}/p_{io}) \cdot w_{io}], \text{ where } w_{io} = p_{io}q_{ip} \bigg/ \sum_{j=1}^{n} p_{jo}q_{jo} \quad (8.5)$$

This is identical with the formulation given in (8.1). Similarly, the price index using average quantity weights could be recast into:

$$AQ\bar{P}_{ko} = \sum_{i=1}^{n} [(p_{ik}/p_{io}) \cdot w_{ia}], \text{ where } w_{ia} = p_{io}q_{ia} \bigg/ \sum_{j=1}^{n} p_{jo}q_{ja} \quad (8.6)$$

This is identical with the formulation given in (8.4). Although the market basket formulation and the price relative formulation can be seen to be algebraically identical, there are significant differences in the two approaches. The market basket approach conceives of the problem as one in which the cost of a fixed list of goods is measured under two different conditions, and the index computed by comparing the two sums. The price relative approach views the price index as a computation of the mean value of the price relatives, weighted according to some measure of their importance. The price relative approach introduces a degree of flexibility, since quantities need not be used as the basis for weighting. For example, expenditure weights may have more relevance to comparisons over time or space than quantity weights.

The use of fixed quantity weights would be completely valid in economic terms, only if the price elasticity of the demand function for each commodity approximate zero. In such a case, the Laspeyres and Paasche quantity weight indexes would coincide. The use of fixed expenditure weights is meaningful only if the price elasticity of the demand function for each commodity approximates one. In such a case the expenditure weight would not change in response to price changes. The use of an average expenditure weight instead of an average quantity weight would for any particular country give greater weight to these items which are cheap in price and consumed in greater quantity, and less weight to those commodities which are high in price and consumed less. The formulation of an arithmetic price index using an average Latin American expenditure weighting system is given below:

$$AEA\overline{P}_{ko} = \sum_{i=1}^{n} [(p_{ik}/p_{io})\cdot w_{ie}], \text{ where } w_{ie} = \sum_{k=1}^{n} p_{ik}q_{ik} \bigg/ \sum_{j=1}^{n} p_{jk}q_{jk} \quad (8.7)$$

$AEA\overline{P}_{ko}$ represents an arithmetic price index for country k with country o equal to 1, and with the price relatives weighted by average expenditures.

Another advantage of the price relative approach is that it can employ methods of aggregation other than the arithmetic mean. The arithmetic mean is influenced by price increases to a greater extent than by equal relative price decreases. With the geometric mean, however, a doubling of price in one area of expenditure would be offset by a halving of price in another area of similar importance. The formulation of the index computed with the geometric mean of price relatives weighted by average expenditures is given below:

$$AEG\overline{P}_{ko} = \prod_{i=1}^{n} (p_{ik}/p_{io})^{w_{ie}} \quad (8.8)$$

$AEG\overline{P}_{ko}$ represents an arithmetic price index for country k with country o equal to 1, and with the price relatives weighted by average expenditures.

In computing price relatives or exchange rates between countries, it is highly desirable that, given a set of fixed weights, the price index computed for country k with country o equal to 1 should be the reciprocal of the price index for country o with country k equal to 1. In other words, the price relation between two countries should not be affected by reversal. This reversal property does hold for both the Laspeyres and the Paasche indexes:

$$L\overline{P}_{ko} = \sum_{i=1}^{n} p_{ik}q_{io} \bigg/ \sum_{j=1}^{n} p_{jo}q_{jo} = 1/LP_{ok} = 1 \bigg/ \left(\sum_{j=1}^{n} p_{jo}q_{jo} \bigg/ \sum_{i=1}^{n} p_{ik}q_{io} \right) \quad (8.9)$$

$$P\overline{P}_{ko} = \sum_{i=1}^{n} p_{ik}q_{ik} \bigg/ \sum_{j=1}^{n} p_{jo}q_{jk} = 1/PP_{ok} = 1 \bigg/ \left(\sum_{j=1}^{n} p_{jo}q_{jk} \bigg/ \sum_{i=1}^{n} p_{ik}q_{ik} \right) \quad (8.10)$$

However, this reversal property does not hold for the arithmetic price index with price relatives weighted by average expenditures:

$$AEA\overline{P}_{ko} = \sum_{i=1}^{n} [(p_{ik}/p_{io})\cdot w_{ie}] \neq 1/AEAP_{ok} = 1 \bigg/ \sum_{i=1}^{n} [(p_{io}/p_{ik})\cdot w_{ie}] \quad (8.11)$$

The geometric price index with price relatives weighted by average expenditures does meet the reversal test:

$$AEGP\overline{_{ko}} = 1/AEGP\overline{_{ok}} = 1\left/\prod_{i=1}^{n} (p_{ik}/p_{io})^{W_{ie}}\right. \qquad (8.12)$$

The price index chosen to compare the relative prices of different countries, therefore, was a geometric price index with price relatives weighted by average expenditures.

4. SELECTION OF COMMODITIES FOR PRICE COMPARISONS

In selecting the commodities to be included in price indexes, the first and most important criterion is, of course, the commodity groups which are to be represented. The classification of commodities into groups itself poses problems. Different kinds of classifications are required for different kinds of economic analysis, and it will be necessary to develop a number of different types of classifications which can serve a wide variety of uses. In setting up classifications which are optimal for price measurement, furthermore, consideration should be given to the determinants of price. Commodities which are grouped together should be as homogeneous as possible with respect to price behavior. This suggests that they should be influenced by similar supply and demand conditions. Most classification systems do reflect such conditions to a greater or lesser degree. Food products have related supply and demand conditions and behave quite differently from consumer durables or services, which are influenced by very different factors. Within food, however, meat may behave quite differently from cereals or fruits. Meaningful economic classifications must be developed to improve the usefulness and accuracy of the price measurements. For this project, the classification system used initially was approximately the same as that used by the OEEC and ECLA. After some work with regression analysis, however, it became clear that other breakdowns might be more appropriate.

As a first approximation, the following categories were used: (1) meat and dairy products, (2) cereals, (3) fruits and vegetables, (4) other foods, (5) clothing, (6) rent, (7) other durables, (8) other semidurables, (9) other nondurables and (10) other services. Subsequent research will probably result in further reclassification, taking into account the behavior and differing importance of the various groups covered. In general, economic classifications should avoid giving a large amount of detail for relatively unimportant groups, or lumping into one classification a number of important groups.

With homogeneous commodity classifications, it should be feasible to determine the number of commodities required within a group to provide the desired degree of accuracy. Because the prices of commodities within a commodity group are highly intercorrelated, it should not be necessary to include all of the important commodities. It should be possible through multivariate analysis to analyze which commodities represent the behavior of given commodity groups best both over time and for groups of countries.

In order to test the redundancy of commodity prices within the classification groups shown above, a stepwise regression technique was employed. The dependent variable in this regression was the average price relative computed for a given set of commodities. The independent variables were the price relatives for each of the individual commodities in the set. The weights used to compute the dependent variable were the average expenditure weights for all Latin American countries derived from the original ECLA data. Since there were 19 countries and two US cities represented, there were 210 different pairs, thus providing 210 observations for each set.

As the first step in the stepwise regression, the correlation coefficients between each of the independent variables (price relatives of commodities in the group) and the dependent variable (computed average price relative) were computed. The commodity with the highest simple correlation was chosen for step 1. The regression equation employing this commodity as the independent variable was computed, and the remaining unexplained variance determined. In step 2, the remaining independent variables were each correlated with the remaining unexplained variance. The commodity with the highest partial correlation coefficient was chosen for step 2. The multiple regression equation using the commodities chosen in steps 1 and 2 as independent variables was computed to obtain the unexplained variance still remaining. This process was continued in succeeding steps until either all of the commodity price relatives were included in the multiple regression equation or it was no longer possible to explain any of the remaining variance by including additional variables.

In this process, the rate at which the correlation coefficient approaches 1.0 is an indication of the redundancy in the data. The results of these calculations are shown in Table 8.1 for the various groups of commodities used. As can be seen, almost all groups approach a correlation of 1.0 long before the list is exhausted, and a correlation of 0.995 ($r^2 = 0.990$) within each of the ten commodity groups can be obtained with a total set of 54 items out of the original 262. This is shown in Table 8.1 by the line drawn under the correlation coefficient in each commodity group at the point where it reaches 0.9950. In all but two commodity groups the stepwise regression exhausted the full set of commodity price relatives as independent variables. In the subgroups 'clothing' and 'other durables', however, one commodity price relative was rejected. In each of these cases, the commodity price relative in question was perfectly correlated with another commodity price relative in the same subgroup. The fully redundant commodities are shown by xxxxxx in the table.

Table 8.1 Correlation Coefficients Derived from Arithmetic Stepwise Regression Analysis

Commodity	Meat and dairy	Bread and cereals	Fruits and vegetables	Other foods	Clothing	Rent and utilities	Other durables	Other semi-durables	Other non-durables	Other services
1	0.9506	0.9690	0.9358	0.9708	0.9763	0.9825	0.9546	0.9514	0.9375	0.9518
2	0.9792	0.9870	0.9647	0.9882	0.9900	0.9930	0.9764	0.9764	0.9698	0.9769
3	0.9897	0.9933	0.9757	0.9936	0.9941	0.9944	0.9832	0.9870	0.9808	0.9874
4	_0.9956_	_0.9984_	0.9843	_0.9958_	_0.9967_	_0.9983_	0.9884	0.9940	0.9859	0.9933
5	0.9997	0.9995	0.9879	0.9966	0.9980	0.9992	0.9906	_0.9959_	0.9904	_0.9954_
6	0.9986	1.0000	0.9922	0.9973	0.9988	0.9999	0.9926	0.9971	0.9937	0.9965
7	0.9989	1.0000	0.9947	0.9980	0.9993	1.0000	0.9938	0.9978	0.9947	0.9973
8	0.9994	1.0000	_0.9959_	0.9984	0.9995	1.0000	_0.9953_	0.9984	_0.9954_	0.9979
9	0.9996	1.0000	0.9970	0.9988	0.9996	1.0000	0.9961	0.9989	0.9961	0.9983
10	0.9997	1.0000	0.9976	0.9990	0.9997		0.9969	0.9993	0.9967	0.9987
11	0.9998		0.9982	0.9992	0.9997		0.9976	0.9998	0.9974	0.9990
12	0.9999		0.9987	0.9994	0.9997		0.9981	0.9999	0.9981	0.9995
13	0.9999		0.9989	0.9995	0.9998		0.9984	1.0000	0.9986	0.9996
14	0.9999		0.9992	0.9996	0.9998		0.9987		0.9990	0.9997
15	1.0000		0.9995	0.9997	0.9998		0.9989		0.9993	0.9998
16	1.0000		0.9997	0.9998	0.9998		0.9992		0.9995	0.9999
17	1.0000		0.9997	0.9998	0.9999		0.9994		0.9997	0.9999
18	1.0000		0.9998	0.9999	0.9999		0.9995		0.9998	0.9999
19	1.0000		0.9999	0.9999	0.9999		0.9996		0.9998	0.9999
20	1.0000		0.9999	1.0000	0.9999		0.9997		0.9999	0.9999
21	1.0000		0.9999	1.0000	0.9999		0.9998		0.9999	0.9999
22	1.0000		0.9999	1.0000	1.0000		0.9998		0.9999	0.9999
23	1.0000		1.0000	1.0000	1.0000		0.9999		1.0000	1.0000
24	1.0000		1.0000	1.0000	1.0000		0.9999		1.0000	1.0000
25	1.0000		1.0000	1.0000	1.0000		0.9999		1.0000	1.0000
26	1.0000		1.0000		1.0000		0.9999		1.0000	1.0000
27	1.0000		1.0000		1.0000		0.9999		1.0000	1.0000
28			1.0000		1.0000		0.9999		1.0000	1.0000
29			1.0000		1.0000		1.0000		1.0000	1.0000
30			1.0000		1.0000		1.0000		1.0000	1.0000
33			1.0000		1.0000		1.0000		1.0000	1.0000
32			1.0000		1.0000		1.0000		1.0000	1.0000
33					1.0000		1.0000			
34					1.0000		1.0000			
35					1.0000		1.0000			
36					1.0000		1.0000			
37					xxxxxx		1.0000			
⋮							1.0000			
44							1.0000			
45							xxxxxx			
Weight (Total = 95)	14.2	9.9	8.5	13.1	13.1	16.9	4.8	1.3	5.7	7.4

Since the general price index to be constructed was a geometric index, it seemed appropriate to utilize a geometric formulation in the multivariate analysis. Table 8.2 presents the correlation coefficients computed on this basis.

In comparison with the arithmetic computation, the correlation coefficients produced by the geometric computation started out very much lower, but rose faster and generally surpassed those obtained from the arithmetic computation.

These results are what would be expected from the difference in the spec- ification of variance in the two methods of computation. In the arithmetic formulation the variance to be explained is that of the *absolute* values of the dependent variable and therefore the stepwise regression will select those price relatives which minimize the absolute unexplained variance. This means that the arithmetic stepwise regression will first select as important those commod- ity price relatives which are most closely related to the high values of the dependent variable. Commodity price relatives which are closely related to low values of the dependent variable will be selected only after the major part of the variance has been explained. The geometric formulation of the stepwise re- gression, in contrast, considers *relative* variance of the dependent variable. In contrast to the arithmetic formulation of the stepwise regression, under the geo- metric formulation any one single commodity price relative is likely to explain less of the total variance, since it must explain both the high and the low values of the dependent variable, not just the high values. Hence, the correlations in the initial steps of the geometric formulation will be smaller than those of the arithmetic formulation. On the other hand, since relative rather than absolute variance is considered, the amount of variance to be explained is reduced. Therefore, it generally takes fewer commodity price relatives to reach a given level of accuracy. For this reason, the geometric stepwise regression generally approaches a correlation of 1.0 with fewer commodity price relatives than the arithmetic stepwise regression. As a result, in almost all commodity groups a significant number of commodity price relatives failed to enter the geometric stepwise regression since they did not explain a significant amount of the re- sidual variance. The number of such commodity price relatives is indicated by xxxxxx in the appropriate columns. For the commodity group 'other durables', the correlation never exceeded 0.9558, and only seven of the 45 commodity price relatives entered the regression. The results were largely accounted for by the extremely high intercorrelation of the commodity price relatives, causing computational difficulties.

The regression coefficients produced by the stepwise regressions represent the weights which should be used for combining the price relatives. The arithmetic computation always resulted in positive regression coefficients, and thus, positive weights. In those cases where all commodity price relatives were included as independent variables, the weights observed at the end of the stepwise regression exactly coincided with those in the original ECLA data.

Table 8.2 Correlation Coefficients Derived from Geometric Stepwise Regression Analysis

Commodity	Meat and dairy	Bread and cereals	Fruits and vegetables	Other foods	Clothing	Other durables	Other services
1	0.6406	0.6886	0.5711	0.5579	0.6501	0.1969	0.4703
2	0.7697	0.8672	0.7768	0.8227	0.8261	0.5648	0.7027
3	0.8894	0.9649	0.8738	0.8859	0.9078	0.7166	0.9525
4	0.9734	0.9794	0.9206	0.9348	0.9796	0.8707	0.9582
5	0.9931	0.9995	0.9425	0.9688	0.9900	0.9536	0.9734
6	0.9964	0.9998	0.9699	00.9924	0.9932	0.9557	0.9826
7	0.9982	1.0000	0.9823	0.9945	0.9963	0.9958	0.9887
8	0.9985	1.0000	0.9879	0.9978	0.9977	xxxxxx	0.9947
9	0.9998	1.0000	0.9952	0.9988	0.9983	xxxxxx	0.9982
10	0.9999	1.0000	0.9985	0.9991	0.9988	xxxxxx	0.9985
11	0.9999		0.9992	0.9995	0.9995	xxxxxx	0.9993
12	1.0000		0.9996	0.9996	0.9998	xxxxxx	0.9995
13	1.0000		0.9998	0.9997	0.9999	xxxxxx	0.9997
14	1.0000		0.9998	0.9998	0.9999	xxxxxx	0.9997
15	1.0000		0.9998	0.9999	1.0000	xxxxxx	0.9998
16	1.0000		0.9999	0.9999	1.0000	xxxxxx	0.9999
17	1.0000		1.0000	0.9999	1.0000	xxxxxx	1.0000
18	1.0000		1.0000	0.9999	1.0000	xxxxxx	1.0000
19	1.0000		1.0000	0.9999	1.0000	xxxxxx	1.0000
20	1.0000		xxxxxx	xxxxxx	xxxxxx	xxxxxx	xxxxxx
21	xxxxxx		xxxxxx	xxxxxx	xxxxxx	xxxxxx	xxxxxx
22	xxxxxx		xxxxxx	xxxxxx	xxxxxx	xxxxxx	xxxxxx
23	xxxxxx		xxxxxx	xxxxxx	xxxxxx	xxxxxx	xxxxxx
24	xxxxxx		xxxxxx	xxxxxx	xxxxxx	xxxxxx	xxxxxx
25	xxxxxx		xxxxxx	xxxxxx	xxxxxx	xxxxxx	xxxxxx
26	xxxxxx		xxxxxx		xxxxxx	xxxxxx	xxxxxx
27	xxxxxx		xxxxxx		xxxxxx	xxxxxx	xxxxxx
28			xxxxxx		xxxxxx	xxxxxx	xxxxxx
29			xxxxxx		xxxxxx	xxxxxx	xxxxxx
30			xxxxxx		xxxxxx	xxxxxx	xxxxxx
31			xxxxxx		xxxxxx	xxxxxx	xxxxxx
32			xxxxxx		xxxxxx	xxxxxx	xxxxxx
33					xxxxxx	xxxxxx	
34					xxxxxx	xxxxxx	
35					xxxxxx	xxxxxx	
36					xxxxxx	xxxxxx	
37					xxxxxx	xxxxxx	
38						xxxxxx	
39						xxxxxx	
40						xxxxxx	
41						xxxxxx	
42						xxxxxx	
43						xxxxxx	
44						xxxxxx	
45						xxxxxx	

Table 8.3 Arithmetic and Geometric Stepwise Regression Coefficients

	Step 5		Step 10		Step 19		
	Arith-metic	Geo-metric	Arith-metic	Geo-metric	Arith-metic	Geo-metric	ECLA weight
BREAD AND CEREAL PRODUCTS							
Multiple R	0.9995	0.9955	1.0000	1.0000			
Regression coefficients:							
1. Rice	2.83	3.70	2.56	2.56			2.6
2. Corn	0.71	0.75	0.77	0.77			0.769
3. Corn meal			0.16	0.16			0.163
4. Corn starch			0.07	0.07			0.074
5. Flour			0.14	0.14			0.143
6. Semolina			0.03	0.03			0.038
7. Macaroni			0.76	0.76			0.766
8. French bread	3.03	10.91	2.69	2.69			2.7
9. English bread	3.25	3.46	2.71	2.71			2.7
10. Oats	1.34	1.31	1.23	1.23			1.2
MEAT AND DAIRY PRODUCTS							
Multiple R	0.9977	0.9931	0.9997	0.9999	1.0000	1.0000	
Regression coefficients							
1. Beef-1	3.72		2.25		0.67	0.48	0.663
2. Beef-2		4.48	1.3	2.64	2.53	3.06	2.4
3. Beef-3	2.24	2.79	2.17	2.36	2.20	2.06	2.2
4. Lamb leg						0.03	0.056
5. Lamb chop							0.056
6. Pork roast				1.09	0.40	0.26	0.351
7. Pork chop					0.25	0.78	0.322
8. Fowl			0.89		1.10	1.16	0.652
9. Chicken							0.288
10. Bacon		1.47		0.69		0.23	0.120
11. Boiled ham	2.84		1.77		0.21	−0.81	0.186
12. Salami				−0.122	0.09	−0.60	0.098
13. Lunch meat		2.35		1.56	0.27	1.46	0.122
14. Canned meat						−0.47	0.063
15. Fish-1				0.99	0.12	0.59	0.264
16. Fish-3			0.39		0.38	0.04	0.380
17. Tuna				0.55		0.33	0.129
18. Sardines					0.12		0.054
19. Milk	5.13	3.30	3.75	4.26	3.76	4.10	3.6
20. Evaporated milk	0.67		0.27	0.16	0.22	0.29	0.117
21. Condensed milk			0.11		0.12		0.124
22. Powdered milk							0.182
23. Milo							0.123
24. Butter			1.35		0.74		0.673
25. Hard cheese					0.21	0.96	0.054
26. Soft cheese					0.37	0.36	0.399
27. Dutch cheese					0.44		0.420

The geometric computation, as has already been indicated, resulted in a closer fit at a much earlier stage in the process, so that zero residual variance was reached well before all commodities were included. Where the list of commodities was small, the geometric computation did include all items in the list, and resulted in exactly the same regression coefficients as provided by the arithmetic computation and the original ECLA data, but where the commodity lists were long the process excluded many commodities and the regression coefficients for many of the commodity price relatives which were included were negative. Table 8.3 shows the regression coefficients which were computed for two commodity groups.

For 'bread and cereals', the commodity price relatives which were selected at step 5 by both methods coincided, and were also the ones which had the highest weights in the ECLA data. The arithmetic and geometric regression weights did, however, differ substantially at step 5. At step 10, all commodity price relatives were included, since there were only ten commodities in this group, and both stepwise regressions reproduced the original ECLA weights.

For 'meat and dairy products', where there were 27 commodities, the situation was quite different. At step 5, only two of the five commodity price relatives selected by the two methods were the same, and step 10 had only four of the ten commodities in common. At step 19, 15 of the 19 commodities were the same. The regression coefficients in the arithmetic stepwise regression were generally quite similar to the ECLA weights, and all important commodities were included. The geometric stepwise regression coefficients were in many cases quite different from the ECLA weights, and were sometimes negative. In subsequent evaluation, both the arithmetic and the geometric regression coefficients were tested.

Both the Brookings lists and the State–ECLA intersection list were also analyzed by means of the arithmetic stepwise regression. The correlation coefficients for these lists are shown in Table 8.4. The correlation coefficients start out very high, but approach the value of 1.0 very slowly. It is interesting to note that the regression coefficients which were generated for these lists by the arithmetic stepwise regression were often negative.

On the basis of the results from the stepwise regression programs, and from the lists provided by Brookings and the Department of State, 18 lists of commodities with different weighting systems were constructed, and price indexes between all pairs of countries were computed for ten commodity groups. The results of these computations were then compared with the price indexes produced by using the full set of ECLA data to see how different commodity lists and different weighting systems affected the price indexes. The summary results of these computations are shown in Table 8.5.

There is a considerable difference in the performance of the different commodity lists and different weighting systems. The list which performed best

Price Measurement

*Table 8.4 Correlation Coefficients Derived from Stepwise Regression
Analysis of Brookings and State Lists*

Com-modities	Brookings lists (Arithmetic)					State lists	
	Argentina	Brazil	Chile	Peru	Uruguay	Arith-metic	Geo-metric
1	0.9637	0.9660	0.9637	0.9569	0.9637	0.9660	0.4678
2	0.9867	0.9855	0.9867	0.9766	0.9855	0.9842	0.7246
3	0.9924	0.9921	0.9917	0.9869	0.9913	0.9928	0.8286
4	0.9944	0.9943	0.9931	0.9908	0.9937	0.9939	0.9408
5	0.9956	0.9951	0.9946	0.9932	0.9948	0.9949	0.9656
6	0.9963	0.9957	0.9956	0.9947	0.9954	0.9955	0.9864
7	0.9971	0.9963	0.9966	0.9957	0.9961	0.9962	0.9967
8	0.9977	0.9969	0.9974	0.9963	0.9966	0.9967	0.9972
9	0.9981	0.9972	0.9980	0.9966	0.9970	0.9970	0.9975
10	0.9983	0.9976	0.9985	0.9972	0.9974	0.9973	0.9983
11	0.9985	0.9978	0.9988	0.9973	0.9977	0.9975	0.9987
12	0.9985	0.9980	0.9989	0.9974	0.9979	0.9980	0.9992
13	0.9986	0.9982	0.9990	0.9975	0.9981	0.9982	0.9993
14	0.9987	0.9983	0.9991	0.9977	0.9982	0.9984	0.9997
15	0.9988	0.9984	0.9991	0.9977	0.9983	0.9986	0.9999
16	0.9989	0.9985	0.9992	0.9978	0.9984	0.9987	1.0000
17	0.9989	0.9985	0.9992	0.9978	0.9985	0.9988	1.0000
18	0.9990	0.9986	0.9992	0.9979	0.9985	0.9989	1.0000
19	0.9990	0.9987	0.9993	0.9979	0.9986	0.9990	1.0000
20	0.9991	0.9987	0.9993	0.9980	0.9986	0.9990	1.0000
21	0.9991	0.9987	0.9993	0.9980	0.9986	0.9991	xxxxxx
22	0.9991	0.9988	0.9993	0.9981	0.9987	0.9991	xxxxxx
23	0.9992	0.9988	0.9994	0.9981	0.9987	0.9992	xxxxxx
24	0.9992	0.9988	0.9994	0.9981	0.9987	0.9992	xxxxxx
25	0.9992	0.9988	0.9994	0.9982	0.9987	0.9993	xxxxxx
26	0.9993	0.9989	0.9994	0.9982	0.9987	0.9993	xxxxxx
27	0.9993	0.9989	0.9995	0.9982	0.9987	0.9993	xxxxxx
28	0.9993	0.9989	0.9995	0.9982	0.9987	0.9993	xxxxxx
29	0.9993	0.9989	0.9995	0.9982	0.9987	0.9994	xxxxxx
30	0.9994	0.9989	0.9995	0.9982	0.9988	0.9994	xxxxxx
31	0.9994	0.9989	0.9995	0.9982	0.9988	0.9994	xxxxxx
32–33	0.9994	0.9989	0.9996	0.9982	0.9988	0.9994	xxxxxx
34–35	0.9994	0.9989	0.9996	0.9982	0.9988	0.9995	xxxxxx
36	0.9994	0.9990	0.9996	0.9982	0.9988	0.9995	xxxxxx
37	0.9994	0.9990	0.9996	xxxxxx	0.9988	0.9995	xxxxxx
38–39	0.9994	0.9990	0.9996		0.9988	0.9995	xxxxxx
40	0.9994	0.9990	0.9996		0.9988	0.9996	xxxxxx
41	xxxxxx	0.9990	0.9996		0.9988	0.9996	xxxxxx
42	xxxxxx	0.9990	0.9996		xxxxxx	0.9996	xxxxxx
43–45		0.9990	0.9996		xxxxxx	0.9996	xxxxxx
46		0.9990	xxxxxx			0.9996	xxxxxx
47–53		0.9990				0.9996	xxxxxx
54		xxxxxx				0.9996	xxxxxx
55–60						0.9996	xxxxxx
61–64						xxxxxx	xxxxxx

was that which used the 54 commodities derived from the stepwise arithmetic regression, using regression weights. It showed an average absolute deviation from the ECLA data of approximately 2 percent. The range of the dispersion from the ECLA price indexes was –4 percent to +4 percent. The use of geometric weights gave approximately the same result, although the two lists differed considerably in terms of the accuracy with which they reported individual countries. The Brookings union list, which included all commodities shown on any of the Brookings lists, did very well in yielding a relatively small average deviation, matching that of the two 'best' lists. The dispersion, however, was somewhat greater, ranging from –5 percent to +7 percent. It should be noted that the Brookings union list has 104 commodities, in contrast with 54 for the 'best' list. For the most part, the other lists yield considerably inferior and somewhat mixed results. Surprisingly enough, the use of equal weights for the 'best' list did not result in a very great loss. Here, the average deviation rose to 4 percent and the range extended from –11 to +9. This performance was in fact superior to the commodity lists and weights provided by Brookings for the different countries.

In order to test the redundancy of different commodity lists, the State list and the different Brookings lists were analyzed by stepwise regression, and those commodities were selected which yielded an R^2 of 0.99. In some instances, the resulting smaller subset with arithmetic regression weights gave results superior to the original set and weights, even though the original sets were about five times as large. In other cases, notably the Argentine list, the results were very much worse, but it is quite possible that raising the number of commodities included would have increased the accuracy of the index substantially.

To put some limit on the range of possibilities, the commodities which were brought into the stepwise regression *last* were selected and a price index was computed using these commodities with equal weights. The items which are excluded by the stepwise regression are for the most part those which are most redundant, with the items chosen first. Therefore, they are not necessarily the worst commodities that could be chosen. Nevertheless, this set of data did give a poor showing. Its average deviation from the ECLA standard was 12 percent, and the range of deviation was from –22 to +29.

The last experiment undertaken was an attempt to duplicate the price relatives for producer durables using consumer durables and service items as independent variables. Unfortunately, this attempt was not successful. Nevertheless, a set of consumer durables and services was derived which seemed to be related to producer durables. This list was then used to estimate consumer price relatives. As might be expected, this list was poorer than any other list tried, since the commodities were restricted to durables and services.

Table 8.5 Alternative Commodity Lists and Weighting Systems Compared
with Full Edited Set of ECLA Price Data
(ECLA Price Indexes = 100)

	List 2	List 3	List 4	List 5	List 6	List 7	List 8
Number of commodities	42	43	46	37	45	54	54
Argentina	113	85	105	107	102	98	100
Bolivia	110	109	100	108	100	97	109
Brazil	112	97	99	100	97	104	99
Chile	112	94	105	108	95	101	95
Colombia	102	99	98	96	87	100	97
Costa Rica	99	107	102	105	96	103	106
Dominican Republic	93	111	99	111	100	99	98
Ecuador	104	112	100	104	103	102	96
El Salvador	90	124	96	108	98	100	100
Guatemala	96	99	98	92	98	98	104
Haiti	85	92	93	90	96	96	95
Honduras	106	106	101	106	107	98	104
Mexico	97	94	99	98	101	109	100
Nicaragua	97	108	108	95	90	98	103
Panama	99	106	94	104	100	96	104
Paraguay	109	106	111	119	107	102	94
Peru	104	93	108	102	107	103	96
Uruguay	107	99	108	100	102	100	89
Venezuela	102	98	103	98	113	101	105
Houston	89	88	92	80	106	102	105
Los Angeles	89	91	89	85	104	101	103
Range of deviation from 100							
High	+13	+24	+11	+19	+13	+4	+9
Low	−11	−15	−11	−20	−13	−4	−16
Average absolute deviation	8	6	5	8	5	2	8

List 2: Brookings Argentine list, Argentine weights.
List 3: Brookings Brazilian list, Brazilian weights.
List 4: Brookings Chilean list, Chilean weights.
List 5: Brookings Peruvian list, Peruvian weights.
List 6: Brookings Uruguayan list, Uruguayan weights.
List 7: 'Best' consumer goods, arithmetic group regression weights.
List 8: 'Best' consumer goods, equal weights.
List 9: State–ECLA intersection list, ECLA weights.
List 10: Brookings union list, ECLA weights.

List 9	List 10	List 11	List 12	List 13	List 14	List 15	List 16	List 17	List 18	List 19
69	104	69	16	10	10	9	13	47	10	18
113	101	96	104	80	100	102	101	116	102	95
99	96	105	91	91	100	90	95	95	99	710
120	102	97	115	136	103	95	104	109	100	143
111	105	98	91	74	104	88	102	95	98	76
103	103	96	96	82	96	89	95	100	96	109
105	100	100	101	116	103	105	106	106	102	72
102	100	100	94	121	104	108	100	88	99	108
91	101	99	100	92	107	109	100	84	103	115
84	98	102	96	156	100	91	98	99	97	93
98	96	100	95	125	100	112	99	100	101	111
101	95	100	107	82	101	123	98	101	100	111
102	101	103	97	98	97	100	102	106	100	83
94	101	98	105	83	97	94	97	101	98	130
109	102	100	98	88	106	107	107	90	108	69
97	100	100	95	96	99	104	102	117	93	100
113	101	99	111	113	99	96	98	78	94	82
92	101	97	116	94	94	103	102	96	99	88
110	107	103	98	108	99	101	95	84	100	90
100	102	101	102	95	91	97	96	119	103	122
89	96	104	96	114	103	98	100	120	105	99
86	95	104	97	140	101	102	104	129	106	93
+13	+7	+5	+16	+56	+7	+23	+29	+6	+6	+610
−16	−5	−4	−9	−20	−9	−12	−5	−22	−7	−41
8	2	2	5	13	3	7	3	12	3	19

List 11: 'Best' consumer goods list, geometric group regression weights.
List 12: State–ECLA intersection list, geometric regression weights.
List 13: Brookings Argentine list, arithmetic regression weights.
List 14: Brookings Brazilian list, arithmetic regression weights.
List 15: Brookings Chilean list, arithmetic regression weights.
List 16: Brookings Peruvian list, arithmetic regression weights.
List 17: 'Worst' consumer goods, equal weights.
List 18: Brookings Uruguayan list, arithmetic regression weights.
List 19: Consumer–producer list, ECLA weights.

In summary, there does appear to be considerable redundancy in price information, and stepwise regression analysis can be useful in exploring this problem, reducing the redundancy and providing weighting systems. It is important, however, to develop classification systems which define commodity groups in terms of their price behavior, and give the kind of detail required for purposes of economic analysis. Generally speaking, if these principles are followed, it would appear that between five and ten commodities are required for each commodity subgroup which is to be distinguished. Further research needs to be done on the exact form of the multivariate analysis which should be employed. It would also be proper to introduce not merely the average of the price observations for each commodity but the raw observations themselves, together with a cost estimate for the collection and processing of different commodity prices. Given this additional detail and cost information, it would then be possible to compute exactly what commodities should be collected and how many observations should be made of each.

Such research does, however, presuppose the existence of larger bodies of data which can be used as a standard of comparison. Basic budget studies and comprehensive price information for benchmark periods are required. The development of different standards of comparison for different countries, regions, or time-periods is very important. This suggests strongly that it would be useful to obtain from different countries the raw price observations underlying their cost-of-living and wholesale price indexes, and subject these data to the kind of experiments indicated. Such research is not only useful for extending our knowledge of price measurement over time and space, but it is essential if countries are to improve their own domestic price indexes and simultaneously reduce the costs involved.

9. Price Indexes and International Price Comparisons

Richard Ruggles
Yale University

1. FISHER'S INTEREST IN PRICE INDEXES

In any collection of studies honoring Irving Fisher, an explicit recognition of the subject of index numbers is quite appropriate. Fisher himself pursued index numbers merely as an instrument for the measurement of the changes of the price level in an economy. He first dealt with the index number problem comprehensively in an appendix to Chapter 10 of his *Purchasing Power of Money* (1911). However, Fisher's interest in this topic could be traced back as far as 1892, to his 'Mathematical investigations in the theory of value and prices' (1892).

In Fisher's analysis (1892, pp. vii–ix), the level of prices depended upon five definite factors: the volume of money in circulation, its velocity of circulation, the volume of bank deposits subject to check, its velocity and the volume of trade. In his view, the branch of economics which analyzed these five elements of purchasing power should be recognized as an exact science, capable of precise formulation, demonstration, and statistical verification. Although Fisher acknowledged that his investigation was a restatement and amplification of the old quantity theory of money, he wished to illustrate and verify those principles by historical facts and statistics. To this end, he needed an empirical measurement of the level of prices, and to him this meant the derivation of the best form of an index number.

This chapter first appeared in W. Fellner (ed.), *Ten Economic Essays in the Tradition of Irving Fisher*, New York: John Wiley and Sons, 1968.

2. PRICE INDEXES BEFORE FISHER

Fisher's aims and objectives were by no means new. As far back as the early 1700s, Fleetwood (1707) made an investigation to find the number of pounds which would have the same exchange value as five pounds formerly had, by asking how much corn, meat, drink and cloth that sum would have purchased originally and what sum would be needed now to purchase the same goods. Over the next century, there were a number of other investigations relating to the measurement of prices. Most took a selection of unweighted (or all equally weighted) price changes and averaged them to get the average change in prices. Arthur Young (1812) was one of the first to object to counting every article as equally important; he recommended that commodities should be weighted by their relative values.

Over the next 50 or 60 years, a considerable number of economists (Lowe, 1822; Scrope, 1833; James, 1835; Porter, 1838; Newmarch, 1884) used both weighted and unweighted averages of price changes to determine the change in the purchasing power of money. Jevons (1884) raised the question of whether the average should be arithmetic or geometric, and he came out in favor of geometric measurement. Laspeyres (1864) took issue with Jevons's geometric average and argued for the arithmetic average. A further controversy developed with M.W. Drobisch (1871) objecting to both Laspeyres's and Jevons's methods and suggesting that instead of weighted price relatives, price aggregates should be used. Laspeyres (1871) admitted the criticism of Drobisch, and finally in 1871, he formulated the rationale for what is now called the Laspeyres price index: the ratio of the value of a collection of quantities existing in the base year to its value in a given succeeding period, with the first period used as the base. Paasche (1874), also influenced by Drobisch, created an index similar to that of Laspeyres except that he used the given year quantities instead of base year quantities.

During the next decade, the number of index numbers proliferated. Writers such as Walras (1889), Sidgwick (1883), and Edgeworth (1883, 1896) came out for the arithmetic or geometric means, although they were often indifferent to the precise formulation used. Palgrave (1886) produced index numbers by weighting the price variations according to values of later periods rather than earlier periods. Finally, by the turn of the century, Walsh (1901) produced a general comprehensive treatise on *The Measurement of General Exchange-Value* which examined most of the index numbers that had been suggested up to that time. For the most part, the indexes examined consisted of different combinations of index formulas employing the arithmetic, harmonic and geometric means, the median and the mode, and different systems of weights. Interestingly enough, Walsh included an index number which was a geometric formulation of price relatives using the mean of value weights for different periods. Much of the future work on price index numbers came to rely on the work Walsh had carried out.

Fisher's work on price indexes in *The Purchasing Power of Money* had drawn heavily upon Walsh's work, and at this juncture he concluded that of the 44 index numbers he examined, he would recommend for practical purposes the median with a simple system of weights (whole numbers) based on expenditures and changing from time to time for the sake of making better year-to-year comparisons. This is interesting since listed among the 44 formulas was the geometric mean of the indexes of Paasche and Laspeyres, which Fisher later espoused as the Ideal Index.

The Making of Index Numbers, published by Fisher (1922), was in spirit a continuation of the index number discussion of *The Purchasing Power of Money*. Despite the magnitude of his effort, Fisher wasted no time defining his problem or establishing an analytic framework. To him, the purpose of index numbers was irrelevant to their construction. An index was defined merely as the average percentage change. As a rationale, he suggested the analogy that if one looks at prices starting at any one time, they seem to scatter or disperse like the fragments of a bursting shell. But just as there is a definite center of gravity of the shell fragments as they move, so there is a definite average movement of the scattering prices. This average is the index number. Moreover, just as in physics the center of gravity is often convenient to use instead of a list of individual shell fragments, so the average of the price movements, called their index number, is often convenient to use in economics (1922, pp. 2–3). It is obvious, of course, that this conception of an index number is intimately related to the assumption that there is a center of gravity, or a price level, from which all price changes vary in some stochastic manner. Fisher did not invent this concept, and it is somewhat puzzling why, given this view, he did not feel that any random observation of unweighted price changes would be satisfactory from a theoretical point of view for determining the mean value of the price level. However, Fisher did not indulge in speculation. Instead, with the patience of a Thomas Edison, he laboriously computed 134 different price indexes for some 36 commodities over a five-year period.

But Fisher had a more difficult task than Edison. In testing light bulbs there are objective criteria such as the brightness of the light and the durability of a filament — objectives which would be readily accepted by all interested in the development of an electric light. Fisher had to develop his own criteria, and those he developed were not immediately obvious to other economists. The tests applied to index numbers in the 1922 *Making of Index Numbers* are quite different from those used in the 1911 work. In his later work, Fisher relied on only two tests: time reversal and factor reversal. The time reversal test states that the percentage change between two years should turn out to be the same irrespective of which year is used as the base. In other words, the computation with one year as base should result in a figure which is the reciprocal of the result obtained using the other year as the base. The factor reversal test states that the index of price multiplied by the index of quantity should equal the change in value between the two periods.

Another widely accepted test for index numbers which had been used by other economists of the period (Walsh, 1901) was the circularity test. This test stated that in a comparison between *A*, *B* and *C*, *A/B* × *B/C* should equal *A/C*. Fisher argued, however, that in comparing any two periods or any two places it was irrelevant to bring into the comparison the effect of a third period or third place. For this reason he felt that the primary considerations should be the binary tests which he set forth, and that only after these were met should one ask how well the different index numbers met the circularity test.

Although Fisher devoted some attention to crossing weights in his index number formulas, he felt that in every case better results could be obtained by crossing formulas, and therefore that indexes with crossed weights were inferior. A cross-weighted index could never pass the factor reversal test. Fisher also rejected unweighted indexes as being too simple and inappropriate. Out of the total of 134 indexes tested, some 47 met both the time reversal and factor reversal tests. Of these, 34 employed the median and mode and so were, according to Fisher, subject to freakishness, or were unweighted. This left 13 indexes which passed both tests and were acceptable to Fisher. Since all 13 formulas met both tests, Fisher felt that they all had an equal probability of being correct. Thus his final error of measurement is based upon the variance among these 13 indexes.

The index which best conformed to the minimum error measurement and ranked very high in the circularity measurement was the geometric mean of the Laspeyres and Paasche indexes. This Fisher referred to as his Ideal Index.

Fisher's work was widely reviewed, and although it was praised for its diligence, it received substantial criticism. Allyn Young (1923) wrote one of the most flattering reviews, but he criticized Fisher for his rejection of the circularity test and cross weights. Bowley (1923), in his review, was considerably more caustic. He charged that the criterion of 'fairness' used by Fisher was vague and did not form an adequate basis for scientific analysis. It is interesting to note that Bowley (1899) himself, as Fisher had recognized, had suggested the Ideal Index as a possible index number formula as early as 1899. Bowley was not against the use of the geometric mean of the Laspeyres and Paasche indexes; rather, he felt that Fisher's treatment was arbitrary and inadequately based on the consideration of the definition and purpose of index numbers and on the principles of weighting. Perhaps one of the most biting reviews was that by Yule (1923). He took issue with Fisher that the purpose to which an index number is put does not affect the choice of formula. Further, he suggested that even the 134 formulas contained in the book were little more than a random collection, and the conclusion reached could not be extended beyond them since an infinite number of other formulas is possible. Fisher replied in detail to each of these reviews (1923a,b, 1924), reiterating his position that the purpose of an index number was irrelevant, that cross weighting was not desirable, and that the circularity test was not valid.

Fisher's work on index numbers came at a time when many countries were embarking upon the development of price indexes. Despite Fisher's contention that the geometric mean of the Laspeyres and Paasche formulas provided the best measure possible, no country used this formulation as a basis for its price measurement. In a sense, Fisher had proved too much. He had shown that in time comparisons between two years the Laspeyres price index did not differ significantly from the Paasche index, and that the use of the geometric mean of both indexes was therefore a refinement which was probably not justified in view of the doubtful accuracy of the basic information. Second, despite Fisher's rejection of the circularity test, the users of index numbers did consider that the circularity test was important. Most statisticians wished to present the price index as a series extending over a period of years, rather than as a set of binary measurements. Finally, because the problem of weights was often a difficult one, there was a strong preference for the Laspeyres index, which could choose a base period when weights were available and not require a new computation of weights for each year for which the comparison was made. Thus the Laspeyres index, despite its inadequacies according to the Fisher measurements, became the standard form of index number in common usage.

3. THE WELFARE BASIS OF INDEX NUMBERS

Although the quantity theory of money had provided the basis and motivation for the development of index numbers, it did not, as many of its critics inferred, provide any theoretical basis or criteria as to the meaning or interpretation of index numbers. Pigou (1920), in his *Economics of Welfare*, however, analyzed the implications of the Laspeyres and Paasche quantity indexes with reference to the measurement of the national dividend. He reasoned that when the Paasche quantity index was greater than 1, an individual could be said to be better off in period 2 than he had been in period 1, since this implied that the quantity of goods consumed in period 2 valued at the prices in period 2 exceeded the worth of the quantity of goods consumed in period 1 valued in the prices of period 2. Conversely, if the Laspeyres quantity index is less than 1 an individual could be said to be better off in period 1. The Paasche and Laspeyres indexes, thus, in Pigou's view, provided the limits within which the choice of an appropriate measure should lie. Although Pigou felt that the choice was more or less arbitrary within this range, he came out in favor of the Fisher Ideal Index as the proper measure.

Haberler (1927) and Allen (1933) pursued the same line of reasoning used by Pigou with reference to price indexes. According to their analyses, the Laspeyres and Paasche price indexes provided the upper and lower limits of a true cost-of-living index. Staehle (1935), however, pointed out that both Allen's and Haberler's analyses rested on the basic assumption that the stand-ard of living was identical in the two periods being compared. Staehle introduced into the discussion the Konüs condition (Konüs, 1939), which was a somewhat less restrictive assumption requiring only that the money value of the quantities purchased in periods 1 and 2 be equal in order for the comparison to be valid. The Staehle contribution resulted in a number of contributions from such authors as Lerner (1935), Allen (1935, 1949) and Schultz (1939), generally verifying Staehle's findings. Staehle (1937) himself used the Konüs assumptions to construct international comparisons of price indexes by equat-ing similar expenditure levels in different countries.

Pigou's (1920) work in *The Economics of Welfare* also initiated a related body of literature concerned with the measurement of real income (Hicks and Hicks, 1939). Hicks (1940) applied the Pigovian criteria to the valuation of social income. This was in the period of the development of the new welfare economics, and there was an increased consciousness of the problems asso-ciated with the development of community indifference curves. Scitovsky (1941) showed the necessity for introducing double criteria with respect to the distribution of income. Kuznets (1948) raised related questions and cast doubt on such elements as government capital formation in the measurement of real income. Little (1949) also commented on the Hicksian position, concluding that the total measures themselves had no significance, and that the concept of net national income at factor cost tries to answer an impossible question and cannot be relied upon. Finally, this phase of the controversy was summarized by Samuelson (1950), reaching the general conclusion that, although the Laspeyres and Paasche index numbers did have relevance to the welfare of a single individual, it was not possible to extend this analysis to groups of in-dividuals and thus to the welfare measurement of real social income.

4. EMPIRICAL INTERNATIONAL PRICE COMPARISONS

The theoretical literature on index numbers referred to comparisons over both time and space. Thus, for example, Fisher rejected the test of circularity on the basis that a comparison of prices between Georgia, Norway and Egypt should not obey the circularity criterion, that is, that any comparison between Norway and Egypt should not take into account their respective relationship to Georgia. Staehle's work, furthermore, was primarily directed toward the comparison of the price of living in different countries. But in empirical terms, by far the greatest part of the literature about index numbers has been directed to measurements over time for a given country or locality, and there has been relatively little discussion of the methodological differences between comparisons over time and comparisons over space.

The comparison of prices of different countries with each other may have many different purposes. Even the most casual tourist, on arriving in a new country, finds himself comparing the prices of goods and services which he can buy with the price that he would pay in his own country. Implicit in such a comparison, of course, is his acceptance of the rate at which he can exchange his money for the foreign currency. It is in these terms that the prices in a particular country may all appear low or all appear high, even to the most casual observer. In the case of an undervalued exchange rate, the tourist will find many bargains and be tempted to stock up before leaving the country. Conversely, a heavily overvalued exchange rate may cause the tourist to leave the country sooner than anticipated because of a lack of funds.

A related but somewhat different purpose motivates organizations wanting to ascertain proper pay scales or expense allowances for its employees in different countries. In the early 1930s, the International Labour Office (ILO) (1932) undertook a special study known as the Ford–Filene inquiry, which had the purpose of determining what wages should be paid to employees of the Ford Motor Company to ensure them comparability of pay wherever they were stationed. This study involved 14 European countries and the United States. A somewhat similar study was carried out by Unilever (1930) about the same time to determine standards of living in Europe equivalent to those in England. The ILO (1952) continued its interest in comparing wage levels in real terms for workers in specific industries and in the early 1950s published material on wages in the textile industry. With the integration of the European coal and steel industries, a study of the wages of workers in these industries was carried out for seven European countries (European Coal and Steel Community, 1955). Finally, many international organizations and individual governments conduct special inquiries to determine cost-of-living or post allowances for their employees abroad. The United Nations (1954) makes periodic surveys of prices relevant to the cost of living of its employees in all of its major posts. The German Foreign Office (Statistisches Bundesamt, 1965) published data on prices in over 50 countries. More generally, governments do not widely publish the data collected, but many foreign offices prepare such information.

Economists have been interested in international price comparisons in order to measure the real standard of living of different countries. One of the earliest studies of this sort was that of Colin Clark (1951), which used the data provided by Unilever, the Ford–Filene study, and other information regarding the level of exchange rates to measure the real standard of living per capita in a large number of countries. The work done by the United Nations (1966) in this area has generally used official exchange rates as the device to convert all currencies to a common base, and thus has implicitly assumed that prices relative to exchange rates are the same in all countries. In the early 1950s, the Organization for European Economic Cooperation (Gilbert and Kravis, 1954) undertook a systematic study of prices for the full range of final products including investment goods and government consumption for the European countries and the United States. This study was the most comprehensive and authoritative conducted to that point. It was extended and updated in 1958 (Gilbert and Associates, 1958), but unfortunately no continuing work has been done in this area for the European countries. Most recently, the Economic Commission for Latin America (1963) undertook a study of purchasing power for 19 different Latin American countries. As in the case of the OEEC studies, the coverage was quite broad, including not only consumer goods but also investment goods and government consumption. The results of this purchasing power study were applied to the problem of obtaining comparisons of real income by Braithwaite (1967).

Besides the main stream of work on international prices, there has been a considerable number of studies focusing on a smaller number of areas or direct comparison between two countries. The Scandinavian countries conducted studies (Nordisk Statistisk Skriftserie, 1954) in the mid-1950s. A comparison between Japan and the United States (Economic Research Institute, 1963) was published in 1963. Many studies have been made comparing the Soviet Union and the United States; one of the major ones was conducted by Bornstein (1959). A somewhat different approach has been utilized by Paige and Bombach (1959) to obtain real output by industrial sector, thus using prices other than those for final goods. Some investigators have preferred to attempt a short-cut to the measurement of real standard of living, using multiple regression techniques applied to various economic indicators. Beckerman (1966) in particular has pursued this approach.

5. THE EFFECT OF METHODOLOGY IN INTERNATIONAL COMPARISONS

Understandably, the methodology of the different investigations has varied widely. In some cases, binary comparisons have been carried out using the equivalent of Laspeyres and Paasche price indexes. In other cases some sort of average quantity weights or average value weights have been utilized. In a few cases, the equivalent of the Fisher Ideal Index has been used. There has, however, been no significant examination of the consequences of using different index number formulas, weighting systems, or numbers of commodities. One of the major reasons for this, of course, is that most investigators were primarily interested in using what seemed to them the best method available to obtain immediately useful results, and the burden of computing various alternative measures under different methodological procedures was excessive before the development of the computer.

The Agency for International Development became interested in the problem of international price comparisons as part of its analysis of economic conditions in different countries which were receiving foreign aid. It recognized that adequate price information was not available, and it therefore undertook to support research aimed at investigating whether existing price information such as that contained in post allowance data of the Department of State might provide a basis for international price comparisons. In order to make such a determination, it was necessary to find a set of data which could serve as a benchmark, and to see whether or not methods could be developed to achieve the same results as were derived from the benchmark data with a smaller subset of data. The Economic Commission for Latin America made its worksheets available for such research and the Department of State also made available its information on prices for the same set of countries.

In attacking this problem, the investigation was broken into three subproblems. First, what form of index numbers and weighting systems should be used for international comparisons? Although the Economic Commission for Latin America had used average Latin American quantity weights, the question needed to be explored to see whether other equally reasonable procedures would result in substantially different answers. Second, after determining a suitable methodology for computing international price indexes, the questions of whether the price index information was redundant and whether a subset of price data for the different countries would have achieved substantially the same result had to be investigated (Ruggles, 1968). Only if this were found to be true would it be possible to consider whether a subset resembling the State Department data was satisfactory or whether some different commodity selection was required.

Finally, the question of whether the price information collected by the Department of State was statistically comparable to that collected by ECLA also needed to be answered. This question involves testing to see whether on average the mean values of the price relationships in the State data and the ECLA data for similar commodities coincide. The question that will be examined in the remaining part of this chapter pertains solely to the first phase of this research project. Specifically, how do different index number formulas and weighting systems compare when applied to the same set of data? This problem is not unlike that examined by Irving Fisher, although no attempt will be made here to cover all the Fisher formulas. Attention will be directed to those price indexes which are in common usage or which are logical extensions of already existing methods. In all, eight index number formulations will be examined. The following notation is employed: p = price, q = quantity, I $(1, ..., n)$ = commodities, and $j, k (1, ..., m)$ = countries.

The Laspeyres Price Index

It has already been noted that in comparisons over time the price index which has been in common current usage is the Laspeyres price index. The reasons for this are, of course, that for a single country it does not differ significantly from other price index formulas over short periods of time and it has the advantage of statistical convenience in the choice of base year weights and provision of circularity over the years covered. In a spatial comparison of country k with country j, the Laspeyres price index uses the quantity weights of the base country as indicated below:

$$\sum_{i=1}^{n} p_{ik} q_{ij} \bigg/ \sum_{i=1}^{n} p_{ij} q_{ij} \qquad (9.1)$$

It is also possible to express the Laspeyres price index in the form of weighted price relatives, where the weights are the value shares of each commodity in the base country j. This formulation is:

$$\sum_{i=1}^{n} (p_{ik}/p_{ij}) \cdot v_{ij} \quad \text{where} \quad v_{ij} = p_{ij} q_{ij} \bigg/ \sum_{i=1}^{n} p_{ij} q_{ij} \qquad (9.1a)$$

The Paasche Price Index

The Paasche price index uses as weights the quantities of country k, the country with which the base country is being compared. This index in time comparisons yields an index number showing smaller changes than the Laspeyres index, since prices and quantities are inversely correlated and thus the Paasche index weights less heavily those items which rise in price and more heavily those items which decline in price. The formula for country comparisons is as follows:

$$\sum_{i=1}^{n} p_{ik} q_{ik} \bigg/ \sum_{i=1}^{n} p_{ij} q_{ik} \qquad (9.2)$$

The Paasche price index expressed in terms of price relatives weighted by value shares would be as follows:

$$1\Bigg/\sum_{i=1}^{n}(p_{ij}/p_{ik})\cdot v_{ik} \quad \text{where} \quad v_{ik} = p_{ik}q_{ik}\Bigg/\sum_{i=1}^{n}p_{ik}q_{ik} \qquad (9.2a)$$

It should be noted that the Laspeyres index for country k relative to country j would be the reciprocal of the Paasche index for country j relative to country k. Unlike time comparisons, there is of course no way of deciding which country is more appropriately a 'base' in the comparison between two countries. Furthermore, from a logical point of view, it is desirable that the comparison between two countries be invariant in terms of which country is used as base. This country reversal requirement is the same as the time reversal requirement suggested by Fisher.

The Palgrave Price Index

In much the same way as the Laspeyres price index can be thought of as the arithmetic mean of price relatives for country k relative to country j, weighted by the value shares of country j, so also is it possible to use country k's value shares as a weighting scheme. The formula which follows is, in fact, the price index recommended by Palgrave (1886) and was tested by Fisher as formula 9:

$$\sum(p_{ik}/p_{ij})\cdot v_{ik} \quad \text{where} \quad v_{ik} = p_{ik}q_{ik}\Bigg/\sum_{i=1}^{n}p_{ik}q_{ik} \qquad (9.3)$$

In terms of economic behavior, one would expect that the Laspeyres and Palgrave indexes would be very much closer together than the Laspeyres and Paasche indexes. The reason for this is that value shares are much less sensitive to changes in prices than are quantities, due to the inverse correlation between price and quantity. In fact, if the elasticity of demand for the different commodities examined were unity, value shares would not change, although quantities might show substantial change. Only in the case of perfectly inelastic demand would the quantity changes be invariant to changes in prices; in this case the value share would be directly correlated with price so that the Palgrave index would report a substantially higher price index than the Laspeyres index.

The Fisher Ideal Price Index

Just as in the case of time comparisons, it is quite possible to take the geometric mean of the Laspeyres and Paasche indexes between two countries and obtain an index. This is shown below:

$$\sqrt{\left[\sum_{i=1}^{n} p_{ik} q_{ij} \bigg/ \sum_{i=1}^{n} p_{ij} q_{ij}\right] \cdot \left[\sum_{i=1}^{n} p_{ik} q_{ik} \bigg/ \sum_{i=1}^{n} p_{ij} q_{ik}\right]} \qquad (9.4)$$

This index does meet the country reversal test previously cited, and if computed for quantities, as well as for prices, it would also meet the factor reversal test of Fisher. This test requires that the price index multiplied by the quantity index equal the change in value observed. As Fisher noted, this index does not meet the circularity test, that is, when more than two countries are involved it will not produce a single-scaled relationship among all countries.

The Theil Price Index

Theil (1965, 1967; Kloek and Theil, 1965) has proposed a variation on the Fisher Ideal Index in terms of a cross of the Laspeyres and Palgrave indexes formulated in logarithmic terms, as follows:

$$\log P_{kj} = \sum_{i=1}^{n} [(v_{ij} + v_{ik})/2] \cdot (\log p_{ik} - \log p_{ij}) \qquad (9.5)$$

In terms of original variables,

$$P_{kj} = \prod_{i=1}^{n} (p_{ik}/p_{ij})^{(v_{ij} + v_{ik})/2} \qquad (9.5a)$$

It should be noted that as in the case of the Fisher Ideal Index, the Theil index does meet the country reversal test. But unlike the Fisher index it does not meet the factor reversal test. Fisher did, in fact, consider the Theil formula among the indexes he examined (formula 123). Theil has termed the residual by which his index does not meet the factor reversal test the 'information difference component'. The Theil formula also does not result in a single scale of relationships when three or more countries are considered.

Walsh Price Index

One of the price indexes favored by Walsh (1901) was a geometric formulation of price relatives weighted by the geometric mean of value shares. Fisher discussed this index as number 1123:

$$\prod_{i=1}^{n} (p_{ik}/p_{ij})^{v_{ix}} \text{ where } v_{ix} = \left[\prod_{i=1}^{n} (p_{ik}/p_{ij})^{1/m} \right] \Big/ \left\{ \sum_{i=1}^{n} \left[\left(\prod_{i=1}^{n} v_{ij} \right)^{1/m} \right] \right\} \quad (9.6)$$

This price index would in Fisher's terms meet the country reversal test and the circularity test, but would not meet the factor reversal test.

Walsh Price Index with Arithmetic Weights

It is also possible, of course, to construct the Walsh index with value share weights arrived at by the arithmetic average of value shares of all countries. This would be as follows:

$$\prod_{i=1}^{n} (p_{ik}/p_{ij})^{v_{iy}} \text{ where } v_{iy} = (1/m) \cdot \sum_{j=1}^{m} \cdot (p_{ij} q_{ij}) \Big/ \sum_{i=1}^{n} p_{ij} q_{ij} \quad (9.7)$$

This index has the same properties as the previous index.

ECLA Price Index

A price index using average quantity weights for all countries was used by ECLA (1963) in its measurement of purchasing power for Latin American countries. This index reflects the market basket concept; the market basket which is being considered is the average quantity consumed of each commodity throughout Latin America:

$$\sum_{i=1}^{n} p_{ik} q_{ia} \Big/ \sum_{i=1}^{n} p_{ij} q_{ia} \text{ where } q_{ia} = (1/m) \cdot \sum_{j=1}^{m} q_{ij} \quad (9.8)$$

This index meets both the country reversal and circularity tests, but does not meet the factor reversal test.

6. THE APPLICATION OF ALTERNATIVE FORMULAS TO THE ECLA DATA

The experiments reported on here made use of basic data collected by the United Nations Economic Commission for Latin America. Although the full set of ECLA data provides information on all final products entering the gross national product, only that portion of the data which relates to consumer goods and services was used. The data for producers' durables and government services present a number of additional problems which would complicate the interpretation of the results and raise questions that would not be particularly germane to the purpose of the experiments. The price and quantity data used covered about 270 consumer goods and services for 19 countries. The information was collected in 1960 and 1961 by UN personnel who visited each of the countries involved and collected the basic information with the cooperation of the national governments. The data were processed at the United Nations office in Santiago, Chile. Subsequently, the worksheets listing the price and quantity for each commodity in each country were put in machine-readable form at the Yale Economic Growth Center and processed on the Yale computer. Among other computations, each of the eight formulas given was applied to the primary data to determine the effect of the different formulas on the resulting index. In making these comparisons, the prices, all of which were reported in national currencies, were converted to a common currency (dollars) through the use of official exchange rates. The price comparisons between any two countries thus contain the assumption that the currencies in question exchange at the official exchange rates. If, for any two countries, all goods and services actually entered into international trade and the prices of these goods and services determined both the equilibrium and official exchange rates, then the price index relating these two countries would be 100. There are, of course, many reasons why prices in two countries may systematically diverge from each other and thus cause the total price index to be greater than or less than 100.

7. COMPARISON OF THE LASPEYRES, PAASCHE AND PALGRAVE INDEXES

One of the first computations which was made was the comparison of the Laspeyres and Paasche price indexes. This comparison involved 684 sets of binary comparisons with each set consisting of the indexes relating a pair of countries for total consumer expenditures and its breakdown into specific subcategories. As already noted, the Laspeyres price index between country *A* and country *B* is equal to the reciprocal of the Paasche price index between country *B* and country *A*. Table 9.1 shows the Laspeyres and Paasche indexes for each of the 19 countries compared with two base countries: Argentina and Venezuela.

The disparity between the Laspeyres and Paasche indexes is quite wide. For example, comparing Haiti with Argentina as a base, the Argentine basket of goods would cost in Haiti 175 percent of what it would cost in Argentina: 75 percent more. But, if the Haitian market basket were purchased in both Argentina and Haiti, the cost in Haiti would be only 79 percent of what it

Table 9.1 Comparison of Laspeyres and Paasche Price Indexes

	Argentina as base			Venezuela as base		
	Laspeyres	Paasche	Laspeyres as percent of Paasche	Laspeyres	Paasche	Laspeyres as percent of Paasche
Argentina	100	100	—	50	36	138
Bolivia	136	89	153	54	39	138
Brazil	115	85	135	48	36	133
Chile	160	134	119	78	50	156
Colombia	149	111	134	61	45	135
Costa Rica	177	113	159	63	52	121
Dominican Republic	227	123	202	96	58	166
Ecuador	139	87	160	56	37	151
El Salvador	204	127	161	70	58	121
Guatemala	211	142	149	80	70	114
Haiti	175	79	222	68	38	179
Honduras	238	139	171	87	76	114
Mexico	139	96	148	52	44	118
Nicaragua	203	125	162	78	59	132
Panama	192	129	148	72	62	114
Paraguay	119	78	153	54	31	174
Peru	123	94	131	48	39	123
Uruguay	105	85	123	50	32	156
Venezuela	275	200	138	100	100	—
Geometric mean, all countries	161	109	148	65	48	135

would be in Argentina: 21 percent less. The magnitude of difference between the Laspeyres and Paasche indexes on the Argentine base is of almost similar magnitude for the Dominican Republic. The two indexes are closest together for the comparison of Argentina with Chile, but even here, the disparity is 19 percent. On average, the difference between the Laspeyres and Paasche indexes using the Argentine base is 48 percent. Using Venezuela as a base, the situation is similar but somewhat less marked. No country in the Venezuelan comparison showed the large difference that was observed for some of the countries in the Argentine comparisons. The average difference between the Laspeyres and Paasche indexes using Venezuela as a base was 35 percent.

The difference between the Laspeyres and Paasche price indexes is always in the expected direction. The difference is due to the fact that prices and quantities tend to be inversely correlated, so that there is a systematic substitution of low-priced goods for high-priced goods in the consumption of each country. It is, therefore, always less expensive to buy what is actually consumed in any country than to buy any other market basket. If prices in two similar countries were equal, one would expect the Laspeyres and Paasche price indexes for these two countries to coincide. The extent of the difference between the

Table 9.2 Comparison of Laspeyres and Palgrave Price Indexes

	Argentina as base			Venezuela as base		
	Laspeyres	Palgrave	Laspeyres as percent of Palgrave	Laspeyres	Palgrave	Laspeyres as percent of Palgrave
Argentina	100	100	—	50	50	100
Bolivia	136	144	94	54	55	98
Brazil	115	118	97	48	51	94
Chile	160	162	99	78	73	107
Colombia	149	149	100	61	58	105
Costa Rica	177	169	105	63	65	97
Dominican Republic	227	223	97	96	102	94
Ecuador	139	127	109	56	51	110
El Salvador	204	191	107	70	79	89
Guatemala	211	201	105	80	87	92
Haiti	175	166	105	68	70	97
Honduras	238	205	116	87	88	99
Mexico	139	127	109	52	55	95
Nicaragua	203	194	105	78	85	92
Panama	192	195	98	72	80	90
Paraguay	119	113	105	54	46	117
Peru	123	125	98	48	50	96
Uruguay	105	113	93	50	52	96
Venezuela	275	269	102	100	100	—
Geometric mean, all countries	161	157	103	65	66	98

Laspeyres and Paasche indexes is an indication of the degree to which prices do diverge and the amount of substitution that has taken place. Table 9.1 thus indicates that relative prices in Argentina vary more from relative prices in other Latin American countries than do relative prices in Venezuela. This may be partly due to the structure of tariffs and subsidy programs in the two countries.

The comparison of the Laspeyres and the Palgrave indexes was carried out primarily to investigate for a binary comparison the effect of using alternative sets of expenditure shares as weights. Since price and output are inversely correlated, the expenditure share for any particular commodity should be more stable than the quantity consumed. If all commodities had price elasticities of unity, expenditure shares would remain constant. When the Palgrave formula yields an index larger than the Laspeyres formula, price elasticities are greater than unity, so that substantial substitution is taking place. Conversely, when the Palgrave index is below the Laspeyres index, the expenditure share weights are inversely correlated with price, so that price elasticities are less than unity. Table 9.2 shows the comparison of the Laspeyres and Palgrave indexes, again with Argentina and Venezuela as bases. The differences between the Laspeyres and Palgrave indexes are quite small and in varying directions from country to country. For Argentina, the Palgrave index averages 3 percent smaller than the Laspeyres index. But for Venezuela, it averages 2 percent larger, thus indicating generally the relative stability of expenditure shares.

8. COMPARISON OF VARIOUS TYPES OF AVERAGE PRICE INDEXES

In view of the wide disparity between the Laspeyres and Paasche indexes, it is apparent that for international comparisons, unlike many comparisons over time, the question of the index number formula and weights is of considerable consequence. Furthermore, unlike comparisons over time, the choice of a proper base is not obvious. The variety of information provided by the different price indexes is very useful, but for many purposes a single figure may be desired for the comparison of prices between two countries, rather than a

Table 9.3a Comparison of Various Types of Average Price Indexes with Argentina as a Base

	Binary country weights		Latin American average weights		
	Fisher Ideal (Quantity weights)	Theil (Expenditure weights)	Walsh (Geometric expenditure weights)	Walsh (Arithmetic expenditure weights)	ECLA (Quantity weights)
Argentina	100	100	100	100	100
Bolivia	110	110	99	104	112
Brazil	99	102	99	100	103
Chile	146	146	145	146	152
Colombia	128	127	118	119	124
Costa Rica	141	137	133	135	140
Dominican Republic	168	169	161	168	186
Ecuador	110	108	102	105	112
El Salvador	161	154	136	141	156
Guatemala	173	172	165	169	174
Haiti	118	122	125	129	143
Honduras	181	179	173	179	189
Mexico	115	113	107	109	111
Nicaragua	159	158	147	151	161
Panama	157	157	153	156	159
Paraguay	96	96	92	96	102
Peru	197	197	103	103	104
Uruguay	94	94	85	89	96
Venezuela	234	233	228	230	233
Geometric mean, all countries	132	132	126	129	135

*Table 9.3b Comparison of Various Types of Average Price Indexes with
Venezuela as a Base*

	Binary country weights		Latin American average weights		
	Fisher Ideal (Quantity weights)	Theil (Expenditure weights)	Walsh (Geometric expenditure weights)	Walsh (Arithmetic expenditure weights)	ECLA (Quantity weights)
Argentina	43	43	—	44	43
Bolivia	46	45	43	45	48
Brazil	42	42	43	44	44
Chile	62	62	63	63	65
Colombia	52	49	52	52	53
Costa Rica	57	56	58	59	60
Dominican Republic	75	72	71	73	80
Ecuador	46	43	45	46	48
El Salvador	64	63	60	61	67
Guatemala	75	74	72	74	75
Haiti	51	51	55	56	61
Honduras	76	75	76	78	81
Mexico	48	48	47	47	48
Nicaragua	68	66	64	66	69
Panama	67	68	67	68	68
Paraguay	41	40	40	42	44
Peru	44	43	45	45	45
Uruguay	40	40	37	39	41
Venezuela	100	100	100	100	100
Geometric mean, all countries	56	55	55	56	58

number of significantly different price indexes. To explore this question, the
five average price indexes discussed in the preceding section were computed
for the ECLA data. Table 9.3a gives the results using Argentina as a base, and
Table 9.3b using Venezuela as a base.

These tables show a considerable degree of correspondence among this
set of indexes. The Fisher Ideal Index, which is the geometric mean of the
Laspeyres and Paasche indexes, is very similar to the Theil index, which uses
expenditure rather than quantity weights. Both the Fisher Ideal and the Theil
indexes use binary country weights and, for this reason, neither produces a
single scale of relationships among countries. Thus, for example, according to
Table 9.3a the Fisher index measures prices in the Dominican Republic as 31
percent above those in Colombia, but in Table 9.3b the same Fisher index
shows the difference as 44 percent. The scale of relationships among countries
depends upon what base is used. The Theil Index has the same characteristic:
for the comparison of the Dominican Republic and Colombia cited, the Theil
index yields differences of 33 percent and 4.7 percent for the Argentine and
Venezuelan bases, respectively. In view of this lack of circularity in his index,

Theil recommends that the geometric average of all binary comparisons between two countries be computed in order to produce a single scale. The remaining three indexes, which employ average Latin American weights, yield the same relationships between pairs of countries regardless of whether the Argentine or Venezuelan base is used. The reason for this is, of course, that for any one of these three formulas, the same weights have been used for all countries. Despite this conceptual difference, the statistical difference between the binary indexes and the constant weight indexes is quite small, and as Fisher noted 45 years ago there seems little basis for choosing among them.

9. PRICE INDEXES FOR MAJOR CATEGORIES OF EXPENDITURE

If, as has been suggested, the differences in the price index numbers for different countries arise from the systematic substitution of lower-priced goods for higher-priced goods in the same expenditure category, any breakdown of the total index into component groups should reveal the same sort of differences as have already been observed for the totals. Table 9.4 examines this question for Argentina and Venezuela, with respect to the Laspeyres, Paasche and

Table 9.4 Comparison of Laspeyres, Paasche and Palgrave Price Indexes for Major Categories of Expenditure (total for all Latin American countries = 100)

	Laspeyres	Paasche	Palgrave	Laspeyres as percent of Paasche	Laspeyres as percent of Palgrave
Argentina					
Total*	62	92	64	67	97
Food	50	79	56	63	89
Clothing and textiles	80	96	79	83	101
Rent	116	116	108	100	107
Other: Durables	69	98	72	70	96
Nondurables	62	84	58	74	107
Services	78	100	60	78	130
Venezuela					
Total*	154	209	151	74	102
Food	154	203	161	76	196
Clothing and textiles	149	168	146	89	102
Rent	227	227	217	100	105
Other: Durables	86	138	97	62	89
Nondurables	158	220	147	72	107
Services	159	250	131	64	121

*Reciprocals of geometric mean lines, Tables 9.1 and 9.2.

*Table 9.5 Comparison of Various Types of Average Price Indexes for
Major Categories of Expenditure (total for all Latin American
countries = 100)*

	Binary country weights		Latin American average weights		
	Fisher Ideal (Quantity weights)	Theil (Expenditure weights)	Walsh (Geometric expenditure weights	Walsh (Arithmetic expenditure weights)	ECLA (Quantity weights)
Argentina					
Total*	75	76	80	78	74
Food	63	62	67	65	62
Clothing and textiles	88	87	88	88	88
Rent	116	116	116	116	116
Other: Durables	82	83	84	84	76
Nondurables	72	73	73	72	70
Services	88	86	83	83	80
Venezuela					
Total*	180	182	181	178	172
Food	177	178	177	174	167
Clothing and textiles	158	158	158	158	154
Rent	227	227	229	229	227
Other: Durables	109	105	113	114	114
Nondurables	186	183	188	183	185
Services	200	206	196	196	197

*Reciprocals of geometric mean lines, Tables 9.3a and 9.3b.

Palgrave indexes. In this table, instead of comparing Argentina and Venezuela with each of the other Latin American countries, they are each compared to the other Latin American countries as a group. The price index for all Latin American countries as a group is considered to be 100, and the Argentine price index is expressed as a percentage of this average. Thus, in Table 9.4, the figures shown in the total line are the reciprocals of the mean figures shown in the geometric mean lines of Tables 9.1 and 9.2, where Argentina and Venezuela, respectively, were set equal to 100. As was expected, the differences between the Laspeyres and Paasche indexes are, with the exception of rent, as substantial for major categories as they are for the total. In the case of rent, ECLA had assumed identical quantity weights for all countries because of the difficulty of measuring the quantity of housing. Similarly, the Laspeyres and Palgrave indexes show that different elasticities were important for different groups of commodities. Since the figures in Table 9.4 are the reciprocals of those in Tables 9.1 and 9.2, the relationships of the Laspeyres index to the Paasche and Palgrave indexes are, of course, also inverted.

Table 9.5 shows the same computations for the five types of averaged price indexes. The indexes for major categories again show a remarkable consistency with each other, and thus they all reveal approximately the same information about the relative price structures.

10. COMPARISON OF INDEX NUMBER FORMULAS FOR SPECIFIC COUNTRIES

The results presented so far have all pertained to computations using Argentina and Venezuela as bases. Similar computations were made for all 19 countries. Table 9.6 gives a summary of the results for the Laspeyres, Paasche and Palgrave indexes. The figures in this table represent the geometric mean of the values for each country in relation to all other countries; thus they show the relationship of each individual country to all other Latin American countries. For Argentina and Venezuela, the figures in Table 9.6 are equal to the total lines shown in Table 9.4.

Since in the comparison of each country with all other countries the geometric mean of all other countries is set equal to 100, one might expect that the

Table 9.6 Laspeyres, Paasche, and Palgrave Price Indexes Average Values for Specific Countries

	Laspeyres	Paasche	Palgrave	Laspeyres as percent of Paasche	Laspeyres as percent of Palgrave
Argentina	62	92	64	67	97
Bolivia	71	99	65	72	109
Brazil	65	94	63	69	103
Chile	82	139	92	59	89
Colombia	82	110	77	75	106
Costa Rica	88	122	87	72	101
Dominican Republic	108	160	109	68	99
Ecuador	70	98	68	71	103
El Salvador	99	133	91	74	109
Guatemala	117	153	113	76	104
Haiti	73	123	79	59	92
Honduras	115	165	116	70	99
Mexico	71	99	73	72	97
Nicaragua	101	139	99	73	102
Panama	102	141	105	72	97
Paraguay	59	90	62	66	95
Peru	70	94	67	74	104
Uruguay	57	87	56	66	102
Venezuela	154	209	151	74	102
Geometric average, all countries	84	120	83	70	99

geometric mean for all such comparisons (the summary line at the bottom of Table 9.6) would also come out to 100 for each type of index. However, this is not the case because of what Fisher called index number bias. When multiplied together, the geometric means for the Laspeyres and Paasche indexes do equal 100, but individually these means do not equal 100, nor does the Palgrave index. From this table, it can be seen that the differences between the Paasche and Laspeyres indexes for some countries are even larger than that for Argentina. Thus, for both Chile and Haiti, the Laspeyres index was only 59 percent of the Paasche index. For all countries together, the Laspeyres index averaged 70 percent of the Paasche index, whereas the Palgrave index almost coincided with the Laspeyres.

Table 9.7 provides a similar comparison among the five types of average price indexes. As in Table 9.6, the price indexes are given for each Latin American country relative to the average of all Latin American countries, the latter equaling 100. The price indexes for Argentina and Venezuela are the

Table 9.7 Various Types of Average Price Indexes: Values for Specific Countries

	Price indexes using binary country weights		Price indexes using Latin American average weights		
	Fisher Ideal (Quantity weights)	Theil (Expenditure weights)	Walsh (Geometric expenditure weights)	Walsh (Arithmetic expenditure weights)	ECLA (Quantity weights)
Argentina	75	76	80	78	74
Bolivia	84	83	79	81	83
Brazil	78	81	79	78	76
Chile	107	108	115	113	112
Colombia	95	94	93	92	91
Costa Rica	104	104	106	105	103
Dominican Republic	132	130	128	131	137
Ecuador	82	81	81	81	83
El Salvador	115	113	108	109	116
Guatemala	134	133	131	131	128
Haiti	94	96	99	100	106
Honduras	138	138	138	139	140
Mexico	84	84	85	85	82
Nicaragua	119	119	117	117	119
Panama	120	120	122	121	117
Paraguay	73	72	73	74	76
Peru	81	81	82	80	77
Uruguay	70	69	68	69	71
Venezuela	180	182	181	178	172
Geometric mean, all countries	100	100	100	100	100

same as those shown as the total line in Table 9.5. In Table 9.7, the Fisher Ideal and the Theil indexes are single scaled, since here a geometric average of the original binary comparisons of the kind shown in Tables 9.3a and 9.3b has been computed. The geometric mean of all countries for each of the price indexes in Table 9.7 is 100, indicating that all of these indexes are single scaled and meet the circularity test. The agreement among all the indexes is quite close. They diverge most for Chile and Haiti, but the differences are small relative to the large spread between the Paasche and Laspeyres indexes. It is interesting to observe that the use of ECLA quantity weights does not produce results very different from those obtained with the other forms of averaging.

11. SUMMARY AND CONCLUSIONS

The concept of a price index as a measure of the level of prices no longer has significant support among economists. Although there are those who still hold to some formulation of the quantity theory of money, it is generally recognized that relative price changes are continually taking place in the system, and that there can be no single acceptable definition of the price level of the economy as a whole. Such a rejection of the price level concept argues against the Fisherian concept of a price index as a summary statistical measure reflecting the center of gravity of widely dispersed price movements. Present income and employment theory does not look upon price behavior as a stochastic process, but rather as systematic behavior conditioned by the changing structure of the economy. General price indexes made up of a variety of price observations are no longer considered meaningful. For example, the Price Statistics Review Committee (1961) criticized the United States Wholesale Price Index for its lack of economic content.

The theoretical basis of the measurement of real income has fared little better than has the concept of the price level. It has come to be recognized that economic welfare does not depend solely upon the level of real national income or real gross national product. Even if it is assumed that welfare is measurable, such factors as the distribution of income, the major divergences between private and social product, changes in taste, and the role of public consumption, all are important for welfare comparisons. It is difficult to find any single aggregate measure which can be supported as an adequate indicator of economic welfare.

Despite this disillusionment with the concepts of price level and economic welfare, the use of price indexes flourishes. To an increasing extent, economists are focusing their attention upon the rates of growth of economies and the role of investment and technology in this growth. Real output measures are constructed in order to develop measures of productivity. Various techniques are employed to measure real gross national product. For some goods and services, physical measures of output change are used; for others, price indexes are used to deflate current value data. The end result is a real product measure. This can then be divided into the current value figures to yield implicit price indexes for each expenditure component of the gross national product. The many problems raised by index number theory in the past have not been solved; they have merely been buried.

There are, in fact, even more serious problems inherent in the measurement of price and output than those already raised in the formal discussion of index number theory. The validity of price and quantity indexes is seriously affected by technological change over time. As the Price Statistics Review Committee (1961) pointed out, in actual practice this problem is generally handled by assuming that there is no quality change over the time-period in question. Such an assumption is, of course, not valid. Technological change results in continuous product improvement, which is not measured as output. For example, Griliches (1961) found by regression analysis that changes in the characteristics of automobiles between 1954 and 1960 were such that if taken into account at their 1954 valuation (Laspeyres), the prices of automobiles could be said to have fallen by 27 percent. If the characteristics of automobiles were priced at their 1960 values (Paasche), the resulting price index would have shown a decline of only 1 percent. Over this period, the official Consumer Price Index for automobiles rose 11 percent. Although this use of a regression analysis of quality change demonstrates the importance of the problem, unfortunately it cannot be applied as a general solution. Much of the quality change comes about as change over time in what is available, with little or no price difference for products of different characteristics at a given point in time. Thus improved alloys, better plastics, new fabric finishes, better electronic components, and the like are often put into use without observable price differences between the old technology and the new technology. In some instances, the new technology may result in lower costs, so that the improved products may sell more cheaply than products produced by the old technology. Even more serious is the introduction of completely new goods and services as substitutes for old. The past 50 years has seen an untold number of these totally new factors enter into our economic life. Such things as air travel, telephones, television and medical discoveries have resulted in a whole new range of products. The fact that these are introduced gradually over a long period of time does not detract from their importance. If, in the long run, such factors are important for measuring changes in prices and output, they are also equally important for measuring the trend of prices and the rate of output growth in the short run.

Partly because it is recognized that technological change and changes in tastes do occur and do affect the validity of price measurements, economists paradoxically have become less sensitive to the price index number problem itself. Generally, for comparisons over short periods of time, the Laspeyres and Paasche price indexes (and almost any other index number formula which might be used) give approximately the same result. The statistical differences among the various index numbers are believed to be inconsequential when compared with the other recognized inadequacies of measurement.

Price index comparisons over space have fared little better. In seeking to compare price levels, much the same problem confronts the economist making comparisons over space as over time. If there is no valid concept of the price level, a price index purporting to measure it will not have much significance. Although international trade theory might suggest that the price levels of two countries would be brought into balance through the operation of international trade and an equilibrium exchange rate, many goods and services do not enter into international trade, and there are factors other than trade which affect the balance of payments and exchange rate.

The use of price indexes to make real income comparisons between countries has also encountered considerable difficulty. All of the restrictions relating to real income comparisons over time apply, and in addition the cultural and institutional differences among countries are likely to be much more severe than those encountered over relatively brief time spans. As a result, few economists take seriously the real per capita income estimates which result from converting national income data to a common currency.

Despite these difficulties, there is considerable pressure for the construction and use of international price indexes. To an increasing extent, economists are appreciating the fact that differences in the price structure of different countries significantly affect the operation and behavior of the economies. Thus, for example, Braithwaite (1967) has recently reported that although Argentina, according to her own national accounts statistics expressed in domestic values, is devoting 23 percent of her total resources each year to capital formation, and thus has a high level of domestic savings, the same figures viewed in terms of the price structure of the United States suggest that only 11 percent of Argentina's total resources are being devoted to capital formation. In this case the difference results from the relatively high price of Argentine investment goods (due to a policy of protection of domestic industry) and the relatively low price of food and services, whereas in the United States producers' durables are relatively low priced and food and services relatively high priced.

In making international price comparisons, there is the same problem of quality as is present in the measurements of price changes over time. Recently Kravis and Lipsey (1967) have employed the regression technique to measure quality differences between countries, but again this technique is applicable only to a relatively small range of products, and cannot deal with the problem of the introduction of new products.

In view of the similarities of the problems relating to price indexes over time and space, it might appear that one would arrive at the same conclusion for space comparisons as for time comparisons with respect to the choice among index number formulas: since the Laspeyres and Paasche indexes yield approximately the same results and since weights are more generally available for the Laspeyres index, the Laspeyres index is quite appropriate and convenient for short-period comparisons. For international price comparisons, however, it has been shown that the Laspeyres and Paasche price indexes produce very different results. The price structures in different countries generally differ substantially from one another, whereas the price structure for any one economy generally changes slowly over a period of time. It is difficult to see any theoretical solution to the problem of resolving these observed differences between the Laspeyres and Paasche indexes, since they are due to real structural differences. In Argentina, the climate and other agricultural conditions favor the raising of cattle, and as a result beef prices are very low and beef consumption very high. In the Dominican Republic, chickens are more plentiful, and chickens are relatively low in price compared to beef. Panama consumes bananas, but Chile consumes apples. The differences between the Laspeyres and Paasche indexes reflect this kind of substitutability at the most detailed product level, rather than gross substitution between major categories of consumption. Some reduction in the range of price differences might be achieved by specifying certain equivalences — potato and rice, wheat and corn and so on — but this approach has not yet been pursued on a systematic basis to obtain more relevant price comparisons.

One way out of the dilemma, of course, is to take an arbitrary average between the Laspeyres and Paasche indexes. This is Fisher's solution to this problem, and Theil also has followed such a procedure. However, neither the Fisher index nor the Theil index meets the circularity test and, therefore, they do not provide a measurement which is single scaled when more than two countries are considered. The lack of a single scale impairs the general usefulness of the indexes for international comparison. Although it is possible by taking the geometric mean of the relevant sets of binary comparisons to generate a single-scale measure based on either the Fisher or Theil indexes, such a procedure is somewhat inefficient, since the computation of the binary indexes requires a substantial amount of detailed weighting information, but the resulting differences in the binary indexes are then suppressed by consolidating them into a geometric mean.

The use of average quantity weights for a group of countries as computed by ECLA is considerably more direct and requires less information. If the number of countries is substantial, the average weights for all countries taken together will be rather stable: therefore, if information on a particular commodity is lacking for any one country, the weighting will not be significantly affected. In contrast, as Theil points out, in both the Fisher and Theil indexes a missing weight for any one country will make it impossible to arrive at any single-scaled answer whatsoever. Some of the binary comparisons can, of course, be made but the full set of binary comparisons is required to compute the geometric mean.

There are, however, a number of other difficulties associated with the use of quantity weights. If every commodity consumed by any consumer were included in the price index, the use of quantity weights would be valid. In actual practice, however, it is of course not feasible to include the thousands or tens of thousands of items this would require. The commodities included in a price index represent composite commodities, and, correspondingly, the quantities assigned as weights must represent composite quantities. But quantity weights conceived in this manner do not have their original meaning; in fact, they must be derived through the use of expenditure figures by taking the price of the commodity representing the composite group and dividing it into the total expenditure for all commodities in the composite group to obtain a pseudo-quantity weight. It has long been recognized, of course, that quantities have little or no meaning when groups of commodities are added together. As Leontief (1936) some 30 years ago pointed out, 'the theoretical problem of lumping together several commodities is essentially the same whether the number is 5,000, 50, or only 2'. Because of this, it seems inherently more reasonable to use a formula which employs expenditure shares directly as weights. The Walsh formulation of the price index does this by averaging expenditure shares for all countries and constructing the price index on a geometric basis so that it is single scaled for all countries being compared. The use of price relatives with expenditure weights also facilitates the derivation of optimal sets of commodities for international comparisons by permitting simple weight reallocation through the use of regression analysis, as Nancy Ruggles (1968) has found.

In summary, there is currently no general theoretical or statistical basis for the development of a price index for measurements over time and space. In practical terms, furthermore, the problems of technological, cultural, and institutional differences pose such major difficulties in measurement and interpretation that minor differences among various index formulas are relatively inconsequential. But for international price comparisons, the Laspeyres and Paasche price indexes present such wide differences that for many purposes some form of averaging device must be employed. Although Fisher rejected the circularity test, a single scale does seem to be desirable when a number of different countries are being compared. A system based upon averaging weights therefore seems more reasonable than one depending upon purely binary comparisons. A formulation which weights price relatives by expenditure shares seems somewhat more flexible than one which uses an international market basket approach, applying artificially constructed quantity weights to price observations.

REFERENCES

Allen, R.G.D. (1933), 'On the marginal utility of money and its application', *Economica*, **40**.

———— (1935), 'Some observations on the theory and practice of price index numbers', *Review of Economic Studies*, 57–66.

———— (1949), 'The economic theory of index numbers', *Economica*, n.s., **41** (63), 197–203.

Beckerman, Wilfred (1966), *International Comparisons of Real Incomes, Development Centre Studies*, Paris: Organization for Economic Cooperation and Development.

Bornstein, Morris (1959), 'A Comparison of Soviet and United States national product', US Congress, Joint Economic Committee, in *Comparisons of the United States and Soviet Economies*, Washington, DC, Part II.

Bowley, A. L. (1899), in R. H. Palgrave (ed.), *Dictionary of Political Economy*, Vol. III, London, p. 641.

———— (1923), 'Review of "The making of index numbers"', *Economic Journal*, **33**, 90–94.

Braithwaite, Stanley N. (1967), 'Comparison of Latin American real incomes', paper presented to the Tenth General Conference of the International Association for Research in Income and Wealth, Maynooth, Ireland, August.

Clark, Colin (1951), *The Conditions of Economic Progress*, 2nd edition, London: Macmillan.

Drobisch, M.W. (1871), 'Über Mittelgrossen und die Anwendbarkeit derselben auf die Berechnung des Steigens und Sinkens des Geldwerths', Berichte über die Verhandlungen der Königlich sachsischen Gesellschaft der Wissenschaften zu Leipzig; Mathematisch-physische Classe, Band XXIII, pp. 25–48.

Economic Commission for Latin America (1963), *A Measurement of Price Levels and the Purchasing Power of Currencies in Latin America, 1960–62*, E/CN 12/653, March.

Economic Research Institute, Economic Planning Agency of the Japanese Government (1963), *Analysis of Price Comparisons in Japan and the United States*, Economic Bulletin No. 13, Tokyo, September.

Edgeworth, F.Y. (1883), 'On the method of ascertaining a change in the value of gold', *Journal of the Statistical Society of London*, **46**, 714–18.

———— (1896), 'A defence of index numbers', *Economic Journal*, 132–42.

European Coal and Steel Community, High Authority (1955), *Informations Statistiques*, **2** (5), Luxembourg.

Fisher, Irving (1892), 'Mathematical investigations in the theory of value and prices', *Transactions of the Connecticut Academy of Arts and Sciences*.

———— (1911), *The Purchasing Power of Money*, New York: Macmillan Company.

———— (1922), *The Making of Index Numbers*, Boston, MA: Houghton Mifflin.

———— (1923a), 'Professor Young on index numbers', *Quarterly Journal of Economics*, **37**, 742–55.

———— (1923b), 'Professor Bowley on index numbers', *Economic Journal*, **33**, 246–51 (March).

———— (1924), 'Mr Udny Yule on Index numbers', *Journal of the Royal Statistical Society*, **87**, 89–98.

Fleetwood, W. (1707), *Chronicon Preciosum*, London.

Frisch, Ragnar (1936), 'Annual survey of general economic theory: The problem of index numbers', *Econometrica*, **4** (1), 1–39.

Gilbert, Milton and Associates (1958), *Comparative National Products and Price Levels*, Paris: Organization for European Economic Cooperation.

Gilbert, Milton and Irving Kravis (1954), *An International Comparison of National Products and the Purchasing Power of Currencies*, Paris: Organization for European Economic Cooperation.

Griliches, Zvi (1961), 'Hedonic price, indexes for automobiles: An econometric analysis of quality change', Staff Paper 3 in Hearings, Subcommittee on Economic Statistics of the Joint Economic Committee, 87th Congress, First Session, Part 1, January 24, pp. 173–96.

Haberler, G. (1927), *Der Sinn der Indexzahlen*, Tübingen.

Hicks, J.R. (1940), 'The Valuation of the Social income', *Economica*, **7**, 105–24.

Hicks, J.R. and U.K. Hicks (1939), 'Public finance in the national income', *Review of Economic Studies*.

International Labour Office (1932), *A Contribution to the Study of International Comparisons of Costs of Living*, Studies and Reports, Series N, No. 17, Geneva.

_____ (1952), *Textile Wages: An International Study*, Studies and Reports, New Series No. 31, Geneva.

James, Henry (1835), *The State of the Nation*, London.

Jevons, W.S. (1884), *A Serious Fall in the Value of Cold Ascertained, and its Social Effects Set Forth,* London, pp. 15–118.

Kloek, T. and H. Theil (1965), 'International comparisons of prices and quantities consumed', *Econometrica*, **33** (3), 535–56.

Konüs, A.A. (1939), 'The problem of the true index of the cost of living', *Econometrica*, **7** (1), 10–29.

Kravis, Irving B. and Robert E. Lipsey (1967), 'The use of regression methods in international price comparisons' (mimeographed, May).

Kuznets, Simon (1948), 'On the valuation of social income — Reflections on Professor Hicks' article', *Economica*, n.s., **15** (57), 1–16.

Laspeyres, E. (1864), 'Hamburger Waarenprise 1850–1863 und die californisch–australischen Goldentdeckungen seit 1848', *Jahrbücher für Nationaloekonomie und Statistik*, Jena, Band III, pp. 81–118.

_____ (1871), 'Die Berechnung einer mittleran Waarenpreissteigerung', *Jahrbücher für Nationaloekonomie und Statistik*, Jena, Band XVI, pp. 296–314.

Leontief, W. (1936), 'Composite commodities and the problem of index numbers', *Econometrica*, **4** (1), 39–59.

Lerner, A.P. (1935), 'A note on the theory of price index numbers', *Review of Economic Studies*, 50–56.

Little, I.M.D. (1949), 'The valuation of the social income', *Economica*, **16** (61), 11–26.

Lowe, Joseph (1822), *The Present State of England in Regard to Agriculture, Trade and Finance*, London.

Newmarch, W. (1884), 'Commercial History and review of 1863', Supplement to *The Economist*, February 20.

Nordisk Statistisk Skriftserie No. 1 (1954), *Levnadskostnader och Reallöner i de Nordiska lluvudstäderna*, Stockholm.

Paasche, H. (1874), 'Über die Preisentwicklung der letzten Jahre, nach den Hamburger Börsennotierungen', *Jahrbücher für Nationaloekonomie und Statistik*, Jena, Band XXIII, pp. 168–78.

Paige, Deborah and Gottfried Bombach (1959), *A Comparison of National Output and Productivity of the United States and the United Kingdom*, Paris: OEEC.

Palgrave, R.H. Inglis (1886), 'Currency and standard of value in England, France and India, and the rates of exchange between these countries', Memorandum laid before the Royal Commission on Depression of Trade and Industry, Third Report, Appendix B, folio, pp. 213–390.

Porter, G.R. (1838), *The Progress of the Nation, in its Various Social and Economical Relations, from the Beginning of the Nineteenth Century*, London.

Pigou, A.C. (1920), *The Economics of Welfare*, London: Macmillan.

Price Statistics Review Committee (1961), in *Government Price Statistics*, Hearings, Subcommittee on Economic Statistics of the Joint Economic Committee, 87th Congress, First session, Part 1, January 24, pp. 5–99.

Ruggles, Nancy (1968), 'Redundancy in price indexes for international comparisons: a stepwise regression analysis', unpublished.

Samuelson, Paul (1950), 'Evaluation of real national income', *Oxford Economic Papers*, n.s., **2** (1), 1–29.

Schultz, Henry (1939), 'A misunderstanding in index-number theory: The true Konüs condition on cost-of-living index numbers and its limitations', *Econometrica*, **7** (1), 1–9 (January).

Scitovsky, T. de (1941), 'A Note on Welfare Propositions in Economics', *Review of Economic Studies*, **9** (1), 77–88.

Scrope, Poulett (1833), *Principles of Political Economy ... Applied to the Present State of Britain*, London.

Sidgwick, H. (1883), 'On the definition and measure of value', Ch. II in *Principles of Political Economy*, London.

Staehle, Hans (1935), 'A Development of the economic theory of price index numbers', *Review of Economic Studies*, 163–88.

_____ (1937), 'A general method for the comparison of the price of living', *Review of Economic Studies*, 205–214.

Statistisches Bundesamt, Weisbaden (1965), *Preise, Löhne, Wirtschafts-rechnungen: Preise für die Lebenshaltung*.

Theil, Henri (1965), 'The information approach to demand analysis', *Econometrica*, **33** (1), 67–87.

_____ (1967), *Economics and Information Theory*, Amsterdam: North-Holland Publishing Co.

Unilever Inquiry (1930), Summarized in *The Economist*, London (November).

United Nations (1954), *Retail Price Comparisons for International Salary Determination*, Statistical Papers, Series M, No. 14.

_____ (1966), *Yearbook of National Accounts Statistics, 1965*, New York.

Walras, L. (1889), *Eléments d'économie politique pure*, 2nd edition, Lausanne, pp. 431–32, 457–68.

Walsh, Correa M. (1901), *The Measurement of General Exchange-Value*, New York: Macmillan Company.

Young, Allyn (1923), 'Fisher's "The making of index numbers"', *Quarterly Journal of Economics*, **37**, 342–64.

Young, Arthur (1812), *An Enquiry into the Progressive Value of Money in England as Marked by the Price of Agricultural Product*, London.

Yule, U. (1923), 'Review of "The making of index numbers"', *Journal of the Royal Statistical Society*, **86**.

10. The Wholesale Price Index: Review and Evaluation

Richard Ruggles
Yale University and The National Bureau of Economic Research

---

1. INTRODUCTION

This report on the Wholesale Price Index was undertaken by the National Bureau of Economic Research with the support of the Council on Wage and Price Stability. The purpose of the project was to provide a general evaluation of the Wholesale Price Index in terms of its appropriateness and adequacy for the uses to which it is being put both within the federal government and by private users outside the federal government. It is hoped that such an evaluation will be useful in assisting the Bureau of Labor Statistics with their anticipated review and revision of the index.

The study is divided into four sections. Section 2 evaluates the scope and coverage of the present Wholesale Price Index in terms of its coverage of the categories of the Standard Industrial Classification system and its suitability for and usefulness to governmental and private users. Section 3, the classification and weighting systems of the Wholesale Price Index, focuses on the relation of the Wholesale Price Index to other price indexes and the methods which are used to combine the price observations into price indexes. Section 4 is concerned with problems of sampling as they relate to the collection of wholesale price data and as they affect the reliability of the price indexes. Finally, Section 5 considers the validity of wholesale price measurements and their consistency with other price information. Section 6 contains the summary and conclusions.

In this review and evaluation of the Wholesale Price Index, the major focus is on the basic price observations collected by the Bureau of Labor Statistics and how they are combined to produce the Wholesale Price Index. The BLS

This chapter first appeared as a Report for The Council of Wage and Price Stability, June 1977.

has been extremely cooperative in providing access to the raw data so that appropriate analyses could be undertaken. Other agencies which are involved in using wholesale price indexes have also cooperated by providing data tapes or tabulations which were directly relevant to the problem of analyzing the Wholesale Price Index.

No attempt was made within this project to cover the general literature on price indexes or on the evaluation of price measurements. The large body of such material would have involved a much more extended research project and would have diverted efforts away from the analysis of the basic wholesale price data.

An advisory committee composed of those persons who are currently involved in research projects related to prices and price indexes at the National Bureau of Economic Research was established to provide guidance and a critical review of the project. The members of this committee are as follows: Philip Cagan (Columbia University and NBER), Murray Foss (NBER), Robert J. Gordon (Northwestern University), Avram Kisselgoff (NBER), Irving Kravis (University of Pennsylvania), Robert Lipsey (Queens College and NBER), Geoffrey Moore (NBER), Milton Moss (NBER), M.I. Nadiri (New York University and NBER), Joel Popkin (NBER) and Irving Rottenberg (NBER).

The research on wholesale price data was carried out at the National Bureau of Economic Research with the assistance of Charlotte Boschan, Orin Hansen, John LeMonnier, Matthew Berman, Sidney Rothstein and Bruce Spencer. This manuscript has not been submitted to the Board of Directors of the National Bureau of Economic Research for critical review. The final text and the conclusions of this review and evaluation remain, therefore, the sole responsibility of the author.

2. SCOPE, USE AND CHARACTERISTICS OF THE WHOLESALE PRICE INDEX

The Wholesale Price Index is one of the oldest statistical series published by the federal government. It was authorized in 1891 by the Senate Committee on Finance for the purpose of investigating the effect of the tariff laws on trade, domestic production and prices. It was first published in 1902 covering the years 1890–1901 (Department of Labor, 1902). Initially, it was an unweighted average of price relatives, covering approximately 200 commodities.

Although the interest in establishing a Wholesale Price Index originated in the relation of international trade to the domestic economy, the prevailing climate of economic theory was such that the goal sought was, in fact, a single number for the value of money: a measure of prices in general. Neither the selection nor the weighting of commodities was considered important, since it was thought that even a random sample of unweighted items would adequately reveal the central tendency of price changes.

Since those early days, the Wholesale Price Index has continued to evolve. By World War I, a weighting system had been introduced and the Wholesale Price Index was calculated by building up aggregates of values based on fixed quantity weights. By 1940, the number of commodities had expanded to approximately 900 and the Index was based on 2,000 individual price quotations. Currently, the Index covers about 2,700 commodities and is based on more than 9,000 observations. Nevertheless, although the number of series and observations in the Wholesale Price Index has been expanded, conceptually it still is remarkably similar to what it was 60 years ago. The major reorientation of the Index, urged by the Price Statistics Review Committee in 1961, never took place, and the Index has continued to evolve along the lines which had previously been established.

Scope of the Wholesale Price Data

One of the first things an investigator learns about the Wholesale Price Index is that it is not based on the prices of wholesalers. Wholesalers, in general, protest the name of the Index, maintaining that it leads to a false impression of their prices. Rather, wholesale price data are collected primarily from producers in mining and manufacturing, with some agricultural price data being provided by the Department of Agriculture. To the extent that the scope of the data has broadened since its inception, it has resulted in more complete coverage of these particular industries, not in coverage of other industries.

It is, of course, not possible to price directly all of the commodities produced in the United States. There are literally millions of commodities and if further dimensions such as region, class of customer, etc., were to be taken into account, it would almost be necessary to obtain a price for every transaction in order to cover all commodities. Any product or commodity which is selected, therefore, serves to represent a much larger set of commodities. Whether it is adequate for this purpose depends on whether its price behavior is similar to the price behavior of the other commodities it represents.

A mere count of the actual commodities priced in relation to the total number of commodities is not really meaningful, since as already indicated the commodity space can be classified into almost as many commodities as there are transactions in the economy. Especially in the manufacturing industries, the products of each establishment differ from those of every other establishment in some degree, and even for a single establishment, products which appear to be similar may differ when sold to different classes of customers. In brief, any specification of the commodity universe in terms of a highly detailed level of commodity classification would be arbitrary and not particularly useful for analyzing the scope and coverage of wholesale price data.

It is reasonable, however, to consider what classes of products are represented by wholesale price data, and what the relative importance of these classes is. In order to determine this, it is helpful to recode the wholesale price commodities into the Standard Industrial Classification (SIC) system which encompasses all areas of economic activity. One source of data where this transformation has been made, which provides considerable insight into the coverage of the Wholesale Price Index, is the data base constructed by the Bureau of the Census for calculating indexes of production in mining and manufacturing.

The extent to which the wholesale price data collected by the Bureau of Labor Statistics are representative of 5-digit SIC product classes is shown in Table 10.1. Since the 1972 Census, Production Index covers the period from 1967 to 1972, a product must have been priced both in 1967 and 1972 in order to serve as a price deflator for the Census of Production value of shipments data. In Table 10.1, the 5-digit product classes and their value of shipments are classified into the 2-digit SIC major industries. The coverage of wholesale price data is measured in two ways: by the percentage of the 5-digit product classes in a given 2-digit major industry that are represented by one or more commodities which are 'directly' priced by the BLS; and by the shipments of these 5-digit product classes as a percentage of the total shipments of all product classes within each 2-digit major SIC industry. The term 'directly priced' is used by the Bureau of Labor Statistics to refer to those SIC products for which there is a directly corresponding WPI commodity which is priced. As can be seen, in terms of numbers, somewhat under half of the product classes were represented, and slightly over half in terms of value.

Some industries such as tobacco were very well covered, while others such as nonmetallic minerals, printing and publishing, petroleum and coal products, and instruments were rather lightly represented. This table does not reflect the recent interest in energy and fuel prices, which are now covered very well by wholesale price data, but were not in 1967. It should be emphasized that this measure of coverage says little about how well any given product class is covered. Direct pricing of one or two commodities within a price class may not constitute sufficient coverage to provide a meaningful and valid price index.

A somewhat different measure of coverage can be obtained by examining the weight diagram which the Bureau of Labor Statistics uses to create the Wholesale Price Index. An analysis of this body of data is shown in Table 10.2. As in Table 10.1, all 5-digit SIC product classes are classified into the 2-digit SIC major industries both in terms of number of classes (col. 1) and in terms of the value of shipments (col. 2). In this case, agriculture, forestry and

Table 10.1 Representation of Wholesale Price Data within 5-digit SIC
Product Classes of the 1972 Census of Production ($bn)

SIC code and title	Total number of product classes		Percent of product classes represented by one or more WPD[a]	
	Number	Value	Number	Value
10 Metal mining	25	3	4	_[b]
11 Anthracite mining	4	_[b]	0	0
12 Bituminous coal and lignite	3	5	0	0
13 Oil and gas extraction	9	24	11	46
14 Nonmetallic minerals, exc. fuels	53	4	2	7
20 Food and kindred products	164	106	68	80
21 Tobacco manufactures	6	5	83	100
22 Textile mill products	103	27	37	49
23 Apparel and other textile products	88	28	44	57
24 Lumber and wood products	59	23	32	26
25 Furniture and fixtures	48	11	47	67
26 Paper and allied products	59	27	59	79
27 Printing and publishing	74	29	0	0
28 Chemicals and allied products	120	53	39	47
29 Petroleum and coal products	17	27	18	8
30 Rubber and plastic products	34	20	59	44
31 Leather and leather products	22	5	46	78
32 Stone, clay and glass products	62	20	45	70
33 Primary metal industries	99	51	60	76
34 Fabricated metal products	119	50	58	57
35 Machinery, exc. electrical	180	61	58	60
36 Electrical equipment and supplies	117	50	64	65
37 Transportation equipment	65	92	17	48
38 Instruments and related products	48	14	15	20
39 Miscellaneous manufactures	57	11	49	59
Total	1,630	746	45	55

Notes
a. Less than $0.5 billion or 0.5 percent.
b. Wholesale price data.

Source: Computed from data tape on 1972 Census of Production, Bureau of the Census.

fishing are shown, in addition to mining and manufacturing industries. Owing to the difference in data sources, the number and value of shipments of 5-digit product classes within the 2-digit SIC industries differ in detail from Table 10.1 to Table 10.2 they are quite similar in general magnitude.

The percentage of the 5-digit SIC product classes in each 2-digit major industry which were directly priced by the Bureau of Labor Statistics in 1976 is shown in column 3, and the percentage importance of the value of shipments of these industries is shown in column 4. In about 47 percent of the 5-digit product classes, there is at least one commodity which is directly priced.

Table 10.2 Five-Digit SIC Product Classes Directly Priced and Price Indexes Published by the Bureau of Labor Statistics ($bn)

SIC code and title	Total product classes		Percent directly priced in WPI		Percent pub-lished by BLS	
	No. (1)	Value (2)	No. (3)	Value (4)	No. (5)	Value (6)
01 Agriculture and crops	20	28	80	91	–	–
02 Agriculture and livestock	12	37	58	99	–	–
08 Forestry	2	1	50	43	–	–
09 Fishing	3	2	33	51	–	–
10 Metal mining	32	4	6	22	6	22
11 Anthracite mining	4	1	25	65	0	0
12 Bituminous coal and lignite	3	5	33	99	33	99
13 Oil and gas extraction	9	26	56	77	33	57
14 Nonmetallic minerals exc. fuels	62	4	11	50	3	18
20 Food and kindred products	169	111	59	85	40	63
21 Tobacco manufactures	6	6	50	76	50	76
22 Textile mill products	111	29	45	71	27	55
23 Apparel and other textile products	89	29	38	60	17	30
24 Lumber and wood products	63	25	37	56	29	51
25 Furniture and wood products	43	11	37	60	30	55
26 Paper and allied products	60	29	53	83	37	69
27 Printing and publishing	75	30	3	5	0	0
28 Chemicals and allied products	123	55	50	78	30	59
29 Petroleum and coal products	17	30	77	97	18	6
30 Rubber and plastic products	34	21	71	63	47	48
31 Leather and leather products	30	7	67	83	37	55
32 Stone, clay and glass products	63	21	56	77	40	64
33 Primary metals industries	107	60	61	88	47	77
34 Fabricated metal products	127	51	54	72	27	45
35 Machinery exc. electrical	190	64	60	62	36	33
36 Electrical equip. and supplies	117	54	62	60	33	36
37 Transportation equipment	71	103	18	68	7	38
38 Instruments and related products	48	16	29	44	6	8
39 Miscellaneous manufactures	60	13	47	57	22	28
Total	1,763	871	47	73	27	42

Source: Bureau of Labor Statistics, *WPI Weight Diagram for 1972* and *Wholesale Prices and Price Indexes*, data for January 1976.

These product classes with at least one directly priced commodity constitute approximately 73 percent of the total value of shipments. Again, it should be emphasized that direct pricing of a single 7-digit product within a given 5-digit product class does not mean that a 5-digit product class is well represented; it only means that it is represented. Conversely, the omission of product representation for a 5-digit product class may not be serious if, in fact, 'imputations' of the prices of similar products can be used satisfactorily as proxies for the price behavior of the nonrepresented products. But there is, of course, no way of knowing whether the imputations which are made for uncovered products are valid or not. In value of shipment terms, the share of 5-digit product classes for which there are wholesale price data is quite high. As already noted, the energy area received considerable attention during the oil crisis and, as a consequence, coal and lignite now have 99 percent coverage and petroleum and coal products 97 percent. Some of the primary industries are also well represented. Agriculture and livestock are both over 90 percent and primary metals 88 percent. Where the coverage is weakest is in metal mining and printing and publishing. It is apparent, both from Table 10.2 and from Table 10.1, that the range of representation of wholesale price data in mining and manufacturing is quite wide.

One measure of the adequacy of coverage of wholesale price data is the willingness of the Bureau of Labor Statistics to publish price indexes for specific 5-digit SIC product classes. The general criterion used by the Bureau of Labor Statistics is that the price index for a 5-digit SIC product class is published if 50 percent or more of its 7-digit products (by value) are 'directly priced'. Usually a single wholesale price will be accepted as sufficient 'direct pricing', but sometimes BLS is more demanding. The percentage of 5-digit SIC product classes for which price indexes are published is shown in column 5 of Table 10.2, and their relative importance in terms of value of shipments is shown in column 6. As can be seen, price indexes for only 27 percent of all 5-digit SIC product classes, accounting for 42 percent of value of shipments, are published. There is fairly high coverage in terms of value of shipments for oil and gas extraction and primary metals.

There is low coverage, amounting to one-third or less of the value of shipments, in such industries as metal mining, nonmetallic minerals except fuels, apparel and other textile products, printing and publishing, petroleum and coal products, machinery except electrical, instruments and related parts and miscellaneous manufactures. By this measure, the coverage of wholesale price data leaves much to be desired.

Uses of Wholesale Price Data

Perhaps the most common use of wholesale price data is its embodiment in the general Wholesale Price Index which, in turn, is used to monitor general price developments. Throughout its long history, the monthly release of the Wholesale Price Index has been newsworthy. Businessmen have looked upon it both as reflecting the current state of affairs and as a harbinger of things to come, and government officials have always devoted attention to explaining it. Although the Consumer Price Index is considered to be important from the point of view of the cost of living of households, it is thought to be less useful as a forward indicator than the Wholesale Price Index because it contains many items such as housing, services and durable goods which do not exhibit large month-to-month variations. The Wholesale Price Index, containing as it does prices of agricultural raw materials and primary production, is thought to reflect changes in economic activity more quickly.

The volatility of the Wholesale Price Index can, nevertheless, be misleading. Those government agencies faced with the conduct of fiscal and monetary policy, such as the Federal Reserve Board, the Council of Economic Advisers and the Treasury Department, have voiced the view that the Wholesale Price Index as presently constructed is ill suited as an indicator of what is taking place in the economy. They argue that the weighting system gives undue influence to certain kinds of prices which behave erratically and that the aggregate index is not meaningful for understanding the behavior of prices.

There is a general consensus that, although there is a need for a monthly price index in addition to the Consumer Price Index for monitoring price developments, the Wholesale Price Index fulfills this function so badly that a major effort should be made to replace it. On a longer-run basis, the implicit price deflator of the gross national product (both of which depend heavily on wholesale price data), or more recently the fixed weight price index of the gross national product, can be used. But these measures are available only with a considerable time lag and on a quarterly basis, and monthly price data available on a current basis are also needed.

A second use of wholesale price data, which in recent years has become increasingly important, is that by business for the escalation of long-term purchases and sale contracts or for direct comparison with changes in their own selling and buying prices. Although some use is made of the All Commodity Wholesale Price Index for this purpose, most users employ those components of the Index which relate to their own industry or to specific commodities. There is evidence that the substantial inflation of the early 1970s has heightened the use of indexation or escalation, so that the detailed components of the Wholesale Price Index are becoming increasingly important in the day-to-day operation of the economy. The increasing use of LIFO inventory accounting and the establishment of replacement cost accounting for equipment also requires the use of components of the Wholesale Price Index for internal pricing and for the determination of profits. The recent regulation by the Securities and Exchange Commission that corporations must provide valuations of their assets at replacement value, as well as book value, means that companies need price indexes which are suitable for making such revaluations. Insofar as the wholesale price data provide measures of changes in the prices of the required specific commodities, they are being used for these purposes, but there is a growing demand for price data which can be applied to plant and equipment categories in the same way that Bulletin F, issued by the Internal Revenue Service, has been used to determine appropriate depreciation rates.

The statistical agencies of the federal government which collect monthly information from enterprises about their sales and purchases of materials are also finding that the high rates of inflation have led to a demand for deflated data showing the change in the quantity of sales and purchases. When monthly price changes were small, changes in sales and purchases provided a good approximation of changes in production. But with the combination of considerable inflation and recession, increasing sales and purchases figures may mask a situation in which actual quantities are declining. In this context, it is quite important that the current value data be deflated by price indexes which directly relate to the industries and products in question; it is not the general Wholesale Price Index which is needed, but rather highly detailed components.

The problem of matching price data from one source with data on sales and purchases collected from other sources makes the deflation problem difficult and often misleading. An interagency committee including representatives of the Bureau of Labor Statistics, the Bureau of the Census and the Federal Reserve Board is now focusing on the problem of bringing together price data and Census shipments data to obtain indexes of production. The fact that the Bureau of Labor Statistics classification system differs from the Standard Industrial Classification used for the Censuses of Manufactures and Mining makes the establishment of correspondence difficult. Since different government agencies are involved, conflicts and inconsistencies cannot be resolved by examining the basic data; this would constitute unauthorized disclosure. Even if a common classification system were used, differences would remain in the classification of specific establishments and their products which would prevent any really meaningful integration of the price data collected by one agency with the shipments data collected by another agency.

Price data on a more comprehensive and complete basis are needed by the Bureau of Economic Analysis of the Department of Commerce for the deflation of the quarterly and annual national income accounts, for both final expenditures on gross national product and gross product originating by industry. For final expenditures, wholesale price data are used to deflate inventories, producers' durable goods, goods purchased by government and certain consumer expenditures not covered by the Consumer Price Index. For gross product originating by industry, wholesale price data are used to deflate both inputs and outputs by industry to obtain a double-deflated gross product originating. The deflation process utilizes all of the wholesale price data available except in those few instances where better price data can be obtained from other sources. As presently collected, however, the wholesale price data are not sufficiently broad or comprehensive to fully meet this need, and their adaptation to this use is often inappropriate and unsatisfactory. Nevertheless, constant price data are needed, and wholesale price data are often the only price data available. Wholesale price data are also used for longer-term analysis of output and productivity. As has already been noted, the Bureau of the Census makes considerable use of wholesale price data in constructing indexes of production over five-year census periods. These data are very important, since they provide the basic benchmarks to which annual and quarterly production data are tied. Many other agencies use the longer-run data as the basis for analyzing long-term economic growth and the trends of productivity in different sectors of the economy.

Finally, the regulatory and administrative agencies use the wholesale price data to follow price developments in specific industries or sectors of the economy. Thus, on a month-to-month basis, the Council on Wage and Price Stability examines wholesale price data to keep track of prices of specific commodities. The Anti-trust Division of the Department of Justice obtains from the Bureau of Labor Statistics a computer tape of wholesale price data at the WPI 8-digit commodity level and processes them to determine which products have had, in relative terms, the largest price increases during the past three, six and 12 months. Those products with very large price increases are then further investigated to see whether the price increase may have been due to a restriction of competition caused either by excessive industrial concentration and/or by collusive behavior of producers. Ideally, the Anti-trust Division would like to have even more detailed commodity price data available at a regional or SMSA level, since for many products such as concrete, lumber, bakery products, etc., prices may differ substantially from place to place; these price differences may arise from differences in production and transport costs or from monopolistic practices. Other government agencies such as the regulatory commissions use wholesale price data more informally, but they do use them to keep track of changes in prices in different sectors of the economy relative to prices observed for their own area of responsibility. Although the Wholesale Price Index is not ideal for all of these applications, it is a major source of data for them.

Relation of the Wholesale Price Data to Other Price Data

As has already been noted, although wholesale price data constitute a major source of price data, they are not the only source. Consumer price data are collected for the Consumer Price Index. Construction prices are used in developing the Housing Price Index. Export and import prices are collected for Export and Import Price Indexes. The Department of Agriculture collects a considerable amount of price data relating to the agricultural sector in addition to what it provides for the Wholesale Price Index. Price data in specific areas are collected by the regulatory and administrative agencies.

For any given commodity, the consumer price data are quite different from wholesale price data in that they are collected at the level of the retail outlet, in contrast with the wholesale price data which are collected at the level of 'the first significant commercial transaction'. Conceptually, the difference between these prices reflects the transport and trade margins between the producer and the final purchaser. Many of the commodities in the wholesale price data, furthermore, are intermediate products which are not purchased by consumers but rather are inputs into the production processes of other producers. Nevertheless, it is generally believed that price changes at the producer level will subsequently be translated into price changes at the retail level and therefore that wholesale price data are predictors of the future behavior of consumer prices. Unfortunately, since completely different classification systems are used for commodities in the consumer price data and commodities in the wholesale price data, it is not generally possible to relate the retail price of a commodity to its price at the producer level. Although both sets of price data are the responsibility of the Bureau of Labor Statistics, the different objectives and price collection methods have thus far prevented any substantial coordination from taking place. There is, however, no major obstacle preventing better integration of consumer price data and wholesale price data. It would be perfectly possible for specific products which are priced at the retail level also to be priced at the producer level and classified in such a manner that comparisons of retail and producer price changes could be made.

The output of the construction industry is not covered by wholesale price data. However, many of the manufactured components going into construction, such as lumber, concrete, hardware, etc., are included in the wholesale price data as products of manufacturing industries. There are formidable problems in the development of price data for construction due primarily to the difficulty of measuring the output of the industry. The changing nature of housing and other structures makes specification pricing largely irrelevant. A variety of techniques including 'hedonic' regression analysis have been used to overcome these difficulties. Currently, the Bureau of the Census does prepare a price index for single-family houses and collects data on other construction. As in the case of the relation between wholesale and consumer price data, better articulation of the prices of materials used by the construction industry to the wholesale price data on these products would improve the possibility of understanding price behavior in this sector.

With respect to import and export price data, it is somewhat ironical that the original impetus to the creation of the Wholesale Price Index came from an interest in relating export and import prices to domestic prices and output. Collection of import and export prices is carried out by the Bureau of Labor Statistics quite separately from wholesale price collection. Price data are collected for approximately 5,000 products from over 1,000 companies and are classified according to the Standard International Trade Classification. Some efforts are currently under-way to develop common classifications so that comparisons between import and export prices and domestic prices can be made, but there is a great need for better integration between wholesale price data and the export and import price data. Only if this is obtained can the questions asked by Congress in 1890 be answered by 1990.

Agricultural price data have an even longer history than the wholesale price data. For many years data have been collected on the prices received by farmers for crops and livestock products and prices paid by farmers for inputs to production and for home consumption. These have been used to construct a parity ratio, which in turn has served as the basis for the stabilization of farm prices. Most of the data on agricultural prices contained in the Wholesale Price Index are in fact collected by the Department of Agriculture and provided to the Bureau of Labor Statistics, so that in this area there has been a greater degree of integration than in other areas.

Finally, there are large quantities of price data available in the regulatory and administrative agencies in the federal government. Thus the Department of Defense has massive amounts of price data relating to the products it purchases. The regulatory commissions in transportation, communication and electric power maintain records of rate changes. The Anti-trust Division of the Department of Justice obtains price data in connection with its investigations, and more recently the Council on Wage and Price Stability has obtained data directly from producers in specific industries for the purpose of monitoring price behavior. In a great many instances these data lie outside the area of coverage of the wholesale price data, but sometimes they can be used to extend the information now being collected in the wholesale price field. However, because much of the information obtained by the administrative and regulatory agencies is of a confidential nature, it is not generally made available to the statistical agencies. Paradoxically, it is often made available to other administrative agencies, so that in actual practice confidentiality is often breached, whereas purely statistical use of such data would not do so. Although such regulatory and administrative sources of price data do not constitute a comprehensive and systematic body of data, they can be particularly useful in providing information in greater depth which can be used to test the validity of prices collected for statistical purposes. It would indeed be helpful if the legitimacy of using such price data for statistical purposes could be specifically recognized.

Sources of Wholesale Price Data and Reporter Characteristics

The Bureau of Labor Statistics gets its monthly price data from a variety of sources. Some are obtained from trade sources, including reports from organized markets, trade associations and trade journals; some are provided in already processed form by other government agencies; but for the most part, price data are collected by questionnaires sent to companies. Table 10.3 gives a tabulation of the sources of wholesale price data as of March 1975. This table is derived from the basic data tape at the observation level used to generate the Wholesale Price Index. There are a few products, e.g., fuel oil, gasoline and electric energy, which depend on special collection efforts outside of the basic data base, and these are not included in this tabulation.

As can be seen in this table, trade sources are currently a very small percentage of the total number of reports, and only assume major importance in metal mining. Government sources, while even smaller in number, do play a

Table 10.3 Sources of Price Reports as of March 1975

Major industry	Price reports			
	Total no. of reports	Percent of total		
		Trade sources	Government agencies	Com-panies
SIC code and title				
01 Agriculture and crops	93	20	36	41
02 Agriculture and livestock	38	3	68	29
08 Forestry	7	0	0	100
09 Fishing	7	0	100	0
10 Metal mining	4	100	0	0
11 Anthracite mining	8	0	0	100
12 Bituminous coal and lignite	53	0	0	100
13 Oil and gas extraction	65	1	0	99
14 Nonmetallic minerals, exc. fuels	121	4	3	93
20 Food and kindred products	583	8	8	84
21 Tobacco manufactures	47	0	0	100
22 Textile mill products	254	9	2	89
23 Apparel and other textile products	122	3	1	96
24 Lumber and wood products	355	5	2	93
25 Furniture and fixtures	156	0	2	98
26 Paper and allied products	233	0	0	100
27 Printing and publishing	2	0	0	100
28 Chemicals and allied products	857	9	1	90
29 Petroleum and coal products	85	1	0	99
30 Rubber and plastic products	276	0	1	99
31 Leather and leather products	96	8	0	92
32 Stone, clay and glass products	334	1	1	98
33 Primary metals	594	6	1	93
34 Fabricated metal products	672	2	1	97
35 Machinery, exc. electrical	1,771	1	1	98
36 Electrical equipment and supplies	992	1	3	97
37 Transportation equipment	191	0	0	100
38 Instruments and related parts	140	1	0	99
39 Miscellaneous manufactures	162	1	3	96
Total	8,318	3	2	95

Source: Computed from data tapes, Bureau of Labor Statistics.

major role in agriculture. In terms of weights, Table 10.3 indicates that the products for which there are direct price reports constituted about 25 percent of the total value of all products. Coverage ranged from printing and publishing and anthracite mining, where there was almost no direct pricing, to a high of 50–60 percent in agricultural products. In the distribution of relative weights by type of reporter shown in Table 10.3, within a product each price observation was generally weighted equally, and relative weights were obtained by assigning to each reporter an equal share of the weight at the product level. Exceptions to this weighting procedure were made for automobiles, refined

Value of shipments				
Total value of shipments ($bn)	Value of shipments of commodities directly priced as percent of total	Percent of directly priced value of shipments		
		Trade sources	Government agencies	Com-panies
28	54	10	87	3
37	61	–	99	1
1	33	0	0	100
2	20	0	100	0
4	18	100	0	0
–	1	0	0	100
5	44	0	0	100
26	40	19	0	81
4	23	4	–	96
111	35	6	33	61
6	56	0	0	100
29	14	18	1	81
29	18	3	1	96
25	12	3	2	94
11	26	0	2	98
29	31	0	0	100
30	–	0	0	100
55	26	6	–	94
30	27	1	0	99
21	12	0	1	99
7	48	13	0	87
21	36	1	2	97
60	15	11	1	88
51	16	2	1	97
64	19	–	–	99
54	24	1	2	98
103	22	0	0	100
16	7	1	0	99
13	10	–	3	97
871	25	5	22	73

petroleum, contract coal and mobile homes. For other than agricultural products, the overwhelming importance of companies as a source of price reports is apparent. The charge that the WPI is based to a large degree on prices provided by trade associations and trade journals is indeed unfounded.

As a basis for further study of the characteristics of the price reporters and the nature of the price data which they provide, a 1-in-14 sample was drawn from the list of WPI price observations. Table 10.4 shows the characteristics of the price reporters tabulated from this sample. For the smaller industries, the sample is obviously not adequate to permit conclusions about the nature of the price reporters, but for a number of industries a sufficient number of reports was obtained to show the characteristics of their price reporters. In general, it can be said that price reports are obtained from the headquarters of companies substantially more often than from the establishments themselves. It is not

Table 10.4 Characteristics of WPI Price Reporters

Major industry		Type of reporter				
SIC code and title	Sample size	Head-quarters	Establish-ments	Trade sources	Govern-ment	Not known
01 Agriculture and crops	7	0	3	3	1	0
02 Agriculture and livestock	3	0	1	0	2	0
09 Fishing	1	0	0	0	1	0
12 Bituminous coal and lignite	6	6	0	0	0	0
13 Oil and gas extraction	5	5	0	0	0	0
14 Nonmetallic minerals, exc. fuels	15	7	0	8	0	0
20 Food and kindred products	47	21	18	4	2	2
21 Tobacco manufactures	3	1	0	0	0	2
22 Textile mill products	16	11	5	0	0	0
23 Apparel and other textile products	9	6	3	0	0	0
24 Lumber and wood products	27	26	0	1	0	0
25 Furniture and fixtures	9	2	7	0	0	0
26 Paper and allied products	18	17	0	1	0	0
28 Chemicals and allied products	65	58	3	4	0	0
29 Petroleum and coal products	9	9	0	0	0	0
30 Rubber and plastic products	23	18	5	0	0	0
31 Leather and leather products	7	0	6	1	0	0
32 Stone, clay and glass products	25	21	4	0	0	0
33 Primary metals	37	30	7	0	0	0
34 Fabricated metal products	49	21	28	0	0	0
35 Machinery, exc. electrical	137	115	22	0	0	0
36 Electrical equipment and supplies	76	32	44	0	0	0
37 Transportation equipment	14	12	1	0	0	1
38 Instruments and related parts	6	3	3	0	0	0
39 Miscellaneous manufactures	15	15	0	0	0	0
Total	629	436	160	22	6	5
Percent distribution	100	69	25	4	1	1

Source: One-in-14 sample drawn from wholesale price observations for March 1975.

quite clear, however, whether reports of single-establishment firms were re-corded as headquarters reports. The most usual employment size is between 100 and 1,000 employees, but a substantial number of reports come from larger firms employing 1,000–5,000 employees, or over 5,000 employees. Although employment size is clearly not an indicator of the amount of a given product produced, it is quite apparent from the statistics on size of reporting unit that the amount of output of a specific product can be expected to vary widely among reporters. The final section of Table 10.4 distinguishes between pro-ducers of the product being priced and purchasers of it. From this, it can be seen that although in principle the BLS recognizes purchasers as a source of price data, in practice they collect relatively few prices from this source. Aside from the oil and gas industry, purchaser prices are used for only a few products such as aluminum ingot.

Size of reporting unit (headquarters or establishment)					Producer or purchaser		
Under 100 employees	100–1,000 employees	1,000–5,000 employees	Over 5,000 employees	Not known	Pro-ducer	Pur-chaser	Not known
1	2	0	0	4	1	1	5
1	0	0	0	2	0	1	2
0	0	0	0	1	0	0	1
0	1	3	2	0	6	0	0
0	0	0	5	0	0	5	0
4	2	0	1	8	6	0	9
7	16	8	10	6	40	0	7
0	2	0	1	0	3	0	0
2	12	1	1	0	13	2	1
2	7	0	0	0	9	0	0
2	9	7	8	1	26	0	1
1	7	1	0	0	9	0	0
0	3	5	9	1	17	0	1
0	21	25	15	4	61	0	4
0	1	2	6	0	9	0	0
2	11	2	8	0	23	0	0
1	2	1	1	2	6	0	1
3	11	8	3	0	25	0	0
2	10	18	7	0	36	1	0
3	28	13	3	2	49	0	0
5	49	46	35	2	137	0	0
2	34	24	16	0	75	1	0
1	4	4	5	0	13	1	0
0	3	3	0	0	5	0	1
3	9	3	0	0	15	0	0
42	244	174	136	33	584	12	33
7	39	27	21	6	92	2	6

The sample was obtained by arranging the reports by WPI code, and taking every 14th case. This list was then submitted to the Bureau of Labor Statistics and detailed information was requested for each individual price report in the list. This was done in such a manner that the confidentiality of the individual reporters was guaranteed. The Bureau of Labor Statistics cooperated by asking its individual commodity analysts to supply the required information from their files about each individual reporter. The character of each series was described as of mid-1976.

Conceptually more is involved than the question of whether purchasers or producers more accurately reflect transaction prices. If prices are collected from producers and averaged without weighting, as is currently done by the Bureau of Labor Statistics, the shifts in volume of sales by different producers will not be reflected in the change in the average price at which products are sold. However, if prices are collected from purchasers both the price changes of different producers and the shift in volume of sales by different producers may be reflected in a price index computed as an average of prices at which goods are purchased. On the other hand, such a purchasers' price index would not, of course, reflect shifts in the volume of purchases by different buyers. While purchaser-based price indexes might be useful and informative for some very homogeneous commodities, for many commodities the detailed specifications differ from producer to producer so that the average price computed from purchasers of a product would be essentially an average unit price reflecting a 'mix' of price and specification changes.

The Characteristics of Wholesale Price Observations

The characteristics of the WPI price observations themselves were also investigated. The attributes focused on are: whether prices are list prices and whether discounts are taken into account, whether prices refer to orders or shipments, and the time lag between orders and shipments of a product.

Over the past 10 years, the Bureau of Labor Statistics has made considerable efforts to obtain transaction prices rather than list prices. They have done this by sending out questionnaires requesting information on both the list price and the various types of discounts given by producers to their customers.

The filled-out pricing forms, which the individual reporters return to the Bureau of Labor Statistics, often show relatively few changes in discounts. It is not unreasonable to assume that the discounts which are reported are the more regularized and standardized discounts which apply to all purchasers. It is often true, however, that different classes of customers will be given quite different discounts depending on their line of business and past or future expected purchases. This sort of information is difficult to quantify on a pricing form and may in fact refer not to a given set of products, but rather to the total billing for a customer. In such cases, it may not be feasible to allocate the discount to the prices of specific commodities.

Even if the structure of prices and discounts for a commodity were to remain relatively stable, the *de facto* discount can change when a producer shifts the criteria on which discounts are granted. Thus, in periods of excess supply and competition among producers, it is reasonable to assume that producers will be more lenient in determining the classes of discounts to which a purchaser may be entitled. Conversely, in periods of tight supply and excess demand, new customers may be classified so that they are not eligible for as large discounts as would be normal, and extras may be charged for services and special orders which were formerly provided free of charge. For these reasons, the list prices adjusted by discounts reported to the Bureau of Labor Statistics may not reflect the actual changes in transaction prices.

The frequency of list prices minus discounts and net realized prices in the price reports is shown in Table 10.5; this table is based upon the same 1-in-14 sample of price reporters discussed above. In this sample less than 20 percent of the prices reported were described as list prices. Two-thirds were list prices adjusted by discounts and less than 10 percent referred to the average realized unit selling prices. Thus, in conceptual terms, the Wholesale Price Index has gone in the direction of reporting as far as possible list prices minus discounts. There is, of course, no way of determining from the questionnaires whether the producers are reporting all of the discounts which they actually give to their customers.

Perhaps an equally important question is whether the prices which are obtained refer to order prices at which future output will be sold or are the shipment prices which reflect the prices at which past output has been sold. This distinction is crucial to understanding the price index and its proper use for monitoring the price behavior of the economy and for the deflation of current price data. Table 10.5 shows that, in fact, the price observations are fairly evenly split between order prices and shipment prices. The proportions vary among industries: some industries, such as food and kindred products, are themselves evenly divided, whereas other industries are predominantly one or the other. Thus prices of lumber and wood products primarily refer to shipments, whereas prices in the machinery industry primarily refer to orders.

This question would be of minor consequence if the lag between goods being ordered and goods being shipped were small. When a producer takes goods off the shelf or out of inventory, it makes little difference whether the price is considered to be an order price or a shipment price. But if the time lag between order and shipment is substantial, it becomes very important indeed whether the price reported is that of orders or shipments. Thus, if the lag between orders and shipments is equivalent to six months, an order price means that the producer is quoting a price which will be paid for a product six months

Price Measurement

Table 10.5 Characteristics of WPI Price Observations

SIC major industry	Type of price			
SIC code and title	List price	List prices minus discounts	Average realized unit selling price	Un-known
01 Agriculture and crops	1	2	2	2
02 Agriculture and livestock	0	0	2	1
09 Fishing	0	0	1	0
12 Bituminous coal and lignite	0	0	6	0
13 Oil and gas extraction	5	0	0	0
14 Nonmetallic minerals, exc. fuels	11	4	0	0
20 Food and kindred products	17	23	4	3
21 Tobacco manufactures	0	3	0	0
22 Textile mill products	4	10	1	1
23 Apparel and other textile products	4	5	0	0
24 Lumber and wood products	1	14	12	0
25 Furniture and fixtures	0	9	0	0
26 Paper and allied products	2	15	1	0
28 Chemical and allied products	12	29	21	3
29 Petroleum and coal products	3	4	2	0
30 Rubber and plastic products	6	17	0	0
31 Leather and leather products	0	6	0	1
32 Stone, clay and glass products	4	20	1	0
33 Primary metals industry	19	15	0	3
34 Fabricated metal products	3	38	0	8
35 Machinery, exc. electrical	2	122	0	13
36 Electrical equipment and supplies	20	52	3	1
37 Transportation equipment	0	14	0	0
38 Instruments and related parts	2	4	0	0
39 Miscellaneous manufactures	0	15	0	0
Total	116	421	56	36
Percent	18	67	9	6

Source: One-in-14 sample drawn from wholesale price observations for March 1975.

hence; while this is useful for indicating anticipated price trends, it is not relevant to deflating the value of the shipments which the producer has made over the past period. Conversely, if the price of shipments is reported, and the order to shipment lag is six months, the shipments price will be useful for deflating output, but since it reflects orders which were placed six months ago it does not provide information on current economic developments. An examination of the order to shipment time indicates that only 21 percent of the producers were judged to have a time lag of less than one month between order and shipment, 51 percent were judged to have a time lag of one month to six months, and another 10 percent had lags in excess of six months. The 18 percent for which information is not available were for the most part in the primary metals, fabricated metal products and machinery industries. Other reporters in these industries all indicate substantial time lags between order and shipment,

Order or shipment price				Order to shipment time					
Order prices	Ship-ment prices	Both	Un-known	Shelf or spot	1 wk to 1 mth	1 mth to 6 mths	6 mths to 1 yr	More than 1 yr	Un-known
0	2	1	4	0	1	2	0	0	4
0	0	0	3	0	2	0	0	0	1
0	0	0	1	0	1	0	0	0	0
0	6	0	0	0	0	6	0	0	0
5	0	0	0	5	0	0	0	0	0
9	6	0	0	0	0	15	0	0	0
20	20	1	6	0	1	19	26	0	1
3	0	0	0	0	0	3	0	0	0
0	1	5	10	0	1	13	0	0	2
1	0	8	0	0	0	8	0	0	1
0	27	0	0	0	26	0	0	0	1
0	0	0	9	0	0	9	0	0	0
0	18	0	0	0	17	0	0	0	1
32	26	3	4	0	28	37	0	0	0
0	9	0	0	6	0	3	0	0	0
9	13	0	0	0	11	10	1	0	1
0	6	0	1	0	0	0	0	0	7
5	19	0	1	0	5	19	0	0	1
0	23	0	14	0	0	19	0	0	18
6	32	0	11	1	0	8	0	0	40
128	8	0	1	13	3	74	20	14	13
54	21	0	1	2	9	57	1	0	7
4	10	0	0	0	0	14	0	0	0
6	0	0	0	0	3	2	0	0	1
11	4	0	0	0	1	4	0	0	10
294	251	18	66	27	109	322	48	14	109
47	40	3	10	4	17	51	8	2	17

so that it seems quite probable that order to shipment time lags may be even more important than indicated by the sample.

The fact that there is almost an equal mixture of order and shipment prices in the Wholesale Price Index and that there are very substantial time lags between orders and shipments means that the Wholesale Price Index is difficult to interpret as an indicator of current price trends and may give misleading results if used to deflate current shipment data. The various government agencies using wholesale price data are well aware of this problem and take these considerations into account. But unfortunately the data deficiency is such that the necessary adjustments cannot really be made.

A more detailed examination of the relation between order and shipment prices and the time lag between order and shipments is provided in Table 10.6. This table shows that for both order and shipment prices the most frequent order-to-shipments lag was one to six months, but that for a substantial number of order prices the time lag for delivery was longer whereas shipment prices were reported only in instances with shorter time lags. For periods of delivery of six months or less, price reports were a mixture of order and shipment prices.

Table 10.6 Relation of Shipment and Order Prices to Time Lag between Orders and Shipments

	Total	Order prices	Shipment prices	Unknown
Spot or shelf	31	16	7	8
One week up to one month	144	51	86	7
One month up to three months	249	113	103	33
Three months up to six months	57	42	4	11
Six months up to one year	34	34	0	0
One year or more	12	12	0	0
Unknown	102	17	51	34
Total	629	285	251	93

Source: One-in-14 sample drawn from wholesale price observations for March 1975.

Wholesale Price Commodity Specifications

The Wholesale Price Index is designed to measure the average change in the prices of commodities sold in the United States. The specification of the commodities which are priced plays a central role in the pricing methodology. From the earliest days of the Wholesale Price Index, the emphasis has been on obtaining prices for major or strategically important commodities as they appear on the market, and this focus has made it important to design specifications in such a way that a meaningful price can be obtained for each of the commodities which are included in the index. This is a very different emphasis from that which would result if the focus of interest were on the prices each producer charges for its products; in such a case, it would be necessary to focus on the producing unit and to adapt the pricing procedure so that what actually is produced by a given producer can in fact be priced. Concentrating on commodities rather than producers may lead to a situation in which the commodities selected do not accurately reflect what is being produced, since it may not be feasible to develop specifications at the commodity level which can successfully embrace the large variety of different products produced.

For many commodities included in the Wholesale Price Index, the specifications are quite detailed, so that it is possible to combine prices of different producers into an average price in a meaningful manner. This is true, for instance, for the specification for wire rods given below:

10-13-01-11.02   Wire rods: 7/32" diameter, coils, hot rolled carbon steel, CI 008 industrial or standard quality, base quantity 20 net tons and over; mill to user, f.o.b. mill, per 100 lbs.

Such a specification refers to a rather standard, identifiable product about which average price information can be published. However, when one moves to more finished consumer goods which are produced in considerable variety, the specification problem becomes somewhat more difficult. For example, consider the specification below for cake mix:

02-12-02-15.04   Flour base cake mix, home layer cake type, sweet, 8 oz. to 20 oz. pkg., case of 12 to 24 pkgs.; manufacturer's price to wholesaler or retail chain, carrots or mixed cars, delivered, per pound.

The first thing to be noted is that the units of measure can differ considerably within the specification. Thus, for cake mixes, the packages can vary from 8 to 20 ounces. While at first blush it might seem that the price per pound is a common unit of measure, much of what is being sold in the different sizes is convenience packaging, which both costs more to produce and has a different utility to the purchaser. Within the general category of cake mixes, furthermore, there are wide differences in the ingredients used, both by different manufacturers and for different types of cake, and in many cases these will be reflected in the price. In this case, therefore, average price has much less meaning than in the case of wire rods.

Even broader specifications are established for some classes of consumer durables. For example, color television receivers have the following specification:

12-52-01-56   Color television receiver, console model, 21", 23", or 25" picture tube, veneer cabinet; manufacturer to dealer or distributor, f.o.b. factory or warehouse, each.

It will be noted in this example that the size of the picture tube, which may vary from 21" to 25", is the only technical specification of the receiver. Some receivers may have automatic and/or remote tuning, others may have special features to synchronize the color, but all would fit within the broad specifications given here. Even the quality of the cabinet can vary in such a way as to lead to variation in the price of the unit. Thus, what really is specified here is a 'product class' rather than a specific commodity.

The use of the average price for each commodity by the BLS in building up the Wholesale Price Index does not, however, lead to a problem of change in product mix, since care is taken to ensure that each individual price series collected from individual producers is represented in both of any two succeeding periods being compared. In other words, it is the individual price series which is the basic pricing vehicle used by BLS. The commodity specification is used to determine which precise product a given producer will report each month. If the producer alters his product in any significant manner, the change is reported to the BLS. The BLS then decides whether the change constitutes a break in the series and whether some adjustment should be made in the quoted price to reflect the specification change. Thus the integrity of each series is maintained, and the average price for the same group of series in two successive periods will be unaffected by either product mix or specification changes.

Nevertheless, this does not dispose of the problem. From the point of view of pricing theory, it is important to ask whether the BLS specifications define homogeneous commodities or heterogeneous product classes. If the specifications successfully define fairly narrow groups of commodities, one would expect that in any market the dispersion of prices for individual commodities would be rather narrow, and price differentials among producers would not persist over time. Producers with low prices would expand and raise their prices, and producers with high prices would be forced to contract and/or lower their prices. If substantial price differentials continue, one could assume that the products involved are somehow different even if their specifications do not appear to differ. Thus there may be a regional difference, suggesting that product location is a significant market factor, or the prices of large and small producers may be different, suggesting that they serve different markets. In many cases, such regional and market differences may be as important as differences in the physical specifications of the commodities themselves. The relative homogeneity of WPI commodity specifications can be evaluated by examining the variance of the individual observations relative to average price within each WPI commodity, comparing this variance with the variance of price relatives within commodities as a percentage of the average price relative and determining within the same commodities whether the relative structure of price observations (i.e., high price reporters vs low price reporters) persists over time. These computations have been carried out in Table 10.7 for 1,609 WPI commodities. The computations were carried out at the 8-digit commodity level and weighted to the 2-digit level by shipment weights. The price observations in industries such as primary metals, tobacco manufactures, and paper and allied products have relatively low coefficients of variation. On the other hand, relatively high coefficients of variation were found in furniture and fixtures, leather and leather products, machinery, electrical equipment, instruments and miscellaneous manufactures. The pattern follows what one would normally expect considering the difficulty of developing specifications narrow enough to describe homogeneous products. For all commodities, the variance of price observations around their average price in January 1974 was almost twice as large as the variance of price relatives around the average price relative from January 1974 to January 1975. Thus the dispersion of price change

*Table 10.7 Relative Dispersion of Prices and Price Relatives within
WPI Commodities, 1974 and 1975*

SIC code and title	$\sigma^2(P_{74})$ as percent of mean	$\sigma^2(P_{75}/P_{74})$ as percent of mean	Correlation coefficient (r) of P_{74} and P_{75}	No. of commodities	No. of obs.
14 Nonmetallic minerals, exc. fuels	22.8	13.1	.75	3	94
20 Food and kindred products	11.1	6.5	.75	101	500
21 Tobacco manufactures	4.0	2.3	.82	9	42
22 Textile mill products	16.9	9.1	.51	63	217
23 Apparel and other textile products	16.5	5.7	.87	35	103
24 Lumber and wood products	12.0	6.2	.64	63	253
25 Furniture and fixtures	41.3	5.8	.98	25	129
26 Paper and allied products	8.6	7.1	.72	44	185
28 Chemicals and allied products	14.8	8.0	.62	167	588
29 Petroleum and coal products	13.7	6.0	.90	10	40
30 Rubber and plastic products	15.7	7.7	.55	71	219
31 Leather and leather products	24.3	6.5	.87	25	68
32 Stone, clay and glass products	17.4	6.6	.78	52	235
33 Primary metals industry	6.5	6.6	.47	121	494
34 Fabricated metal products	16.1	11.1	.73	155	579
35 Machinery, exc. electrical	24.6	15.5	.64	380	1,269
36 Electrical equipment and supplies	18.7	6.9	.77	193	626
37 Transportation equipment	16.0	7.6	.79	21	83
38 Instruments and related products	21.6	7.6	.45	29	83
39 Miscellaneous manufactures	29.5	7.9	.81	42	139
Total	14.4	7.9	.71	1,609	5,946

Source: Computed from data tape of wholesale price observations from Jan. 1974 to Jan. 1975.

was in general much narrower among industries than the dispersion of absolute prices within commodities.

Between 1974 and 1975, there was a positive correlation of the prices of individual series within commodity group for a substantial number of industries. Within a commodity specification, price series which reported relatively high prices in January 1974 tended to report relatively high prices in 1975. In other words, price differentials tended to persist even with the relatively sharp price changes which occurred between 1974 and 1975. This finding tends to confirm the view that for most industries, the WPI commodity specifications describe product classes rather than specific commodities. This is not intended to be a criticism of WPI specification pricing; rather, it is a statement of observed fact which has broad implications for the design of the system of classification to be used for price collection, the methods to be used for computing price indexes and the sampling strategy to be used for obtaining a more comprehensive coverage of manufacturing and mining production. These specific issues will be examined in subsequent parts of this report.

3. CLASSIFICATION AND WEIGHTING SYSTEMS FOR PRICE INDEXES

Classification Systems for Price Indexes

The basic classification of the commodities in the Wholesale Price Index consists of an 8-digit code built around market groupings rather than around industries. The general approach of the Wholesale Price Index has been to collect price data for specific commodities in primary markets, and in order to be able to define each commodity precisely for purposes of accurate price measurement, rather detailed commodity codes were used. The coding system for wholesale price commodities existed before the establishment of the detailed 7-digit commodity code of the Standard Industrial Classification. Although the WPI codes do not correspond to the SIC, they, like the SIC, are hierarchical in structure. The first four digits of the code refer to a group of products. The next two digits are used to classify a subgroup of products and the last two digits refer to the detailed products themselves. It is, of course, possible to build concordances between the WPI codes and the SIC codes, and in fact this has been done by the BLS in order to use data from the Censuses of Manufactures and Minerals as weights to combine the prices of the specific commodities into prices for subgroups and groups. The Bureau of Census also uses a concordance to determine which price indexes should be used to deflate the value of shipments of different products contained in the Censuses of Minerals and Manufactures in order to obtain indexes of production. However, because of differences in basic definitions between the WPI codes and the SIC, the concordances do not provide a one-to-one relationship. A given 8-digit WPI code can often equally well be fitted into a number of different 7-digit SIC codes, since the two classification systems are based on different character-istics. These differences are usually minor, but in a substantial number of cases the various 7-digit product codes into which an 8-digit WPI code fits may fall into a number of different 5-digit product classes. This means the same WPI price is being used to represent prices for several different SIC 5-digit product classes.

This lack of direct correspondence between the WPI classification system and the SIC makes the use of WPI prices in conjunction with other data diffi-cult. As already noted, the Bureau of Labor Statistics does publish some of its data classified in 4- and 5-digit SIC classifications. But a considerable amount of information is lost in this transformation. There is growing consensus that the Bureau of Labor Statistics should shift entirely to the Standard Industrial Classification used elsewhere throughout the federal government.

The adoption of the Standard Industrial Classification for the WPI would make it easier to harmonize all of the different price indexes now compiled, and would provide a basis for developing a more general system of price indexes for the economy as a whole. Table 10.8 shows how such a system of price indexes might be structured. It is arranged in terms of an input–output table based on the Standard Industrial Classification.

Table 10.8 Structure of the System of Price Indexes (percent of 1975 GNP)

	Inter-industry sales (producer)	Final sales (purchaser)				
		Con-sumer	Govern-ment	Gross invest-ment	Ex-ports	Im-ports
Inter-industry Purchases						
Agriculture	4%					
Mining	2%					
Construction	4%					
Manufacturing	23%					
Transportation, utilities	9%	64%	22%	12%	10%	8%
Wholesale, retail trade	18%					
Finance, insurance, real estate	14%					
Services	12%					
Public administration	12%					
Gross Product Originating						
Capital consumption allowances	9%					
Compensation of employees	} 61%					
Operating surplus						

The stub of this table lists the 2-digit SIC industries, plus the components of gross product originating: capital consumption allowances, compensation of employees and operating surplus. The columns in this table refer to the inter-industry and final sales of the industries listed in the rows. The indexes relating to inter-industry sales would measure producers' prices, and those for final sales, purchasers' prices. Total final sales equals gross national product, but the total of any column or any row for a specific industry equals the total value of product of that industry. Out of this comprehensive system, the present Wholesale Price Index, as was shown in Table 10.2, covers primarily agriculture, mining and manufacturing. Agricultural prices, furthermore, are, as noted above, largely obtained from the Department of Agriculture and are not collected by the Bureau of Labor Statistics.

Each of the different sets of price indexes shown in the table would pose substantially different problems of measurement. The agricultural producers' price index would involve seasonal production and seasonal price fluctuations. The mining producers' price index would pose problems of integrated operations which may use artificial transfer prices primarily influenced by the tax laws. The construction price index must deal with the problem of measuring price change where unique goods are produced. The manufacturing producers' price index would be closest to the present Wholesale Price Index, but it would require much greater coverage than now exists and it would need to be more closely integrated with other data about the manufacturing sector, for example, shipments, inventories, etc., at a detailed level. The producers' price indexes for the remaining major categories of gross product originating (transportation, utilities, wholesale and retail trade, finance, insurance and real estate, services and public administration) all pose major unsolved problems of price measurement, and compiling such indexes would call for new types of information. Some of the needed information may be available from regulatory and administrative agencies, but some would have to be developed from sources outside of the government. Thus, to compile an index on wholesale and retail trade it would be necessary to collect information about wholesale and retail trade activity, costs, and sales that is not now available. Finally, price indexes for capital consumption allowances and wage and salary price indexes on an industry-specific basis, which are needed in order to obtain a better understanding of the relation between wages, prices, productivity and profits, would require a new compilation effort.

Considering the disposition of gross product, it would be highly desirable to be able to trace a commodity from producer to final consumer so as to obtain a better understanding of the relationship between the producers' price for a commodity and the consumer price. The Consumer Price Index covers a major segment of final sales. However, since the Consumer Price Index focuses on components of the consumer budget, it is not easy to relate the commodities purchased by consumers to those produced by producers. Similarly, though many of the goods purchased by the government are identifiable as products of agriculture, mining and manufacturing, for many products such as defense procurement there are severe problems of measurement and in other cases the government obtains special prices so that what it pays is not necessarily the price for which the same product sells in the private sector. Gross investment (construction and purchase of producers' durable equipment) contains elements that are partially included in the price indexes of the producing sectors, but it also includes costs of getting the gross investment into place, and the final price to the purchaser may be quite different from the producers' price of the construction and the equipment. Finally, the problem of relating import and export prices to domestic prices is well recognized. Export and import price indexes are currently being developed by the Bureau of Labor Statistics. Much of the value of these price indexes will depend on how well the integration with domestic prices can be carried out.

Viewed in these terms, the Standard Industrial Classification cast in the form of an input–output table could provide the framework for a system of price indexes. Such an approach would not only facilitate the fitting together of existing price indexes by providing the basis for their harmonization, but by revealing major gaps in the price data, it could help ensure complete and cohesive coverage of the economy as a whole. If price indexes were compiled for the products of the Standard Industrial Classification at the 7-digit level, the data could be aggregated in a number of different ways. The Bureau of Labor Statistics currently publishes price data, not only in terms of WPI commodity groups, but also by stage of processing and by durability of product. The stage of processing classification is particularly useful for tracing through the repercussions of price changes at one stage of processing on the price behavior at subsequent stages, though the present BLS presentation is only partially successful in this effort since rather broad commodity groupings are used as the basis of the classification. Reorganizing the basic input–output table according to stage of processing, however, permits a more systematic and comprehensive approach based on industrial classifications. This approach to stage of process classification has been adopted in a study recently carried out by Joel Popkin. It is based on the 1967 input–output table as shown in Table 10.9. In this table, industries have been arranged according to their involvement in specific stages of processing. The validity of the arrangement is demonstrated by the relatively small percentage of output which falls below the main diagonal. Such a classification system can show how the prices at higher stages of processing are related to the inputs from lower stages of processing, and it thus provides information on the transmission of price changes at one stage of processing to later stages of processing.

Other forms of aggregation are also useful. If users wish to monitor prices in specific market areas or for specific types of products, indexes can be developed by bringing together with appropriate weights the detailed industry or product class prices which are relevant to the purpose at hand. There are, however, major problems involving the harmonization of different classification systems which need to be resolved. The Standard Industrial Classification consists of 4-digit industries within which there are product classes, but since only one digit is used to designate the product class, not more than nine product classes can be defined within any 4-digit industry. Below the product class are detailed product codes. Since two digits are allowed for this section of the code, up to 99 different products can be distinguished within each product class. For purposes of input–output classification, the most detailed classification used is that at the 4-digit industry level. The SIC classification was not designed primarily for input–output analysis, so that some reclassification is required in order to obtain suitable industry classifications. The national income accounts utilize the SIC industry classification for gross product originating, but the classification of final expenditures by type bears little relationship to the SIC. Trade data for the most part are based on the Standard International Trade Classification, and this in turn can be related to the SIC classifications only partially and with considerable difficulty.

Table 10.9   *US Input–Output Table for 1967 Distribution of Total Transactions (Joel Popkin, March 1, 1976, Preliminary, for comment and review only)*

Producer	Consumer 1	2	3	4	5	6	7	8	9
Imports	.000	0.066	*	0.001	0.004	0.072	0.004	0.007	0.001
Dummy		–	0.023	0.010	0.014	0.012	0.004	0.007	0.029
Business services		–	0.060	0.044	0.034	0.014	0.008	0.013	0.064
Finance, insurance, real estate		*	0.044	0.013	0.028	0.168	0.010	0.042	0.052
Communications		–	0.074	0.007	0.016	0.001	0.003	0.011	0.015
Crude oil, natural gas		–	–	0.001	–	0.025	0.048	–	–
Utilities		–	0.004	0.005	0.008	0.011	0.185	0.004	0.006
Intermediate transport		0.297	0.006	0.008	0.002	0.010	0.015	0.125	0.016
Wholesale trade		*	0.010	0.005	0.004	0.008	0.004	0.029	0.019
Petroleum refining		0.001	0.002	0.005	0.003	0.002	0.007	0.039	0.011
Crude food, tobacco		0.009	–	0.015	–	–	–	0.001	0.002
Crude nonfood		0.003	*	0.001	*	*	0.024	*	*
Primary, indus. chem., pigments		*	0.003	0.001	*	0.010	0.001	0.001	0.003
Primary, wood		*	–	*	–	–	*	*	0.001
Primary, pulp, paperboard mills		*	0.001	0.001	*	–	*	*	0.001
Primary, nonferrous metals		0.010	–	*	*	–	*	*	0.001
Primary, blast furnaces, steel mills		0.012	*	*	–	0.008	0.001	*	*
Primary, stone clay, glass		*	0.002	*	*	0.004	*	*	0.002
Primary, textiles		0.004	*	*	*	*	*	*	0.001
Primary, fertilizers		–	–	0.001	–	–	*	*	0.001
Intermediate		0.187	0.095	0.007	0.007	0.029	0.005	0.023	0.030
Machinery, equipment		0.008	0.013	0.004	0.009	0.013	*	0.002	0.009
Automotive		0.001	0.001	*	*	*	*	*	0.001
Consumer home goods		0.030	0.007	0.001	0.001	0.001	*	*	0.006
Consumer staples		0.013	0.104	0.002	*	*	*	0.002	0.008
Consumer food, tobacco		0.198	–	0.001	–	–	*	0.001	0.013
Ord. ship, railroad, aircraft		0.005	*	*	–	–	*	0.005	0.002
Maintenance, repair		–	0.005	0.045	0.025	0.032	0.030	0.025	0.001
Government enterprises		–	0.011	0.014	0.004	*	0.150	0.007	0.004
Nonbusiness services		0.106	0.020	0.011	0.051	0.002	0.003	0.027	0.020
Final transport		–	–	–	–	–	–	–	–
Retail trade		0.047	0.009	0.009	0.005	0.004	0.001	0.011	0.016
Construction		–	–	–	–	–	–	–	–
Special		–	–	–	–	–	–	–	–
I.V.A.		–	–	–	–	–	–	–	–
Value added	0.000	–	0.507	0.688	0.782	0.573	0.474	0.618	0.665
Column totals (billion $)	0.000	15.8	57.3	161	22.5	15.0	37.3	17.3	64.8
Purchases from industries below main diagonal as proportion of total purchases and value added	0.000	0.93	0.413	0.144	0.119	0.136	0.241	0.173	0.133
Purchases from industries below the main diagonal (billion $)	0.0	14.7	23.7	23.2	2.7	2.0	9.0	3.0	8.6

*Between –.00049 and +.00049.

10	11	12	13	14	15	16	17	18	19	20	21	22	23
0.040	0.009	0.121	0.027	0.057	0.123	0.091	0.050	0.020	0.042	0.017	0.018	0.024	0.007
0.002	0.001	0.007	0.011	0.003	0.022	0.041	0.024	0.008	0.005	0.004	0.012	0.013	0.003
0.029	0.021	0.025	0.029	0.015	0.022	0.012	0.025	0.024	0.011	0.019	0.022	0.023	0.013
0.033	0.050	0.059	0.027	0.014	0.012	0.012	0.007	0.026	0.012	0.020	0.018	0.021	0.007
0.001	0.002	0.001	0.003	0.002	0.002	0.002	0.002	0.005	0.002	0.002	0.004	0.007	0.001
0.448	–	–	0.002	–	–	–	–	–	–	–	*	–	–
0.017	0.005	0.022	0.032	0.009	0.027	0.019	0.024	0.031	0.010	0.010	0.009	0.005	0.003
0.051	0.019	0.022	0.023	0.032	0.037	0.024	0.047	0.052	0.017	0.034	0.016	0.008	0.018
0.008	0.029	0.018	0.021	0.031	0.026	0.032	0.026	0.025	0.030	0.020	0.024	0.026	0.022
0.063	0.017	0.014	0.087	0.008	0.007	0.002	0.003	0.005	0.001	0.006	0.005	0.002	0.001
–	0.309	0.035	0.003	0.009	–	–	–	–	0.012	–	0.010	–	–
*	0.003	0.074	0.032	0.075	0.013	0.048	0.082	0.048	0.062	0.062	0.003	*	–
0.022	0.012	0.009	0.169	0.007	0.034	0.008	0.011	0.012	0.021	0.047	0.032	0.002	0.004
*	*	0.003	*	0.297	0.104	0.003	0.002	0.005	0.002	*	0.004	0.004	0.008
–	*	–	0.002	0.001	0.147	–	–	0.004	0.001	0.001	0.037	0.002	–
0.002	*	0.002	0.019	*	–	0.188	0.020	0.004	*	–	0.033	0.025	0.007
*	*	0.012	0.007	0.002	–	0.004	0.264	0.009	–	–	0.075	0.037	0.012
*	*	0.010	0.003	0.008	0.002	0.002	0.003	0.133	0.005	0.003	0.008	0.005	0.012
–	0.002	0.004	*	0.001	0.008	*	–	0.005	0.327	–	0.007	0.003	0.003
–	0.024	0.010	0.010	*	–	*	–	*	–	0.216	*	*	*
0.013	0.019	0.042	0.086	0.043	0.052	0.054	0.055	0.075	0.125	0.073	0.197	0.208	0.482
0.004	0.005	0.020	0.015	0.003	0.008	0.002	0.007	0.010	0.006	0.002	0.018	0.122	0.029
–	*	0.001	–	*	–	*	*	–	–	–	0.006	0.002	0.057
*	0.001	*	0.001	0.008	0.001	0.001	0.001	0.004	0.003	*	0.005	0.016	0.009
0.003	0.002	0.001	0.011	0.002	0.001	0.001	0.001	0.002	0.011	0.009	0.006	0.003	0.019
*	0.054	0.002	0.001	*	0.008	*	–	*	0.002	0.002	0.005	–	–
–	*	*	*	*	–	*	–	*	–	–	0.003	0.014	0.002
0.014	0.010	0.009	0.007	0.005	0.009	0.003	0.009	0.009	0.003	0.004	0.003	0.003	0.002
0.001	*	0.001	0.001	0.001	0.001	0.001	0.001	0.002	0.001	0.004	0.001	0.001	0.001
0.001	0.007	0.004	0.003	0.005	0.001	0.001	0.002	0.004	0.001	0.002	0.003	0.003	0.021
–	–	–	–	–	–	–	–	–	–	–	–	–	–
*	0.018	0.005	0.003	0.002	*	0.001	0.001	0.002	0.001	0.002	0.004	0.006	0.001
–	–	–	–	–	–	–	–	–	–	–	–	–	–
–	–	–	–	–	–	–	–	–	–	–	–	–	–
0.249	0.382	0.464	0.369	0.361	0.332	0.248	0.332	0.457	0.289	0.236	0.409	0.419	0.255
25.8	60.6	13.2	20.0	13.4	10.9	22.6	27.6	11.6	19.2	3.5	162	66.3	31.7
0.060	0.157	0.137	0.143	0.081	0.091	0.070	0.080	0.113	0.153	0.098	0.054	0.048	0.055
1.5	9.5	1.8	3.7	1.1	1.0	1.6	2.2	1.5	2.9	0.3	8.7	3.2	1.7

(cont)

Table 10.9 (cont)

Producer	24	25	26	27	28	29	30	31	32
Imports	0.045	0.004	0.024	0.007	0.001	0.020	0.001	0.040	*
Dummy	0.007	0.010	0.005	0.012	0.007	0.004	0.017	0.006	0.005
Business services	0.038	0.054	0.034	0.022	0.023	0.031	0.026	0.018	0.044
Finance, insurance, real estate	0.019	0.032	0.011	0.014	0.009	0.035	0.048	0.040	0.078
Communications	0.004	0.006	0.003	0.008	0.002	0.004	0.010	0.009	0.008
Crude oil, natural gas	–	–	–	–	–	–	–	0.001	–
Utilities	0.005	0.004	0.004	0.005	–	0.073	0.022	0.008	0.021
Intermediate transport	0.013	0.009	0.024	0.006	0.020	0.072	0.006	0.095	0.002
Wholesale trade	0.035	0.023	0.030	0.014	0.033	0.009	0.024	0.020	0.007
Petroleum refining	0.001	0.002	0.002	0.003	0.008	0.008	0.007	0.037	0.007
Crude food, tobacco	0.001	*	0.263	–	0.001	0.003	0.004	0.001	*
Crude nonfood	0.001	0.003	0.005	*	0.011	0.028	*	*	–
Primary, indus. chem., pigments	0.012	0.021	0.003	0.004	0.038	0.004	0.001	0.002	*
Primary, wood	0.027	0.001	*	0.001	0.017	–	*	*	*
Primary, pulp, paperboard mills	0.002	0.029	*	–	–	0.001	*	*	0.001
Primary, nonferrous metals	0.028	*	*	0.025	0.009	*	*	0.002	–
Primary, blast furnaces, steel mills	0.024	*	*	0.027	0.010	*	*	*	–
Primary, stone, clay, glass	0.009	*	*	0.002	0.034	*	0.003	0.001	*
Primary, textiles	0.040	0.140	*	0.001	*	*	*	0.001	*
Primary, fertilizers	*	0.001	*	*	–	0.001	0.001	*	*
Intermediate	0.185	0.092	0.093	0.119	0.116	0.012	0.058	0.023	0.017
Machinery, equipment	0.017	0.002	0.001	0.052	0.020	0.002	0.005	0.003	–
Automotive	0.001	*	–	*	*	–	*	0.001	–
Consumer home goods	0.080	0.009	0.001	0.004	0.012	0.001	0.009	0.001	0.001
Consumer staples	0.005	0.164	0.004	0.001	*	0.004	0.024	0.002	0.013
Consumer food, tobacco	*	0.003	0.210	–	–	0.005	0.005	0.004	*
Ord. ship, railroad, aircraft	0.001	*	–	0.240	–	*	*	0.017	–
Maintenance, repair	0.003	0.002	0.003	0.003	*	0.102	0.011	0.024	0.004
Government enterprises	0.001	0.006	0.001	0.001	*	0.001	0.007	0.040	0.021
Nonbusiness services	0.002	0.004	0.004	0.005	0.003	0.006	0.047	0.013	0.14
Final transport	–	–	–	–	–	–	–	–	–
Retail trade	0.003	0.004	0.002	0.008	0.041	0.002	0.011	0.006	0.004
Construction	–	–	–	–	–	–	–	–	–
Special	–	–	–	–	–	–	–	–	–
I.V.A.	–	–	–	–	–	–	–	–	–
Value added	0.390	0.372	0.272	0.412	0.547	0.569	0.634	0.544	0.763
Column totals (billion $)	31.1	58.3	99.8	39.9	23.4	17.3	93.8	35.9	98.6
Purchases from industries below main diagonal as proportion of total purchases and value added	.015	.019	.010	.017	.044	.008	.011	.006	0.000
Purchases from industries below the main diagonal (billions $)	0.005	1.1	1.0	0.7	1.0	0.1	1.0	0.2	0.0

33	34	35	37	38	39	40	41	42	43	44	45	46
0.001	0.019	0.000	0.020	0.004	−.010	−7.95	0.040	0.056	*	–	*	*
0.007	–		0.003	−.026	−.012	0.113	−.002	*	0.004	0.003	*	0.033
0.055	–		0.009	–	–	0.009	0.026	0.042	0.016	0.028	0.015	0.016
0.015	–		0.194	0.019	*	0.130	0.002	0.010	0.009	0.011	0.005	0.012
0.004	–		0.016	0.010	–	0.027	0.004	0.007	0.004	0.003	0.007	0.009
–	–		–	–	0.026	0.016	–	–	–	–	–	–
0.001	–		0.028	–	–	0.014	0.004	0.003	0.027	0.007	0.009	0.013
0.027	–		–	–	–	–	–	–	–	–	–	–
0.041	–		0.054	0.033	0.051	0.500	0.016	0.013	0.009	0.012	0.009	0.005
0.011	–		0.021	–	0.053	0.146	0.013	0.007	0.004	0.003	0.005	0.003
0 003	–		0.012	–	0.104	0.556	*	−.004	0.001	0.002	0.001	0.002
0.008	–		0.001	–	0.030	0.223	*	−.047	*	0.000	–	*
0.004	–		0.001	–	0.024	0.259	0.006	0.021	*	0.002	*	*
0.057	–		0.001	*	0.012	0.072	*	*	*	*	*	*
–	–		*	–	0.014	0.110	*	0.001	0.002	0.001	0.001	0.001
0.027	–		*	*	0.033	0.139	0.001	−.002	*	–	–	–
0.014	–		*	–	0.050	0.043	0.003	*	*	–	*	–
0.079	–		0.001	–	0.017	0.058	*	*	0.001	0.002	*	–
*	–		0.001	–	0.020	0.043	0.001	*	*	0.001	*	*
–	–		*	–	0.008	0.039	0.001	0.001	*	*	–	0.002
0.064	–		0.018	0.059	0.160	1.077	0.055	0.031	0.011	0.010	0.007	0.009
0.025	–		*	0.236	0.172	1.171	0.099	0.068	0.015	0.012	0.005	0.007
*	–		0.034	0.063	−.031	0.244	0.009	0.008	0.004	0.002	0.015	0.015
0.010	–		0.037	0.013	0.049	0.177	0.008	0.008	0.006	0.006	0.003	0.002
0.001	–		0.066	–	0.070	0.176	0.008	0.007	0.020	0.029	0.005	0.002
–	–		0.133	–	0.107	0.374	0.003	0.023	0.002	0.020	0.011	0.002
–	–		0.001	0.041	0.219	0.444	0.218	0.145	–	–	0.001	*
*	–		–	–	–	–	0.014	0.025	0.020	0.011	0.011	0.111
0.001	–		0.004	–	–	0.021	0.003	0.017	0.001	0.004	0.002	0.004
0.006	–		0.143	–	−.006	0.045	0.026	0.064	0.001	0.175	0.014	0.009
–	–		0.023	0.006	0.023	0.758	0.042	0.017	0.016	0.008	0.006	0.007
0.041	–		0.149	0.026	–	0.010	*	*	−.011	0.007	–	*
–	–		–	0.492	–	0.003	0.014	0.128	0.156	0.129	0.042	0.475
–	–		0.005	–	–	1.790	0.380	0.371	0.683	0.510	0.824	0.257
–	–	0.000	–	–	−.184	–	–	–	–	–	–	–
0.399	0.981	1.00	0.000	–	–	–	–	–	–	–	–	–
79.9	92.4	−1.8	490.7	110.4	10.0	5.1	71.3	19.5	19.5	13.3	6.3	29.3
0.000	0.000											
0.0	0.0											

37. Personal consumption
38. GPF capital formation
39. Net inventory change
40. Net exports
41. Fed. gvt purchase, defense
42. Fed. gvt purchase, other
43. Fed. gvt purchase, education
44. S&L gvt purchase, health, etc.
45. S&L gvt purchase, safety
46. S&L gvt purchase, other

The classification problem arises because different kinds of information, though highly interrelated, have been developed on the basis of classification systems which are designed for different purposes. In the international area this can be seen if one looks at the list of classification systems currently under development by the United Nations. Some of these are listed below.

ISIC   *International Standard Industrial Classification of All Economic Activities* (E.68XVII.8)

ICGS   *International Classification of All Goods and Services* (Draft E/CN.3/457 Parts I and II)

SITC   *Standard International Trade Classification* (EC.61.XVII.6 and Draft E/CN.3/456)

BEC   *Broad Economic Categories* (E.71.XVII.12)

SNA   *A System of National Accounts* (E.69XVII 3)

ISCO   *International Standard Classification of Occupations* (ILO, Geneva, 1969)

ISCED   *International Standard Classification of Education* (UNESCO COM-74/ISCED/3)

CSTE   *Commodity Classification for Transport Statistics in Europe* (ECE W/Trans/WP6/194/Rev 1)

This list covers only some of the more general classification systems; more specialized classifications exist in special fields such as energy and public health. Continuing efforts are being made to harmonize these systems in such a way that each of the various classification systems can be obtained by different aggregations of commonly agreed upon detailed classifications.

In the classification of prices, every effort should be made to provide a system of classification which will meet the needs of different users of price information and make it possible to relate different types of price index information to one another. As Wassily Leontief (1971, pp. 5–6) stated in his presidential address to the American Economic Association, the establishment, maintenance and enforcement of coordinated uniform classification systems is an especially urgent need. He argued that incompatible data are useless data and pointed out that because of differences in classification domestic output data cannot be compared with corresponding export and import figures or even with employment statistics. An unreasonably high proportion of the material and intellectual resources devoted to statistical work is now spent not on the collection of primary information but on a frustrating and wasteful struggle with incongruous definitions and irreconcilable classifications.

In order to meet the objective of harmonized classifications, greater coordination is needed within the federal statistical system. Federal statistical agencies involved in collecting basic information should have common access to basic data, so that common classifications and definitions can be uniformly applied to data from specific establishments and companies.

Combining Price Observations at the Reporter Level

As was noted in the discussion of the specification of wholesale price commodities in Section 2, the Bureau of Labor Statistics bases its price index on average prices for each commodity. In computing this average, each price reporter is weighted equally and each must be represented in both of the periods for which a price comparison is to be made. The average prices for the two periods are then combined into a price relative which shows the change in price between the two periods.

In Section 2 of this report, it was shown that for many commodities widely different prices are reported, and that these price differences persist over time. On the basis of this evidence it was concluded that the different price reporters were in fact reporting on different commodities and that, in practice, the WPI commodity specification was usually serving as a product class specification rather than as a definition for a homogeneous commodity. In such cases, the concept of average price may have little or no meaning. Although the BLS procedure ensures that the same price series are represented in the computation of average prices for both periods, the rationale of computing a relative of the average prices disappears if the series do not refer to identical commodities. Where each price series is more properly thought of as referring to a separate commodity, it would be more reasonable to compute the price relative for each price series and then to combine these relatives into an average price relative for all the price series represented in a WPI commodity classification.

For homogeneous products where an average price is desired for purposes of publication, it can be argued that the method of computation now used by the BLS is more meaningful. In such cases, however, the variance among the price reports is likely to be very much smaller, and the correlation between the pairs of prices for individual price series is likely to be very much lower. The difference between the relative of average prices and the average of relative prices will not then be significant.

Table 10.10 shows a comparison of the actual computations of the relative of average prices $\Sigma_{i=1}^{n} P_{it} / \Sigma_{i=1}^{n} P_{i(t-1)}$ and the average of price relatives $\Sigma_{i=1}^{n} (P_{it} / P_{i(t-1)})$ carried out at the WPI commodity level and weighted up to the 2-digit level. It will be noted that for most categories, despite the considerable change in price from January 1974 to January 1975, the two methods of computation yield quite similar results. In only four industries did the difference between the two computations exceed 1 percent, and in all these cases the variance of price observations as a percentage of average price as indicated in Table 10.7 of Section 2 was quite large, suggesting that for the commodities in

Table 10.10 Comparison of Price Indexes Computed as Relatives of
           Average Prices and as Averages of Price Relatives
           (January 1974 = 100)

SIC code and title	No. of products	No. of obser- vations	Relative of average prices[a]	Average of price relatives[b]	Percent difference
01 Agriculture and crops	7	39	102.4	102.0	−0.4
02 Agriculture and livestock	3	10	64.4	64.4	0.0
08 Forestry	1	4	80.7	76.6	−5.4
11 Anthracite mining	2	8	192.7	192.7	0.0
12 Bituminous coal and lignite	5	36	212.6	212.7	0.1
13 Oil and gas extraction	13	53	124.9	124.9	0.0
14 Nonmetallic minerals, except fuels	3	94	114.4	113.0	−1.2
20 Food and kindred products	112	500	121.7	121.7	0.0
21 Tobacco manufactures	9	42	120.0	119.8	−0.1
22 Textile mill products	68	217	100.1	99.6	−0.5
23 Apparel and other textile products	36	103	110.8	110.7	−0.1
24 Lumber and wood products	65	321	98.7	98.7	0.0
25 Furniture and fixtures	25	129	113.6	114.0	0.4
26 Paper and allied products	47	185	128.5	128.6	0.1
27 Printing and publishing	1	2	120.4	120.5	−0.1
28 Chemicals and allied products	168	588	149.4	148.9	−0.5
29 Petroleum and coal products	10	40	134.7	134.2	−0.4
30 Rubber and plastic products	73	219	129.2	128.8	−0.3
31 Leather and leather products	25	70	110.5	110.4	−0.1
32 Stone, clay and glass products	53	259	119.6	119.7	0.1
33 Primary metals industry	124	494	129.0	128.5	−0.5
34 Fabricated metals products	160	579	131.2	130.8	−0.4
35 Machinery, except electrical	385	1,207	126.4	122.8	−2.9
36 Electrical equipment and supplies	195	626	119.7	119.3	−0.3
37 Transportation equipment	21	83	124.1	124.0	0.1
38 Instruments and related parts	29	83	112.4	112.7	0.3
39 Miscellaneous manufactures	46	139	116.5	117.7	1.1
Total	1,686	6,146	126.0	125.6	−0.4

Notes:
a. $\sum_{i=1}^{n} P_{it} / \sum_{i=1}^{n} P_{i(t-1)}$.
b. $\sum_{i=1}^{n} P_{it} / P_{i(t-1)}$.

Source: Computed from data tape of wholesale price observations, Bureau of Labor Statistics.

these industries the WPI specifications cover a wide range of products — a
result which, given the nature of these industries, is not at all surprising. In
other words, the two different methods of computation give significantly different results only in those instances where it would be more appropriate to use
the average of price relatives as the technique of computation.

   As has been noted, the individual price reports within a commodity are all
equally weighted by the BLS. In large part, this procedure has been followed

for want of appropriate weights. It has not been possible for BLS to determine how important a given producer is in the production of a specific commodity. It does not follow, however, that equal weighting is the best solution. A small number of large producers may often account for a large share of total production, and the price reaction of large and small producers to changing market conditions may differ substantially. Giving equal weight to all producers, therefore, may distort the price index by overweighting the price behavior of small producers. Given its resources and lack of access to census reports, BLS may not have any other alternative. But integration of the price collection effort with the collection of other information about the reporting establishments would permit a better system of weighting to be devised, either through more detailed questions on industrial censuses about the importance of the products which are being priced or in some cases through the current industrial reports collected on a monthly basis.

In summary, then, if, as appears to be appropriate, each price series should be treated as a separate commodity, the computation of price indexes should be based upon price relatives calculated at the series level, and weighted appropriately up to the product class level to which they contribute. This would then provide a systematic treatment of price observations which would be independent of the classification system.

System of Weighting Used for the Wholesale Price Index

After computing the price relative of average prices at the commodity level, the BLS then weights these price relatives by value of shipments in order to obtain price indexes for commodity groups, 5-digit product classes, and 4-digit industries. The shipments data are primarily obtained from the economic censuses. For the period from January 1967 to January 1976, the shipment weights referred to the year 1963. Although there was an economic census in 1967, no revision of weights using shipments data from this census was made because of a lack of funds to carry out the revision. Starting with January 1976, the shipments data obtained from the 1972 economic censuses are being used. The base reference period which is set equal to 100 is the year 1967, and this was not changed with the recent shift to 1972 base year weights.

In effect, the weighting system used by the BLS results in a Laspeyres index, weighted by the quantity of goods shipped in the base year. The actual calculation is carried out by multiplying the base year value of shipments by the change in price (i.e., the price relative) since the base year. This is in contrast to a straightforward application of the Laspeyres formula which would multiply the quantity of a product in the base year by its current year price. If systematically carried out at the most detailed level, the two computations would yield identical results. Since the base reference period in the BLS index is different from the weight base year, the index must also take into account the price relative between the reference year and the weight base year. As is shown below for an index for the year 1975, these calculations do in fact reduce to a Laspeyres index in which the quantity weights refer to the year 1963 and the reference year is 1967:

$$\frac{\sum_{i=1}^{n} (P_{i75}/P_{i63}) \cdot P_{i63} Q_{i63}}{\sum_{i=1}^{n} (P_{i67}/P_{i63}) \cdot P_{i63} Q_{i63}} = \frac{\sum_{i=1}^{n} P_{i75} Q_{i63}}{\sum_{i=1}^{n} P_{i67} Q_{i63}} \qquad (10.1)$$

In the longer run, such factors as growth of the economy, introduction of new products, changes in types of goods demanded by consumers and new technologies for producing them will lead to a difference between Laspeyres and Paasche indexes. In the shorter run, however, the major difference between the Laspeyres and Paasche indexes results from the inverse correlation that commonly exists between changes in price and changes in quantity. Those products whose prices rise the most tend to decline in relative sales, and products which fall in price or rise the least enjoy a relative expansion of sales. Because of this relationship, the Laspeyres weighting system will result in heavier weights for commodities that rise in price and lighter weights for commodities that fall in price than will the corresponding Paasche indexes. Consequently, quite aside from the long-run obsolescence of any fixed weight index, the Laspeyres index will report a larger cyclical increase than will the Paasche index. It is often argued that because of this substitution process the 'true' price index lies somewhere between the Laspeyres and Paasche indexes, and it was on this basis that Irving Fisher chose the geometric mean of the two as his 'ideal' index. The literature of price index theory offers a wide range of alternative weighting schemes, based on many different models of economic behavior.

One relatively simple alternative which would overcome some of the problems of Laspeyres quantity weights is the use of expenditure weights instead of quantity weights. Fixed quantity weights are unrealistic because they assume that the quantity of goods purchased is not affected by relative price changes, that is, that all demand curves are completely inelastic. In contrast, the use of fixed expenditure weights assumes that it is the share of expenditure on an item that is fixed. This is equivalent to a price elasticity of unity, i.e., a situation in which an increase in price results in an exactly offsetting decline in quantity so that the relative amount spent remains unchanged. Although the fixed expenditure assumption is obviously not valid for all commodities, on average it is true by definition, and it may be a good approximation for many individual commodities. An expenditure-weighted index will lie between the Laspeyres and Paasche indexes, and will not necessarily have either an upward or downward bias.

The same weighting information used for the Laspeyres index can be used to weight price relatively by relative expenditures, as shown below:

$$\sum_{i=1}^{n} \frac{P_{i75}}{P_{i67}} \cdot \frac{P_{i63} Q_{i63}}{\sum_{i=1}^{n} P_{i63} Q_{i63}} \qquad (10.2)$$

It should be noted that this analysis applies to comparisons between two years other than the base weight year. When a given year is being compared with the base weight year, the expenditure-weighted index reduces to the Laspeyres index, as shown below:

$$\sum_{i=1}^{n} \frac{P_{i75}}{P_{i63}} \cdot \frac{P_{i63} Q_{i63}}{\sum_{i=1}^{n} P_{i63} Q_{i63}} = \frac{\sum_{i=1}^{n} P_{i75} Q_{i63}}{\sum_{i=1}^{n} P_{i63} Q_{i63}} \qquad (10.3)$$

Gross and Net Output Weights

At the present time, the Wholesale Price Index is weighted by data obtained from the Census of Manufactures on value of shipments excluding the value of interplant transfers, military products and goods sold at retail directly from producing establishments. For different levels of aggregation, the weights are added, and thus the Wholesale Price Index as a whole reflects the influence of raw materials and intermediate products both as separate price indexes and as part of more highly fabricated products for which there are also price indexes. It is apparent that given this system of weighting the behavior of the index as a whole will depend to a major degree on how many such raw materials and intermediate products are included in the index.

The Stigler Committee Report in 1961 urged that the prices of individual commodities should be weighted according to their sales to other industries. This was termed 'net output' weighting since it represented value of shipments net of sales made within the industry. It was proposed that input–output relationships be used to determine how much of each commodity was sold outside a given industry. In more recent years, the name 'ring fence' has occasionally been given to such price indexes, which are constructed so that only the prices of the products leaving a given industry or sector are measured. It should be noted that the net output or ring fence weighting system is not the result of a process of aggregation — rather the weights are obtained through consolidation. Examples of various levels of net output weights are shown in Table 10.11 for specific 4-digit industries.

Table 10.11 Examples of Various Levels of Net Output Weights

		Total shipments	Shipments outside 2-digit industry ($mn)	Shipments outside mining and manufacturing
2011	Meat packing	13,237	10,826	10,486
2086	Soft drinks	3,000	2,966	2,966
2092	Soybean oil	1,753	683	323
3312	Blast furnaces	22,206	17,050	2,234
3411	Metal cans	2,639	2,625	176
3441	Fabricated structural steel	2,614	2,570	2,494

In this illustration, it can be seen that the gross and net output weights of different industries have very different relationships. Thus, in meat packing, approximately 30 percent of all shipments go to industries in food and kindred products, but very few sales are made to other 2-digit industries. In contrast, the soft drink industry sells little to either food and kindred products or any other industry in mining and manufacturing, while almost two-thirds of the value of shipments of soybean oil is sold within food and kindred products and half of the remainder is sold to other 2-digit industries, leaving less than 20 percent to be sold outside of mining and manufacturing. In primary metals and fabricated metal products, a basic industry such as blast furnaces sells a substantial portion of its product within its own 2-digit industry and most of the remainder to other 2-digit industries in mining and manufactures. Metal cans, however, sell practically nothing within their own 2-digit industry, and make almost all of their shipments to other 2-digit industries in mining and manufacturing. Finally, fabricated structural steel sells most of its output outside of mining and manufacturing, presumably to the construction industry.

In order to derive the various levels of gross and net output weights required for different levels of aggregation, it is necessary to use an input–output table to compute the appropriate weights at the finest level of aggregation possible. Ideally, one would like to have an input–output table at the 7-digit product level, since it is at this level that weights are to be applied. Such detail is not available, however, and sufficient homogeneity generally exists at the 4-digit level to catch most of the inter-industry transactions. A practical procedure, therefore, is to use gross value of shipments weights at the 7-digit level to produce 4-digit industry price indexes. The Bureau of Labor Statistics has indicated that they intend to review each 7-digit product and develop the best net weight possible. Then at the 4-digit level, net output weights can be used to obtain various higher levels of aggregation which may be desired.

Table 10.12 compares the results of applying gross output and net output weights to the wholesale price data, using as a basis the 1967 input–output table. In this exercise, it should be borne in mind that the wholesale price data are for the 2-digit industries or for the manufacturing sector as a whole. The weights which have been applied relate to the available data, and the 4-digit industries for which price data are not available have been omitted. The computation was made, however, to show the effect of the two different systems of weighting on the indexes. As can be seen, the difference for the period January 1974 to January 1975 was not large. The greatest difference was for the leather and leather products industry, where the net output weighted index rose substantially more than the gross output weighted index. In most of the other industries, there was relatively little difference between the indexes. The total

Table 10.12 Comparison of Price Indexes Computed with Gross Output Weights (Total Shipments) and Net Output Weights (Net Shipments Outside of Industry), January 1974–January 1975, with January 1974 = 100

SIC code and title	Gross output weights, 1967[10]	Net output weights, 1967[10]	Percent difference
20 Food and kindred products	111.4	112.4	0.8
21 Tobacco manufactures	120.8	120.8	0.0
22 Textile mill products	107.0	105.7	−1.2
23 Apparel and other textile products	105.9	106.0	0.1
24 Lumber and wood products	94.4	95.6	1.3
25 Furniture and fixtures	114.5	114.5	0.0
26 Paper and allied products	143.9	141.0	−2.0
27 Printing and publishing	142.3	142.3	0.0
28 Chemicals and allied products	137.8	136.1	−1.2
29 Petroleum and coal products	156.8	156.3	−0.3
30 Rubber and plastic products	131.4	131.4	0.0
31 Leather and leather products	101.5	106.5	5.0
32 Stone, clay and glass products	119.2	119.3	0.1
33 Primary metals industry	135.2	135.4	0.1
34 Fabricated metal products	133.6	133.8	0.1
35 Machinery except electrical	126.6	126.7	0.1
36 Electrical equipment and supplies	117.9	118.1	0.2
37 Transportation equipment	118.8	117.3	−1.3
38 Instruments and related parts	113.0	112.7	−0.3
39 Miscellaneous manufactures	116.5	116.5	0.0
Total	124.6	122.8	−1.4
WPI Industrial commodities (1963 BLS weights)	123.8		
WPI All commodities (1963 BLS weights)	117.1		

Sources: 1967 input–output table at 4-digit level, Bureau of Economic Analysis, and data tapes for wholesale price observations, Bureau of Labor Statistics.

for all manufacturing was obtained by using net output weights reflecting shipments outside of mining and manufacturing, and even in this instance the difference between the gross and net output weighting systems was not very large. It is also interesting to note that the BLS Wholesale Price Index for industrial commodities using 1963 weights came out to be approximately the same as the gross and net output weighted indexes shown in Table 10.12, for which 1967 weights were used.

Although this table does not show a sharp difference between the gross and net output weights, this does not mean that the weights used are a matter of indifference. The BLS wholesale price commodity index (in contrast to the constructed example of SIC industry price indexes in Table 10.12) includes commodities at many different levels of production, and the aggregate index is very much influenced by agricultural products and raw materials. In large part these agricultural products and raw materials account for the well-known sensitivity of the Wholesale Price Index. But at the same time they give a distorted view of price behavior for the economy as a whole. In an index of producers' prices it is indeed desirable to include price information on raw materials as well as finished products, but the weighting system used to obtain aggregate indexes should not permit these commodities to have an undue influence. The use of net output weights makes it possible both to provide the full amount of detail desired and to ensure that the prices of commodities are correctly weighted at each level of aggregation. The use of such net output weights is contemplated in the BLS's future plans.

Price Indexes of Value Added

In addition to constructing net output price indexes for industries or sectors, it is also possible to develop price indexes which refer to the value added by the industry or sector. The Bureau of Economic Analysis of the Department of Commerce now carries out a double deflation of value added by 2-digit industry, using prices of the inputs into an industry and prices of the outputs of the same industry. The result is a value added measurement in constant dollars. This measure of real value added for each industry is then divided into value added in current prices to derive an implicit deflator for value added. This implicit deflator is in fact a Paasche weighted price index, since it has been derived using current values. It would have been equally possible to develop a fixed-weight Laspeyres price index of value added directly by compiling base year output in current prices and subtracting from it base year input in current prices, thus obtaining base year value added in current prices.

A price index of value added, unlike the net output price index, measures the contribution of a specific industry to the change in prices taking place in the economy. If an industry faced with a price increase of raw materials changes its output prices only sufficiently to cover the increased raw materials cost, there would be no change in its value added price index although its net output price index would increase. Conversely, if the price of raw materials falls and this fall is not reflected in output prices, the net output price index would remain constant but the value added price index would increase. In other words, the value added price index measures the extent to which a given industry or sector is dampening the inflationary pressures in the economy or contributing to them. Value added price indexes are thus very useful for the analysis of inflation in order to determine the sectors and industries where the price increases are originating. It would be possible, of course, to go further and analyze the effect of increases in wages, changes in productivity and/or changes in the gross margins of producers within an industry or sector. For such analysis, however, price data relating to input and output prices need to be carefully matched with information relating to wage costs, inventories, shipments and capital consumption allowances measured at replacement cost.

Unfortunately, the present wholesale price data are too incomplete to permit the computation of value added price indexes and comparable net output indexes at a detailed industry level. Nevertheless, some rough idea of the difference between the present Wholesale Price Index for industrial commodities and an implicit value added price deflator for the manufacturing sector can be obtained. This is shown in Figure 10.1 for the years 1947–75. Both indexes use 1967 as a reference base. During the period from 1947 to approximately 1959 the WPI of industrial commodities rose more slowly than did the implicit value added price deflator for manufacturing. This reflects the fact that during this period the prices of raw materials used by the manufacturing sector were rising more slowly than the prices of the sector's output. For the period from 1959 to 1969, although there was some fluctuation of the two indexes they generally moved together. Since 1971, however, the WPI has risen far more sharply than the implicit value added price deflator for manufacturing, indicating that raw material prices have risen faster than manufactured goods prices.

Thus it is apparent that no single system of weighting is appropriate for all purposes. Using value of shipments weights on a gross output basis, as is presently done, is nevertheless misleading, and inappropriate at higher levels of aggregation. Net output weights would correct this deficiency. At more detailed levels net output weights yield essentially the same price indexes as are obtained with the present gross output weights, but at higher levels of aggregation the double counting of intermediate outputs is eliminated and the price indexes for industries and sectors more accurately reflect the prices of the output which they produce. Value added price indexes are not a substitute for net output price indexes; rather, they provide an additional type of information which is extremely useful for understanding the price behavior of the economy. When related to measures of output, productivity, wage cost and margins, value

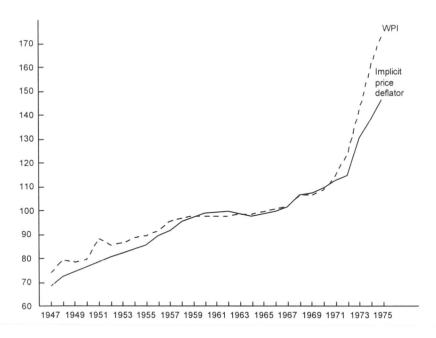

Sources: WPI, Bureau of Labor Statistics and Implicit Deflator, Bureau of Economic Analysis.

Figure 10.1 The Wholesale Price Index for Industrial Commodities and the
Implicit Price Deflator for the Manufacturing Sector, 1947–75
(1967 = 100)

added price indexes contribute to an understanding of price behavior which is essential for the development of economic policy to stabilize prices, promote economic growth and ensure full employment.

In order to meet these needs, the Wholesale Price Index would have to be transformed into a system of industrial prices of the type which has been described under the discussion of classification systems. It should be possible to use the individual price measurements with different weighting systems to produce a wide variety of interrelated price indexes, and to relate the industrial price data directly to price data collected for other parts of the economy. Thus it should be possible to link the prices of industrial products to those of consumer goods, producers' durables and exports and imports, so that the transmission of price changes through the various sectors of the economy can be observed. This approach does, of course, necessitate a high degree of integration between the collection of price data and the collection of other economic information relating to establishments engaged in producing the products which are priced.

4. SAMPLING AND RELIABILITY

Current Methods of Price Collection

The current methods of collecting wholesale price data have evolved gradually over the past 75 years as the Wholesale Price Index has grown both in number of commodities covered and number of price reporters surveyed. As has already been noted in the discussion of classification systems, the classification system used for the Wholesale Price Index is unique and is not directly related to other industrial or product classification systems. Since the wholesale price classification system covers only those commodities which are directly priced by the Bureau of Labor Statistics, it changes with changes in the coverage of the Wholesale Price Index, and cannot be used as a framework for defining the universe of the price data to be covered.

Although the Bureau of Labor Statistics (1971, p. 98) defines the universe of the Wholesale Price Index as consisting 'of all commodities sold in commercial transactions in primary markets of the United States,' there has been no formal attempt to sample this universe on a probability basis. Rather, 'judgmental' selection has determined which products are to be priced and which price reporters are to be queried. Commodity specialists responsible for specific commodity groups use census data to determine the relative importance of different industries and product classes, but despite this, as has already been shown, the relative coverage of different industries and products varies widely. In part, this is due to the lack of a systematic framework for data collection, and the evolutionary development of the index which has been shaped by the demands of different users for prices of specific products. In part, the choice of products to be included is a reflection of the organization and staffing of the price collection and data processing work within the Bureau of Labor Statistics. The commodity specialists become well acquainted with the trade associations and major firms in a given area of specialization. They obtain a 'feel' for deciding which commodities are best to price from the industry and user point of view. This same approach also determines which producers are to be queried with reference to a given commodity. Trade associations or firms already being surveyed can usually supply the names of other firms producing a given commodity. The determination of both the commodity selection and the price reporter thus, in large measure, depends on the diligence of the commodity specialist, and the personal contacts which he can build up. Just as in most libraries the collection of books in various areas of specialization is a direct reflection of the scholars working in those areas, so also are the prices collected by Bureau of Labor Statistics a reflection of the commodity specialists in different areas.

Since the selection of both commodities and price reporters is carried out on a judgmental basis, it is not possible to compute meaningful estimates of sampling errors. The equal weighting of all price reports and the irregularity of coverage makes any judgment relating to reliability very difficult to justify. This does not mean that the Wholesale Price Index is unreliable; rather it means that given present information it is not possible to judge its reliability. One of the strongest reasons for going to probability sampling is to provide the basis for measuring sampling errors.

The Need for a Sampling Frame

Probability sampling requires a suitable sampling frame which can identify what commodities are produced and what firms or establishments produce the commodities. Although such information is provided by industrial censuses, the Bureau of the Census is forbidden by law under the confidentiality provisions of Title 13 of the US Code from revealing the names of respondents to the census. Currently, discussion is under way on the possibility of making an industrial register generally available to federal statistical agencies. Such a register would be helpful, in that it would provide the names of firms and establishments, their general industrial classification and their employment size class, but this information alone would not furnish an adequate basis for developing a probability sample.

Although the Bureau of Labor Statistics is contemplating the use of a variety of sources of information as the basis for its sampling, including unemployment insurance and even Dun and Bradstreet credit data, it should be generally recognized that these are at best makeshift substitutes and provide a 'second best' basis for a complete probability sampling frame. If the Bureau of Labor Statistics were to try to obtain suitable information on its own through independent surveys it would in essence be conducting a second industrial census, in large part duplicating the industrial census collected by the Bureau of the Census. To carry out such an independent survey in the manner required would not only involve considerable expense, but it would raise serious questions about reporting burdens and wasteful duplication of effort within the federal government. In other words, if the Bureau of Labor Statistics accepts the present limitations on data confidentiality, it cannot effectively carry out probability sampling; but if an attempt is made to remedy the situation directly it would result in uneconomic duplication of information gathered already by the federal government. From all points of view, it is apparent that the development of a sampling frame for probability sampling needs to be a cooperative effort that would involve both the Bureau of Labor Statistics and the Bureau of the Census. What is needed, furthermore, is not merely a single occasion, one-time arrangement, since the essence of probability sampling is that the sample should reflect the introduction of new products and new producers and the disappearance of old products and old producers. The sampling frame is needed not only for the selection of individual commodities, but also to provide the basic weighting system for price indexes. In order to develop net output price indexes, information is needed on the sales of individual products to other industries and to final sales in the economy.

Classification and Sampling Stratification

The Standard Industrial Classification (SIC) system is hierarchical in nature. Individual commodities are identified at a 7-digit product level and grouped into 5-digit product classes. The 5-digit product classes are combined into 4-digit industries, and these in turn are further aggregated into 3-digit and 2-digit industry groupings. The classifications of products and industries are based on such considerations as the types of raw material inputs, the similarity of production processes, and the nature of the market for the output. Although it is essential to base the collection of price data and the development of price indexes on the Standard Industrial Classification system, it is neither feasible nor desirable to implement it fully at the most detailed 7-digit product level. On the one hand the 7-digit product detail would require price indexes for over 12,000 products, many of which may be relatively unimportant or may behave very similarly to other products. Thus, in the current Wholesale Price Index, the price behavior of common wire nails and fence staples is quite similar and probably does not need to be distinguished in separate price indexes. On the other hand, other 7-digit products may from the point of view of price behavior be too broadly defined. For example, there may be regional differences in the price behavior of locally produced products such as lumber, concrete, or other building materials, or price differences for a product such as coal which is sold to different classes of purchasers (e.g., contract vs spot).

For these reasons, the classification system used for sampling prices should be based on the similarity of price behavior of the products within the industry and/or product classifications. This can reduce the sample size which is needed to achieve a given level of sampling reliability. First, stratified sampling would permit the use of relatively small samples in those cases where there is considerable homogeneity in price behavior and larger samples where there are wide differences in price behavior. Second, by combining product classes which exhibit similar price behavior, a single sample can be used to measure price behavior where a number of different samples would otherwise have been required — each of the same size as the sample for the combined group — to achieve the same level of reliability at the individual product class level. Third, in cases where detailed price data are not required, similarity of price behavior may make it possible to use price indexes at higher levels of aggregation to indicate the general price behavior. This latter technique may be applied for 'miscellaneous' or 'not elsewhere classified' products in a given industry.

The Need for Benchmark Data

The WPI is currently based on approximately 8,500 monthly price reports. The monthly sample size is in principle kept constant, and the price indexes for monthly, quarterly, annual and five-year periods are all derived from the same sets of data. This procedure is in contrast with that employed in the collection of other economic data for manufacturing, which employs comprehensive economic censuses every five years, annual surveys of all large manufacturing establishments and samples for smaller establishments and monthly current industrial reports on selected information from a monthly sample. The use of comprehensive benchmarks supplemented by sampling for intervening periods has two rather obvious advantages. First, the benchmark periods provide detailed and comprehensive information which permits certain types of analysis that could not be carried out otherwise. Thus, for example, quality adjustments, and checks with purchaser prices and unit values could be carried out. Second, the benchmark data also provide the basis for designing efficient samples for the intervening periods. They provide the frame for sampling and can be used to test the validity of specific sampling procedures.

There is a corresponding need in the Industrial Price Index program for more comprehensive collection of price data at benchmark periods and for the development of samples of different sizes for annual, quarterly and monthly price measurement. The comprehensive benchmark price data are needed for the design of appropriate classification systems and for the stratification of sampling and selection of products and reporters on a probability basis. Without such benchmark price data, sampling will be less efficient and more costly; perhaps even more importantly, it will not be possible to test the validity of specific sampling procedures. Furthermore, as in the other economic data on manufacturing, it does not follow that the same sample size should be used for annual, quarterly and monthly price indexes. Annual price indexes are used primarily for deflation of national income and product accounts and the measurement of real output at fairly detailed industry and product levels. It may be that in some cases monthly pricing is helpful in arriving at within-year price variation to provide more accurate deflation, but in other instances price changes may be more regular and less frequent.

Although quarterly price indexes are also used for deflation of national income accounts, much less detail is available on a quarterly basis. Finally, monthly price indexes are primarily used for monitoring prices and indexation. For these purposes, even less detail may be required. By definition, all monthly price data will be available for quarterly price comparisons, and all quarterly price data will be available for annual comparisons. The implication of this is that additional series should be added to the monthly sample for quarterly price measurement, and additional price series should be added to the quarterly price data for annual price measurement. However, in some instances, it may be that monthly price collection does not add to the workload significantly and that interaction with the reporter improves the quality of response and helps to capture product change.

Redundancy of Price Data

Probability sampling can provide estimates of sampling error, but in many cases it may not be feasible to develop true probability samples. Difficulties in developing suitable product specifications, the existence of industrial concentration and regional differences may make probability sampling difficult and consequently may introduce bias into the measurement of sampling error. Another way of approaching the sampling problem is to ask whether there is redundancy in the price data within a given product class. If redundancy exists, this would mean that some of the price series could be omitted with no loss of information. In other words, the price index that is obtained for a product class could have been obtained by using a smaller set of observations than was actually used. In such a case it follows that the additional observations have no significant effect on the price index.

In empirical terms, it is possible to test for this kind of redundancy by using stepwise regression analysis to determine how many observations are required to estimate the actually observed price index with a correlation coefficient of 1.0. If all the observations are required, the correlation coefficient of 1.0 will not be reached until the last step in the stepwise regression analysis. On the other hand, if there is redundancy the correlation coefficient of 1.0 will be reached before the last step and in fact the stepwise regression will stop since the residual variance to be explained will become too small to compute. Examples of the pattern taken by the stepwise regression coefficient in successive steps for redundant and nonredundant product classes are shown in Figure 10.2. In this figure, the correlation coefficients (r^2) are plotted on the vertical axis and the number of observations used at each step in the regression are shown on the horizontal axis. For product class A, a correlation coefficient of 1.0 is reached only by using the full set of N observations and there is thus no redundancy. For product class B, the correlation coefficient of 1.0 is reached at X observations and the observations from X to N can be considered redundant.

To test the degree of redundancy in the present wholesale price data, such calculations were made using wholesale price observations for commodities within 5-digit product classes over the period 1967–72. For this experiment, the price series used were limited to those which were continuous over the full period and were not linked or adjusted. The results of the experiment for seven

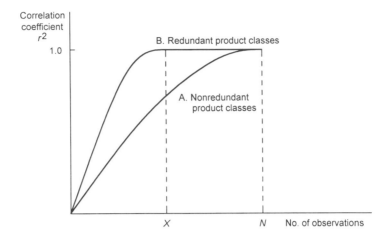

*Figure 10.2 Stepwise Regression Patterns of Redundant and
Nonredundant Product Classes*

5-digit product classes is shown in Table 10.13. For the first three product classes, softwood lumber, concrete blocks and steel forgings, the correlation coefficient of 1.0 was not reached until the last observation. In the case of softwood lumber, the correlation with even the first observation was nevertheless very high and a correlation of over 0.99 was reached by the fifth observation. In contrast, concrete blocks started with a very low correlation coefficient and by the next to the last observation had only reached 0.96. With respect to the last four product classes, steel pipe, power valves, primary batteries and glass containers, some redundancy appeared. There were wide differences, however, in the pattern and the degree of redundancy. Primary batteries, for example, started off with low correlations and achieved a correlation of 1.0 with eight out of the ten observations. In contrast, glass containers started off with a correlation of over 0.98 and achieved an r^2 of approximately 1.0 at step 8, indicating that the remaining nine observations were redundant.

For this analysis, reporter price series have been pooled for different commodities within a given product class. However, in practical terms, the distinctions between reporter price series, commodities and product classes are all somewhat arbitrary and depend upon what specific definitions and classifications are used. Although, for practical reasons, it may be useful to compile price indexes at the 5-digit product class level, in many industries there may be less difference between 5-digit product classes than between reporter price series and commodities within product classes. Where this is true, it would be reasonable to pool all reporter price series within a 4-digit industry to see to what extent they can be used to estimate all of the 5-digit product classes within the 4-digit industry. In the stepwise regression analysis, this means that instead

Table 10.13 *Stepwise Correlation Coefficients for Individual Product Classes*

Number of obser- vations	Softwood lumber 24212	Concrete blocks 32170	Steel forgings 34621	Steel pipe 33176	Power valves 34943	Primary batteries 34573	Glass containers 32210
1	0.859998	0.342853	0.352587	0.774985	0.678913	0.372166	0.984675
2	0.963505	0.588714	0.631847	0.964282	0.985524	0.740008	0.994897
3	0.978796	0.689256	0.792047	0.996008	1.000000	0.846823	0.997867
4	0.988063	0.795010	0.858825	0.999763	xxxxxxxx	0.963844	0.999291
5	0.995316	0.859549	0.923011	0.999999	xxxxxxxx	0.981510	0.999863
6	0.996749	0.917472	0.952753	xxxxxxx	xxxxxxxx	0.998864	0.999892
7	0.997750	0.963150	0.968858	xxxxxxx	xxxxxxxx	0.999722	0.999977
8	0.998510	1.000000	0.983546			1.000000	0.999997
9	0.999154		0.992340			xxxxxxxx	xxxxxxx
10	0.999507		0.995594			xxxxxxxx	xxxxxxx
11	0.999765		0.997790				xxxxxxx
12	0.999869		1.000000				xxxxxxx
13	1.000000						xxxxxxx
14							xxxxxxx
15							xxxxxxx
16							xxxxxxx
17							xxxxxxx

Source: Computed from Wholesale Price Reporter Series 1967–72.

of estimating a single dependent variable, i.e., the 5-digit product class, there will be a number of different dependent variables to be predicted, i.e., all the 5-digit product classes within a 4-digit industry. The independent variables would include all the reporter price series within the 4-digit industry which in effect would be used with different regression coefficients to estimate each of the price indexes for the 5-digit product classes.

The result of such stepwise regression analysis for the 5-digit product classes in the 4-digit paper and steel industries is shown in Table 10.14. In the case of the paper industry the 5-digit product classes pertain to newsprint (26211), printing paper (26213), book paper (26214), writing paper (26216) and raft paper (26217). It was possible to estimate the price indexes for these 5-digit product classes with a correlation coefficient of 1.0 by using seven reporter price series out of the 12 which existed in this 4-digit industry. In the case of steel, six 5-digit product classes were distinguished. They were coke oven and blast furnace products (33121), steel ingot and semi-finished shapes (33122), hot rolled sheet and strip (33123), hot rolled bar shapes (33124), steel wire (33125) and steel pipe (33126). In all some 51 reporter price series were available for these products but using only 18 resulted in a correlation coefficient of over 0.99 for the price indexes for all six 5-digit product classes; with 34 observations the correlation reached 1.0.

*Table 10.14 Stepwise Correlation Coefficients for All Product Classes in
4-digit SIC Industries*

Number of observations	Paper 2621	Steel 3312	Number of observations	Paper 2621	Steel 3312
1	0.369283	0.427573	19		0.995968
2	0.431817	0.571979	20		0.996344
3	0.451080	0.661872	21		0.996868
4	0.564523	0.691034	22		0.996904
5	0.806137	0.714781	23		0.997433
6	0.964373	0.724923	24		0.997977
7	1.000000	0.729477	25		0.998032
8	xxxxxxxx	0.818137	26		0.998268
9	xxxxxxxx	0.869453	27		0.998278
10	xxxxxxxx	0.899005	28		0.998298
11	xxxxxxxx	0.902981	29		0.998303
12	xxxxxxxx	0.904480	30		0.998983
13		0.904818	31		0.999258
14		0.906025	32		0.999587
15		0.906359	33		0.999932
16		0.961074	34		0.999993
17		0.986395	⇓		xxxxxxx
18		0.992384	51		xxxxxxx

Source: Computed from Wholesale Price Reporter Series 1967–1972.

What the stepwise regression analysis of redundancy suggests is that it may be possible to make efficient use of smaller sets of reporter price series and thus increase the sampling efficiency. This is especially true if, as suggested, different sizes of samples are used for benchmark periods, annual, quarterly and monthly price indexes. Stepwise regression analysis can be used to determine where redundancy exists and can indicate what reporter price series are redundant and how weighting systems should be altered to redistribute the weights of those reporter price series which are redundant. It is not proposed that stepwise regression analysis be used to design the price indexes for benchmark periods or even annual periods; where stepwise regression is primarily useful is in reducing the sample size required for short-term price measurement. Since, by definition, redundant prices can be substituted for nonredundant prices, if for operational or analytical reasons specific reporter price series are considered to be essential, the stepwise regression analysis can be constrained to enter these reporter price series first. Stepwise regression analysis cannot, of course, be used to determine what additional prices need to be collected to improve the index; only the utilization of a suitable sampling frame and probability sampling can accomplish this. The major use of stepwise regression analysis is to indicate where similarities in price behavior permit certain prices to be used successfully as proxies for others.

Operational Considerations

In the discussion of the need for a sampling frame it was pointed out that it was not practical for the Bureau of Labor Statistics to collect the information needed for the development of such a sampling frame. In the collection of price data the question must also be raised whether it is practical or sensible to collect price information separately from other economic information. On the one hand, it is apparent that the data on prices, value of shipments, inventory and other related economic variables are ultimately used in relation to one another. If such relationships can be established at the level of the firm or establishment, this will have important implications for the accuracy of measurement at more aggregative levels. From an analytical point of view, it is not reasonable that one government agency should collect one type of information from producers and another government agency should collect related information from the same producers, with each government agency separately processing its own information. From the point of view of sampling and data processing also, a combined effort would result in a smaller reporting burden for producers, and more reliable and internally consistent data, due to more efficient editing and processing procedures. For all these reasons, it is important that price data should be collected in conjunction with other economic information.

5. VALIDITY OF THE WHOLESALE PRICE INDEX

Product Change and Price Adjustments

Valid price measurement depends to a major degree on the availability of observations of prices for identical products over a period of time. A significant turnover of products or a change in their characteristics makes the problem of price measurement more difficult and the interpretation of the results more questionable. But, in the process of economic change, new products appear on the market, old products disappear and the specifications of existing products may change significantly. It is appropriate, therefore, to examine the impact of such changes on the wholesale price observations. This has been done in Table 10.15 for the year 1974.

During 1974, there were almost 104,000 separate price observations. Of these, approximately 102,000 were for price series that were continuous from month to month, i.e., for which there was a price report for the current month and the previous month, and no adjustment was needed for changes in specification. Linked prices to fill in missing observations or to adjust reported prices for changes in product specifications were established for approximately

Table 10.15 Monthly Continuity of Price Observations during 1974

SIC code and title	Continuous series	Linked series	New series	Discontinued series
01 Agriculture and crops	1,163	1	0	0
02 Agriculture and livestock	476	0	0	2
08 Forestry	84	0	0	0
09 Fishing	84	0	0	0
10 Metal mining	60	0	0	0
11 Anthracite mining	144	0	0	0
12 Bituminous coal and lignite	484	3	9	5
13 Oil and gas extraction	730	0	17	8
14 Nonmetallic minerals, exc. fuels	2,264	2	0	0
20 Food and kindred products	7,934	6	35	14
21 Tobacco manufactures	561	3	0	0
22 Textile mill products	3,862	39	10	20
23 Apparel and other textile products	1,775	23	7	7
24 Lumber and wood products	4,648	11	14	13
25 Furniture and fixtures	1,937	30	0	7
26 Paper and allied products	2,757	15	17	13
27 Printing and publishing	72	0	0	0
28 Chemicals and allied products	9,668	36	33	29
29 Petroleum and coal products	791	35	34	11
30 Rubber and plastic products	3,304	34	1	25
31 Leather and leather products	1,134	21	4	5
32 Stone, clay and glass products	3,439	16	35	12
33 Primary metal products	7,668	46	17	27
34 Fabricated metal products	8,960	93	27	55
35 Machinery, exc. electrical	21,418	293	139	105
36 Electrical equipment and supplies	10,023	116	37	70
37 Transportation equipment	2,365	105	5	8
38 Instruments and related parts	1,667	32	4	2
39 Miscellaneous manufactures	2,460	32	8	17
Total	101,944	994	453	455
Monthly average	8,495	83	38	38

Source: Computed from data tape of wholesale price observations, Bureau of Labor Statistics.

1,000 observations, less than 1 percent of the total, and new commodities introduced and old commodities dropped each amounted to approximately 450 observations, less than one-half of 1 percent of the total. While the number of product changes is quite small, the magnitude of their effect is probably some-what larger since in many product areas major changes in prices coincide with model changes. Nevertheless, it does not appear likely that the price index over a one-year period is seriously influenced by product discontinuation or adjust-ments of price data made by the Bureau of Labor Statistics.

There is, however, a broader aspect to the question of whether the Whole-sale Price Index captures the dynamic quality of product change. BLS adjusts the price observations only in those cases where the change in the specification of the product is directly associated with a change in price reflecting the cost change. Thus if new features are added to a product which increase its cost of production, a price adjustment will, in principle, be made to deduct the cost of the improvements from the stated price. The estimate of the cost change is usually obtained directly from the producer. It is also true that a change in specifications eliminating special features with an accompanying lower price would result in a downward adjustment of price to take into account the reduction in the costs of production.

On the other hand, where there are design changes which affect the performance of a product but are unrelated to the cost of production, there is no recognition of this fact other than the publication of the new specification. In practical terms, there is no easy way to introduce price adjustments if the changes in specification are not directly related to cost or had not previously been available as special features with known prices.

The introduction of new products and the dropping of old products do not in themselves affect the price index. New products are brought into the index only after observations have been obtained for the new product for both the current month and the previous month. Similarly, products are dropped when there is no price for the current month. A necessary consequence of this procedure, however, is that if new products come in at lower prices and are substituted for old products at higher prices, this *de facto* reduction is not captured by the price index. Thus, for example, integrated circuit pocket calculators are considered to be a new product, displacing an old product, mechanical calculators. The fact that the new product both is available at a fraction of the cost of the old product and represents a major improvement in efficiency is not captured by the price index.

Although the month-to-month change in specifications of the products included in the price index is relatively small, these changes are of a cumulative nature; over a period of time they do become significant. Table 10.16 shows the degree of continuity over the whole period 1967–75 for both products and reporters. There were approximately 1,800 products which were reported continuously over the period. New products were equal to more than 50 percent of the continuous products. A somewhat smaller number of products was dropped, reflecting the fact that the number of products included in the Wholesale Price Index was expanding over this period. Different industries showed quite different patterns of product continuity and replacement. In food and kindred products, for example, new products represented less than 10 percent of the continuous products, whereas in machinery the number of new products substantially exceeded the number of continuous products. As might be expected, the areas where technological change was great were also the areas where the most product change took place. To the extent that the new products were superior to the products which disappeared, this dimension of price change remains unmeasured and is assumed to be nonexistent.

Price Measurement

*Table 10.16 Continuity of Products and Reporter Series, January 1967–
January 1975*

SIC code and title	Products			Reporter series within continuous products		
	Contin-uous	New	Dropped	Contin-uous	New	Dropped
01 Agriculture and crops	61	0	27	83	10	6
02 Agriculture and livestock	27	4	0	34	0	2
08 Forestry	4	0	0	7	0	0
09 Fishing	7	0	0	7	0	0
10 Metal mining	3	1	2	3	0	0
11 Anthracite mining	2	0	0	0	18	12
12 Bituminous coal and lignite	2	3	3	4	5	3
13 Oil and gas extraction	8	7	0	17	13	6
14 Nonmetallic minerals, exc. fuels	6	1	2	149	6	16
20 Food and kindred products	188	16	22	466	127	154
21 Tobacco manufactures	9	0	0	47	0	1
22 Textile mill products	83	31	36	186	62	109
23 Apparel and other textile products	35	10	21	73	37	82
24 Lumber and wood products	72	22	2	173	82	117
25 Furniture and fixtures	28	0	2	140	22	63
26 Paper and allied products	45	21	13	138	52	32
27 Printing and publishing	1	0	0	4	0	0
28 Chemicals and allied products	241	92	99	432	81	93
29 Petroleum and coal products	8	17	30	29	14	12
30 Rubber and plastic products	36	54	2	71	48	51
31 Leather and leather products	30	8	5	55	19	19
32 Stone, clay and glass products	43	27	18	177	22	37
33 Primary metal products	139	36	21	408	105	106
34 Fabricated metal products	142	41	24	410	41	24
35 Machinery, exc. electrical	241	304	159	562	345	159
36 Electrical equipment and supplies	165	91	28	468	133	146
37 Transportation equipment	63	44	15	78	65	14
38 Instruments and related parts	50	11	1	79	23	16
39 Miscellaneous manufactures	56	1	2	145	45	36
Total	1,795	842	518	4,425	1,497	1,444

Source: Computed from data tape of wholesale price observations, Bureau of Labor Statistics.

Within products which were continuously reported, new price reporters were added and old price reporters disappeared. This turnover does not necessarily cause discontinuity in the price observations since, as in the case of new products, new price reports are linked in only after their prices have been reported for two successive months. For price reporters as a whole, replacements came to approximately one-third of the continuous reporters. Again, there was considerable variation by industry but not to the same degree as was observed for products. As in the case of product turnover, the turnover of reporters may result in a failure to reflect an actual price change in the index. If low-cost producers enter the market and successfully drive out high-cost producers, the result is a real fall in the price of the commodity. Given the way new reporters are brought into the index, however, such an introduction of new low-price reporters and elimination of old high-price reporters will have no effect on the price index. Furthermore, the normal operation of markets which results in a shift of sales to existing low-price producers away from existing high-price producers also is not reflected in the price index. This is, of course, a characteristic of any price index where the weight is fixed at the producer level, the fixed weight being part of the index assumption of base year technology. In such a case, although it is true that, seen from the producer's point of view there would be no change in prices, from the purchaser's point of view, prices would fall.

As has been indicated, the Bureau of Labor Statistics adjusts reported prices to take into account changes in commodity specifications which may result from a producer changing the design of his product, altering the terms of sale, quoting a price for a different unit of quantity, etc. In such cases the Bureau adjusts the price reported for the previous month so as to make it more comparable to the price of the commodity as it is currently being reported. Thus, for example, if a commodity is improved by adding a new feature which also raises the price, then instead of comparing the currently reported price with the previous month's price, an adjusted 'link price' is computed for the previous month and the price index is based on the relation between the current price and the link price. In those instances where there has merely been a change in the unit of quantity on which the price report is based (e.g., gross to dozen or 1 lb. to 100 lb.), the adjustment required to obtain the link price is straightforward, but it may be quite large. Over the period from January 1967 through January 1975, the Bureau of Labor Statistics made adjustments to compute link prices for approximately 6,400 observations out of the total of 470,000. Table 10.17 shows the distribution of link prices as a percentage of reported prices. A link price which is higher than the reported price indicates that the price of the previous period was adjusted upward to be more comparable with the current month's price; such an adjustment would lower the price index over what it would have been if no adjustment had been made.

For a number of industries, the upward and downward adjustments are roughly balanced, but this is not true for all. For industries which produce more highly fabricated products, e.g., transportation equipment, machinery, instruments, apparel and textile products, the upward adjustment of reported prices to take into account new product features is apparent. The only industry in which reported prices were substantially more often adjusted downward was the lumber industry, and this for the most part reflected unit of quantity adjustments. It is undoubtedly true that the price adjustments which the Bureau of Labor Statistics introduces do substantially improve the quality of price measurement for specific commodities, but as has already been pointed out, they

*Table 10.17 Relation of Link Price Adjustments to Original Reported
Prices over the Period January 1967–January 1975*

		Link price as percent of quoted price						
SIC code and title	0.1– 9.9	10.0– 89.9	90.0– 99.9	100	100– 109.9	110– 999.9	Over 1,000	Total
01 Agriculture and crops	0	1	12	1	6	7	0	27
02 Agriculture and livestock	0	0	13	1	10	0	0	24
08 Forestry	0	0	0	0	0	0	0	0
09 Fishing	0	0	0	0	0	0	0	0
10 Metal mining	0	0	2	0	0	0	0	2
11 Anthracite mining	0	0	0	0	0	0	0	0
12 Bituminous coal and lignite	0	1	0	0	1	1	1	4
13 Oil and gas extraction	0	0	1	0	1	0	0	2
14 Nonmetallic minerals, exc. fuels	0	6	9	5	0	7	0	27
20 Food and kindred products	2	34	49	36	54	34	0	209
21 Tobacco manufactures	0	2	0	0	1	3	0	6
22 Textile mill products	0	54	62	13	42	88	1	260
23 Apparel and other textile products	1	12	25	8	40	88	0	174
24 Lumber and wood products	0	9	508	34	21	10	0	582
25 Furniture and fixtures	0	61	42	4	42	92	0	241
26 Paper and allied products	0	7	16	11	16	7	0	57
27 Printing and publishing	0	0	0	0	0	0	0	0
28 Chemicals and allied products	6	37	42	23	30	47	5	190
29 Petroleum and coal products	0	12	34	2	27	3	0	78
30 Rubber and plastic products	0	28	28	9	20	10	0	95
31 Leather and leather products	0	6	31	16	24	17	0	94
32 Stone, clay and glass products	4	22	43	6	63	27	1	166
33 Primary metal products	4	74	111	15	110	59	3	376
34 Fabricated metal products	3	93	104	57	101	90	1	449
35 Machinery, exc. electrical	82	266	182	131	429	434	19	1,543
36 Electrical equipment and supplies	1	144	125	58	193	227	4	752
37 Transportation equipment	2	32	74	57	482	87	3	737
38 Instruments and related parts	6	23	11	14	29	44	1	128
39 Miscellaneous manufactures	1	38	19	35	30	50	1	174
Total	112	962	1,543	536	1,772	1,432	40	6,397

Source: Computed from data tape of wholesale observations.

affect an almost insignificant fraction of all price reports. There is, of course, no way of determining the number or magnitude of the price adjustments that would be required to ensure true comparability in commodity prices over time.

Thus this examination of the product continuity and price adjustment of wholesale price data strongly suggests that the BLS treatment does result in an index that is little different from what would have resulted if there had been no product turnover and no price adjustment.

Nevertheless, the question remains whether this omission of the effect of changes in products and prices that actually do take place in itself constitutes a bias. It is sometimes possible to make some estimate of the consequences of this procedure. In a few instances, hedonic price indexes can be computed to take specification changes into account, but this technique is quite limited since it can only measure those aspects of quality change for which price data exist in previous periods. In other instances, it is possible that a functional or performance approach can be taken to specific products. Thus an automobile tire which can be used for 50,000 miles instead of 25,000 could be thought to provide twice as much service, so that the cost of the service of auto tires could be considered, in one sense, to have fallen by half. Unfortunately, the number of products for which performance or efficiency can be measured is very limited since, in most cases, subjective valuations are involved. Even in the case of tires, a 50,000-mile tire is not necessarily equal in value to two 25,000-mile tires, since it can be used on only one wheel at a time. There does not seem to be any satisfactory way to make adjustments for all the quality changes resulting from new products and product improvements. It is not at all clear that inadequate adjustments are better than none. Such a partial approach may capture only a small and unpredictable fraction of actual quality change, although giving the impression to the user that the price and quantity indexes have indeed been adjusted for quality change.

For these reasons, statistical agencies of the federal government have generally taken the position that quality improvements which are unrelated to cost of production should not be taken into account in the measurement of price change. In general this has meant a rather rigid adherence to specification pricing. The rationale behind this decision is both practical and theoretical. It is practical in the sense that it is the easiest and most operational procedure. It is theoretical in the sense that specification pricing provides a measure which is based on a single well-defined assumption, rather than on many individual, subjective or arbitrary assumptions made in the course of estimation. The major difficulty with such specification pricing is that the resulting price indexes will have a substantial upward bias since they do not capture the effect of new products and product improvements. For many types of analysis, this defect may not be serious, but the user should be fully aware of the implication of this method of measurement in the interpretation of real output and productivity.

Evaluation of Wholesale Price Data

Evaluations as to whether the wholesale price measurements collected by the Bureau of Labor Statistics represent 'true' price changes have been made by a number of different investigators. An Interagency Committee on the Measurement of Real Output (1970) headed by Alan Searle investigated the relation of the Wholesale Price Index data to unit price information in the Census of Manufactures. Stigler and Kindahl (1970) carried out a study of the behavior of industrial prices in which comparisons between the WPI and a set of prices specially collected by them were analyzed. Robert J. Gordon (1977) has recently completed a study on the measurement of durable goods prices in which he analyzed the validity of wholesale price measurements in this area. The Bureau of Economic Analysis of the Department of Commerce is currently constructing price indexes of goods purchased by the government and is comparing these indexes to the wholesale price indexes for the same commodities. Finally, the Council on Wage and Price Stability is conducting special studies for specific products and industries in order to determine the validity of the wholesale price measurement as the basis for government price policy in those areas. These studies are discussed briefly below.

The Interagency Committee on the Measurement of Real Output

This committee represented a combined effort by the Bureau of Labor Statistics, the Office of Business Economics, the Bureau of the Census and the Federal Reserve Board to improve the deflators used to measure changes in output at the quinquennial benchmark periods of the Census of Manufactures. Primary attention was focused on the comparison of detailed 7-digit unit value data from the Census of Manufactures and price data from the Wholesale Price Index for measuring the change in output from 1954 to 1958 and 1958 to 1963. Two basic studies were undertaken. One summarized, at the major industry (2-digit) level, comparisons of the 7-digit census unit value with matched wholesale price data. This study concluded that any gains in measurement which unit values might offer because they reflected transaction prices and more complete coverage were more than offset by the problems of changing product and transaction mixes, which were found to be substantial from census year to census year.

The second study was an in-depth analysis of 25 items at the 7-digit product level, which analyzed the reasons for the differences between the wholesale price data and census unit values. This in-depth study supported the general conclusion of the first study but, in addition, it found that in a substantial number of cases some of the difference between unit values and wholesale prices indexes could be accounted for by the fact that the Wholesale Price Index tended to reflect changes in list prices rather than changes in transaction prices including discounts. On the basis of these two studies, it was concluded that specification pricing such as that represented by the wholesale price data should be used for deflation in the absence of positive evidence of its unsuitability in specific instances. It was also recognized, however, that there were circumstances in which unit value indexes might be preferred to price indexes, and the committee noted what these might be. In essence, these included cases where there was a central tendency in the unit values and no wholesale price data were available, or where the wholesale price data which were available had known faults. Thus, if the wholesale price data came from trade sources where only list prices were reported, or were known to be based on delivered prices rather than f.o.b. prices, or did not adequately cover the products contained in the 7-digit census classification, then the unit value might be used if there was a strong central tendency among unit values in the 7-digit product class.

Although this report did reverse the order of preference from the previous practice which had been to use unit values except where they seemed unreasonable, it did not constitute a vote of approval for the Wholesale Price Index. Rather, it emphasized the lack of suitability of deflators based on census unit values. The superiority of the wholesale price data was only relative. Examination of the report's findings leaves the impression that for many reasons the wholesale price data are also very inadequate on any absolute scale. Thus the report points out that in the tire industry the wholesale price data cover only rayon cord tires, whereas during the period under review nylon cord tires had been falling in price and increasing in quantity. In a number of industries, it was found that the wholesale price data failed to pick up all applicable discounts. In some cases, the Wholesale Price Index had an upward bias because it did not sufficiently represent the lower-priced products of smaller companies which were growing in importance. Because the committee concerned itself only with the material at hand, it was not possible for it to undertake large-scale investigations of the bias in the Wholesale Price Index as a whole.

The Stigler–Kindahl report
This report was primarily concerned with determining whether the administered price thesis of Gardiner Means was borne out by price data other than the Bureau of Labor Statistics wholesale price data. The analysis rests on approximately 1,300 newly collected price observations for 70 commodities over the period 1957–67. In the course of their analysis, the authors made a careful comparison between their price series and those of the BLS. The Stigler–Kindahl prices were collected primarily from purchasers rather than sellers. In many cases the amount paid as reported on invoices was obtained, thus ensuring that the price would be closer to transaction price than to list or quoted price. There were also other differences from the BLS data. Many of the purchasers from whom prices were obtained had contracts, and in these cases the price obtained was the contract price, sometimes adjusted by escalation features. This is in contrast with the BLS practice of collecting list, discounted list, spot, or order prices. Finally, the Stigler–Kindahl report focused more narrowly on specific commodities, so that many more prices were obtained for a single commodity than were obtained by the BLS for the corresponding Wholesale Price Index.

In the short run, the movements of the Stigler–Kindahl index and the Wholesale Price Index differed substantially at both the aggregate level and the detailed level. The BLS index had larger, jerkier movements and the variance of its monthly changes was much larger than that of the changes in the Stigler–Kindahl index. During the first five years of the period, the trend of the two indexes was substantially the same, but from 1961 on the BLS index rose about 0.7 percent a year relative to the Stigler–Kindahl index. Stigler and Kindahl concluded from this evidence that there was no systematic trend difference between the BLS index and their prices when their prices were stable or rising, but that when their prices fell the BLS index failed to reflect the full decline. The explanation which they offered was that the quoted prices on which the BLS index is based are not revised immediately when market conditions change, whereas the transaction prices on which their indexes were based do reflect changed conditions promptly. Furthermore, Stigler and Kindahl argue that it is more prudent for a businessman to be slow in authenticating price reductions and prompt in authenticating price increases.

The Stigler–Kindahl work has often been cited as confirming the need to move to transaction pricing from list or quoted prices. It is argued that obtaining prices from buyers yields the actual amount paid for a given item, so that all discounts or add-on charges will be fully reflected. To the extent that producers use discounts and add-on charges to vary their quoted or list prices, this argument is reasonable. But the difference between the BLS index and Stigler–Kindahl prices also reflects a number of additional factors.

One consequence of going to buyers rather than producers is that a different market is being priced. Stigler and Kindahl obtained prices from a large variety of purchasers, many of whom bought from brokers, wholesalers, or distributors, rather that directly from producers. Prices in these secondary markets will not move in perfect consort with producers' prices; at the least, they can be expected to reflect inventory variations.

In addition, brokers, jobbers and other wholesalers buy from producers and resell to other purchasers. In periods of short supply, the producer price may in fact behave very differently from the price charged by intermediate wholesalers. Producers may be concerned with long run pricing and may have contracts with many of their main customers. Purchasers from brokers may be paying spot prices for products which are in short supply. Thus, from the point of view of collecting price information, the differences between producers' prices and purchasers' prices may be quite substantial and reflect many factors other than the difference between 'list' and 'transactions' prices.

Second, since the Stigler–Kindahl index reflects prices which purchasers have actually paid for commodities they have already received, the timing of the price measurement may be very different indeed from that of the BLS index which may reflect spot or order prices of the same date. If the order-to-shipment lag is lengthy, the difference in timing may be very substantial. This difference in timing cannot in fact, however, account for the difference between the BLS index and the Stigler–Kindahl prices. If timing alone were the major consideration, it might have been expected that in a period of falling prices, the Stigler–Kindahl index would lag behind the BLS index, rather than falling faster. Thus it may be that the actual difference between the two indexes is understated.

Third, for the price information to be valid, the purchaser needs to be a continuous purchaser of the product in question, and must be capable of separating out the other costs charged by the producer. Problems of interpretation arise when a purchaser changes his supplier. Such a change may reflect dissatisfaction with the existing source of supply in terms of quality of product, promptness of delivery, conditions of sale, or price. The new supply may be purchased from a producer who has not changed his own price over the past period, so that the apparent change in the purchaser's price may be due to a shift in the source of supply rather than to price changes by individual producers.

The Gordon study

The study on the measurement of durable goods prices by Robert J. Gordon sets out to create a new set of price indexes which differ radically in methodology of measurement and sources from the BLS Wholesale Price Index. His data indicate a decline of 16 percent in the price of durable goods over the period 1947–70, whereas the official BEA deflator (which is primarily based on the BLS index) shows an increase of prices for these goods of 73 percent. The sources of Gordon's data are: mail order catalog prices; unit value indexes for narrowly defined commodities as collected in the Census of Manufactures; prices of used automobiles and tractors from appraisal manuals; records of equipment purchases from individual steam electric generating stations; rental data for electronic computers; internal company price indexes for equipment sold by Western Electric Company to the Bell Telephone Company; and a calculation of the value of all quality changes on full-sized Chevrolet automobiles for the period 1956–68. Almost all price data on which the results are based were newly assembled for this study, and the final durable goods price index was a weighted average of over 15,000 separate price quotations which were selected to satisfy the 'twin criteria of adequate adjustment for quality change and measurement of transactions rather than list price'.

In the analysis of the behavior of unit values relative to wholesale price for a number of narrowly specified product classes, Gordon found that the ratio of unit value to wholesale prices for all product groups varied over the cycle, with significant discounting of list prices in recession. He considered secular deviations between changes in unit values and the WPI to be important 'signaling devices' suggesting the need for further investigation. In some cases the WPI may be found to be supported by outside data, but in other cases the unit value

data may be confirmed. Gordon feels that some unit value data, properly analyzed, can be a valuable source of price information, and can pinpoint areas
where further research on prices is likely to have a high payoff.

Perhaps the most striking feature of the Gordon study is his measurement
of the 'quality bias' in the BLS indexes. The criterion used as the basis for
quality measurement is that two items are identical if their ability to produce
services is the same. Hedonic regression techniques were used to correct for
changes in overall dimensions or other major physical characteristics, and
further adjustments were made in the prices of different models for changes in
features which are introduced simultaneously on all models. The final measurement of bias in the official figures which Gordon arrives at is very substantial, as is shown in Table 10.18.

*Table 10.18 Producers' Durable Equipment Deflators (annual percentage
            rates of change)*

	1947–57	1957–70	1947–70
BEA deflator	3.5	1.7	2.4
Gordon deflator	–0.2	–1.2	–0.7
Difference	–3.7	–2.9	–3.1

If the Gordon deflator is taken to be correct, the bias of the BEA deflator,
which is primarily based on the BLS index, amounts to an overstatement of
price increases by over 3 percent a year for the period 1947–70.

The Bureau of Economic Analysis would argue, however, that the appropriate measure of quality change in producers' durable equipment should be
based solely on its resource costs rather than its performance in order for
measurement of capital productivity to have any economic meaning. To define
the quantity of capital purely in terms of its performance would render the concept of capital productivity meaningless. For this reason, they would maintain
that a cost-oriented type of quality adjustment is correct for producers' durable
equipment. Although in principle this argument seems persuasive, it is also
true that in an economy with high rates of technological change, many products
such as computers and communication satellites may have striking increases in
their performance without additional cost, and these, because of the difficulty
in measuring the output effect of new products and quality change of existing
products, are never included in real output.

Whether or not Gordon's ringing indictment of the Wholesale Price Index
is fully justified, it is certainly true that there are major differences between
Gordon and BLS in product coverage and pricing methods. First, it is generally recognized that the BLS index does not provide the basic coverage
needed to deflate producers' durable equipment. Despite the fact that a great
many prices are collected in the area of machinery and electrical equipment,

many of the prices refer to components and parts, rather than finished producers' durables. This makes it difficult to use the price data for deflating final sales of producers' durable equipment. Second, as has been noted above in the discussion of product change and price adjustments, the BLS specification pricing method leads to measuring the price change of those products where specifications do not change, so that, as Gordon charges, the effect of product improvement is completely lost. Even where a product of changing quality is priced, the pricing technique used eliminates the quality change from the price measurement rather than including it as a price reduction.

Gordon has provided provocative and convincing examples of the effect which a different treatment of quality change would have on prices of specific products. Thus his analysis of adding machines and computers demonstrates the bias which results from using specification pricing in an area where specifications are changing rapidly. The measurement of quality change is also important for other areas of pricing. For example, in the pharmaceutical area, the introduction of new drugs such as penicillin is a dramatic product change. But as has already been observed, there is no easy or objective way to measure such quality change. Different investigators using different methods and different assumptions can and will arrive at widely different measurements of quality change, so the measurement process ceases to be an objective investigation. The very definition of what is a product group, what are the attributes of the product, and what function it serves can lead to very different estimates of quality change.

What Gordon's analysis does successfully show is that the BLS Wholesale Price Index does not provide a satisfactory measure of prices of producers' durable equipment if changes in quality and/or new products are to be considered as a dimension of output. This finding casts serious doubt on our ability to measure real capital stock and in fact on our measurement of real product in general. It demonstrates that reasonable assumptions can yield answers that are very different from the answers obtained by using the BLS Wholesale Price Index. Unfortunately, Gordon has been in one sense too successful: he has not only demonstrated the fallibility of the BLS Wholesale Price Index, but has provided the basis for questioning almost any measurement which could be devised. By introducing additional dimensions into the analysis, such as additional benefits or reductions in costs which may accompany new products or changed specifications of old products, an imaginative economist could easily out-Gordon Gordon.

Nevertheless, Gordon's results must be taken seriously. Although he may not have fully succeeded in developing definitive procedures for measuring quality change accurately, he has demonstrated that the introduction of quality change into the price index can make substantial differences in the measurement of real output.

The BEA government price project

The Bureau of Economic Analysis has currently undertaken, with the support of funds from the Department of Defense, a research project on the development of price indexes for goods purchased by the Department of Defense. Since the federal government is a major purchaser of goods and services, such price indexes are very important, and a comparison between these indexes and the corresponding wholesale price indexes can cast light on whether the prices paid by the government change in the same way as prices which producers charge in the private sector of the economy.

The wholesale price data purposely exclude goods sold to the government, and in view of government procurement practices, it is quite reasonable to expect that producers may sell products to the government at different prices than to other buyers. For many products, government purchases are determined by bids from many producers. In periods of slack demand, producers might be willing to take government contracts below market price in order to utilize their capacity more fully and keep their labor force employed. In periods of high demand, producers could be expected to bid at more nearly market prices, since they could expect to sell all they could make at that price.

At this stage, the BEA project has only preliminary results for a few industries. The relation of the wholesale price indexes to the price index of defense purchases of clothing and textiles and footwear is shown in Figure 10.3. In both of these cases, the Wholesale Price Index shows a fairly continuous upward trend from the first quarter of 1974 through the second quarter of 1976. In contrast, the defense purchase price index shows a substantial decline from the third and fourth quarter of 1975 to the second quarter of 1976. This suggests that the prices paid by the Defense Department may have been more responsive to the depressed production levels which existed in the textile and leather industries in 1975. In any case, these results strongly indicate that separate price indexes are required for the goods and services purchased by the government. It may also be true, however, that in the same period other large purchasers obtained special prices or discounts which were also not adequately reflected in the wholesale price data.

The Council on Wage and Price Stability

This agency has the responsibility for monitoring prices and restraining inflation. For this reason it has been concerned as to whether the BLS Wholesale Price Index does accurately reflect what is taking place in specific industries. Although the Council does not have access to the price observations which are reported to the Bureau of Labor Statistics, it can and does request information directly from individual producers, and in many cases producers voluntarily provide it with copies of the pricing forms which they have also turned in to the BLS.

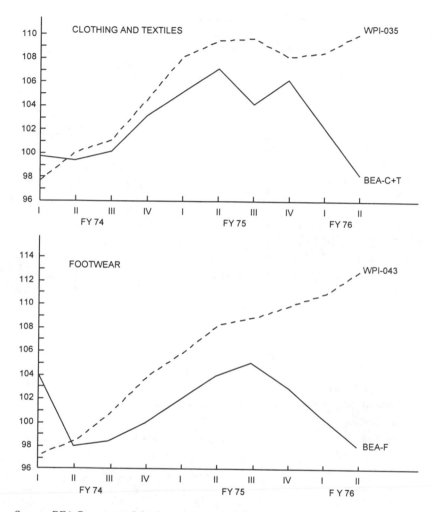

Source: BEA Government Price Project, Preliminary Results.

Figure 10.3 Price Indexes of WPI and BEA (fiscal year 1974 = 100)

For some industries, the Council has carried out investigations to determine the suitability of the BLS wholesale price data for its purposes. One of the more intensive of these studies was concerned with steel prices. From this study, the Council on Wage and Price Stability (1975) concluded the following:

> The published BLS wholesale price indexes for finished steel products in 1974 simply did not satisfactorily inform us on what was happening to steel prices. First, the existence and array of the multitier structure of mill prices and of the array of

nonmill prices were not visible in the steel WPI's. Second, a simple unweighted arithmetic average of three to nine unknown respondents may mislead, if small suppliers are averaged with large ones. Of the twelve major steel firms, the three largest have 45 percent of capacity and the three smallest 3 percent. Third, one does not know what role, if any, the higher West Coast mill prices play in the average, nor are regional differentials visible. Fourth, in the absence of specific prices, it is not possible to reconcile the WPI steel index information with company price lists, data collected from steel companies by the Council, buyers' information, implicit prices in other data and other sources. These comments on the short-comings of the WPI steel indexes for Council purposes describe an unsatisfactory situation relating to confidentiality and limited disclosure, and are not necessarily criticism of BLS. They raise the question of whether confidentiality is necessary or desirable for the list prices at which goods are sold in the market place.

By comparing the information which it received from steel companies with the copies of the BLS price reporting forms which were voluntarily given to it by the companies, the Council found that what were reported to the BLS were essentially list-based prices including only a few narrowly defined extras. Actual prices moved differently from the prices reported to BLS in 1974 because in that period of short supply companies increased or devised new price extras and surcharges beyond the base list price provided to the BLS. For example, the Council calculated a composite realization price for a number of specific steel products, weighted on the basis of company shipments per quarter using information received from steel companies on shipments for the four quarters of 1974. This was then compared with the BLS price for the same period. This comparison is shown in Table 10.19 for sheet steel.

Table 10.19 Sales Realization Price Indexes Compared to BLS WPI, 1974 (January 1974 = 100)

	IQ	IIQ	IIIQ	IVQ
BLS WPI	100	111.0	133.2	134.1
Company composite	100	119.3	138.7	140.2
Highest price	100	121.7	132.4	143.0
Lowest price	100	131.5	150.4	149.2

It is interesting to note here that the lowest prices rose more rapidly than the highest prices, and that the company composite generally rose more slowly than either the highest price or lowest price.

The Council's comparison between the prices of cold rolled sheet steel from independent brokers and service centers as compared with the BLS Wholesale Price Index is also interesting. This is shown in graphical form in Figure 10.4. From this figure it is apparent that the prices of the independent brokers rose considerably faster than either the BLS price or service center prices up to the

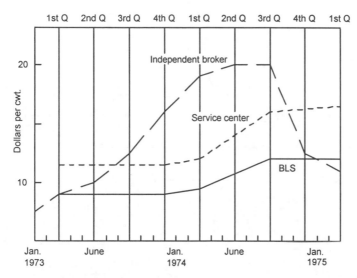

Sources: Bureau of Labor Statistics published data and confidential company data collected by the Council on Wage and Price Stability.

Figure 10.4 Price Index for Cold Rolled Steel

third quarter of 1974, and dropped sharply thereafter, in sharp contrast with the prices of both service centers and the BLS WPI. Service centers in this context are defined as intermediaries which buy steel from the mills in bulk and then cut, shape, or otherwise prepare it for resale in smaller lots. Approximately 25 percent of the total steel sold is handled by service centers. Although the price level of service centers is higher than the BLS price, the two series run parallel throughout the period. This figure emphasizes the point made in connection with the Stigler–Kindahl study that the price behavior for a given commodity may in large part depend upon the exact point in the channel of distribution at which it is priced.

The Council (1976a) provided additional information on the relation of realized prices to the BLS Wholesale Price Index in a report on steel price increases issued in June 1976. This document included a chart on the realized prices and wholesale prices of steel sheet, reproduced in Figure 10.5. It is apparent that realized prices rose faster than the BLS Wholesale Price Index. This may reflect the fact that an increase of, say, $10.00 per ton at list may also be added directly without further discount to a lower discounted price, thereby causing a larger percentage increase.

Finally, a recent study by the Council on Wage and Price Stability (1976b) on price behavior in the aluminum industry investigated the WPI for primary aluminum ingot. This case is particularly interesting since it represents one of the few commodities for which the Bureau of Labor Statistics collects

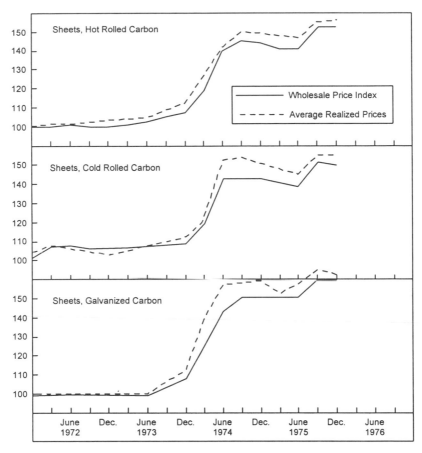

Sources: Bureau of Labor Statistics published data and confidential company data collected by the Council on Wage and Price Stability.

Figure 10.5 Realized Prices vs Wholesale Price Index (first quarter 1972 = 100)

purchasers' prices. The use of purchasers' prices was instituted in 1971 when it was discovered that the list price of primary aluminum ingot reported to BLS by producers was 29¢ per pound, but users were in fact purchasing it for 22¢ per pound. The BLS price index for aluminum ingot was compiled on the basis of prices obtained from five purchasers and a price listed for aluminum ingot in *Metals Week*. Since January 1976, the BLS aluminum ingot price index has been based solely on purchasers' prices. The Council on Wage and Price Stability obtained list prices from four producers and compared them with the WPI. This comparison is shown in Table 10.20.

Table 10.20 Recent Price History of Aluminum Ingot, 99.5 Percent Pure (all prices are indexed January 1974 = 100)

Date (1)	Wholesale Price Index (2)	WPI (recalculated without spot prices)[a] (3)	Weighted average four reporters[b] (4)	*American Metal Market* average price (5)
7/71	97.5	n.a.[c]	100.0	n.a.
1/74	100.0	100.0	100.0	100.0
2/74	100.0	100.0	100.0	100.0
3/74	117.3	121.4	100.0	100.8
4/74	124.2	127.1	108.6	108.6
5/74	125.5	127.2	108.6	108.6
6/74	128.9	131.7	115.5	115.1
7/74	131.5	134.7	115.5	115.5
8/74	139.1	143.9	124.8	123.9
9/74	143.0	150.5	134.7	133.4
10/74	138.1	150.1	135.6	134.4
11/74	137.5	150.7	135.6	134.4
12/74	137.5	150.9	135.6	134.4
1/75	134.1	147.9	135.4	134.4
2/75	133.3	147.9	135.4	134.4
3/75	133.3	147.9	135.4	134.4
4/75	131.7	145.2	135.4	134.4
5/75	131.0	144.2	135.4	134.4
6/75	132.7	146.9	135.0	134.4
7/75	133.9	148.4	135.0	134.4
8/75	135.2	149.5	141.9	141.3
9/75	137.6	152.4	141.9	141.3
10/75	137.1	152.4	141.9	141.3
11/75	136.7	152.4	141.9	141.3
12/75	137.8	153.9	141.9	141.3

Notes:

a. This is *not* an official index used by the Bureau of Labor Statistics.

b. The reported prices were weighted by totaling the primary capacity of the four reporting companies and dividing this into the company's capacity. This fraction was multiplied by the quoted price for each reporter, and the resulting products were summed to arrive at a weighted average price. This was then converted to an index with a January 1974 base.

Source: Bureau of Labor Statistics, company submittals, *American Metal Market*.

If the Wholesale Price Index is computed on the basis of buyers' prices only (col. 3), it rises very much faster than the prices reported by producers. The Council on Wage and Price Stability attributes this to the fact that buyers were obtaining their metal from brokers or smaller aluminum companies who were taking advantage of supply shortages and charging higher prices, whereas the major producers, taking into account long-term relationships with their customers, did not raise prices above list. The Council recognizes that the gap between the change in purchasers' prices and that in producers' prices may be somewhat misleading if, as is alleged, the producers in periods of short supply draw up their contracts to buy back scrap from their customers at prices below market price, and in periods of recession, shading from list price is achieved by agreeing to buy back scrap at prices above market price.

The criticisms which the Council on Wage and Price Stability makes of the WPI are well supported by the evidence which it provides. The BLS prices do not appear to capture the changes in discounts, extra charges, etc. which accompany changes in market conditions. This confirms the evidence of Stigler–Kindahl and Gordon. Despite the fact that net realized prices refer to actual shipments, whereas presumably the BLS prices at least sometimes refer to orders, the net realized prices seem to lead the BLS Wholesale Price Index. For this reason, for some commodities it may well be that the BLS should place more emphasis on obtaining average net realized prices instead of relying on list prices less discount. For other commodities where different prices are charged to different customers, the use of net realized price can cause rather wide swings in the series which are unrelated to *price* change.

Thus it is evident that the wholesale price data alone are not adequate for monitoring price behavior. It should also be recognized, however, that the requirements of the Council on Wage and Price Stability for basic price information exceed what can reasonably be expected of the data collected for the WPI. As the Council points out, it needs to know such things as the prices of large producers as against small producers, or of producers in one region of the country as against purchasers in another region of the country. The quantity of price data required for such analysis greatly exceeds what the BLS can reasonably be expected to collect. Furthermore, the confidentiality assurances which BLS gives to the suppliers of price information prevent the data in its most detailed form from being given to the Council, and any aggregation of the data into indexes further reduces its usefulness to them. For this reason, the Council should expect to have to develop its own price collection program in those areas where it is specifically concerned with monitoring prices and developing policies to contain inflation. The most the BLS WPI can be expected to do is to give a broad general picture of price developments throughout the economy. Even for this use, however, the deficiencies of the present BLS WPI which the Council has pointed out need to be corrected.

Comparisons of Census Unit Values and the Wholesale Price Index

The report of the Interagency Committee on the Measurement of Real Output, which was written in June 1970, was primarily intended as the basis for the 1963–67 index of production for mining and manufacturing. Since that time, calculations have also been completed on the price deflators for the period 1967–72. The Committee has continued to function and the result of its work is embodied in the data for these two periods. Although the production index has been published for the years 1963–67, there has been no report on further evaluation of wholesale prices and census unit values for either the 1963–67 or 1967–72 period. Computer tapes containing the basic data at the 7-digit SIC product levels are available, and it has been possible to tabulate information from these tapes to obtain more up-to-date evaluations about the use of census unit value data relative to wholesale price data.

The 1963–67 index of production of manufacturing and mining

As was indicated in the discussion of the 1970 report of the Interagency Committee, it was decided that wholesale price data should be used in preference to census unit value data in all cases except those where there was clear evidence that the wholesale price data were inadequate. This procedure was closely adhered to in the 1963–67 deflation of value of shipments. Despite this, as indicated in Table 10.20, the wholesale price data still accounted for the deflation of only 45 percent of the total value of shipments. Unit values continued to be used for almost 25 percent and for some industries such as coal mining, oil and gas extraction, and petroleum and coal products, unit values were the major source of information. Other government agencies were the source of deflators for 14 percent of the value of shipments, with higher-level indexes being used to deflate the final 15 percent.

The basic data contained on the computer tapes permit a direct comparison at the 7-digit product level between unit values and wholesale price indexes where both of these kinds of deflators were available. In all, there were 725 such products. Direct comparisons at the 7-digit product level, on average, showed less than 1 percent difference between the unit value index and the Wholesale Price Index. This is shown in Table 10.21.

The average difference between the unit value index and the Wholesale Price Index does, however, hide the fact that for individual 7-digit products there were wide differences. In part, this is evident in the striking differences among the 2-digit SIC major industries. A more detailed examination of some of the specific 5-digit product classes is shown in Table 10.22. The difference between the unit value index and the Wholesale Price Index appears in large measure to stem from the extremely wide variation in unit value indexes. Thus industrial pumps and vacuum cleaners increased sharply in unit value when, in terms of wholesale price data, pumps showed only a moderate increase and vacuum cleaners showed a decline. In the case of freight cars, the sharp decline in unit values was not at all reflected in the price index, which was relatively stable. Clocks and watches also showed large drops in unit value, perhaps reflecting the introduction of cheaper clocks and watches. These cases, particularly industrial pumps and vacuum cleaners, seem to support the conclusion of the original report of the Interagency Committee, that changes in the mix of products within even the 7-digit product class were such as to make census unit

Table 10.21 Sources of Deflators of Census Value of Shipments, 1963–67 (as percentage of value of shipments)

SIC code and title	Unit value	Wholesale prices	Other gvt prices	Higher-level prices	Total
10 Metal mining	88	5	1	6	100
11 Anthracite mining	12	88	0	0	100
12 Bituminous coal and lignite mining	100	0	0	0	100
13 Oil and gas extraction	100	0	0	0	100
14 Nonmetallic minerals, exc. fuels	36	62	0	2	100
20 Food and kindred products	38	57	0	5	100
21 Tobacco manufactures	36	62	0	2	100
22 Textile mill products	26	60	4	10	100
23 Apparel and other textile products	19	54	2	25	100
24 Lumber and wood products	18	58	7	17	100
25 Furniture and fixtures	11	59	0	30	100
26 Paper and allied products	35	48	6	11	100
27 Printing and publishing	14	0	30	66	100
28 Chemicals and allied products	27	23	26	24	100
29 Petroleum and coal products	82	17	0	2	100
30 Rubber and plastic products	62	23	1	24	100
31 Leather and leather products	17	69	0	14	100
32 Stone, clay and glass products	27	49	8	16	100
33 Primary metals industries	28	64	1	17	100
34 Fabricated metal products	7	52	16	25	100
35 Machinery, exc. electrical	9	57	9	25	100
36 Electrical equipment and supplies	24	30	23	23	100
37 Transportation equipment	1	60	35	4	100
38 Instruments and related products	8	40	32	20	100
39 Miscellaneous manufacturers	8	31	22	39	100
Total	26	45	14	15	100

Sources: Indexes of Production; 1967 Census of Manufactures and Mineral Industries, Table A-1.

Table 10.22 Examples of Differences between Unit Value Index and WPI

Code	Product class	Unit value index	WPI
35611	Industrial pumps	191.3	104.8
36350	Vacuum cleaners	171.4	91.1
37422	Freight train cars	45.1	103.7
38711	Clocks	64.7	102.4
38715	Watches	34.8	102.1

values unreliable as indicators of price change. For the other categories, the concentration of production on lower-priced units may well also reflect the substitution of new cheaper units for older higher-priced units.

Since the Interagency Committee examined the adequacy of the Wholesale Price Index as a deflator for each 7-digit product separately, it is possible to look at those cases where the WPI was rejected in favor of some other price measurement. This tabulation is shown in Table 10.23. In all, there were only 113 cases in which wholesale prices at the 7-digit product level were rejected, and in almost all of these cases, substitute wholesale prices were chosen. The exceptions were prices of chemical and allied products, which were obtained from the Tariff Commission, and some other prices obtained from various other government agencies, including the Office of Business Economics. In only eight cases were unit values substituted for wholesale price indexes, and these also were in the area of chemicals and allied products. On average, the substitute deflators were somewhat lower than the Wholesale Price Index, suggesting that wholesale price data may have been rejected because they did not sufficiently capture transaction prices. The most striking case is electrical

Table 10.23 Comparison of Unit Values and Wholesale Price Indexes for 7-digit SIC Products, 1963–67 (1963 = 100)

SIC code and title	No. of 7-digit SIC products (1)	Unit value index (1967) (2)	Wholesale Price Index (1967) (3)	Percent difference (3–2)/3
10 Metal mining	2	109.7	105.3	−4.2
11 Anthracite mining	1	96.1	96.7	+0.1
12 Bituminous coal and lignite	3	106.4	107.3	+0.8
13 Oil and gas extraction	2	108.6	116.7	+6.9
14 Nonmetallic minerals, exc. fuels	9	107.7	107.5	−0.1
19 Ordinance	5	124.9	108.8	−14.8
20 Food and kindred products	86	109.0	109.2	+0.1
21 Tobacco manufactures	7	105.5	107.3	+1.6
22 Textile mill products	21	102.6	95.6	−7.3
23 Apparel and other textile products	27	115.8	105.4	−9.9
24 Lumber and wood products	13	110.1	103.4	−6.5
25 Furniture and fixtures	24	115.9	108.2	−7.1
26 Paper and allied products	27	104.8	105.2	+0.4
28 Chemicals and allied products	97	91.5	98.0	+6.6
29 Petroleum and coal products	11	105.5	105.6	+0.1
30 Rubber and plastic products	17	107.2	106.1	−1.0
31 Leather and leather products	13	120.0	112.6	−6.6
32 Stone, clay and glass products	30	104.8	103.4	−1.4
33 Primary metal industries	80	106.8	108.5	+1.6
34 Fabricated metal products	66	108.5	108.0	−0.5
35 Machinery, exc. electrical	89	118.9	109.9	−8.2
36 Electrical equipment and supplies	60	99.6	98.5	−1.1
37 Transportation equipment	5	56.6	102.4	+44.7
38 Instruments and related products	5	81.6	102.1	+20.0
39 Miscellaneous manufactures	25	109.8	105.7	−3.9
Total	725	107.2	106.4	−0.8

Source: Computed from data tapes on 1963–67 Census of Production, Bureau of the Census.

machinery, and the major item in this category was electronic computing equipment. In this case, the Interagency Committee rejected the use of the WPI of 102.2 for office machines and substituted instead a price index of 60 which, in their view, more adequately reflected the increase in efficiency which resulted from technological change in the computer industry.

The 1967–72 index of production for manufacturing and mining

Although the report by the Bureau of the Census on the index of production for manufacturing and mining for the period 1967–72 is not yet finished, a tape of the basic data is now available so that further comparisons can be made of census unit values and wholesale prices. Table 10.24 shows the number of 7-digit products which were deflated by unit values, wholesale prices, other government prices and higher-level prices for the period 1967–72. This is the same data shown for the earlier period in Table 10.19. In total, over 7,800 products were deflated, and wholesale price data were used for approximately half. Unit value data and other government prices were not used as extensively as they had been for the period 1963–67, but higher-level indexes were used more extensively. This greater use of the Wholesale Price Index in part reflects the increase in the amount of wholesale price data available.

In developing the computer tapes for the deflation of value of shipments for the period 1967–72, the Interagency Committee made a direct substitution on the tape of alternative deflators for wholesale prices in certain cases where a deflator was obtained from an outside source. Unfortunately, in such cases the

Table 10.24 Analysis of Wholesale Prices for 7-digit Products Rejected as Deflators by Interagency Committee, 1963–67

SIC code and title	Number of products	Wholesale Price Index	Substitute deflator	Percent difference
19 Ordinance	7	106.7	107.6	0.8
21 Tobacco manufactures	1	100.1	100.4	0.3
22 Textile mill products	2	80.4	89.3	11.0
23 Apparel and other textile products	6	100.8	107.8	7.0
24 Lumber and wood products	3	107.5	108.5	0.9
26 Paper and allied products	2	106.0	107.1	1.0
28 Chemicals and allied products	47	97.4	92.2	−5.3
29 Petroleum and coal products	2	100.5	101.0	0.4
30 Rubber and plastic products	2	101.4	106.3	4.9
31 Leather and leather products	1	128.9	120.0	−6.8
33 Primary metals industry	19	115.5	112.4	−2.4
34 Fabricated metals products	13	114.3	107.2	−6.2
35 Machinery, exc. electrical	8	106.1	85.0	
Total	113	103.1	99.1	−3.9

Source: Computed from data tape on 1963–67 Census of Production, Bureau of the Census.

wholesale price data were eliminated from the computer record; what remains is the deflator actually used. Where no substitution was made, the wholesale price data do, of course, remain in the computer record. The census unit value data always remain in the record, so it is possible to make a comparison between the census unit value at the 7-digit product level and the deflator actually chosen to represent this 7-digit product level. Since the wholesale price data were in fact most commonly used instead of census unit values for deflators, this is for the most part a comparison between the wholesale price data and census unit data at the 7-digit product level. This tabulation is shown in Table 10.25. As was the case with the comparison between unit value and wholesale price data for the period 1963–67, on average, there was again less than 1 percent difference between the two indexes. However, there was considerable variation from industry to industry, and the 2-digit industry figures mask a much wider variance at the 7-digit product level. As was also true for the

Table 10.25 Sources of Deflation of Census 7-Digit Products, 1967–72

SIC code and title	Unit value	Wholesale prices	Other gvt prices	Higher-level prices	Total
10 Metal mining	19	2	1	9	31
11 Anthracite mining	4	0	0	1	5
12 Bituminous coal and lignite mining	2	1	0	0	3
13 Oil and gas extraction	17	1	0	1	19
14 Nonmetallic minerals, exc. fuels	50	3	1	14	68
20 Food and kindred products	223	494	0	129	846
21 Tobacco manufactures	0	18	0	5	23
22 Textile mill products	82	125	0	85	292
23 Apparel and other textile products	72	139	0	97	308
24 Lumber and wood products	35	106	2	73	216
25 Furniture and fixtures	29	140	0	34	203
26 Paper and allied products	72	147	0	42	261
27 Printing and publishing	0	0	277	31	308
28 Chemicals and allied products	186	270	105	194	755
29 Petroleum and coal products	22	28	0	15	65
30 Rubber and plastic products	8	81	87	32	208
31 Leather and leather products	22	36	0	14	72
32 Stone, clay and glass products	77	147	12	77	313
33 Primary metals industries	91	128	8	59	286
34 Fabricated metal products	75	339	37	157	608
35 Machinery, exc. electrical	157	921	66	185	1,329
36 Electrical equipment and supplies	94	453	148	151	846
37 Transportation equipment	48	53	66	61	228
38 Instruments and related supplies	30	86	50	69	235
39 Miscellaneous manufactures	16	131	24	104	275
Total	1,430	3,848	884	1,641	7,803
Percent	18	49	11	21	100

Source: Computed from data tape on 1967–72 Census of Production, Bureau of the Census.

1963–67 data, the variability is due to unit value indexes taking on extreme values; the wholesale price data exhibit somewhat more consistent patterns. There does not seem to be any evidence, as Gordon had suggested, of substantial upward bias in wholesale price data compared to unit value data.

It is also possible to make a direct comparison of those instances where the census unit value was chosen as the deflator at the 7-digit product level even when a Wholesale Price Index was available, since in these cases both values remain on the tape. For the period 1967–72, there were a substantial number of these cases (341), in marked contrast with only eight cases for the period 1963–67. A comparison of these data in Table 10.26 indicates that, on average, it is true here that unit values were significantly lower than the corresponding wholesale price indexes. For some products such as bituminous coal and lignite and rubber and plastic products, the differences were substantial. There were, nevertheless, a few other cases, such as textile mill products and

Table 10.26 Comparison of Unit Values with Corresponding WPI or Census Deflators, 1967–72

SIC code and title	Number of products (1)	Unit value index (2)	WPI or census deflator (3)	Percent difference of (3)
10 Metal mining	2	93.9	105.9	+11.3
12 Bituminous coal and lignite	1	169.3	197.2	+14.1
13 Oil and gas extraction	1	116.2	113.5	+0.6
14 Nonmetallic minerals exc. fuels	10	119.3	120.1	+5.9
20 Food and kindred products	336	120.9	121.8	+0.7
21 Tobacco manufactures	5	111.5	111.5	0.0
22 Textile mill products	47	107.5	105.6	−1.8
23 Apparel and other textile products	49	124.2	115.8	−7.3
24 Lumber and wood products	19	136.4	125.8	−8.4
25 Furniture and fixtures	46	121.8	117.7	−3.5
26 Paper and allied products	75	112.7	113.9	+1.1
28 Chemicals and allied products	143	102.3	108.2	+5.5
29 Petroleum and coal products	17	107.3	107.2	−0.1
30 Rubber and plastic products	28	108.2	111.9	+3.3
31 Leather and leather products	15	130.0	128.6	−1.1
32 Stone, clay and glass products	45	125.2	126.1	+0.7
33 Primary metals industries	101	114.5	124.1	+7.7
34 Fabricated metal products	114	127.2	121.6	−4.6
35 Machinery, exc. electrical	146	132.5	121.6	−9.0
36 Electrical equipment and supplies	143	111.8	109.2	−2.3
37 Transportation equipment	17	140.7	119.5	−17.7
38 Instruments and related supplies	4	130.7	104.2	−25.4
39 Miscellaneous manufactures	20	128.0	114.5	−11.8
Total	1,383	117.4	118.4	+0.8

Source: Computed from data tape on 1967–72 Census of Production, Bureau of Census.

machinery except electrical, where the wholesale price which was rejected had shown a similar price rise to the unit value.

Although the general utility of census unit values as deflators is still open to serious question, they are increasingly being used to check the validity of wholesale price data. It seems quite reasonable, furthermore, that if efforts are made to collect more highly specified unit value data, greater use can be made of them in the future. For certain types of products, such as chemicals, coal and primary metals, unit value data may more fully reflect the net effect of discounts, long-term contracts and special charges related to specific products.

6. SUMMARY AND CONCLUSIONS

Scope, Uses and Characteristics of Wholesale Price Data

Scope and coverage
The Wholesale Price Index is one of the oldest statistical series published by the federal government. The universe of prices it is intended to represent consists of all commodities sold in primary markets in the United States. Over the past 75 years the data base of the Wholesale Price Index has expanded so that at present over 8,300 price observations representing about 2,300 commodities are collected monthly. Although the wholesale price commodity classification system is unique and not directly compatible with other major classification systems, both the Bureau of the Census and the Bureau of Labor Statistics have provided reclassifications of the wholesale price commodities to fit as well as possible into the Standard Industrial Classification system. Approximately half of the 5-digit SIC product classes are represented by at least one wholesale price commodity. The BLS publishes price indexes for 5-digit SIC product classes in those instances where more than 50 percent of the value of shipments is covered by WPI commodities. According to this criterion, only 27 percent of the 5-digit SIC product classes, accounting for 42 percent of the value of shipments, are adequately covered by wholesale price data. Within the 2-digit mining and manufacturing industries, coverage is very uneven.

Thus, despite the general breadth of representation of wholesale price data in agriculture, mining and manufacturing, their coverage is grossly inadequate and falls far short of what is needed to provide comprehensive price indexes for these industries.

Uses
Despite their limited scope, the wholesale price data are widely used for many different purposes. The aggregate Wholesale Price Index is used by both business and government to monitor general price developments in the economy.

The recent inflationary price rises have resulted in increased use of wholesale price data for indexation of contracts. Both the Bureau of the Census and the Bureau of Economic Analysis rely on wholesale price data to deflate current values to obtain measurements of production and real output. Regulatory agencies such as the Anti-Trust Division of the Justice Department and the Council on Wage and Price Stability use wholesale price data to determine where unwarranted price increases may be taking place. The Council of Economic Advisers, the Treasury Department and the Federal Reserve Board make use of wholesale price data in setting fiscal and monetary policy.

None of the users consulted felt that the wholesale price data satisfactorily met their needs. The wholesale price index was often considered misleading as a general price index and wholesale price data were considered to fall short of what is required for the deflation of current value data. The lack of integration of price data with other basic economic data such as wages and profits makes the analysis of price behavior difficult or meaningless. There is a pressing need for a comprehensive, systematic and detailed set of industrial prices which can be integrated with other relevant economic data, and can be used to produce multipurpose price indexes at different levels of aggregation.

Relation to other price indexes
There are, of course, other price data available besides wholesale price data. Consumer prices, export and import prices and construction prices are collected for use in constructing other price indexes. Unfortunately, there has been very little integration of the various types of price data, with the consequence that it is not possible to develop a systematic analysis of the relationships of prices in different parts of the economy. Thus the commodities which are priced at the consumer level are not generally identifiable in the Wholesale Price Index, so that it is not possible to trace the effect of costs and prices at the producer level on prices of the same commodities at the retail level. Similarly, the repercussions of changes in demand for a commodity at the retail level cannot be traced back to their effects on producer prices. Import and export prices for specific commodities cannot generally be related to prices at either the producer or the retail level. But it is only through the analysis of such relationships that change in the economy can be understood and policies developed for maximum price stability without recession.

Thus the Wholesale Price Index should not be considered in isolation from the other major price indexes; the major bodies of price data should be linked together in a systematic manner so that the interrelation of prices in different parts of the economy can be analyzed.

Sources of wholesale price data
Although some wholesale price data are obtained from other government

agencies such as the Department of Agriculture, most wholesale price data are collected by the Bureau of Labor Statistics directly from companies and establishments. Relatively few prices are obtained from either trade associations or trade journals. In the case of a few products, notably aluminum ingots, prices are obtained from the purchasers of the products rather than from the producers on the grounds that producers' prices for these products tend to be list prices and do not reflect discounts and extra charges, and it is believed that purchasers' prices are closer to transaction prices. The use of purchasers' rather than producers' prices may, however, introduce other ambiguities.

To the extent that purchasers buy from jobbers, brokers, or wholesalers, the prices reported may reflect the fluctuations of prices of distributors rather than producers. The basic principle of the Wholesale Price Index, as stated by the Bureau of Labor Statistics, that it should reflect the first commercial transaction for a specific commodity (i.e., the producer's price), may thus be violated by using purchasers' prices. This does not mean, of course, that purchasers' prices are unimportant or uninteresting, but simply that the Wholesale Price Index should not be a mixture of producer and purchaser prices obtained from different points in the wholesale and retail distribution chain where there may be wide differences in price behavior.

Characteristics of wholesale price observations

Although the Bureau of Labor Statistics tries to obtain information from producers about the discounts they give and/or extra charges they impose, there is strong evidence to indicate that reported price changes do not fully reflect changes in transaction prices. Equally serious is the fact that some of the prices reported refer to order prices while others refer to shipment prices. Since there is often a substantial time lag between orders and shipments, the period of time to which a price report is related will differ greatly depending on whether it is an order price or a shipment price. Order price data should not be used to deflate current value of shipments and conversely shipment price data may not reflect the current prices being charged by producers. The situation is further complicated by the fact that in many cases it is not known whether the prices being collected are in fact order or shipment prices, and for most products, order and shipment prices are averaged together in the construction of the indexes. Spot prices are also obtained for some products; although these prices reflect current economic conditions, they cannot be used as the basis for deflation in cases where an appreciable amount of the product is sold on a longer-term contractual basis. The price which most nearly conforms to the transactions price at the producer level is the average net realized price. This price appears to be more sensitive to discounts and extra charges than order prices.

In view of the relative insensitivity of order prices and the major use of price indexes for the deflation of current value data, it is suggested that average net realized prices should be obtained where this would be possible and would not reflect changes in price mix. Where it is felt that the order-to-shipment lag is unusually long, order prices may be collected in addition, but these should not be combined with average net realized prices in the construction of general price indexes.

Wholesale price commodity specifications

The Bureau of Labor Statistics draws up commodity specifications as the basis for its price collection. There is, however, considerable question as to whether even fairly detailed specifications can successfully delimit homogeneous commodities. Examination of price reports for individual wholesale price commodities indicates that in a large number of instances there is considerable variance in the levels of prices observed. Furthermore, these differentials persist over time, suggesting that the commodities are, in fact, not homogeneous but rather represent a collection of different products having different prices.

The lack of homogeneity within commodities has major implications for the development and use of specifications. As a general rule, specifications can do no more than designate product classes, rather than individual commodities. For the purpose of price measurement, the individual commodity should be defined in terms of the price series reported at the establishment or company level. Any significant change in the specifications of a price series should be considered to be a break in that price series requiring an adjustment to be made or the series to be treated as a new product.

Classification and Weighting Systems for Price Indexes

Classification systems

As has already been noted, the present classification system used for the Wholesale Price Index is unique and unrelated to other major classification systems. Furthermore, it is not comprehensive, but covers only selected products. For these reasons, it is difficult to relate wholesale price data to other economic data and integration of the Wholesale Price Index with other price indexes is not possible.

The Standard Industrial Classification (SIC) is widely used by government agencies for the collection and aggregation of economic data, and it is logical that this classification should also be used as a basis for developing a system of price indexes into which the Wholesale Price Index would fit.

Specifically, an input–output table based on the Standard Industrial Classification should be used as a framework for price indexes relating to both industries and final products. In such a context an integrated industrial price program could be developed. The Wholesale Price Index could be recast and expanded to cover the products of the mining and manufacturing industries in a systematic and comprehensive manner. Agricultural products are currently priced by the Department of Agriculture. The other major industries — construction, transportation and utilities, wholesale and retail trade, finance, insurance and real estate and public administration — are not now covered by the Wholesale Price Index, and they pose such major problems of methodology and additional collection efforts that they would require separate new price measurement programs. The industrial price program as a whole should be designed so that the industrial price indexes can be integrated with the consumer price index, the import and export price indexes, and with new price indexes developed for government purchases of goods and services and for gross investment expenditures. Finally, it would be helpful to be able to relate wage–price data to other price and output data at the industry level. All of this will require, of course, a much better integration between the collection and processing of related economic data. It may well be that these different collection activities should be combined into a single effort, which would not only ensure the integration of the different kinds of data, but would also reduce reporting burdens on the respondents and provide for more consistent, valid and economical data processing.

In developing classification systems, the need should be recognized for appropriately detailed subclassifications to permit data to be recast into the form most suitable for a specific kind of analysis. Thus, for instance, a stage of processing classification system based on the SIC can be used to show how price and cost changes are transmitted through the economy.

Combining price observations at the reporter level

In computing the price change for a given commodity, the Bureau of Labor Statistics averages the price observations of all reporters in each period and expresses the price change as the relative of the average prices. Although the problem of mix changes does not arise, since the averages which are computed refer to the same price reporters in both periods, the rationale of this method of computing price change does depend on the existence of identifiable and homogeneous commodities. Where each price reporter is in fact producing a different commodity, it would be more appropriate to compute price change as the average of the price relatives computed at the reporter level. As was noted in the discussion of wholesale price commodity specification, the magnitude of the price variance within most wholesale commodity specifications suggests that the different prices which are reported do reflect product differences.

An experimental computation of price indexes for the year 1974 found no difference between an index based on the relative of average prices and one based on the average of relative prices for commodities with relatively small variances in absolute price observations. Where the variance of prices within commodities was large, however, the two methods did yield different results.

In these instances, since there is reason for believing that the large variance implies that single commodity specifications really admit different products, the method of computing price change as the average of price relatives appears to be the more appropriate. In operational terms, therefore, the safest method would be to compute price relatives at the reporter level and then combine them into price indexes.

Under the current Bureau of Labor Statistics procedure, all price reporters within a commodity are weighted equally, mainly due to lack of information on their relative importance. It would be preferable, however, to make an effort to determine the relative importance of the different price reporters' production of the commodity being priced and to weight them accordingly. This is important since the prices of small producers may change differently from those of larger producers and a serious bias would result if all producers were weighted equally.

Quantity weights and expenditure weights

For the period 1967–75, the Bureau of Labor Statistics used the quantity of goods shipped by producers in the year 1963 as the basis of the weighting system. Beginning in 1976, the weights were shifted to reflect the quantity of goods shipped in 1972. In terms of reference year, however, the year 1967 has been set equal to 100 and this reference year was not changed when the weight base was changed.

One of the characteristics of a base year quantity-weighted price index is that it will tend to overweight prices which increase and underweight prices which fall relative to a price index based on given-year quantity weights. This results from the fact that commodities which rise in price tend to decline in quantity and those which fall in price tend to increase in quantity. Because of this phenomenon, base year quantity-weighted indexes tend to report larger price rises than do given-year quantity-weighted indexes.

It is often recommended that chain indexes based on frequent changes in base year weights be used to overcome this problem. If the measurement of short-run price change is the major function of a price index, there is much to be said for the use of more nearly current weights which are more relevant to the periods being compared. But chaining does not solve the basic dilemma, i.e., whether to use weights referring to the period before a price change has taken place or after it has taken place; it merely shortens the period being considered. In actual practice, the difficulty of obtaining the data for a system of current year weights and the costs associated with implementing it normally rule out its use.

Instead of weighting prices by quantities, it is also possible to weight price relatives by values or expenditures. For the case where the period used for weights and reference base are the same and comparisons are made only with the base year, the two methods are identical, but where the base reference period is different from the weight period, or comparisons are made between years other than the base year, the results will differ. The use of value- or expenditure-weighted price relatives is equivalent to making the assumption that all products have unitary elasticity of demand, whereas price indexes based on fixed quantity weights make the assumption of zero elasticity of demand.

Since the major interest in price measurement lies in short-run price behavior, it seems desirable that weighting systems should be updated more often than they have been in the past. Furthermore, price relatives weighted by value or expenditure weights seem to be a reasonable alternative to prices weighted by quantities as the basis for construction of price indexes.

Gross and net output weights

The Wholesale Price Index as currently compiled by the Bureau of Labor Statistics is based on the aggregation of total shipment weights. This means that raw materials and intermediate products are represented both as separate price series and as part of products which are priced at higher stages of fabrication. One of the most frequent criticisms made of the WPI is that this gross output weighting system results in disproportionate representation of the prices of raw materials and intermediate products, and that it is this feature which prevents the general index from being generally representative of industrial prices.

It is quite possible, however, to develop a net output weighting system which would make use of the same indexes at the individual product level as are now computed, but would employ nonduplicative weighting for higher levels of aggregation. This can be accomplished by using an input–output table to determine the shipments of specific products among industries. Thus a price index for a raw material product might have a substantial weight at the detailed product level, but at successively broader industry aggregations it would have smaller and smaller weights as less and less of it is sold outside the industry being considered.

In contrast with the gross output weighting system which is based on *aggregation* of fixed weights, the net output weighting system is based on *consolidation* of weights in accordance with inter-industry purchases of specific products. For higher levels of aggregation, the net output weighting system has much to recommend it. At the lowest level of product detail it is, of course, very close to the present gross output weighting system.

Price index of value added

For a specific industry, a value added price index which is based on the measurement of price changes of both the industry's output and its inputs is very useful for analyzing the contribution of that industry to the overall price change in the economy. A value added price index differs from a net output price index for an industry, since the latter merely shows the change in the output price of an industry and does not take into account how much of that price change reflects changes in costs of raw materials and other purchased products used by the industry.

In examining price–cost behavior of the economy, a full set of value added price indexes can identify those industries where price changes are originating, and analysis of the demand and supply conditions, wage behavior, productivity and profits in those industries can illuminate the reasons for the price changes. Such information is basic to the development of policy designed to ensure price stability and full employment. Actual analysis of price behavior may, of course, be complicated by index number problems arising from input substitution, technological change and/or changes in the mix of output. In such cases, Laspeyres weighting systems may give very different results from Paasche weighting systems and neither may adequately describe the actual price behavior taking place.

Although the input prices for some industries are a reflection of the output prices of other industries, different industries purchasing the same product as inputs may, in fact, pay different prices. Thus electric power companies that purchase their coal on the basis of long-term contracts may pay a price which behaves differently from the spot price paid for coal by other industries. Also, input prices reflect purchasers' rather than producers' prices. To construct appropriate input price indexes, trade and transport margins need to be included as part of the cost of materials purchased. Materials may also be purchased from brokers or importers, who may charge quite different prices from domestic producers, depending upon demand and supply conditions. For these reasons, it may be necessary to develop specific price indexes of inputs in some industries, so that the value added price index will accurately reflect the changes in input prices paid and output prices received. The same sort of price data are required for value added price indexes as are needed to develop real output measures by industry originating in the national income accounts.

In view of the importance of value added price indexes and real output measures by industry, any program of collecting industrial price data should be oriented to providing the data required for both input price indexes and output price indexes. If, as has been suggested, the input–output framework is used as the basis for the industrial price index, both input prices and output prices will automatically result.

Sampling and Reliability

Current methods of price collection
The collection of wholesale price data has evolved gradually over the past 75

years. Commodity specialists in the Bureau of Labor Statistics use tabulated data from the industrial censuses supplemented by industry data from trade sources and companies to determine on a judgmental basis the commodities for which price indexes are to be constructed and the reporters from whom price observations are to be obtained. By its very nature, this process results in uneven coverage and prevents the computation of meaningful estimates of sampling errors.

The need for a sampling frame

The Bureau of Labor Statistics recognizes that probability sampling is desirable, and that for this purpose a sampling frame is required. Unfortunately, such a sampling frame is not available due to the confidentiality restrictions under which the Bureau of the Census now operates. It would not be efficient or desirable for the Bureau of Labor Statistics to develop its own sampling frame; it would result in an increased reporting burden on respondents and duplication of effort within the federal government. Since an appropriate sampling frame is essential for the collection of price data, the solution must lie in a cooperative effort within the federal government, which will necessitate some change in present bureaucratic arrangements.

Classification and sampling stratification

The Standard Industrial Classification system needs to be adapted in order to provide a satisfactory framework for the collection of price data. The stratification of samples in order to take advantage of differences in the price behavior in different parts of the economy would greatly increase the efficiency of sampling. The development of the necessary classifications and stratification should be based upon detailed analysis of price behavior in different industries, regions and markets.

The need for benchmark data

At the present time, the same number of observations are collected for the Wholesale Price Index each month. In order to be able to design a more efficient price index, it would be useful to have a much larger collection of benchmark price data from time to time. It is also reasonable that samples of different sizes would be appropriate for annual, quarterly and monthly price indexes since their uses are substantially different. Greater detail is needed in the annual data for the deflation of the national income and product accounts; somewhat less detail is needed in the quarterly data and even less detail is needed in monthly data which are primarily used for monitoring the general price behavior of the economy. Special indexation requirements may, however, require specifically designed price indexes at a detailed level on a monthly basis.

Redundancy of price data

Stepwise regression analysis indicates that price indexes at the 5-digit product class level can in many cases be produced with subsets of the data now collected. This suggests that in some cases it may be possible to obtain the same level of accuracy with samples which exclude observations which are similar to those already collected. Stepwise regression analysis can be used to pinpoint the specific areas where this is possible and to specify weighting systems which will eliminate the redundant data.

Operational considerations

The collection of price data separately from other related economic data has a number of disadvantages. First, the reporting burden on respondents is increased since they are asked to report similar information to different government agencies, and each government agency in turn must independently process the reports which they collect. Second, from an analytic point of view, the separation of price data from shipments, orders, inventory and other related economic data makes both the price information and the other economic information less useful than they could be. For these reasons, it is important that the collection of price information should be integrated with the collection of other economic data.

The Validity of the Wholesale Price Index

Product change and price adjustments

Price indexes are based on measurements of the prices for identical products from one period to another. But unfortunately from the point of view of price measurement, new products are introduced, old products disappear, and the specifications of existing products change. Whether a price index is seriously affected by this process of product change depends in large degree on how rapid the change is and what adjustments are made for the changes.

Examination of the introduction of new products, the dropping of old products, and the price adjustments introduced by the Bureau of Labor Statistics indicates that less than one-half of 1 percent of the wholesale price observations each month are altered as a consequence of product change. Product change and breaks in price series are of course cumulative over time, however, so that only about half of the price series collected were continuous over the nine-year period, 1967–75, in terms of both product and reporter. In terms of products, approximately three-quarters of the initial products continued throughout the period, but due to expansion of the number of products, approximately one-third of the products currently priced have been introduced since 1967. Thus, from a longer-run point of view, there is considerable change in the price series collected and in the products represented.

For the measurement of month-to-month price change, it does not appear that either the product turnover or the adjustments which the BLS makes for changes in specifications significantly affect the price measurement. This is not equivalent to saying, however, that the month-to-month price change adequately reflects product and specification changes. New products are generally introduced in such a way that they do not affect the index. Thus, if a new product is in fact a cheaper and better substitute for an old product, this will not appear as a price decline; the only price change considered will be that of the new product itself. Under current practice, furthermore, the introduction of new products into the price index is purely judgmental. There is no automatic way to ensure that new products are covered, and as a consequence important products may not be introduced into the index soon enough and obsolete products may be kept in longer than justified. Price adjustments for changes in specifications are generally introduced only in those cases where the specification change has resulted in a cost change which is reflected in the price of the product. Thus, if new features are added to a product at an additional cost, a cost adjustment will be made, but a new feature that improves quality without increasing cost will have no effect. As already noted in actual practice, because of price adjustments, specification changes are relatively minor.

From a longer-run point of view it is apparent that the Wholesale Price Index does not capture the quality change which comes about through the introduction of new products or through product improvement which is not the direct result of increased costs. This is, however, not necessarily a deficiency, since it is not clear that it is either possible or desirable to attempt to do so. Hedonic price indexes and/or judgmental appraisals of quality change would generally result in a fragmentary and somewhat arbitrary adjustment which in all probability would capture only a small fraction of the dynamic change taking place. And if reliable and objective measures of quality change are not feasible, it is far preferable to produce price indexes which do not attempt to measure quality change at all, but adhere to objective and well-established criteria for price measurement. The resulting price indexes should, of course, not be used uncritically in contexts where real output measures including quality change are desired. There are, however, many uses where the more restricted concept of a price index which does not reflect quality change is quite appropriate. Certainly in periods of high inflation, an understanding of the price behavior of products as defined by conventional specification pricing is very useful indeed.

Evaluations of wholesale price data
There have been a number of different studies which have attempted to evaluate the validity of wholesale price data. An Interagency Committee on the Measurement of Real Output analyzed the relationship between census unit

value data and corresponding wholesale price data, and came to the conclusion that, in general, wholesale price data were better measures of price changes than the census unit values. This conclusion was not so much a vote of confidence for the wholesale price data as it was a recognition that the mix effect in the census unit value data impaired its usefulness for price measurement. In the process of analyzing wholesale price data and census unit value data, the Committee did find that in many instances wholesale price data were grossly deficient in capturing discounts from list price.

The Stigler–Kindahl report collected price data from purchasers rather than producers, in the hope that these would more truly reflect transaction prices. They found that purchasers' prices were more cyclically sensitive than producers' prices, confirming their belief that the wholesale price data did not accurately reflect discounts. These findings are clouded somewhat, however, by the fact that purchasers' prices may also differ from producers' prices because they reflect a different point in the transaction chain. Thus brokers and wholesalers may charge different prices for their products than producers, depending upon demand and supply conditions.

A study by R.J. Gordon on the measurement of durable goods prices came to the conclusion that the Wholesale Price Index does not reflect the change in quality which comes about through the introduction of new products and product improvement. Gordon's data are quite persuasive in showing that very different price measurements result if the criterion of performance is used as a basis for pricing. The differences which Gordon shows are so very large that it is apparent that the necessary adjustments are not merely matters of detail. As already suggested in the discussion of product change and price adjustments, however, it is somewhat questionable whether it is possible to capture objectively all quality change occurring in new products and product improvement, and the attempt to do so may result in incomplete and arbitrary choices which are difficult to interpret. In these circumstances, there is a strong case for continuing the use of the criteria now employed in compiling the Wholesale Price Index, as far as quality change is concerned.

The BEA government price project represents an effort to determine whether the government pays the same prices for the goods it purchases as other purchasers of the same products. The evidence thus far suggests that the government indeed does pay different prices, and that a separate price collection effort is needed to provide the basic data to deflate goods and services purchased by the government.

Finally, the Council on Wage and Price Stability has conducted a number of special studies which indicate that the wholesale price data do not capture the changes in discounts and charges for extras which actually occur under changing demand conditions. This reinforces the conclusions of the Interagency Committee, the Stigler–Kindahl study and the Gordon study. It points up the fact that the Wholesale Price Index cannot be used by regulatory agencies as an accurate indication of price behavior in a given industry. It also strongly suggests that more emphasis should be placed on obtaining net average realized unit prices for narrowly specified commodities where mix effects can be minimized.

Interagency deflators for production indexes, 1963–67 and 1967–72
Since the 1970 report of the Interagency Committee on the Measurement of Real Output, deflators have been developed for the minerals and manufacturing industries for the periods 1963–67 and 1967–72, and these reflect the implementation of the recommendations of the Interagency Committee that wholesale data should be used as deflators wherever possible instead of unit value deflators. Analysis of the results of these efforts continues to reflect the inadequacy of the coverage of mineral and manufacturing industries in the Wholesale Price Index. It becomes quite apparent that greater integration is needed between the collection of price data and that of other economic data. Without such integration it will not be possible to obtain accurate and valid measurements of real output and productivity.

Conclusions

The wholesale price data collected by the Bureau of Labor Statistics constitute a very important body of economic information. As incorporated in the Wholesale Price Index, they are used to monitor the inflation of prices and to serve as an early warning system. As deflators, they are used with current value data to measure real output and productivity. To an increasing extent business and labor are using wholesale price data for the indexation of contracts or the adjustment of accounting records. Finally, those concerned with monetary and fiscal policy use wholesale price data in economic models which seek to analyze the behavior of prices, output and employment. In view of the central role of wholesale price data in the federal statistical system, it is important that they should be critically evaluated to determine whether or not they provide satisfactory measurements of price behavior. In these terms this report concludes that there are deficiencies which need to be corrected before the wholesale price data will provide an adequate and reliable basis for measuring price behavior.

The scope and coverage of the body of wholesale price data are not adequate for the uses made of the data The Wholesale Price Index is not a general price index; even in terms of the Bureau of Labor Statistics definition it is only intended to cover prices of 'commodities sold in commercial transactions in primary markets of the United States'. Essentially that has meant in practice

that coverage is limited to producers' prices in agriculture, mining and manufacturing. Agricultural prices are supplied for the most part by the Department
of Agriculture, so that the wholesale prices which the Bureau of Labor Statistics collects refer almost entirely to mining and manufacturing. This should
be explicitly recognized by renaming the set of wholesale price data collected
by BLS 'industrial sector prices' and steps should be taken to develop new sets
of price data for the other sectors of the economy.

Even within the industrial sector, wholesale price data cover adequately
only 25 percent of the 4-digit SIC industries, accounting for somewhat under
half of the production in mining and manufacturing. A substantial increase in
price collection is required if the objective of adequate coverage is to be
achieved for industrial sector prices.

The classification system on which the Wholesale Price Index is based is in-
appropriate The wholesale price commodity classification system is unique,
and is not directly related to the Standard Industrial Classification (SIC) system
which is used by other federal statistical agencies. This makes it difficult to
relate wholesale price data to other economic data, and thus, the usefulness and
relevancy of the wholesale price program is seriously impaired. In developing
industrial sector prices, the Standard Industrial Classification should be used
as the basic classification system. This can be done within the input–output
framework which is used for other economic data. Special attention should
also be given to providing a stage of processing classification within the input–
output framework which will permit price behavior to be traced through the
economy. Such analysis is very important for linking raw material and intermediate price changes with price changes of final output.

The lack of integration between wholesale price data and other related eco-
nomic data increases the reporting burden on the private sector and seriously
impairs the analytical usefulness of the federal statistical system The present
practice of collecting price data separately from other related economic data
means that many firms and establishments are required to report their price data
to the Bureau of Labor Statistics at the same time as they are reporting sales,
inventories, wages, profits and other economic data to other agencies. The lack
of integration has disturbing consequences both for the efficiency of the data
collection program and for the usefulness of the result. The most serious
problems arise from the separation of the BLS program from the program of
the Bureau of the Census. Much of the information needed by BLS to establish
an adequate industrial classification of establishments and as a basis for
probability sampling is contained in the data already collected by the Bureau
of the Census in its *Current Industrial Reports*, its *Annual Surveys of Manu-*
factures, etc. Collection of the same types of information by BLS would

clearly constitute excessive duplication, both in terms of cost to the federal government and in terms of burden on respondents. Conversely, the price data collected by the Bureau of Labor Statistics is central to the deflation of value of shipments and the adjustment of inventory data obtained by the Bureau of the Census. It is apparent that integration of these collection programs would greatly improve the efficiency of the data collection program of both agencies.

The same considerations apply to the use of the data for analysis. Collection and compilation of the different types of economic data independently by different government agencies makes it impossible to observe interrelationships at the reporter level, and introduces incomparabilities due to different classification and data processing procedures. For the analysis of productivity, for example, compatible data are needed not only on prices, shipments and inventories, but also on wage costs and other inputs. Owing to the fragmentation of the data collection program, such compatible data are not now obtainable. A systematic effort is needed to make it possible for each of the data collecting agencies to draw on a wider range of statistical sources, including the data collected by the regulatory agencies. Such a program would reduce the burden on respondents and make better use of the data collection efforts of the whole federal statistical system, and it should go forward.

The present intermingling of order and shipment prices results in data which are difficult to interpret The wholesale prices now collected by the Bureau of Labor Statistics are a mixture of order prices and shipment prices. Despite a substantial order-to-shipment lag, these are combined into the Wholesale Price Index. Current order prices are not suitable for deflating current shipments if an appreciable order-to-shipment lag exists. Similarly, shipment prices may not serve well as an early warning of future price inflation. Combining the two types of data into one index is no solution, however.

As a first step, the Bureau of Labor Statistics needs to determine for each price series whether it is, in fact, an order price or a shipment price. The lag between orders and shipments is different at different stages of the business cycle, and it is important to obtain information on the order-to-shipment lag in various industries as a part of the analysis of price behavior. Ideally, one would like to have both order and shipment prices for each product in each industry. Where the order-to-shipment lag is nonexistent only a single price is needed, and where the lag is very short it may be possible to adjust order prices by the order-to-shipment time lags to obtain valid current price deflators. Where the lag is lengthy and variable, however, it may be necessary to collect both order and shipment prices, since changed economic conditions may lead to different discounts, rebates or other conditions of sale between the initial order and final billing. To the extent that more and more contracts are subject to escalation, the discrepancy between the current shipment prices and order prices may be expected to narrow. It is not possible *a priori* to judge what specific areas will require both shipment and order prices, but a study on a pilot basis would be helpful in determining this.

In some instances wholesale price data fail to capture changes in transactions prices Although the Bureau of Labor Statistics tries to obtain transaction prices, the prices reported to them often do not fully reflect changes in discounts and rebates or the special prices which producers offer to their customers. As a result, in some cases the Wholesale Price Index does not show the softening of price increases which may occur in a period of oversupply or declining economic activity, and conversely it may underestimate the increase in prices with increasing economic activity and the tightening up of supplies. Numerous studies seem to suggest that this is a serious deficiency of the present Wholesale Price Index. Unfortunately, there does not appear to be any simple or straightforward solution to this problem. Recourse to purchaser prices may result in introducing into the producer price index fluctuations of prices which occur at other points in the distribution system, and the current practice of averaging the reports from the different kinds of sources into one commodity series prevents the user from knowing the type of information on which the price measurement is based. Nor do unit values necessarily provide a measure of change in transaction prices, because of product mix effects. Net realized prices may be useful where these are available on a narrow enough basis, but here again the resulting change in price may be due to the change in the mix of customers who pay different prices. Although no single type of information can be relied upon to provide transactions prices, monitoring of a number of different types of price information can help in keeping track of the direction and magnitude of the bias from this source. For this reason it is urged that in areas where there is likely to be a major difference between the wholesale price data and actual transaction prices, additional collection of other kinds of data should be undertaken to provide a basis for explicit adjustment of the reported prices.

Current use of specification pricing and the manner in which new products are brought into the Wholesale Price Index results in measures which omit most of the quality change taking place in the economy Specification pricing is used by the Bureau of Labor Statistics to ensure that the same product is priced in each of two periods being compared. In a situation where products do not change in quality and no new products are introduced, this procedure results in correct price measurement. Where changes in product specifications result in a corresponding change in the price of the product, the BLS does introduce a price adjustment so that the changed specification does not result in a price change. However, if specification changes do not appear to be directly related to price changes, no adjustment is made. Therefore, quality improvements which do not cause equivalent cost increases are not taken into account. Similarly, new products are not introduced into the price index in such a way that they are linked to the products which they are replacing, and therefore, the effect of product improvement due to the introduction of new products is excluded.

It is very difficult to find appropriate methods of taking quality change and new products adequately into account. Hedonic price indexes are useful where prices can be attached to the different characteristics of products. For many types of quality change, however, this is not possible. In other areas, functional specifications rather than physical specifications may be found helpful. But here again, functional specifications are often highly subjective and where a product has many different uses the importance of its different attributes may differ in these different uses. As in the case of the transactions price problem, what is required in this area is the exploration of a number of different methods which can be used to develop adjustment factors. At the present time, there does not seem to be any general consensus on the appropriate methods. But in view of the overwhelming importance of this problem, systematic research should be undertaken on how quality change due to product change and the introduction of new products can best be measured.

System of weighting wholesale price data used by the Bureau of Labor Statistics results in general price indexes which are misleading The use of value of shipment weights to combine commodity price data into aggregate price indexes results in overweighting raw material inputs and intermediate outputs. As a consequence, the behavior of the general Wholesale Price Index unduly reflects the behavior of these commodities. In order to develop appropriate indexes for different levels of aggregation, e.g., product, product class, 4- and 2-digit industry, a system of net output weights should be used which would weight the commodity price data by the amount of the commodity sold outside of the grouping for which the index is being compiled. At the more disaggregated levels, net output weights would correspond quite closely to those presently used for the WPI. At higher levels of aggregation, however, the duplication of raw materials and intermediate products would be eliminated.

In addition to indexes based on net output weighting, it would also be useful to compile value added price indexes at a fairly detailed industry level. This requires both an input price index and an output price index for each industry, from which an index of value added prices can be constructed. Such prices indexes are useful in analyzing the degree to which a given industry is absorbing, passing along, or initiating price changes. The input prices and output prices for each industry are also a necessary ingredient in the process of developing real value added measures by industry.

The use of judgmental data collection rather than probability sampling prevents statistical estimation of sampling errors and reduces the efficiency of the collection effort The present system of price collection used by the Bureau of Labor Statistics results in uneven and often inadequate coverage. Unfortunately, since the sampling is not done on a probability basis, it has not been possible to determine how efficient the present system of collection is. By the same token, however, the BLS has no way of determining where it should concentrate its efforts in order to improve the sampling reliability of the wholesale price data. A sampling frame is needed as the basis for developing a probability sample. This already exists in other statistical agencies of the federal government, and it should be obtained through cooperation with them.

The current method of price collection involves collecting the same number of series each month. It should be recognized that the needs for benchmark, annual, quarterly and monthly price indexes are different, and the samples for these different periods should be designed accordingly.

REFERENCES

Council on Wage and Price Stability (1975), *A Study of Steel Prices*, Staff Report, July.
_____ (1976a), *Report on Steel Price Increases*, June.
_____ (1976b), *Aluminum Prices 1974–75*, September.
Department of Labor (1902), 'Course of wholesale prices 1890–1901', *Bulletin of the Department of Labor*, **39**, 205–9.
Department of Labor, Bureau of Labor Statistics (1971), *Handbook of Methods*, Washington, DC.
Gordon, Robert J. (1977), 'The measurement of durable goods prices', NBER Transcript.
Interagency Committee on the Measurement of Real Output (1970), 'Considerations on the choice of price or unit value deflators for census benchmark production indexes', June 15 (mimeographed).
Leontief, Wassily (1971), 'Theoretical assumptions and nonobserved facts', *American Economic Review*, 5–6.
Stigler, George J. and James K. Kindahl (1970), *The Behavior of Industrial Prices*, National Bureau of Economic Research, General Series No. 90.

PART THREE

PRICE BEHAVIOR

11. The Relative Movements of Real and Money Wage Rates

Richard Ruggles
Harvard University

Recent discussions of the movements of real and money wage rates (Dunlop, 1938; Tarshis, 1939; Richardson, 1939) have seemed to confuse rather than clarify the problem. This article will attempt three things. First, an analysis of the various studies will be made in order to find the source of disagreement between the different writers. Second, a new statistical approach will be attempted in an effort to reveal more clearly than, heretofore, the actual relation between real and money wage rate movements. Finally, the bearing of these lines of reasoning upon the conclusions of traditional theory will be examined. The validity of the methods used in the studies considered will be questioned, rather than the primary reliability of the data on which the conclusions are based. In cases of this kind, it is not enough merely to give a convincing argument; unless we also show why other arguments, though apparently convincing, are not valid, the answer will be as indeterminate as before.

1. DUNLOP'S STUDY OF REAL AND MONEY WAGE RATES

Mr Dunlop's study (1939) was directly stimulated by a passage in Mr Keynes's *General Theory* (1936, pp. 9–10) describing the probable relation between real and money wage rates:

> It would be interesting to see the results of a statistical inquiry into the actual relationship between changes in money wages and changes in real wages. In the case of a change peculiar to a particular industry one would expect the change in real wages to be in the same direction as the change in money wages. But in the case of changes in the general level of wages, it will be found, I think, that the change

This chapter first appeared in *Quarterly Journal of Economics*, **55** (1), 1940.

in real wages associated with a change in money wages, so far from being in the same direction, is almost always in the opposite direction. When money wages are rising, that is to say, it will be found that real wages are falling; and when money wages are falling, real wages are rising.

In contradiction of this view, Dunlop submitted data covering the period in England from 1860 to 1937 inclusive, with the omission of the years 1913–19. His conclusion concerning the English experience was that 'increases in wage rates have usually been associated with increased real wage rates, while decreases in wage rates have equally often been associated with a rise or fall in real wage rates' (Dunlop, 1938, p. 421).

Mr Dunlop first computed the link relatives of money wage rates and real wage rates for the 70 years examined, and by this method indicated the direction of change in both variables for each year. In addition to computing the link relatives of real wage rates from the cost-of-living indexes of G.E. Wood and A.L. Bowley, Mr Dunlop devised a 'corrected' series of link relatives of real wages. This correction was made to take terms of trade into consideration, inasmuch as changes in import prices affect the cost of living in England, and thus factors of external conditions are reflected. Since the Keynesian statement was to apply to a closed economy, he corrected the food and clothing elements of the cost of living in accordance with changes in the terms of trade (see Dunlop, 1938, ftn, pp. 417–18). Further correction involved trend elimination from the real wage rate relatives. Then by classifying the money wage rate changes into three groups (increasing, unchanging, and decreasing), he examined real wage rate movements with reference to money wage rate movements. For example, between 1860 and 1913 there are 25 years in which money wage rates increased, and he found the real wage rate movements for these 25 years to be as follows (Dunlop, 1938, p. 414): in 17 years real wage rates increased, in three years real wage rates were unchanged and in five years real wage rates decreased. From this he concluded that when money wage rates rose, real wage rates also tended to rise.

But is such a conclusion justified? Table 11.1 gives the actual distribution of real and money wage rates over the whole 70-year period. By using these figures, we can tell whether the structure in any specific group differs significantly from the other groups or from the distribution throughout the whole 70-year period. This has been done in Table 11.2.

Here column A gives the distribution of real wage rates as presented by Mr Dunlop's data; column B gives the distributions that would be expected if each of the three groups of money wage rate movements showed the same distribution of real wage rate movements as the whole 70-year period. Such analysis is valuable since we are interested in discovering in what way the movement of real wage rates is different in periods of rising and of falling money wage rates.

Table 11.1 Yearly Changes in Real and Money Wage Rates*

| | Money wage rates | | | Real wage rates | |
	No. of years	Percent		No. of years	Percent
Increased	31	44.4	Increased	39	55.8
Unchanged	15	21.4	Unchanged	10	14.2
Decreased	24	34.2	Decreased	21	30.0
Total	70	100.0	Total	70	100.0

*Dunlop (1938), computed from the table on p. 416. All figures in this chapter are taken directly from the various articles rather than the original sources. This ensures the use of precisely the same material as the author in each instance. The figures are approximations, since in many cases computation was done by slide rule. Further refinement seemed unnecessary and would have given a misleading idea of the accuracy of the material concerned.

Table 11.2 Distribution of Real Wage Rate Movements According to Money Wage Rate Movements*

| | Uncorrected | | Corrected for terms of trade | | Corrected also for trend | |
Real Wage Rate	A	B	A	B	A	B
For the 30+ years money wage rates increase						
Years increase	19	17.3	24	20.4	22	18.1
Years unchanged	4	4.4	1	1.2	0	0.5
Years decrease	8	9.3	6	9.4	9	12.4
Total	31	31.0	31	31.0	31	31.0
For the 15 years money wage rates do not change						
Years increase	6	8.4	9	9.8	7	8.8
Years unchanged	4	2.1	5	0.7	1	0.2
Years decrease	5	4.5	1	4.5	7	6.0
Total	15	15.0	15	15.0	15	15.0
For the 24 years money wage rates decrease						
Years increase	13	13.4	15	15.8	12	14.2
Years unchanged	2	3.4	0	1.0	0	0.2
Years decrease	9	7.2	9	7.2	12	9.6
Total	24	24.0	24	24.0	24	24.0

*Dunlop (1938), computed from the table on p. 416.

The deviation of the empirical results from the theoretical frequencies in Table 11.2 is less than would have been expected in the light of Mr Dunlop's conclusion. In other words, real wage rate movements in periods of rising money wage rates are not very different from those in other periods. Furthermore, the breakdown of the 70-year period into three groups renders the significance of the discrepancies even more doubtful, since now the groups are quite small. This seriously weakens his proof that real and money wage rates move together. The movement of real wage rates in the various periods analyzed is not highly differentiated, and the reliability of such differentiation as we do find is impaired by the smallness of the sample.

But even if he could show that real and money wage rates tend to rise together, this would not necessarily mean that it was the rise of money wage rates which caused the corresponding movement in real wage rates. The reason for this is to be found in the definition of the real wage rate. If money wage rates and the cost of living move in opposite directions, real wage rates must of necessity move in the same direction as money wage rates. For example, when money wage rates rise and the cost of living falls, real wage rates will rise, since the two variables tend to reinforce rather than counteract each other. Likewise, if money wage rates fall and the cost of living rises, then real wage rates will fall, the influence of both variables being in the same direction in this case also.

Now, what would be the correspondence of real and money wage rates if money wage rates and the cost of living were randomly associated as to direction and amplitude of movement? (Here money wage rates and the cost of living are considered merely as two independent variables with equal and unrelated tendencies as to direction and degree of movement.) Under these assumptions, money wage rates and the cost of living will move in the same direction 50 percent of the time and in opposite directions 50 percent of the time. Furthermore, money wage rates will fluctuate to a greater extent than the cost of living 50 percent of the time, and this 50 percent will be distributed equally between the period in which cost of living and money wage rates move together and the period in which they move opposite to each other. In the period in which money wage rates and the cost of living move together, real wage rates will move with money wage rates whenever the amplitude of money wage rate movement exceeds that of the cost of living. Under the above assumptions, this would be for 50 percent of this period; in other words, for 25 percent (50 percent of half) of the whole period. As for the other period — that in which money wage rates and the cost of living move opposite to each other — we have already seen that whenever money wage rates and the cost of living move opposite to each other, real and money wage rates will move in the same direction. Thus it follows under the above assumptions that real and money wage rates would move in the same direction 75 percent of the whole period.

A random relationship as to direction between the movement of real wage rates and that of the cost of living is probably an unreal condition, and yet they do not move in the same direction as often as is implicitly assumed by most economists. When money wage rates and the cost of living are regarded as a part of the general price level, economists quite often consider them as moving in the same direction. However, if attention is directed to the growth element in an economy, then the upward trend in real wage rates may easily occur through a rise in money wage rates accompanied by falling prices due to increased productivity. In Mr Dunlop's data, money wage rates and the cost of living move in opposite directions approximately 24 percent of the time. Therefore, the fact that real and money wage rates move together does not necessarily lead to the conclusion at which he has arrived — that in the upswing (before the top of the boom) money wage rates tend to outstrip the movements of the cost of living (Dunlop, 1938, p. 430). In some instances the rise in real wage rates is to be attributed rather to the fall in the cost of living. It would seem then, that Mr. Dunlop attempts to support his argument with statistics involving cost-of-living movements that are inconsistent with the assumptions implied. This, it must be admitted, might be of minor importance if the statistics were more conclusive; but since there is little difference between real wage rate movements in the various periods into which money wage rate movements may be divided, this erratic movement of cost of living assumes a major role. Hence, we must conclude that even if he could show a reliable difference in real wage rate movements in periods of rising money wage rates, he still would not have produced completely convincing evidence as to the relations of real and money wage rates.

Mr Tarshis (1939) seems to support Dunlop's conclusion by analyzing monthly data pertaining to the period 1932–38 in the United States. He found in this instance that there was a high positive correlation between the direction of change of real and money wage rates. The movement of both variables here is upward throughout most of the period. His proof, however, is also open to question.

In the first place, the coefficient of association which he used for determining the relationship is of doubtful validity. This measure utilizes only those months in which both real and money wage rates exhibit movement. In other words, those months in which money wage rates did not change are dropped from the analysis, but those months in which the cost of living did not change are included. Naturally, in periods when money wage rates do not change and the cost of living does change, real wage rates will move exactly opposite to the cost of living and will not 'follow' money wage rates. The coefficient of association which Mr Tarshis obtained is for this reason spuriously high.

Furthermore, a random relationship between money wage rates and cost-of-living movements, as defined previously in this paper, would yield a coefficient of association of 0.80 between real and money wage rate movements. This arises from the fact that real and money wage rates move in the same direction whenever money wage rates and the cost of living move opposite to each other. Although there is a general tendency for money wage rates and the cost of living to move in the same direction, it seems quite reasonable to suspect that Mr Tarshis's coefficient of association of 0.86 is to be accounted for, in part, by the periods (24 percent of the time) in which this tendency does not hold true.

There is also the objection that the period analyzed is very short and not even one complete cycle. It is a well-known fact that real wage rates have had an upward trend. The purpose of analysis here is to discover whether the movement of real wage rates during periods of rising money wage rates is very different from what it is in periods of falling money wage rates. Were the coefficient of association a valid measure, it would merely show that real wage rates went up in a period of rising money wage rates; it could not indicate whether this movement was more marked than in periods of falling money wage rates.

The significance of Mr Tarshis's analysis, therefore, is impaired both by the statistical measure used and by the nature of the period examined. Its relevance to the general problem of real and money wage rate relationship is highly questionable, and it by no means supports the conclusion reached by Mr Dunlop.

Professor J.H. Richardson (1939) considered the problem from a different angle. Using the same basic data (to 1900) as Mr Dunlop, he directed his attention 'first to changes in the cost of living and then in real wages'. The link relative method of comparing real wage rates from year to year he considered 'less satisfactory in some ways than index numbers calculated on a suitable base year' (p. 135). His reason was that in Mr Dunlop's use of the link relative method, direction only was considered and amplitude disregarded. In his analysis, however, Professor Richardson has implicitly used the direction test, inasmuch as he determines the number of years in which the cost of living and real wage rates move together. Using a fixed-base index number does not alter the analysis, since only the direction of change in the variables from year to year is being considered. The procedure followed by Professor Richardson is quite similar to that of Mr Dunlop, except that cost of living is substituted for the money wage rate. His conclusion was that 'in the whole period of thirty-nine years there were changes in the cost of living in thirty-five years, and in thirty-one of these years real wage rates moved in the opposite direction to the cost of living or remained unchanged, thus strongly supporting the traditional conclusion' (p. 430).

Just as Mr Tarshis took periods in which money wage rates changed, so Professor Richardson with no greater justification has taken periods in which the cost of living changes. Certainly, if the cost of living never changed, we could rightly say that real wage rates moved with money wage rates. Moreover, it seems quite unreasonable to say that the traditional conclusion is strengthened when real wage rates remain unchanged while the cost of living moves. In this case the movements of money wage rates and the cost of living balance each other. Correcting for these two factors we find that there are: 23 years in which real wage rates and the cost of living move opposite to each other, eight years in which real wage rates do not move and eight years in which real wage rates do not move opposite to the cost of living.

Furthermore, in 11 of the 23 years in which real wage rates and the cost of living move opposite to each other, money wage rates move opposite to the cost of living. This point is the converse of the point made earlier in regard to Dunlop's analysis. It is obvious that whenever money wage rates and the cost of living move in opposite directions, real wage rates must of necessity move opposite to the cost of living. The combination of the above factors explains the difference between Mr Dunlop's and Professor Richardson's results. The case in support of the traditional conclusion is not strong, since the deviating years are more numerous than Professor Richardson realized.

The three studies examined above have been found to be of doubtful significance, because their approaches lacked validity. Confusion and ambiguity have been revealed. To avoid these pitfalls it will be better to reexamine the data by a new approach, rather than to attempt a correction of the methods there used. I now turn to this problem.

2. RE-ANALYSIS OF THE ENGLISH DATA

By examining these earlier studies of the problem of real wage rate relationships, we have obtained more in the way of understanding the determining factors than if we had set up definitions at the outset. Analysis stated only in terms of the direction of real and money wage rate movement is inadequate, since it is impossible to tell what part of the relation discovered is to be attributed to movements in the cost of living. For example, if the cost of living went up 15 percent and money wage rates went down 0.1 percent, then according to Mr Dunlop's analysis we should say that real wages followed the money wage rate movement. This, however, would overlook the fact that practically all the movement in the real wage rate could be accounted for by the movement in the cost of living. We ought not to be content with the apparent facts, but should seek their significance. An apparent correspondence of real and money wage rate movement does not indicate that in these periods real wage rates tended to be governed by the movements of money wage rates. The question, indeed, was originally considered because money wages were believed to be more rigid than the cost of living. Naturally, if the cost of living tends to move in the same direction as the money wage rate, but fluctuates more, then the real wage rate will move opposite to the money wage rate.

A statistical investigation should start at the source, rather than at the conclusion of this problem. In other words, the fluctuations of the basic variables, cost of living and money wage rates, should be compared. Link relatives are suitable for this purpose, since the changes in money wage rates are to be compared with the changes in the cost of living. This method will allow direct year-to-year comparisons. It does have the fault, mentioned by Professor Richardson, of not taking into account cumulative changes, but these cumulative changes may conceal as well as reveal peculiarities of the data. In order

Price Behavior

to obviate the difficulty of cumulative change, the data have been roughly divided into cyclical periods as suggested by Mr Keynes (1939, p. 38) and Mr Dunlop (1938, p. 419). The data in Table 11.3 have been computed from the material presented in the studies by these writers. The letter 'C' indicates that the percentage change in the cost of living exceeds that in the money wage rate, 'O' indicates an equivalence of percentage changes, and 'M' indicates that the percentage change in money wage rates is greater.

Table 11.3 Change of Money Wage Rates and the Cost of Living in Richardson's and Dunlop's Data

		Dunlop			Richardson		
		Money wage rates	Cost of living*		Money wage rates	Cost of living	
Depression	1860–61	0	2.9	C	0	2.4	C
	1861–62	1.8	–3.2	C	1.8	–2.4	C
	1862–63	0.9	–2.9	C	0.9	–2.8	C
Prosperity	1863–64	6.0	–1.3	M	6.0	–1.0	M
	1864–65	1.6	1.6	O	1.6	1.0	M
	1865–66	4.8	5.7	C	4.8	5.6	C
Depression	1866–67	–0.8	5.2	C	–0.8	5.3	C
	1867–68	–0.8	–1.7	C	–0.8	–1.8	C
	1868–69	0	–4.5	C	0	–4.0	C
	1869–70	2.3	–0.3	M	2.3	0	M
Prosperity	1870–71	3.8	1.3	M	3.8	0.4	M
	1871–72	5.8	5.0	M	5.8	4.5	M
	1872–73	6.2	1.3	M	6.2	1.1	M
	1873–74	0.6	–3.3	C	0.6	–2.2	C
	1874–75	–1.3	–2.8	C	–1.3	–3.1	C
	1875–76	–1.3	–2.8	C	–1.3	–1.8	C
Depression	1876–77	–0.7	2.2	C	–0.7	1.8	C
	1877–78	–2.0	–1.2	M	–2.0	–1.8	M
	1878–79	–1.4	5.2	C	–1.4	–4.7	C
	1879–80	0.7	2.9	C	0.7	2.8	C
Prosperity	1880–81	0	–3.6	C	0	–1.4	C
	1881–82	4.2	2.2	M	0	0.5	C
	1882–83	0	0.1	C	1.4	–1.9	C
	1883–84	0	–4.6	C	0.7	–1.9	C
Depression	1884–85	–2.7	–5.9	C	–0.7	–3.5	C
	1885–86	–1.4	–2.2	C	–0.7	–3.1	C
	1886–87	1.4	–2.3	C	0.7	–2.1	C
	1887–88	2.7	–0.3	M	1.3	0	M
Prosperity	1888–89	6.7	2.4	M	3.3	2.1	M
	1889–90	3.8	1.4	M	4.5	0	M
	1890–91	0	0.7	C	0	1.1	C
	1891–92	0	0	O	–0.6	0	M
	1892–93	0	–2.3	C	0	–2.6	C
Depression	1893–94	0	–2.6	C	0	–1.6	C
	1894–95	0	–2.0	C	0	–2.1	C
	1895–96	0	–0.3	C	0.6	–0.6	C
	1896–97	1.2	3.0	C	1.8	2.1	C

		Dunlop			Richardson		
		Money wage rates	Cost of living*		Money wage rates	Cost of living	
Prosperity	1897–98	3.6	2.6	M	0.6	1.6	C
	1898–99	2.3	–1.8	M	3.0	–0.1	M
	1899–1900	5.6	7.6	C			
	1900–01	–1.1	–0.8	M			
	1901–02	–2.2	–2.0	M			
Depression	1902–03	0	2.1	C			
	1903–04	–2.2	–0.4	M			
	1904–05	0	–0.5	C			
Prosperity	1911–12	3.2	2.7	M			
	1912–13	1.1	1.8	C			
	1920–21	–3.4	8.7	C			
Depression	1921–22	–25.3	–17.4	M			
	1922–23	–8.2	–5.5	M			
	1923–24	1.5	–0.9	M			
Prosperity	1924–25	1.7	–0.7	M	0.5	–2.9	C
	1925–26	–0.4	–0.2	M	0.4	0	M
	1926–27	–0.6	–2.4	C	–0.9	–4.0	C
	1927–28	–1.6	–1.5	M	–1.0	–0.6	M
	1928–29	–0.3	–0.7	C	–0.3	–0.5	C
Depression	1929–30	–0.4	–1.5	C	–0.7	–7.9	C
	1930–31	–1.9	–2.3	C	–2.3	–3.9	C
	1931–32	–1.9	–2.7	C	–1.5	–3.5	C
	1932–33	–0.7	–1.0	C	–0.5	–0.0	M
	1933–34	0.4	0.3	M	0.5	–0.8	C
	1934–35	1.2	–0.1	M	1.3	2.8	C
Prosperity	1935–36	2.8	1.3	M	3.1	2.9	M
	1936–37	3.3	2.7	M	4.6	5.2	C

*Corrected for terms of trade.

Table 11.3 does not necessarily support the conclusion advanced by Keynes that the traditional argument is refuted, since real wage rates rise in prosperity and fall in depression. It is important to note that money wage rates move quite consistently with the phases of the cycle, but that the cost-of-living movements are somewhat inconsistent within each cycle phase. The years 1876–80, for example, include three years in which the cost-of-living movements are downward, and two years in which they are upward. An analysis of cycle phases, therefore, would make the money wage rate movements cumulative, whereas the cost-of-living movements would tend to balance out. In fact, in 19 of the 35 years considered depression years, the movement of the cost of living is such that the real wage rate was above that of the preceding period of prosperity. It is true that this is uncorrected for trend, but in 15 of these years the increase is above any reasonable allowance for trend.

Mr Dunlop (1938, p. 425) observed this and explained it by saying that the 'policy of no wage reduction seems to have been successful until a phase of the depression is reached when great pressure is characteristically brought to bear by the employers against wage rates. Then real wage rates might be expected to fall.' This theory is not very well borne out by the statistical analysis, since such a movement of money wage rates occurs in Mr Dunlop's data only in the period 1884–86. Mere summary of the movements of real and money wage rates in prosperity and depression is inadequate, since it does not consider movements within a cycle phase. Yearly changes, as given in Table 11.3, do reveal the nature of the movements more fully.

Examination of money wage rate movements in this way indicates that the tendency to rise greatly exceeds the tendency to fall. A trend such that the range of movement (6.7 to –2.7, 1921–23 excepted) would appear to be equally distributed would exaggerate the rate of secular increase. In other words, the movement of money wage rates is such that the degree of variation upward is greater than that downward, aside from the allowance for secular trend. In fact, it might be easier to explain the secular trend by reasoning that money wage rates tend to move up in the prosperity phase, and then consolidate this gain in the depression phase by not falling so violently. This seems to suggest that what appears to be a secular movement may not necessarily be wholly the result of any distinct trend forces, but partly the effect of the cycles upon money wage rates which are flexible upward.

The cost of living does not lend itself to any such specific generalization. A glance at the link relatives, in fact, emphasizes the irregularity of this variable. Attempts to find suitable lags or leads have proved fruitless. But it is this very irregularity that accounts for the fact that real wage rates are often found to be higher and lower at different times in the same depression than they were in the preceding period of prosperity. Since money wage rates move consistently with the cycle's phases, but the range of movement upward is greater than the range of movement downward, the irregularity of the cost-of-living movement can easily explain why real wage rates are found increasing throughout the prosperity period and during a large part of the depression period. It is unfortunate that such great irregularity exists, since we can reach no definite conclusion as to the relative variation upward and downward. From the dynamics of the situation we should expect upward fluctuations in the cost of living to be more marked, since the violent increases in money wage rates would themselves be a factor in causing the cost of living to rise. In addition, the forces causing money wage rates to rise may also be present in the prices which enter into the cost of living. Yet no comparison of the range of fluctuations in money wage rates and in the cost of living is significant in the light of the irregularities just mentioned.

If a secular trend analysis were applied to the money wage rate movement, it would be found that its rate of increase is much greater than the rate of decrease in the cost of living. Although statistically one could apparently conclude that money wage rates have been a greater force than the cost of living in the creation of the real wage rate, theoretically this position would not be the only alternative. Money wage rates might be accelerated in their rise by the rise in the cost of living, and then consolidate this gain by not falling when the cost of living falls. In this way the cost of living could be a large determinant in the movement of real wages in spite of having a smaller trend than money wage rates. Such a relationship between cost of living and money wage rates does not seem at all unreasonable, and might serve better than the more simple explanation as to the correspondence of the cost of living and money wage rate movements.

The crucial point of the investigation is still undecided. It can be fairly safely stated that money wage rates tend to rise above the cost-of-living movement in the prosperity phase, but this does not conclude the argument. In order to support Mr Dunlop's contention, the rise of money wage rates above the cost of living must be shown to be greater than the fall of the cost of living below the decline in money wage rates (i.e., that real wages increase more in prosperity than in depression). Irregularities in the cost of living are so numerous that their influence on the data should not be overlooked, since the various periods in our data are in disagreement on this point. Certainly it should be recognized that these statistics do not satisfactorily prove the original implications of Mr Dunlop's conclusion.

Mr Tarshis's short-run study can be analyzed by the same method as was used on Mr Dunlop's and Professor Richardson's material. This has been done in Table 11.4. The link relatives were derived from his data, and the letters after the cost-of-living relatives have the same significance as they had in Table 11.3. The 'corrected' cost-of-living index was computed by Mr Tarshis in order to allow for the changes in the cost of living which were due to changes in the prices of agricultural commodities. The results yielded by this analysis do not seem to verify the high correlation between real and money wage rates which he found.

Mr Tarshis's data were presented as a study of the short-run relationship between real and money wage rates. The purpose of his analysis was to examine monthly change, rather than the cumulative summaries which longer periods present. In Table 11.4 we should attempt to discover whether the change in real wage rates has been influenced more by the change in money wage rates than by the change in the cost of living. Real wage rates will be correlated more closely with the series having the greater amplitude of fluctuation. A summary of Table 11.4 given below is in positive contradiction of any conclusion to the effect that real wage rates are more highly related to changes in money wage rates than to changes in the cost of living for the short-run period considered.

	Months money wage rate movement exceeds cost-of-living movement	Months cost-of-living movement exceeds money wage rate movement
Uncorrected	36	35
Corrected	39	32

Table 11.4 Monthly Link Relatives of the Money Wage Rates and Cost of Living in Tarshis's Data

	Money wage rates	Cost of living	Cost of living correction		Money wage rates	Cost of living	Cost of living correction
1932				**1935**			
J–F	−1.5	−1.6 C	−1.4 M	D–J	1.8	0.9 M	−0.3 M
F–M	−2.3	−0.3 M	−0.2 M	J–F	1.2	0.4 M	0.8 M
M–A	−0.8	−0.8 O	−0.7 M	F–M	−0.9	0.1 M	−0.2 M
A–M	−0.4	−1.2 C	−0.6 C	M–A	1.0	0.8 M	0.3 M
M–J	−1.6	−1.4 M	−0.6 M	A–M	0.0	−0.4 C	−0.4 C
J–J	−0.8	−0.3 M	−0.7 M	M–J	0.2	−0.3 C	1.8 C
J–A	−1.6	−0.7 M	−0.9 M	J–J	−0.5	−0.3 C	−0.2 C
A–S	−2.3	−0.5 M	−0.8 M	J–A	−0.7	−0.1 M	1.0 C
S–O	−0.6	−0.9 C	−0.2 M	A–S	0.0	0.3 C	0.2 C
O–N	−0.2	−0.5 C	−0.5 C	S–O	0.0	0.3 C	0.4 C
N–D	−0.6	−1.1 C	−0.4 M	O–N	0.2	1.9 C	0.6 C
1933				N–D	−0.2	0.5 C	0.2 O
D–J	0.2	−1.7 C	−0.1 M	**1936**			
J–F	−0.6	−1.9 C	−2.4 C	D–J	1.7	0.8 M	−0.1 M
F–M	−0.2	−1.2 C	−1.6 C	J–F	−0.3	−0.8 C	−1.0 C
M–A	−1.1	−0.1 M	−0.6 C	F–M	0.2	−0.3 C	0.3 C
A–M	0.4	0.6 C	−1.9 C	M–A	−0.3	0.1 M	0.0 M
M–J	−1.5	1.0 M	1.7 C	A–M	0.3	0.4 C	0.8 C
J–J	1.8	2.3 C	1.2 M	M–J	0.2	1.3 C	0.7 C
J–A	10.0	1.7 M	2.5 M	J–J	0.0	0.0 O	−0.1 C
A–S	3.4	0.8 M	0.8 M	J–A	0.0	0.4 C	−0.7 C
S–O	2.1	−0.4 M	−0.1 M	A–S	−0.2	0.2 O	0.2 O
O–N	−0.2	−0.6 C	−0.8 C	S–O	0.2	−0.4 C	−0.3 C
N–D	−1.1	−1.0 M	−0.7 M	O–N	1.0	0.1 M	−0.2 M
1934				N–D	0.0	0.3 C	−0.5 C
D–J	4.0	0.3 M	−0.6 M	**1937**			
J–F	−0.2	1.0 C	0.3 C	D–J	1.5	0.8 M	0.3 M
F–M	−0.4	0.3 M	0.2 M	J–F	0.7	0.1 M	0.1 M
M–A	1.5	−0.3 M	0.1 M	F–M	0.8	0.0 M	0.1 M
A–M	0.9	0.2 M	0.3 M	M–A	2.8	0.3 M	0.9 M
M–J	0.4	−0.5 C	−0.7 C	A–M	1.6	0.5 M	1.1 M
J–J	0.9	−0.1 M	−0.2 C	M–J	0.3	−0.1 M	0.2 M
J–A	0.2	0.5 C	−1.0 C	J–J	0.9	0.0 M	0.7 M
A–S	0.5	1.2 C	0.5 C	J–A	0.6	0.2 M	0.5 M
S–O	−0.2	−0.5 C	3.1 C	A–S	0.0	0.4 C	0.5 C
O–N	0.0	−2.5 C	0.3 C	S–O	0.8	0.1 M	0.0 M
N–D	−0.5	−0.1 M	−0.3 M	O–N	0.0	−0.4 C	0.9 C
				N–D	−1.8	−0.3 M	0.1 M
				1938			
				D–J	0.6	−1.1 C	−0.8 C
				J–F	−0.2	−0.6 C	−0.3 C
				F–M	−0.5	−0.1 M	0.2 M

Further consideration of Table 11.4 shows that when a period of a year is broken down into months, the relation between money wage rates and the cost of living is not constant. Although this is to be expected, it makes clear an important point. The answer to the problem with which we are concerned in this paper may depend in large degree on the length of the period chosen. For example, if a period of 20 years were used, the movements of money wage rates would almost invariably be greater than those of the cost of living, since money wage rates show a stronger secular trend than the cost of living for the periods studied. The apparent conclusion would then be drawn that money wage rates are of greater importance in determining the real wage rate changes than the cost of living. Likewise, if cycle phases were the periods utilized, it can easily be seen that it would be possible for the one variable to move more than the other in every year except at the peak or bottom, where the other variable's movement might be such that for that phase of the cycle it would exceed the first variable's movement. In such cases, obviously, an analysis of cycle periods is not sufficient, since the contrary-to-fact assumption is often made that further analysis would lead to constant relations within the given period. The data which Mr Tarshis has presented should caution statisticians against too positive use of yearly figures as representing a constant change of money wage rates and the cost of living.

Unfortunately, the period which Mr Tarshis studied is extremely short, and does not cover even one complete cycle. Since the variables involved are greatly affected by the cycle, no definite conclusion can be reached on the basis of these figures. Furthermore, seasonal relationships cannot be ascertained, or even their presence made known, in such a brief period. The period is therefore neither representative, reliable, nor capable of being studied by the proper tools of analysis. These factors, coupled with the above-mentioned relations between money wage rates and the cost of living, render the value of the study very dubious.

3. THE CONCEPT OF REAL WAGE RATES

In the preceding part of this paper, it has been taken for granted that the cost of living and money wage rates are the variables with which the 'traditional theory' concerning wage rates and prices is concerned. This assumption, it must now be noted, is of doubtful validity. Mr Keynes stated (1939, p. 37) the traditional conclusion by quoting Marshall's final statement (Bk VI, Ch. viii, § 6) of the matter as given in a passage in the *Principles*. It is unfortunate that he did not include more of the quotation, for the inappropriateness of using cost-of-living figures would have been immediately obvious. The complete quotation is as follows:

In the first place the undertaker's profits bear the first brunt of any change in the price of those things which are the product of his capital (including his business organization), of his labour and of the labour of his employees; and as a result fluctuations of his profits generally precede fluctuations of their wages, and are much more extensive. For, other things being equal, a comparatively small rise in the price for which he can sell his product is not unlikely to increase his profit manyfold, or perhaps to substitute a profit for a loss. That rise will make him eager to reap the harvest of good prices while he can; and he will be in fear that his employees will leave him or refuse to work. He will therefore be more able and more willing to pay the high wages; and wages will tend upwards. But experience shows that (whether they are governed by sliding scales or not) they seldom rise as much in proportion as prices; and therefore they do not rise nearly as much in proportion as profits.

The wage rates employed in the studies discussed above apply mostly to manufacturing industries. Consequently, if the Marshallian argument is to be considered, the prices required will not be cost-of-living prices, but rather wholesale prices. The term real wage has been loosely used mainly because economists speak in general terms about an economy. But when an attempt is made to solve a problem statistically, the analysts should not fall into the same error. Mr Dunlop corrected the cost-of-living figures for terms of trade in order to make the prices more applicable to his problem. Mr Tarshis omitted agricultural commodities in his cost-of-living index for the same reason. Mr Keynes (1939, p. 44), in fact, writes: 'It is important, therefore, if we are to understand the situation, that statisticians should endeavor to calculate wages in terms of the actual product of the labor in question.' It seems strange, therefore, that cost of living should have been used. Certainly it seems no more justified to exclude the product of the farmer than the product of the retailer. If the goods which labor produced are valued at retail prices, they are no longer the same goods, since they now contain the value added by the retailer. Inasmuch as a large part of the traditional conclusion is concerned with wage *cost*, wholesale prices are more relevant than cost-of-living data. The fluctuations of wholesale prices are much wider than those of the cost of living; and since this problem of real and money wage rate relationship deals with the relative fluctuation of variables, the use of cost-of-living figures will have major effects on the results of the analysis. But mere substitution of wholesale prices for the cost of living does not adequately solve the wage cost problem. For example, it would be entirely possible for wage cost to change, even though there were no change in either wholesale prices or money wage rates. With shifts in the degree of plant utilization, there will be shifts in the productivity of given units of labor. An increase in the productivity of labor without a corresponding increase in money wage rates would naturally lower the labor cost to the entrepreneur. Likewise an increase in the real wage rate relative to wholesale prices is quite possible with decreasing wage costs. To develop a refined method of attack on this question is beyond the scope of this paper. It is enough for our purpose to point out the errors involved in these earlier attempts to test the traditional conclusion statistically.

What, then, is the significance of the relationship between money wage rates and the cost of living? Since, as has been shown above, the cost of living is not the variable assumed in the traditional conclusion, it is difficult to see what the relevance of such analyses as the foregoing may be. It is my conclusion that the relation between real and money wage rates is not of a constant nature. The interrelation of wholesale and retail prices, the degree of monopoly, and the changing economic structure continually interact upon the relationship and render it unstable. Furthermore, external conditions such as wars, inflations, and exceptional harvests are major factors in causing unpredictable shifts. The results obtained in Section 2 would tend to support this point of view, since no clear-cut relation was discovered. Any relation that might be assumed would not be strongly supported by the whole period, and without a theoretical explanation would have little meaning.

It may be felt, however, that the use of the *corrected* cost-of-living data presents another case. Aside from the reliability of the corrections made by Mr Dunlop and Mr Tarshis, the purpose itself is somewhat questionable. As explained above, if the traditional theory is being examined statistically, the corrections are inadequate since retail prices are not the prices required. As a historical description of the relation of welfare to money wage rates, moreover, the correction is of minor importance, since such things as the general level of employment and the number of hours worked are not included in the analysis. Real wage rates must not be considered alone when the welfare of labor is being studied. The real wage rate might be the same in a period of prosperity as in a depression, but the welfare of labor as a whole would be quite different.

Our conclusion, then, is that the statistical studies to date have not produced any convincing evidence concerning the interrelations between money wage rates, wage costs, and welfare. Further study of pay rolls in relation to output and to the wholesale price of this output should be undertaken, in order to analyze the problem from the point of view of the producer. To gain insight into the problem of welfare, the flexibilities of the prices of consumers' products should be studied. The long-run assumptions of price movement are not applicable to the cycle, and this in turn may affect the long-run elements, inasmuch as it is quite possible that the cycle is not merely a fluctuation around a secular trend. For these reasons statisticians and theorists should unite in studying the cyclical relationships of the above variables.

REFERENCES

Dunlop, John T. (1938), 'The movement of real and money wages', *Economic Journal*, September.

Keynes, J.M. (1936), *The General Theory of Employment, Interest and Money*, Harcourt Brace and Company.

_____ (1939), 'Relative movements of real wages and output', *Economic Journal*, March.

Richardson, J.H. (1939), 'Real wage movements', *Economic Journal*, September.

Tarshis, L. (1939), 'Changes in real and money wages', *Economic Journal*, March.

12. The Nature of Price Flexibility and the Determinants of Relative Price Changes in the Economy

Richard Ruggles
Yale University

Discussions of price flexibility in the literature of economics are not all concerned with the same subject matter. Three quite different topics can be distinguished. The first two deal with the effects of price flexibility or inflexibility on the operation of the system as a whole; the third deals primarily with the nature and causes of price flexibility itself, and only secondarily with its consequences.

The first topic considers the effect of price flexibility or rigidity on the level of economic activity. Discussions in this area have frequently been concerned either with the analysis of the Keynesian and classical models (see, for example, Bissell, 1940; Lange, 1944; Patinkin, 1948) or with the development of certain other specific aggregative models. On the more empirical side, a great deal has been written about the effects which might have been expected to flow from greater price flexibility or greater price rigidity in specific historical instances. Much of both the theoretical and empirical work has been predominantly concerned with the flexibility of the wage rate and its repercussions on prices, output and employment.

The second topic contemplates price flexibility from a long-run point of view. Interest in this area has been focused primarily on the efficiency of the economic system in allocating its resources — i.e., whether in the long run prices do tend to be determined by competitive forces. The literature in this area is not so extensive as that in the preceding area, perhaps because economists have, in recent years, been preoccupied more with problems of income and employment than with those of resource allocation.

This chapter first appeared in *Business Concentration and Price Policy*, National Bureau of Economic Research, 1955.

The third category of price-flexibility literature is considerably less homogeneous with respect to final objectives than either of the two preceding groups. It is rather the common starting point which suggests the treatment of this segment as a unified body of literature. Writers in this area usually start from a consideration of the empirical fact that during economic fluctuations there is substantial variance in the relative price changes of different products and factors of production, and they propose to investigate the causes of this variance. Branching out from this starting point are a number of different definitions of price flexibility and a number of different analyses of causal factors.

It is this third topic with which this paper will be concerned. To the extent that this literature also attempts to evaluate the significance of existing price flexibility or inflexibility, it does have some relation to the first two topics, but the following discussion will not be primarily concerned with the effects of price flexibility on either the level of activity of the economic system or the efficiency of resource allocation. Attention will be focused on an examination of definitions and measures of price flexibility in the literature, a restatement of the problem of price flexibility in terms of traditional value theory and a discussion of the determinants of relative price changes, an empirical investigation of relative price changes and price–cost interrelationships in various sectors of the economy and the application of the foregoing analysis to certain specific problems. This chapter is divided into four sections corresponding to this general outline.

Section 1 will examine the various definitions and measurements of price flexibility which appear in the literature. These concepts differ considerably, and no attempt will be made in this section to present a comprehensive picture of the entire literature; the focal point of the discussion will be the differences among the concepts, so that where one concept has been discussed by a number of writers only one or two of such writers will be mentioned.

Section 2 will attempt to evaluate the various definitions of price flexibility discussed in Section 1 in the light of a restatement of the problem in terms of the traditional theory of the firm. This discussion will be especially concerned with developing an analysis which will be applicable to existing empirical material. The section will have two parts: it will explore the nature of price flexibility itself, and pursuing the question somewhat further, it will consider the determinants of relative price changes in the economy.

Section 3 will apply the analysis developed in Section 2 to the observed price behavior of various sectors of the economy in an effort to explain why the relative price changes in the various sectors differ. Since output prices for earlier stages of production become costs for later stages of production, the sectors will be classified as far as possible according to the flow of goods through the channels of production; the price–cost interrelationships in agriculture, agricultural processing industries, mining, mineral processing industries and the distributive trades will be considered in turn. The analysis will not be primarily statistical, although use will be made of readily available empirical material.

Section 4 will test the theory of price behavior presented in Section 3 in yet another way. The behavior of various aggregative price indexes will be examined to see whether their general movement and relative differences can be explained readily in terms of the theory. First, the actual behavior of the components of the cost-of-living index will be examined to see whether their relative differences conform to what would be expected in terms of the theory of the determinants of price behavior. Second, the Wholesale Price Index will be similarly examined, and its general movements will be contrasted with those of the cost-of-living index. The process of analyzing these two price indexes necessarily raises the question of the meaningfulness of an aggregate index, given the systematic changes in the components which will occur if the postulated theory is found to be tenable. Finally, the index of real wages will be examined in the light of this theory of price behavior. Although it will not of course be possible in this brief analysis to offer a complete statistical test of the theory, it will be studied in relation to past statistical literature.

1. DEFINITIONS AND MEASUREMENTS OF PRICE FLEXIBILITY IN THE LITERATURE

In the mid-1930s, Gardiner C. Means (1935a,b, 1936) published a statistical study of price inflexibility in the American economy which stirred up considerable interest. A number of writers (Nelson and Keim, 1940) were concerned with various aspects of this subject before that time, but none of the publications had the explosive effects of Means's study. Means's (1935a, p. 1) chief interest was in pointing out the presence in the economy of inflexible administered prices, which, he claimed, had highly disruptive effects on the functioning of the economy and were largely responsible for the failure of *laissez-faire*. As proof of the existence of inflexible administered prices, Means presented a chart showing the results of a tabulation of the frequency of price change for 747 of the items included in the Bureau of Labor Statistics monthly Wholesale Price Index over a 95-month period from 1926 to 1933. The frequency distribution of the numbers of price changes for individual items was found to be U-shaped. To Means, this U-shaped distribution indicated that prices could be divided into two quite different types. The highly flexible prices grouped at one end of the distribution (i.e., prices which changed frequently) he interpreted as those which, for the most part, were market determined and around which traditional economic analysis was built. The inflexible prices at the other end of the distribution (i.e., prices which changed infrequently) he interpreted as those which were administratively established and held for appreciable periods of time. Considering the frequency of price change as a measure of price flexibility thus enabled Means to satisfy himself that two quite different pricing systems existed: flexible prices, resulting from many forces continually interacting in that part of the economy in which markets existed; and inflexible prices, set by administrative action and held constant.

One of the first comments on Means's analysis of price inflexibility was that it did not and could not show whether the economy as a whole had been shifting from market to administered prices. It was suggested that the differences in the frequency of price change found by Means might be a normal phenomenon, and that the period examined was no different in this respect from previous periods. A number of writers (Humphrey, 1937; Tucker, 1938; Mason, 1938; Backman, 1948) undertook to discover whether any evidence could be found that, in recent periods, an increasing proportion of prices had fallen into Means's 'infrequent change classification. For this purpose, distributions of the frequency of price changes were made for periods as far back as 1837 (Tucker, 1938, p. 43). The proportion of items falling into the rigid category in different periods was not found to differ greatly and did not reveal a trend toward rigidity in the more recent periods. Furthermore, over the period 1890–1936, there was no trend in the actual changes observed in the component series for each year expressed as a percentage of the total changes which would have taken place if each series had changed each month during the year (Mason, 1938, p. 59). These negative results seemed to indicate that there was no adequate statistical basis for believing that the price system was becoming any more rigid than it had been in any previous period for which data were available.

The frequency of price change as a measure of relative price flexibility or inflexibility was quickly supplemented by the amplitude of price change. In his original presentation, Means had shown that the frequency of price change was highly correlated with its amplitude. However, he did not use amplitude as a measure of flexibility, but rather considered it an accompanying characteristic with further economic implications. Means demonstrated the relationship between the frequency and the amplitude of price change in two ways. First, he presented a conventional scatter diagram of the two variables, which showed the existence of a correlation. Then he separated the items in the BLS index into ten groups on the basis of their frequency of price change, and for each of these groups he drew up charts showing the distribution of amplitude of change. For those groups with relatively infrequent price changes, he found that the amplitude of change was relatively small.

This discussion of the relation of frequency of price change to amplitude of price change was continued by a number of other writers (Mason, 1938;

Nelson and Keim, 1940), and the focus of interest quickly shifted to the amplitude of price change alone, on the ground that this element was theoretically more significant for the incidence of price distortion in the economy. But a simple distribution of the relative amplitude changes of the various items in the Bureau of Labor Statistics Wholesale Price Index similar to that which Means had made for frequency of price change proved to be unhelpful, since the distribution usually came out unimodal (Mason, 1938, p. 61) and so did not provide any convenient means of distinguishing between flexible and inflexible prices. With a unimodal distribution it was of course impossible to say what amplitude of price change represented true price flexibility. Therefore, although a great deal was written about price flexibility in terms of the amplitude of price change and its effect in distorting the price structure, it was not very successfully developed into a tool of analysis. In practice, the amplitude of price change was primarily used for the comparison of the relative flexibility of specific groups of commodities — that is, the flexibility of chemicals and drugs as a group compared with that of farm products as a group (Mason, 1938, p. 62; Nelson and Keim, 1940, p. 30; Backman, 1948, p. 432). In this sense it was possible to speak of one group as more or less flexible than another, but Means's original concept, that of a 'market' sector of the economy operating with perfectly flexible market prices, could not be explored by this method.

A third concept of price flexibility concerns the change in price per unit of a commodity relative to its change in quantity. A wealth of statistical material on the price–quantity behavior of various commodities and products has been provided by F.C. Mills (1927, 1934, 1936, 1946a,b) in his various studies of price behavior, but these actual statistical measures did not become a subject of discussion in the general price-flexibility literature. Instead, writers on this subject usually confined themselves to setting out lists of commodities or making scatter diagrams wherein the amplitude of price change and the amplitude of quantity change were shown explicitly. Means (1935a, p. 8), for example, in his original study listed ten industries, for which he showed both the percentage drop in prices and the percentage drop in production. As was the case in his use of the amplitude of price change, Means did not consider the price– quantity relationship to be a measure of price flexibility; rather he used it as a part of the description of the differences in the attributes of market and administered prices. Similarly, scatter diagrams of price–quantity relationships have been widely used in the literature to show similarities or differences in the reaction of prices of products having different attributes, for example, the pattern of price–quantity reactions of concentrated versus nonconcentrated industries and of durable versus nondurable goods (Thorp and Crowder, 1941; Backman, 1939; Nelson and Keim, 1940). Like the study of the amplitude of price change, the study of price–quantity reactions did not yield a meaningful definition of absolute price flexibility, but rather was used to establish differences in relative price flexibility.

A quite different measure of price flexibility was introduced into the discussion by J.T. Dunlop (1939). Employing Lerner's (1933) measure of the degree of monopoly, that is, the ratio of the gap between marginal cost and price to price (price minus marginal cost divided by price), Dunlop proposed the change in the degree of monopoly as a measure of price flexibility. (In order that the gap between marginal cost and price divided by price shall be equivalent to the inverse of the elasticity of demand and thus measure the degree of monopoly in Lerner's sense it is, of course, necessary for the firm to be at the point of maximum profits so that marginal cost will equal marginal revenue.) He argued that the degree of monopoly (thus measured) was more significant analytically than other existing measures of flexibility because of its relation to the determinants of output and employment. An increase in Lerner's degree of monopoly for a given commodity during a period of falling prices would mean that the marginal cost of the producer of the commodity fell faster than the price of the final output. A decrease in Lerner's degree of monopoly in such a situation would mean that marginal cost did not fall as fast as the price of the final output. Dunlop's measure thus attempts to relate the amplitude of the change in marginal cost to the amplitude of the change in price of the final output. His analysis of price flexibility thus differed from the preceding analyses in that it attempted to take into account the price–cost relationship within an industry. Where input prices and output prices move together, the price of the final good is said to be as flexible as costs. For the industries which he studied, Dunlop concluded that the degree of monopoly increased in the depression of the thirties, i.e., that the cost elements fell faster than the prices of the finished goods.

Another analysis of price flexibility in terms of price–cost relationships was made by A.C. Neal (1942) in an effort to discover the importance of industrial concentration to price flexibility. On the basis of changes in costs, Neal calculated, for a number of industries from 1929 to 1933, what the price would have been if the overhead margin had been kept a constant absolute amount per unit of output. He called this calculated price the expected price. Actual prices that matched this expected price, he reasoned, could be considered flexible. It should be noted that there is a conceptual difference between Dunlop's and Neal's measures. Dunlop's measure of flexibility depended on the equality of *percentage* changes in costs and prices, whereas Neal's measure required that *absolute* changes in costs be exactly reflected in price, so that the dollar amount of the producer's overhead margin per unit of output would remain unchanged. Neal's study covered a much larger number of industries than had Dunlop's and the close relationship which he found between his expected prices and the actual prices led him to believe that the differential price behavior among industries could be explained for the most part by differential direct cost behavior, rather than by concentration of industry.

More recently, Sho-Chieh Tsiang (1947) has made yet another analysis of price flexibility that relies on price–cost relationships. Starting from Lerner's measure of the degree of monopoly, Tsiang further develops the idea that the percentage gross profit margin (total value of product minus prime costs expressed as a percentage of the total value of product) is an expression of the inverse of the elasticity of demand. In this respect, his approach is in fact a combination of those used by Dunlop and Neal. He follows Dunlop in that he singles out Lerner's degree of monopoly as a starting point, and as a result considers the percentage margin between price and marginal cost rather than the absolute margin used by Neal. On the other hand, Tsiang follows Neal in conceiving of the problem in terms of a margin concept, which Dunlop did not do. Tsiang is concerned with the computation of the gross profit margin for the aggregate of all United States manufacturing for the period 1919–37. This aggregative analysis is in marked contrast with the interproduct and inter-industry studies of price flexibility discussed above. With the term 'price flexibility' thus interpreted, Tsiang (1947, p. 85) found that there was some evidence for the widely held view that the price system in United States manufacturing industries was becoming less flexible. On the basis of his data, he felt that there had been a persistent tendency since 1923 for the average gross profit margin in manufacturing industries as a whole to be negatively associated with the average unit prime cost, i.e., that there had been a persistent tendency for the average value per unit of output to change less than proportionally to the changes in average prime cost.

A number of other definitions of price flexibility have appeared in the general literature, but most of them have been incapable of application as tools of empirical analysis. Mason (1938), in his survey of price flexibility, has given an excellent summary of these concepts. He points out that price flexibility is often used in a normative sense, flexible prices being said to exist where actual price behavior coincides with desirable price behavior, on some definition of desirable. In this context, prices would be considered rigid not because they change infrequently or fail to respond to changes in certain economic forces, but rather because they do not behave as they should behave if economic stability or some other desirable economic objective is to be achieved. Mason (1938, p. 56) also considers price flexibility in terms of the rate or degree of movement of a price in response to the changes in price-determining variables. At this point Mason takes up Gunnar Myrdal's notion of price flexibility which would 'group all prices statistically according to the speed with which they change under the influence of a changing impulse'. As he indicates, however, if all the factors which influence prices were included in the list of price-determining variables, actual price movements would by definition be completely explained and there would be no such thing as either flexibility or inflexibility. For a concept of price flexibility to have any meaning, therefore, the analysis can include only some of the price-determining variables. To the extent that any of these definitions depend on either perfect knowledge of all price-making factors or on elaborate normative judgments, they are of course not relevant to empirical analysis.

2. CONCEPT OF PRICE FLEXIBILITY AND DETERMINANT OF RELATIVE PRICE CHANGE

Despite the large volume of literature on the subject of price flexibility, there has been no very significant cumulative development, and the majority of readers may well agree with R.S. Tucker (1938, p. 54) that the discovery of differences in price flexibility in the system is 'no more important and no less ridiculous than the discovery by Molière's bourgeois gentilhomme that he had been speaking prose all of his life'. If one were to take into account all of Jules Backman's (1940) factors and conditions which may affect price flexibility, the subject might be found to be of such a complex institutional nature that it would defy any simple theoretical model. There are, furthermore, many quite serious criticisms, both theoretical and empirical, which can be made of much of the discussion in the literature. Before proceeding further, it will be useful to consider some of the criticisms.

One of the most serious questions regarding Means's U-shaped distribution of the frequency of price changes in the components of the BLS Wholesale Price Index was raised by Tibor Scitovsky (1941, p. 681). He pointed out that the U-shaped distribution may be due only to the particular form in which the data happen to be available, and that the distribution of the number of *actual* price changes need not be U-shaped at all. His argument runs as follows.

Means's frequency distribution is based upon the changes which occur in the BLS monthly series. If the price of a commodity changes many times during a month, the BLS figure, which represents one monthly observation, obviously would not show it. Therefore, although there is no limit to the *actual* number of times that a price could have changed during the 95-month period studied by Means, the largest number of changes that can appear in the data is 94. In other words, the 94-change class interval would include all commodities from those which actually did change just once a month up to all those which changed daily (i.e., roughly 2,900 changes in the 95 months) or more often. The lower frequencies of price change would be affected only slightly by shifting from a monthly to, say, a daily reporting of prices; a price with zero change throughout the period would have zero change regardless of the time interval between observations, and prices which changed only a few times in the 95 months would have months of zero change in which the daily changes would also be zero. As the frequency of change increases, however, Means's monthly observations would correspond less and less to actual price changes, and at high frequencies it is quite apparent that price changes would be greatly understated. On a daily observation basis, the high-frequency end of the distribution would be extended. The cases which now occur in the high-frequency area, say from 80–94 monthly changes (181 cases), would be distributed over all the frequencies from 80 to 2,850. There seems to be no adequate reason to believe that the distribution would remain U-shaped, although again a slight cluster might occur at the high frequencies for the same reason — prices which changed more than once daily would be lumped with those which changed only once daily. If, instead of daily changes, all actual price changes were recorded for each commodity, it seems reasonable that there would be a continuously decreasing number of cases, even at the very highest frequencies of change.

By raising doubts about the validity of Means's U-shaped distribution, Scitovsky in effect destroyed much of the meaningfulness of the dichotomy between rigid and flexible prices. Without a significant cluster at the high end of the distribution, there is no adequate criterion of perfect price flexibility, so that Means would be forced back into the same position as the writers who discussed amplitude of change: frequency of change can serve only as a relative measure, and no judgment can be made on whether a price is or is not flexible.

There have been other criticisms of Means's basic data. A number of them attack the assumptions in the use of the BLS Wholesale Price Index. One such criticism points to the prevalence of quality changes, with nominal price kept the same. For example, according to the National Resources Committee (1939, p. 182), during the Depression a shirt of quality and workmanship that originally sold for $1.95 could be purchased by the consumer for $1.69 or less. Yet the quoted prices of shirts apparently remained rigid. Changes in price took the form of changes in workmanship and style, rather than in the traditionally established wholesale price. Furthermore, Neal (1942, pp. 40–42) has pointed out that the BLS price quotations do not always include all the discounts which sellers give their customers, so that the quoted price may not be representative of the actual price. Thus, in the BLS quotations, salt and fertilizer prices remained stable at a time when in point of fact vigorous price competition existed in the form of exceptional discounts. In considering the validity of the BLS price data, the National Resources Committee (1939, p. 185) concluded that it was imperative to use caution whenever individual price series were involved. In analyses of price rigidity, they felt, it was essential that emphasis be placed upon broad and consistent relationships and that reliance upon small differences in absolute figures be avoided.

A theoretical criticism of Means's use of frequency of change as a measure of price rigidity and price flexibility was raised by D.H. Wallace (1936, p.

347). He pointed out that in cases where no price-determining factor had changed, the price, by definition, should not change either, yet by Means's definition such a price would be considered rigid. Furthermore, by his definition, a price might well be flexible even though it moved in the direction opposite from that which would have been indicated by normal price-determining forces. Means's measure is therefore not really relevant to an analysis of the economic forces in the system.

The use of amplitude as a measure of price flexibility is open to many of these same criticisms. It has already been pointed out that the amplitude of change of a price series gives no clue to the absolute flexibility or rigidity of the series; price flexibility in this sense is purely relative. Most of the studies of the amplitude of price fluctuation, furthermore, used the same BLS data which were used in the studies of frequency of change, and there is reason to believe that the difference between actual prices and prices quoted in the BLS index introduces a more serious distortion in amplitude than in frequency. In a period of depression, the divergence between actual and quoted price may increase cumulatively. Lloyd Reynolds (1939, p. 33) has shown that in a few cases there are major divergences. The drop in the price of aluminum from 1929 to 1933, for example, was reported as 5 percent by the BLS, but according to census information it amounted in fact to 35 percent. In the price of sulfuric acid, a zero drop reported by the BLS was a 12 percent drop according to the Bureau of the Census. Further examples of disparities were cited by the National Resources Committee study (1939, p. 183). Although these disparities are probably the exceptions rather than the general rule, they are nevertheless serious enough to raise questions about the suitability of the BLS data for any refined analysis. Finally, with amplitude as with frequency, it does not seem valid to consider a price inflexible just because it does not change, if there has been no change in price-determining factors. The fact that prices have different actual amplitudes of change does not mean that they are differentially sensitive to specific price-determining forces, yet this is how the findings on amplitude have often been interpreted.

Mills's price–quantity ratio has never seriously been proposed as a measure of price flexibility, in the sense that this term is understood in the literature; Mills himself considered it to be a description of the general patterns of price–quantity movements. Given the demand curve, Mills's ratio is the reciprocal of the Marshallian elasticity of demand, but when both demand and supply schedules shift, the resulting coefficient is somewhat ambiguous. The more usual use of price–quantity relationships as a measure of price flexibility, as was indicated in Section 1, has been in terms of scatter diagrams for different categories of goods, and to this use many of the objections raised with respect to amplitude and frequency also apply. When the BLS wholesale price data are used, some of the price–quantity relationships which appear will be spurious.

Furthermore, the price–quantity relationships again provide only relative and not absolute measures of price flexibility, and the measure obtained is not directly relevant to the question of the correspondence of price to price-making forces.

Dunlop's measure of price flexibility, as was noted above, represents a considerable departure from the measures which had been used in other empirical studies. Unlike them, Dunlop's measure does set up an absolute criterion for a flexible price. By this criterion, prices are flexible when they move with costs. If price does not change when marginal cost is rigid, the price is stable but not necessarily inflexible. The fuller implications of this concept will be taken up later in this paper, but it will be useful at this juncture to consider some possible criticisms of the empirical side of Dunlop's work. To obtain marginal cost for an industry, Dunlop took the National Industrial Conference Board index of average hourly earnings for the industry and the Bls Wholesale Price Index for one representative raw material for the industry, and weighted these according to the respective importance of wages and materials in value of product in 1933, as given in the *Biennial Census of Manufactures*. The ratio of the change in marginal cost computed in this manner to the change in the BLS wholesale price he considered to be an approximation to Lerner's degree of monopoly, and thus, a measure of the flexibility of prices. If the ratio was greater than 1 (i.e., if the change in computed marginal cost exceeded the change in the BLS price), the degree of monopoly would have increased, and prices would be inflexible. If the ratio was less than 1, the opposite would obtain. Dunlop made yearly comparisons for six industries for the period 1929–35; and for eight industries (four of which were included in the first six) changes in the gap between marginal cost and price were shown through the phases of the cycle (1929–33 and 1933–36) rather than from year to year. Dunlop's statistical methods are thus certainly open to criticism. He used data from a variety of sources which employ different industrial classifications and have special unmatched definitions. Changes in average hourly earnings, furthermore, have been shown to be a rather poor indicator of changes in unit wage costs (Committee on Price Determination, 1943, pp. 131–43). The use of one representative raw material for each industry (for example, the fall in the price of pig iron as an indicator of the decline in all raw material costs in the steel industry) requires heroic assumptions. Reliance on the BLS wholesale price data for both raw material and finished goods prices requires just that sort of dependence on the accuracy of individual series which the National Resources Committee advised against. And finally, in spite of Dunlop's conclusion that the gap between price and marginal cost widens in a depression, by his own analysis this was true in only four of the eight cases examined. However, Dunlop did recognize the limitations of his data, and he intended the article as a first approximation rather than a detailed statistical analysis of the problem. It is certainly true that he brought to the subject a completely new orientation, one which promised to be much more useful than previous approaches.

Neal's work bears a marked resemblance to Dunlop's. However, although Neal wrote some three years after Dunlop, there does not seem to be much evidence that he was in fact developing Dunlop's original ideas. Both Neal and Dunlop attempted to study the relationship between marginal cost and price, but Dunlop was interested in the percentage difference between marginal cost and price, while Neal was interested in the absolute difference. Statistically, Neal's study was very much the more comprehensive of the two. Neal analyzed a group of 106 industries from the Census of Manufactures data. Since he used matched data from one major source, his results probably have greater statistical significance than Dunlop's, and the census data are probably also more pertinent to the study of the effects of actual prices on producers' net receipts than are the BLS wholesale price statistics. Neal derived an expected price for each industry by computing the price changes implicit in the direct costs of the industry and assuming a constant absolute margin over these direct costs. He then took the position that the extent to which his computed 'expected' price was *correlated* with the actual price was a measure of the degree to which changes in direct cost could be used to explain changes in price. There is, however, one major objection to this procedure. Although the correlation between his expected price and the actual price was high, there was a systematic difference between the two: for the period 1929–31, in 82 out of the 106 industries, Neal's expected price was higher than the actual price, and for the period 1929–33 the same was true for 72 out of 84 industries. When the expected price exceeds the actual price, of course, the assumption of constant absolute margins is not in fact borne out by the data; in absolute terms margins for the majority of industries declined. But Neal was interested primarily in the subject of industrial concentration and its relation to price flexibility, so that when he had proved to his own satisfaction that the degree of industrial concentration was only a minor factor in price inflexibility, he went no further. He considered only manufacturing in his study, and made no effort to see how the other parts of the economy — such as agriculture, mining and the distributive trades — fitted into the analysis. He was thus not concerned with the question of why prices and costs actually did move differently from one another, but only with establishing that the reason was not related to concentration.

Tsiang used the same source as Neal for his statistical data: he analyzed the data on direct costs and value of product given in the Census of Manufactures. There were two major differences in his approach, however. First, Tsiang considered only four sets of data: the aggregated data for all United States manufacturing, and summary data for each of three broad industry groups — cotton textiles, paper and pulp and iron and steel. This is in marked contrast to the 106 industries studied by Neal. Secondly, instead of deriving estimates of expected value per unit on the basis of constant absolute margins and correlating the expected values with actual value per unit as Neal did, Tsiang derived percentage margins and analyzed their changes from period to period in relation to changes in direct costs. In other words, Tsiang was interested in the behavior of percentage margins as direct costs rise and fall.

The chief weakness of Tsiang's analysis lies in its aggregative nature; this becomes especially important when it is recalled that the differences in price and cost changes among the various industries are very great indeed. Tsiang did try one test of aggregation; he examined the gross profit margins of four different groups of industries: capital goods, consumer goods, construction materials and producers' supplies. Because the average gross profit margins of these industries were all about the same in 1929, Tsiang concluded that the aggregate gross profit margin for all United States industry would not be changed by a shift in the composition of industry due to differential rates of expansion and contraction over the cycle. However, many other types of aggregation difficulties might be encountered. Within an industry, for instance, it is quite possible that producers with large margins would have a different rate of expansion or contraction than producers with small margins. Rather than attempting to prove that the process of aggregation is legitimate by making various partial tests, it would be simpler to use somewhat less aggregated data and study the behavior of gross profit margins at more homogeneous levels. In attacking the problem on such an aggregative level, furthermore, Tsiang also neglected any explicit discussion of the differential behavior of prices and costs in different industries.

Despite these criticisms, and despite the diversity of the approaches of the various writers discussed above, certain common elements do emerge. The major concern of all these economists is with the differences in the relative amplitude of price change in the economy during periods of economic fluctuation. Price flexibility as Means conceived it became a subject of study because it was obvious from even a casual examination that during periods of economic fluctuation the price behavior of some sectors of the economy was quite different from that of other sectors. Means would not have considered differences in the frequency of change significant if in terms of amplitude all prices had moved approximately together during the period 1926–33.

The importance of economic fluctuations as a frame of reference for this consideration of price flexibility cannot be overemphasized. The writers in this group gave very little attention to the long-run type of flexibility mentioned at the beginning of this paper, nor did they concern themselves with the question of how changes in productivity are transmitted through the system in the form of higher wage rates for labor, increased profits for the producer, or lower prices for the consumer, or with the manner in which the secular growth or decline of an industry affects factor returns and prices in that industry. Instead, they were interested in trying to see to what extent differences in the short-run cyclical price behavior of the different sectors of the economy could be explained by the method of price fixing (market or administered), the degree of fabrication of the good (raw material or finished goods), the durability of the good and other attributes which appeared to be related to differential price behavior. Dunlop, Neal and Tsiang, for example, were interested in the extent to which the price changes of various industries in the manufacturing sector of the economy could be explained by changes in direct cost as the single determinant. Backman, on the other hand, listed a great many possible determinants of price and implied that he felt most price changes could be explained only in terms of a variety of determinants. Thus, in the context of the literature the study of price flexibility has been the study of the short-run determinants of price behavior in different sectors of the economy during periods of economic fluctuation.

A mere review of this literature, however, still leaves much to be desired. It is clear that the next step should be some consideration of the type of price behavior that might be expected under various assumptions, and an investigation of the extent to which this expected behavior corresponded to what actually took place. The remaining portion of Section 2 will, therefore, be devoted to the consideration of the major determinants of price. Sections 3 and 4 will then examine price data for the various sectors of the economy to see whether or not the differences in relative price change which are in fact found can be adequately explained in terms of these major determinants of price.

It has already been pointed out in the review of Mason's discussion of the various measures of price flexibility that a definition of price flexibility that took into account *all* the determinants of price would be meaningless. Divergence between actual and expected price in such a circumstance would not be an indication of price inflexibility; rather it would simply indicate that some of the price-determining factors had inadvertently been left out of the analysis in the computation of the expected price. In other words, any concept of price flexibility, except a purely normative one, must be defined in a partial sense. A price can be called inflexible only if it does not change when an expected price computed on the basis of certain specified partial determinants changes. Before any analysis can be made, therefore, the specific determinants which are to be taken into account must be decided upon.

In traditional value theory, the major specific determinants of price are generally considered to be cost and demand. Economists have long recognized that cost and demand are not the only elements in price determination; such factors as expectations, the temperament of the producer, and even public opinion may have an effect on price, and in some instances inertia due to the difficulty of changing prices once they are set may be important. If we exclude all such factors in considering the determinants of individual prices, however, the term 'price flexibility' can be given analytic meaning. To the extent that these excluded factors are in fact operative and seriously influence the actual price changes, prices can be considered inflexible or perverse. As a first approximation, therefore, prices will be considered flexible if they react as would be expected in response to changes in cost and demand conditions, inflexible if they do not change as much as would be expected, and perverse if they move in the direction opposite to that expected. As the analysis develops, certain modifications will be made in this definition.

The framework of traditional value theory can be used in developing the expected reaction of price to various types of change in cost and demand. The analysis will start by reviewing the price behavior of an individual firm or industry that is supposed to follow various types of change in cost and demand under the usual assumption of profit maximization in perfect competition and monopolistic competition; the problem of oligopoly will be considered briefly at the close of the discussion. For simplicity in studying price behavior under perfect and monopolistic competition, cost and demand changes will be considered separately. Two questions will therefore be distinguished: how changes in demand would affect price in a situation in which cost conditions do not change and how changes in cost would affect price in a situation in which demand conditions do not change.

Under the principle of profit maximization, equilibrium price and output will occur where marginal cost equals marginal revenue, and the relation between marginal cost (which equals marginal revenue) and price (which equals average revenue) will be determined by the elasticity of demand. (This is the basis of Dunlop's use of Lerner's degree of monopoly as a measure of price flexibility.)

From this general observation, it follows that if demand shifts but the *elasticity* of demand remains the same, the firm should, in order to maximize its profits, keep the same percentage mark-up over marginal cost and sell whatever it can at that price. With a horizontal marginal-cost curve, for example, even though demand falls drastically it would be in the interest of the firm to keep its price unchanged as long as costs do not change and the elasticity of demand remains the same. With a rising marginal cost curve, a fall in demand without a change in elasticity would require a price drop proportional to the drop in marginal costs which would accompany the reduced level of output. Thus, if the elasticity of demand does not change, a shifting level of demand would trace out a pattern of equilibrium prices above the marginal cost curve and in fixed ratio to marginal cost at every point; any change in marginal cost resulting from operation at a different level of output would be directly reflected in an equivalent percentage change in price. If the marginal revenue curve for the firm intersects the marginal cost curve at a point where marginal cost is vertical (i.e., discontinuous), a fall in marginal revenue within this range with no change in the elasticity of demand would result in a fall in price and maintained output in the firm. If the elasticity of demand changes, the relation between price and marginal cost must also change. An increase in elasticity would narrow the range between price and marginal cost, and a decrease in elasticity would widen the range.

In a competitive industry, price is determined by the intersection of the industry demand curve and the industry marginal supply price. With a constant marginal supply price, any shift in demand would leave price unchanged. With a rising marginal supply price, a falling demand would trace out a falling pattern of equilibrium prices along the supply curve. With a falling supply curve that was compatible with competition (e.g., economies of scale external to this industry), a fall in demand would actually raise price.

In summary, then, for the individual firm faced with a sloped demand curve, a shift in demand which left elasticity unchanged would require a price change directly proportional to any change in marginal cost resulting from movement along the marginal cost curve. For a competitive industry, a shift in demand would move price along the marginal supply price curve. In either case, the ratio of price to marginal cost would change following a shift in demand only if the elasticity of demand also changed.

If demand is kept constant and cost is permitted to change, consideration of the elasticity of demand is again necessary. In the case of the individual firm faced with a sloped demand curve, a change in cost would be directly reflected in a proportional change in price if the elasticity of demand at the new point of equilibrium is the same as at the old. If, with a movement along the demand curve, demand becomes less elastic and the marginal cost curve is horizontal, an upward shift of the marginal cost curve would result in a more than proportional price rise, and a downward shift would result in a less than proportional price fall. Any movement along the demand curve which increases elasticity would, of course, operate in the opposite direction.

Under competitive conditions, shifts in the marginal supply price schedule would lead to equilibrium prices which lie on the demand curve, and the equilibrium price would equal marginal supply price at every point. Thus, when the elasticity of demand for the individual firm remains constant, and in all cases of pure competition, the equilibrium price will move directly proportionally with marginal cost. Price and marginal cost will diverge only when the elasticity of demand for the individual firm at the new point of equilibrium is different from that at the old. When demand becomes less elastic, a fall in marginal cost will not be matched by a proportional fall in price, and a rise in marginal cost will lead to a price rise which is more than proportional. The obverse would hold when demand becomes more elastic.

This analysis throws some light on the question of the relative price behavior of firms in monopoly and competition during economic fluctuations. As Scitovsky (1941, p. 663) has pointed out, the belief that prices are more variable under competition than under monopoly probably sprang from the fact that competitive producers tend to undercut one another's price in response to flagging demand and falling costs, while the monopolist in a similar situation can keep up his price. But, as Scitovsky says, the heart of the question is not whether the monopolist can maintain prices which are less variable than those which would obtain under competitive conditions, but whether it is really in his interest to do so.

Tsiang (1947, pp. 23–4), for example, observes that under imperfect competition the prices of individual products are more or less under the control of the individual producers. From this he suggests that a rise in demand need not imply a rise in market price, as is necessarily the case under perfect competition where the demand confronting each producer is horizontal. In this connection it should be noted, however, that if the elasticity of demand for the product did not change and if marginal costs were constant over the relevant range of output for the producer in imperfect competition, no change in price could be expected to occur with a rise in demand, that is, the reaction in imperfect competition would differ from the reaction in perfect competition only because of the assumed difference in cost structure.

To the extent that producers do not maximize profits in the short run, prices may move differently (more or less) from what would be expected on the basis of changes in costs and demand. In perfect competition producers may refrain from placing goods on the market or conversely may dump their stocks, thus producing prices different from what would be expected on the basis of change in current costs and demand. If producers in perfect competition feel that a drop in demand is temporary, goods may be held off the market, and prices will not drop as much as would have been expected in terms of the fall in demand and marginal costs in the individual plants.

It has already been noted that under pure competition if the marginal supply price schedule is horizontal, any change in factor costs would be directly reflected in price. For the individual firm faced with a sloped demand curve and a horizontal marginal cost curve, price would not equal marginal cost but would move exactly with it, if the elasticity of demand did not change. The relevant question, therefore, is whether in economic fluctuations a fall in demand would be associated with an increase or a decrease in the elasticity of demand.

According to Harrod (1936, pp. 84–8), a fall in demand will make people more sensitive to price differences. In his view the imperfection of competition is due to habit, inertia and lack of knowledge. The pressure of poverty is necessary to drive people to the trouble of avoiding waste; why, he asks, should a man in more comfortable circumstances make as much effort to find the cheapest market? 'With an expanding income a man may slip by imperceptible stages into careless habits. A contraction recalls him to his senses. He is loath to relinquish enjoyments to which he has been accustomed and immediately begins to cast about for means of meeting adversity with the least inconvenience to himself. . . . He seeks to economize with the smallest possible loss in substantive utility' (p. 87). Thus Harrod argues that demand will become more elastic in times of depression and less elastic as prosperity returns.

The validity of Harrod's argument has been questioned a number of times and Galbraith (1936) has gone so far as to state the opposite. He says (p. 463): 'Where the decrease in demand is the result of depression an increase in elasticity may be considered improbable. People with decreased money incomes and increased concern for their economic security are less rather than more responsive to lower prices. Producers and consumers alike tend to postpone purchases of durable equipment.'

Of the two arguments, Harrod's seems the more persuasive. Galbraith has not given any reason why people who have increased concern for their economic security feel that they can afford to neglect price considerations. The fact that producers and consumers tend to postpone their purchases of durables has more to do with the level of demand than with its elasticity.

Whether or not Harrod is correct as a general rule, however, it is obvious that for different goods the elasticity of demand will be affected differently by economic fluctuations. A situation which increases people's price sensitivity between bread and potatoes may make the demand curve for train rides from New Haven to New York more inelastic by taking away from it a large portion of the rather elastic demand of those who travel for pleasure and leaving as the major element the rather inelastic demand of those who travel on business. Without much more knowledge of a great many more variables, it does not seem likely that the change in elasticity of demand to be expected in any particular instance can be predicted. It does not follow, therefore, that a monopoly would always have less variable prices during periods of economic fluctuation than would a purely competitive industry. Indeed, to the extent that Harrod's arguments are valid, in order to maximize profits the monopolist should have the more variable prices.

It is apparent from the discussion above that the determination of changes in elasticity for any individual producer might be very difficult (if not impossible). If change in the elasticity of demand is included as one of the factors determining the expected change in price, therefore, it would be impossible to compute the expected price behavior. Furthermore, under certain forms of industrial organization the change in the elasticity of demand is one of the key factors determining the expected reaction of price to a change in cost. In assessing the flexibility of prices associated with various types of industrial organization, it is important not to include in the measure of expected prices elements which are implicitly correlated with a specific form of industrial organization, and the effect of a change in the elasticity of demand is just such an element. Under perfect competition, changes in the elasticity of demand for various products will not affect the expected price; it will remain equal to marginal cost. For the individual firm faced with a sloped demand curve, however, any shift in the elasticity of demand will cause the expected price to rise or fall faster or slower than marginal cost. The inclusion of changes in elasticity as one of the factors determining the expected change in price will, therefore, obscure the influence of industrial organization on price behavior.

For these reasons, the definition of price flexibility given above will be modified so as to relegate changes in the elasticity of demand to the same category as changes in expectations, etc. discussed above. The expected change in price will be determined on the basis of the change in marginal cost only; a change in the elasticity of demand, like a change in expectations, will (if profits are maximized) result in what will be defined as price inflexibility. Perfect price flexibility will then be a situation in which price changes by the same percentage as marginal cost. If price moves less than marginal cost, the price is inflexible; if it moves more than marginal cost, it is excessively flexible; and if it moves in the opposite direction from marginal cost it is inversely flexible. This definition corresponds to that implicit in Lerner's measure of the degree of monopoly, which both Dunlop and Tsiang used. Constancy in the percentage margin between price and marginal cost would indicate that prices and marginal costs moved by the same percentage.

Thus far, the discussion of price behavior has been couched entirely in terms of perfect and monopolistic competition, and the more complex area of oligopoly has not been considered. In an oligopolistic market, it would not necessarily be true that if profits are to be maximized the prices charged for a product will change in response to changes in the elasticity of demand and changes in marginal cost; that kinked demand curves can lead to price inflexibility has often been pointed out. For a discussion of the possible role of the kinked demand curve and other oligopolistic influences, see Stigler (1947, pp. 432–49) and Tsiang (1947, pp. 69–74). However, the determination of the effect of the exact conditions and assumptions under which an oligopolist is operating is not unlike the problem of change in the elasticity of demand in monopolistic competition. In the first place, the actual assumptions made by the different firms in an oligopolistic industry cannot be derived empirically, so that it is virtually impossible to establish any norm for expected price behavior in these instances. Furthermore, the very difference in behavior between firms in oligopoly and firms in perfect competition is an element which it would be interesting to measure. With the definition of price flexibility suggested above, the effects of oligopolistic conditions would tend to appear as price inflexibility, so that the importance of such an industrial organization in this respect could be assessed.

The following section will apply this definition of price flexibility to the various sectors of the economy. The statistics are purely illustrative. No attempt has been made to carry out a comprehensive empirical survey; such a study would absorb considerable resources and would involve extensive detailed analyses. Section 3 will only show what general indications do exist with respect to the empirical facts of price flexibility, and suggest the directions in which further work might proceed.

3. COST, PRICE AND OUTPUT BEHAVIOR OF VARIOUS SECTORS OF THE AMERICAN ECONOMY, 1929–32

The Depression of the 1930s affords an opportunity for studying the reaction of different industrial sectors of the economy to a sharp and deep contraction in the level of income and demand. It is essential to confine this sort of analysis to short periods of time, in order to minimize the influence of such secular factors as technology, institutional change and the growth and decline of industries. For this reason, the empirical analysis in this section will generally be restricted to the period 1929–32. For some sectors (agriculture and distributive trades) data for a few years after 1932 will be presented in order to throw some light on the relation of cycle to trend. For manufacturing, only 1929 and 1931 will be considered, since the basic source of data is the *Biennial Census of Manufactures*.

In the following presentation, the flow of goods will be followed through the different stages of the production process, and in each stage the relationship among the changes in costs, prices and output will be examined. The production of agricultural goods will be considered first, and then that part of manufacturing which is concerned with the processing or fabrication of agricultural materials. A few of the major mineral products will then be examined, and from this the analysis will proceed to the manufacturing industries which utilize mineral products. Finally, finished goods will be followed through the distributive channels to the consumer. The exact form of the discussion will differ among sectors, depending on both the special problems arising in the particular sector and the nature of the available statistical material.

Agriculture: Field Crops

In agriculture, any analysis of output and prices must take into account the special role played by variations in harvests. The effect of overall economic fluctuations is overlaid on a pattern of good and bad harvests, so that an analysis of the effect of a fall in demand on price and output must take account of variations in crop size due solely to weather. No simple correction can be made to eliminate the influence of weather and predict what would have occurred under 'normal' conditions. Even for years which can be considered 'normal', the effect of previous abnormal years will be reflected in the level of stocks, and this in turn will influence prices. Rather than attempt a correction of agricultural price and output data, therefore, an indirect approach will be utilized. From an examination of the nature of cost conditions for various products, the reactions of farmers to economic fluctuations in terms of altered *inputs* will be predicted. Data on agricultural inputs will then be consulted to see how far the actual statistics agree with what would be expected.

In crop production, farmers generally provide much of the necessary labor themselves and receive as compensation the residual after other costs are paid. Hired labor is relatively unimportant; in 1929 it amounted to only 8.5 percent of the gross cash income from marketings (US Department of Agriculture, 1941, p. 9, 1939, Part II, Sec. 1, p. 5). The farmer attempts to maximize his residual share, so that from the point of view of cost–output determination his own labor return becomes part of overhead, like his other fixed costs and the return on his capital. Marginal costs for the individual producer of agricultural crops involve primarily such things as seed, fertilizer, gasoline, twine, sacks and small amounts of hired labor. Data for the year 1938 (US Department of Agriculture, 1940, p. 568) indicate that for most agricultural crops marginal costs would not be more than 15–20 percent of total costs. Of course, when the farmer reaches capacity in the sense that all the land available to him is in full use, the marginal cost curve will rise sharply, becoming discontinuous at this point. In the production of crops, therefore, the marginal cost curve will be very low at points below full cultivation and will become vertical at the point of full cultivation. The farmer does produce at the point where marginal cost equals price: the vertically rising marginal cost curve at full capacity will cut the horizontal demand curve at that point, so that it pays the farmer to produce as much as he can. With a fall in demand, the demand curve for the individual farmer will move downward, but it will still be horizontal, and unless demand should fall far enough so that price would be below the farmer's minimum marginal cost, it will still be in his interest to maintain capacity production. Even if the prices to the farmer of the elements going into marginal cost should change, the vertical portion of the marginal cost curve will remain the same, so that regardless of changes in cost and demand, the farmer will generally find it to his profit to cultivate his land fully.

Not only will the individual farmer maintain his output but, in the face of a general fall in income and demand, marginal farmers will not leave the industry. Those marginal farmers who would, if demand falls, receive an inadequate residual return for their labor and fixed costs should under normal conditions be attracted away from agriculture by superior opportunities elsewhere. But when there is a general fall in income and demand in the economy, there are no employment opportunities elsewhere, and the farmer finds that he has little or no possibility of getting out of agriculture.

It seems reasonable to expect, therefore, that the number of acres harvested by farmers should not decline in a depression. Statistics on the total number of acres harvested by farmers and the acres of various crops harvested are given in Table 12.1.

Table 12.1 Indexes of Acres Harvested of Various Crops, 1929–39

Year	Total of 46 crops	Corn	Wheat	Hay	Cotton	Oats	Barley	Potatoes
Total acres (thousands)								
1929	356,989	97,805	63,332	55,728	43,232	38,153	13,526	3,019
Indexes (1929 = 100)								
1930	101	104	99	97	98	104	93	103
1931	100	109	91	100	90	105	83	115
1932	102	113	91	100	83	109	97	118
1933	93	108	78	100	68	96	72	113
1934	83	94	69	100	62	77	48	119
1935	94	98	81	100	64	104	91	117
1936	88	95	77	103	69	88	62	101
1937	95	96	102	98	78	93	74	105
1938	96	94	110	102	56	94	78	100
1939	91	91	85	105	55	87	93	100

Source: US Department of Agriculture, *Agricultural Statistics, 1940*, pp. 541–2.

The total quantity of crops harvested did not change appreciably in the sharp decline of income and demand from 1929 to 1932. Governmental restriction of production shows up in the year 1934. The statistics for individual crops show considerable variation, but it would be difficult to tell without further detailed analysis whether the variations are in fact due to changes in income and demand. Some of the changes, such as the decline in cotton, are probably due to secular influences. Insofar as other crops are substituted for cotton, they too will show a secular influence. Furthermore, to the extent that farmers do react to differential price changes due to different weather conditions in various regions, the actual analysis becomes very complex. But it seems clear that the depression directly following 1929 did not cause farmers as a group to contract the total number of acres harvested.

As noted above, differences in the year-to-year yield of the various crops make it almost impossible to analyze the impact of changes in demand on price changes of agricultural goods. Nevertheless, an examination of the price indexes for the crops whose acreage was given in Table 12.1 can illustrate the general magnitude of the impact which the Depression had upon these prices. These price indexes are shown in Table 12.2. It can be seen from this table that a price drop of 60 percent was not unusual — the smallest price drop for any crop was 30 percent, and even this was large compared with the acreage changes shown in Table 12.1.

Table 12.2 Indexes of Season Average Prices Received by Farmers,
*   1929–39 (1929 = 100)*

Year	Corn (1)	Wheat (2)	Hay (3)	Cotton (4)	Oats (5)	Barley (6)	Potatoes (7)
1930	75	65	104	56	77	75	70
1931	40	38	74	34	51	61	35
1932	40	37	55	39	38	41	29
1933	65	72	67	61	80	81	63
1934	102	85	115	74	115	127	34
1935	82	80	64	66	63	70	45
1936	130	99	93	73	107	145	87
1937	65	93	75	50	72	100	40
1938	63	54	59	51	57	68	42
1939	70	65	65	54	71	82	52

Source: Department of Agriculture, *Agricultural Statistics, 1940.*

Agriculture: Livestock Production

Farmers who are primarily engaged in raising livestock may face a cost situation somewhat different from that described for the producers of field crops. To the extent that cattle are grazed on grasslands or the farmer grows his own feed, marginal cost still may be small relative to total value of product until full capacity is reached, becoming discontinuous at that point. However, if the farmer purchases his feed, marginal cost may be high relative to total value of product at all levels of output. The individual producer cannot afford to stay in business if the price of his output falls below his marginal costs, so that it might seem that price could not fall very far without causing a contraction in output. But according to the analysis of field crops presented above, the quantity of feed grown does not contract in depressions. The demand for feed is entirely derived from the demand for livestock, so that the price of feed will fall proportionally to the price of livestock. Any contraction in livestock production would immediately leave surplus feed which would drive the price of feed down until it would all be taken. Thus, taking into account the effects on the price of feed, the volume of livestock production would not be expected to contract in a depression, although, of course, there may be substitution among types of livestock, or perhaps even between some field crops and livestock. Table 12.3 gives the production of various kinds of livestock; from these

Table 12.3 Indexes of Livestock and Dairy Products, 1929–39

Year	Cattle on farms (1)	Slaughtered Cattle (2)	Slaughtered Calves (3)	Slaughtered Hogs (4)	Hogs on farms (5)	Chickens on farms (6)	Eggs (7)	Milk (pounds) (8)
Total number (thousands)								
1929	58,877	12,038	7,406	71,012	59,042	449,006	37,921,000	98,976,000
Indexes (1929 = 100)								
1930	104	100	104	95	94	104	103	101
1931	107	100	108	98	93	100	101	104
1932	112	99	106	101	100	97	96	105
1933	119	108	114	103	103	99	94	106
1934	126	129	135	97	97	97	91	103
1935	116	122	129	65	65	87	88	103
1936	115	134	137	83	83	89	90	104
1937	113	127	136	76	76	94	99	104
1938	112	123	123	83	83	86	98	108
1939	113	120	119	93	93	92	101	110

Source: US Department of Agriculture, *Agricultural Statistics, 1940*, pp. 344, 359, 364, 375, 461, 476, 428.

figures it does not appear that the fluctuations in production in the period 1929–32 were any more significant in magnitude than they were in other parts of the 1929–39 period.

Agriculture, then, because of the nature of its marginal costs, would be expected to maintain its output in the face of a fall in demand, and this expected behavior is in fact borne out by the statistics on crops and livestock. The whole impact of a contraction in demand falls on price; price will decline until the full quantity produced can be absorbed by the economy.

Manufacturing: Agricultural Raw Materials

Manufacturing plants that process agricultural raw materials are, of course, related to agriculture but the nature of the relationship between price and marginal cost is quite different. In order to examine whether the price behavior of agricultural processing plants corresponds to what would be expected on the basis of changes in their marginal costs, it will be necessary to give attention to the nature and shape of their cost functions, the price changes in the elements of cost and the changes in their output prices.

Exact determination of the shape of the marginal cost curve is not feasible for each individual industry. No reliable methods are at present available for measuring the shape of marginal cost curves from empirical data (Staehle, 1942, p. 349). However, another attack on the problem is possible. By making a simple arbitrary assumption about the nature of marginal cost, the process as a whole can be made operational, and any results which are derived can then be reconsidered in terms of possible alternative assumptions about the shape of marginal costs. For the purpose of the preliminary analysis, therefore, it will be assumed that marginal cost was constant over the relevant range of output, and that in the periods studied the technical coefficients of the input factors were also fairly constant. In this connection, user cost of plant and equipment will be neglected, both because it is impossible to measure and because its influence on marginal costs is probably very minor. These assumptions imply that within relevant production ranges each additional unit of output would require a specific fixed amount of labor and materials irrespective of the output level, and the relative changes in the prices of capital, labor and materials would not in the short run cause significant substitutions among the input elements. At the end of the analysis, these assumptions will be reviewed by considering what effect other kinds of assumptions would have on the analysis.

With an assumed constancy of marginal cost and fixed relations among the input factors of labor and materials for incremental changes in output, it is possible to construct a price index of the change in marginal cost from available empirical materials, as follows. Under the given assumptions, labor and materials costs would have approximately the same relative importance in both marginal costs and average direct costs.

In the following discussion the term 'direct costs' will be used to denote the census classifications of wages paid to direct labor, plus cost of materials used. Changes in average direct costs can be obtained by dividing the total change by an index of output change. It is assumed that these direct costs do not contain any overhead labor or materials costs.

In Tsiang's terminology these direct costs are referred to as prime costs. Therefore, if the price change in labor cost per unit and the price change in materials cost per unit were combined according to their relative importance in direct costs, an approximation of the price change in marginal cost should be obtained. This procedure is somewhat similar to Dunlop's calculation of the price changes in marginal cost by using census weights for combining price indexes of wages and raw materials. The main difference between the two approaches is that instead of utilizing Dunlop's indexes for wage rates and raw materials, the present calculation derives average labor cost per unit and average materials cost per unit from the census statistics. In contrast with Dunlop's assumptions, it is interesting to note that Neal and Tsiang make the assumption that average direct cost is equal to marginal cost, and thus use the census statistics directly for computing the change in marginal cost. The actual statistical result achieved by this process is identical with the other method. However, it should be pointed out that their assumption that average direct cost equals marginal cost is overly restrictive, since for the process to be legitimate it is only necessary that the change in average direct cost be equal to the change in marginal cost.

The changes in output prices can best be computed from the same body of statistical data that was used to derive direct costs. It is more meaningful to consider value per unit of output than quoted prices. Such factors as shifts in the composition of output, the importance of discounts and the existence of special prices for some customers will affect total receipts and so will be reflected in value per unit of output, whereas they might well be omitted in an analysis of quoted prices. In the census statistics, furthermore, the value of product which is recorded for an industry is from the same set of plant questionnaires that furnish the data on cost of materials and wages paid. The use of a matched set of data makes more reasonable the assumption that the same industrial classifications, the same time period, and the same concepts of output were used in obtaining both costs and receipts. It was on this basis that the data in the Census of Manufactures were used to obtain approximations of the changes which took place in marginal cost, price and output for various industries in the period 1929–31.

Table 12.4 shows the percentage changes in labor cost per unit, materials cost per unit, direct cost per unit, value per unit and output for a number of manufacturing industries which process agricultural goods. Labor cost in this table relates to production workers only. The wage and salary payments made to administrative, sales, technical, office and supervisory personnel (with the exception of working foremen and gang bosses) are all excluded. The output data given in Table 12.4 have been taken from Solomon Fabricant (1940, Appendix B). They may not be fully satisfactory for many industries; to the extent that the quality of a product changes while the unit in which output is measured does not change, the real output rate may be obscured. Fortunately,

Table 12.4 Percentage Change in Unit Costs and in Output, Various Agricultural Processing Industries, 1929–31

Industry	Labor cost (per unit)	Materials cost (per unit)	Direct cost	Value	Output
Flour	−15	−42	−41	−38	−9
Meat packing	−14	−35	−33	−33	−5
Butter	−25	−39	−39	−39	+2
Cane-sugar refining	0	−12	−11	−10	−13
Cotton goods	−13	−42	−32	−34	−22
Woolen and worsted goods	−12	−32	−27	−36	−19
Women's clothing	−24	−25	−25	−26	+3
Textile, gloves	−16	−31	−27	−27	−33
Cloth hats	−18	−20	−19	−21	−40
Leather	−3	−37	−32	−30	−39
Leather boots and shoes	−13	−22	−20	−20	−16

Source: Cost and value data, Bureau of the Census (1933a), pp. 42–44; 133–5; output data, Solomon Fabricant (1940), pp. 385, 387, 395, 404, 427, 430, 436, 347, 457, 462, 474.

it is not crucial that the output indexes be truly valid. The major point of the analysis is to examine the *relative* changes in labor cost, materials cost and value per unit within each industry; the output index is used only to reduce the total figures to averages. The relationship among labor cost, materials cost and value per unit will be the same regardless of the output index, since for any one industry the total figures are all divided by the same constant. The only reason for using an output index at all was to get some idea of similarities and differences among the different industries. Only if the output indexes possess a relatively high degree of validity will these inter-industry comparisons be meaningful, and in any case very little accent should be placed on small differences among industries.

The industries shown in Table 12.4 were chosen because they involve the use of a number of different agricultural products, and also because they illustrate a number of different analytic points. The most outstanding findings which emerge from the table as a whole are that labor cost dropped less than materials cost in all instances, and that together these direct costs dropped by about the same percentage as price. Thus if the change in direct costs is taken to be an approximation of the change in marginal cost, price in the industries shown moved directly with marginal cost.

A more detailed examination of Table 12.4 brings out some additional points of interest. There is considerable variation among the industries in the extent of the drop in labor costs, and no simple explanation of the causes of such variation is apparent. Differential changes in wage rates or in the wage structure might account for some of the variation, but probably of equal importance are the differences in productivity changes among industries, the substitution of the owner's labor for hired labor in small firms (for example, the butter industry), the differential rate of contraction of firms having high labor costs compared with firms having lower labor costs, and finally the doubtful validity of the output index as an indicator of real output changes.

The variations among the industries in the changes in materials cost are somewhat more easily explained. The drop in materials cost is greatest for those industries that directly consume unprocessed farm products, and is less for those industries that utilize partly processed agricultural products. Thus the drop in materials cost was substantial for flour, meat packing, butter, cotton goods and leather, and somewhat less for women's clothing, textile gloves, cloth hats and boots and shoes. The woolen and worsted industry is hard to classify because it is composed of a number of different sub-industries, some of which supply various intermediate products to later processing stages, and so represents a mixture of plants at various stages of processing. Cane-sugar refining has been included to illustrate what happens in an agricultural processing industry when materials prices are less variable. Most cane sugar for refining is imported, and since this import price did not drop as much as the prices of other agricultural materials, the price of refined sugar did not drop as much as the prices of the other processed agricultural goods shown.

A separate examination of the drop in labor costs and the drop in materials costs is not sufficient to account for all the variations in final goods prices in the various industries. The relative importance of labor and materials in the production process must be taken into account, in order to give an accurate appraisal of the change in direct costs. The significance of this point is well illustrated by a comparison of the butter and the cotton industries. The percentage drop in labor costs for the butter industry (25 percent) was considerably greater than it was for the cotton industry (13 percent). The drop in materials costs was about the same for the two industries (butter, 39 percent; cotton, 42 percent). Because of the greater importance of labor in the cotton industry, the output price of cotton goods dropped somewhat less (34 percent) than it did for butter (39 percent). Materials were so much more important than labor in the butter industry that the output price of butter changed by exactly the same percentage as did materials.

Finally, there are significant differences in the degree to which prices (value per unit) dropped in the various industries shown in Table 12.4; these differences can all be explained adequately in terms of changes in labor costs and materials costs and the relative importance of labor and materials in the production process. The higher the degree of fabrication, the more important labor becomes in relation to materials and the more closely will price change follow the change in labor cost. The prices at which processed agricultural goods are sold to distributors, therefore, will depend in large part on how highly they are fabricated before they are ready for the consumer. The variations in relative price changes even within the agricultural processing industries are not inconsiderable. Excluding cane-sugar refining, the drop in finished goods prices in Table 12.4 ranges from 20 percent for boots and shoes to 39 percent for butter. But, insofar as output prices shown in Table 12.4 do tend to move with cost, they can all be called flexible, despite the fact that the amplitude of change differs considerably from industry to industry.

As noted above, the use of the change in direct cost per unit as an indicator of the change in marginal cost involves the assumptions of constant marginal costs and a lack of substitution among capital, labor and materials in the period under study. It will be useful at this juncture, therefore, to examine the effects of different assumptions about marginal cost upon the analysis.

If the marginal cost curve, instead of being constant, were upward sloping (for example, marginal cost increasing with increases in output), the drop in direct costs shown in Table 12.4 would be an understatement of the actual drop in marginal costs. Under such circumstances, instead of the roughly equivalent movement of marginal costs and prices indicated in Table 12.4 by the change in direct costs and prices, marginal cost would in fact generally have fallen more than prices, so that according to the definition of price flexibility adopted above prices would be somewhat inflexible. Conversely, if marginal costs were downward sloping (for example, marginal costs decreasing with increasing output), the fall in direct costs shown in Table 12.4 would overstate the actual drop in marginal costs, and prices would be overly flexible.

In assessing the suitability of the assumptions made earlier with respect to the probable shape of the marginal cost curves for the industries shown in Table 12.4, the following points should be borne in mind. For a good many industries, it does not seem reasonable to expect that the amount of materials required per unit of output should vary in any manner except directly with output — especially, for example, in such industries as flour, butter and cane-sugar refining. In these industries, too, labor costs are not a very large proportion of direct costs, so that any variation in the amount of direct labor required per unit of output as output increases would have relatively little influence on the level of marginal cost. And in certain other industries, it may be true, as Reynolds (1942, esp. p. 277) has suggested for cotton textiles, that the fixed factors which are usually assumed to be indivisible are in fact highly divisible. Many plants are made up of batteries of similar machines, each of which can be operated as an independent unit. If the machines are of equal efficiency, the putting into use of successive units need not involve any increase or decrease in marginal cost. Finally, shifts in the marginal cost function due to technological changes are somewhat less likely to have taken place in the downswing period under consideration (1929–31) than in other periods. All things considered, an attempt to arrive at more realistic assumptions about the shape of the marginal cost function (and technological change) in many of the agricultural processing industries would probably result in refinements which would be matters of detail rather than of consequence. This would not be true in every case, but it would be true in the majority of cases.

Mining

The minerals industries present yet a different set of problems. Unfortunately, in this sector any analysis is seriously hampered by the lack of adequate data. The various types of mining, furthermore, cannot be treated as one homogeneous group in the way agricultural crop production was. Each particular branch of the mineral industry has its own peculiarities.

In coal mining, labor cost is even more important than it is in most manufacturing industries. For the year 1929, labor costs represented about 60 percent of the value of the product in both the anthracite and bituminous industries (Bureau of the Census, 1933b, p. 583). Materials costs amount to about 15 percent of the value of the product. It is difficult to find data showing how materials costs changed from 1929 to 1932 or what materials were used, but very probably few if any direct products of agriculture were involved. To the extent that materials used were highly processed goods, their costs should change in about the same way as labor costs. And in any case, since labor costs constitute 80 percent of the total direct cost in coal mining, a relatively small error would be introduced by assuming that total direct costs moved about the same way as labor costs. The data in Table 12.5 have been drawn from this assumption.

This table shows that prices and labor costs did move together for the period 1929–32, a period in which production of coal was cut back sharply. The data on iron-ore production are difficult to interpret because of the vertical integration of the industry. Quoted prices of iron ore did not change at all throughout the Depression, but even though these unchanging prices did nominally appear on the books of vertically integrated firms, their significance may be questioned. The separation of the accounts of the operation of iron-ore mining from the production of steel within the same firm is of necessity an arbitrary procedure, and the resulting statistics represent imputations which are irrelevant from the point of view of the total profits of the firm.

The production of petroleum and nonferrous metals differs from coal production in that the differing richness of deposits is a very important factor. No generalization can be made about cost curves in either industry. Some oil wells or mines utilize low-grade deposits and have relatively high marginal costs in the form of labor and some materials. Other wells or mines are much richer, having very low marginal costs and yielding considerable rent. With a fall in demand, high-cost producers will be forced to abandon operations completely,

Table 12.5 Indexes of Labor Cost and Value per Unit in the Extractive Industries, 1929–32 (1929 = 100)

Industry	1930	1931	1932
Anthracite coal:			
Labor cost per unit	102	95	82
Value per unit	98	95	84
Output	94	81	68
Bituminous coal:			
Labor cost per unit	95	86	71
Value per unit	95	87	72
Output	87	71	58
Crude petroleum:			
Labor cost per unit	97	73	56
Value per unit	94	51	68
Output	89	84	78
Metalliferous mining:			
Labor cost per unit	104	90	84
Value per unit	90	78	73
Output	75	50	26

Sources: US Department of Commerce, *Statistical Abstract of the United States, 1939*, p. 340; *Statistical Abstract of the United States, 1940*, pp. 784, 791, 804.

while the low-cost producers can continue to operate. This situation is well illustrated by the Michigan copper-mining industry. In 1929, the yield of copper per ton of ore was 24.5 pounds; in 1930, 25.4 pounds; in 1931, 33.1 pounds; and finally in 1932, 47.6 pounds (US Bureau of Mines, 1933, p. 146). Similarly, output per man-hour in the production of crude petroleum was 35 percent greater in 1932 than it was in 1929, and in lead and zinc mining it was 68 percent greater (Works Project Administration, 1938, p. 63; 1940, p. 74). High-yield deposits thus account for a relatively larger share of the total output of the industry when demand falls. The cost curves of a high-yield producer are very much like those of a farmer. Marginal costs are relatively low, becoming discontinuous (i.e., vertical) at capacity production. With a fall in demand, a high-yield mine, in order to maximize *present* income, should continue full production; although price has fallen, price would still be equal to marginal cost. In some cases the owner of a very valuable natural resource might prefer shutting down operations long before price fell to the point where it equaled direct operating costs. Since minerals are exhaustible resources, mining involves a cost akin to user cost, and if the mine is very rich and the producer has high future expectations this user cost might be great.

In considering how price should move relative to *direct* cost actually incurred with a fall in demand, however, one would expect price to come closer to direct cost, since direct cost actually incurred lies on the portion of the curve just before the vertical rise. Thus the fall in price would tend to be greater than that in actual direct cost. Exact prediction of the movement of price relative to direct cost would require engineering knowledge of the difference in the richness of deposits in the industry and economic knowledge of the structure of the industry. The data for petroleum and metalliferous mining in Table 12.5 show that, as would be expected in these industries, if the change in labor cost is again taken as an index of the change in direct costs, prices fell faster than direct costs.

It will be apparent that this discussion of the mineral industries has in fact been concerned with the shape of the supply curves in the various industries. For coal mining and probably also for quarrying, the abundance of deposits of roughly similar productivity leads to supply curves for these products that are almost horizontal for a wide range below capacity production. If costs do not change, a fall in demand would probably result in a fall in output rather than in price. It is only if the supply curve shifts downward due to falling labor costs that any significant price decline can take place. In contrast, those minerals which are found in deposits of widely varying richness will have rising industry supply curves, and a fall in demand will intersect the supply curve at a lower point, thus permitting a price fall as well as a contraction in output. Any downward shift in costs, of course, would increase the price drop and permit a larger output than would otherwise be possible.

Manufacturing: Mineral Raw Materials

The processing of mineral materials by manufacturing industries can be examined in a manner similar to that used for the processing of agricultural materials. Table 12.6 presents the relevant data for a number of different industry groups. Like the agricultural processing industries, the mineral processing industries in the table show a correspondence between direct costs and prices, with one significant exception. This exception is manufactured heating and illuminating gas; in this industry direct costs dropped 12 percent while price dropped only 1 percent. The reason for this discrepancy is obvious: gas is a public utility and its rates are fixed. It has been included in the selection of industries in Table 12.6 to show how an inflexibility of prices relative to costs would show up, even in a case where costs were not particularly flexible.

The mineral processing industries are very different from the agricultural processing industries with respect to the magnitude and consistency of the drop in materials cost. For the agricultural processing industries, it was noted that materials costs dropped considerably and in all cases more than labor cost. In contrast, the materials costs for lime, clay products, fertilizer, tin cans, buttons, clocks and watches and manufactured gas dropped less than for any agricultural processing industry, and in some of these cases fell less than did labor costs. The industries which exhibit this smaller drop in materials costs are either those which obtain a significant portion of their materials from those extractive

Table 12.6 Percentage Change in Unit Costs and in Output, Various Mining Processing Industries, 1929–31

Industry	Labor cost	Materials cost (per unit)	Direct cost (per unit)	Value	Output
Lime	−18	−17	−18	−20	−22
Clay products	−14	−7	−11	−11	−52
Petroleum refining	−10	−34	−33	−36	−9
Fertilizer	−13	−15	−14	−15	−22
Tin cans	−20	−16	−17	−18	−8
Wire drawn from purchased rods	−4	−29	−24	−24	−49
Nonferrous metal products	−20	−45	−41	−38	−41
Washing machines	−24	−24	−24	−22	−21
Buttons	−14	−18	−16	−17	−12
Pens	−1	−24	−17	−16	−17
Clocks and watches	−4	−5	−5	−3	−26
Manufacturing heating and illuminating gas	−12	−12	−12	−1	−8

Source: Cost and value data: Bureau of the Census (1933a), pp. 308, 358, 397, 427, 428, 491, 492, 523, 631, 632; output data: Solomon Fabricant (1940), pp. 497, 517, 531, 522, 552, 553, 556, 559, 578, 593, 596.

industries in which the price drop would be expected to be small, or else those which use more highly fabricated materials, which already have a considerable amount of labor cost in them. Petroleum refining and nonferrous metal products behave differently from the industries just listed, in that their material costs do drop significantly. Again, this is what would be expected, because of the nature of the mineral industries supplying them.

The remaining industries require further explanation. Wire drawn from purchased rods uses both steel and copper. The drop in materials cost for the wire industry, therefore, should fall somewhere between those of these two raw materials. If the fall in materials cost for tin cans and the fall in price of nonferrous metal products are taken as indicators for steel and copper, respectively (since nothing better is available), materials cost in the wire industry does behave as expected. For washing machines, labor cost declines more than it does for any other industry in Table 12.6, which is hardly to be expected. The explanation here may lie in the lack of validity of a production index which does not take into account a change in the quality of the product. If cheaper washing machines were produced in 1931, the real output would have fallen more than indicated by the production index, and the declines in both labor cost and materials cost would have been smaller than appear here.

The conclusion that is reached from an examination of these mineral processing industries, then, is in accord with that reached for agricultural processing industries. The prices of producers tend to move in accordance with their direct costs, computed as the weighted average of labor and materials costs. In some of the mineral processing industries, a fall in demand does not produce a sharp decline in materials cost; instead the decline in materials cost is about equal to the decline in labor cost so that price, materials cost and labor cost all move together. In those cases where materials cost does decline sharply, the reaction will be like that in the agricultural processing industries. The higher the degree of fabrication, the more closely the change in the price of the product will approach the change in labor cost, since labor cost is relatively a more important part of the total value of the product.

Again, it should be noted that the use of the change in direct cost as an indicator of marginal cost in this analysis implies all the restrictive assumptions that were discussed above with reference to the agricultural processing industries. It is quite possible that a number of the industries listed in Table 12.6 did not have constant marginal costs and fixed technical coefficients among their inputs in this period. If the quantitative importance of these deviations was not overly great, however, the changes in direct costs may still reflect the approximate change in marginal costs. In some instances, it may even be true that some of the discrepancies shown in Table 12.6 would disappear if a better approximation to the change in marginal costs could be obtained. Thus, if the marginal cost function in nonferrous metal products actually declined with expanding output, the drop in direct cost shown in Table 12.6 would overstate the actual drop in marginal cost, so that marginal cost and price might have moved more closely together than did direct cost and price.

Manufacturing: Summary

Up to this point in the analysis, specific industries in manufacturing have been discussed to illustrate particular points, but there has been no discussion of how well manufacturing as a whole fits this pattern. It would not be meaningful to combine all of manufacturing, for reasons which have already been pointed out. The aggregation of agricultural processing industries with mineral processing industries, and materials producing industries with those making highly fabricated goods, would, because of the relative shifts in the importance of these various groups, obscure the very relationships which were being investigated. Some disaggregation is therefore necessary. To cover all of manufacturing, and yet preserve to some extent the differences among the different major industries, the 16 major industry groups used in the census classification are presented in Table 12.7. For three of the industry groups, production indexes are not available.

Generally speaking, the correspondence between the drop in direct costs and the drop in prices for the various industries is quite close. In seven of the

Table 12.7 Percentage Change in Unit Costs and in Output, Major Industry Groups, 1929–31

Industry	Labor cost	Materials cost (per unit)	Direct cost (per unit)	Value	Output
Food and kindred products	−11	−30	−28	−25	−9
Textiles and their products	−18	−32	−28	−28	−13
Forest products	−13	−10	−11	−15	−45
Paper and allied products	−14	−18	−17	−16	−14
Printing, publishing and allied industries	+1	−10	−6	−6	−16
Chemicals and allied products	−9	−23	−21	−15	−15
Products of petroleum and coal	−4	−27	−25	−25	−17
Rubber products	−22	−37	−33	−21	−31
Leather and its manufactures	−12	−28	−24	−25	−18
Stone, clay and glass products	−13	−10	−11	−11	−34
Iron and steel and their products	+2	−7	−5	−8	−50
Nonferrous metals and their products	−8	−41	−37	−33	−42
Transportation equipment	+9	+3	+5	+5	−55
Industries with no output indexes					
Machinery	−48	−44	−46	−48	
Railroad repair shops	−68	−54	−62	−58	
Miscellaneous	−61	−63	−62	−68	

Sources: Cost and value data: Bureau of the Census (1933a), pp. 42, 133, 218, 262, 280, 307, 358, 372, 380, 397, 426, 491, 522, 593, 618, 630; output data: Solomon Fabricant (1940), pp. 410, 460, 475, 481, 485, 486, 514, 519, 535, 543, 556, 565, 592.

16 industries, the drop in price was within one percentage point of the drop in direct cost. In five industries prices dropped more than direct costs, and in four industries less. The two industries in which the discrepancy was greatest were chemicals and rubber; in both of these price would have been expected to fall more than it did. In forest products, iron and steel and nonferrous metal products, price dropped somewhat more than would have been expected. There does not seem to be any single simple explanation that can account for these divergences.

Aggregation like that shown in Table 12.7 has both advantages and disadvantages in drawing conclusions regarding the behavior patterns of individual firms. Since many firms are included in the aggregate, the effect of normal random variance is reduced and the average change for the group as a whole takes on more significance. On the other hand, aggregation combines what are essentially inhomogeneous groups. Any single industry includes a variety of products and some of these products will have wider margins between direct cost and price than others (margin in this sense equals price minus direct cost divided by price). If with a fall in demand the rates of contraction of high-margin and low-margin products are different, the aggregate would show a change in the average margin even if the margin for every individual product remained unchanged. The use of finer industry classifications in Tables 12.4 and 12.6 was in part an attempt to avoid some of these aggregation problems. Even with a single homogeneous industry, however, the aggregation problem would not be entirely overcome. Margins in large firms may differ from those in small firms, and the rate of contraction of firms in a depression may be related to size. Or, margins for plants in one part of the country may be different from margins in another part, and the contraction in output may be more severe in one section of the country than in others. For an accurate appraisal of the behavior of the relation between direct costs and prices, it would in fact be necessary to make the analysis product by product and plant by plant throughout the country. Examination of a few representative individual plants, furthermore, would not be sufficient; every plant has special conditions, and there is ample evidence that the change in margins from year to year is highly variable in individual cases. What would be required would be distribution curves of margins for all the plants and products in a given industry. Preliminary investigation along these lines has indicated that, although there is wide dispersion in the behavior of individual plants, there is a central tendency, and this central tendency is normally around the point of zero change in margins (i.e., the gap between price and direct cost is a constant percentage of price).

This discussion is not intended to imply that all the discrepancies between the changes in direct costs and the changes in price which appear in Table 12.7 can in fact be explained by problems of aggregation. On the contrary, some of the actual correspondence between direct cost and price change may well be the result of the fact that a number of essentially dissimilar groups have been combined, and in doing so their differences have been averaged out.

There are a number of other considerations, besides that of aggregation, which should be taken into account in appraising these statistics. First, the records upon which the statistics are based are accounting records, and for small firms especially, records of labor cost and materials cost are not kept uniformly and consistently from year to year or from firm to firm; similarly, the valuation of inventories on different bases will obviously lead to difficulties in interpretation. Second, price would be expected to move with marginal cost only when there have been no technological changes, no significant institutional changes, and no secular growth or decline. Over a two-year period some such changes are bound to occur, and to the extent that they do, margins could be expected to shift. Finally, it has been assumed that marginal cost corresponds to direct cost, with direct cost computed as average labor and materials cost per unit of output (i.e., that all production functions are linear). In actual fact, the productivity of labor in many industries is affected by the scale of output, and in such cases the change in direct cost may not be a good indicator of the change in marginal cost and so should not necessarily agree with the change in price. Any adequate analysis of the discrepancies between the change in direct costs and the change in prices in manufacturing industries must take all of these factors into account. In this connection, see *The Studies of the Production in Employment and Productivity in 59 Manufacturing Industries* (Works Progress Administration, 1939).

Distributive Trades

The products processed by the manufacturer, and some of the products coming direct from the farmer, must pass through the channels of distribution. Direct costs in the distributive trades are primarily the goods purchased for resale to other distributors or to consumers. The labor costs and other materials costs and the rent can generally be considered fixed over rather wide ranges of output, so that the purchase price of goods for resale (including transportation) is fairly closely identified with the industry's marginal cost. Here again, the analysis is hampered by the fact that very little information is available, but something can be done with the concept of gross margins. In the distributive trades, the difference between the prices paid by the distributors for goods and the prices received by them for the same goods is normally expressed as a percentage of final price and is termed gross margin. This concept differs from mark-up in that it is calculated on the basis of actual receipts (including discounts, sales, etc.) rather than on the basis of quoted prices. Table 12.8 gives the percentage gross margins for a variety of different distributors.

For almost all groups there is no significant change in gross margins in the period 1929–32. The one major exception is Chicago meat markets; gross

Table 12.8 Percentage Gross Margins in the Distributive Trades, 1929–32

Type of establishment	Number of stores	Percentage gross margin			
		1929	1930	1931	1932
Wholesale grocers, Ohio	17	12	11	11	10
Wholesale machinery supply	35–44	24	24	24	25
Meat markets, Chicago	34–50	22	25	28	29
Food chains	17,754–33,147	20	n.a.	22	22
Clothing stores, sales, to $100,000	n.a.	35	36	34	33
Specialty stores	70–85	34	34	33	32
Chain shoestores	611–1,361	34	n.a.	n.a.	33
Variety chains	1,579–2,188	33	n.a.	32	31
Dept. stores, sales, to $10 million	21–30	34	34	34	34
Dept. stores, sales, to $4–10 million	44–54	34	34	33	33
Dept. stores, sales, to $1–4 million	110–142	32	32	32	32
Dept. stores, sales, to $500,000–1,000,000	57–95	31	31	31	31
Dept. stores, sales, to $250,000–500,000	115–167	29	30	29	29

Source: McNair, Teele and Mulhearn (1941), pp.112–13, 105–9, 222, 285, 288, 387, 419, 431, 583.

margins here rose from 22 percent in 1929 to 29 percent in 1932. Whether or not meat markets are a significant exception cannot really be determined on evidence at present available but, by and large, it does not appear that the gross margins in the distributive trades change violently with a contraction in demand and costs. In other words, prices charged by the distributive trades tend to follow closely the prices they have to pay for the goods they sell.

Summary

This examination of the different industrial sectors of the economy during the period 1929–32 indicates that their actual behavior was consistent with the explanations which would be offered by a student taking his first course in value theory. At no stage in the discussion has it been necessary to consider the effect of industrial concentration to explain the relation between the fall in direct costs and the fall in price. The major determinants of price changes, according to both the theory and the empirical findings, should be the relative importance of agriculture in the economy, and the extent to which demand for agricultural goods falls; the nature of mineral resources and the importance of labor cost in mining, coupled with the extent to which demand for mineral goods falls; the fall in the wage rate and its effect on labor cost; and the shape of production functions. To the extent that differences in the behavior of the wage rate might be explained by differences in industrial concentration, however, it is still possible that industrial concentration would in fact affect prices. For an analysis of monopoly as a possible determinant of inter-industry wage structure, see Joseph W. Garbarino (1950, pp. 282–305).

Generally speaking, economists are accustomed to taking as given the technological and institutional elements of the economic system. The relative magnitude of agriculture in the economy, the distribution of mineral resources and the shape of production functions are all of this nature. The change in demand and the change in the wage rate and its relation to labor cost, however, are more properly economic problems. Income analysis in its more recent forms attempts to predict the changes in the patterns of consumption and investment in the economy; if this attempt becomes successful it should be possible by studying behavior patterns to predict changes in demand for various kinds of final goods and trace these back to the derived demands for agricultural and mineral goods.

An adequate theory of the wage rate is, however, still lacking. This lack is much more serious than might at first appear. Throughout the analysis up to this point, it has been implicitly assumed that when changes in direct costs agreed with changes in prices, it was not because the direct costs themselves were determined by prices. Should the causality run in the opposite direction, i.e., should direct costs be determined by prices instead of by other forces, the question of what determines prices would still remain open. It is probable that the price of a producer's final product does not affect the cost of his materials except through its effect on his demand for the materials, but this is not necessarily true of labor cost. If the wage rate in a plant is sensitive to the price of the final good which the plant produces rather than to the profit or loss of the plant or to the change in output, it may well be that costs will cease to be an explanation of prices, and that instead it will be possible to predict wage changes by changes in prices. This matter would bear further looking into, and until some adequate explanation of what wage rates do depend on can be given, the theory itself is incomplete.

As a final qualification of the empirical findings, it should be noted that the relationships observed for the period 1929–32 may no longer be relevant. The empirical evidence for the period 1929–32 does not throw any light on what would happen with rising income and demand. Periods of upswing are more difficult to analyze because the movement tends to be slower and technology is more apt to change. An examination of the relatively rapid upswing of 1921 to 1923 has been made, however, and it appears that price behavior in this upswing was in general accord with what would be expected. If, for example, there is considerable public pressure to limit the profits of producers, it would be quite possible that producers would not operate so as to maximize profits in the short run. Furthermore, it may no longer be true that the price of agricultural materials will rise and fall more than labor cost. Industry-wide bargaining and the sensitivity of labor to changes in the cost-of-living index may render wages more highly variable, at least in the upward direction, and in the downward direction agricultural price supports may prevent the normal fall in agricultural prices. In this connection the significance of guaranteed annual wages is interesting. Insofar as guaranteed annual wages remove some of the cost-of-production workers from marginal cost and make their wages a fixed cost which must be paid regardless of the level of operation, the importance of labor in marginal cost would be reduced over certain ranges of output. At points of production above the level consonant with the guaranteed wage, however, the normal relation of price to direct labor and materials cost would continue. If materials costs in the industry in question are variable, prices with guaranteed annual wages would tend to be more variable at points under 'normal' output, but not different at points above 'normal' output. Finally, governmental action in imposing rationing and price control might have a strong effect on price–cost relationships. For all these reasons, today's pattern may be quite different from the pattern of 20 years ago.

The relevance of the findings in this section for the topic of price flexibility as it was conceived by Means and those who came after him needs no particular elaboration. The major patterns of price behavior in the economy can be adequately explained in terms of factors other than industrial concentration. This is not to say that in some instances the consideration of the industrial organization of an industry might not be necessary, nor that in explaining wage–price relationships monopoly and monopolistic relationships need not be explored. What can be said, rather, is that even if monopoly did not exist a price system very similar to the existing one would emerge as long as wages were less flexible than agricultural prices and some mineral prices.

4. THE THEORY OF PRICE BEHAVIOR AND AGGREGATIVE PRICE INDEXES

In the preceding section, the theory of price behavior has been analyzed in terms of a disaggregation of the economy. There still remains, however, the question whether this theory of price behavior is compatible with the aggregative price indexes covering the economy as a whole. For an explanation of price behavior to be completely satisfactory, it is necessary to show that it can in fact explain both micro- and macroeconomic behavior. This final section, therefore, will consider whether or not the theory of price behavior outlined in the preceding section provides a valid explanation of the behavior of component prices in consumer price indexes, the behavior of the wholesale price index and the relative movements of real and money wage rates.

The Consumer Price Index

The major components of the Consumer Price Index which are available for the United States are food, apparel, rent, gas and electricity, other fuels, ice, house furnishings and miscellaneous. The price indexes for these components are shown in Table 12.9 for the period 1929–51, along with the cumulative decline from 1929 to various stages of the Depression and the cumulative rise from 1933 to various stages of recovery.

The price indexes for food show the greatest cumulative movement in each stage. This is, of course, what would be expected, since foods are agricultural

Table 12.9 Consumer Price Indexes by Commodity Groups, 1929–51 and Cumulative Percentage Changes, 1929–41

Year	Total	Food	Apparel	Rent	Gas and electricity	Other fuels	Ice	House furnishings	Miscellaneous
Indexes (1935–39 = 100)									
1929	123	133	115	141		113		112	105
1930	119	126	113	138		111		109	105
1931	109	104	103	130		109		98	104
1932	98	87	91	116		103		85	102
1933	92	84	88	100		100		84	98
1934	96	93	96	94		102		93	98
1935	98	100	97	94	103	99	n.a.	95	98
1936	99	101	98	96	191	199	n.a.	96	98
1937	103	105	103	101	99	191	n.a.	104	101
1938	101	98	102	104	99	101	n.a.	103	102
1939	99	95	101	104	99	99	100	101	101
1940	100	97	102	105	98	102	100	101	101
1941	105	106	106	106	97	108	104	107	104
1942	117	124	124	109	97	115	110	122	111
1943	124	138	130	108	96	121	114	136	116
1944	126	136	139	108	96	126	116	136	121
1945	128	139	146	108	95	128	116	146	124
1946	139	159	160	109	92	137	116	159	129
1947	159	193	186	111	92	156	126	184	140
1948	171	210	186	117	94	183	135	195	150
1949	169	202	190	121	97	188	140	189	155
1950	172	205	188	131				190	157
1951	186	228	205	136				211	165
Cumulative percentage changes									
1929–30		−5	−2	−2		−2		−3	0
1929–31		−22	−10	−8		−4		−12	−1
1929–32		−35	−31	−18		−9		−24	−3
1929–33		−37	−34	−31	−44	−13		−25	−7
1933–34		+11	+9	−6	−44	+2		+11	0
1933–35		+19	+10	−6	−44			+13	0
1933–36		+20	+11	−4				+14	0
1933–37		+25	+17	+1				+24	+3
1937–38		−7	−1	+3				−1	+1
1933–39		+13	+14	+4				+20	+3
1933–40		+15	+16	+5				+20	+3
1933–41		+26	+20	+6				+27	+6

n.a. (not available).

Source: US Department of Commerce (1950), p. 285; US Federal Reserve System (1952), p. 548.

products that reach the consumer without any very great degree of processing by labor. The indexes for apparel move somewhat less than those for food; again, this would be expected since most of the materials involved come from agriculture, and the goods go through more processing by labor before they reach the consumer. House furnishings are somewhat similar to apparel, but contain more nontextile components. In the first two years of the decline, house furnishings did drop more than apparel, but by 1932 and 1933 the drop in apparel was very much greater. Rent presents a special problem. In the earlier stages of the Depression, the rent index did not drop as much as food, apparel, or house furnishings, but by 1933 it had dropped considerably more than house furnishings and it continued to drop in 1934, reaching a level 44 percent below that of 1929 — a greater drop than that shown by any other component. Rents could be expected to be somewhat sticky in their response to a decline in economic activity, because they are contracted on a longer-term basis than most consumer prices. However, it would appear that the relatively fixed stock of housing makes rent very sensitive to demand if the period of adjustment is long enough. For gas and electricity, fuel and ice, only a combined index is available for the period 1929–33. It is evident from inspection of the component indexes for later years, however, that this index combines a number of different types of price behavior. Gas and electricity show very little variability, as would be expected in view of public utility price-setting procedures. Ice uses as materials primarily electricity and water — both utilities — and these combined with some labor would determine its price behavior. As would be expected the price of ice is, next to gas and electricity, the least variable of the consumer price components. The fuel index is based largely upon price changes in coal and fuel oil. The price of coal would be expected to be considerably less variable than that of fuel oil, since it has a much larger labor component; thus the fuel index combines a fairly invariant price index with a more variable one to yield an index of about the same variability as those of apparel and house furnishings. The index for miscellaneous items, finally, is composed of such prices as street-car and bus fares, upkeep of automobiles, medical care, newspapers, radios, motion pictures, other recreation, barber and beauty shop services and toilet articles. These prices tend to be relatively less variable because of such factors as rate regulation and customary prices, as well as the importance of labor services and the high degree of fabrication.

The behavior of the different components of the index followed somewhat the same pattern after 1939 as before, except that the effects of price control are quite evident. Food prices did not rise as much as would have been expected in terms of the rise in apparel and house furnishings. From 1941 to 1945, in fact, the prices of both apparel and house furnishings rose by 37 percent, whereas food rose by only 31 percent. This is probably due to the greater ease of controlling food prices — the lower-priced lines in apparel and house furnishings tended to disappear from the market. With the end of the war and the removal of price control, the prewar relationship among the components in the consumer price index was restored.

It is thus apparent that the relative movements of the various components of the consumer price index do behave approximately as would be expected on the basis of the preceding analysis of the determinants of relative prices. Any detailed analysis of the exact year-to-year movements would of course have to take into account such factors as the relative sizes of the agricultural harvests, the extent of government and foreign demand for agricultural products, the various rounds of wage increases, and the secular changes in productivity in different parts of the economy. Each of these elements has a role in determining relative price movements. But the basic structure of consumers' prices and the major changes that can be expected in this structure during periods of economic fluctuation do emerge quite clearly from this relatively simple analysis.

The Wholesale Price Index

The BLS Wholesale Price Index is based on some 900 price series and 1,700 price quotations (US Department of Labor, 1951, p. 117). Prices for the same commodity at several different stages of production are often included. For example, cotton appears in the index as raw cotton, cotton yarn, cotton gray goods, cotton piece goods and cotton clothing. For each of these stages a representative commodity sample has been selected and priced at the primary market level of distribution. In the remaining space of this paper, it would not be feasible to go through each of these series in the manner that was done for the cost-of-living index. Instead, it will be useful to give some brief attention to the general aggregative nature of the series. The wider variability of the Wholesale Price Index over the cost-of-living index is well known. In terms of the theory of price behavior suggested by this paper, this greater variability would be expected.

As was pointed out in Section 3, the prices of agricultural raw materials and semi-finished goods would be expected to exhibit greater variability than the prices of finished goods. This expectation is based on the observation that the labor-cost element tends to be less variable than the prices of agricultural raw materials and the higher the degree of fabrication, the more important labor costs become relative to the cost of the original agricultural raw materials in the total direct cost. Since price tends to move with direct cost, the larger the influence of labor costs in direct cost, the more the variability of final output prices will tend to decline to that of labor costs. Many agricultural raw materials and semi-finished products are included in the Wholesale Price Index, whereas these same items are excluded from the Consumer Price Index, since only fully processed goods reach the consumer. Since the theory of price behavior outlined in Section 2 would thus produce a greater variability for the Wholesale Price Index, and since this greater variability is in fact found, there is no evidence from this test that there is any basic contradiction between the general nature of the Wholesale Price Index and the theory of price behavior.

The wholesale price concept originated in the period when economic theory was concerned with the relation between the 'price level' and the quantity of money. Economic statisticians regarded the Wholesale Price Index as a sampling of prices in the system, and thus in some sense a measure of the level around which prices tended to cluster. Economists tried to differentiate between situations in which relative prices in the price structure changed and those in which the general level of price itself changed. Changes in the price level were considered to involve only random changes in the price structure. But such a dichotomy is possible only if changes in the level are not systematically related to changes in the structure. According to the foregoing analysis of the determinants of price change, any price movement in the system necessarily involves relative price changes; a change in level without a change in structure is impossible. With a change in income the primary response will be in the prices of agricultural goods, and the repercussions will diminish as the goods become more and more highly fabricated. The 'price level' of agricultural materials and some mineral materials is thus always in flux, being affected by such things as the level of income, foreign demand and weather conditions. But the 'price level' of highly processed goods may hardly vary at all.

As an indicator of the 'level' of prices, therefore, the Wholesale Price Index is not a meaningful economic construct; rather it is merely a conglomeration of those price quotations which are easiest to get. Vertically unintegrated industries will provide a much greater number of price quotations, and even if these more numerous prices are weighted by value added at each stage, the result will not be the same as that which would be obtained using the final goods price of an integrated industry. Whenever a product contains materials of agricultural origin or of mineral origin with variable prices, the price variation will be dampened as the degree of fabrication increases, approaching the variation of labor cost. The variability attributed to an industry's prices in the Wholesale Price Index, therefore, will depend upon the particular stages in the fabrication process for which price quotations are included. It is probably no exaggeration to say that the Wholesale Price Index is no better as an indicator of inflation and deflation than freight-car loadings are of the deflated gross national product — if as good.

Relative Movement of Real and Money Wage Rates

Statistical information on the movement of an index of the real wage rate has appeared in the economic literature from time to time, but the conclusions to be drawn from this data were never very clear. In his original article on this topic, Keynes (1936, pp. 9–10) stated that prices would rise faster than money wages in recovery because in perfect competition a producer would be faced with a rising marginal cost function, and prices of output would therefore have to rise faster than the wage rate as output expanded.

In attempting to test this hypothesis for the economy as a whole, a number of economists (Dunlop, 1939; Tarshis, 1939; Richardson, 1939) used the cost-of-living index as a measure of price change, but these are in fact not the prices which are germane to the theoretical discussion (Ruggles, 1940). Prices in this context should have been restricted to the selling prices of the producers who actually paid the wage rates. The cost-of-living index is a conglomeration of prices which are paid by consumers. It includes agricultural prices, import prices, rent and prices of consumer services. Although the cost-of-living and money wage rate controversy was not meaningful in terms of its original problem, it is still interesting to ask how real wage rates behave at different phases of economic fluctuations.

The analysis of the determinants of relative price changes presented in the body of this paper is related to this discussion and can throw some light on what should be expected in terms of the relation between the Consumer Price Index and the money wage rate.

With a fall in the money wage rate and a contraction in income, the components of the Consumer Price Index can be divided into groups of commodity and service prices which will fall faster than the wage rate, fall with the wage rate and fall less than the wage rate. Goods whose value contains an appreciable proportion of agricultural or variable-priced mineral materials will vary more than the money wage rate. Goods which are highly fabricated or whose value is mostly in labor services will vary directly with the money wage rate. Finally, goods whose prices are administratively fixed, i.e., utilities, will change less than the money wage rate. Rent is the one element in consumers' expenditures which cannot be classified in this manner. As noted above, in the short run rent may be fairly inflexible because of contractual obligations, but in the longer run it becomes extremely flexible. The question whether a decrease in the money wage rate will cause an increase or a decrease in the real wage rate will thus depend on the importance in terms of weights and degree of variability of the prices which are more variable than the money wage rate compared with the prices which are less variable than the money wage rate. The relative variability of the different prices will depend on the magnitude of the total income decline which accompanies the decline in the money wage rate. For an exact prediction in any particular instance, it would be necessary to know the amount of investment, government expenditures and the propensities of various groups to consume change, as well as changes in foreign demand for agricultural goods and the influence of changes in weather conditions. But some general conclusions can be drawn. In a mild recession or in the early phases of a major depression, it would be quite possible for the real wage rate to decline, largely because of the lag in the response of rent to changes in income. In a deeper, more prolonged depression, however, it seems likely that the real wage rate would rise. Rent becomes more variable than money wage rates in the longer run, so that the only components of expenditures whose prices remain less flexible than money wage rates are a few public utilities.

An adequate empirical investigation of this problem would be particularly hard because of the difficulty of obtaining a measure of the money wage rate for an economy as a whole. In addition, retail-price quotations always involve the problem of the failure to take adequate account of the change in the quality of goods. For these reasons, the problem of the movement of real and money wage rates will probably remain in the sphere of pure theory for some time.

REFERENCES

Backman, Jules (1939), 'Price inflexibility and changes in production', *American Economic Review*, September, 480–46.

_____ (1940), 'The causes of price inflexibility', *Quarterly Journal of Economics*, May, 474–89.

_____ (1948), 'Price inflexibility — War and post war', *Journal of Political Economy*, October, 428–37.

Bissell, R.M.S., Jr (1940), 'Price and wage policies and the theory of employment', *Econometrica*, July.

Committee on Price Determination, Conference on Price Research (1943), *Cost Behavior and Price Policy*, National Bureau of Economic Research.

Dunlop, John T. (1938), 'The movement of real and money wages', *Economic Journal*, September.

_____ (1939), 'Price flexibility and the degree of monopoly', *Quarterly Journal of Economics*, August, 522–33.

Fabricant, Solomon (1940), *The Output of Manufacturing Industries, 1899–1937*, National Bureau of Economic Research.

Galbraith, J.K. (1936), 'Monopoly power and price rigidities', *Quarterly Journal of Economics,* May, 463.

Garbarino, Joseph W. (1950), 'A theory of interindustry wage structure variation', *Quarterly Journal of Economics*, May, 282–305.

Harrod, R.F. (1936), 'Imperfect competition and the trade cycle', *Review of Economic Statistics*, May, 84–8.

Humphrey, Don D. (1937), 'The nature and meaning of rigid prices, 1890–1933', *Journal of Political Economy*, October, 651–66.

Keynes, J.M. (1936), *The General Theory of Employment, Interest and Money*, Harcourt, Brace and Company.

_____ (1939), 'Relative movement of real wages and output', *Economic Journal*, March, 34–51.

Lange, Oscar (1944), *Price Flexibility and Employment*, Cowles Commission Monograph No. 8, Principe Press.

Lerner, A.P. (1933), 'The concept of monopoly and the measurement of monopoly power', *Review of Economic Studies*, 1, 51–61.

Mason E.G. (1938), 'Price inflexibility,' *Review of Economic Statistics*, **20**, 53–64.

Means, Gardiner C. (1935a), *Industrial Prices and Their Relative Inflexibility*, Senate Document 13, 74th Congress, First Session.

_____ (1935b), 'Price inflexibility and the requirements of a stabilizing monetary policy', *Journal of the American Statistical Association*, June, 401–13.

_____ (1936), 'Notes on inflexible prices', *Proceedings, American Economic Review*, March Supplement, 23–4.

McNair, M.P., S.F. Teele and F.G. Mulhearn (1941), *Distribution Costs*, Harvard University Press.

Mills, F.C. (1927), *The Behavior of Prices*, National Bureau of Economic Research.

_____ (1934), *Changes in Prices, Manufacturing Costs and Industrial Productivity, 1929–1934*, Bulletin 53, National Bureau of Economic Research.

_____ (1936), *Prices in Recession and Recovery*, National Bureau of Economic Research.

_____ (1946a), *Price–Quantity Interactions in Business Cycles*, National Bureau of Economic Research.

_____ (1946b), 'Elasticity of physical quantities and the flexibility of unit prices in the dimension of time', *Journal of the American Statistical Association*, December, 439–46.

National Resources Committee (1939), *The Structure of the American Economy*, Part 1, Chap. VIII, pp. 122–52.

Neal, Alfred C. (1942), *Industrial Concentration and Price Inflexibility*, American Council on Public Affairs.

Nelson, Saul and Walter G. Keim (1940), *Price Behavior and Business Policy*, Temporary National Economic Committee Monograph 1; Chap. 11, pp. 11–53 and Appendix 1, pp. 165–241.

Patinkin, Don (1948), 'Price flexibility and full employment', *American Economic Review*, September, 543–64.

Reynolds, Lloyd G. (1939), 'Producers' goods prices in expansion and decline', *Journal of the American Statistical Association*, March.

_____ (1942), 'Relations between wage rates, costs, and prices', *American Economic Review*, March Supplement, 275–301.

Richardson, J. Henry (1939), 'Real wage movements', *Economic Journal*, September.

Ruggles, Richard (1940), 'The relative movements of real and money wage rates', *Quarterly Journal of Economics*, November, 130–49.

Scitovsky, Tibor (1941), 'Prices under monopoly and competition', *Journal of Political Economy*, October.

Staehle, Hans (1942), 'The measurement of statistical cost functions: An appraisal of some recent contributions', abstracted in *American Economic Review*, November Supplement, 349.

Stigler, George J. (1947), 'The kinky oligopoly curve and rigid prices', *Journal of Political Economy*, October, 432–49.

Tarshis, L. (1939), 'Changes in real and money wages', *Economic Journal*, March.

Thorp, Willard L. and Walter F. Crowder (1941), 'Concentration and product characteristics as factors in price–quantity behavior', *American Economic Review*, February, Supplement, 390–408.

Tsiang, Sho-Chieh (1947), *The Variations of Real Wages and Profit Margins in Relation to the Trade Cycle*, Pitman.

Tucker, R.S. (1938), 'The reasons for price rigidity,' *American Economic Review*, March, 41–54.

United States Department of Agriculture (1939), *Income Parity for Agriculture*, Part II, Section I, p. 5.

_____ (1940), *Agricultural Statistics, 1940*.

_____ (1941), *Material Bearing on Parity*, p. 9.

United States Department of Commerce, Bureau of the Census (1933a), *Biennial Census of Manufactures: 1933*.

_____ (1933b), *Abstract of the Fifteenth Census of the United States, 1933*.

_____ (1939, 1940, 1950), *Statistical Abstract of the United States, 1939, 1940 and 1950*.

United States Department of Interior, Bureau of Mines (1933), *Minerals Yearbook, 1932-33*.

United States Department of Interior, Geological Survey (1934), *Mineral Resources of the United States, 1931*, Part 1.

United Sates Department of Labor (1951), *Handbook of Labor Statistics, 1950*.

US, Federal Reserve System (1952), *Federal Reserve Bulletin*, May 1952.

Wallace, D.H. (1936), 'Monopoly prices and depression', in *Explorations in Economics*, McGraw–Hill.

Works Project Administration (1938), *Production, Employment, and Productivity in the Mineral Extractive Industries, 1880–1938*, National Research Project.

_____ (1939), *Studies of the Production, Employment, and Productivity in 59 Manufacturing Industries*, National Research Project.

_____ (1940), *Employment and Output per Man in the Mineral Extractive Industries*, National Research Project, Report S–2.

13. Price Stability and Economic Growth in the United States

Richard Ruggles and Nancy D. Ruggles
Yale University and United Nations

Since World War II, there has been considerable concern in the United States about rising prices, on the one hand, and the relatively slow rate of growth of the economy, on the other. Considerable controversy about the proper role of monetary and fiscal policy has developed both among academic economists and among government officials. A number of congressional investigations have been launched to determine whether monopolies or labor unions have acted irresponsibly or whether the government itself has been inept in pursuing the goals of price stability and growth.

There have been charges that stability and growth are incompatible. The cost of full employment and growth, it has sometimes been argued, is an ever-rising price level. The economy is depicted as being on a kind of knife-edged equilibrium where additional demand would result in a price spiral upward and less demand would result in a recession with its attendant unemployment. The fact that price rises continue in periods of recession has been attributed, by many, to a lagged response to excess demand in the previous period. Others, dissatisfied with this thesis, have labeled the situation one of cost push, caused by excessive labor demands or by the administered prices of monopolies.

This, in brief, is the general area of problems which will be examined in this paper. Analysis of these questions is very important in evaluating the adequacy of orthodox economic theory as an explanation of the price behavior and economic development of industrial economics. It should be recognized, of course, that the models developed for the industrial economics may not be directly relevant to the nonindustrial economics. At the same time, however, as the economic development of nonindustrial economics proceeds, it may be expected sooner or later to bring these economics face to face with the same

This chapter first appeared in German in *Konjunkturpolitik*, 8 (3), 1962 and in Spanish in *Economia*, 20 (71), 1962.

types of problems with which the industrial economics are now concerned. Furthermore, in many cases it may be found that certain policies which superficially seem advisable on the basis of orthodox economic theory are not in fact appropriate even in the industrial economies.

The discussion of price stability and growth will be developed in three parts. The first part will consider the price behavior of an industrial economic system under varying conditions. In this analysis, the determinants of the price behavior of individual producers will be examined together with their implications for the performance of the price system as a whole. In the second part, the actual price performance of the US economy since World War II will be examined to see to what extent various explanations of the price movements are valid. Finally, the mechanism of growth as it is directly related to price behavior will be analyzed. In this analysis, special attention will be given to the interaction of changes of prices, incomes, and production in the system, and to the process by which growth is achieved.

1. PRICE BEHAVIOR AND ITS DETERMINANTS IN AN INDUSTRIAL ECONOMIC SYSTEM

In analyzing the price behavior of an economic system, some disaggregation will be useful in order to show the different sets of forces which operate in different parts of the economy. For this purpose, a broad industrial breakdown will be used, on the grounds that it will reveal the major differences in price behavior among the different sectors and at the same time will ensure coverage of the entire economy.

Agricultural prices are the easiest to understand. This is because the farmer does not find it to his advantage to change his rate of output even when there are wide swings in the prices of agricultural goods. The individual farmer can seldom influence the price of his product by restricting his output, so that if he were to cut his output when price fell he would merely be cutting his own income by more than was necessary. The farmer's income is essentially a residual return, determined by the difference between his receipts from cash marketing and his out-of-pocket costs for production. Since, for the most part, the out-of-pocket costs are relatively small, price rarely falls to the point where it does not pay him to buy such things as seed and fertilizer, which he would need if he is to produce as against not producing. Statistics on the number of acres harvested and planted during the Great Depression in the 1930s show that US farmers did not contract their output until the Agricultural Adjustment Act forced them to do so in 1933. In fact, from 1929 to 1932 there was a 2 percent increase in the number of acres harvested, despite the fact that farm prices dropped on an average of 60–70 percent.

It might be thought that when farm prices fall, farmers would find it desirable to move off the farm and seek other employment. During a fall in the level of economic activity, however, such a move is not very realistic, since the farmer who leaves his farm would be likely to find himself an unemployed worker without any income whatsoever. Evidence on migration of farmers to the cities indicates that it is in good times that farmers decide to leave the farms and go into other occupations. For these reasons, therefore, the supply of agricultural goods is relatively insensitive in the short run to fluctuations in demand. Of course, the weather and other similar factors affect farm yields in the short run, and this in turn will have an impact on prices, but by and large major changes in the level of demand will be directly observable as fluctuations in farm prices.

Pricing in industries other than agriculture involves a number of other considerations. For the most part, the business enterprise is an organization that combines labor and materials in order to make a product or provide a service. Generally speaking, a business enterprise purchases raw materials from another enterprise, hires employees to process these materials, and in turn sells its products or services to other groups in the economy. Unlike the farmer, many of these enterprises have very high out-of-pocket or direct costs of production materials and direct labor that may add up to as much as 80 or even 90 percent of the total value of the final products created. In such instances, it is obvious that a 10 or 20 percent drop in price would force these enterprises to shut down completely since otherwise they would be paying out more money for materials and direct labor than they were taking in as receipts from sales, and they could minimize their losses by stopping production altogether.

Traditional value theory does provide tools whereby we can attain a better insight into how producers react to changes in cost and changes in demand. According to traditional theory, the producer will continue to expand his production until he reaches a point where the cost of an increment of output is just equal to the receipts which are generated by the sale of that increment of output. Since the producer faces a sloped demand curve, production beyond this point would mean that the cost of the increment of output would exceed the amount which it would bring in the form of receipts, and the producer would be making an actual loss on each additional unit he produced. In conventional terms, therefore, the producer will be in equilibrium when his marginal cost is equal to his marginal revenue. The relationship of this point to price would be given, of course, by the elasticity of demand. Marginal revenue at the point of equilibrium will be below price by an amount which will vary with the elasticity of demand at that particular point. The more inelastic the demand, the wider will be the gap between the equilibrium marginal cost of the producer and his price. The more elastic the demand, the smaller the gap between marginal cost and price. In other words, a producer can be thought of as establishing a mark-up over his marginal cost which will be determined entirely by the elasticity of demand for his product.

Several interesting implications follow from this. Suppose, for example, that the producer was operating under conditions of constant marginal cost. Suppose, furthermore, that his demand expanded but that the elasticity of his demand curve did not change. Under such circumstances it would not be in the interest of profit maximization for the producer to change the relation of his price to his marginal cost, and therefore he would not raise his price despite the fact that demand had increased. Similarly, a fall in demand under these conditions would not result in a price decline. Instead, if the elasticity were constant, a fall in demand would have its entire impact in a drop in output of the producer. Changes in cost, furthermore, would be reflected in proportionate changes in price if the elasticity of demand at the new point of equilibrium were the same as the elasticity at the old point. In other words, if the elasticity of demand is relatively constant over the range of normal operation, shifts in the cost of production will be directly reflected in price changes.

The big question, then, which we must answer with respect to price behavior, is how the elasticity of demand changes. Unfortunately, it is not possible for economists or businessmen to ascertain with any degree of accuracy whatsoever how the elasticity of demand shifts over short periods and with changes in the level of demand. Most studies of the elasticity of demand have been content to assign a given value which it is assumed pertains over a part of the demand curve and is valid for a period of time.

There have been suggestions in the economic literature that the elasticity of demand should change systematically from prosperity to depression. Harrod, for instance, suggests that a fall in demand will make people more sensitive to price differences. In his view, the imperfection of competition is due to habit, inertia and lack of knowledge. The pressure of poverty is necessary to drive people to the trouble of avoiding waste. Why, he asks, should a man in more comfortable circumstances make as much effort to find the cheapest market? With expanding income, a man may slip by imperceptible stages into careless habits. A contraction recalls him to his senses. Thus, Harrod argues that demand will become more elastic in times of depression and less elastic as prosperity returns. The validity of this argument has often been questioned, and Galbraith has gone so far as to state the opposite. He suggests that where the decrease in demand is the result of depression, an increase in elasticity may be considered improbable. People with decreased money incomes and increased concern for their economic security are less, rather than more, responsive to lower prices. Producers and consumers alike tend to postpone all purchases that they can. These arguments suggest strongly that the elasticity of demand may behave differently for different products. For some products, a depression may make demand more elastic while for other products it tends to make demand less elastic. It is quite possible, furthermore, that producers within the same industry producing somewhat similar products may find themselves differently affected if they appeal to different classes of consumers.

If economists cannot agree as to how elasticity will behave in different periods, there seems no reason to believe that businessmen approaching the same problem in somewhat different terms will have very much clearer ideas as to what repercussions a change in demand may have on the price sensitivity of their consumers.

It is possible, however, to make the problem somewhat more operational with the aid of some simplifying assumptions. Let us assume, for example, that marginal cost is approximately horizontal over the range of output variation that normally takes place in business. In addition, let us assume that the materials used in production and direct labor constitute the variable costs of the enterprise. The difference between these total direct costs and the total receipts of the enterprise can be used as a measure of the mark-up or gross margin of the firm. In other words, the gross margin shows the amount over direct costs which producers are charging for their products.

Given this concept of gross margin, it is then possible to examine the price behavior of the firm relative to its costs by asking whether this gross margin increases or decreases with changes in economic activity. If gross margin stays unchanged, this is an indication that producers are changing their prices in exactly the same percentage as they are experiencing changes in their direct costs. It is useful to examine various industries — mining, contract construction, manufacturing, public utilities and the distributive trades to see how they react at various phases of economic activity.

The mining industry covers a great many different types of economic activity. In some cases, the industry is essentially applying labor to resources of little value in the ground, and producing raw materials for further manufacture — for example, iron, coal mining, quarrying and the mining of low-grade iron ores. In other cases, mining may involve the exploitation of valuable ores or petroleum resources. In these cases the richness of the deposit will play an important role in determining whether it continues in operation with a fall in the price of the product. High-cost mines may be forced to shut down when the price of the product falls below their direct costs of operation.

The data for coal mining and other similar low-value mining industries show that prices move quite closely with the wage cost per unit of output. Thus, for example, from 1929 to 1932 the price of bituminous coal dropped 28 percent in the United States, and labor cost per unit of coal produced dropped 29 percent. Output for this industry had fallen 42 percent in this period. This suggests strongly that producers on the average kept a fairly constant margin between price and direct cost, so that changes in cost were reflected directly as changes in prices. In metalliferous mining, however, where the ores are valuable, the labor cost per unit of output dropped only 16 percent, but the value per unit of output dropped 27 percent. In this industry, the shutdown of marginal mines with higher labor costs was an important factor, and with the exodus of high-cost firms from the industry it became possible for price to fall more than labor cost.

The analysis of the manufacturing sector is considerably simpler than that of the mining industries. As a general rule, manufacturers purchase raw materials from other producers and, by combining these materials with direct labor, produce products which they in turn sell to other manufacturers or to other purchasers in the economy. In any given industry, different producers will have different levels of gross margin. There will be a few producers with very narrow margins and a few producers with quite wide margins. There will, however, be a tendency for most producers to cluster around what may be considered a typical or average margin for the industry as a whole. In other words, if gross margins for an industry are plotted in a frequency distribution a unimodal curve results, and the variance of this distribution would be highly related to the size distribution of plants or firms in the industry. Where there are many small producers, the variance of the distribution tends to be quite wide. Where there are mainly large producers, the central tendency of the distribution is very strong and the variance around this central tendency tends to be quite small. If these distributions of gross margins are examined for different periods, very little change is found in either the central tendency of the distribution or the degree of variance, even though demand has changed substantially. Thus, for example, the very great change in demand from 1929 to 1931 left the distributions of margins for plants in various industries almost completely unchanged. Looking at the problem another way, one can say that the distribution of the change in margins produces a unimodal curve which has a central tendency of zero. Some producers find it advisable to increase their margins from one period to another, while other producers are thinking it advantageous to narrow their margins. It is interesting to note in this connection that the producers with the widest margins have a tendency in succeeding periods to reduce the size of their margins, while those having the narrowest margins tend to increase them. There is, thus, a tendency for a regression towards the mean of the margin for the industry.

A general constancy of margin for an industry implies that changes in labor costs and materials costs tend to get passed along directly in the form of final product price changes. While this is not true of every single producer, it is true by and large for producers as a group. Looked at another way, one could say that the price of the product of a manufacturer moves as a weighted average of the change in his material costs and the change in his labor costs. Thus a producer who is fabricating raw materials that come from agriculture will have a price that will behave somewhere between the change in the wage cost and the change in the agricultural material cost which he experiences. For example, in the meat packing industry in the United States from 1929 to 1931 the price of materials dropped by 35 percent and labor cost dropped by 14 percent, making it such that the weighted average of these two together dropped by 33 percent, and the output price also dropped by 33 percent. In industries where the degree of fabrication of the original agricultural materials is greater, the materials themselves become manufactured products. Thus, for example, in the cloth hat industry, the materials cost dropped only 20 percent from 1929 to 1931, labor cost dropped 18 percent, altogether direct cost dropped 19 percent, and price dropped 21 percent. As the degree of processing of agricultural materials becomes greater, the changes in prices of the products approach the changes in labor costs, since cumulatively labor becomes the major component in direct costs. For those manufacturers whose chief materials are of mineral origin, material cost may behave similarly even when it is not highly fabricated to wage costs since, as already seen, the chief cost of many mineral industries is for labor to process low-valued ores. Thus, for example, in the manufacture of lime, materials costs dropped 17 percent from 1929 to 1931, labor costs dropped 18 percent, average direct cost dropped 18 percent, and output price dropped 20 percent. Again in fertilizers, raw material cost dropped 15 percent, labor cost dropped 13 percent, average direct cost dropped 14 percent, and output price dropped 15 percent. In the cases of those industries that process ores which have more value in the ground, the situation is much more analogous to that of the industries processing agricultural materials. Thus, in the case of nonferrous metal products raw material, price dropped 45 percent, labor cost dropped 40 percent, average direct cost dropped 41 percent, and output price dropped 38 percent.

As a first approximation, therefore, producers may be considered essentially to pass along the impact of cost changes. This general constancy of margin seems to hold, furthermore, irrespective of whether an industry has a high or low degree of industrial concentration. It is in the interest of a producer to maximize his profits, and there is no reason to believe that monopolies or highly concentrated industries are any more lax in doing this than their more competitive counterparts.

Analysis of the distributive trades in terms of margins has been carried out for many years, and it is well recognized in this sector of the economy, that it is a common pricing practice to add a mark-up or margin to the wholesale price of goods. This practice at the individual establishment level tends to give very considerable stability to the gross margins of large sectors of the distributive trades. Thus, for example, department stores do not show even a 1 percent point change in gross margin over the period of the Great Depression from 1929 to 1932. Large department stores, for example, remained at gross margin of 34 percent, whereas the smaller department stores kept equally constant at somewhat lower margins.

In the service industries, the price of the service is customarily considered to be the price of the product. Thus, for example, the price of haircuts is identical with what the barber receives. Likewise, domestic servants and the professional charges of doctors and lawyers may be thought of in these terms. In this area, therefore, price not only moves with cost, but is exactly equal to cost. A somewhat similar situation statistically appears in the construction industry, where price indexes generally are based upon a weighted average of the materials cost and labor cost in the industry. It is recognized that such a price index is quite unsatisfactory, since it does not reflect the productivity change that takes place in the industry, but the lack of meaningful output price data has led us to depend upon cost as the measure of price in these areas.

Finally, in the area of public utilities it should be noted that prices do not necessarily follow costs. Insofar as the prices of public utilities are the result of government regulation, they may behave quite sluggishly, failing to reflect changes in cost as they take place. For example, in the manufactured heating and illumination gas industry from 1929 to 1931, there was a 12 percent drop in labor cost and a 12 percent drop in material cost, thus constituting a total 12 percent drop in direct costs, but output price in this industry dropped by only 1 percent.

Given the kinds of price behavior described above, it is now possible to develop a theory of the determinants of price behavior in the economic system as the level of economic activity rises or falls. A fall in the level of economic activity and demand will cause a sharp drop in the prices of agricultural goods and those mineral goods which have as their basis a valuable ore. The price changes in these commodities will have an impact upon the raw material costs of industries processing them. The prices of the processing industries will follow a weighted average of the change in the material cost and the change in the labor cost involved in the processing. The distributive trades and the services will likewise pass along any increases or decreases in their costs. The only significant stickiness in the system seems to lie in the area of public utility and other regulated prices, where the regulated price does not change as quickly as the underlying cost conditions. In other words, broadly speaking, prices depend upon the level of demand and the behavior of wages. This is, of course, a first approximation, as it does not take into account the situation for those industries which do not have constant marginal costs, and does not adequately indicate what happens when changes in productivity take place. For the period 1929–31, the theory fits quite well since productivity changes were not particularly great in that period.

Since the war, however, the periods of increasing economic activity were also periods of increasing productivity, and it is necessary to examine further what the impact of productivity increase is upon price formation. Analysis of productivity changes in the fifties seems to indicate that increases in productivity are clustered in the first part of cyclical upswings. The increase in productivity at this stage is usually more than sufficient to offset the increase in wage rates that takes place. In this initial period of upswing, therefore, the producer finds himself with falling costs despite rising material prices and rising wage rates. The prices that the producer charges, therefore, do not rise in this period, but it is interesting to note that they do not fall either, and there is a tendency for gross margins to widen as costs drop.

The period of widening margins, however, is quite short-lived. As the rate of increase of the economy begins to slacken, the rate of productivity increase also slackens, and soon it is insufficient to offset the continuing increase in wage rates and material costs. At this juncture the producer's costs per unit of output will begin to rise, and he will increase his price somewhat to meet this increase in costs. The statistics seem to indicate, however, that the increase in the price which the producer charges is not as great as the increase in costs so that gross margin tends to narrow during this later part of the upswing. When the top of the boom is reached, the increase in material cost generally stops, but the increase in wages continues. The increase in productivity at this time is very small so that wage cost continues to rise and the producer's margin narrows further. As the level of economic activity turns down, there is an actual decline in material cost but this is in some degree offset by the continued rise in wage rates during the recession and by the tendency of productivity to fall. There is some evidence, therefore, that the producer's margin continues to narrow through the downswing, and does not begin to widen again until the start of the upswing.

If this analysis of the behavior of productivity is valid, it strongly suggests that prices are not fully responsive to all changes in cost, but that this lack of responsiveness is confined to a slight stickiness which prevents them from rising as much as might be expected under cost pressures, and prevents them from falling as they might in the first part of the upswing. From the point of view of price behavior, however, the importance of these changes in margins should not be magnified. The changes in margins are very slight, and the price system would have approximately the same shape even if such minor variations in margins did not take place. The major impact of the changes in margins falls upon profits: they tend to increase profits relatively speaking in the first part of the upswing and to curtail them as the upswing continues.

In summary, therefore, one can say that changes in the level of economic activity will have an impact upon agricultural and mineral raw material prices, and these, together with changes in wages rates and productivity, will directly determine the price behavior of the economy, conditioned only by a minor price stickiness on the part of producers, which prevents the full amount of price declines from taking place in the early upswing in response to the productivity changes. It produces somewhat smaller increases in prices than costs in the later phases of the upswing of the cycle and in the early downswing. Given this hypothesis as a basis, it will now be useful to examine the price behavior of the US economy in the postwar period to ascertain the kinds of forces at work in the economy.

2. PRICE BEHAVIOR OF THE US ECONOMY: 1947–60

Before analyzing the price behavior of the postwar US economy, it will be useful to give some consideration to the problem of price measurement and the meaning of the price indexes with which the analysis must be done. One of the most comprehensive forms of price data about the economy is to be found in the implicit price deflators calculated from the gross national product by the Department of Commerce.

In order to show how much of the change in the gross national product is due to changes in price and how much is due to changes in output, the Department of Commerce undertakes the deflation of each category of final expenditures on a highly detailed basis. The deflators are based primarily upon price information collected by various government agencies. This price information cannot always be relied upon to reflect the true behavior of prices, however. Prices are obtained for items of fixed specifications, although new items continually appear on the market and old items change in quality. When improvements in quality cannot be measured, or new products appear which are more desirable than those they replace, price indexes, which must leave these factors out of account, will show too much price increase.

In pricing consumer goods, the Bureau of Labor Statistics does attempt to take into account those improvements in quality which result in increased costs, but improvements in quality may also occur at no increase in cost, so that the consumer gets more value for his money. In such cases, no adjustment is made in prices and the price indexes do not reflect quality improvements in any way. It is, however, quite obvious that the change in quality in consumer goods has been very considerable. If one were given $1,000 to spend on consumer goods, and given the choice of purchasing the goods available in 1950 at the prices of 1950 or the goods presently available at current prices, it is extremely doubtful whether one would in fact prefer the 1950 goods. In 1950 many goods which are common today were not available. Synthetic fabrics were not as common, and the introduction of plastics has improved the quality of many other products. There has been considerable development in such household appliances as automatic washers and dryers, electric razors, television and hi-fi. The packaging of frozen foods and the development of semi-prepared foods have add to the price of food, but have also substantially reduced the time required for meal preparation.

The fact that most people feel, despite the rise in the price index for this category of goods, that they will get more for their money in the present period suggests a flaw in the manner in which we measure prices over time. Conceptually there are two methods by which a more accurate measurement of real price changes might be made. Omitting from consideration all differences in values arising from style changes and changes in consumers' taste, it would be interesting to inquire how consumers would value an item produced in 1950 against its 1960 counterpart or successor. Since progress is made over time in the design and function of goods, it is reasonable to presume that on an average the 1950 goods would receive a lower valuation that the 1960 goods. If the valuation of the 1960 product (including new items) exceeded the valuation of the 1950 product (including obsolete items) by more that the 20 percent by which the price index has risen, prices must really be lower in 1960 than they were in 1950.

As an alternative measure, individuals might be asked what percentage they would require to be added to their present level of expenditures to make them willing to restrict their purchases to the exact goods available in 1950, priced at today's prices. If on average they would require more than 20 percent additional, this would again indicate that prices have actually fallen since 1950. The difficulties encountered in measuring price changes in consumer goods also exist for consumer services. Generally speaking, the compensation of the person performing the service is taken as the indicator of price. It is obvious, however, that it is possible for the quality of services to improve. Thus, for example, medical service is better than it used to be because medical knowledge has increased, but this is not taken into account in measuring the price change in medical services. Similarly, quality changes in such services as housing and education cannot be measured and are not reflected in their prices. It is a serious error, as a moment's reflection will indicate, to assume that if teachers do not improve, education as a product does not improve over the years.

We have only to ask ourselves whether we would be content to give children today exactly the same education as was given 50 years ago, using the same books and the same fund of knowledge. Education, like other products, is a combination of factors of production, and should not be assessed only in terms of an intuitive judgment about the contribution of any one of these factors of production.

Nor are consumer goods and services the only areas that present pricing problems. For producers' durable goods, it is well recognized that equipment produced today is far more productive than that produced even five years ago. But such increases in efficiency are extremely difficult to take into account in price indexes. In terms of the ability of the capital goods to yield productive services, there can be little doubt that the increase from year to year is substantial. But price indexes of producers' durable equipment generally reflect changes in the cost of production rather than changes in the performance of the equipment itself.

Residential and commercial construction also poses problems. Again, price indexes are constructed by determining what a structure of standard specifications would cost. Improvements in design and cost-reducing changes in specifications are not taken into account in the price comparison, so that the price index tends to have an upward bias.

Finally, the measurement of changes in prices of goods and services purchased by government is very difficult. For military equipment, it is often impossible to determine what happens to prices when design changes radically. Yet few would argue against the proposition that military equipment produced in the past is definitely inferior to present military equipment. For the services of government employees, like the services in general, it is assumed that there is no change in output per man, so that all increases in salary are in effect increases in the price of government gross product.

By this measure, the price of government services in the US has risen by an average of over 5 percent a year since 1946. There is good reason to believe, however, that the productivity of government workers has increased substantially in this period. For one thing, the introduction of data handling machines and computers speeds up the operation of many stages of government work. Statistics in the US government are now in large part handled mechanically rather than by clerks. The mechanization which is so characteristic of current developments in business is also occurring in government.

There is, thus, an upward bias in the price indexes for almost every category of expenditures. For commodities, it exists because quality changes and new products cannot be adequately integrated into the price data. For services, it exists because by and large the value of services is assumed not to increase, although there is strong evidence that it does. By ignoring the upward bias of the price indexes, we are likely to be basing policy conclusions on a mistaken impression. Since we are forced to use inflexible and inadequate assumptions to arrive at specific price indexes, we may create price indicators which are more the result of our assumptions than of the real world.

If this upward bias in the price indexes is taken into account, a rather interesting picture emerges. The large price increases of the three postwar years, 1946–48, and the Korean War year of 1951 stand out. However, up through 1955, the other years — 1949, 1950, 1952, 1953, 1954 and 1955 — exhibit overall price changes which are probably smaller than overall quality improvement, so that in fact from the end of the postwar inflation through 1955, the American economy did not show an overall upward price movement in any period except the Korean boom. The same is also true of 1959 and 1960. For the eight years involved, the average annual price increase was only 1.2 percent; for consumer goods alone, it averaged 0.7 percent. Price index changes of these magnitudes were probably considerably less than the actual quality changes taking place.

For the period from 1956 to 1958, the picture was somewhat different. The price increases indicated by the indexes averaged about 3 percent, and even when output was declining in 1958, the price index still showed a rise. The importance of this price rise may have been somewhat overstressed, but there can be little doubt that it has been this which has created such grave concern on the part of so many people; and the question of why the price indexes behaved the way they did and what kind of price behavior we can expect in the future is important.

In the early postwar period and during the Korean War, the existence of excess demand is sufficient to explain the price movements that occurred. Immediately after the war, the combination of long-postponed expenditures and accumulated liquid funds resulted in a rapid increase in demand for consumer goods, which were still in short supply in an economy that had not fully reconverted from war production. During the Korean War, expenditures by the federal government on national security increased from $18.5 to 37.3 billion in one year alone, thus pumping into the economy almost $19 billion in additional expenditures. At the same time, the increase in armed forces reduced the civilian labor force so that the normal increment of labor due to population growth did not occur. In a period of two years, the real output of the economy rose by over 17 percent and employment rose only 4 percent. Under such conditions, it is not at all surprising that the increase in real output could take place only with rising prices.

But the absence of a significant price rise, on average, in the other years prior to 1956 did not mean that there were no rising prices anywhere in the economy. During this period, agricultural prices were generally falling. These falling agricultural prices were offset in most of these years by rising wages, so that prices on an average were quite stable. From 1951 to 1955, there was a decline of almost 19 percent in the wholesale prices of farm products, while average hourly earnings in manufacturing rose by 18 percent. But in the commodity-producing industries, wage costs rose more slowly than hourly earnings, because productivity increased. In manufacturing as a whole wage costs rose only 2 percent. Thus the pattern of price behavior in these years can be explained in terms of the behavior of agricultural prices, wages and productivity. The movement of agricultural prices, together with the growth in productivity, tended to hold down the increase in product prices by keeping both material costs and labor costs below what they would otherwise have been. Wage rates, on the other hand, exhibit an upward influence, increasing somewhat more than in proportion to the productivity gain. The net result was comparative price stability. The evidence of the forces at work can be seen, however, in the changing price structure as revealed by the performance of the cost-of-living index, or by the implicit price deflators of gross national product. These indexes show that the prices of durable goods where productivity increases were greatest actually declined from the end of the Korean War through 1955. Prices of nondurable goods using agricultural materials, for example food processing and clothing, were relatively stable; although productivity gains in these industries probably were not as large as in the durable goods industries, agricultural raw material costs fell. In such areas as construction, productivity gains were less pronounced and material costs, being mainly non-agricultural, did not fall. Prices in this sector, therefore, rose from 1951 to 1955 by 10–15 percent, a considerably greater price rise than that exhibited by other commodity-producing sectors. The largest price increases occurred in consumer services and government services. Here price increases from 1951 to 1955 ranged from 15–27 percent. Services, in fact, accounted for most of the upward price movement that occurred in this period.

In the last two years, 1959 and 1960, farm prices have again been declining, and wages have continued upward. In 1959, productivity gains offset some of the increases in wage costs. In 1960, the productivity increase was dampened with the result that the total price increase was somewhat greater.

Most of the concern of public officials and economists with the inflationary problem derives, however, from price behavior during 1956, 1957 and 1958. Raw material costs, which had been falling up to 1955, were stabilized and productivity increases were, for the most part, much smaller than those which had helped offset price increases up to 1955. On the average, prices for the economy as a whole rose about 3 percent per year over this period. And what seemed most disturbing was the fact that the price increases were not confined to services; during 1956 and 1957, prices of producers' durable equipment rose by more than 6 percent in each year.

In view of these sharp price increases, the question was immediately asked whether in manufacturing in general price increases were in excess of the rise in the costs which producers were facing. The early impetus for the administered price argument came largely from the belief that there were unjustified price increases in the manufacturing sector.

It can be seen that in 1956 and 1957, the rise in the wage and salary bills of manufacturing firms greatly exceeded the increase in their output, so that per unit of output there was a substantial increase in labor costs. In 1956, labor cost per unit of output rose by 4.4 percent and in 1957, it rose by 3.1 percent. Even in the year 1958, when the wage and salary bill declined, the index of production declined even faster, so that in this year also there was a slight increase in wage and salary cost per unit of output. The price index for materials used in manufacturing behaved quite similarly. By 1958, labor costs had risen 8.8 percent, material costs by 7.6 percent, and wholesale prices by 7.6 percent. Thus the prices of manufactures did not fully reflect the higher cost of labor.

The increases in the wage and salary bills exceeded the increases in production considerably, causing labor costs per unit of output to rise 7.7 percent in 1956 and 3.9 percent in 1957, and even 4.7 percent in 1958. Materials cost also rose substantially from 1957. For the period from 1955 to 1958 as a whole, labor costs rose by 16.5 percent, material prices by 10.5 percent, but wholesale prices of durable goods by about 8 percent.

This same phenomenon of costs rising faster than the price indexes is also evidenced by the fact that corporate profits reached their peak in the fourth quarter of 1955. Although in absolute amount profits remained at the same in 1956, profits dropped sharply in relation to the wage bill; thus the relative share of profits was squeezed by rising wage costs. During 1957 and 1958, absolute profits also declined, showing the effect of rising costs and falling demand. The periods when profits rose in relation to wages were actually the periods of price stability.

It has been argued that the fact that wage increases have outstripped the increases in productivity was due to demand pressure. This hypothesis suggests that the level of unemployment during 1956 and 1957 was below the frictional level, and that it was the excessive demand for goods which made it possible for labor to get excessive increases in wages. There is a clear implication in this argument that if the economy is working too near to full capacity, a wage creep will ensue and wages are quite likely to rise faster than productivity. There has been considerable discussion about how much unemployment is required to keep wages in line to maintain price stability. But this analysis leaves out of account the effect which any improvement in economic conditions will have upon wage rates.

Few would say that a level of unemployment above 10 percent was required to keep the wage rate in line. Yet, in the recovery from the Great Depression of the 1930s, there were years of substantial increases in average hourly earnings, despite the fact that the economy had a level of unemployment which varied from 14 to 20 percent of the labor force.

The increases in average hourly earnings in 1934 may have been considered to be due to structural changes, but in 1937 there were also substantial increases, despite the fact that unemployment was 14 percent of the labor force. In this connection, it is interesting to note that the rise of prices during the recovery from the recession of the 1930s was at about the same rate as it has been in recent years.

I would like to suggest, therefore, that focusing on the wage rate as the major culprit in the price rise is as erroneous as focusing on the prices charged by the manufacturers. Productivity did not increase significantly from 1956 to

1958; thus, if wage increases were not on balance to exceed productivity increases, it would have been necessary that no wage increases be permitted during these three years. Thus, by this dubious reasoning, the increase in pay given government workers and university professors either should not have been given or else such wage increases should have been offset by equivalent wage declines elsewhere in the economy.

In pursuing price stability as measured by price indexes, we thus may be in danger of trying to achieve the impossible. If the wage rate depends, not on the actual level of unemployment, but on the change in economic conditions, it may only be possible to curtail increases in the wage rate when the economy is going into a decline. In these same periods, productivity increases will also be dampened, so that even modest increases in wage rates may still outstrip productivity increases. I do not believe that an economy which would provide the proper conditions for wage stability would be a healthy one. It would probably mean that deterioration of the economy is the only effective way to obtain a sufficient restraining influence on wages. As the history of the 1930s shows, even partial recovery from a deep depression normally and properly brings with it price increases. Only a deteriorating economy will achieve price stability or price declines by affecting the wage rate rather than productivity.

The picture of price behavior in the US economy can be somewhat clarified by looking at the behavior of the various components of the Consumer Price Index, and the question of administered price behavior on the part of business can be further analyzed. During the period from 1947 to the Korean boom, all the major components of the Consumer Price Index moved upward. Even agricultural prices rose with the increase in demand, so that in 1951, food prices were some 13 percent over the 1947–49 average. The component of the Consumer Price Index which rose the least was apparel. It moved up only 7 percent, reflecting a basic change in the buying habits of the American public, coupled with depressed world textile markets. As those in the textile industry know only too well, clothing no longer accounts for as high a percentage of consumer expenditures as it did several decades ago. The prices of most of the components of consumer expenditures rose some 10–13 percent during this period. The only major component showing a larger increase than this was transportation, both public and private. Private transportation (that is, automobiles and the cost of running them) rose 17 percent. But public transportation (street cars, buses, and railroads) rose over 30 percent. Except for this substantial price rise in public transportation, the disparity in price behavior was not wide. Throughout the economy the response to the increases in demand was a general rise in prices.

The situation in the period from 1951 to 1957 contrasts greatly with what went on before. The Consumer Price Index, as a whole, rose about 7 percent in this period. An examination of the individual components of consumer prices indicates that two elements rose substantially more than the others. These were public transportation again, which rose about 34 percent, and medical care, which rose over 22 percent. Neither of these components can be considered to have privately administered prices, at least in the usually accepted meaning of the term. Fuel rose almost 20 percent, and it is especially interesting to note that over half of this increase took place in 1956, reflecting, of course, the impact of the Suez crisis on fuel oil prices. This may or may not be a case of privately administered prices in the usual sense. Certainly the situation differs from that in other industries, in that it followed upon a special increase in demand, and it is problematical whether such a spurt in price would have taken place without the Suez crisis. The increase in demand even affected the price of coal through its substitution for oil. The price of coal had risen only 3 percent from 1951 to early 1956, but it rose about 10 percent during 1956. The next largest increase was in rent, which rose almost 19 percent from 1951 to 1957. Again, it is difficult to conceive of rent as a price administered privately by large companies. The next largest increase, 15 percent, was in household operation. The major components of this category are dry cleaning, laundry, soap and detergents, telephone and water rates. The only one of these that might be considered to arise in an industry with privately administered prices is soap and detergents. But the detailed price data for this group show that its price rose only 5 percent from 1951 to 1957, the other elements of household operation being responsible for the larger price increase in the group as a whole. Including soap and detergents actually reduces the price increase shown for this group as a whole. These five components of the Consumer Price Index (public transportation, medical care, fuel, rent and household operation) constitute less than 30 percent of consumers' budgets, yet together they were responsible for raising the cost of living by almost 6 percent and this amounted to over 85 percent of the total rise in consumer prices. In contrast, the goods and services which constitute the remaining 70 percent of consumers' budgets contributed less than 1 percent to the increase in the cost of living from 1951 to 1957.

Examination of those elements of consumer prices which rose least during the period from 1951 to 1956 brings out some additional points that are relevant to this question. One category, house furnishings, showed an absolute drop of approximately 6 percent. This drop reflects two influences. First, that part of house furnishings composed of textiles dropped sharply in price. This price behavior in part reflects the relatively depressed state of the textile industry and of agriculture in general. But secondly, house furnishings also include the major durable household appliances, and here the rise in wage cost was offset to some degree by increases in productivity. Prices in this sector therefore did not have to cover wage rate increases to the same extent that they did in industries such as services, where productivity increases did not have as great an influence on the price index. The house furnishings category includes a great many products that can be considered to have administered prices — more probably than any other component of consumer budgets except private transportation. Its behavior again failed to support the contention that industrially administered prices forced up the cost of living. One other category, apparel, registered a very slight price decline over this period. Here, the fall in raw material costs, combined with technological change, probably balanced the increased wage cost, so that price increased did not materialize. Food prices also remained virtually unchanged. This again can be attributed to two influences. Agricultural prices fell, but wage prices in the food processing industries rose, with the result that final prices to the consumer remained about constant. All of the other major components of consumer prices rose during this period, but one other category rose less than the average. Private transportation rose about 6 percent. Again, as with household appliances, the behavior of the price of private transportation did not bear out the generalization that administered prices were responsible for the inflationary price rise.

If there is any general pattern to be found in these price changes, it is that prices of service items in consumer budgets have risen, whereas those of commodities have not. Dividing the consumer budget into these two groups, the data show that from 1951 to 1956 services rose 21 percent, and commodities rose only 2 percent.

The data on wages, prices of manufactures, corporate profits and the various components of consumer prices thus present a consistent picture. They do not lead to the conclusion that the price rises in the period from 1951 to 1957 can be attributed primarily to the presence of administered prices in the economy, at least not in the sense of prices privately administered by large companies. Manufacturers did not pass on to the public the full effect of the increases in their costs, and corporate profits did not increase as a share in the value of output. This result should not, of course, be attributed to virtue and restraint on the part of big companies, but rather to the general softness of the economy as a whole, and the lack of demand strong enough to support price increases of the sort that occurred during the Korean boom. The behavior of the individual components of the Consumer Price Index also bears out the same conclusion, since the elements that rose fastest were either personal services or public utilities.

What the data for this period do indicate is that costs, and in particular wage costs, rose more than prices. Wages rose faster than real output. In real terms, gross national product rose about 11.5 percent in the five years from 1951 to 1956, or about 2 percent a year. In contrast, wages rose 32.5 percent in the same period, which is a rate of almost 6 percent a year. Thus the increase in productivity did not match the increase in wages and the result was a rise in costs. These rising costs, however, were not accompanied by an excessive demand for goods. The economy did not face significant shortages. In fact, in 1954, and again in 1958, an actual fall in demand occurred. Gross national product in real terms declined at the same time that the gross national product price deflator rose. Thus, despite the fall in output, prices continued to rise in many sectors of the economy. The lack of demand pressure accompanying the price rise indicates that the price increases were not due to inflationary pressures from the demand side but rather to rising costs.

The cost-of-living components also reflect the relative price shifts that have been taking place. As the economy grows, the one element which becomes more and more costly is, of course, personal service. The changing price structure reveals this. The prices of services have risen relative to other prices. To try to prevent such relative price rises would indeed be to frustrate the allocative mechanism of the price system. Rising prices serve a dual function. On the one hand, they encourage people to enter this area by giving them a higher rate of remuneration. On the other hand, increased prices discourage the use of these services by people who are at the margin. Whether the price system is equitable or not may be a matter for debate, but this is the basic principle on which it operates. It may be too much to require also from the price system that, in achieving a reallocation of resources in producing goods and determining who consumes the goods, it also achieves an exact balance between price rises in the sectors of the economy where they are necessary to effect such a reallocation, and price declines in other sectors. There is no natural mechanism which would tend to make the change in the price index come out to be zero. It is rare, in fact, that the wage rates in declining industries actually fall. What happens instead is that the wage rate is maintained, and there is unemployment in those sectors of the economy. The relative inflexibility of the wage rate downward is something that we must cope with. Reallocation of labor is not achieved by lowering its remuneration, but rather by causing unemployment; the people who lose their jobs must find other occupations. Given such a system of prices, it would be natural for a period of change on balance to cause a rise in prices. An attempt to achieve price stability must, therefore, be at the cost of either preventing the allocative mechanism from working or forcing wage and price declines in specific sectors of the economy.

3. STABILITY AND GROWTH

In the past decade, the American economy has experienced three recessions and a substantial secular price rise. The recessions are commonly considered to be temporary phenomena which, although capable of being influenced by public policy, are either unavoidable losses or normal readjustments required by the economy. The secular price rise, in contrast, is considered a long-run problem of a serious nature, indicating a lack of moral fiber on the part of the government for not maintaining price stability, or irresponsibility on the part of monopolies who administer prices, or self-seeking unions who demand unwarranted price increases. The goal of price stability has been cloaked in an air of morality that does not seem to apply to the maintenance of employment.

The main reason recessions are considered temporary is that if we wait long enough, they will cure themselves and prosperity will return. There is much truth in this point of view. Nevertheless, the record of the seven years since the Korean boom raises some serious questions about it. Only two of these years, 1955 and 1959, can be termed years of prosperity and growth. In this period there were three years of declining output, 1954, 1958, and 1960.

In two other years, 1956 and 1957, there was no appreciable change in actual output per man-hour, despite the rapid pace of technological change and the expansion of capacity. If the economy continues to exhibit this kind of behavior any growth that is achieved must be crowded into a small space of time; all the rest of the time will be recessions, recovery from recession, or leveling off prior to going into recession. In these terms, recession is *not* a temporary problem. It may be that prosperity is just around the corner, but so is the next recession.

There has been little attempt to evaluate the welfare implications of moderate secular price rises quantitatively. Specifically, one may well ask how a 2 or 3 percent annual price rise would compare in importance with unemployment 2 or 3 percent over the frictional level. The inequities that are introduced by a price rise relate to that fraction of the population which holds assets in the form of money and/or depends upon a fixed income. In this category there are, of course, banks, pension holders, and college professors. It is possibly true that it is the more articulate portion of the population that is affected most by price rises and least by unemployment, and that this influences the amount of attention devoted to the two problems. There can be no doubt that secular price rises produce real inequities, but a very mild degree of unemployment, 2 or 3 percent above the frictional level, may produce far more hardship. In the first place, such unemployment must, by definition, hit specific individuals more heavily than others. Those who have job security, like bankers and college professors, are not harmed at all. Other people, however (and they are the people whose incomes were lower to begin with), may be totally unemployed for many weeks or even months. In contrast, the worst-hit group in a moderate secular price rise will suffer a reduction in real income of only 2 or 3 percent. It may be argued that unemployment tends to hit different people at different times, but this is not necessarily true. The marginal workers in industries highly sensitive to changes in output will continually be laid off in times of soft demand. Furthermore, even in the case of a secular price rise, many of the so-called fixed incomes are not absolutely fixed. College professors eventually do get increases in pay, and social security benefits do rise. Furthermore, from an empirical point of view, price indexes tend to overstate the amount of price rise, since a large part of quality change is ignored. In contrast, unemployment figures understate the degree of unemployment, since a cut in hours worked is not reflected in the number of unemployed.

Moreover, a consideration merely of the level of unemployment misses another large element of the picture. There has been an unfortunate tendency to measure the degree of utilization of capacity by the degree to which there is full employment, but recent developments in our economic system have been in the direction of increasing the proportion of overhead labor. Automation, for instance, demands technicians rather than operatives. Even when the level of operation falls considerably below capacity, technicians are still necessary to maintain and repair the machines, and employment cannot be cut down as much as output falls. A considerable drop in the utilization of capacity thus may occur with small changes in unemployment. Similarly, in certain parts of the economy that are growing in importance, such as communications, public utilities, transportation and retail trade, employment does not vary significantly with short-run variations in output. As the utilization of capacity is increased, the efficiency with which the already employed labor is used also increases. Thus, from 1949 to 1950, man-hours employed increased 2.4 percent, while output increased 10.5 percent. Unemployment only dropped from 5.9 to 5.3 percent of the civilian labor force.

In terms of opportunity costs, the question is how much lower our standard of living is than it could be if the economy were operating at a reasonable level of capacity. The inequities involved are in missed opportunities for a higher standard of living for a large proportion of the people. For example, the lost production in the recession of 1958 was very considerable and exceeded what would normally be estimated by looking at the unemployment figures. The Board of Governors of the Federal Reserve System prepares a combined index of the degree of capacity utilization in industries producing such major materials as iron and steel, aluminum, copper, cotton yarn, synthetic fabrics, cement, wood pulp, paper, petroleum products, coke and industrial chemicals. At the beginning of 1958, the combined capacity in these industries exceeded output by about 35 percent. It is true that these were some of the industries that were hardest hit, but they represent a substantial proportion of the private economy. The Federal Reserve Board index of industrial production indicates that in the first quarter of 1958 industrial production was at the level which had previously been attained five and a half years before, in the last quarter of 1952. Furthermore, when fewer goods are produced, the output of retail and wholesale distribution will also fall. For the economy as a whole, it is not unrealistic to suggest that output was a good 20–25 percent below physical capacity. At current prices, this means that we could have produced one hundred billion dollars' worth of goods and services more than we did.

Given an estimate of this magnitude, the question naturally arises whether we would have had the capacity in terms of manpower as well as plant and equipment to produce such an additional volume of goods. Unemployment was about 7 percent of the labor force. The length of the average work week, however, dropped by another 4 or 5 percent, so that the total level of unemployment, taking part-time work into account, might have been as high as 10 or 12 percent. Moreover, the labor force grew more slowly owing to lack of employment opportunities than would be normal for good times. During 1957, the labor force increased by only 0.6 percent. With full employment an additional 2 percent increase in the labor force could have been expected. Taking all of these figures together, man-hours could probably have increased at least 10 or 12 percent without exceeding the full employment level. This would still leave 2 or 3 percent frictional unemployment.

Could such a 10–12 percent increase in man-hours result in a 25 percent increase in output if, as already suggested, the physical capacity to produce such output exists? An answer to this question may be sought by looking at the relationship between the changes in man-hours and the changes in output that have actually occurred in years of recovery from a recession or depression. In the most striking instance, a 2.4 percent increase in man-hours in 1950 achieved a 10 percent increase in output. In the least favorable case, a 3.5 percent increase in man–hours in 1955 resulted in a 7.9 percent increase in output. Thus the increase in output generated per man-hour exceeded that which would be needed to produce an increase of one hundred billion dollars in output, given 1958 unemployment.

For 1960, it now begins to appear that the economy may be in a recession equal to if not larger than the 1958 recession. Unemployment is now (October 1960) estimated at 6.4 percent of the labor force and this figure is expected to increase in the next few months.

The severity of postwar recessions has, of course, been sharply reduced by the automatic stabilizers that have evolved. In the 1958 recession, the $18 billion fall in gross national product resulted in a drop of only $4 billion in personal disposable income. The fall in corporate profits and in government revenue and the increase in transfer payments absorbed three-quarters of the total decline. Insofar as disposable income and consumer expenditures are insulated from sharp declines in output, the spiral will not be reinforced by declines in consumer spending. The decline in gross national product will be lessened and the recession will not be as deep.

But these same stabilizers not only prevent income from going down; they also stabilize it in an upward direction, making it difficult for gross national product to rise. The gross national product rose significantly in 1951, 1955 and

1959. The year 1951 reflects the Korean boom. The years 1955 and 1959 were periods of recovery from recession. The increase in gross national product in 1951 was larger than that for either 1955 or 1959. The reason for this was that the government's expenditures increased by $21.4 billion in 1951, in contrast with an increase of only $0.5 billion for 1955 and 1959.

The years 1955 and 1959 were remarkably similar in the magnitude of the increase in gross national product, the manner in which it was generated and the way it was distributed. In both years, the rise in producers' expenditures on durable goods and inventories sparked the rise and accounted for about 45 percent of the total increase. Tax rates were not changed during these years, yet the government received, as increased tax revenues, 37 percent of the increase of gross national product and government surplus increased by $10 billion. Income retained by producers increased by $6.5 billion. Although consumers received about $20 billion of additional income, their saving actually decreased so that consumer expenditures rose by more than disposable income.

In other words, taxes and profits syphoned off more than 50 percent of the increase in gross national product, and prevented the upward movement from becoming larger. This may lesson the danger of demand inflation, but it may also prevent the economy from achieving full utilization of its potential capacity. Looking at it another way, the income generated by private economic activity may not be sufficient to buy the product of that activity if the government removes 37 percent of these funds as it did in these periods, and does not return an equivalent amount to the economy. In other words, growth in an upswing may be frustrated before it can take place because of the syphoning off of the increase in income by increased tax payments. We are, in fact, in the position of being strangled by automatic stabilizers. The result is not stability, but recession.

The problem of secular price stability is not independent of this dilemma of automatic stabilizers and growth. The dampening effect of the automatic stabilizers has resulted, when coupled with the inevitable recession, in a low rate of productivity increase. Low rates of productivity increase, coupled with even moderate increase in wages, will result in the long run in steady price increases caused by rising costs. To the extent that the higher costs and prices mean a higher gross national product in money terms for the same level of output, growth becomes even more difficult, since the automatic stabilizers operate on the level of money flows in the economy rather than on the amount of real output. Thus we are caught in a vicious circle where low productivity means higher wage costs, and higher wage costs mean rising prices, and rising prices mean, given the automatic stabilizers, further dampening of growth.

Many economists imply that an economy operating close to capacity will be under more demand pressure than one where growth is dampened, and thus that the secular price rise in such a case would tend to be accelerated. This argument overlooks the role of productivity in the price mechanism. At high levels of capacity utilization, the economy is more efficient and productive and a high level of investment tends to ensure the continuation of productivity increases in future periods. The last few years are eloquent testimony to the fact that cost-inspired price rises can be appreciable even where there is excess capacity. In contrast, the considerable rise in output in 1955 was achieved without significant price rise, despite a relatively high level of demand.

Nevertheless, the attempts to stop rising prices have employed primarily policies that are appropriate for demand inflation rather than for rising costs. Specifically, it has been argued that the economy was spending too much and that what was required was monetary controls to prevent consumers and business from overspending. Such policies would only succeed in stopping the price rise if they prevented wages from continuing to rise faster than productivity. In a situation where businessmen expect good profits, are making investments that would yield increases in productivity and generally believe in extending markets, they are apt to give in to labor's demands for wage increases. Labor, similarly, is likely to make significant demands on the grounds that such wage increases are justified, given the level of profits and the optimistic expectations of the future.

To stop the wage rise by monetary means, it is necessary to reverse these expectations, to make businessmen hesitant about giving wage increases, and labor less insistent about asking for them. But such a result is not healthy for the economy either. It will not only retard wage increases, but because it makes businessmen pessimistic about the future, it will make them unwilling to undertake investments to increase productivity and provide for growth. When a price rise is not accompanied by excessive demand, tight money can achieve stability in prices only at the cost of reducing the rate of growth of the economy and perhaps risking stagnation. There is no assurance that a tight money policy will slow down the increase of wages more than it will dampen productivity increases and the investment needed to provide for an expanding output. In fact, if productivity is more sensitive than wages to depressed conditions, a tight money policy may, in the initial stages before it results in unemployment, not reduce the price rise at all, but rather, by retarding productivity gains more than wages, cause an actual increase in wage cost which in turn will necessitate additional price rises. Thus a tight money policy may well be self-defeating. The very elements that permit wages to increase are the same things that stimulate investment and increase productivity. The use of monetary policy to prevent wage increases may also kill the goose that lays the golden egg.

What, then, is the solution to this problem of chronic recessions, slow growth and secular price rise? The wellspring of our economic growth and productivity increase lies in the investment that we are willing to make in productive plant and equipment. For the immediate future, an expanded level of investment of a productivity-increasing nature would help to cure the present recession by providing additional demand in the hard-hit durable goods industries. An increase in consumer expenditures achieved by tax reductions, on the other hand, would be likely to go into other sectors of the economy, such as services and nondurables, where demand has not fallen to the same degree.

Similarly, even expanded public works might tend to cause excess demand in the construction sector of the economy, without spreading fully to other types of durable goods and equipment. From a longer-range point of view, stimulation of the right kind of investment would increase productivity and this in turn would tend to lessen the rise in wage cost and thus in prices, and at the same time the expansion of capacity in productivity would make possible a higher rate of growth. I do not mean to suggest that there should be no tax reductions. It may well be that as additional capacity is generated, some stimulation of consumer demand would be required. Similarly, I do not wish to suggest that there should be no increase in public expenditures. There are many pressing needs in the economy for such things as urban renewal, highways, education and health, but there are good reasons why, in addition, we should expand investment of a productivity-increasing nature beyond the level it has averaged in the postwar period. Our rate of growth in this period has been small relative to many other countries' and this will inevitably be taken as a reflection on the efficiency of our system. Countries just entering the stage of economic development may well question whether a system such as ours would be adaptable for their needs. Furthermore, we may well require in the coming period more resources than would be available to us if we continued at our present rate of growth. Problems, not only of defense, but of world economic development and a rising standard of living should lead to growing drains upon our future output. A growing economy permits adjustments to take place easily, but if growth is so slow that the demands upon our resources exceed our available output, frictions are bound to develop.

If for these reasons a high level of investment is the desirable goal, how can it be attained under present conditions? In this connection we can learn from the experience of other countries in dealing with this problem. A number of other industrial countries have used various forms of accelerated depreciation or fast tax write-off quite successfully to stimulate investment.

In some cases the charge-what-you-wish system, as in Sweden, proved to be such a powerful stimulant that the level of investment had to be held in check by a supplementary tax. The United Kingdom, a few years ago, tried a system of giving an initial allowance of 40 percent of capital expenditure, chargeable against profit in the first year. Over the life of the asset, an amount equal to 120 percent of the original purchase price could be charged off. Such a device, of course, amounts to direct subsidy, and it may not be necessary or desirable to go that far. Care would have to be exercised that less productive forms of investment were not unduly stimulated and that the fast tax write-off did not degenerate into a major tax loop-hole.

In summary, I would like to reemphasize the point that the problems of recurrent recession, secular price rise, and low rates of growth are all highly interrelated and should not be considered separately. To this end, serious consideration should be given to raising the level of investment. Such a step would not only increase demand in a part of the economy which is presently hard hit, but would also lessen the pressure of cost on prices and stimulate long-run growth. The use of fast tax write-offs as a device for encouraging investment would constitute a significant offset to the automatic stabilizers in the upward direction, since corporate profits and profit taxes are the largest elements in such stabilizers. It may be, of course, that fast tax write-offs would in some periods prove too powerful a tonic for investment. In such cases, a supplementary investment tax or variation in the speed of write-off might be used to keep investment at a viable level, in much the same manner that the Federal Reserve System now controls the availability of credit and the rate of investment.

14. Chronic Inflation in the United States, 1950–73

Nancy D. Ruggles and Richard Ruggles
United Nations and Yale University

Felipe Pazos's study of chronic inflation in Latin America does more than analyze the historic relation of prices, output and employment in specific Latin American countries: it provides a different and more appropriate way of viewing the inflationary process. First, and perhaps most important, Pazos emphasizes that the long duration of the inflationary processes in Latin America makes it clear that the price increases are not merely temporary disturbances. Rather, they are chronic phenomena that have developed self-perpetuating mechanisms to keep them going, as well as compensatory devices that make them tolerable for the societies in which they occur. He points out that such chronic price rises do not have many of the features generally associated with inflations. Over a period of 20 years or more, an economy cannot be expected to be continuously overstimulated, or real wages continuously reduced. Such features, which are conventionally associated with the inflationary process, reflect essentially short-term disequilibria that cannot be maintained for many years. Thus Pazos argues very persuasively that the chronic inflation observed in Latin America does not entail the behavior or the consequences predicted by the conventional macroeconomic models of inflation.

The usefulness of the Latin American experience for analyzing inflation in the United States depends upon whether the mechanisms operating in the Latin American countries are similar to those operating in the United States, where the increases in prices are considerably more moderate. It is distinctly possible that the more moderate price fluctuations to which the United States is subject may be similar in basic character to those observed for the Latin American countries. The purpose of this paper, therefore, is to examine the evidence

This chapter first appeared in Carlos Diaz-Alejandro, S. Teitel and V. E. Tokman (eds), *Politica Economica en Centro y Periferia*, Fondo de Cultura Economica, Mexico, 1976.

further to see what the chronic inflations experienced by Latin American countries indicate about the mechanism of prices, output and employment, and whether the price fluctuation in the United States during the last two decades is similar in its mechanisms to that found for Latin American countries.

1. THE LATIN AMERICAN EXPERIENCE

Pazos finds that one of the basic characteristics of the chronic inflations in Latin America is that the substantial annual price increases are not very closely related to fluctuations in output. The annual changes in prices and output for Argentina, Brazil, Chile and Uruguay shown in Table 14.1 for the period 1950–70 strongly support this view.

The average annual rates of price increase for these countries are quite similar, ranging from 26 to 31 percent, but the average growth rates are very different, ranging from a low of 1.5 percent for Chile to a high of 5.7 percent

Table 14.1 Annual Changes in Prices and Real GNP, 1949–70 (percent change in cost of living and real GNP from preceding year)

	Argentina		Brazil		Chile		Uruguay	
Year	Price	Real GNP	Price	Real GNP	Price	Real GNP	Price	Real GNP
1949	31	−4.6	5	5.6	19	−0.6	5	3.5
1950	26	1.5	9	5.0	15	4.8	−5	3.1
1951	37	3.9	12	5.1	22	4.3	12	8.2
1952	39	−5.0	17	5.6	22	5.7	17	−5.3
1953	4	5.4	14	3.2	26	5.2	5	6.5
1954	4	4.0	22	7.7	56	0.4	5	5.7
1955	12	7.2	23	6.8	76	−0.1	8	1.6
1956	13	2.8	21	1.9	66	0.6	7	1.7
1957	25	5.1	16	6.9	29	10.5	15	1.0
1958	32	6.3	15	6.6	26	2.7	18	−3.6
1959	114	−6.6	39	7.3	39	−0.5	40	−2.8
1960	27	8.0	29	6.7	12	6.5	39	3.3
1961	14	7.1	33	7.3	8	6.1	23	1.9
1962	26	−1.7	52	5.4	14	4.9	11	−2.6
1963	26	−2.4	70	1.6	44	4.7	21	−2.0
1964	22	10.4	92	3.1	46	4.1	43	4.1
1965	29	9.2	66	3.9	29	5.0	57	0.9
1966	32	0.7	41	4.4	23	7.0	74	2.6
1967	29	1.0	31	5.0	18	2.3	89	−5.7
1968	16	4.6	22	8.4	27	2.9	125	0.2
1969	8	7.9	22	9.0	31	3.1	21	5.3
1970	14	4.8	23	9.5	33	1.7	16	4.6
Average	26	3.5	30	5.7	31	3.6	29	1.5

Source: Felipe Pazos (1974), Table 7, p. 31.

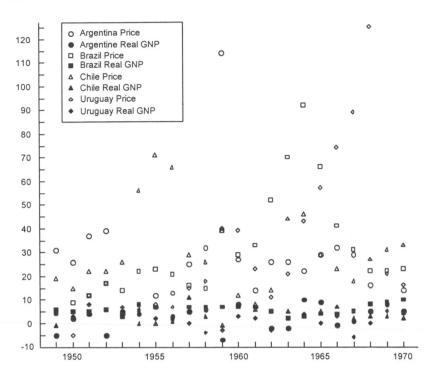

Figure 14.1 Price and Real GNP Changes, 1949–70

for Brazil. Within each country, the year-to-year fluctuations in price and output are quite large, but a scatter diagram (Figure 14.1) reveals no meaningful
relation between price and output changes.

The slight negative r^2s which do result from correlating price and output
changes (Argentina, −0.34; Brazil, −0.18; Chile, −0.26; Uruguay, −0.10) are
primarily due, in Pazos's view, to the exchange crises and/or the deflationary
monetary and fiscal policies which accompany extreme price increases. Aside
from the declines or stagnation in output which accompany the periods of
largest price increases, there does not appear to be any significant relationship
between the changes in prices and the changes in output. In any event, there
is clearly no positive relationship; the hypothesis that the price increases in
these Latin American economies reflect aggregate demand pressure does not
seem to be borne out. Nor does there appear to be any evidence that the inflationary process is one in which an initial excess demand sets off a price–cost
spiral which ultimately results in hyperinflation and collapse.

Unfortunately, it is difficult to relate the changes in prices to changes in
wages in Latin America, since the evidence is deficient. Data on money wages

are very fragmentary; often they refer only to the legal minimum wage, and how well this corresponds to changes in money wages for the economy as a whole is not known. The changes in the official minimum wage rates are of the same general magnitude as the changes in prices, since governments take the price changes into account in setting the minimum official wage, but there is no precise information on the behavior of real wages. However, both the official minimum wages and collective wage agreements are often tied to the cost-of-living price index, thus automatically building a wage–price spiral into the system. The fact that certain sectors of the economy are not covered by such agreements may reduce the strength of this relationship, but even the non-covered sectors are likely to be strongly influenced by what is taking place in the covered sectors of the economy.

The relation of money wages to the level of employment is even less clear. Although the level of unemployment in these Latin American countries is known to be substantial, reliable information on the change in unemployment from year to year does not exist for most countries. Pazos does present some data 'for Argentina and Chile which demonstrate a lack of relationship between wage changes and unemployment levels. He argues, however, that such evidence does not refute the Phillips curve analysis, because unemployment in these countries is always at levels where the Phillips curve is supposed to be flat. Nevertheless, the Phillips curve must be discounted as an explanation of wage–price behavior for Argentina and Chile, since a wide variety of changes in money wage rates is found for many observed levels of unemployment.

The Monetarist and Structuralist Explanations of Inflation

The traditional explanations of inflation in Latin America have usually been cast in either monetary or structural terms. The monetarists have sought to explain the inflation by laying the blame on monetary instability or fiscal irresponsibility. It is argued that inappropriate monetary expansion permits large wage increases, and large government deficits expand aggregate demand beyond the level of available resources. The structuralists, on the other hand, lay primary blame on sectoral bottlenecks which generate price increases as the rest of the economy grows and population increases. Two sectors are usually singled out as the culprits. Agriculture is seen as a sluggish sector which cannot provide the basic food requirements for an expanding economy; the consequent rise of agricultural prices triggers an inflationary response. The foreign trade sector is also seen in many cases as causing sectoral imbalance, due to the behavior of export prices for raw materials and agricultural products, on the one hand, and the import prices of highly fabricated goods, on the other. The structuralists also point out that with economic growth import demands grow faster than export industries, thus bringing pressure upon the exchange rate which in turn results in internal inflationary pressures.

Pazos's Explanation of Chronic Inflation

Pazos considers the role of both monetary and structural factors in the inflationary process in Latin America. He recognizes that in specific instances these factors may play a significant part, but he sees them as the end result of the process rather than, as stated by their proponents, the basic underlying causes. It is Pazos's view that there is a multiplicity of causes which can trigger a chronic inflation, but that the central problem is why and how the chronic inflation achieves its continuity. In other words, both internal and external disturbances may have an impact upon the economic system, but what needs to be explained is why the reaction of the economies in Latin America is such that these result in chronic inflation.

According to Pazos, the essential part of the mechanism of chronic inflation lies in the determination of wage contracts and other commitments. He points out that labor contracts and other time commitments (such as contracts for materials) are fairly evenly scattered through time, and since in the Latin American economies labor contracts are negotiated on the basis of the change in cost of living, and other contracts are often related to other prices, wages and materials costs are raised in accordance with the prior rise in prices. Producers' costs reflect these increases, and this in turn is again reflected in higher prices. The interaction of wages, costs, and prices is therefore such as to ensure continuous wage and price increases.

In contrast, Pazos considers that changes in aggregate demand have much more of an effect on the quantity of output and the volume of imports than on prices, except when full capacity is approached. Until productive capacity is approached (which Pazos points out has seldom if ever occurred in the four countries studied) or import capacity is reached (which has occurred more frequently), the expansion in aggregate demand above the rise in costs is not met by price rises, but by increases in output and imports. In fact, Pazos points out that the rise in prices frequently decelerates when output is increasing because cost per unit decreases with fuller utilization of capacity and increased productivity. Only when import capacity is reached does the expansion in demand bring about an acceleration of price rises, first of import prices and then of all prices. When aggregate demand increases by a smaller proportion than the rise in costs, enterprises restrict sales and output rather than reducing their prices. This leads to a decline in output. With this decline, costs per unit of output rise, and productivity becomes stagnant, giving a further push to prices.

In Pazos's model, the factors influencing changes in aggregate demand are much the same as those which operate in economies with mild inflation or no inflation at all, such as private investment, public expenditure, taxes, saving and foreign trade. The one difference he sees is that in the countries with chronic inflation which he is examining, monetary policy works much more rapidly, owing to the lower cash ratio at which the economy operates and its continuous need for larger amounts of money. Monetary policy is therefore very effective in inducing contraction and expansion in real investment and consumption. However, since it operates entirely through aggregate demand it is not effective in decelerating price rises.

Pazos, in summarizing, states that his model has been devised to fit a number of facts that are not explained well by other theories. These he lists as follows:

1. Continuation of price and wage rises throughout wide fluctuations in the volume of production, which swing from deep contractions to rapid expansions.
2. Continuation of price and wage rises throughout wide fluctuations in exports, agricultural production, and capital inflows.
3. Continuation of price rises in the face of unused production capacity.
4. Continuation of wage rises in the face of heavy unemployment.
5. Lack of correlation between price rises and budget deficits.
6. Low correlation in some countries between price rises and monetary expansion. And finally,
7. Odd behavior of stock market quotations.

It will be useful now to turn to the United States experience during the period 1950–72 to see whether the United States experienced in lower degree similar price and output fluctuations, and whether Pazos's description of the process is valid for the United States economy.

2. UNITED STATES EXPERIENCE

Price and Output Relationship

The US economy has, of course, not experienced the large price increases which characterized the four countries in Latin America. As indicated in Table 14.2 and Figure 14.2, the changes in prices and output which have occurred do not seem to bear much relation to each other.

The first price rise in the 1950s took place at the outbreak of the Korean War in 1951, at a time when there was substantial unemployment and the economy was operating considerably below full capacity. Output and prices both rose sharply. There is little doubt but that fear of possible future shortages,

*Table 14.2 Implicit Price Deflators of GNP and GNP in 1958 Dollars,
United States, 1950–73 (percentage change from preceding
period)*

Year	Implicit price deflator	GNP in 1958 dollars	Year	Implicit price deflator	GNP in 1958 dollars
1950	1.3	9.6	1962	1.1	6.6
1951	6.8	7.9	1963	1.3	4.0
1952	2.1	3.0	1964	1.6	5.4
1953	1.0	4.5	1965	1.8	6.3
1954	1.5	−1.4	1966	2.8	6.5
1955	1.4	7.6	1967	3.2	2.6
1956	3.4	1.8	1968	4.0	4.7
1957	3.7	1.5	1969	4.8	2.7
1958	2.5	−1.1	1970	5.5	−0.5
1959	1.7	6.4	1971	4.7	2.7
1960	1.6	2.5	1972	3.2	6.1
1961	1.3	1.9	1973	5.3	5.9
			Average	2.7	4.0

Source: *Economic Report of the President*, February 1974; Implicit Price Deflators, Table C4, p. 254; GNP in 1958 Dollars, Table C2, p. 250

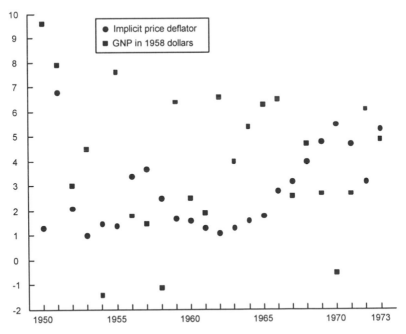

Figure 14.2 Price and Real GNP Changes, United States, 1950–73

largely induced by memories of World War II, forced prices up as both producers and consumers bought up existing stocks of goods to ensure future supplies. As production increased and shortages did not materialize, the rate of price increase slackened.

The next period of significant price increase was from 1956 to 1958. At the time, this caused considerable public debate and several Congressional inquiries were undertaken. Some economists blamed the price rise on a lagged response to the expansion of demand in 1954 and 1955, and a generally tight economy. In view of the slower overall rate of growth, however, other economists blamed excess sectoral demand: specifically, it was alleged that lack of capacity in the heavy industries generated price responses in these industries which then spread to the whole economy. Still others blamed the price rise primarily on costs rather than demand, especially wage increases which exceeded productivity gains. Although considerable heat was generated by these controversies, no generally accepted explanation emerged.

In the period 1963–65, a high rate of growth was accompanied by an exceptionally low rate of price increase. In terms of price–output behavior, it was argued, on the one hand, that the large increases in output generated large productivity gains which more than offset wage increases. On the other hand, it was also argued that what was taking place was a gradual absorption of the underutilized capacity that resulted from the slow growth and recessions of the late 1950s, so that throughout the early 1960s the economy was only catching up to full capacity.

From 1967 to 1970, the rate of price increase accelerated, despite the slower increase in output. It was argued by some economists that the Vietnam War had led to excess demand, and that the rapid output increases of the early 1960s had to come to an end as full capacity was approached. The large price increase in 1970 was again attributed to a lagged response to earlier increases in demand. Although it does appear that agricultural prices did respond to demand inspired by the Vietnam War, there is no clear support for the thesis that the economy at this time was pressing on full capacity. The largest price increase occurred in 1970, when output actually declined.

Since 1971, rates of price increase higher than those previously experienced have continued, accompanied in 1972 and 1973 by relatively high output increases. Special contributory factors of high wheat prices due to world supply conditions and high oil prices due to the Middle East War have been held responsible for much of the price increase. Nevertheless, the official government position has been that there is general excess demand, and that it is this that has been responsible for rising prices. However, the price increase continued unabated in late 1973 and 1974 despite actual output declines, and this has led to some questioning of whether excess demand has indeed been responsible.

Thus the lack of close relation between the behavior of prices and that of output which Pazos observed for Latin American countries also seems to be reflected in the US data. The price increases are of a much lower order of magnitude in the United States than in Latin America, but the causes of fluctuations in relative prices seem to be as much in doubt for the United States as they are for the Latin American countries.

It is very probable that the average level of price increase shown in Table 14.2 is overstated; the introduction of new products and technological changes which permit the improvement of existing products are not adequately reflected in the price indexes. This happens because specification pricing is used to determine price changes, and thus only existing products with unchanged specifications enter into the price measurements. Even a little reflecting on the impact of new products such as radio, television and air conditioning, and technical improvements resulting from the development of plastics, transistors, printed circuits, etc. will indicate the importance of these developments. Given the importance of technology and new products, it is not unreasonable to suggest that the price indexes may be overstated by at least 2 percent a year. If this criterion were applied to the data shown in Table 14.2, there would have been price declines in 11 out of the 24 years shown, and the rate of economic growth would be 50 percent greater. It is quite possible, therefore, that if prices were measured correctly, the United States economy could not be characterized as having had continuous price increases, and from this point of view it would not be correct to characterize the price behavior of the United States economy in the last two decades as chronic inflation.

Nevertheless, from the point of view of many consumers, chronic inflation in the cost of living seems to be a reality. On the one hand, they find that certain expenses such as bus fares and doctors' bills continue to increase sharply over time, and the prices of old familiar products also seem to rise continuously. On the other hand, the introduction of new products and quality improvements do not take the form of observable price reductions so that, for all practical purposes, chronic inflation in the cost of living does seem to be taking place. As was noted for Latin America, the different rates of price increase do not appear to be closely related to fluctuations in output, so that the basic factors responsible for year-to-year price changes in the United States may not be different from those observed for the Latin American countries. Furthermore, during the last five years the price increases in the economy have been larger than can be accounted for by quality change, and it may well be that the US economy during this most recent period has suffered from a somewhat milder form of the same type of chronic inflation which Latin America has had for much longer.

Wage–Price Relationships

Examination of the relationship between wages and prices is much easier for the United States than for Latin America, since better data are available. In recent years, the Council of Economic Advisers has published data on changes in compensation per man-hour, output per man-hour, unit labor cost, and the implicit price deflator for the private nonfarm sector of the national economy. These figures are given in Table 14.3.

Table 14.3   *Compensation per Man-hour, Output per Man-hour, Unit Labor Cost and Implicit Price Deflator for the Private Nonfarm Sector of United States Economy, 1950–73 (percent change from preceding period)*

Year	Compensation per man-hour	Output per man-hour	Unit labor cost	Implicit price deflator	Year	Compensation per man-hour	Output per man-hour	Unit labor cost	Implicit price deflator
1950	5.5	6.3	−0.8	1.1	1962	4.0	4.6	−0.5	0.9
1951	8.7	2.0	6.6	6.5	1963	3.6	3.1	0.5	1.2
1952	5.5	0.9	4.5	2.6	1964	4.7	3.7	1.0	1.3
1953	5.6	2.9	2.6	1.8	1965	3.7	2.9	0.8	1.4
1954	3.2	2.3	0.9	1.7	1966	6.1	3.5	2.5	2.2
1955	3.5	4.4	−0.9	1.3	1967	5.7	1.6	4.0	3.3
1956	5.8	−0.6	6.4	3.4	1968	7.3	2.9	4.3	3.5
1957	5.7	2.2	3.4	3.7	1969	7.0	−0.1	7.2	4.5
1958	3.8	2.5	1.3	1.7	1970	7.3	0.7	6.6	5.0
1959	4.3	3.4	0.9	1.8	1971	7.0	4.0	2.8	4.4
1960	4.1	1.2	2.8	1.4	1972	6.9	4.2	2.6	2.3
1961	3.2	3.0	0.2	0.9	1973	7.6	3.1	4.4	4.0
					Avg.	5.3	2.3	2.6	2.5

Source: Economic Report of the President, February 1974, Table C-33, p. 287.

Over the 23 years examined, compensation per man-hour rose by an average of 5.3 percent per year, whereas output per man-hour increased by only 2.3 percent per year. This meant that unit labor costs rose on average by 2.6 percent per year, and it is interesting to note that the implicit price deflator for the private nonfarm sector rose by a similar amount (2.5 percent per year). In other words, for the period as a whole, according to the implicit price deflator, the increase in prices in the private nonfarm sector was equal to the difference between the increase in wages and the increase in productivity. The year-to-year correspondence between unit labor cost and the implicit price deflator is also high, but changes in the implicit price deflator show considerably less variance than do those in unit labor costs. At no time did the implicit price deflator decline, but unit labor costs declined in 1950, 1955 and 1962. Similarly, in some periods when unit labor costs rose substantially, the rise was not fully reflected in the implicit price deflator. Thus in 1956 unit labor costs rose 6.4 percent, while the implicit price deflator rose only 3.4 percent, and in 1969 unit labor costs rose 7.2 percent while the implicit price deflator rose only 4.5 percent. Nevertheless, productivity changes, by directly affecting unit labor costs, do affect the year-to-year behavior of prices.

The role of productivity in determining relative prices can also be seen in the data on consumer prices. For the most part, it may be presumed that durable consumer goods such as automobiles, television sets, refrigerators and other household appliances are produced in industries where technological changes and economies of scale operate in such a manner as to generate large productivity increases. In contrast, in many of the service industries, individuals are employed in providing personal services to the public, such as public transportation, barber shops, laundries, domestic service, medicine, recreation, etc. In these industries productivity change is much less rapid. Table 14.4 shows the consumer price index changes from 1950 to 1972 for durable goods and for services other than rent.

Table 14.4 Consumer Price Indexes for Durable Goods and for Services, United States, 1950–73 (percent change from preceding period)

Year	Durable goods	Services (less rent)	Year	Durable goods	Service (less rent)	Year	Durable goods	Services (less rent)
1950	1.0	2.8	1958	1.5	4.2	1966	0.1	4.1
1951	7.6	6.0	1959	1.5	3.4	1967	1.5	4.7
1952	1.0	4.7	1960	−0.5	3.7	1968	3.1	5.7
1953	−0.7	4.1	1961	−0.1	2.4	1969	3.7	7.6
1954	−2.5	2.9	1962	1.0	1.9	1970	4.5	8.6
1955	−2.0	2.3	1963	0.3	2.1	1971	4.2	5.7
1956	0.0	2.7	1964	0.9	2.2	1972	2.1	3.9
1957	3.2	4.6	1965	−0.4	2.5	1973	2.5	4.3
						Avg.	1.3	4.0

Source: *Economic Report of the President*, February 1974, Table C-45, p. 301.

The difference in the price behavior for these two series reflects to a considerable degree productivity differences. It should be noted, however, that the differences in the observed price behavior for different sectors may, in part, be illusionary due to the difficulties in measuring quality change that have already been discussed in connection with the implicit price deflator of the gross private nonfarm product. In the case of durable goods, no allowance is made for new products or the substantial improvement in quality which has occurred in many existing products. On the other hand, services also exclude quality improvements and the use of new techniques in the provision of services such as the use of computers, new drugs, or the increase in medical knowledge. Nevertheless, the observed differences in productivity change are obviously an important element in explaining how price indexes behave.

Wage–Employment Relationships

The question of what determines the behavior of money wage rates is of central importance to an explanation of the inflationary process. It is often suggested that the Phillips curve, which relates the change in money wages to the level of unemployment, provides an adequate explanation: at high levels of unemployment the excess supply of labor keeps the money wage rate down, and at low levels of unemployment the bidding for the limited supply of labor by producers forces money wage rates upward.

The appeal of the Phillips curve explanation is its apparent reasonableness. The empirical support for the hypothesis, however, leaves much to be desired. The evidence for the whole economy is shown in Table 14.5 and Figure 14.3. From this, no very clear picture emerges. Although it is true that the relatively low increases in average hourly earnings in the early 1960s occurred in a period of relatively high unemployment, it is also true that in the last few years unemployment levels which are similarly high have been accompanied by large

Table 14.5 *Changes in Average Hourly Earnings, Unemployment Levels and Changes in Employment, United States, 1950–73 (changes expressed as percent of preceding year)*

Year	Changes in avg. hourly earnings Current dollars	1967 dollars	Unemployment as % of labor force	Changes in employment	Year	Changes in avg. hourly earnings Current dollars	1967 dollars	Unemployment as % of labor force	Changes in employment
1950	3.7	2.7	5.3	2.3	1962	3.3	2.2	5.5	1.5
1951	7.4	−0.4	3.3	1.9	1963	2.9	1.6	5.7	1.6
1952	5.0	2.8	3.0	0.5	1964	3.1	1.7	5.2	2.2
1953	5.7	4.9	2.9	1.7	1965	3.7	2.0	4.5	2.6
1954	3.5	3.0	5.5	−1.8	1966	4.0	1.2	3.8	2.5
1955	3.2	3.7	4.4	3.5	1967	4.6	1.6	3.8	2.0
1956	5.2	3.7	4.1	2.6	1968	6.6	2.3	3.6	2.0
1957	4.9	1.3	4.3	0.5	1969	6.6	1.2	3.5	2.6
1958	4.1	1.3	6.8	−1.7	1970	6.7	0.7	4.9	0.9
1959	3.6	2.7	5.5	2.5	1971	7.0	2.6	5.9	0.6
1960	3.4	1.8	5.5	1.9	1972	6.3	3.0	5.6	3.3
1961	3.1	2.0	6.7	0.0	1973	6.0	0.0	4.9	3.3
					Avg.	4.7	2.2	4.8	1.5

Source: *Economic Report of the President*, February 1974: Average Hourly Earnings, Table C-30, p. 284; Unemployment, Table C-26, p. 279; Employment, Table C-24, p. 220.

Price Behavior

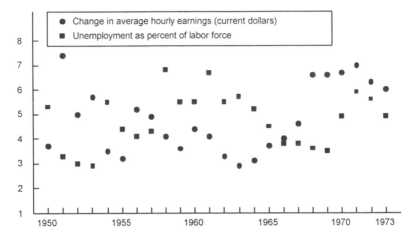

Figure 14.3 Change in Average Hourly Earnings and Level of
Unemployment, United States, 1950–73

wage increases. The proponents of the trade-off hypothesis suggest that there has been a shift of the Phillips curve upward, but the wide scatter in the relationship even before the most recent period does not suggest any clearly definable relationship. It seems highly probable that a wide variety of different hypotheses would be consistent with the observed aggregate data on average hourly earning and unemployment levels.

Price–Cost Behavior of Manufacturing Establishments

Considerable insight into the mechanism of price change can be obtained by analyzing the price–cost behavior of specific producers under different economic conditions. Aggregative data by their very nature reflect the combined effect of behavioral and structural changes and so cannot distinguish among alternative hypotheses relating to microeconomic behavior. But if valid economic models are to be developed to explain the inflationary process, more information on the price–cost behavior of producers at different phases of the inflationary process is required.

For the period 1954–59, a special study was made of the price–cost behavior of manufacturing establishments in the United States. This study was jointly sponsored by the Social Science Research Committee and the Bureau of the Census. The basic data used for this study were the individual establishment reports (approximately 80,000) collected each year by the Bureau of the Census for the Annual Survey of Manufactures. The data for identical establishments were linked from year to year, so that the price–cost behavior of each establishment could be examined. For most years, the percentage of the sample which was successfully matched was quite high — around 90 percent. But for the link from 1957 to 1958, when a new sample was introduced, the matched establishments fell to approximately 60 percent. In addition to the establishment data, some broader industry data at the 4-digit classification level were developed. In particular, output price indexes and material price indexes were created from the existing wholesale price information.

For each establishment, the basic data on value of shipments, inventories, cost of materials, production workers' wages, man-hours, salaries and employment were processed to generate: the change in output as measured by double-deflated value added; the change in employment as measured by full-time equivalent employees; the change in average hourly earnings as measured by production workers' wages divided by man–hours; the change in real value added per man-hour; and the price–cost behavior of establishments as measured by the first difference change in their gross margins. Gross margin is defined as the amount by which the value of output exceeds direct costs. Direct costs in this context refer to cost of materials and production workers' wages. If the prices of an establishment's products are rising faster than its combined material and labor costs, its gross margin will increase. On the other hand, if material prices and labor costs per unit together rise at a faster rate than price per unit, margins will decline. It is important to note that this price–cost behavior can be observed even in the absence of price information for specific establishments, since the gross margin computed from the total value of product, materials costs, and production workers' wages is equivalent to the mark-up of price above unit direct costs. Value added weights were used to combine the establishment measurements into indexes for all of manufacturing. The results of this computation for manufacturing establishments are shown in Table 14.6.

Table 14.6 Manufacturing Establishment Behavior, United States, 1954–59

	1954–55	1955–56	1956–57	1957–58	1958–59	1955–59
Output price index	2.2	4.6	3.4	1.5	1.2	11.3
Materials price index	2.4	4.8	2.6	1.0	1.2	11.0
Output (real value added)	15.1	6.2	–1.2	–13.9	13.1	6.2
Employment (full-time equivalent)	6.6	1.7	0.0	–9.1	6.6	–5.3
Average hourly earnings	4.3	6.6	6.8	7.2	4.2	22.5
Real valued added per man-hour	9.7	17.5	7.1	–3.1	7.9	19.7
Gross margin (1st difference change)	0.2	1.1	–1.7	–5.4	–0.8	0.3
Level of gross margin as percentage of value of product in initial year	32.3	33.0	37.3	38.2	34.9	32.8

Source: Matched Establishment Data Files, Decile Tabulations, Annual Survey of Manufacturers, United States Bureau of the Census.

As was observed in the data for the private nonfarm sector, there is also considerable year-to-year variation in the manufacturing price increase during this period; it amounted to as much as 4.6 percent from 1955 to 1956, and as little as 1.2 percent from 1958 to 1959. Even more striking, however, is the year-to-year change in output observed for manufacturing establishments. From 1954 to 1955 there was an increase of 15.1 percent, whereas from 1957 to 1958 there was a decline of 13.9 percent. In other words, this period does show substantial change in the level of activity of manufacturing establishments. Employment also shows considerable variability, rising by 6.6 percent in the upswing, and declining by 9.1 percent in the downswing. During this period, the rate of increase in average hourly earnings continued to rise from the beginning of the upswing (1954–55) through the downswing (1957–58), dropping back again to a lower rate only during the next upswing from 1958 to 1959.

Although it is true that these average hourly earnings changes are measured at the establishment level with fixed value added weights, and thus are not affected by shifts among industries or establishments, this does not mean that the measurements are free from other kinds of biases. Establishments with expanding employment tend to hire lower-paid employees, and therefore they will show a smaller average hourly earnings increase than establishments that are reducing their employment by laying off lower-paid employees. Such changes in employment will have an effect upon average hourly earnings independent of wage rate changes. The importance of this effect can be seen in Table 14.7, where the changes in average hourly earnings are shown for establishments with different employment experience.

In constructing this table, establishments were classified into ten groups ranked by the change in employment within the establishment. Those establishments with the largest decreases in employment are shown in the first decile, and those with the largest increases are shown in the tenth decile. Each decile contains 10 percent of total value added in manufacturing. The table shows that average hourly earnings in establishments which increased employment rose less than average hourly earnings in establishments which decreased employment. From this, it follows that in years in which employment in manufacturing establishments as a whole is increasing, the observed change in average hourly earnings for all of manufacturing will be biased downward. Conversely, in periods of declining employment, the change in average hourly earnings will be biased upward. The underlined figures in Table 14.7 identify the change in average hourly earnings for the decile of establishments which came closest to zero change in employment, and thus presumably reflected with somewhat less bias the actual change in wage rates.

The analysis is complicated by the further fact that within establishments adjustments have not been made for overtime payments and occupational shifts

Table 14.7 *Behavior of Average Hourly Earnings of Manufacturing Establishments (DWW/MH) Ranked in Deciles According to their Percentage Change in Full-time Equivalent Employment (DFE), United States, 1954–59 (year-to-year percentage changes)*

Declines	1954–1955 DFE	1954–1955 DWW/MH	1955–1956 DFE	1955–1956 DWW/MH	1956–1957 DFE	1956–1957 DWW/MH	1957–1958 DFE	1957–1958 DWW/MH	1958–1959 DFE	1958–1959 DWW/MH
1	-31.4	7.5	-34.9	22.6	-33.3	22.2	-47.4	10.4	-28.2	8.0
2	-10.1	6.0	-14.6	9.8	-15.1	7.1	-28.3	12.0	-9.9	6.5
3	-4.1	4.9	-7.5	8.2	-9.6	6.9	-20.7	10.0	-4.0	5.7
4	-0.4	4.8	-3.6	5.3	-5.6	7.2	-15.3	7.4	-0.6	4.9
5	2.2	4.7	-0.6	3.6	-2.6	6.5	-11.1	10.7	1.8	4.4
6	5.1	3.8	1.7	4.4	-0.2	4.9	-7.4	9.7	5.0	4.3
7	9.5	3.8	5.1	4.3	2.0	5.6	-3.9	6.5	8.9	3.5
8	15.0	3.7	9.5	3.5	5.7	6.8	-0.1	6.2	14.3	3.3
9	23.7	3.0	16.5	2.9	12.6	4.8	5.4	6.8	22.8	2.0
10	55.8	1.3	44.3	2.0	45.1	-3.8	36.9	-8.2	56.5	-0.8
Average	6.6	4.3	1.7	6.6	0.0	6.8	-9.2	7.2	6.6	4.2

Source: Matched Establishment Data Files, Decile Tabulations, Annual Survey of Manufactures, United States Bureau of the Census.

in employment. What Table 14.7 does demonstrate, however, is that the data on average hourly earnings, even when computed at the establishment level, should not be used as a proxy for a wage rate index.

The change in productivity as reflected by the change in real value added per man-hour shown in Table 14.6 varies widely, the largest increase coming in the years from 1954 to 1956 and from 1958 to 1959 when output was increasing, and an actual decline taking place from 1956 to 1958 when output was falling. Since increasing productivity reduces unit costs, this means that in periods of rising output cost increases are offset in some degree by the accompanying increases in productivity; these offsets do not exist in periods of declining output.

Price–cost behavior, as reflected by the change in gross margins, is also shown in Table 14.6. The slight increase in gross margins from 1954 to 1955 indicates that prices rose slightly more than costs (2.2 percent compared with 2.0 percent). Such a difference is probably within the probable error of the data. In the second period, with output and productivity still rising, gross margins increased more substantially; had margins not increased, in fact, the output price index would have risen only 3.5 percent instead of the 4.6 percent shown. From 1956 on, however, gross margins narrowed, indicating that costs were rising faster than prices. Had it been possible for establishments to maintain their gross margins intact going into the recession from 1957 to 1958, the output price index would have risen by 6.9 percent instead of the 1.5 percent increase which actually occurred. In other words, in the upswing gross margins increased only slightly, and for establishments as a whole the major gain in profits came not from prices rising more than costs, but rather from the fact that as volume expanded overhead became a smaller percentage of the gross margin, and profits (i.e., gross margin minus overhead) increased as a percentage of the total value of output. In contrast, in the recession, establishments increased prices substantially less than the increase in their unit costs, thus not only absorbing some of the cost increases, but because of the lower scale of operations drastically reducing their profits; in many cases overhead costs may have exceeded gross margins so that profit became negative.

Table 14.6 shows that prices increased with the expansion of output in 1955–56, but it throws no light on whether this price rise was generated primarily by establishments expanding their output to meet the increased level of demand. An analysis of this question is provided in Table 14.8, where for the period 1955–56 establishments have been classified in deciles ranked by the change in their output.

It is interesting that, even in this period of moderate expansion, approximately half of all manufacturing establishments had declines in output. From this table it can be seen that establishments with the largest increases in output were not located in industries with the largest price rises. In fact, the expanding

*Table 14.8 Behavior of Output Prices and Margins of Manufacturing
Establishments Ranked in Deciles According to their
Percentage Change in Real Value Added, 1955–56
(year-to-year percentage changes)*

Decile	Change in real value added	Change in output prices	Change in gross margin
1	−54.6	4.9	−15.3
2	−26.9	5.2	−4.7
3	−14.6	5.4	−2.2
4	−7.0	5.0	−1.1
5	−2.0	4.7	−0.2
6	3.4	4.6	1.2
7	9.6	4.2	1.6
8	7.8	4.1	3.6
9	33.4	4.5	6.7
10	97.2	3.5	20.3
Average	5.4	4.6	1.1

Source: Matched Establishment Data Files, Decile Tabulations, Annual Survey of Manufactures, United States Bureau of the Census.

establishments were located in industries where prices rose less than average, and the contracting establishments were in industries where prices rose more than average. It was still true, however, that in terms of price–cost behavior, the establishments with increases in output increased their margins, and those with declining output decreased their margins.

Summary of Findings

In summary, this examination of the behavior of prices, output, wages and employment in the United States economy from 1950 to 1973 tends to support the following conclusions:

1. There has been a continual rise in the implicit price deflator and average hourly earnings throughout the period, even for years in which output and employment declined. With the exception of the most recent period, these apparent increases may, however, in part be due to faulty measurement of prices which does not sufficiently reflect quality change.
2. There does not appear to be a significant relation between the magnitude of price and wage increases and the magnitude or direction of the concurrent change in output.
3. During periods of substantial unemployment, money wages have continued to rise.
4. Productivity data for manufacturing establishments indicate a strong positive relationship between changes in output and changes in productivity.

5. The behavior of gross margins of manufacturing establishments indicates that price increases do not result from producers raising prices more than costs.

6. Paradoxically, in an expanding economy prices rise most in the more stagnant sectors; the faster-growing establishments generate productivity increases which tend to offset cost increases.

These conclusions are quite consistent with Pazos's findings on the relationship of wages, prices, and employment in Latin America. Because the price changes in Latin America are very much larger and the empirical data available for the United States is very much richer, the US experience has been presented in somewhat different terms. Pazos was concerned with economies which are more agricultural and more open than the United States. Therefore, he focused somewhat more on these sectors of the economy, and in view of the monetarist arguments on the causes of inflation, he was concerned with government deficits, monetary expansion, and the stock market. The above examination of the US experience has focused much more on price–cost behavior at the establishment level in years of differing levels of economic activity. Yet there is nothing contradictory in the conclusions arising from these different countries' experiences. What remains to be done is to see whether there is some reasonable model of prices, output and employment which can account for the price behavior observed for both Latin America and the United States.

The Mechanism of Chronic Inflation

In traditional income theory, inflation is generally considered to result either from excess aggregate demand or a cost–push price rise resulting from wage increases that are in excess of productivity increases.

The excess demand explanation depends upon final purchasers wishing to buy more output than can be produced, and in consequence bidding prices up. This behavior is observed during periods of war, when the government is buying a large fraction of total output and in the process creating purchasing power greatly in excess of the remaining goods available. Such price increases occurred in the United States during World War II, and also in the immediate postwar period when there was substantial accumulated purchasing power and the economy had not fully returned to peacetime production. It is also probable that the price rise in the United States at the outbreak of the Korean War in 1950–51 can be attributed to a surge in demand by producers and consumers who anticipated mobilization for war and sought to buy up the goods which were currently available on the market. This latter situation differed somewhat from that in World War II because the economy in 1950 was not at full employment, and in point of fact the expectations of future shortages were not borne out. The rapid growth of output was able to supply both civilian and military demands without further price increases. The initial period of rapid price rise was, therefore, very short-lived.

Pazos has expressed skepticism that there has been any period of general excess demand in Latin America since 1950. This seems quite possible, but a variant of the excess demand explanation may be relevant in these countries. Proponents of the excess demand theory of inflation suggest that the mechanism may operate by causing price rises in those sectors of the economy which cannot expand; for example, a large increase in income can cause agricultural prices or import prices to rise, and this price increase then spreads to other parts of the economy. Pazos does recognize that such a mechanism may have operated in specific instances in Latin America, but there are many other periods of price rise where there was no such sectoral excess demand.

In both Latin America and the United States, there have been periods when output was declining and unemployment increasing, yet prices continued to rise. Attempts to explain this phenomenon sometimes rely on lags in economic response, but these explanations are not very convincing. Such periods, when no excess aggregate or sectoral demand exists and price rises continue, are frequently referred to as cost–push inflation arising from the increase in wages. This, of course, immediately raises the question why wages should increase when there is no excess demand for labor. The answer has usually been couched in terms of the Phillips curve. It is argued that at every level of unemployment there will be a level of money wage rate change which is normal. Reducing the level of unemployment will lead to a faster rise in the money wage rate, and increasing unemployment will slow it. In order to keep the increase in the money wage rate in line with the long-run productivity increase in the economy, the appropriate level of unemployment (read from the Phillips curve) will be required. At this level of unemployment, price stability will result. If the required level of unemployment is unacceptable, some price rise must be accepted instead: thus there is a trade-off between the amount of price rise and the level of unemployment. However, the Phillips curve hypothesis does not adequately account for the observed variations of money wage rate change accompanying the same levels of unemployment, in either Latin America or the United States. For Latin America, what evidence there is seems to indicate very little relationship of any sort between wage changes and unemployment. For the United States, there have been attempts to explain away the wide variation in money wage rate changes for given levels of unemployment by suggesting that the Phillips curve has shifted from time to time. But no satisfactory explanation has been provided as to why such shifts take place, and whether they are endogenous to the system.

Thus the major features of price behavior observed in both Latin America and the United States are not well explained either by the presence of excess demand or by a trade-off between the change in the money wage rate and the level of unemployment. An explanation is needed which explicitly recognizes the mechanism of chronic inflation.

In considering the mechanism of chronic inflation, the major question which needs resolving is why a chronic inflation does not either escalate into a hyperinflation or result in a major depression. This question can be examined in four steps: the impact of increases in money wages on real aggregate demand, the relation of wages, productivity and wage costs, the impact of increases in wage costs on prices and the extent to which increases in prices affect money wages.

Wage increases and real aggregate demand
Increases in the wage bill resulting from an increase in money wage rates will generate a less than proportional increase in purchasing power, due to the operation of the automatic stabilizers in the economy. There are many sources of leakage. First, a portion of the increased wage bill will go, not to the employees, but to the government in the form of payroll or social security taxes. Some part of the increased wage bill may also go into pension funds. A substantial additional portion will be withheld for income taxes. Thus, even before the worker receives his take-home pay, a significant portion has been removed. Some workers may then save a portion of their increased pay, or use it to repay debts. But even if they spend it all, some of it will be syphoned off into sales taxes. Producers will, therefore, receive back in the form of consumer expenditures only a fraction of the increased wage bill which they have been forced to pay out. Unless the other sectors — government and those responsible for capital formation — have simultaneously responded by increasing their outlays by an amount equal to all the leakages, producers will not receive enough additional funds to pay the increased wage bill. The agricultural sector may receive additional income, since the wage increases will result in bidding up food prices, but if any of the increased farm income is saved, the amount of aggregate spending flowing back to the other producing sectors will be even further reduced.

In the case of the government sector, an increase in government revenues does not often result in an equal increase in government expenditures, since both tax rates and government expenditures are determined by legislative actions. A change in tax revenue which is the result of more income and spending in the economy will, in the absence of specific offsetting legislative action, increase the government surplus or reduce the deficit. A decline in income and spending will, of course, have the opposite effect, reducing the government surplus or increasing the deficit. Although the government could alter this behavior through conscious fiscal policy decisions, the usual tendency is quite the opposite. When prices are rising, governments tend to restrict their own spending, despite rising revenues. When increasing unemployment and declining output reduce government revenues, governments often do increase spending, but seldom by as much as spending in other sectors has fallen.

Capital formation, in turn, responds to two major influences: the demand for the goods produced with the capital and profits. If the demand for goods is growing and profits are high, capital formation will be high since producers will wish to provide for future growth and will have the funds to do so. But an increase in wage costs which results in a reduction of real aggregate demand will reduce both the rate of growth and the level of profits. Both of these facts mean that an increase in wages beyond the increase in productivity will tend to depress real capital formation.

As a consequence of these responses, the producers who raise their prices enough to meet their increased costs at the previous level of output will find that their sales have fallen and they will be forced to reduce output and employment. Such a decline could, of course, be offset by increased government spending or increased outlays on capital goods. In the absence of such positive actions, however, chronic underemployment may accompany the chronic price rise.

Major depression tends to be prevented by the same automatic stabilizers that frustrate the growth of real aggregate demand. Wage earners who are laid off do not suffer a complete cut-off in purchasing power, since unemployment compensation and relief provide them with some funds, and they may be able to draw upon accumulated saving or to borrow. Therefore, when producers reduce their output and employment, their sales do not decline as much as their wage bills. Furthermore, as Pazos points out, governments tend to become actively responsive to economic conditions when they threaten to get out of hand. In periods of acute unemployment, governments are much more willing to run deficits and thus prevent further declines in aggregate demand. Similarly, in periods of extreme price increase, governments move to control prices and wages, and so reduce the interaction between them.

This type of mechanism explains why increases in money wage rates and prices do not result in excess aggregate demand, and in turn to hyperinflation, but it does not throw any light on why wages tend to increase and how such increases affect prices.

Wages, productivity and wage costs

It is generally recognized that wages tend to increase even when output and employment are declining. This aspect of wage behavior has been called wage stickiness, and has been attributed to the unwillingness of workers to accept lower money wages or the inability of employers to break contractual arrangements with employees. From a longer-run point of view, the secular increase in wages is considered normal as long as it reflects productivity changes. Wages will respond to the general productivity change occurring in the economy, since producers in the high-productivity sectors will bid wages up to attract workers from the sectors with lower productivity. Given the normal growth in productivity, wage earners become accustomed to positive wage increases; this is how they obtain their share of the increased output of the economy. Wages can thus be expected to increase even in the absence of a price rise, as part of the normal adjustment to the long-run forces of economic growth. However, an increase in wages beyond the increase in labor productivity for any sector or industry will increase wage costs, and will be reflected in price increases in that sector or industry.

In most economic models, the rate of productivity increase is considered to be a general long-run secular phenomenon, pervasive throughout the economy and continuing in all periods, but somewhat obscured by fluctuations in income and employment. There is strong evidence, however, that productivity change does not occur at a fixed and immutable rate that is the product solely of long-run economic forces, but may be more concentrated in some sectors or industries and may be highly sensitive to economic conditions in the short run. To the extent that labor-saving machines and new technology are introduced in periods of expanding capacity, new products are introduced in periods of high demand, and the productivity change itself is partly a learning process, productivity may be strongly influenced by both the level of economic activity and its rate and direction of change, and may, therefore, be considerably more responsive to changes in output than is the money wage rate. Thus, in a period of rapidly rising output and increasing wages, the increased rate of productivity change may, for a considerable time, result in falling unit labor costs and output price stability. But, if output and employment are falling, productivity will lag and the previously normal increase in money wages will now exceed productivity change, resulting in rising unit labor costs. In this manner, fluctuations in productivity can affect the behavior of wage costs.

In specific instances, of course, wages are not the sole element of cost; material prices may also be important. Thus, for agricultural products, it is well recognized that higher levels of demand do result in higher prices, at least in the short run. As Pazos suggests, import prices may play an important role in some industries. Finally, some raw material prices such as copper, oil or other natural resources may behave more like farm prices than prices of manufactured products. Nevertheless, for the United States economy as a whole, the importance of these materials is relatively small. In national accounts terms, agriculture constitutes approximately 3 percent of the United States economy, merchandise imports 5 percent and mining (including crude petroleum) accounts for about 1.5 percent. In contrast, employee compensation is equal to 63 percent of the gross national product. It is evident that for most producers the major element of costs is labor, either directly in the form of wages paid or indirectly as embodied in materials purchased from other producers. Wage behavior thus is a major determinant of prices.

The relation of wage increases to price increases
The extent to which producers increase their prices in response to wage increases depends in considerable degree on the state of the economy. If real aggregate demand is rising, the increase in money wage rates will be accompanied by substantial increases in productivity so that unit wage costs will not rise as much as money wage rates. Since producers do not generally increase their gross margins substantially during such periods, the rise in price will be less than the rise in money wages. But, if real aggregate demand is stagnant or decreasing, productivity will be increasing more slowly or may even decline, so that unit wage costs may rise sharply. In the face of falling output, however, producers reduce their gross margins since they are reluctant to raise prices as much as costs, so again the increase in money wages will not be translated into an equivalent price increase. Thus wage rate changes are not fully translated into price changes, and the wage–price spiral tends to be attenuated rather than accelerated.

The effect of prices on wage costs
The final link in the spiral is the sensitivity of money wages to increases in the cost of living. It seems apparent that increases in the cost of living do cause money wages to rise more than they would otherwise, but it is difficult to predict whether the additional wage increases tend to fall short of or to exceed the cost-of-living increases. Undoubtedly, the rate of growth of real income and the level of unemployment condition the response of money wages to increases in the cost of living, but many other factors are also important, including legislated increases in minimum wages, strong union pressure for an increasing standard of living, the general political climate, and expectations as to the future growth of the economy. Certainly in the mid-1930s in the United States, the recovery from the Great Depression, accompanied by increases in the cost of living, led to large increases in money wages even though a substantial fraction of the labor force (15–20 percent) was still unemployed. Improved expectations and increases in profits may lead to money wage rate increases even when the economy is not at full capacity or full employment.

Understanding the determinants of wage behavior is central to the explanation of chronic inflation. Current theories of wage change cast in terms of the level of unemployment cannot explain the observed variance in wage behavior. There is, of course, no shortage of wage theories; many involve such considerations as the value of human capital, opportunity costs of nonmarket activities, and job search strategies, but the increased sophistication of the theoretical models of wage behavior unfortunately has not resulted in any better understanding of observed wage behavior. As has already been pointed out, part of the problem lies in the fact that the currently available data on average hourly earnings do not adequately measure wage behavior. In order to test alternative hypotheses of wage behavior, data are required on wage and employment changes of employees in relation to their social and demographic characteristics and the economic and organizational characteristics of the establishments which hire them.

The Policy Implications of Chronic Inflation

The mechanism of chronic inflation described here has major policy implications for the achievement of price stability. If the wage–price spiral does not result either from excess aggregate demand or from a trade-off between money wage rate increases and unemployment, the attempt to control price increases by operating on aggregate demand will be doomed to failure. Reducing aggregate demand will affect the level of output and employment, but it will not lessen the wage–price spiral. In many instances, a reduction in aggregate demand will only make the difficulty worse. Since productivity change is more sensitive to changes in aggregate demand than is the money wage rate, slowing the rate of real growth will result in increased wage costs, which are likely to be passed along as increased output prices. Conversely, an acceleration in aggregate demand may stimulate productivity to the point where it will offset the changes in money wages, resulting in greater price stability.

As a long-run solution to the problem of chronic inflation, more attention needs to be directed to the relation of changes in wage rates to changes in productivity. If productivity is increasing rapidly, these increases can be passed along in high wage rate increases without producing inflation. But if productivity increases are smaller than wage rate increases, chronic inflation will ensue, and it will be accompanied by insufficient aggregate demand, slower growth and unemployment. Attempting to deal with this sort of chronic inflation by keeping aggregate demand down will not restore price stability, but rather will only further reduce output and employment.

3. EQUITY IMPLICATIONS OF CHRONIC INFLATION

Continual price increases do pose serious problems of equity. The real value of fixed monetary incomes declines steadily, and the real capital value of monetary assets erodes. In contrast, holders of both real assets and fixed monetary debt experience capital gains. There is no doubt that chronic inflation does redistribute income, in ways that are coming to be considered inequitable.

There is a growing recognition of this problem in many countries, and various steps have been taken to redress the inequities. In the US, wage contracts often include cost-of-living adjustments designed to protect wage earners from real income erosion, and recently a cost-of-living adjustment has been introduced into the social security system.

A more systematic and comprehensive indexing has been undertaken in Brazil where a monetary correction has been introduced not only for wages and pensions, but for financial instruments as well. In the ordinary situation, interest rates reflect anticipated inflation, so that the monetary interest rate serves to compensate the lender for the decline in the real value of his capital sum as well as to provide him with a real rate of return. When a large price rise is anticipated, the monetary interest rate will be correspondingly high. Since the future course of price increases is seldom predicted exactly, there will still be windfall gains and losses when the actual price change does not correspond to that anticipated. Under the monetary correction scheme established in Brazil, however, in addition to the usual adjustment of wages and pensions, all monetary assets and monetary liabilities are adjusted at appropriate intervals by a price index for the economy as a whole. This means that the monetary interest rate can approximate the real interest rate, since capital values will be adjusted separately according to the general price level.

This monetary correction technique has important implications for the functioning of financial markets. Because the rate of interest reflects the real rate of interest only, and the capital sum is separately adjusted to reflect price changes, the borrower does not face the problem of paying each year both the real interest and the whole amount by which the capital value has declined. It is as if the lender made an additional loan in monetary terms each year to compensate for the price rise; the amount of the debt in real terms, of course, remains unchanged. Without the monetary correction, the borrower is forced, in a period of rapid inflation, to reduce his real debt by a considerable amount each year. The rapid repayment schedule this implies often makes borrowing useless, if not impossible. The monetary correction, in contrast, makes it possible for the borrower to have the use of the real value of the sum borrowed for whatever the period for which it was borrowed. From the point of view of the lender, the upward adjustment of capital values compensates for the effect of the inflation to preserve his real equity, without the necessity for anticipating the rate of price rise. Consequently, there is no motive for a flight to real assets. In equity terms, the protection afforded to small asset holders — individuals with savings accounts and holders of government bonds — is especially important.

Many economists feel that full indexing would accelerate the rate of price inflation. There is, however, no indication that this has happened in Brazil. Wherever cost-of-living adjustments for wages and pensions have already been introduced, as in the United States, the basic reliance on wage and fixed incomes to slow an inflation may already have been effectively abandoned, and the introduction of full indexing may redress the inequities which are created under a partial system without further impact on the rate of inflation. Even in the absence of formal cost-of-living wage adjustments, furthermore, the desire of workers to maintain their real incomes leads them to respond, in making wage agreements, not only to past price increases but also to anticipated future increases. In such a situation, a formal cost-of-living adjustment might be either more or less than the increase resulting from wage bargaining taking anticipated future increases into account. Expectations of future price increases do tend to be self-fulfilling when they influence wage settlements, owing to the effect of wage costs on product prices. Similarly, the monetary interest rate in an unindexed economy, as noted above, must take anticipated inflation into account, and such anticipations may be either an over- or underestimate.

Full indexing may, therefore, be a useful device to offset some of the inequities produced by chronic inflation. If the chronic inflation is minor, the effect of indexing will also be small. Nevertheless, over a period of time it will prevent the cumulative erosion of equity, and reduce the magnitude of capital gains and losses. If the chronic inflation is severe, full indexing may serve not only to maintain equity, but also to promote greater stability in the economy.

Both the Latin American countries which were examined by Pazos and the United States have experienced chronic inflation. Although the rate of inflation in the United States has been very much smaller, it has not responded any better to traditional monetary and fiscal measures. Attempts to slow it have resulted in the loss of real income to society, and the cumulative effects of chronic inflation have produced inequities. In view of the failure to eliminate chronic inflation, perhaps a more effective strategy could be one which attempted to reduce the inequities resulting from it. Monetary and fiscal policies could then be directed to the more positive goals of improving social and economic welfare, rather than the elusive goal of price stability.

15. The Anatomy of Earnings Behavior

Nancy D. Ruggles and Richard Ruggles
*National Bureau of Economic Research
and Yale University*

1. INTRODUCTION

Earnings from wages and salaries constitute two-thirds of the total personal income received by households and more than half of the total of all payments generated by the gross national product. As the economy grows and develops, wage and salary earnings also change. Increases in the population bring more wage and salary earners into the labor force. Retirements and deaths reduce the labor force. Productivity increases lead to increased earnings, and changes in labor force participation also have major effects. In the shorter run, changes in the level of economic activity and differences in the rate of inflation affect the behavior of total earnings and of the earnings of different social and economic groups. A better grasp of these relationships is needed, to understand both why total wage and salary earnings as they appear in the national accounts change as they do and how different socio-economic groups gain or lose, both in absolute terms and relative to one another.

The degree of disaggregation currently available in the national income accounts is not sufficient to provide a basis for this type of analysis. Although wage and salary earnings are given quarterly by industry, no information is provided on the age, sex and race of the wage and salary recipients; on the size distribution of wage and salary earnings; on exits from and entrants into the labor force; or on the distribution of changes in earnings among different socio-economic groups. Information of this type is needed in order to elucidate the processes of evolutionary economic change and the effects upon such

This chapter was first presented at the Conference on Research in Income and Wealth, Ann Arbor, May 1974 and then published in *The Distribution of Economic Well-Being*, Studies in Income and Wealth, Vol. 41, National Bureau of Economic Research, 1977. The tables in this chapter are based on Appendix Tables A-1 through A-3 of the volume.

evolutionary change of short-run changes in the level of economic activity and inflation. However, abandonment of the national income accounting approach is no solution. Independent studies of age profiles, lifetime earnings patterns, sex and race differentials in earnings, labor force participation, size distribution of earnings and changes in income of different socio-economic groups would lead to a maze of conflicting observations that would be impossible to integrate into a cohesive whole. Ideally, one would like to be able to disaggregate total wage and salary earnings into components that would permit evaluation of the importance of different factors relative to one another and to the behavior of total earnings.

2. THE NATURE OF THE LEED FILE

A partial solution to this problem can be found in the LEED file of the Social Security Administration (SSA). The SSA has created a 1 percent sample of the social security files in such a way that it yields a Longitudinal Employee–Employer Data (LEED) file. In each year, the reports by employers for all social security numbers ending in a given series of digits are selected and matched over time to provide a complete set of employee–employer records for each individual in the sample. Such a procedure not only brings together all of the information pertinent to a given individual, but it also automatically brings in the new entrants into the labor force in the proportion in which they occur, and the absence of employee–employer records automatically reflects exits. The basic information provided on each individual includes age, sex and race, and for each quarter of every year, the amount of wages paid to the individual by each employer. There is, however, a cut-off point established in the social security law beyond which wages are no longer reported. Since the Federal Insurance Contribution Act (FICA) tax is applied against total earnings as they are paid, the effect of this provision is to stop the reporting of income at the point in the year when the limit for any one employer is reached. If an individual is receiving earnings from several employers, each would be reported separately, and the limit would apply to each individually. Although the Social Security Administration does compute an estimate of total earnings for the year in those instances where the limit is reached before the end of the year, it is obvious that the early part of the year will be more fully reported than the later part, and the estimates for these early quarters will more fully reflect the national totals. For the purposes of this study, therefore, the analysis will be confined to the first-quarter data, which are relatively unaffected by the taxable limit, and which, in addition, reduce the influence of seasonality.

It should be pointed out that the LEED file does not contain various sorts of social and demographic information which would be very useful in the analysis of earnings behavior. Thus, for example, no information is provided on education, occupation or marital status of individuals; the data, furthermore, refer solely to total earnings paid, and no information is provided on the number of hours worked. Thus earnings may be low either because the wage rate is low or because the employee worked for only a fraction of the period or on a part-time basis.

Despite these deficiencies, however, the LEED file is still a rich source of data. It is an extremely large sample, equal in magnitude to the 1 percent Census Public Use Samples. In contrast to the Public Use Samples, however, it follows each individual over a substantial period of time (1957–69), so that year-to-year changes for specific individuals or groups can be observed. Although other panel history sample surveys are being developed, most of them cover very much smaller samples and cannot be successfully disaggregated to show the anatomy of the total wage bill in the national economy.

The social security system covers about 90 percent of total wage and salary employment. Certain government employees are excluded, and there is a small number of other groups who, like the railroad employees, have their own pension system, or who are not covered by any system. As is indicated in Table 15.1, the percentage of wage and salary earners covered by social security rose from 87 to 90 percent over the period covered by the LEED file. This table

Table 15.1 Coverage of Social Security LEED File

	Percent of total employment			Wage and salary earnings		
Year	Total reported to SSA	Not reported to SSA		BEA total ($bn)	LEED file ($bn)	LEED as percent of BEA
		Government	Other			
1957	87	8	5	237	189	80
1958	88	7	5	235	190	81
1959	88	7	5	253	204	81
1960	89	6	5	269	219	81
1961	89	6	5	271	223	82
1962	89	7	4	290	241	83
1963	89	7	4	305	252	83
1964	89	6	5	324	270	83
1965	89	6	5	347	285	82
1966	89	6	5	380	315	83
1967	90	7	3	412	347	84
1968	90	7	3	448	379	85
1969	–	–	–	492	417	85

Sources: Percentage of total employment: Social Security Administration, 1971, p. 3; BEA wage and salary earnings: *The Survey of Current Business* (various years); 1957–64: August 1966, Table 2.1, pp. 34–5; 1965–67: July 1969, Table 2.1, p. 26; and 1968–69; July 1971, Table 2.1, p. 26. LEED wage and salary earnings: Tabulated from LEED 1% file — summary figures multiplied by 100.

Price Behavior

also compares the total wage and salary figures reported in the national accounts by the Bureau of Economic Analysis (BEA) with the wage and salary figures derived from the LEED file. The LEED coverage gradually increased from 80 percent of the national accounts wage and salary earnings total in 1957 to 85 percent in 1969. This total is somewhat lower than the social security employment coverage, partly because of the processing procedures used in the creation of the LEED file. The Social Security Administration points out that it creates the LEED sample in September of the year following the year to which the data refer, and that any items that are posted after this date are excluded. It is difficult to estimate the exact amount of under-coverage which results from this procedure, and it may differ considerably from year to year, but it is likely to be from 2 to 4 percent. Another source of difference may lie in the fact that the government employees who are not included in the LEED file have higher than average earnings.

From the point of view of year-to-year change, the earnings reflected in the LEED file track the national accounts wage and salary earnings very well. The gradual rise in the percentage of earnings covered from 80 to 85 percent in all probability reflects the combined effect of the increased number of people covered by the social security system and changes in the timing of updating procedures. In terms of sampling reliability, the LEED 1 percent sample is, of course, quite large, starting with 515,000 cases in 1957 and rising to 700,000 cases in 1969.

3. SPECIFIC QUESTIONS TO BE INVESTIGATED

The LEED file provides a basis for investigating a wide variety of questions. In view of the lack of information on such things as hours worked, education and family status, it is not possible to develop a full-fledged model of wages and labor force participation with the LEED material alone. Nevertheless, the LEED file is capable of providing new insights relating to certain specific aspects of earnings and labor force participation. This paper will confine itself to four sets of questions relating to specific variables. These are: age–earnings profiles and birth cohort lifetime patterns of earnings; sex and race differentials in both age–earnings profiles and birth cohort patterns of earnings; work history at different points in the life cycle for different sexes and races; and the distribution of earnings by size for different age–race–sex groups, its change over time, and the effect of changes in the level of economic activity and in prices on the distribution of earnings and labor force participation.

Age

Age–earnings profiles have been the focus of considerable interest by economists. It has long been recognized that earnings rise with age up to a point, and then level off and decline. This phenomenon underlies many of the human-capital models which attempt to explain the observed differentials in terms of human investment by both the wage earner and the employer. The most comprehensive and reliable age profiles available up to now have come from the Census records, although even small samples do reveal the general patterns in broad outline. What has been lacking is an understanding of how the age–earnings profiles shift from year to year as the age composition of the population changes and as the level of economic activity and prices change, and as long-run economic growth takes place. Since the LEED file is available yearly for the period 1957–69, it can be used to ask how age–earnings profiles do shift over time, and whether these shifts are sensitive to differing sizes of entering cohorts and different economic conditions.

A second question with respect to age is how earnings change from the point of view of birth cohorts, rather than from the perspective of age– earnings profiles. In recent years, the topic of lifetime earnings of specific birth cohorts has aroused increasing interest because of the realization that individuals are, in fact, treated quite differently at different points in the life cycle, receiving different levels of income and having different financial responsibilities. The LEED file is particularly well suited to analyze the pattern of earnings for a 12-year segment of the lives of individual cohorts, and to discover whether there is a significant difference in these lifetime patterns. There is a real need to link the analysis of shifts in age–earnings profiles over time with the relative behavior of different birth cohorts over time. These two questions are in fact different aspects of the more central question of the relation of age to earnings.

Sex and Race

Questions relating to sex and race differentials have also been central to the analysis of earnings and labor force participation. There have been many studies of such differentials, some of which have attempted to assess the extent of discrimination, defined in terms of differences in earnings of individuals with similar qualifications in the same occupation but with different race and sex characteristics. This sort of analysis is outside the scope of the present study. The sex–race differentials which are observed in the LEED file may result from a large variety of factors, including differences in occupation, education, labor force participation, and discrimination, and it is not possible to isolate the different factors. It is important, however, to recognize that, whatever their roots, there are major sex and race differentials, which result in different amounts of earnings for different individuals. With the LEED data, it is possible to ask how age–earnings profiles differ for the different sex and race groups and how these profiles have shifted over the period from 1957 to 1969. The answer to these questions can throw considerable light on whether or not the gross differentials between sex and race groups are, in fact, being systematically reduced by increased educational opportunities and a reduction in discrimination. In this connection, it is also possible to trace out the lifetime earnings patterns of different birth cohorts for individual race and sex groups, to ascertain whether there are characteristic differences in the shapes of these functions, and whether generalizations can be made about such patterns in terms of the nature of the groups involved.

Work History

There are a number of questions relating to work history that can be answered by the data in the LEED file. For example, it is useful to ask how the different sex and race groups enter and exit from employment over their life cycle. Men traditionally enter the labor force in their teens or early twenties, and leave it only through death or retirement. Women, on the other hand, may leave the labor force during the childbearing years, and then may or may not reenter it. Detailed evidence on the age pattern of entrance and exit based on a large sample has not been readily available. The LEED data can cast considerable light upon the nature of this pattern for both white and nonwhite females.

There are also other questions relating to work history to which the LEED data can provide answers. For each individual, it can be ascertained whether he is working at all in a given quarter, and whether his employer is the same or different from the one reported in some other specific period. Thus a work history can be developed which reflects exits from and entrants to employment from one year to the next, and shows as separate groups those individuals who retain the same employer and those who change employers. The question of exits and entrants is highly related to employment turnover or instability, and to the pattern of younger people coming into the labor force and older people leaving it. Differences in age, race and sex patterns throw light on questions of labor force participation by different groups at different stages in their life cycles. For instance, is it true that it is the tendency for labor force entrants to come in at a low wage and for those who exit to leave at a high wage that makes possible increases in wages to all workers without a corresponding increase in the total wage bill? Although hours worked are not available in the LEED file, it is possible to see whether an individual's total earnings increased or decreased from one period to the next. Such increases and decreases will, of course, reflect changes in both wage rates and hours worked. Moving from part-time to full-time work may result in very large increases in earnings, and from full-time to part-time will result in large decreases. Changes in overtime work may also have a major impact on the change in earnings. Changes in wage rates should, in general, result in increases in earnings rather than decreases, but on the average, such increases would not be expected to be large. Examination of the increases and decreases in earnings for individuals with unchanged employers can, therefore, cast some light on the question of how important changes in labor force participation are for individuals who remain employed. Such questions are central to analyzing why the wage bill changes as it does under different economic conditions.

Distribution of Earnings by Size

The distribution of average annual earnings by size is, of course, directly related to the question of earnings differentials according to age–sex–race groups. Specifically, it may be asked whether the observed higher male wages come about through a greater variance in the size distribution of their income. In other words, does the male distribution include low- as well as high-income earners, or is the whole range of male earnings higher? Does the size distribution of earnings become more unequal with advancing age, and is this true for all sex and race groups?

Finally, does the size distribution of income differ significantly over time, and at different levels of economic activity? This final set of questions relates to the effects of changes in the level of economic activity and the price level upon earnings and labor force participation. The questions which will be asked relate to who benefits and who loses in periods of slow growth and small wage increases, compared with periods of higher growth and larger wage increases. In all periods, some individuals gain and others lose. The question which is being asked here relates to differences in the number of people who gain and lose, and the differential effects on different age, sex and race groups. Only by such analysis, expressed in real terms, can the loss or gain resulting from dampening down or speeding up economic activity be assessed.

Age and Earnings

Age–earnings profiles for the period 1957–69 can be derived from the LEED file by single years of age. These are shown in Figure 15.1. The successive age–earnings profiles for the different years shift upward, the lowest representing the year 1957, and the highest the year 1969. From this figure, it becomes apparent that the shift from year to year is highly dependent upon economic conditions. The year 1958, for example, shows no significant upward shift over the year 1957; in fact the two age–earnings profiles overlap. Similarly, in the mild recession of 1961 the age–earnings profile also failed to

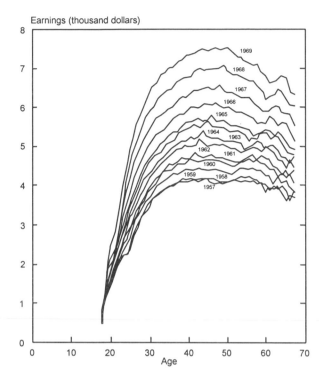

Figure 15.1 Age–Earnings Profiles, 1957–69 (current dollars)

shift upward significantly. In contrast, in each year from 1966 through 1969 there was a strong upward shift in the profile reflecting a sharp rise in earnings for all age levels.

From Figure 15.1, it would appear that the profile is considerably less flat in the ages from 35 to 60 in more recent years than it was in 1957. In other words, those in the middle age groups would appear to have gained relatively more than those either younger or older. The age–earnings profiles shown in Figure 15.1 are, however, not completely smooth and regular. Inasmuch as they are based on a very large sample, the irregularities deserve consideration.

Thus, for example, the profile for 1969 shows a sharp dip in earnings for those of age 58, born in 1911, relative to those immediately older or younger. This dip can in fact be traced back for this birth cohort in the profiles for previous years, suggesting that for some reason this cohort was retarded relative to those around it. This was the birth cohort which entered the labor force in approximately 1930, and it is not unreasonable to assume that the labor market conditions at the time of their entry had a significant depressing effect on their earnings, relative to those who preceded them and were already established in the labor market. In contrast, the cohort who were born a decade

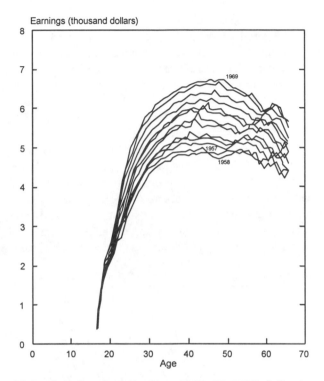

Figure 15.1a Age–Earnings Profiles, 1957–69 (1957 dollars)

later and came into the labor market in 1940 are high earners relative to the cohorts surrounding them and seem to have enjoyed this advantage continuously. Especially sharp peaks for this birth cohort can be seen in the profiles for the period 1961–65.

The average earnings shown in Figure 15.1 are in terms of current year prices and to the extent that consumer prices were rising, it overstates the upward shift of age–earnings profiles in real terms. In Figure 15.1a, average earnings of each year are deflated by the Consumer Price Index using 1957 as a base. The successive annual profiles are much closer together than those in Figure 15.1, indicating that a substantial part of the observed earnings increases from 1957 to 1969 did not reflect increases in real earnings.

It is interesting to note that in real terms the age–earnings profile for the year 1958 is lower than that for 1957, indicating that even the employed workers in the 1958 recession suffered a real decline in income.

The earnings patterns for all birth cohorts born in the period from 1904 to 1941 are shown in Figure 15.2. Each line in this figure shows the average earnings over the period 1957–69 for a single-year birth cohort. The points plotted in this figure are, of course, the same as those in Figure 15.1. In Figure 15.1, however, the points for all ages in a given year are connected, yielding a cross-section picture. In Figure 15.2, points for a given birth cohort for all years are connected, thus tracing out the experience of given groups through time. The relation between Figures 15.1 and 15.2 can be easily seen if one considers that the age profile shown for the year 1969 can be obtained by connecting the end points of the birth cohort earning patterns.

In Figure 15.2, the lack of change in earnings from 1957 to 1958 appears as a sideways movement in earnings patterns; this same sideways movement is exhibited again for the period 1960–61. The ripples in the earnings pattern lines indicate slackening in the rate of increase of earnings due to slowing down of economic activity. The earnings patterns for the cohorts born in 1911 and 1921 are labeled explicitly on Figure 15.2; as can be seen, these are the cohorts which respectively lagged behind and led adjacent cohorts, and appeared as dips and peaks in Figure 15.1. If the age cohort earnings patterns are deflated by the Consumer Price Index, the individual age cohort earnings patterns rise

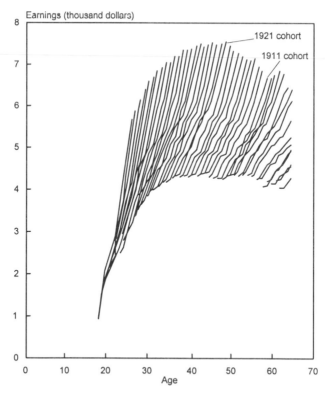

Figures 15.2 Age–Cohort Earnings, 1957–69 (current dollars)

much more slowly, and the difference in the rate of increase with age becomes more apparent. This is shown in Figure 15.2a. From 1957 to 1958, the earnings of all cohorts 35 years old and over declined.

Less drastic slowdowns in the increase in earnings can be seen for a number of other years. The interrelation of the earnings patterns of different birth cohorts can be seen more easily when they are plotted by calendar year, rather than age. Figure 15.3 shows the earnings patterns for people who were born in 1940, 1928, 1916 and 1904.

At the beginning of the period, these people were aged 17, 29, 41 and 53. By the end of the period, they were 29, 41, 53 and 65. In 1957, the average earnings of the 1904 and 1916 cohorts were almost identical, and they exhibited the same pattern of growth for the next two years. After that, however, the 1904 cohort rose somewhat more slowly, and in 1963, when its members were 59 years old, its earnings were equaled by those of the faster-rising 35-year-olds of the 1928 cohort. This 1928 cohort was also increasing faster than the

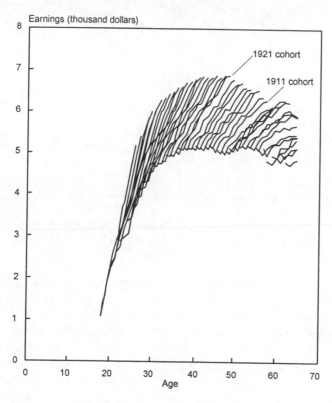

Figure 15.2a Age–Cohort Earnings, 1957–69 (1957 dollars)

1916 cohort, and caught up with the latter by 1965, going on to be the top in much more slowly, and the difference in the rate of increase with age becomes average earnings from then on. The 1940 cohort, which of course started out the lowest of all in 1957 when they were 17 years old, increased rapidly throughout the period, catching up with the 1904 cohort in 1968 when they were 28 and those in the older group were 64. The striking point of Figure 15.3 is that younger cohorts successively overtake older cohorts, and in turn are themselves overtaken by still younger cohorts. The variance which existed among cohorts when they were at ages ranging from 17 to 53 became considerably reduced when they all advanced to the age range 29–65.

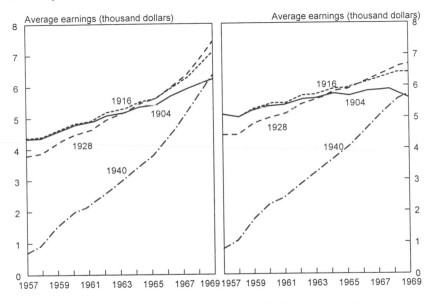

Figure 15.3 Earnings Patterns of   *Figure 15.3a Earnings Patterns of*
Four Birth Cohorts, 1957–69   *Four Birth Cohorts, 1957–69*
(current dollars)   *(1957 dollars)*

In relating the age–earnings profiles to the earning patterns of specific birth cohorts, the leveling off and decline in average earnings shown by the cross-sectional age–earnings profile is in marked contrast with the continual rise in earnings exhibited by every birth cohort up to the point of retirement at age 65.

The shape of the age–earnings profile results from the differential rates of earnings increase at different points in the life cycle. The effect of economic conditions appears in a substantially reduced rate of earnings increase for all birth cohorts in periods of recession and unemployment, but substantial increases in output and employment do not appear to have as much influence. If the earning patterns of specific birth cohorts are measured in real terms (as shown in Figure 15.3a), the rate of increase for all of the cohorts is substantially reduced, and for the oldest cohort (those born in 1904) an actual decline in real earnings takes place in the last several years, i.e., after age 65. No significant real decline takes place prior to that age, however, except in periods of recession.

Sex and race differentials

The discussion of age–earnings profiles and birth cohort earnings patterns to this point has treated the population as a whole, without respect to either sex or race. It is well known, however, that significant sex and race differences do exist. The differences in age–earnings profiles are striking. Figure 15.4 shows the age–earnings profiles by race and sex for the year 1969; this figure is a decomposition of the total age–earnings profile shown in Figure 15.1.

For white males, the peak average earnings in 1969 were received by those in the late forties, and substantial differentials existed over the ages from 30 to 65. For nonwhite males, the highest income was received in 1969 by those in their late thirties. Although the level of nonwhite male earnings is lower than that for white males, the general shape of the age profile is quite

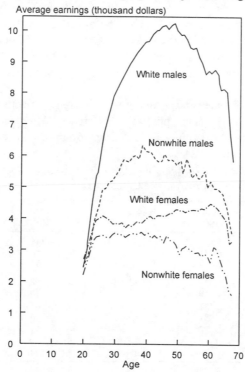

Figure 15.4 Age–Earnings Profiles by Race and Sex, 1969

similar. For all ages and both races, male earnings are substantially greater than female.

Besides being substantially below that for both groups of males, the age–earnings profile for white females is very different in shape. After an initial rise up to the mid-twenties, the age–earnings profile drops until the mid-thirties, after which time there is a gradual rise to age 60. This pattern is undoubtedly influenced by the withdrawal of women during the childbearing ages. There appears to be a mix effect in which the net exit of women with higher incomes is greater than the net exit of women with lower incomes. Table 15.2 illustrates this pattern for white women aged 24. It should be pointed out that this decline in the age–earnings profile of white females does not mean that there is a corresponding decline in the lifetime patterns of birth cohorts passing through these age groups. During the year 1963, more than 27 percent of the women 24 years old exited from employment, while only 18 percent of the women employed in the first quarter of 1964 had not been employed in the first quarter of 1963. Thus, of women who were 24 years old in 1963, the number employed declined by approximately 9 percent from 1963 to 1964. As Table 15.2 shows, this decline was sharper for women in higher earnings groups than for those in lower earnings groups. It seems reasonable that this effect may be due to the higher family-income status of women who are themselves receiving higher earnings. The decision to leave employment because of childbearing is probably related to the level of income enjoyed by the family. Women in low-income families who themselves are receiving low incomes cannot afford to stop working.

For nonwhite females, the ages of highest income are between 30 and 40, a range over which there is no appreciable difference. After that, as in the case of nonwhite males, the earnings for older age groups are lower. It should be

Table 15.2 Number of White Women Aged 24 in Social Security Covered Employment by Income Class

Income group, $	Number 1963	Exits 1963	Entrants 1964	Percent net change
1–999	585	292	261	−5.3
1,000–1,999	535	194	156	−7.1
2,000–2,999	814	206	139	−8.2
3,000–3,999	932	204	105	−10.6
4,000–4,999	730	129	55	−10.1
5,000–5,999	275	48	21	−9.8
6,000–6,999	82	10	6	−4.9
7,000–7,999	20	6	1	−25.0
8,000 and over	4	0	0	0
Total	3,979	1,089	744	−8.7

Source: Based on detailed tabulations of Appendix Table A-3.

pointed out that the age–earnings profiles reflect the influence of historical changes on lifetime patterns. It is doubtless true that the occupations and industries in which the different sex and race groups are employed have different lifetime patterns. It is also true, however, that in recent years these occupations and industries have been changing, especially for the younger age groups, which suggests that the age profiles can be expected to change in the future.

A comparison of the percentage change in average earnings by sex and race over the period 1957–69 for specific age groups is shown in Table 15.3. This table provides a measure of the extent to which gross differentials among the various groups have changed. The most striking feature of this table is the relative improvement in the position of nonwhite females. They averaged an increase of 107 percent over the period 1957–69, and in almost every age group exceeded the increases shown for other groups. In contrast, the position of white females improved the least. Overall, their earnings rose by only 67 percent. From age 55 onward, however, white females did better than white males, and after 60 even better than nonwhite males. Nonwhite males did better than white males at all ages, increasing by over 90 percent between the ages of 25 and 54. In general, then, the gross differentials by race narrowed in the period 1957–69 for all age groups, with black women making the largest relative gains. White females, however, dropped behind; the gross differential between them and white males increased for all ages up to 55.

Table 15.3 Percent Change in Average Earnings by Age, Sex and Race, 1957–69

Age	White male	White female	Nonwhite male	Nonwhite female
20–24	54	52	77	106
25–29	75	66	90	124
30–34	74	59	92	110
35–39	76	59	92	109
40–44	80	67	90	107
45–49	84	64	92	108
50–54	76	64	99	98
55–59	71	72	79	105
60–64	69	86	83	130
Average	73	67	86	107

Source: Based on Appendix Table A-1.

The earnings patterns for specific birth cohorts can also be broken down by race and sex. This is done in Figures 15.5 and 15.5a. The four sectors of the figures represent a disaggregation by race and sex of the earnings patterns for birth cohorts shown in Figures 15.3 and 15.3a. It is apparent that the sex and race differentials in earnings patterns are established in the early years; as the

Price Behavior

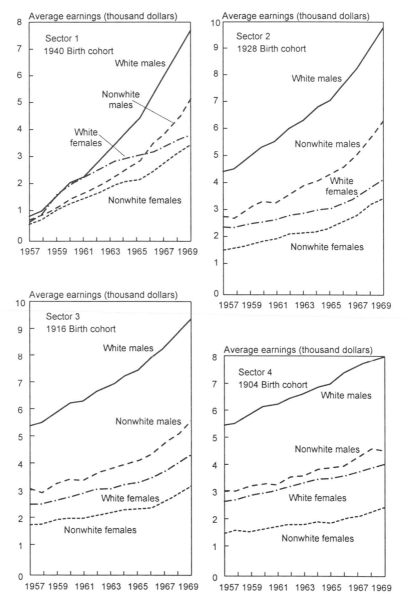

*Figure 15.5 Earnings Patterns by Race and Sex for Selected Birth Cohorts,
1957–69 (current dollars)*

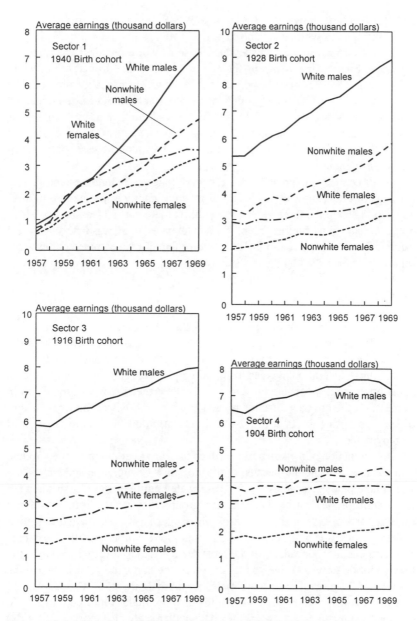

Figure 15.5a Earnings Patterns by Race and Sex for Selected Birth Cohorts, 1957–69 (1957 dollars)

1940 birth cohort shows, well before age 29. White female earnings are on a par with those of white males up to age 22, after which time the earnings of white males increase much faster than those of white females; the latter are surpassed by nonwhite males by the age of 26. The rate of increase of white and nonwhite females over the period as a whole was remarkably similar. The patterns for all race and sex groups in the older cohorts reveal the expected slowing in the rates of increase, but again it is striking that no birth cohort for any race or sex suffers a decline in earnings over any part of its life cycle, and the relative positions of the different sex and race groups are essentially maintained throughout.

In this connection, it may be noted from Figure 15.5a that the average real earnings of older nonwhite males do drop significantly in periods of mild recession. Thus in the three older birth cohorts there is a substantial decline in both 1958 and 1961 for this group. For white males, there was a decline in real earnings for the oldest cohort in 1958, but for females the earnings patterns are relatively undisturbed by the recessions.

Work History

Individuals' employment history varies considerably over their lifetimes. The LEED file cannot capture the complete pattern in all of its detail; it does not include the self-employed, many of the employees of state and local governments, most federal employees, railroad employees, and those employed in some other small uncovered occupations. Nevertheless, as was indicated in Table 15.1, the coverage is quite high, so that an analysis of the work history of specific birth cohorts does provide information on the lifetime pattern of employment.

Determination of the size of the birth cohort raises certain problems. Actual birth data are not suitable, because of the mortality, immigration and emigration which take place prior to the age of legitimate employment. Census data are more appropriate, but for younger age groups they suffer from substantial underreporting. In the 1970 Census, for example, it is estimated that total underreporting was of the order of 2.5 percent, for example, 5 million persons, and it is generally conceded that the most serious underreporting occurs in the highly mobile groups — the young, the male, the nonwhite. For instance, the number of 20-year-old nonwhite males reported in the 1960 Census was 23 percent below the number of 30-year-old nonwhite males reported in the 1970 Census. Understatement on a somewhat smaller scale also exists in the 1960 Census for young whites (12 percent for males, 9 percent for females), but for older age groups the discrepancy between the 1960 and 1970 censuses is in line with expected mortality. Although it would be possible to adjust the birth cohort size to reflect mortality, it is perhaps more useful to treat it as a form of withdrawal from employment, somewhat analogous to permanent retirement.

The expected lifetime employment pattern for males is one in which the percentage employed increases during the initial years due to individuals entering the labor force for the first time, levels off in the adult years, declines somewhat due to mortality in the middle and later years, and declines sharply at the point of retirement. For females, childbearing can be expected to have a significant impact on the lifetime employment pattern. Figure 15.6 presents the observed lifetime employment patterns for four different birth cohorts. These cohorts have been selected so that, taken all together, they cover the ages from 17 to 65. The pattern within a cohort reflects the actual experience of that cohort in the years from 1957 to 1969.

For males, the expected pattern does emerge. The break between the 1940 and 1928 cohorts may be due in large part to census understatement of the size of the younger population cohort. If the cohort is, in fact, larger than shown in the census, the percentage of this cohort employed in covered occupations would be correspondingly lower, and would be more in line with the 1928 cohort. It is, of course, quite legitimate for employment percentages for these two cohorts to be different at the point of the break, since one represents the situation for 29-year-olds in 1969, whereas the other represents 29-year-olds in 1957. In the experience of the 1928 birth cohort, it can be seen that the employment of nonwhite males dropped in the recession of 1958, but rose substantially above that of white males in the subsequent prosperity of the late 1960s. The striking feature of the 1916 and 1904 birth cohorts is the substantial decline in the percentage employed, similar for both nonwhite and white males. The decline starts in the early forties, and increases thereafter, until at the conventional retirement age of 65 only about a quarter of the cohort is still employed in covered occupations.

For white females, the percentage employed declines from age 21 through age 28, reflecting withdrawals from raising families. Starting in the early thirties, the percentage employed increases continually to the mid-fifties. Only after that does the decline set in, and it is more gradual than that of males. During the childbearing ages, the percentage employed dropped from 46 to 27 percent. Since, in fact, the data shown here pertain only to covered employment, the actual percentage employed probably exceeded this by at least another 6 or 7 percentage points. Thus approximately three-fifths of the number of women initially employed are employed throughout this period. Although the higher percentage of women employed at the end of the 1940 birth cohort, in comparison with the beginning of the 1928 birth cohort, may be explained in part by census underenumeration, underenumeration is substantially less for women, and this same relation between cohorts can be observed between the other pairs of cohorts as well. This suggests that there is a successive increase in the percentage employed by each successive younger cohort.

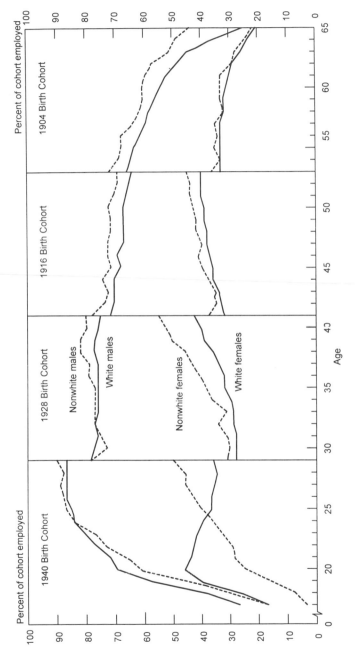

Figure 15.6 Percent of Cohort Employed by Race and Sex for Selected Birth Cohorts, 1957–69

Nonwhite women do not follow the pattern either for white women or of males. Their employment in the earlier years is substantially lower, but it increases steadily even during the childbearing ages. At age 25, it equals that of white women, and it continues to rise thereafter. As in the case of white women, this increase extends into the mid-fifties. In the oldest cohort, the employment of nonwhite women is almost identical with that of white women.

The percent-employed data, however, do not adequately reveal the year-to-year work-history changes. It is interesting to ask how people move in and out of employment in the various age groups, and to determine the relative importance of workers with single employers over time. Table 15.4 presents this information by race and sex for three age groupings in 1957–58 and 1968–69. An exit, for the purposes of this table, is a person who was employed in the first quarter of the initial year, but for whom there is no record of employment in the first quarter of the following year. An entrant is a person for whom there is no record of employment in the first quarter of the initial year, but who is employed in the first quarter of the following year. Persons having unchanged single employers in both years can also be identified, since the establishment identification number is given in the social security records. It should be borne in mind that the observations relate to a period of one quarter, and the absence of an employer report signifies that an individual was not employed in social-security-covered employment at any time during the quarter. On the other hand, the presence of an employer report does not necessarily mean that the person was fully employed during the whole quarter. Even a single week of employment within the quarter would be sufficient to generate an employer record. In view of this extended period over which the employment measurement is made, the number of exits and entrants is quite high. As many as 30 percent of females under age 24 exit in a single year; the smallest percentage of exits shown for any group in Table 15.4, about 7 percent, relates to males in what is presumably their period of highest employment, ages 25–59. Predictably, entrants are highest in the early age groups and lowest in the ages after 60. About 35–40 percent of the younger age groups, and 60–70 percent of the middle and older age groups, have single, unchanged employers in successive years. The older age group does not appear to have significantly lower continuity of employment than the middle group.

With respect to sex differences, females do have a higher level of entrants and exits than do males. A more detailed age grouping would, of course, reflect the initial high entry, subsequent exit during the childbearing period, and gradual reentry from age 30 onward. In the period over age 60, the work-history pattern of females is amazingly similar to that of males.

In terms of race, nonwhites also have higher entry and exit rates, and a somewhat lower percentage with single employers, but these racial differences also fade out in the most advanced age group.

Table 15.4 Work History of Employed Workers, 1957–58 and 1968–69
        (percent)

	Total initial year	Exits	Entrants	Unchanged single employers	Changed and multiple employers
1957–58, under 25					
White male	100	17	26	44	40
White female	100	30	38	41	29
Nonwhite male	100	22	29	40	38
Nonwhite female	100	37	52	38	24
1957–58, 25–59					
White male	100	9	7	66	25
White female	100	17	18	64	19
Nonwhite male	100	11	11	55	43
Nonwhite female	100	21	20	59	20
1957–58, 60 and over					
White male	100	21	8	66	13
White female	100	21	12	67	12
Nonwhite male	100	20	7	63	17
Nonwhite female	100	20	12	61	17
1968–69, under 25					
White male	100	12	32	36	51
White female	100	25	45	37	38
Nonwhite male	100	16	39	32	52
Nonwhite female	100	28	41	36	36
1968–69, 25–59					
White male	100	7	6	73	20
White female	100	14	16	64	22
Nonwhite male	100	10	10	52	38
Nonwhite female	100	15	18	56	29
1968–69, 60 and over					
White male	100	18	7	66	16
White female	100	19	8	69	12
Nonwhite male	100	11	7	58	30
Nonwhite female	100	21	11	59	20

Source: Based on detailed tabulations of Appendix Tables A-1 and A-2.

The work-history data thus suggest substantial churning of individuals in and out of employment, and the LEED data undoubtedly understate the actual amount of this churning, since lapses of employment which are less than one quarter are not captured. These changes in employment have implications for the change in total earnings. The employer is relieved of paying anything to those who leave his employment. On the other hand, he now becomes responsible for paying those who enter employment. In a static system, one would expect that the salaries of those who were retiring would be larger than those of new entrants, so that, on balance, employers would make a saving, which would be distributed among the employed workers as seniority increases. In this manner, everyone could receive an increase in pay without any increase in total earnings. In an expanding system, however, the larger size of new cohorts will mean that employment will be expanding, so that the payment to those entering may be larger than the saving on those retiring. In periods of increasing unemployment, on the other hand, one would expect that exits due to layoffs and reduced hirings would result in some net saving to the employer. The extent and magnitude of these changes in earnings are reflected in Table 15.5. In three years, 1957, 1960 and 1962, the reduction through exits did, in fact, exceed the increase through new entrants; this effect was primarily the result of recession and increasing unemployment. In two additional years, 1958 and 1963, there was an exact balance. In the remaining years, entrants' earnings exceeded exits' earnings, for some years by a substantial amount.

Payments to persons employed by unchanged single employers also contribute to the change in total earnings. It is illuminating to divide these people into two groups: those whose earnings decreased from one year to the next and those whose earnings increased. Decreases in earnings come about mainly by reduction in overtime or shifting to part time. As Table 15.5 shows, decreases in earnings are not insignificant. From 1957 to 1958, the magnitude of decreases in earnings was almost equal to that of increases in earnings, and even in the most expansionary year, decreases were over one-third the size of increases. What this suggests is that the earnings of a substantial body of individuals are actually reduced even in periods of expansion. The net change in

Table 15.5 Year-to-Year Change in Total Earnings by Type of Change, 1957–69 (billions of dollars)

Initial year	1957	1958	1959	1960	1961	1962	1963	1964	1965	1966	1967	1968
Initial total earnings	189	190	203	218	222	241	252	270	285	315	347	379
Earnings of exits	–16	–14	–13	–16	–15	–16	–16	–16	–16	–19	–22	–24
Earnings of entrants	+14	+14	+15	+13	+16	+15	+!6	+18	+21	+23	+24	+27
Decreases by unchanged employers	–10	–7	–7	–10	–7	–9	–8	–11	–11	–10	–12	–12
Increases by unchanged employers	+11	+16	+15	+14	+18	+16	+19	+18	+26	+27	+31	+34
Net change by changed and multiple employers	+1	+4	+5	+3	+7	+5	+7	+6	+10	+11	+11	+13
Final total earnings	190	203	218	222	241	252	270	285	315	347	379	417

Source: Based on Appendix Tables A-1 and A-2.

the earnings of people with changed or multiple employers also shows the same sort of pattern.

The process by which the total earnings in one year change to a new level of total earnings in the following year thus includes a variety of factors. The change from 1957 to 1958, for example, appears to be quite minor, from $189 to 190 billion, but the component elements involved in this change are quite large. Certainly the patterns of work history and the change in the structure of employment are considerably more important in determining total earnings than the average movement of the wage rate.

The size distribution of earnings

As a first approach to analyzing the behavior of the size distribution of earnings, it is useful to determine the effect upon that distribution over time of those individuals who leave employment (exits), and those who enter (entrants), as well as the changes in earnings of those who are continuously employed. Given the age profile of earnings, one might expect that those who exit from employment would have quite a different distribution of income from those who enter. Specifically, it would seem reasonable that those who leave employment would, on the average, have substantially higher incomes, and the variance of the size distribution of their earnings would be larger. Those who

Table 15.6 Quartile Distributions of Earnings, 1957–58 and 1968–69, for Exits, Entrants and Persons Employed Both Years, by Race and Sex

	1957–58			1968–69		
	Bottom quartile	Median	Top quartile	Bottom quartile	Median	Top Quartile
White males						
Entrants	$700	$1,700	$3,600	$800	$1,900	$4,500
Exits	800	2,100	4,000	900	2,700	5,900
Employed both years	2,900	4,500	6,000	4,200	6,900	9,500
White females						
Entrants	500	1,300	2,400	700	1,800	3,400
Exits	600	1,400	2,500	700	1,900	3,700
Employed both years	1,600	2,600	3,500	2,300	3,800	5,200
Nonwhite males						
Entrants	500	1,200	2,300	700	1,700	3,500
Exits	500	1,300	2,300	600	1,700	3,600
Employed both years	1,700	2,700	4,000	2,400	4,300	6,400
Nonwhite females						
Entrants	500	1,000	1,700	700	1,700	3,200
Exits	500	1,000	1,700	600	1,400	2,800
Employed both years	1,000	1,700	2,500	1,600	3,000	4,300

Source: Based on detailed tabulations of Appendix Table A-2.

enter employment might be expected to be similar to each other, with lower earnings and smaller variance. An examination of what actually takes place, however, is presented in Table 15.6. The surprising finding is that, for all groups, exits and entrants have very much lower levels of income than do those who remain employed. This strongly suggests that the exits and entrants are not primarily those entering the labor force for the first time and those retiring from it permanently, but rather lower-paid individuals who come in and go out of employment on a transient basis. It is true that for white males the level of earnings for exits is generally higher than for entrants, but for white females the difference is very much smaller, and it is practically nonexistent for nonwhite males and females.

Abstracting from the effect of exits and entrants, Figure 15.7 shows the change in the size distribution over time for employees with unchanged employers. In general, there has been some increase in inequality in the size distribution over time. Using the interquartile range as a percentage of the mean as a measure, dispersion increased from 1957 to 1968 from 0.69 to 0.77 for white males, from 0.73 to 0.76 for white females, from 0.85 to 0.93 for nonwhite males, and from 0.88 to 0.90 for nonwhite females. Such changes in inequality are not large, but they all are in the same direction. The differences among race and sex groups in inequality are also not large, with white males and females being the most equal and nonwhite males and females the most unequal.

The age composition of the various race–sex groups obviously affects this measure of the dispersion of the size distribution of earnings. As Table 15.7 shows, if the quartile distributions are examined within specific ages for the different race–sex groups, there is a significant decline in the amount of observed inequality for some groups. As might be expected, the greatest reduction in inequality appears for males, since for them the age profile rises and falls more steeply. For females, there is less reduction in inequality, and in fact, for nonwhite females of age 60 the dispersion is greater than the average for all groups combined. What Table 15.7 does suggest is that the differential observed in the average level of male and female earnings does not result from a highly unequal male distribution consisting of both lower-paid males and higher-paid males, contrasted with a cluster of females who tend to receive approximately the same earnings. In point of fact, female earnings by age are more unequal than male earnings. Male earnings do become more unequal with advancing age, but even at their most unequal point, they are more equal than those of females at any of the ages shown. This finding may well be attributable in part to a larger incidence of part-time work among females.

Although examination of the interquartile differences and the median levels of income does show the substantial differences in the size distribution of income for the different races and sexes, an actual comparison of the percentage

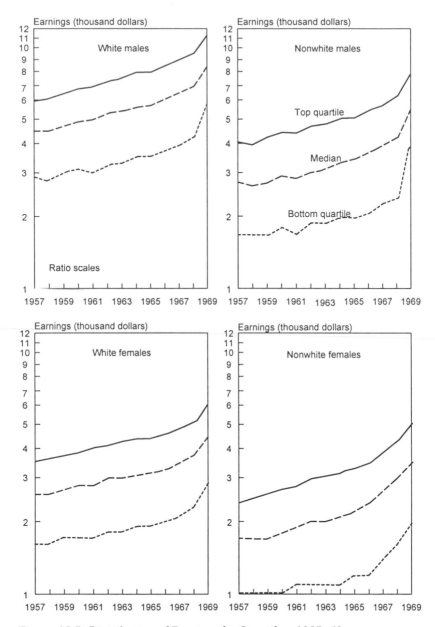

Figure 15.7 Distribution of Earnings by Quartiles, 1957–69

of individuals in the different income size classes by race and sex provides a sharper contrast. This is done in Table 15.8. Twenty-four percent of white males had incomes over $10,000 in 1968, whereas only 2 percent of white

Table 15.7 Dispersion of Earnings by Age, Sex and Race, 1968
(persons employed in both 1968 and 1969)

	First quartile	Median	Third quartile	Quartile difference as percent of mean
White males				
Age 60	$5,200	$7,400	$10,000	65
Age 45	6,200	8,500	11,500	62
Age 30	5,300	7,300	9,300	55
All ages	4,200	6,900	9,500	77
White females				
Age 60	2,900	4,100	5,700	68
Age 45	2,300	3,400	4,700	71
Age 30	2,500	4,000	5,500	75
All ages	2,300	3,800	5,200	76
Nonwhite males				
Age 60	3,300	4,700	6,600	70
Age 45	3,700	5,400	7,600	72
Age 30	3,500	4,800	6,700	67
All ages	2,400	4,300	6,400	93
Nonwhite females				
Age 60	1,100	2,300	3,600	109
Age 45	1,800	3,000	4,400	87
Age 30	2,100	3,400	4,800	79
All ages	1,600	3,000	4,300	90

Source: Based on detailed tabulations of Appendix Table A-2.

Table 15.8 Percentage of Individuals in Earnings Size Classes

	Under $3,000	$3,000–10,000	Over $10,000	Total
White males	20	56	24	100
White females	39	59	2	100
Nonwhite males	34	60	6	100
Nonwhite females	51	47	2	100

Source: Based on Appendix Table A-3.

females were in this class. Nonwhite males do considerably better than white females, having 6 percent in the over $10,000 class, but the percentage of nonwhite females matched that of white females exactly at this income level. However, 51 percent of nonwhite females were found in the lowest income class, i.e., under $3,000.

The apparent stability of the size distribution of earnings hides the churning at the level of the individual wage earner, which has already been mentioned in connection with the examination of work history. This effect is summarized in Table 15.9 for race and sex groups for two different periods.

Table 15.9 Percentage Distribution of Employees by Change in Earnings,
*   1957–58 and 1965–66*

		Employed both years			
	Exits	With decreases	No change	With increases	Entrants	Total
1957–58:						
White male	10	29	10	42	9	100
White female	17	21	9	36	17	100
Nonwhite male	15	30	9	34	12	100
Nonwhite female	19	19	14	29	19	100
1965–66:						
White male	7	21	6	56	10	100
White female	12	18	7	44	18	100
Nonwhite male	9	21	5	48	17	100
Nonwhite female	14	17	9	37	23	100

Source: Based on Appendix Tables A-1 and A-2.

In the recession period from 1957 to 1958, individuals who left employment, or suffered decreased or unchanged earnings, constituted approximately 50 percent of all workers, somewhat less for white males and females, and somewhat more for nonwhites. In contrast, in the period 1965–66, which was a period of upswing, between 60 and 65 percent of all individuals received increases, but even in this period the percentage with a decline or no change was appreciable, ranging from 25 to 30 percent over and above those who actually exited from employment. It should be recognized that the decreases in earnings are in most cases the result of individuals leaving employment during the course of the quarter, moving to a more part-time basis, or eliminating overtime. Some of the increase in earnings is due to a reversal of these factors. Whatever the cause, however, it is apparent from Table 15.9 that a substantial percentage of individuals is subject to earnings fluctuations due to the exits, decreases, increases, and entrances which take place.

The magnitude of the increases and decreases in earnings of individuals is, on the average, quite large. This is shown in Table 15.10, together with the percentage of employees in each year receiving increases and decreases. The interesting aspect of these figures is the relative stability of both the average decrease in earnings and the average increase. While both tend to fluctuate, as would be expected, with economic conditions, the amount of fluctuation of either the average decreases or the average increases does not seem large relative to their average level, but the difference between them does fluctuate considerably. In the recession year of 1958, the average decline was 14 percent, whereas the average increase was 17 percent. In contrast, in 1967, the average decline fell to 10 percent, and the average increase rose to 20 percent. Perhaps even more important was the fact that only 52 percent of the

Table 15.10 Percentage of Employees with Decreases and Increases in Earnings and Percentage Change in Earnings, 1957–69

| | No change or decrease | | Increase | | Net percent change in average earnings |
	Percent of employees	Changes in earnings	Percent of employees	Percent change in earnings	
1957–58	48	−14	52	17	1.0
1958–59	38	−14	62	19	6.6
1959–60	42	−12	58	19	5.4
1960–61	43	−14	57	18	2.9
1961–62	36	−11	64	19	6.9
1962–63	42	−12	58	17	4.1
1963–64	36	−11	64	18	6.2
1964–65	44	−11	56	18	3.8
1965–66	33	−11	67	20	7.5
1966–67	31	−10	69	20	8.0
1967–68	29	−12	71	19	8.2
1968–69	31	−12	69	20	8.4

Source: Based on Appendix Table A-2.

individuals employed in both years received increases from 1957 to 1958, whereas 69 percent did so from 1966 to 1967. In other words, the net change in average earnings is the result of the level of decreases, the level of increases, and the relative number of employees receiving decreases and increases. If the analysis of wage behavior is to be meaningful, such structural characteristics as these must be explicitly built into the analysis; it cannot be based on the change in average earnings, assuming it to be representative of most employees, when in fact it is a net result of widely differing behavior. As has been pointed out, the LEED data do not permit an analysis of hours actually worked, so that it has not been possible to take this element into account in analyzing wage behavior. Nevertheless, it again seems apparent from the nature of the earnings distributions and their changes over time that variations in hours worked may be fully as important as the behavior of wage rates.

4. SUMMARY AND CONCLUSIONS

This study of the anatomy of earnings behavior has focused on four aspects: age–earnings profiles and birth cohort earnings patterns, sex and race differences in age profiles and earnings patterns, work-history experience as related to age, sex and race, and the size distribution of earnings in terms of age, sex, and race, and its change over time.

The LEED data make it possible to trace both the shifts in age–earnings profiles over time and their relation to birth cohort patterns. For the period 1957–69, each birth cohort enjoys a continual rise in average earnings over its lifetime. The shape of the age–earnings profile results from faster growth for younger generations than for older generations, each generation passing those older than itself and in turn being passed by still younger generations. In this way, the rise and fall observed in the age–earnings profile can be fully reconciled with ever-rising birth cohort earnings patterns.

The disaggregation of the age–earnings profiles and birth cohort patterns by race and sex reveals striking differences among the different groups. White males not only have substantially higher overall earnings, but their age–earnings profiles show a substantially faster rise to a peak and a greater subsequent decline to retirement age than is true for other groups. The age profile for nonwhite males is of similar shape, but it is substantially lower, and peaks earlier. White females, in contrast, have age–earnings profiles which decline slightly at the beginning of the childbearing ages, but subsequently continue to rise even during the period when the age–earnings profiles for both white and nonwhite males are declining, although white female earnings never attain even the nonwhite male level. The profile for nonwhite women does not reflect the childbearing decline observed for white females, but a decline does set in at approximately the same age as for nonwhite males. The level of the age–earnings profile for nonwhite females is lower than for any other group.

Over time, age–earnings profiles have been shifting upward. In relative terms, the nonwhite profiles have shifted upward faster than the profiles for either white males or white females, thus narrowing the differential between the race groups. The age–earnings profile of white females, however, has shifted up more slowly than that of white males, thus causing the differential between white male earnings and white female earnings to widen.

The birth cohort earnings patterns for the different sex–race groups demonstrate that the differentials do result from differential rates of growth in earnings. After the early twenties, earnings of females grow at an appreciably lower rate than those of males. Nonwhite males grow at a slower rate than white males, but pass white females in the mid-twenties. Like the birth cohort earnings patterns for the population as a whole, the individual sex–race birth cohort patterns do not decline, except for brief periods in recessions; recessions tend to affect males and in particular nonwhite males more than females. This recession effect may well be due to greater involvement of males in direct production work, which entails layoffs in periods of declining output.

Male work history exhibits the expected pattern of a rising percentage of employment as youths enter the labor force, a period of steady high-level employment, and subsequent slow decline as a result of mortality and eventual retirement. For white females, in the childbearing years the percentage employed is reduced, although even at the lowest point the percentage employed is three-fifths as high as at its earlier peak. After the childbearing years, the percentage of women employed continues to rise until the mid-fifties, a good ten years longer than for men. Nonwhite females do not follow the pattern of white females, but instead the percentage employed rises steadily up to the mid-fifties.

Behind the percentage employed figures, there are in all cohorts a rather large number of both exits and entrants. Since the LEED data are based on quarterly employer reports, an exit is an individual who is employed in the first quarter of one year but not in the first quarter of the following year. Similarly, an entrant is a person who was not employed in the first quarter of one year but who was employed in the first quarter of the subsequent year. These definitions, of course, understate the actual amount of in and out movement that goes on; it is possible to be unemployed for several months and still be considered employed in both periods if the period of unemployment does not contain a complete calendar quarter. Data on the percentage of employed individuals whose earnings increase or decrease from one year to the next provide additional evidence of the importance of such changes in employment. Not only is the percentage of individuals whose earnings decline between two periods large, but the absolute level of the average decrease and average increase in earnings between two periods is also quite large. The usually fairly small average change in earnings is the net result of much larger movements in exits and entrants from employment, and decreases and increases in earnings. Substantial fluctuations in earnings do occur even in periods when there is little apparent change in average earnings.

The size distribution of earnings moves upward in level over time, and, on the average, has become marginally more unequal. It is not true, however, that the differences in average income between males and females can be explained in terms of greater variation in male earnings. As measured by the interquartile difference in earnings in relation to the mean, the earnings of females in specific age groups vary more than those of males.

Deflation of current earnings by the Consumer Price Index does not alter the general conclusions, either for the year-to-year changes or for the whole period 1959–69. As would be expected, the deflated 'real' changes in earnings are smaller than the current value changes, but since the same price deflator was used for all income levels and for all social and demographic groups, the structure of earnings behavior was unaffected by the deflation process.

The findings of this study have two important implications. First, demographic characteristics are central to an understanding of earnings differentials and the behavior of earnings over time. Second, work-history experience, its sensitivity to economic conditions, and its effect on earnings are important considerations for the analysis of policies related to income.

The importance of demographic factors for the determination of earnings has been generally recognized. A number of studies have adjusted age–sex–race groups for education, occupation, intelligence, skills, and other forms of human capital investment in an effort to explain, and in some cases to justify, the observed differentials. It may well be that cultural differences, differences in life-styles, differences in opportunities and rational or irrational discrimination do account for the observed differences; it is not the function of this paper to discuss causality. Whatever the cause, however, it is important to recognize that some entire groups of individuals do receive less for their employment activities, and such differences are important in determining the distribution of income in our society.

The existence of substantial fluctuations in individual incomes from period to period is important because these irregularities do not necessarily reflect transitory elements. It has been popular for economists to concentrate on longer and longer time horizons, and to concern themselves with lifetime or permanent income. But for many members of the lower income classes it is not possible to shift resources easily from one time-period to another. To be out of employment for a whole quarter may be quite serious for low-income individuals, and it is not possible for them to dip into savings to maintain consumption on a temporary basis. In point of fact, their major form of saving may be payments on installment debt, or in some cases on home mortgages. To the extent that such commitments are fixed in the short run, the individual may be forced, paradoxically, to curtail his current consumption in order to maintain his saving rate. The LEED data, of course, do not aggregate individuals into family units, and do not consider other sources of income such as transfer payments or income in kind. Where there are several wage earners in a family or other kinds of family income are available, the impact of the fluctuations in earnings on living standards may be less severe, but it seems reasonable that for families in the lower income groups it is quite substantial. Perhaps for lower income groups it would be more reasonable to think in terms of a current income hypothesis, which would suggest that what is received is what is spent, and that current living standards fluctuate directly with current income. In contrast, the permanent income hypothesis is a rich man's theory. Consumption can only be determined in terms of long-run income expectations and the pattern of life-cycle needs when the lack of correspondence between current income and outlay can be made up either by using existing assets or by borrowing against the expectation of future income. For the lower income groups, it is quite possible that next month's income is irrelevant, to say nothing of next year's.

16. The Measurement of the Supply and Use of Labor

Richard Ruggles
Yale University

Existing employment and unemployment statistics play a central role in: measuring the supply and use of labor, defining full employment in terms of the trade-off between the level of unemployment and the change in wages, and analyzing productivity change and the level of potential capacity of the economy. This paper examines different aspects of these three topics with the aid of data sets made available by the Bureau of Labor Statistics.

To examine the measurement of the supply and use of labor, the Current Population Surveys for the five periods from May 1973 through May 1977 were retabulated to measure employment and unemployment in terms of man-hours rather than persons. The chief adjustment involved taking part-time employment and unemployment into account. This analysis indicated that unemployment in terms of man-hours is significantly greater than the more conventional measure in terms of persons, suggesting that in order to obtain a better understanding of labor utilization employment and unemployment statistics should be compiled in terms of man-hours as well as persons.

The trade-off between unemployment and wages has usually been analyzed using time series data on unemployment levels and wage changes. Because of the nature of the data and the relatively small number of observations, the results of such analyses have generally been unsatisfactory. Another possible approach is to utilize cross-section data on unemployment levels and wage changes for different standard metropolitan areas available for the years 1973 and 1974 from the Current Population Survey and the Bureau of Labor Statistics Hours and Earnings Data. These data indicate that the average wage change in labor market areas with high levels of unemployment is not very different from the wage change in labor market areas with low levels of

This chapter first appeared as a background paper for the National Commission on Employment and Unemployment Statistics, 1979.

unemployment. Although such evidence is not conclusive, it does suggest that wages may not be highly sensitive to a relatively wide range of labor market conditions.

Finally, in measuring potential capacity it is important to take productivity change into account. The currently accepted analysis of recent productivity change concludes that the long-term trend has slowed. However, analysis of data provided by the BLS for 390 manufacturing industries indicates that the lower rate of productivity change observed in the recent period may be cyclical rather than long term. No slowdown was observed for the period through 1973, and even for the period through 1975 the rate of productivity change did not decline for industries having similar changes in output. This suggests that the observed decline in the rate of aggregate productivity change may well have been due to the sharp decline in output in the recession of 1974–75.

The overall conclusion that can be drawn from this paper is that presently available employment and unemployment statistics are inadequate for the analysis of major policy questions. Existing aggregate time series data cannot provide the information needed to analyze such questions as the supply and use of labor, the trade-off between unemployment and wages or the relation between productivity and potential output. What is required is the development of a comprehensive and integrated data base of both household and enterprise microdata that will permit analysis of interrelated economic questions at a highly disaggregated level. Attention needs to be directed to obtaining more meaningful integrated sets of data, rather than to collecting separate and independent time series.

1. INTRODUCTION

The economic events of the past decade have emphasized the need for accurate and valid measurements of economic activity and capacity utilization. The recession of 1974–75 was the most severe since the 1930s, and the persistence of inflation in periods of recession and sluggish growth has been unprecedented.

Few would deny the importance of employment and unemployment statistics as indexes of economic activity and capacity utilization. Since the Depression of the 1930s the public, the media, the Congress and government officials have all attached great importance to the monthly release of information on employment and unemployment, its only rival in the public view among government statistics being the Consumer Price Index. There is general agreement that the available employment and unemployment statistics have served well as indicators of changes in economic activity, but there is less agreement on how well they measure the degree of capacity utilization. In part, this reflects the fact that employment and unemployment statistics may seem to give conflicting indications of what is taking place at any given time. In some periods both employment and unemployment may rise, suggesting that the increase in activity is not keeping pace with the growth in the supply of available labor. To keep capacity fully utilized, it is not sufficient that the economy grow; it must grow enough to absorb the increase in the number of people wanting to work.

To evaluate the adequacy of employment and unemployment statistics for measuring economic activity and capacity utilization, three specific topics need to be investigated. These are: the measurement of labor supply and its use, the concept and measurement of full employment and the relation of employment and productivity to the measurement of capacity utilization. In all of these measurements, the employment and unemployment statistics play a central role.

2. MEASUREMENT OF SUPPLY AND USE OF LABOR

Available Data on Labor Force, Employment and Unemployment

Each month the Bureau of the Census collects for the Bureau of Labor Statistics a Current Population Survey (CPS) of a sample of households, which asks the labor force status of each individual over the age of 16 in the household. This survey serves as the basis for the most widely used measures of the labor force, employment and unemployment in the United States. The published statistics include measures classified in terms of a variety of demographic, social and economic characteristics. In recent years the size of the sample surveyed has been increased to provide more information on the labor force conditions in different geographic areas.

Table 16.1 summarizes the information on the employment status of the civilian noninstitutional population 16 years of age and older for the period 1973–77. The data shown refer specifically to the month of May in each year; comparable data are of course available for every month.

Concepts Used in Present Measures of Labor Supply

As is apparent from Table 16.1, each individual reporting employment status is classified into one of three categories: employed, unemployed or not in the labor force. The definition of an employed worker includes all of those who during the survey week did any work at all as paid employees or in their own business; all of those who did not work but had jobs from which they were temporarily absent due to illness, bad weather, vacation, labor–management disputes or various personal reasons, whether or not they were paid by their

Table 16.1 Employment, Unemployment, and the Labor Force —
Noninstitutional Civilian Population 16 Years of Age and Over
(thousands of persons, seasonally adjusted, May figures)

	1973	1974	1975	1976	1977
1. Employed	84,021	86,062	84,379	87,527	90,267
2. Unemployed	4,304	4,691	8,442	7,041	6,894
Total civilian labor force	88,325	90,753	92,821	94,568	97,161
Unemployment as a percent of the civilian labor force	4.9%	5.2%	9.1%	7.4%	7.1%
3. Not in the labor force	57,281	57,525	58,049	59,001	58,939
Total noninstitutional civilian population 16 years & older	145,606	148,278	150,870	153,569	156,100
Labor force participation rate	61.3%	61.8%	61.5%	61.6%	62.2%

Sources: 1973 and 1974: *Economic Report of the President* (1975), Table C24, p. 277. 1975, 1976 and 1977: *Economic Report of the President* (1978), Table B27, p. 289; U.S. Department of Labor, Bureau of Labor Statistics, *Handbook of Labor Statistics.*

employers or were seeking other jobs; and unpaid family workers working 15 or more hours a week. Each employed person is counted only once, even if he held more than one job. Unemployed persons include those who did not work at all during the survey week, and were waiting either to be called back to a job from which they had been laid off, or to report to a new job scheduled to start within 30 days or had actively looked for work within the preceding four-week period. Persons not in the labor force are defined as all civilians 16 years of age and over who are not classified as either employed or unemployed. This includes persons engaged in doing their own housework or going to school, those unable to work, the retired, and 'other'. The 'other' group includes voluntarily idle seasonal workers for whom the survey fell in an off season and who were not looking for other work.

By classifying each individual exclusively into one of the categories of employed, unemployed, or not in the labor force, individuals who work part-time or want part-time employment are not adequately accounted for. Thus an individual whose working hours have been cut back below what is usual by his employer is, on the basis of presently accepted definitions, classified as employed. Conversely, an individual who is looking for only a part-time job is classified as fully unemployed. The CPS does, however, contain sufficient information to determine the exact nature of each individual's employment status, and BLS provides numerous tabulations showing voluntary and involuntary part-time employment, as well as the reasons why individuals are not employed or looking for work. In one of its many measures of unemployment, BLS does take part-time employment into account in calculating the supply of available labor not utilized. This measure is called 'labor force time lost', and is defined as the aggregate number of hours lost by the unemployed and persons on part-time for economic reasons as a percentage of potentially available labor force hours. Relatively little attention has been directed to this measure, and in fact in 1978 the Council of Economic Advisers dropped it from the *Economic Report of the President* where it had traditionally been presented in Table B7. Instead CEA substituted the civilian labor force participation rate, which shows the civilian labor force as a percentage of the civilian noninstitutional population. In view of the growing importance of part-time job holders in recent years, however, it has become more important to present employment, unemployment and labor force data which fully reflect the activities of part-time job holders and job seekers, rather than classifying them as wholly employed or wholly unemployed.

A Proposed Reformulation of Labor Supply Measurement

It is possible to reformulate the concepts of 'employment', 'unemployment' and 'not in the labor force' in terms of total supply of man-hours in each of these categories rather than number of persons, not only to reflect the role of part-time workers but also to give additional information on such categories as discouraged job seekers, individuals uncertain as to whether they want jobs, and individuals who want jobs but are unable to take them. All of this information is contained in the CPS, and the additional data required to subclassify 'employed', 'unemployed' and 'not in the labor force' and to convert the data to a man-hours basis can be obtained by reprocessing the survey for each year. A summary is given in Table 16.2.

This table resembles Table 16.1 in its general form, but additional breakdowns are provided for each of the categories 'employed', 'unemployed' and 'not in the labor force', and the unit of measurement is man-hours rather number of persons. As in Table 16.1, the month referred to in each year is May. Unlike Table 16.1, however, no seasonal adjustment has been applied.

The CPS figures show that during this period full-time employed persons worked approximately 42 hours per week. While there was some variation by race, age and sex, the average did not change significantly over the years from 1973 to 1977. For white fully employed workers, the figure was identical in 1973 and 1977 and for nonwhites it increased only slightly. Part-time workers who were voluntarily working part-time because they did not want full-time jobs show somewhat greater year-to-year fluctuations but averaged approximately 19 hours per week, less than half that of full-time workers. Part-time workers who were working part time because full-time work was not available averaged about 31 hours per week, but there was some decline in this figure

Price Behavior

Table 16.2 Employment, Unemployment, and the Labor Force —
Noninstitutional Civilian Population 16 Years of Age and Over
(millions of man-hours, seasonally adjusted, May figures)

	1973	1974	1975	1976	1977
1. Employed man-hours					
Working full-time	2,883	2,942	2,832	2,960	3,066
Working part-time voluntarily	250	246	247	263	270
Working part-time involuntarily	64	69	113	87	85
Total	3,197	3,255	3,193	3,310	3,421
2. Unemployed man-hours					
Unemployed full-time workers	140	157	294	242	233
Unemployed part-time workers	18	17	27	24	26
Partially unemployed workers	25	29	46	41	48
Discouraged workers	24	29	41	37	42
Total	207	232	408	344	349
Total civilian labor force man-hours	3,404	3,487	3,601	3,654	3,770
Unemployment man-hours as a percent of the civilian labor force	6.0%	6.6%	11.3%	9.4%	9.3%
3. 'Uncertain workers' man-hours	215	217	243	240	238
Total potential civilian labor force man-hours	3,619	3,704	3,844	3,894	4,008
Not employed man-hours as a percent of potential labor force man-hours	11.4%	12.1%	16.9%	15.0%	14.6%
4. Not in labor force man-hours					
Wants job but unavailable for work	157	145	131	153	171
Does not want job	2,016	2,025	2,016	2,042	2,030
Nonworking hours of voluntary part-time workers:					
Employed	316	328	298	317	331
Unemployed	23	23	33	13	32
Total	2,515	2,521	2,478	2,525	2,564
Total man-hours of noninstitutional civilian population 16 years and older	6,131	6,225	6,322	6,419	6,572
Potential labor force participation rate	59.0%	59.6%	60.8%	60.7%	61.0%

Sources: Based on retabulation and analysis of the Current Population Surveys for May 1973, 1974,
1975, 1976 and 1977. The retabulated CPS data were used to provide more detailed breakdowns
of the seasonally adjusted data in Table 16.1.

over the period from 1973 to 1977. The total number of man-hours for all
employed is the sum of the man-hours of these three groups.

Although it is, of course, not possible to determine the number of hours the
unemployed failed to work, it is reasonable to assign to the different categories
of unemployed the same number of man-hours as were worked by those who
were employed in that category. Thus those who were laid off from or were
looking for full-time work were assumed to have been unemployed for 42
hours. Those laid off from or looking for part-time work were assumed to be
unemployed for 19 hours. In counting unemployment, furthermore, it is necessary to include the unemployed hours of those who were not fully employed but

had wished to be so. For 1973, this came to approximately 11 hours. It is quite possible that those who indicated that they wanted full-time work did not, in fact, want to work the 42 hours full-time workers did. On the other hand, it is also probably true that some of those who did work the 42-hour average would have preferred to work less, but for job-related reasons could not. While 42 hours per week may not be a sustainable rate for any single worker or group of workers, it is interesting to note that for all full-time workers this rate did not fluctuate significantly from 1973 to 1977.

Finally, there is still another group that should be considered to be unemployed. These are the individuals who indicated that they would like a regular job but were discouraged from looking for work because they did not believe any was available in their line of work or area, or because they felt that they lacked the necessary schooling, training, skills or experience to get a job in the current job market. These are generally known as discouraged workers.

The sum of the employed man-hours and the unemployed man-hours add up to the total man-hours in the labor force, and the unemployed man-hours can be shown as a percentage of total labor force man-hours. This is done in Table 16.2. It will be noted that after introducing the part-time category and taking discouraged workers into account, the level of unemployment calculated in man-hours is considerably higher than that computed on the basis of persons alone and shown in Table 16.1.

It is apparent, furthermore, that the concept of individuals not in the labor force is not quite as definite as would be suggested by the trichotomy 'employed'/'unemployed'/'not in the labor force'. When individuals who are not classified as either employed or unemployed are asked whether they would like a regular job, a substantial number of them respond that they do not know. In other words, these individuals are uncertain whether they would accept a job if it were available. To some extent, this response may reflect an unwillingness to make a commitment, either for the respondent or for others about whom the respondent may be reporting. This may be especially true if the respondent perceives that a negative response would meet with the enumerator's disapproval. While it would be incorrect to classify these individuals as unemployed, it is also incorrect to classify them as not part of the labor force. Certainly a substantial number of them would be willing to accept a job if it were offered. For this reason, this category has been shown separately in Table 16.2. Relative to actual unemployment the 'uncertain' category is surprisingly large, suggesting that there is an available labor supply over and above those who are classified as unemployed. By adding the man-hours of those who are uncertain whether they want work to the total actual labor force, a new figure for the potential labor force can be obtained, and the percentage of the potential labor force not employed can be shown. These figures are substantially higher than the conventional unemployment percentages, suggesting that the supply of labor may be larger than is indicated by current measures. The term 'potential' as used here does not refer to the labor supply that might be available under alternative conditions; rather, it measures the maximum labor supply under current market conditions. If 'uncertain' and 'discouraged' workers do not want full-time jobs, the estimate of the potential labor supply will, of course, be excessive. But it is equally in error to assume that the 'uncertain' and 'discouraged' workers do not contribute anything to the potential labor supply.

The category 'not in the labor force' can be broken down into three sub-categories. First, there are those individuals who indicate that they would like a regular job but are not available for work because of other commitments such as schooling, child care, family responsibilities, etc. Second, the largest category are those who say they do not want a job and thus have ruled themselves out of the labor market. Third, in a similar manner those who indicate that they want to work part-time only must have the remainder of their time classified as not in the labor force. The potential labor force as a percentage of the total civilian noninstitutional population over the age of 16 years does show a somewhat larger increase from 1973 to 1977 than does the labor force participation rate shown in Table 16.1.

The reformulated labor supply measurements shown in Table 16.2 thus provide a significantly different picture of employment conditions from that shown by the conventional measures. The major change results from taking more accurately into account the role of part-time workers, both those who wish to work part-time and those who are forced to work part-time due to lack of full-time employment. The other elements introduced into the table, discouraged workers and individuals who are uncertain whether they want employment, are less important quantitatively, but they are useful in that they remind the user that the distinction between being unemployed and not being in the labor force is a difficult one to make, and the measurement of potential labor supply may therefore be imprecise.

3. THE CONCEPT OF FULL EMPLOYMENT AND ITS MEASUREMENT

The Concept of Full Employment

As has already been noted, if an economy is operating at full employment this does not imply that unemployment will be zero. Some measurable frictional unemployment will always exist, because of normal labor turnover and new entrants into the labor force. In addition, there may be some structural unemployment that does not easily respond to a generalized increase in the demand for labor. Certain individuals may be unqualified for the jobs employers have to offer, or in some regions there may be declining industries which are forced to lay off workers because of competition from expanding industries in other regions. Thus determination of what constitutes 'full employment' is an empirical question.

The Council of Economic Advisers identifies certain periods in the past when the economy was operating at full employment, generally at or near the top of cyclical expansions. The CEA argues that the level of unemployment observed in these periods is that which could be expected when the economy is operating satisfactorily without substantial inflation, and on this basis it has developed benchmark unemployment rates corresponding to 'full employment'. For the period from 1952 to 1958, the benchmark rate was put at 4 percent, on the ground that the economy approached full employment during 1955 and at that point it achieved an unemployment rate of this level. The unemployment level of about 3 percent in 1952 and 1953 was attributed to the Korean War boom, and was considered to be at over-full employment. In extrapolating the benchmark unemployment rate to other years, the CEA has taken the changing demographic composition of the labor force into account. Unemployment rates for younger people and women are higher than for adult males, and because of the increase in the proportion of younger people in the population and the greater labor force participation of women, these groups have become a larger proportion of the labor force. CEA argues that such a demographic shift should be reflected in a higher benchmark unemployment rate since each group should be weighted by what is considered to be its 'normal' full employment unemployment rate. For this reason, therefore, the benchmark unemployment rate for 1977 is estimated by CEA to be 4.9 percent.

It is, however, not necessarily valid to assume that each demographic group has its own 'normal' unemployment rate. If, as their unemployment rates and wage scales imply, young adults and women represent less preferred labor, the unemployment rate for adult males will always be lower. While the young adults and women may exhibit more movement in and out of the labor force and fill jobs with higher turnover rates and seasonality, it is difficult to measure either how much of such behavior is voluntary or how much, if any, of their higher level of unemployment is accounted for by such behavior. As these groups become a larger proportion of the labor supply, they may very well develop employment patterns closer to those of adult males (given an adequate level of demand) and hence their 'equilibrium' unemployment rates may appear to change. Nevertheless, even under present conditions, the young adult population and the women represent a reserve supply of labor that can be drawn on as the adult male supply is used up. The proper full employment concept should be one that does not assume a completely segregated labor force. (It is interesting to note that CEA does not assume a segregated market for nonwhite labor, though the same statistical argument would apply.)

The benchmark rate, once determined, plays a crucial role in the Council's analysis of the problem of combating inflation. The CEA considers that the current inflation had its roots in the late 1960s. They state that, 'During this period the economy reached very high levels of employment and resource utilization. The unemployment rate was less than 4 percent in every year from 1966 to 1969, when it reached 3.5 percent, the lowest rate since the Korean War. The major factor initiating the inflation was the traditional one of excess demand' (*Economic Report of the President*, 1978, p. 139). Such a view has as its basis a belief that there is a trade-off between the level of unemployment and the rate of increase in wages and prices. It is argued that in tight labor markets, wages will rise substantially faster than in labor markets where there is high unemployment. Empirical verification of this phenomenon is difficult since it is generally agreed that wages are sensitive not only to the demand for labor but also to prices; many wage contracts contain explicit escalator clauses tied to the cost of living. Time series analysis cannot easily determine the relative importance of labor market tightness and cost-of-living increases in determining wage increases, and recent arguments that for institutional and other reasons the trade-off curve between unemployment levels and wage changes shifts significantly over time further complicates the analysis.

Possibility of Analyzing the Trade-off Between Unemployment Levels and Wage Changes

In recent years, the expansion of the Current Population Survey has made it possible to measure the relative levels of unemployment in different labor market areas. The hours and earnings data collected by the BLS can be used to measure the changes in hours and earnings in different labor market areas by specific industry. Bringing these two bodies of data together makes it possible to ask whether the behavior of average hourly earnings differs in those labor markets with low unemployment relative to those where unemployment is high. Because the changes in consumer prices are quite similar for different geographic areas, the cross-sectional analysis of the relationship between unemployment levels and changes in average hourly earnings is not subject to the identification problem that exists with time series analysis. The results of the cross-sectional analysis for different years are shown in Table 16.3.

As can be seen in Table 16.3, the tapes provided by BLS contained reports on unemployment and changes in average hourly earnings for a considerable number of SMSAs in 1973 and 1974, and for a small number in 1975. For 1973, approximately a third of the SMSAs had unemployment rates below 4 percent, and another third had unemployment rates in excess of 6 percent. With the recession in 1974, there was a substantial increase in unemployment, but it was still true that 20 percent of the SMSAs reporting had unemployment

Table 16.3 *Change in Average Hourly Earnings in Manufacturing for Standard Metropolitan Areas Classified by Unemployment Level, 1973, 1974 and 1975 (percent)*

Unemployment level	1973		1974		1975	
	No. SMSAs	Percent change	No. SMSAs	Percent change	No. SMSAs	Percent change
Under 2%	1	7.3	0	–	–	–
2 to 3%	18	9.9	6	7.7	–	–
3 to 4%	20	7.3	23	10.0	–	–
4 to 5%	37	8.3	23	8.2	–	–
5 to 6%	20	7.5	39	9.6	3	7.6
6 to 7%	24	6.8	25	8.1	2	10.1
7 to 8%	13	7.2	23	8.7	4	8.4
8 to 9%	3	7.6	9	9.4	1	8.0
Over 9%	2	7.5	4	8.5	2	10.4
Total	138	7.7	152	9.0	12	8.7

Source: Computer tapes provided by BLS on unemployment by area and hours and earnings by area and industry.

of less than 4 percent. None of the small number reporting has such low levels in 1975. Although the change in average hourly earnings varied greatly among individual SMSAs, ranging from 1 or 2 percent to as high as 24 percent, the averages shown in Table 16.3 for various levels of unemployment show relatively little variation. Some slight tendency to larger increases in average hourly earnings can be seen for very low unemployment levels in 1973, but the remainder of the table lends no support to the existence of a trade-off in either 1973 or 1974.

A regression analysis relating the percentage change in average hourly earnings to the percentage unemployment level for individual SMSAs gave the results shown in Table 16.4.

Table 16.4 *Regression Analysis for SMSAs, 1973–75*

	1973	1974	1975
R^2	0.11	0.06	0.17
Regression coefficient	–0.40	–0.11	+0.57
Standard error of coefficient	0.10	0.20	0.40
T	–3.99	–0.55	+1.42

The correlation between unemployment levels and the changes in wages is very low in all years. For the year 1973, however, the relation was statistically significant, and the sign of the regression coefficient was negative, indicating that there were larger changes in average hourly earnings at lower levels of unemployment.

There is, of course, no reason to assume that the relationship between unemployment levels and the change in average hourly earnings is linear. In order to test this, two separate regressions were computed for each year, one for very low unemployment levels and one for higher unemployment levels. These results are shown in Table 16.5 for the years 1973 and 1974; insufficient data were available for 1975.

Table 16.5 Regressions for Low and Higher Employment Levels, 1973 and 1974

	1973		1974	
	Below 3.5%	Above 3.5%	Below 3.5%	Above 3.5%
R^2	0.05	0.03	0.07	0.00
Regression coefficient	−1.14	−0.24	+1.68	−0.02
Standard error of coefficient	0.44	0.12	0.52	0.13
T	−2.60	−1.95	+3.23	−0.16

A steeper negative relation does emerge at very low unemployment levels for the year 1973. However, for the year 1974, the relationship reverses (i.e., below 3.5 percent unemployment lower unemployment levels are associated with *smaller* increases in average hourly earnings). This latter result is in part due to a single outlying observation: Witchita Falls, Texas, with a 3.4 percent level of unemployment, reported a 23.7 percent increase in average hourly earnings, far larger than observed in any other SMSA with either lower or higher unemployment. What emerges most strongly is that for unemployment levels above 3.5 percent, where the majority of the observations lie in both years, no significant relationship existed in either 1973 or 1974 between unemployment levels and changes in average hourly earnings.

Different SMSAs do have different types of labor markets, and other factors besides the unemployment rate may enter into the categorization of what is tight or loose. Furthermore, recorded changes in average hourly earnings in manufacturing reflect factors other than changes in wage rates. The mix of workers within industries, the amount of overtime, and the relative change in employment in different industries would all affect the observed average hourly earnings figures. The relation between the level of unemployment and changes in wages may also be considerably more complex than the simple relation described above. For example, lags in the relationship or other factors may be important. It is thus possible that a relationship may exist between labor market tightness and change in average hourly earnings that the available data do not reveal. If there were a significant trade-off between labor market tightness and wage change, however, it seems likely that it would have been apparent even in such rough data. Certainly it can be argued that although the CPS unemployment data for SMSAs may have a high error component, they do adequately distinguish those SMSAs which have high unemployment levels from those where there is little or no unemployment. Thus the large cities in the northeast have expectedly higher unemployment levels than the faster-growing areas in the sunbelt and the west. Furthermore, there is no reason to believe that 'inflationary expectations', which are often cited as important factors influencing wage behavior, should differ among SMSAs, since the change in prices does not differ much among them. It is significant therefore that the available data do not contain any evidence of a trade-off between the level of unemployment and the increase in average hourly earnings. Although a possible relation between unemployment levels and the change in average hourly earnings is suggested for 1973 at very low levels of unemployment, even here it accounts for a very small share of the observed change in average hourly earnings. In the year 1974, no relationship at all could be observed.

Given existing information, it does not seem possible to arrive at a satisfactory measure of what level of unemployment constitutes 'full employment'. To answer satisfactorily the question of whether a significant trade-off actually exists over observed variations in the level of unemployment, considerably more research with better information than is now available would be needed. As already suggested, the changes in average hourly earnings data reflect many factors in addition to changes in wage rates. They are unit value measures rather than properly constructed price indexes for wages, and reflect demographic shifts in the labor force and other changes in labor mix. The BLS has long recognized this, and in recent years has supplemented the average hourly earnings figures with an employment cost index which attempts to measure the change in average hourly earnings of employees in specific occupations. The employment cost index is not available for SMSAs, but even if it were it would still suffer from many of the faults of the average hourly earnings index. What is needed is measurement of actual changes in straight-time average hourly earnings computed at the level of the individual employee. Such measurements for individual employees could then be combined to provide a true price index for wages, much in the way prices of individual commodities are combined into a commodity price index. Furthermore, if, in addition to collecting hours and earnings for each individual employee, information were also obtained on the individual's occupation, age, sex and employer, more sophisticated analyses of wage and employment behavior could be carried out. For any occupation, for example, it would be possible to analyze the effect on the average wage change of exits, entrants, and the wage change of those who remained employed. Thus collecting information for individual employees does not preclude occupational analysis of wage change, but the current Employment Cost Index does preclude adequate analysis of either occupational or individual wage behavior.

4. THE RELATION OF EMPLOYMENT AND PRODUCTIVITY TO THE MEASUREMENT OF CAPACITY UTILIZATION

The Relation of Changes in Employment to Changes in Output

Fluctuations in employment over the cycle tend to be smaller than fluctuations in output. There are a number of reasons for this. During recessions producers are able to lay off only those workers directly employed on the production operations that are being cut back. Other workers performing overhead functions or in supervisory roles may be redundant, but cannot be dispensed with because of the nature of their functions. Producers may also consider that for future production reasons it may be advisable to continue the employment of certain individuals even though their services may not be required during slack periods. In other words, for a given cutback in output, producers may find it neither possible nor desirable to cut employment back equally. By the same token, in recovery from recession output can and does increase very much faster than man-hours, not only through better utilization of existing labor and the spreading of overhead labor, but also because many industries may be subject to decreasing costs with increased output.

Apart from its cyclical variation, over longer periods of time productivity can be expected to increase due to long-run technological change, learning by doing, increased skills of the labor force and use of more and better capital equipment. Economists have traditionally considered that such long-term productivity change is of quite a different nature from short-run cyclical change, and that it reflects persistent long-term forces.

The Concept of Productivity and its Measurement

For analyzing the process of production, productivity measurement should reflect the contributions of all the factors of production, including both capital and labor. Furthermore, the different qualities of the factors of production should also be taken into account in the measurement of inputs. Although many private researchers have constructed productivity measures based upon such principles, the productivity measures published by BLS generally refer solely to labor input in terms of employment or man-hours, without regard to differences in the quality of labor used and without taking capital into account, and it is these measures that are the basis for most policy discussions. The current employment statistics collected by BLS serve as the basis for the measurement of labor inputs, and these are used in conjunction with various output measures to yield different measures of productivity change. The three most commonly used productivity measures are the BLS productivity indexes published for selected industries, which are based for the most part on physical measures of output; productivity measures based on deflated gross output data obtained by deflating census production data by BLS wholesale prices data; productivity measures based on the real gross product estimates of the Bureau of Economic Analysis.

Although the BLS productivity indexes published for selected industries may, in fact, be the most reliable and accurate measures of productivity, they are somewhat fragmentary, representing eight mining, 44 manufacturing and 12 other industries. Individual indexes are compiled for selected 2-, 3- and 4-digit industries, but no general productivity index is attempted. Productivity measures based on the deflated gross output measures are more comprehensive, but these are also restricted to mining and manufacturing.

The industry output measure is based on value of shipments adjusted for inventory change and does not take into account the goods and services firms purchase from one another. Therefore, in any given industry, the productivity figures can be seriously affected by shifts in the organization of production involving vertical integration, the extent of subcontracting, and sources of material supply. The method of deflation also presents serious problems. The available wholesale price information does not and cannot adequately reflect quality change or the introduction of new products. The Wholesale Price Index, furthermore, adequately covers only a small fraction of manufacturing and mining.

In contrast with the gross output measures of productivity, the real gross product measures based on the national accounts data provided by BEA are comprehensive in that they cover all industries and all sectors of the economy. Furthermore, the BEA gross product measures only that output that originates within a given industry, and does not involve double counting. There are, however, other difficulties with the real gross product measure. The same deflation problem exists for real gross product as for the census gross output, namely. the price information on which the deflation is based is severely inadequate. The inadequacy is more important for the BEA real gross product measure, however, since it is more comprehensive and the price information outside mining and manufacturing is of an even poorer quality. In addition, the measurement of real output is conceptually much more difficult in nongoods-producing sectors. In the distributive trades, finance, insurance and real estate and services, it is often necessary to assume that outputs are best measured by inputs, so that the resulting productivity measure is meaningless if input directly corresponds to output productivity change is constrained to be zero.

The Current View of Productivity and Capacity Utilization

Despite the major deficiencies in productivity measurement, considerable use is made of the existing estimates since they are all that is available. Figure 16.1, for instance, is taken from the *Economic Report of the President, January 1978* and shows productivity in the private nonfarm business economy from 1950 to 1977. The CEA uses these figures in constructing a measure of the total capacity of the economy at full employment levels. They point out that from 1950 to 1968, private nonfarm productivity expanded by about 2.6 percent annually, but that from 1968 to 1977, it rose by only about 1.4 percent per year. They recognize that part of this difference in performance was caused by the incomplete recovery from recession, noting that productivity tends to grow faster than its long-run trend when the economy is on the upswing of a cycle, and slower during the downswing. But after correcting for cyclical factors, the CEA still finds a difference — 2.5 percent in the earlier period as against 1.6 percent in recent years. They argue that this slowdown in productivity growth is one of the most significant economic problems of recent years, and in light of this apparent decline in the rate of productivity increase, they have lowered their estimate of potential output. They now estimate that the economy was operating in 1977 at about 95 percent of its potential capacity.

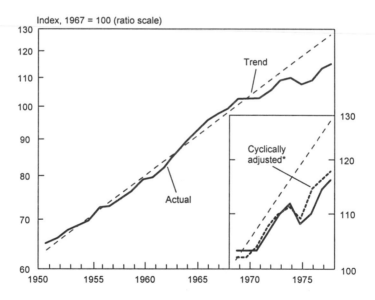

*The cyclical adjustment is based on a regression of productivity on the current and lagged unemployment rate from 1950 to 1980.

Sources: Department of Labor and Council of Eocnomic Advisers.

Figure 16.1 Productivity in the Private Nonfarm Business Economy

The CEA puts forth a variety of reasons to explain such a drop in the rate of productivity increase. For example, they suggest that the slower growth of the capital stock explains at least some of the slower growth in productivity after 1968, and that the accelerated introduction of government regulations dealing with environment, health and safety may also have been responsible for some of the slowdown. Finally, they suggest that much of the recent slow growth in productivity may be attributed to the effect of the extreme instability of the economy since 1968 on investment.

It is a matter of considerable importance as to whether the views about employment and productivity set forth by the CEA are, in fact, based upon valid and reliable analysis. If there has been a decline in the long-term rate of productivity increase, the economy may indeed be operating as close to capacity as is suggested by the Council. If on the other hand the observed decline in productivity is of a cyclical nature, potential output may be quite different from that estimated by CEA and the degree of underutilization of capacity may be substantially underestimated. Thus it will be useful to analyze in somewhat more detail what has happened to productivity in the various sectors over these periods.

Analysis of Productivity Change in Manufacturing Industries

BLS provides productivity measurements for 390 different manufacturing industries and these data constitute some of the best information that is available on productivity. Like the CEA productivity estimates, they do in the aggregate show a higher rate of productivity increase from 1958 to 1968 (3.5 percent per year) than in the more recent period, 1968–75 (2.2 percent per year).

Part of the problem in comparing productivity change since 1968 with that prior to 1968 is that the period since 1968 includes two recessions, whereas the period from 1958 to 1968 included only one. As is indicated in Table 16.6, the average productivity change for the period from 1968 to 1973 is 3.4 percent, and thus is not significantly different from the change of 3.5 percent observed for the period 1958–68.

The apparent decline in the rate of productivity increase in manufacturing thus is accounted for by extending the period of comparison to include the two recession years of 1974 and 1975. Comparing the two periods, 1958–68 and 1968–75, it can be seen in Table 16.6 that during the period 1958–68 the number of industries with high rates of output growth was much larger than the number with high rates of output growth during 1968–75. Conversely, only 22 industries showed actual declines in output from 1958 to 1968, whereas 167 industries showed declines in output from 1968 to 1975. As would be expected, productivity change is closely related to the rate of change in output. Industries which had an average rate of growth of 10 percent or more a year

Table 16.6 Relation of Average Output Change to Average Annual
Productivity Change in Manufacturing Industries, 1958–68,
1968–73 and 1968–75

Output change	1958–68		1968–73		1968–75	
	No. industries	Productivity change	No. industries	Productivity change	No. industries	Productivity change
< –5%	3	1.2	30	2.0	39	1.2
–5 to 0%	19	2.7	60	1.8	128	1.2
0 to 1%	17	3.2	32	2.5	56	1.9
1 to 2%	23	2.6	38	2.3	33	1.8
2 to 3%	34	2.3	35	2.9	40	3.0
3 to 4%	56	2.5	29	2.9	19	2.9
4 to 5%	56	3.3	36	3.5	25	4.3
5 to 7%	91	3.0	69	4.1	23	4.0
7 to 10%	60	4.1	31	5.5	17	5.3
> 10%	31	5.3	30	6.2	10	5.7
Total	390	3.5	390	3.4	390	2.2

Source: Based on tabulations of 'Deflated value of output per hour industries series' computer tapes provided by the Bureau of Labor Statistics. Average annual productivity changes combined by 1969 value added weights.

had productivity increases of over 5 percent a year, whereas those experiencing actual declines showed productivity increases of only 1 or 2 percent a year. In terms of the relative productivity change shown for the two periods, however, the most important finding shown in the table is that for each class of average annual output change above 2 percent per year, the increase in productivity in the later period was larger than that for the earlier period, suggesting strongly that for industries experiencing substantial rates of growth the productivity trend has not, in fact, declined. Most of the difference in the average productivity trend observed for all of manufacturing is attributable to the fact that far fewer industries were growing at the higher rates during the later period.

In contrast with the high-growth industries, the productivity change for industries growing slowly or declining is lower in Table 16.6 for the later period than the earlier one, and it would be useful to analyze this problem of slow growth in somewhat greater detail. Industries experiencing a low average growth over a period of years may exhibit two types of pattern. On the one hand, they may be experiencing slow, gradual long-term change which reflects an adjustment to new demand and supply conditions. One of the reasons for slow growth may, in fact, be lower productivity increases than those of competing industries. On the other hand, low average rates of growth may result from major fluctuations caused by recession and recovery. One might expect that the productivity behavior of industries with these different patterns would be quite different. To examine this question, industries have been analyzed in

Table 16.7 Annual Productivity Changes Observed in 390 Manufacturing Industries for 1958–68 and 1968–75, Classified by Type of Output Change (combined by 1969 value added weights)

Classification of industries by annual change in output	Percent of total observations		Percent change in output		Percent change in productivity	
	1958–68	1968–75	1958–68	1968–75	1958–68	1968–75
1. Industries with output decline	24	43	–6.2	–10.0	–0.5	–0.9
2. Industries with output increase less than 1%	8	7	0.1	0.1	1.6	1.8
3. Industries recovering from decline in output						
a. Increase to level below previous peak	9	15	6.5	8.0	4.0	6.6
b. Increase to level above previous peak	10	11	12.1	15.4	5.4	9.2
4. Industries expanding beyond previous peak						
a. 1 to 1.9 %	3	2	1.5	1.5	2.2	3.8
b. 2 to 4.9%	11	5	3.5	3.5	2.1	3.0
c. 5 to 10%	15	8	7.4	7.3	4.3	3.8
d. 10 to 25%	18	7	15.4	15.1	6.4	6.7
e. Over 25%	2	2	34.7	30.9	10.4	10.3
Total, all industries	100	100			3.5	2.2

Source: Based on tabulations of 'Deflated value of output per hour industries series' computer tapes provided by Bureau of Labor Statistics. Average annual productivity changes combined by 1969 value added weights.

terms of their year-to-year output change. This analysis is shown in Table 16.7, where the annual output changes of industries are classified as declines, no change, recovery from a previous decline and expansion beyond the previous peak.

Table 16.7 again shows that for comparable annual output changes annual productivity changes in the period 1968–75 were generally higher than in the previous decade. The absolute decline in productivity in the later period was greater than in the previous decade for industries experiencing actual output declines. This, no doubt, was due in part to the fact that the output declines in 1968–75 averaged 10 percent, as against only 6.2 percent in the earlier period. The only other category in which the productivity increase in 1968–75 was significantly lower than in the previous decade was that of annual output increases in the range of 5–10 percent. Aside from this, for each category of output change, productivity increase in the later period equaled or surpassed that of the earlier decade.

It is logical that the rate of productivity change should be closely related to the change in output, as has been shown in Tables 16.6 and 16.7. In industries with rapid output growth, there must of necessity be expansion of capacity. This will generally take the form of new capital equipment employing more recent technology and more modern production techniques. This introduction of new machinery, new technology and new production facilities in itself gives an opportunity for additional learning experience that can then be applied to future expansion of output. In stagnant or slowly growing industries, the opportunities for introducing new technology or applying superior production methods are much more limited. Where there is already excess capacity, producers are reluctant to increase the excess further by adding new capacity. It is more difficult for new firms to enter such slowly growing fields if the existing producers have ample capacity to supply all the output that is required. Because new capacity and new production techniques are not added, the experience with new techniques is much more limited, and the learning process is slowed.

This same mechanism by which productivity change is linked to growth in output strongly suggests that the periods of recession or sluggish growth may permanently depress the long-run level of productivity; to the extent that productivity gains are not achieved in the short run, productivity may be permanently lower. This would result in a downward shift in the level of the productivity trend line, but it would not necessarily alter its slope in the manner postulated by CEA.

For the manufacturing industries, therefore, it may be concluded that the apparent decline in the productivity trend from 1968 to 1975 can be attributed to the fact that productivity increases depend on output increases, and in recent years output has not increased as rapidly as in the previous decade. If it had been found either that the recent growth in output had been restricted by the availability of resources or that, for a given level of output change, productivity increases were lower, it would indeed be possible that the slower increase in output could be the result rather than the cause of the slower advance of productivity. But in view of the recession of 1970 and the major recession of 1975, and the finding that productivity change did not decline relative to output change, it seems more likely that these recessions were instrumental in substantially reducing the growth of output over this period than that either capacity or reduced productivity potential was a limiting factor. In this connection it should be noted that if the period 1968–73 is compared with the earlier decade, the productivity trend observed for manufacturing as a whole shows no significant change, i.e., it is 3.5 percent for 1958–68 and 3.4 percent for 1968–73. This suggests that the whole of the decline in average productivity can be attributed to the recession of 1974–75.

Productivity Change in the Nonmanufacturing Sectors

Unfortunately, information similar to that examined for manufacturing is not available for the nonmanufacturing sectors. There is no industry data, and the only available information is the BEA real gross product data on a relatively aggregated basis. As has been pointed out above, the measurement of output in the service-producing industries is very difficult indeed, and the meaning of the productivity figures derived for these sectors is highly questionable.

There has in recent years been a significant shift in employment to the service-producing industries. This is shown in Table 16.8. As can be seen, employment in the service-producing industries has increased much more rapidly than in the goods-producing industries. While this was true even in the period 1958–68, it was more marked in the period 1968–76. In fact, there was an absolute decline in employment in the goods-producing industries from 1968 to 1976, at the same time almost 12 million more people were employed in the service-producing industries.

Table 16.8 Employees on Nonagricultural Payrolls by Industry Division, 1958, 1968 and 1976

	1958	1968	1976
Total employment	51,363	67,951	79,443
Goods-producing industries	19,474	23,693	23,332
Mining	751	606	783
Contract construction	2,778	3,306	3,594
Manufacturing	15,945	19,781	18,956
Service-producing industries	31,890	44,258	56,111
Private	24,051	32,413	41,163
Transportation and utilities	3,976	4,311	4,509
Wholesale and retail trade	10,750	14,099	17,694
Finance, insurance and real estate	2,519	3,381	4,316
Services	6,806	10,622	14,644
Government	7,839	11,845	14,948
Federal	2,191	2,737	2,733
State and local	5,648	9,109	12,215

Source: Handbook of Labor Statistics, 1977, US Department of Labor, Bureau of Labor Statistics, *Bulletin*, 1966, Table 38, p. 88.

One of the reasons CEA confined its attention to the nonfarm private business economy was a recognition of the difficulty of measuring real output change in government. However, it is equally difficult to measure the change in real output and productivity of wholesale and retail trade, finance, insurance and real estate and a large portion of other services, and, as noted above, for many of them output is measured by employment. As the proportion of the economy where productivity change is thus defined to be zero increases, the average rate of productivity change will be correspondingly lowered. But this is, of course, an assumed result, and it does not seem appropriate to base policy conclusions upon it when it has no basis in observed empirical data.

Thus, for the measurement of capacity utilization, it becomes apparent that methods based upon relating existing employment and unemployment statistics to aggregate output measures can produce misleading results. It may not be possible, at the present time, given the conceptual and statistical problems involved, to develop valid and meaningful overall measures of capacity utilization. However, within specific sectors of the economy and for certain kinds of activities productivity measurement can be very useful. For this purpose, it is essential that the employment and unemployment statistics should be developed in such a manner that they can be directly related to other production information at the level of the individual establishment.

5. CONCLUSION

It was suggested in Section 1 that employment and unemployment statistics are useful indexes of economic activity, but are less successful as measures of capacity utilization. This contention has been generally borne out by the examination of the existing measures. The available measures of employment and unemployment are sensitive barometers of economic activity. For measuring the labor supply, however, the usual measures involving the number of persons employed and unemployed are not fully satisfactory. The role of part-time workers, both voluntary and involuntary, is not adequately reflected. Furthermore, account should be taken of discouraged workers and those who are uncertain as to whether they want jobs. A major improvement in measuring the labor supply could be achieved by presenting, in addition to the number of persons employed and unemployed, man-hour measurements that would show the role of part-time employment and unemployment. The data for such measurement are contained in the present Current Population Survey. Cast into this form, the underutilization of the labor supply appears to be considerably larger than is reported by the conventional measures of unemployment.

For the measurement of capacity and capacity utilization, the existing measures are quite unsatisfactory. The present employment and unemployment statistics are an inadequate basis for determining what constitutes full employment. The selection of the benchmark unemployment rate of 4.9 percent as full employment in 1977 rests on a combination of casual empiricism and heroic assumptions. There is no evidence to support the contention that wage increases become significantly larger at unemployment levels below the benchmark unemployment rate. Examination of cross-sectional unemployment and wage data suggests that over the observed range of labor market variation, the rate of change in average hourly earnings does not appear to be very sensitive to varying degrees of labor market tightness. Unfortunately, the deficiencies of wage measurement are such that little can be ascertained about the behavior of actual wage rates (rather than average hourly earnings) under different labor market conditions.

The analysis of how much output is, in fact, lost at given levels of unemployment is also based on inadequate analysis and arbitrary assumptions. The argument that the trend of productivity has declined, so that at any given rate of unemployment the economy is now operating much nearer to capacity than formerly, has not been borne out by an examination of the relation between output changes and productivity changes in individual industries. Generally, for the same rates of output change manufacturing industries enjoyed the same or greater productivity increases in the recent period as a decade earlier. Current aggregate productivity increases are low due to the slower growth of the economy. For the nonmanufacturing sectors of the economy, output (and therefore productivity) is very difficult to measure, and in major areas outputs are measured on the basis of inputs. Under such circumstances, productivity gains are automatically assumed to be zero.

The deficiencies in the determination of what is full employment and the measurement of capacity utilization cannot be attributed solely to the inadequacies of employment and unemployment statistics. The lack of success also reflects the compartmentalization of employment and unemployment statistics as independent time series, unrelated to statistics on wages, prices and output, owing to the decentralization of the federal statistical system. The Bureau of the Census is responsible for reporting on production in the economic censuses. The Bureau of Labor Statistics reports on employment, wages and prices. Even within BLS, responsibility is divided and the different statistical series are collected independently by different methods from different sources. Many of the statistics are actually collected by state agencies in cooperation with BLS. Important related bodies of administrative data such as social security employment and wage data are not integrated with the BLS data. The decentralization of data sources means that the relation between employment, wages, prices, output and productivity can only be observed at fairly aggregated levels, and the lack of comparable classifications, coverage and concepts introduces many types of error and ambiguity. Different government agencies are not permitted to relate data at the establishment reporting unit level in order to obtain greater comparability.

To obtain a better understanding of the interrelationships involved, what is needed is an integrated set of data containing information on employment, wages, and output related at the establishment level. Furthermore, given the importance of regional differences in labor markets and labor supply the analysis needs to be carried out within a regional context. Much of the success of the Current Population Survey as a source of useful data arises from the fact that it has generated a microdata set containing a large body of information for each household. Such a body of data makes it possible to analyze both micro-behavior and the effect of demographic shifts. A similar microdata set is needed for establishments.

The inadequacy of the current measures of capacity utilization has had very serious consequences for economic policy. On the basis of present measures of capacity utilization it has been concluded that the economy is operating close to full employment levels, and that an expansionary policy would lead to rising wages, resulting in increased inflationary pressures, rather than increasing employment. In view of the supposed reduction in the trend of productivity increase, furthermore, it is argued that relatively little additional output could be generated. If, however, as suggested by the analysis in this paper, wages are relatively insensitive to increased labor market tightness but productivity change is highly sensitive to the rate of growth of output, it is quite possible that an expansionary policy would have more impact upon productivity than upon wage increases, and thus might reduce inflationary pressures. If, furthermore, the economy is not as close to full capacity as had been supposed, there may be room for such expansion.

It is apparent that considerably more research is needed on the topic of wage behavior and labor market tightness, and on productivity behavior. This research cannot be carried out without better basic data on employment, wages, prices, output and productivity at the establishment level. There may be large areas where output and productivity measurements are not possible, further-more, because of quality change, new products, or the nature of the output produced. In such cases, it is important that arbitrary assumptions should not be introduced by statisticians in such a manner that they bias the results of policy analysis.

Bibliography

Nancy D. Ruggles and Richard Ruggles

Key to articles included:
P = *Pricing Systems, Indexes, and Price Behavior*
N = *National Accounting and Economic Policy*
M = *Macro- and Microdata Analyses and their Integration*

'Recent Applications of the A-S Reaction Study', Richard Ruggles with Gordon W. Allport, *Journal of Abnormal and Social Psychology*, **34** (4), October 1939.

P11 'The Relative Movements of Real and Money Wage Rates', Richard Ruggles, *Quarterly Journal of Economics*, **55** (1), November 1940.

'The Concept of Linear Total Cost–Output Regressions', Richard Ruggles, *American Economic Review*, **1** (2), June 1941.

M6 'An Empirical Approach to Economic Intelligence in World War II', Richard Ruggles and Henry Brodie, *Journal of the American Statistical Association*, **42**, March 1947.

P3 'Discriminatory and Competitive Pricing', Nancy D. Ruggles, unpublished Ph.D. dissertation, Radcliff College,1949.

An Introduction to National Income and Income Analysis, Richard Ruggles, McGraw-Hill, 1949.

N1 *National Income Accounting and Its Relation to Economic Policy*, Richard Ruggles, Office of the Special Representative in Europe, Economic Cooperation Administration, Paris, 1949.

P2 'Recent Developments in the Theory of Marginal Cost Pricing', Nancy D. Ruggles, *Review of Economic Studies*, 1949.

P1 'The Welfare Basis of the Marginal Cost Pricing Principle', Nancy D. Ruggles, *Review of Economic Studies*, 1949.

La Contabilidad del Ingreso Nacional y su Relacion con la Politica Economica, Richard Ruggles, Pan American Union, 1951.

European National Accounts, Richard Ruggles and Nancy D. Ruggles, Economic Cooperation Administration, 1951.

'The French Investment Program and Its Relation to Resource Allocation', Richard Ruggles, in *Modern France, Problems of the Third and Fourth Republics*, Princeton University Press, 1951.

National Accounts Data Book, Richard Ruggles and Nancy D. Ruggles, Economic Cooperation Administration, 1951.

'Concepts, Sources, and Methods of U.S. National Income Statistics', Richard Ruggles, *Econometrica*, July 1952.

Volkseinkommen und Volkswirtschaftliche Gesamtrechnungen, Richard Ruggles, Humboldt-Verlag, Wien–Stuttgart, 1952.

M11 'Methodological Developments', Richard Ruggles, in B.F. Haley (ed.), *Survey of Contemporary Economics*, Vol. II, Richard D. Irwin, Inc., 1952.

'Economies of Europe Prior to and During World War II', Richard Ruggles, paper presented March 18, 1953 at Industrial College of the Armed Forces, Washington DC (published with discussion).

National Income Accounts and Income Analysis, 2nd edition, Richard Ruggles, translated into Chinese by Mr Leon S. Geoffery, Agency for International Development, United States Aid Mission to China, McGraw-Hill, 1953.

P4 'The Value of Value Theory', Richard Ruggles, *American Economic Review*, May 1954.

P12 'The Nature of Price Flexibility and the Determinants of Relative Price Changes in the Economy', Richard Ruggles, in *Business Concentration and Price Policy*, National Bureau of Economic Research, 1955.

Primary responsibility for the following sections of the United Nations *World Economic Surveys*, Nancy D. Ruggles:

'The Balance of Payments Experience of Industrial Countries: The Impact of Structural Change', 1956.

'Inflation in the Nineteen Fifties: The Character of Recent Price Inflation', 1957.

'Recent Trends in Industrial Countries: Developments in Foreign Trade and Payments', 1958.

Graduate Training in Economics, Richard Ruggles, Yale University Press, 1956.

National Income Accounting and Income Analysis, Richard Ruggles and Nancy D. Ruggles, revised edition, McGraw-Hill, 1956.

'Tendencias Recientes en la Contabilidad del Ingreso Nacional', Richard Ruggles, *Boletin del Banco Central de Venezuela*, **16**, 1956.

'Government Budgets and their Relation to National Accounts', Richard Ruggles and Nancy D. Ruggles, paper prepared for the Subcommittee on Fiscal Policy of the Joint Economic Committee and Statement November 18–27, 1957.

'The Nation's Income and Product Accounts', Richard Ruggles, The Executive Program in Business Administration, Columbia University, 1958.

'Objectives of National Economic Accounts and Their Implications for the General Form of the Accounts', Richard Ruggles, Chapter V of *The National Economic Accounts of the United States*, Report of the National Accounts Review Committee, published in Hearings, Subcommittee on Economic Statistics, Joint Economic Committee; also reprinted by the National Bureau of Economic Research, General Series, No. 64, 1958.

'Prices, Costs, Demand and Output in the United States,1946–1957', Richard Ruggles and Nancy D. Ruggles, Paper prepared for the Joint Economic Committee and Statement, May 15, 1958.

'Recent Price Increases and their Relation to Administered Prices', Richard Ruggles, Hearings, Subcommittee on Antitrust and Monopoly, Committee on the Judiciary, US Senate, July 9–16, 1957; reprinted in part in Richard Mooney and Edwin L. Dale Jr (ed), *Inflation and Recession*, Doubleday and Co., 1958.

'Prices, Costs, and Profits in the United States Economy, 1947–1957', Richard Ruggles and Nancy D. Ruggles, in Hearings before the Joint Economic Committee, US Congress, September, 1959.

'Public Sector Accounts and National Economic Accounts', Richard Ruggles, Paper for United Nations Workshop on Classification of Government Accounts, Santiago, Chile, published by the United Nations, 1960.

M7   'Study of Differential Fertility Based on Census Data', Richard Ruggles and Nancy D. Ruggles, in *Demographic and Economic Change in Developed Countries*, National Bureau of Economic Research, 1960.

N2   'Concepts of Real Capital Stock and Services', Richard Ruggles and Nancy D. Ruggles, in *Output, Input, and Productivity Measurement*, National Bureau of Economic Research, 1961.

P6   'Measuring the Cost of Quality', Richard Ruggles, *Challenge*, November 1961.

'Regional Breakdowns of National Economic Accounts', Richard Ruggles and Nancy D. Ruggles, in W. Hochwald (ed.), *Design of Regional Accounts*, Johns Hopkins Press, 1961.

P5   'The Wholesale Price Index', Richard Ruggles, Chapter V of *The Price Statistics of the Federal Government*, Report of the Price Statistics Review Committee, published in Hearings, Subcommittee on Economic Statistics of the Joint Economic Committee, 1961.

Comparison of National Accounts Data for the United States Classified According to the Concepts of the United Nations System of National Accounts and the Material Product System, Richard Ruggles and Nancy D. Ruggles, a study prepared for the Office of Statistical Standards, US Bureau of the Budget, and submitted to the Conference of European Statisticians of the United Nations, February 1962.

Contabilidada Nacional e Análise Macroeconómica, Richard Ruggles and Nancy D. Ruggles, Livraria Sá da Costa, Lda., Lisboa, 1962, copyright 1956 by McGraw-Hill Book Company, Inc.

P13   'Price Stability and Economic Growth in the United States', Richard Ruggles and Nancy D. Ruggles, published in German in *Konjunkturpolitik*, **8** (3), 1962, also published in Spanish in *Economia*, **20** (71), 1962.

'Relation of the Undergraduate Major to Graduate Economics', Richard Ruggles, *American Economic Review*, Proceedings, May 1962.

'Contabilidad Economica Nacional y Contabilidad del Sector Publico', Richard Ruggles and Nancy D. Ruggles, in M. Balboa (ed.), *El Ingreso y la Riqueza*, Mexico: Fondo de Cultural Economica, 1963.

Evaluation of the Venezuelan Plan, Richard Ruggles, Report of the Committee of Nine of the Organization of American States, 1963.

'Summary of the Conference on Inflation and Growth in Latin America', Richard Ruggles, in W. Baer and I. Kerstenetszky (eds), *Inflation and Growth in Latin America*, Richard D. Irwin, Inc., 1964.

A System of National Accounts and Historical Data, Richard Ruggles and Nancy D. Ruggles, Yale University Press, 1964.

An Economic Data Reporting System for the Agency for International Development, Richard Ruggles and Nancy D. Ruggles with W. Abraham, Yale University Press, 1965.

A Generalized Economic Information Retrieval System, Richard Ruggles and Nancy D. Ruggles, Economic Growth Center, Yale University Press, 1965.

P7   'Domestic Price Statistics: Their Reliability as History and Their Usefulness for Economic Policy', Richard Ruggles, Statement before the Subcommittee on Economic Statistics of the Joint Economic Committee, May 26, 1966.

'Economic Data and the Invasion of Privacy', Richard Ruggles, Hearings, Subcommittee of the Committee on Government Operations, House of Representatives, 89th Congress, 2nd Session, July 26–28, 1966, *The Computer and the Invasion of Privacy*.

P8		'Redundancy in Price Indexes for International Comparisons: A Step-wise Regression Analysis', Nancy D. Ruggles, Progress Report for the Agency of International Development and the Yale Growth Center, November 15, 1966.

Report of the Committee on the Preservation and Use of Economic Data to the Social Science Research Council, Richard Ruggles, April 1965, published in Hearings, Subcommittee of the Committee on Government Operations, House of Representatives, 89th Congress, Second Session, July 26–28, 1966, *The Computer and the Invasion of Privacy.*

'The Co-ordination and Integration of Government Statistical Programs', Richard Ruggles, Hearings, Subcommittee on Economic Statistics of the Joint Economic Committee, May 15–17, 1967.

'Data Files for a Generalized Economic Information System', Richard Ruggles and Nancy D. Ruggles, *Social Sciences Information*, 6, August 1967.

'The Federal Government and Federalism: Past and Future', Richard Ruggles, in *Revenue Sharing and the City*, Committee on Urban Economics of Resources for the Future, Inc., Johns Hopkins Press, 1967.

'History and Development of Economic Data', Richard Ruggles, in *International Encyclopedia of the Social Sciences*, 1967.

'The Role of a National Data Center in Economic Statistics', Richard Ruggles, Federal Statistical Users' Conference, October 14, 1966, Washington, DC.

'Economic Data', Richard Ruggles, *Encyclopedia of the Social Sciences*, 1968.

'Ethical Problems of Privacy and Information Needs in Modern Society', Richard Ruggles, Paper presented at University of Minnesota, 1968.

N3		'The Evolution and Present State of National Economic Accounting', Richard Ruggles and Nancy D. Ruggles, Center for International Education and Research in Accounting, University of Illinois, 1968.

'How Will It Work?', Richard Ruggles, Statement for Joint Economic Committee, October 29, 1968

'On the Needs and Values of Data Banks', *Symposium: Computers, Data Banks and Individual Privacy*, Richard Ruggles, University of Minnesota, May 2, 1968.

P9   'Price Indexes and International Price Comparisons', Richard Ruggles, in W. Fellner (ed.), *Ten Economic Studies in the Tradition of Irving Fisher*, John Wiley and Sons, 1968.

'The Adequacy of the National Data Base for Economic and Social Research and the Design and Evaluation of Public Policy', Richard Ruggles, 1969

'How a Data Bank Might Operate', Richard Ruggles, *Think*, May 1969.

'The National Data Bank: Privacy and Freedom', Richard Ruggles, *Science and Society Seminar,* Brown University, February 19, 1969.

'The Preservation and Use of Machine Readable Records', Richard Ruggles, National Archives, 1969.

The Design of Economic Accounts, Richard Ruggles and Nancy D. Ruggles, National Bureau of Economic Research, 1970.

Economics: The Behavioral and Social Sciences Survey, Nancy D. Ruggles (ed.), Report of the Economics Panel of the Behavioral and Social Sciences Survey of the National Academy of Sciences and the Social Science Research Council, Englewood Cliffs, NJ: Prentice-Hall, 1970.

'Income Distribution Theory', Richard Ruggles, *Review of Income and Wealth*, **16** (3), September 1970.

M12 'Macro Accounts and Micro Data Sets', Richard Ruggles and Nancy D. Ruggles, *Proceedings of the Business and Economic Statistics Section*, American Statistical Association, 1970.

'National Income Accounting', Richard Ruggles, *Encyclopedia Britannica*, 1970.

N8   'The Evolution of National Accounts and the National Data Base', Richard Ruggles and Nancy D. Ruggles, *Survey of Current Business*, Part II, July 1971.

M13 'The Relation of Methodology to the Technology of Economic Research', Richard Ruggles and Nancy D. Ruggles, American Statistical Association and Biometric Society Meetings, Montreal, Canada, August 15, 1972.

'Communication in Economics: The Media and Technology', Richard Ruggles and Nancy D. Ruggles, *Annals of Economic and Social Measurement*, **1** (2), April 1972.

'A Proposal for a System of Economic and Social Accounts', Richard Ruggles and Nancy D. Ruggles, in Milton Moss (ed.), *The Measurement of Economic and Social Performance*, National Bureau of Economic Research, 1973.

The Role of the Computer in Economic and Social Research in Latin America, Nancy D. Ruggles (ed.), proceedings of a conference held in Cuernavaca, Mexico, National Bureau of Economic Research, 1974.

'The Role of the Computer in Economic and Social Research in Latin America: Summary of the Conference', Richard Ruggles in Nancy D. Ruggles (eds), *The Role of the Computer in Economic and Social Research in Latin America*, National Bureau of Economic Research, 1974.

M15 'Social Indicators and a Framework for Social and Economic Accounts', Richard Ruggles and Nancy D. Ruggles, *Proceedings of the Social Statistics Section*, American Statistical Association, 1974.

M8   'A Strategy for Merging and Matching Microdata Sets', Richard Ruggles and Nancy D. Ruggles, *Annals of Economic and Social Measurement*, **3** (2), April 1974.

M16 'The Measurement of Economic and Social Performance: A Progress Report on a National Bureau of Economic Research Project', Richard Ruggles and Nancy D. Ruggles, paper presented at the 14th General Conference of the International Association for Research in Income and Wealth, Aulanko, Finland, August 1975.

M1   'Recession and Recovery in the United States, 1929–1974, and Sectoral Saving and Investment Accounts', Richard Ruggles, in *Nasjonalregnskap Modeller og Analyse* (*National Accounts Models and Analysis*), Oslo, Norway, 1975.

M14 'The Role of Microdata in National Economic Accounts', Richard Ruggles and Nancy D. Ruggles, *Review of Income and Wealth*, **21** (2), June 1975 (also published as 'El Papel de los Microdatos en las Cuentas Nacionales Economicas y Sociales', *Estadistica*, **113**, December 1975).

M2   'Economic Growth in the Short Run: Its Behavior and Measurement', Richard Ruggles in *U.S. Economic Growth from 1976 to 1986: Prospects, Problems and Patterns*, Vol. 2, *The Factors and Processes Shaping Long Run Economic Growth*, Studies for the Joint Economic Committee, 94th Congress, 2nd Session, November 10, 1976.

P14 'Chronic Inflation in the United States, 1950–73', published as 'La Inflacion Cronica en los Estados Unidos, 1950–1973', Richard Ruggles and Nancy D. Ruggles, in Carlos Diaz-Alejandro, S. Teitel and V.E. Tokman (eds), *Politica Economica en Centro y Periferia*, Mexico: Fondo de Cultura Economica, 1976.

P15 'The Anatomy of Earnings Behavior', Richard Ruggles and Nancy D. Ruggles, presented at the Conference on Research in Income and Wealth, Ann Arbor, May 1974 and published in *The Distribution of Economic Well-Being*, Studies in Income and Wealth, Vol. 41, National Bureau of Economic Research, 1977.

     Distributive Impacts of the Budget and Economic Policies', Richard Ruggles, statement and testimony before the House Committee on the Budget, September 29, 1977.

     Guidelines on Principles of a System of Price and Quantity Statistics, Nancy D. Ruggles, United Nations Publication, Series M, No. 59, New York, 1977.

M9   'Merging Microdata: Rationale, Practice and Testing', Richard Ruggles and Nancy D. Ruggles with Edward N. Wolff, *Annals of Economic and Social Measurement*, **6** (4), October 1977.

P10 'The Wholesale Price Index: Review and Evaluation', published as *Review and Evaluation of the Wholesale Price Index*, Richard Ruggles, Report for the Council on Wage and Price Stability, Washington, DC, 1977. (Also published in Joint Economic Committee Hearings, 1977.)

'Review of the Implementation of the Revised System of National Accounts', Nancy D. Ruggles, United Nations document (mimeo), E/CN.3/507, 1978.

M17 *The Development of Integrated Data Bases for Social, Economic and Demographic Statistics*, Nancy D. Ruggles, United Nations Publication, Series F, No. 27, New York, 1979.

Employment and Unemployment Indexes as Measures of Economic Activity and Capacity Utilization, Richard Ruggles, Background Paper No. 28, National Commission on Employment and Unemployment Statistics, April 1979.

P16 'The Measurement of the Supply and Use of Labor', Richard Ruggles, Background paper for the National Commission on Employment Statistics, 1979.

Studies in the Integration of Social Statistics, Nancy D. Ruggles, Part 2, 'Strategy for Further Work on the Framework for the Integration of Social and Demographic Statistics', United Nations publication, Series F, No. 24, New York, 1979.

'Future Directions for Work on the System of National Accounts', Nancy D. Ruggles, United Nations (mimeo), E/CN.3/541, 1980.

'The Role of Macro and Micro Data Structures in the Integration of Demographic, Social and Economic Statistics', Nancy D. Ruggles, United Nations document (mimeo), E/CN.3/552, 1980.

Instructions and Definitions for the National Accounts Questionnaire, Nancy D. Ruggles, United Nations and Organization for Economic Co-operation and Development, 1980.

'The Conceptual and Empirical Strengths and Limitations of Demographic and Time Based Accounts', Richard Ruggles, in F.T. Juster and K.C. Land (eds), *Social Accounting Systems: Essays on the State of the Art*, Academic Press, 1981.

N10 'Integrated Economic Accounts for the United States 1947–1980', Richard Ruggles and Nancy D. Ruggles, *Survey of Current Business*, **62** (5), May 1982.

N11 'Integrated Economic Accounts: Reply', Richard Ruggles and Nancy D. Ruggles, *Survey of Current Business*, **62** (11), November 1982.

'The National Accounts', Richard Ruggles, *Aspects of Italian Official Statistics: Review and Proposals*, Report of the International Statistical Commission, February 1982.

'Price Indexes and Statistics', Nancy D. Ruggles, *Aspects of Italian Statistics: Review and Proposals*, Report of the International Statistical Commission, February 1982.

N12 *The System of National Accounts: Review of Major Issue and Prospects for Future Work and Short Term Changes*, Richard Ruggles, Expert Paper for the United Nations Statistical Office, ESA/STAT/AC.15/2, April 15, 1982.

'Guide to the Yearbook of National Accounts Statistics', Nancy D. Ruggles, *Handbook of National Accounting*, Vol. 1, United Nations Statistical Office, 1983.

'Gross Domestic Product', Nancy D. Ruggles, *Handbook of National Accounting*, Vol. 2, United Nations Statistical Office, 1983.

'Public Sector Accounts', Nancy D. Ruggles, *Handbook of National Accounting*, Vol. 4, United Nations Statistical Office, 1983.

Reference Documentation for Longitudinal Establishment Data (LED), Richard Ruggles and Nancy D. Ruggles with CatherineViscoli, prepared for the Bureau of the Census, December 1983.

Review and Development of the System of NationalAccounts (SNA), Richard Ruggles, Report for the Statistical Commission of the United Nations, E/CN.3/1983/5, July 21, 1982, for the 22nd Session 7–16 March 1983.

'The Treatment of Pension and Insurance Transactions in the United Nations System of National Accounts (SNA)', Nancy D. Ruggles and Richard Ruggles, report prepared for OECD Meeting on National Accounts, Paris, May 1983.

N5 'The Treatment of Pensions and Insurance in National Accounts', Nancy D. Ruggles and Richard Ruggles, *Review of Income and Wealth*, **29** (4), December 1983.

N9   'The United States National Income Accounts, 1947–1977: Their Conceptual Basis and Evolution', Richard Ruggles, in Murray Foss (ed), *The U.S. National Income and Product Accounts: Selected Topics*, Chicago: University of Chicago Press for NBER, 1983. (Paper presented at Conference on Income and Wealth, Washington, 1979.)

M10   'The Analysis of Longitudinal Establishment Data', Richard Ruggles and Nancy D. Ruggles, Presentation at the Bureau of the Census and NSF Conference on Longitudinal Establishment Data File and Diversification Study, Alexandria, Virginia, October 17–18, 1984.

'The Current Review of International Standards for National Accounting', Nancy D. Ruggles, Presentation to Statistics Canada, Ottawa, Canada, April 30, 1984.

'Financial Accounts and Balance Sheets: Issues for the Revision of SNA', Nancy D. Ruggles, Study prepared for the United Nations Statistical Office, January 1984.

'Possible Future Directions for National Accounting', Richard Ruggles, Presentation to Statistics Canada, Ottawa, Canada, April 30, 1984.

'Recent Developments in International Standards for National Accounting', Nancy D. Ruggles, Presentation to Statistics Canada, Ottawa, Canada, November 15, 1984.

N4   'The Role of the National Accounts in the Statistical System', Richard Ruggles, Presentation to Statistics Canada, Ottawa, Canada, November 15, 1984.

'The System of National Accounts: Review of Major Issues', Richard Ruggles, *Statistical Journal of the United Nations ECE*, **2**, 1984.

'The Treatment of Noncash Benefits in Measuring Poverty and Income', Richard Ruggles and Nancy D. Ruggles, Presentation at the First Annual Research Conference, Bureau of the Census, Reston, Virginia, March 22, 1985.

M18   'The Integration of Macro and Micro Data for the Household Sector', Richard Ruggles and Nancy D. Ruggles, *Review of Income and Wealth*, **32** (3), September 1986.

'Social Accounting', Nancy D. Ruggles and Richard Ruggles, *The New Palgrave: A Dictionary of Economic Theory and Doctrine*, Macmillan, 1986.

N13 'Financial Accounts and Balance Sheets: Issues for the Revision of SNA', Nancy D. Ruggles, *Review of Income and Wealth*, **33** (1), 1987.

'Saving and Capital Formation of Enterprise Sectors: A Market Trans-actions View', Nancy D. Ruggles and Richard Ruggles presented at Conference of Income and Wealth, Baltimore MD, March 29, 1987 (not published in conference volume).

M3 'Theoretical Concepts and Empirical Measurement of Saving and Invest-ment', Richard Ruggles, Paper Presented at AEA Meetings, December 30, 1987

N14 'A Note on the Revision of the United Nations System of National Accounts', Richard Ruggles, *Review of Income and Wealth*, **36** (4), December 1990.

'Review of *The Total Incomes System of Accounts*, by Robert Eisner', Richard Ruggles, *Review of Income and Wealth*, **37** (4), December 1991.

N15 'Statistical Measurements for Economic Systems in Transition: Strategy for Implementing the UN System of National Accounts (SNA)', Richard Ruggles, *Economies in Transition Statistical Measures Now and in the Future*, Proceeding of the Sochi International Forum, October 1990, Editor Petr O. Aven with the assistance of Christoph M. Schneider, CP-91-4, September 1991.

M4 'Household and Enterprise Saving and Capital Formation in the United States: A Market Transactions View', Nancy D. Ruggles and Richard Ruggles, *Review of Income and Wealth*, **38** (2), June 1992.

M5 'Accounting for Saving and Capital Formation in the United States, 1947–1991', Richard Ruggles, presented at the ASSA meetings Ana-heim, California, January 6, 1993; published in *Journal of Economic Perspectives*, **7** (2), Spring 1993 and in Philip D. Oliver and Fred W. Peel (eds), *Tax Policy*, The Foundation Press, 1996.

N6 'National Income Accounting Concepts and Measurement: Economic Theory and Practice', Richard Ruggles, *Economic Notes*, by Pashi di Siena, **22** (2), 1993.

N16   'Issues Relating to the UN System of National Accounts and Developing Countries', Richard Ruggles, *Journal of Development Economics*, **38**, 1994.

'The United Nations System of National Accounts (SNA): Its Implementation for Developing Countries', Richard Ruggles, *Journal of Development Economics,* **44,** 77–85, 1994.

N17   'The United Nations System of National Accounts (SNA), and the Integration of Macro and Micro Data', Richard Ruggles, in John Kendrick (ed), *Socio-Economic Accounts*, Klower, 1995.

N7   'The Value Added of National Accounting', Richard Ruggles and Patricia Ruggles, *Review of Income and Wealth,* **41** (2), 1995.

'Factor Cost', Richard Ruggles, articles for *The Encyclopedia Americana*, Grolier, 1998. Also available on CD-ROM.

'The Middle Ages of the International Association for Research in Income and Wealth', Richard Ruggles, Paper presented at the IARIW 50th Anniversary Conference, Cambridge, England, August 1998.

'National Income', Richard Ruggles, articles for *The Encyclopedia Americana*, Grolier, 1998. Also available on CD-ROM.

'Saving and Capital Formation', Richard Ruggles, articles for *The Encyclopedia Americana*, Grolier, 1998. Also available on CD-ROM.

'The International Association for Research in Income and Wealth: Its First 50 Years', Richard Ruggles, *Review of Income and Wealth*, forthcoming, 1999.

Index